ASPECTS of
WESTERN
CIVILIZATION

Problems and Sources in History

ASPECTS of WESTERN CIVILIZATION

Problems and Sources in History

Volume I

Fourth Edition

Edited by

PERRY M. ROGERS

The Ohio State University

Prentice Hall, Upper Saddle River, New Jersey 07458

Library of Congress Cataloging-in-Publication Data

Aspects of Western civilization: problems and sources in history /
edited by Perry M. Rogers. —4th ed.
   p.   cm.
   Vols. 1 and 2.
   ISBN 0–13–083202–2 (vol. 1).—ISBN 0-13-083203-0 (vol. 2)
   1. Civilization, Western—History. 2. Civilization, Western—
History—Sources.   I. Rogers, Perry McAdow.
CB245.A86   2000
909′ 09812—dc21   96–26935
                                                     CIP

Editor-in-chief: Charlyce Jones-Owen
Executive editor: Todd Armstrong
Assistant editor: Emsal Hasan
Editorial assistant: Holly Jo Brown
Managing editor: Jan Stephan
Production liaison: Fran Russello
Editorial/production supervision: Bruce Hobart (Pine Tree Composition)
Prepress and manufacturing buyer: Lynn Pearlman
Cover director: Jayne Conte
Cover designer: Kiwi Design
Cover art: De Architectura di Vitruvio by Leonardo da Vinci/Art Resource, NY.
Director, Image Resource Center: Melinda Lee Reo
Manager, rights & permissions: Kay Dellosa
Image specialist: Beth Boyd
Photo researcher: Teri Stratford
Marketing manager: Sheryl Adams

This book was set in 10/11½ Baskerville by Pine Tree Composition, Inc.,
and was printed and bound by Courier Companies, Inc.
The cover was printed by Phoenix Color Corp.

10 9 8 7 6 5 4 3 2 1

ISBN 0-13-083202-2

Prentice-Hall International (UK) Limited, *London*
Prentice-Hall of Australia Pty. Limited, *Sydney*
Prentice-Hall Canada Inc., *Toronto*
Prentice-Hall Hispanoamericana, S.A., *Mexico*
Prentice-Hall of India Private Limited, *New Delhi*
Prentice-Hall of Japan, Inc., *Tokyo*
Pearson Education Asia Pte. Ltd., *Singapore*
Editora Prentice-Hall do Brasil, Ltda., *Rio de Janeiro*

For Ann
Elisa, Kit, and Tyler

Brief Contents

Contents

Democracy and Empire: The Golden Age of Athens 76

Social and Intellectual Aspects of the Pax Romana   239

Failure and Decline (180–500 C.E.)   250

Mind and Society in the High Middle Ages   333

SECTION III: THE LATE MIDDLE AGES (1300–1450)   *345*

The Waning of The Medieval Church   345

Disease and History: The Black Death   353

The Catholic Reformation   449

Resolution: The Bloody Wars of Religion   458

Preface

The Roman orator Cicero once remarked that "History is the witness of the times, the torch of truth, the life of memory, the teacher of life, the messenger of antiquity." In spite of these noble words, historians have often labored under the burden of justifying the study of events that are over and done. Human beings are practical, more concerned with their present and future than with their past. And yet the study of history provides us with unique opportunities for self-knowledge. It teaches us what we have done and therefore helps define what we are. On a less abstract level, the study of history enables us to judge present circumstance by drawing on the laboratory of the past. Those who have lived and died, through their recorded attitudes, actions, and ideas, have left a legacy of experience.

One of the best ways to travel through time and perceive the very "humanness" of history is through the study of primary sources. These are the documents, coins, letters, inscriptions, and monuments of past ages. The task of historians is to evaluate this evidence with a critical eye and then construct a narrative that is consistent with the "facts" as they have been established. Such interpretations are inherently subjective and open to dispute. History is thus filled with controversy as historians argue their way toward the truth. The only effective way to understand the past is through personal examination of the primary sources.

Yet, for the beginning student, this poses some difficulties. Such inquiry casts the student adrift from the security of accepting the "truth" as revealed in a textbook. In fact, history is too often presented in a deceptively objective manner; one learns facts and dates in an effort to obtain the right answers for multiple-choice tests. But the student who has wrestled with primary sources and has experienced voices from the past on a more intimate level accepts the responsibility of evaluation and judgment. He or she understands that history does not easily lend itself to right answers, but demands reflection on the problems that have confronted past societies and are at play even in our contemporary world.

Aspects of Western Civilization offers the student an opportunity to evaluate the primary sources of the past in a structured and organized format. The documents provided include state papers, secret dispatches, letters, diary accounts, poems, newspaper articles, papal encyclicals, propaganda fliers, and even wall graffiti. Occasionally, the assessments of modern historians are included. Yet this two-volume book has been conceived as more than a simple compilation of sources. The subtitle of the work, *Problems and Sources in History*, gives true indication of the nature of its premise. Students learn from the past most effectively when faced with problems that have meaning for their own lives. In evaluating the material from *Aspects of Western Civilization*, the student will discover that issues are not nearly as simple as they may appear at first glance. Historical sources often contradict each other, and truth then depends upon logic and upon one's own experience and outlook on life. Throughout these volumes, the student is confronted with basic questions regarding historical development, human nature, moral action, and practical necessity. The text is therefore broad in its scope, incorporating a wide variety of political, social, economic, religious, intellectual, and scientific issues. It is internally organized around eight major themes that provide direction and cohesion while allowing for originality of thought in both written and oral analysis:

1. *Imperialism.* How has imperialism been justified throughout Western history, and what are the moral implications of gaining and maintaining empire? Is defensive imperialism a practical foreign policy option? This theme is often juxtaposed with subtopics of nationalism, war, altruism, and human nature.

2. *Church/State Relationships.* Is there a natural competition between these two controlling units in society? Which is more influential, which legacy more enduring? How has religion been used as a means of securing political power or of instituting social change?

3. *Beliefs and Spirituality.* The Judeo-Christian heritage of Western Civilization forms the basis of this theme. How have religious values and moral attitudes affected the course of Western history? To what extent have spiritual reform movements resulted in a change of political or social policy? Are ideas more potent than any army? Why have so many people died fighting for religions that abhor violence? Does every society need a spiritual foundation?

4. *Systems of Government.* This theme seeks to introduce the student to the various systems of rule that have shaped Western Civilization: classical democracy, representative democracy (republican government), oligarchy, constitutional monarchy, divine-right monarchy, theocracy, and dictatorship (especially fascism and totalitarian rule). What are the advantages and drawbacks to each? This rubric also includes the concepts of balance of power and containment, principles of succession, geopolitics, and social and economic theories such as capitalism, communism, and socialism.

5. *Revolution.* This theme seeks to define and examine the varieties of revolution: political, intellectual, economic, and social. What are the underlying and precipitating causes of political revolution? How essential is the intellectual foundation? Are social demands and spontaneity more important elements in radical action?

6. *Propaganda.* What is the role of propaganda in history? Many sections examine the use and abuse of information, often in connection with absolute government, revolution, imperialism, or genocide. How are art and architecture, as well as the written word, used in the "creation of belief"? This theme emphasizes the relativity of truth and stresses the responsibility of the individual in assessing the validity of evidence.

7. *Women in History.* The text intends to help remedy the widespread omission of women from the history of Western society and to develop an appreciation of their contributions to the intellectual and political framework of Western Civilization. At issue is how women have been viewed—or rendered invisible—throughout history and how individually and collectively their presence is inextricably linked with the development and progress of civilization. This inclusive approach stresses the importance of achieving a perspective that lends value and practical application to history.

8. *Historical Change and Transition.* What are the main determinants of change in history? How important is the individual in effecting change, or is society regulated by unseen social and economic forces? What role does chance play? What are the components of civilization, and how do we assess progress or decline? Are civilizations biological in nature? Is a crisis/response theory of change valid? This theme works toward providing the student with a philosophy of history and against the tendency to divide history into strict periods. It stresses the close connection between the past and the present.

Structure of the Book

Each chapter begins with a timeline chronology so that students may visualize the historical parameters of the chapter. This is followed by a series of quotations from various historians, diplomats, philosophers, literary figures, or religious spokespersons who offer insight on the subject matter of the chapter. These quotations may well be used in conjunction with the study questions at the end of the unit. After the quotations, chapter themes are listed and framed by several questions that direct the reader to broader issues and comparative perspectives with ideas and events in other chapters. This feature acknowledges the changing perspectives of different eras while linking historical problems that emphasize the continuity of history. A general introduction then provides a brief historical background and focuses the themes or questions to be discussed in the chapter.

Following this general introduction, the primary sources are presented with extensive direction for the student. A headnote explains in more detail the historical or biographical background for each primary source and focuses attention on themes or interrelationships with other sources. Each chapter concludes with a chronology designed to orient the student to the broader context of history, and a series of study questions that can form the basis of oral discussion or written analysis. The questions do not seek mere regurgitation of information, but demand a more thoughtful response based on reflective analysis of the primary sources.

Use of the Book

Aspects of Western Civilization offers the instructor a wide variety of didactic applications. The chapters fit into a more or less standard lecture format and are ordered chronologically. An entire chapter may be assigned for oral discussion, or sections from each chapter may satisfy particular interests or requirements. Some of the chapters provide extensive treatment of a broad historical topic ("The Sword of Faith: Western Civilization During the Middle Ages"; "'I Am the State!': The Development of Absolutism in England and France"; "'Dare to Know!': The Revolution of the Mind in the Seventeenth and Eighteenth Centuries"; "'Liberty, Equality, Fraternity!': Romanticism and Revolution"). In order to make them manageable and effective, I have grouped them into topical sections (with correspondingly labeled study questions) that can be utilized separately, if so desired.

The chapters may also be assigned for written analysis. One of the most important concerns of both instructor and student in an introductory class is the written assignment. *Aspects of Western Civilization* has been designed to provide self-contained topics that are problem-oriented, promote reflection and analysis, and encourage responsible citation of particular primary sources. The study questions for each chapter should generally produce an eight- to ten-page paper.

Acknowledgments

I would particularly like to thank friends and colleagues at Columbus School for Girls who contributed their expertise and enthusiasm to this book. Susan Altan lent her perspective and sensitive awareness of women's issues at critical moments when new avenues of thought were most needed. Daniel Hall and Thomas Tappan advised me on several scientific and technological matters that broadened the scope of the text immeasurably. Anne Lodge and Mary Ann Leonard offered their unique perspectives regarding ethical issues that often caused me to pause and certainly forced the introduction of new questions into the discussion. Mary Alice Fite provided me with material and literary insight that added greatly to the accuracy of the text, and Jack Guy and Patricia Niehoff-Smith read drafts of some chapters, offering sterling commentary throughout. Thanks also to the students of Columbus School for Girls, who continue to "test" the chapters in this book with their typical diligence and hard work; the final product has benefited greatly from their suggestions and ideas. This revision has also benefitted from the insight and suggestions of Eleanor McCluskey, Broward Community College, Florida and Charles Parker, University of St. Louis, who reviewed the text in its preliminary stages. Finally, I owe an immeasurable debt to my wife, Ann, who suffered all the outrageous fortune and disruption that goes into writing a book of this kind over a period of years—she did it with me.

P. M. R.

PART I

THE EARLIEST CIVILIZATIONS

1

Civilization in the Ancient Near East: Mesopotamia, Egypt, and Israel

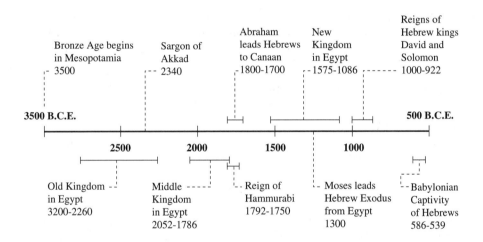

Bronze Age begins in Mesopotamia
- 3500

Sargon of Akkad
-- 2340

Abraham leads Hebrews to Canaan
-1800-1700

New Kingdom in Egypt
-1575-1086

Reigns of Hebrew kings David and Solomon
1000-922

3500 B.C.E.   500 B.C.E.

2500   2000   1500   1000

Old Kingdom in Egypt 3200-2260

Middle Kingdom in Egypt 2052-1786

Reign of Hammurabi 1792-1750

Moses leads Hebrew Exodus from Egypt 1300

Babylonian Captivity of Hebrews 586-539

If a man destroy the eye of another man, they shall destroy his eye.

—*Code of Hammurabi*

You are a lifespan in yourself; one lives by you.

—*Hymn to Aton*

Can you see anything? Yes, wonderful things!

—Howard Carter (upon opening King Tut's tomb)

3

In the beginning, God created heaven and earth.

—Genesis 1:1

And what does the Lord require of you, but to do justly, and to love
mercy, and to walk humbly with your God.

—Micah 6:8

CHAPTER THEMES

- *Systems of Government:* How did the monarchies in Mesopotamia, Egypt,
  and Israel differ from one another? What is the best form of government
  for primitive societies?

- *Beliefs and Spirituality:* How did the belief systems of the ancient Near
  East contribute to the unity of society? In what ways were these societies
  primarily spiritual in nature? How radical a conception is monotheism?

- *Historical Change and Transition:* What were the main contributions of
  ancient Near Eastern societies to Western Civilization? In what specific
  ways did civilization progress during this time?

- *The Big Picture:* What are the most important political, social, and spiritual characteristics that each society must possess in order to lay the foundations for the transmission of culture?

It is difficult to trace the origins of a culture and even more so to pinpoint the
conditions that fostered the growth and development of Western Civilization.
Still, most historians agree that our contemporary world owes a great deal to the
Near Eastern societies of Mesopotamia, Egypt, and Israel. We look to them for
the conception of organized government, writing, law, complex religious ideas,
and ethical values—the cornerstones of modern society.

Beginning about 3500 B.C.E., there was an influx of people into the region of
the Fertile Crescent, the land north of the Persian Gulf that now encompasses
Iran and Iraq. This area was devoid of natural barriers, such as mountain ranges,
and so provided easy access for nomadic peoples. It was here that Western Civilization first began, in the land watered by the flooding of the Tigris and Euphrates Rivers, whose silt allowed for abundant harvests and prosperity. The region became known as Mesopotamia ("the land between the rivers"), and it
fostered many distinct cultures. The Sumerians, who occupied the southern area
at the confluence of the two rivers, assumed cultural leadership over the region
by developing a syllabic writing script called cuneiform. Although conquerors
would establish military control over the region, Sumerian literary and religious
ideas and values proved a continuing influence.

Mesopotamia, at least initially, was organized on the basis of independent city-states. Each city had its own king and priests and conducted its own foreign policy, often in alliance with other city-states. The king's responsibilities included political and military leadership as well as supervision of the priests and their sacrifices to the gods. It is important to note that Mesopotamian kings were not considered to be divine themselves, but rather acted as representatives of the gods. The independence of the city-states often gave way to conquerors like Sargon the Great, who united the area briefly about 2300 B.C.E. Because of the open geographical access to the region, Mesopotamia was overrun by a succession of invaders, such as the Babylonians, Kassites, Assyrians, and finally Persians in the sixth century B.C.E. But the insecurity of the region did not limit the development of literature and law, which were its special contributions.

The second great civilization of the ancient Near East was Egypt. While Mesopotamia suffered from the uncertainties of invasion and swift transition, Egypt was generally secure and isolated because of the surrounding, prohibitive deserts. Egypt remains a land with an aura of mystery, reinforced by a fascination for the colossal statues of Ramses II at Abu Simbel, the Temple of Karnak at Luxor, the overwhelming presence of the pyramids, mummification, and the wealth of Tutankhamon's tomb. But it is perhaps the Egyptian religion with its emphasis on death and the netherworld that most reflects the endless order and regulation of life. Just as the Nile River promotes unity within the country and its annual flooding symbolizes the recurring cycle of life, so too did the Pharaoh serve as a unifying presence. He was a god incarnate and was worshiped as such while he was living; in death he rose to the sky to be born anew each day with the cycle of the sun. Thus the Egyptians' close connection between state and religion, a theocracy of sorts, serves as a foundation for one of the more enduring themes in history.

Nowhere, however, did religion play a greater role than in the development of Hebrew civilization. The Hebrews were a nomadic people whose wanderings and eventual establishment in the promised land of Canaan (modern-day Israel) form the narrative story of the Old Testament of the Bible. But more than this, the story concerns the relationship of Yahweh (or God) to his chosen people, the Hebrews. Many other Near Eastern conquerors held more land and ruled more people, but no one influenced the course of Western Civilization more emphatically than did the Hebrews. Their concern with moral law, right action, and adherence to monotheistic principles has formed the basis for Christianity and Islam in the modern world.

This chapter investigates the three main civilizations of the ancient Near East, with special concern for the relationships between kingship and religion. For it is through adherence to principles of government and religion that society is ordered and civilization proceeds.

Mesopotamian Civilization

Secular Authority and Order

The Reign of Sargon

The city-states that developed in the region of Mesopotamia after about 3500 B.C.E. were ruled by various kings who established local control. One of the first kings to successfully conquer and control the region was Sargon of Akkad, who ruled around 2300 B.C.E. The following excerpt from a tablet in the British Museum recounts his authority.

Sargon, King of Akkad, through the royal gift of Ishtar was exalted, and he possessed no foe nor rival. His glory over the world he poured out. The Sea in the East he crossed, and in the eleventh year the Country of the West in its full extent his hand subdued. He united them under one control; he set up his images in the West; their booty he brought over at his word. Over the hosts of the world he reigned supreme. Against Kassala he marched, and he turned Kassala into mounds and heaps of ruins; he destroyed the land and left not enough for a bird to rest thereon. Afterward in his old age all the lands revolted against him, and they besieged him in Akkad; and Sargon went forth to battle and defeated them; he accomplished their overthrow, and their widespreading host he destroyed. Afterward he attacked the land of Subartu in his might, and they submitted to his arms, and Sargon settled that revolt, and defeated them; he accomplished their overthrow, and their wide-spreading host he destroyed, and he brought their possessions into Akkad. The soil from the trenches of Babylon he removed, and the boundaries of Akkad he made like those of Babylon. But because of the evil which he had committed, the great lord Marduk was angry, and he destroyed his people by famine. From the rising of the sun unto the setting of the sun they opposed him and gave him no rest.

The Code of Hammurabi

From 2000 to 1600 B.C.E., the city-states of Mesopotamia endured a period of nearly continuous warfare which saw shifting alliances and frequent chaos. The most dominant personality of the age, Hammurabi, established his control over the region from about 1800 to 1750 B.C.E. and ruled from the city of Babylon. His great contribution to Western Civilization was a series of laws that sought to establish justice within his empire. This concept of equity, which remedied a large

"The Reign of Sargon" is from George W. Botsford, ed., *A Source-Book of Ancient History* (New York: Macmillan, 1912), pp. 27–28.

"The Code of Hammurabi" is from Robert F. Harper, trans., *The Code of Hammurabi* (Chicago: University of Chicago Press, 1904).

number of abuses, influenced law codes yet to come, most notably those of Greece and Rome. In the following passages, note the continual emphasis on fairness in the regulation of property, trade, debt, family relations, and personal injury.

When the lofty Anu, king of the Anunnaki gods, and Enlil, lord of heaven and earth, he who determines the destiny of the land . . . pronounced the lofty name of Babylon; when they made it famous among the quarters of the world and in its midst established an everlasting kingdom whose foundations were firm as heaven and earth; [they] . . . named me, Hammurabi, the exalted prince, the worshiper of the gods, to cause justice to prevail in the land, to destroy the wicked and the evil, to prevent the strong from oppressing the weak, to go forth like the sun over the black-headed people, to enlighten the land to further the welfare of the people. Hammurabi, the shepherd named by Enlil, am I, who brought about plenty and abundance; . . . the powerful king, the sun of Babylon, who caused light to go forth over the lands of Sumer and Akkad; the king who caused the four quarters of the world to render obedience; the favorite of Ishtar, am I.

When Marduk sent me to rule the people and to bring help to the country, I established law and justice in the language of the land and promoted the welfare of the people. At that time [I decreed]:

1. If a man bring accusation against another man, charging him with murder, but cannot prove it, the accuser shall be put to death.
3. If a man bear false witness in a case, or does not establish the testimony that he has given, if that case be a case involving life, that man shall be put to death.
4. If he bear [false] witness concerning grain or money, he shall himself bear the penalty imposed in that case.
5. If a judge pronounce a judgment, render a decision, deliver a verdict duly signed and sealed, and afterward alter his judgment, they shall call that judge to account for the alteration of the judgment which he has pronounced, and he shall pay twelve-fold the penalty in that judgment; and, in the assembly, they shall expel him from his seat of judgment, and with the judges in a case he shall not take his seat.
22. If a man practice robbery and is captured, that man shall be put to death.
23. If the robber is not captured, the man who has been robbed shall, in the presence of god, make an itemized statement of his loss, and the city and the governor in whose province and jurisdiction the robbery was committed shall compensate him for whatever was lost.
24. If it be a life [that is lost], the city and governor shall pay one mina [about one pound] of silver to his heirs.
53. If a man neglects to maintain his dike and does not strengthen it, and a break is made in his dike and the water carries away the farmland, the man in whose dike the break has been made shall replace the grain which has been damaged.

54. If he is not able to replace the grain, they shall sell him and his goods, and the farmers whose grain the water has carried away shall divide [the results of the sale].

55. If a man opens his canal for irrigation and neglects it and the water carries away an adjacent field, he shall pay out grain on the basis of the adjacent field.

109. If bad characters gather in the house of a wine seller and he does not arrest those bad characters and bring them to the palace, that wine seller shall be put to death.

110. If a priestess who is not living in a convent opens a wine shop or enters a wine shop for a drink, they shall burn that woman.

117. If a man be in debt and sell his wife, son, or daughter, or bind them over to service, for three years they shall work in the house of their purchaser or master; in the fourth year they shall be given their freedom.

128. If a man takes a wife and does not arrange a contract for her, that woman is not a wife.

129. If the wife of a man is caught lying with another man, they shall bind them and throw them into the water.

138. If a man wishes to put away his wife who has not borne him children, he shall give her money to the amount of her marriage price and he shall make good to her the dowry which she brought from her father's house and then he may put her away.

142. If a woman hates her husband and says, "You may not have me," the city council shall inquire into her case; and if she has been careful and without reproach and her husband has been going about and greatly belittling her, that woman has no blame. She may take her dowry and go to her father's house.

143. If she has not been careful but has gadded about, neglecting her house and belittling her husband, they shall throw that woman into the water.

168. If a man set his face to disinherit his son and say to the judges, "I will disinherit my son," the judges shall inquire into his record, and if the son has not committed a crime sufficiently grave to cut him off from sonship, the father may not cut off his son from sonship.

195. If a son strike his father, they shall cut off his hand.

196. If a man destroy the eye of another man, they shall destroy his eye.

197. If he break another man's bone, they shall break his bone.

199. If he destroy the eye of a man's slave or break a bone of a man's slave, he shall pay one-half his price.

200. If a man knock out a tooth of a man of his own rank, they shall knock out his tooth.

229. If a builder build a house for a man and does not make its construction sound, and the house which he has built collapses and causes the death of the owner of the house, that builder shall be put to death.

233. If a builder build a house for a man and does not make its construction sound, and a wall cracks, that builder shall strengthen that wall at his own expense.

[These are] the just laws which Hammurabi, the wise king, established and by which he gave the land stable support and good government. Hammurabi, the perfect king, am I. . . .

The great gods called me, and I am the guardian shepherd whose scepter is just and whose beneficent shadow is spread over my city. In my bosom I carried the people of the land of Sumer and Akkad; under my protection they prospered; I governed them in peace; in my wisdom I sheltered them.

In order that the strong might not oppress the weak, that justice be given to the orphans and the widow, in Babylon, . . . for the pronouncing of judgments in the land, for the rendering of decisions for the land, and to give justice to the oppressed, my weighty words I have written upon my monument, and in the presence of my image as king of justice have I established it.

Mesopotamian Thought and Religion
The Epic of Gilgamesh

The Sumerians who inhabited the southern region of Mesopotamia were the first people in Western Civilization to produce epic tales about deities and human heroes. The Epic of Gilgamesh dates from about 2000 B.C.E. and is a collection of stories about the Sumerian king of Uruk. In the following passages, Gilgamesh, confronted with the reality of his friend Enkidu's death, sets out to find Utnapishtim, the only man to whom the gods have given eternal life. Gilgamesh discovers that he must accept the inevitability of his own death.

There follows the Mesopotamian tale of the Flood and the biblical account contained in the Old Testament. Flood epics were quite common in ancient literature and represented a cleansing of the community in accordance with a higher ethical law. But compare the two accounts closely, especially with regard to the attitudes and actions of the deities.

The Quest for Eternal Life

Bitterly Gilgamesh wept for his friend Enkidu; he wandered over the wilderness as a hunter, he roamed over the plains; in his bitterness he cried, "How can I rest, how can I be at peace? Despair is in my heart. What my brother is now, that shall I be when I am dead. Because I am afraid of death I will go as best I can to find Utnapishtim whom they call the Faraway, for he has entered the assembly of the gods." So Gilgamesh travelled over the wilderness, he wandered over the grasslands, a long journey, in search of Utnapishtim, whom the gods took after the deluge; and they set him to live in the land of Dilmun, in the garden of the sun; and to him alone of men they gave everlasting life. . . .

"The Epic of Gilgamesh" is from N. K. Sandars, trans., *The Epic of Gilgamesh* (Baltimore, Md., and Harmondsworth, Middlesex: Penguin Classics, 1960), pp. 94, 102–110. Copyright © N. K. Sandars, 1960, 1964. Reproduced by permission of Penguin Books Ltd.

Gilgamesh said to him [Utnapishtim], "Why should not my cheeks be starved and my face drawn? Despair is in my heart and my face is the face of one who has made a long journey. It was burned with heat and with cold. Why should I not wander over the pastures? My friend, my younger brother who seized and killed the Bull of Heaven and overthrew Humbaba in the cedar forest, my friend who was very dear to me and endured dangers beside me, Enkidu, my brother whom I loved, the end of mortality has overtaken him. I wept for him seven days and nights till the worm fastened on him. Because of my brother I am afraid of death; because of my brother I stray through the wilderness. His fate lies heavy upon me. How can I be silent, how can I rest? He is dust and I shall die also and be laid in the earth for ever. . . . Oh, father Utnapishtim, you who have entered the assembly of the gods, I wish to question you concerning the living and the dead, how shall I find the life for which I am searching?"

Utnapishtim said, "There is no permanence. Do we build a house to stand for ever, do we seal a contract to hold for all time? Do brothers divide an inheritance to keep for ever, does the flood-time of rivers endure? It is only the nymph of the dragon-fly who sheds her larva and sees the sun in his glory. From the days of old there is no permanence. The sleeping and the dead, how alike they are, they are like a painted death. What is there between the master and the servant when both have fulfilled their doom? When the Annunaki, the judges, come together, and Mammetun the mother of destinies, together they decree the fates of men. Life and death they allot but the day of death they do not disclose." . . .

The destiny was fulfilled which the father of the gods, Enlil of the mountain, had decreed for Gilgamesh: "In nether-earth the darkness will show him a light; of mankind, all that are known, none will leave a monument for generations to come to compare with his. The heroes, the wise men, like the new moon have their waxing and waning. Men will say, 'Who has ever ruled with might and with power like him?' As in the dark month, the month of shadows, so without him there is no light. O Gilgamesh, this was the meaning of your dream. You were given the kingship, such was your destiny, everlasting life was not your destiny. Because of this do not be sad at heart, do not be grieved or oppressed; he has given you power to bind and to loose, to be the darkness and the light of mankind. He has given unexampled supremacy over the people, in victory in battle from which no fugitive returns, in forays and assaults from which there is no going back. But do not abuse this power, deal justly with your servants in the palace, deal justly with the face of the Sun."

The Story of the Flood

Then Gilgamesh said. . . . "I look at you now, Utnapishtim, and your appearance is no different than mine; there is nothing strange in your features. . . . Tell me truly, how was it that you came to enter the company of the gods and to possess everlasting life?" Utnapishtim said to Gilgamesh, "I will reveal to you a mystery, I will tell you a secret of the gods."

"You know the city Shurrupak, it stands on the banks of Euphrates? That city grew old and the gods that were in it were old. There was Anu, lord of the firmament, their father, and warrior Enlil their counsellor, Ninurta the helper, and Ennugi watcher over canals; and with them also was Ea. In those days the world teemed, the people multiplied, the world bellowed like a wild bull, and the great god was aroused by the clamour. Enlil heard the clamour and he said to the gods in council, 'The uproar of mankind is intolerable and sleep is no longer possible by reason of the babel.' So the gods in their hearts were moved to let loose the deluge; but my lord Ea warned me in a dream. He whispered their words to my house of reeds, . . . 'O man of Shurrupak, . . . tear down your house and build a boat, abandon possessions and look for life, despise worldly goods and save your soul alive. . . . These are the measurements of the barque as you shall build her: let her beam equal her length, let her deck be roofed like the vault that covers the abyss; then take up into the boat the seed of all living creatures.'

"When I had understood I said to my lord, 'Behold, what you have commanded I will honour and perform, but how shall I answer the people, the city, the elders?' Then Ea opened his mouth and said to me, his servant, 'Tell them this: I have learnt that Enlil is wrathful against me, I dare no longer walk in his land nor live in his city; I will go down to the Gulf to dwell with Ea my lord. But on you he will rain down abundance, rare fish and shy wild-fowl, a rich harvest-tide. In the evening the rider of the storm will bring you wheat in torrents.'

"In the first light of dawn all my household gathered round me, the children brought pitch and the men whatever was necessary. . . . On the seventh day the boat was complete. . . .

"I loaded into her all that I had of gold and of living things, my family, my kin, the beasts of the field both wild and tame, and all the craftsmen. I sent them on board, for the time that Shamash had ordained was already fulfilled when he said, 'In the evening, when the rider of the storm sends down the destroying rain, enter the boat and batten her down.' This time was fulfilled, the evening came, the rider of the storm sent down the rain. I looked out at the weather and it was terrible, so I too boarded the boat and battened her down. . . .

"With the first light of dawn a black cloud came from the horizon. . . . One whole day the tempest raged gathering fury as it went, it poured over the people like the tides of battle; a man could not see his brother nor the people be seen from heaven. Even the gods were terrified at the flood, they fled to the highest heaven, . . . they crouched against the walls, cowering like curs. . . . The great gods of heaven and of hell wept, they covered their mouths.

"For six days and six nights the winds blew, torrent and tempest and flood overwhelmed the world . . . like warring hosts. When the seventh day dawned the storm from the south subsided, the sea grew calm, the flood was stilled; I looked at the face of the world and there was silence, all mankind was turned to clay. The surface of the sea stretched as flat as a roof-top; I opened a hatch and the light fell on my face. Then I bowed low, I sat down and I wept, the tears streamed down my face, for on every side was the waste of water. . . . I threw everything open to the four winds, made a sacrifice and poured out a libation on the mountain top. . . . When the gods smelled the sweet savor, they gathered like flies over the sacrifice. . . .

"When Enlil had come, when he saw the boat, he was wrath and swelled with anger at the gods, the host of heaven, 'Has any of these mortals escaped? Not one was to have survived the destruction.' . . . Then Ea opened his mouth and spoke to warrior Enlil, 'Wisest of gods, hero Enlil, how could you so senselessly bring down the flood?

> " 'Lay upon the sinner his sin,
> Lay upon the transgressor his transgression,
> Punish him a little when he breaks loose,
> Do not drive him too hard or he perishes;
> Would that a lion had ravaged mankind
> Rather than the flood,
> Would that a wolf had ravaged mankind
> Rather than the flood,
> Would that famine had wasted the world
> Rather than the flood,
> Would that pestilence had wasted mankind
> Rather than the flood.

It was not I that revealed the secret of the gods; the wise man learned it in a dream. Now take your counsel what shall be done with him.'

"Then Enlil went up into the boat, he took me by the hand and my wife and made us enter the boat and kneel down on either side, he standing between us. He touched our foreheads to bless us saying, 'In time past Utnapishtim was a mortal man; henceforth he and his wife shall live in the distance at the mouth of the rivers.' Thus it was that the gods took me and placed me here to live in the distance at the mouth of the rivers."

The Biblical Flood

God said to Noah, "I have decided that the end has come for all living things, for the earth is full of lawlessness because of human beings. So I am now about to destroy them and the earth. Make yourself an ark out of resinous wood. Make it of reeds and caulk it with pitch inside and out. This is how to make it: the length of the ark is to be three hundred cubits, its breadth fifty cubits, and its height thirty cubits. . . .

"For my part, I am going to send the flood, the waters, on earth, to destroy living things having the breath of life under heaven: everything on earth is to

"The Biblical Flood" is from Genesis 6.13–9.1, from *The Jerusalem Bible* by Alexander Jones, ed., pp. 24–26. Copyright © 1966 by Darton, Longman & Todd, Ltd., and Doubleday, a division of Bantam, Doubleday, Dell Publishing Group, Inc. Reprinted by permission.

perish. But with you I shall establish my covenant and you will go aboard the ark, yourself, your sons, your wife, and your sons' wives along with you. From all living creatures, from all living things, you must take two of each kind aboard the ark, to save their lives with yours; they must be a male and a female. Of every species of bird, of every kind of animal and of every kind of creature that creeps along the ground, two must go with you so that their lives may be saved. . . ." Noah did this, exactly as God commanded him. . . .

The flood lasted forty days on earth. The waters swelled, lifting the ark until it floated off the ground. . . . The waters rose higher and higher above the ground until all the highest mountains under the whole of heaven were submerged. . . . Every living thing on the face of the earth was wiped out, people, animals, creeping things and birds; they were wiped off the earth and only Noah was left, and those with him in the ark. . . .

Then God said to Noah, "Come out of the ark, you, your wife, your sons, and your sons' wives with you. Bring out all the animals with you, all living things. . . ." Then Noah built an altar to Yahweh and, choosing from all the clean animals and all the clean birds, he presented burnt offerings on the altar. Yahweh smelt the pleasing smell and said to himself, "Never again will I curse the earth because of human beings, because their heart contrives evil from their infancy. Never again will I strike down every living thing as I have done. . . ." God blessed Noah and his sons and said to them, "Breed, multiply and fill the earth."

The Mesopotamian View of Death

Historians can often tell much about a civilization by the way it regards the finality of death or the existence of an afterlife. The following poems are good examples of the Mesopotamian view.

The Mother Sings

Hark the piping!
My heart is piping in the wilderness
　　where the young man once went free.
He is a prisoner now in death's kingdom,
　　lies bound where once he lived.
The ewe gives up her lamb
and the nanny-goat her kid.
My heart is piping in the wilderness
　　an instrument of grief.
Now she is coming to death's kingdom,
she is the mother desolate

"The Mesopotamian View of Death" is from N. K. Sandars, trans., *Poems of Heaven and Hell from Ancient Mesopotamia* (Baltimore, Md., and Harmondsworth, Middlesex: Penguin Books, 1971), pp. 163–164. Copyright © N. K. Sandars, 1971. Reproduced by permission of Penguin Books Ltd.

in a desolate place; where once
he was alive, now he lies
like a young bull felled to the ground.
Into his face she stares, seeing
what she has lost—his mother
who has lost him to death's kingdom.
O the agony she bears,
shuddering in the wilderness,
she is the mother suffering so much.
    'It is you,'
she cried to him,
    'but you are changed.'
The agony, the agony she bears.
Woe to the house and the inner room.

The Son's Reply

There can be no answer
    to her desolate calling,
it is echoed in the wilderness,
    for I cannot answer.
Though the grass will shoot
    from the land
I am not grass, I cannot come
    to her calling.
The waters rise for her,
I am not water to come
    for her wailing,
I am not shoots of grass
    in a dead land.

A Prayer to the Gods of Night

Dating from about 2000–1500 B.C.E., this prayer reflects the contemplative peace of night, when the gods and stars seemed near.

They are lying down, the Great Ones,
the bars have fallen, the bolts are shot,
the crowds and all the people rest,
the open gates are locked.
The gods of the land, the goddesses,

"A Prayer to the Gods of Night" is from N. K. Sandars, trans., *Poems of Heaven and Hell from Ancient Mesopotamia* (Baltimore, Md., and Harmondsworth, Middlesex: Penguin Books, 1971), p. 175. Copyright © N. K. Sandars, 1971. Reproduced by permission of Penguin Books Ltd.

Shamash Sin Adad Ishtar,
sun, moon, turmoil, love
lie down to sleep in heaven.
The judgment seat is empty now,
for no god now is still at work.
Night has drawn down the curtain,
the temples and the sanctuaries are silent, dark.
Now the traveller calls to his god,
defendant and plaintiff sleep in peace,
for the judge of truth, the father of the fatherless,
Shamash, has gone to his chamber.
'O Great Ones, Princes of the Night,
Bright Ones, Gibil the furnace, Irra
war-lord of the Underworld,
Bow-star and Yoke, Orion, Pleiades, Dragon,
the Wild Bull, the Goat, and the Great Bear,
stand by me in my divination.
By this lamb I am offering,
may truth appear!'

Egyptian Civilization

The Authority of the Pharaohs

The king of Egypt, or Pharaoh (meaning "Great House"), possessed an authority rarely achieved in Western Civilization. He was regarded as a god incarnate who upon death rose to take his place in the sky as the deity, Horus. In the Old Kingdom (3200–2260 B.C.E.), pharaonic authority was great and the pyramids were built to house the body of the dead king. Egyptians considered preservation of the body essential for use in the afterlife, so they perfected the art of mummification. The following selections from the Greek historian Herodotus show the great authority of the Pharaoh in the Old Kingdom. Herodotus describes the commitment demanded by Cheops, for whom the Great Pyramid is named. An account of the process of mummification follows.

Building the Pyramids
HERODOTUS

After Cheops had ascended the throne, he brought the country into every manner of evil. First closing all the temples, he forbade sacrificing there, then ordered all the Egyptians to work for him. Some he told to draw stones

"Building the Pyramids" is from Herodotus, *History*, 2.124, in *A Source-Book of Ancient History*, ed. George W. Botsford (New York: Macmillan, 1912), pp. 6–8.

from the quarries in the Arabian mountains about the Nile; others were ordered to receive them after they had been carried over the river in boats, and
to draw them to the Libyan mountains. And they worked in groups of
100,000 men, each group for three months continually. Ten years of oppression for the people were required for making the causeway by which they
dragged the stones. This causeway which they built was not a much inferior
work to the pyramid itself, as it seems to me; . . . it is made of polished stones
and engraved with the figures of living beings. Ten years were required for
this, and for the works on the mound, where the pyramids stand, and for the
underground chambers in the island, which he intended as sepulchral vaults
for his own use, and lastly for the canal which he dug from the Nile. The
pyramid was built in 20 years; it is square; each side measures 800 feet and its
height is the same; the stones are polished and fitted together with the utmost exactness. Not one of them is less than 30 feet in length.

The pyramid was built in steps, in the manner of an altar. After laying the
base, they lifted the remaining stones to their places by means of machines,
made of short pieces of wood. The first machine raised them from the ground
to the top of the first step; and when the stone had been lifted thus far, it was
drawn to the top of the second step by another machine; for they had as many
machines as steps. . . . At any rate, the highest parts were finished first, then the
next, and so on till they came to the parts resting on the ground, namely the
base. It is set down in Egyptian writing on the pyramid how much was spent on
radishes and leeks and onions for the workmen; and I remember well the interpreter read the sum of 1600 talents of silver. Now if these figures are correct,
how much more must have been spent on the iron with which they worked, and
on the food and clothing of the workmen, considering the length of time which
the work lasted, and an additional period, as I understand, during which they
cut and brought the stones, and made the excavations.

Mummification

HERODOTUS

There are a set of men in Egypt who practice the art of embalming, and make it
their proper business. These persons, when a body is brought to them, show the
bearers various models of corpses made in wood, and painted so as to resemble
nature. . . . The mode of embalming, according to the most perfect process, is
the following:—They take first a crooked piece of iron, and with it draw out the
brain through the nostrils, thus getting rid of a portion, while the skull is
cleared of the rest by rinsing with drugs; next they make a cut along the flank
with a sharp Ethiopian stone, and take out the whole contents of the abdomen,
which they then cleanse, washing it thoroughly with palm wine, and again

"Mummification" is from Herodotus, *History*, 2.86, 87, 90, in *The History of Herodotus*, trans.
George Rawlinson (New York: E. P. Dutton, 1910), pp. 154–156.

frequently with an infusion of pounded aromatics. After this they fill the cavity with the purest bruised myrrh, with cassia, and every other sort of spice, except frankincense, and sew up the opening. Then the body is placed in natron [hydrated sodium carbonate] for seventy days, and covered entirely over. After the expiration of that space of time, which must not be exceeded, the body is washed, and wrapped round, from head to foot, with bandages of fine linen cloth, smeared over with gum, which is used generally by the Egyptians in the place of glue, and in this state it is given back to the relations, who enclose it in a wooden case which they have had made for the purpose, shaped into the figure of a man. Then fastening the case, they place it in a sepulchral chamber, upright against the wall. Such is the most costly way of embalming the dead.

If persons wish to avoid expense, and choose the second process, the following is the method pursued:—Syringes are filled with oil made from the cedar-tree, which is then, without any incision or disemboweling, injected into the abdomen. The passage by which it might be likely to return is stopped, and the body laid in natron the prescribed number of days. At the end of the time the cedar-oil is allowed to make its escape; and such is its power that it brings with it the whole stomach and intestines in a liquid state. The natron meanwhile has dissolved the flesh, and so nothing is left of the dead body but the skin and the bones. It is returned in this condition to the relatives, without any further trouble being bestowed upon it.

The third method of embalming, which is practised in the case of the poorer classes, is to rinse out the intestines and let the body lie in natron the seventy days, after which it is at once given to those who come to fetch it away. . . .

Whensoever any one, Egyptian or foreigner, has lost his life by falling prey to a crocodile, or by drowning in the river, the law compels the inhabitants of the city near which the body is cast up to have it embalmed, and to bury it in one of the sacred repositories with all possible magnificence. No one may touch the corpse, not even any of the friends or relatives, but only the priests of the Nile, who prepare it for burial with their own hands—regarding it as something more than the mere body of a man—and themselves lay it in the tomb.

Ramses the Great

Ramses II (1301–1234 B.C.E.) was one of the greatest of all Egyptian Pharaohs. His reign has been immortalized by his magnificent construction projects, such as the temple of Karnak at Luxor and the enormous statues of Abu Simbel. In addition, his fame is recorded in the Old Testament as the Pharaoh under whom the Exodus of the Hebrews took place. His mummy has been remarkably well preserved; we can tell that he died in his nineties and that he suffered from acne, tuberculosis, and poor circulation of the blood. His tomb had been plundered by

"Ramses the Great" is from George W. Botsford, ed., *A Source-Book of Ancient History* (New York: Macmillan, 1912), pp. 10–12. Translation modernized by the editor.

ancient grave robbers, and one can only imagine its former gold and splendor. The following passage is from an inscription found on the temple at Abu Simbel. In it, the god Ptah speaks to his son, Ramses.

Thus speaks Ptah-Totunen with the high plumes, armed with horns, the father of the gods, to his son who loves him. . . .

Num and Ptah have nourished your childhood, they leap with joy when they see you made after my likeness, noble, great, exalted. The great princesses of the house of Ptah and the Hathors of the temple of Tem are in festival, their hearts are full of gladness, their hands take the drum with joy, when they see your person beautiful and lovely like my Majesty. . . . King Ramses, I grant you to cut the mountains into statues immense, gigantic, everlasting; I grant that foreign lands find for you precious stone to inscribe the monuments with thy name.

I give you to succeed in all the works which you have done. I give you all kinds of workmen, all that goes on two or four feet, all that flies and all that has wings. I have put in the heart of all nations to offer you what they have done; themselves, princes great and small, with one heart seek to please you, King Ramses.

The temple of Ramses II at Abu Simbel is remarkable for its four colossal figures of the Pharaoh. They reflect the great authority of the famous Egyptian king. *(Eugene Gordon/Pearson Education/PH College)*

You have built a great residence to fortify the boundary of the land, the city of Ramses; it is established on the earth like the four pillars of the sky; you have constructed within a royal palace, where festivals are celebrated to you as is done for me within. I have set the crown on your head with my own hands, when you appear in the great hall of the double throne; and men and gods have praised your name like mine when my festival is celebrated.

You have carved my statues and built my shrines as I have done in times of old. You reign in my place on my throne; I fill your limbs with life and happiness, I am behind you to protect you; I give you health and strength; I cause Egypt to be submitted to you; and I supply the two countries with pure life. King Ramses, I grant that the strength, the vigor, and the might of your sword be felt among all countries; you cast down the hearts of all nations; I have put them under your feet; you come forth every day in order that foreign prisoners be brought to you; the chiefs and the great of all nations offer you their children. I give them to your gallant sword that you may do with them what you like. King Ramses, I grant that the fear of you be in the minds of all and your command in their hearts. I grant that your valor reach all countries, and that the dread of you be spread over all lands; the princes tremble at your thought, and your majesty is [evident]; they come to you as supplicants to implore your mercy. You give life to whomever you please; the throne of all nations is in your possession. . . .

King Ramses, . . . the mountains, the water, and the stone walls which are on the earth are shaken when they hear your excellent name, since they have seen what I have accomplished for you; which is that the land of the Hittites should be subjected to your rule. . . . Their chiefs are prisoners, all their property is the tribute in the dependency of the living king. Their royal daughter is at the head of them; she comes to soften the heart of King Ramses; her merits are marvelous, but she does not know the goodness which is in your heart.

The Tomb of King Tut

HOWARD CARTER

One of the most famous dramas of exploration of the ancient world took place in November 1922, when the archaeologist Howard Carter discovered and opened the tomb of Tutankhamon. King Tut, as he is familiarly called, was a rather unimportant king of the Eighteenth Dynasty of the New Kingdom (ca. 1350 B.C.E.) who achieved more fame in death than he ever did in life. Carter's discovery in the Valley of the Kings of a tomb which had not been plundered by ancient grave robbers was a find of unparalleled dimension. Apart from the artistic and

Archaeologist Howard Carter gazes into the tomb of the Pharaoh Tutankhamon—a sight no one had beheld for over three thousand years. *(Photography by Egyptian Expedition, The Metropolitan Museum of Art)*

historical significance of the discovery, the magnificent artifacts of gold and al-abaster that were recovered captured the popular imagination and created a pas-sion for things Egyptian as well as a renewed interest in Egyptian history. Stories of curses and violations of a sacred tomb spawned rumors and even movies in the 1930s. But Carter, a methodical archaeologist, maintained the integrity of his find through detailed cataloguing and scholarly commentary.

In the following passage, Carter narrates his discovery of Tutankhamon's tomb. Together with Lord Carnarvon, who privately financed the excavation, he beheld what no one had seen for over three thousand years.

It was clear by now beyond any question that we actually had before us the en-trance to a tomb, but doubts, born of previous disappointments, persisted in creeping in. There was always the horrible possibility . . . that the tomb was an unfinished one, never completed and never used: if it had been finished there was the depressing probability that it had been completely plundered in ancient times. On the other hand, there was just the chance of an un-touched or only partially plundered tomb, and it was with ill-suppressed ex-citement that I watched the descending steps of the staircase, as one by one they came to light. . . . Work progressed more rapidly now; step succeeded step, and at the level of the twelfth, towards sunset, there was disclosed the upper part of a doorway, blocked, plastered, and sealed.

A sealed doorway—it was actually true, then! Our years of patient labour were to be rewarded after all, and I think my first feeling was one of congratu-lation that my faith in the Valley had not been unjustified. With excitement growing to fever heat I searched the seal impressions on the door for evi-dence of the owner, but could find no name: the only decipherable ones were those of the well-known royal necropolis seal, the jackal and nine cap-tives. Two facts, however, were clear: first, the employment of this royal seal was certain evidence that the tomb had been constructed for a person of very high standing; and second, that the sealed door . . . was sufficiently clear proof that at least from that date it had never been entered. With that for the moment I had to be content. . . .

It was a thrilling moment for an excavator. Alone, save for my native work-men, I found myself, after years of comparatively unproductive labour, on the threshold of what might prove to be a magnificent discovery. Anything, liter-ally anything, might lie beyond that passage, and it needed all my self-control to keep from breaking down the doorway, and investigating then and there.

One thing puzzled me, and that was the smallness of the opening in com-parison with the ordinary Valley tombs. The design was certainly of the Eigh-teenth Dynasty. Could it be the tomb of a noble buried here by royal con-sent? Was it a royal cache, a hiding-place to which a mummy and its equipment had been removed for safety? Or was it actually the tomb of the king for whom I had spent so many years in search? . . . If we had actually found, as seemed almost certain, the tomb of that shadowy monarch, whose tenure of the throne coincided with one of the most interesting periods in the whole Egyptian history, we should indeed have reason to congratulate ourselves.

Naturally my wish was to go straight ahead with our clearing to find out the full extent of the discovery, but Lord Carnarvon was in England, and in fairness to him I had to delay matters until he could come. Accordingly, on the morning of 6 November I sent the following cable: "At last have made wonderful discovery in Valley; a magnificent tomb with seals intact; recovered same for your arrival; congratulations."

[Three weeks later, November 26,] was the day of days, the most wonderful that I have ever lived through, and certainly one whose like I can never hope to see again. . . . We were firmly convinced by this time that it was a cache that we were about to open, and not a tomb. The arrangement of stairway, entrance passage and doors reminded us very forcibly of the cache of Akhenaten and . . . seemed almost certain proof that we were right in our conjecture. We were soon to know. There lay the sealed doorway, and behind it was the answer to the question.

Slowly, desperately slowly it seemed to us as we watched, the remains of passage debris that encumbered the lower part of the doorway were removed, until at last we had the whole door clear before us. The decisive moment had arrived. With trembling hands I made a tiny breach in the upper left-hand corner. Darkness and blank space, as far as an iron testing-rod could reach, showed that whatever lay beyond was empty, and not filled like the passage we had just cleared. Candle tests were applied as a precaution against possible foul gases, and then, widening the hole a little, I inserted the candle and peered in. Lord Carnarvon, Lady Evelyn and Callender were standing anxiously beside me to hear the verdict. At first I could see nothing, the hot air escaping from the chamber causing the candle flame to flicker, but presently, as my eyes grew accustomed to the light, details of the room within emerged slowly from the mist, strange animals, statues, and gold—everywhere the glint of gold. For the moment—an eternity it must have seemed to the others standing by—I was struck dumb with amazement, and when Lord Carnarvon, unable to stand the suspense any longer, inquired anxiously, "Can you see anything?" it was all I could do to get the words, "Yes, wonderful things." Then, widening the hole a little further, so that we both could see, we inserted an electric torch.

I suppose most excavators would confess to a feeling of awe—embarrassment almost—when they break into a chamber closed and sealed by pious hands so many centuries ago. For the moment, time as a factor in human life has lost its meaning. Three thousand, four thousand years ago maybe, have passed and gone since human feet last trod the floor on which you stand, and yet, as you note the signs of recent life around you—the half-filled bowl of mortar for the door, the blackened lamp, the finger-mark upon the freshly painted surface, the farewell garland dropped upon the threshold—you feel it might have been but yesterday. The very air you breathe, unchanged throughout the centuries, you share with those who laid the mummy to its rest. Time is annihilated by little intimate details such as these, and you feel an intruder.

This is perhaps the first and dominant sensation, but others follow thick and fast—the exhilaration of discovery, the fever of suspense, the almost overmastering impulse, born of curiosity, to break down seals and lift the lids of boxes, the thought—pure joy to the investigator—that you are about to add a page to history, or solve some problem of research, the strained expectancy—why not confess it?—of the treasure-seeker.

Surely never before in the whole history of excavation had such an amazing sight been seen as the light of our torch revealed to us. The photographs which have subsequently been published were taken afterwards when the tomb had been opened and electric light installed. Let the reader imagine how the objects appeared to us as we looked down upon them from our spyhole in the blocked doorway, casting the beam of light from our torch—the first light that had pierced the darkness of the chamber for three thousand years—from one group of objects to another, in a vain attempt to interpret the treasure that lay before us. The effect was bewildering, overwhelming.

I suppose we had never formulated exactly in our minds just what we had expected or hoped to see, but certainly we had never dreamed of anything like this, a roomful—a whole museumful it seemed—of objects, some familiar, but some the like of which we had never seen, piled one upon another in seemingly endless profusion.

Gradually the scene grew clearer, and we could pick out individual objects. First, right opposite to us—we had been conscious of them all the while, but refused to believe in them—were three great gilt couches, their sides carved in the form of monstrous animals, curiously attenuated in body, as they had to be to serve their purpose, but with heads of startling realism. Uncanny beasts enough to look upon at any time: seen as we saw them, their brilliant gilded surfaces picked out of the darkness by our electric torch, as though by limelight, their heads throwing grotesque, distorted shadows on the wall behind them, they were almost terrifying. Next, on the right, two statues caught and held our attention; two life-sized figures of a king in black, facing each other like sentinels, gold kilted, gold sandalled, armed with mace and staff, the protective sacred cobra upon their foreheads.

These were the dominant objects that caught the eye at first. Between them, around them, piled on top of them, there were countless others—exquisitely painted and inlaid caskets; alabaster vases, some beautifully carved in openwork designs; strange black shrines, from the open door of one a great snake peeping out; bouquets of flowers or leaves; beds; chairs beautifully carved; a golden inlaid throne; a heap of curious white oviform boxes, staves of all shapes and designs; beneath our eyes, on the very threshold of the chamber, a beautiful lotiform cup of translucent alabaster; on the left a confused pile of overturned chariots, glistening with gold and inlay; and peeping from behind them another portrait of a king.

Such were some of the objects that lay before us. Whether we noted them all at the time I cannot say for certain, as our minds were in much too excited and confused a state to register accurately. Presently it dawned upon our bewildered brains that in all this medley of objects before us there was no coffin or trace of mummy, and the much-debated question of tomb or cache began to intrigue us afresh. With this question in view we reexamined the scene before us, and noticed for the first time that between the two black sentinel statues on the right there was another sealed doorway. The explanation gradually dawned upon us. We were but on the threshold of our discovery. What we saw was merely an antechamber. Behind the guarded door there were to be other chambers, possibly a succession of them, and in one of them, beyond any shadow of doubt, in all his magnificent panoply of death, we should find the Pharaoh lying.

We had seen enough, and our brains began to reel at the thought of the task in front of us. We re-closed the hole, locked the wooden grille that had been placed upon the first doorway, left our native staff on guard, mounted our donkeys and rode home down the Valley, strangely silent and subdued.

Egyptian Values

Egyptian literature abounds with didactic writings intended to instruct an individual on right action or proper conduct in life. A sense of "limit" and thoughtful discretion pervade the following suggestions to a royal administrator named Kagemni by a sage whose identity is unknown. These maxims were found on a piece of papyrus dating from the Old Kingdom. The love songs in this section date from the New Kingdom and reveal a private side to the Egyptian.

Instructions of Kagemni

The respectful man prospers,
Praised is the modest one,
The tent is open to the silent,
The seat of the quiet is spacious.
Do not chatter!
Knives are sharp against the blunderer,
Without hurry except when he faults.

When you sit with company,
Shun the food you love,
Restraint is a brief moment,
Gluttony is base and is reproved.
A cup of water quenches thirst,

"Instructions of Kagemni" is from Miriam Lichtheim, trans. and ed., *Ancient Egyptian Literature: A Book of Readings*, vol. 1 (Berkeley: University of California Press, 1973), pp. 59–60. © 1973 The Regents of the University of California. Reprinted by permission.

A mouthful of herbs strengthens the heart,
One good thing stands for goodness,
A little something stands for much.
Vile is he whose belly covets when [meal]-time has passed,
He forgets those in whose house his belly roams.

When you sit with a glutton,
Eat when his greed has passed,
When you drink with a drunkard,
Take when his heart is content.
Don't fall upon meat by the side of a glutton,
Take when he gives you, don't refuse it,
Then it will soothe.
He who is blameless in matters of food,
No word can prevail against him;
He who is gentle, even timid,
The harsh is kinder to him than to his mother,
All people are his servants.

Let your name go forth,
While your mouth is silent,
When you are summoned, don't boast of strength
Among those your age, lest you be opposed.
One knows not what may happen,
What god does when he punishes.

The vizier had his children summoned, after he had understood the ways of men, their character having become clear to him. Then he said to them: "All that is written in this book, heed it as I said it. Do not go beyond what has been set down." Then they placed themselves on their bellies. They recited it as it was written. It seemed good to them beyond anything in the whole land.

Love Song: "Would You Then Leave Me?"

If good fortune comes your way, [you still cannot find]
    happiness.
But if you try to touch my thighs and breasts,
[then you'll be satisfied.]

Because you remember you are hungry
    would you then leave?

"Love Song: 'Would You Then Leave Me?'" is from William Kelley Simpson, ed., *The Literature of Ancient Egypt* (New Haven: Yale University Press, 1972), p. 298. Copyright © 1972 by Yale University Press. Reprinted by permission.

Are you a man
    thinking only of his stomach?
Would you [walk off from me
    concerned with] your stylish clothes
and leave me with the sheet?

Because of hunger
    would you then leave me?
    [or because you are thirsty?]
Take then my breast:
    for you its gift overflows.
Better indeed is one day in your arms . . .
    than a hundred thousand [anywhere] on earth.

My love for you is mixed throughout my body
like [salt] dipped in water,
like a medicine to which gum is added,
like milk shot through [water]. . . .

So hurry to see your lady,
like a stallion on the track,
or like a falcon [swooping down] to its papyrus marsh.
Heaven sends down the love of her
as a flame falls in the [hay].

Love Song: "I Am Your Best Girl"

I am your best girl:
I belong to you like an acre of land
which I have planted
with flowers and every sweet-smelling grass.

Pleasant is the channel through it
which your hand dug out
for refreshing ourselves with the breeze,
a happy place for walking
with your hand in my hand.

My body is excited, my heart joyful,
at our traveling together.

"Love Song: 'I Am Your Best Girl'" is from William Kelley Simpson, ed., *The Literature of Ancient Egypt* (New Haven: Yale University Press, 1972), pp. 308–309. Copyright © 1972 by Yale University Press. Reprinted by permission.

Hearing your voice is pomegranate wine,
for I live to hear it,
and every glance which rests on me
means more to me than eating and drinking.

Egyptian Religion

The Pyramid Texts

The Pyramid Texts date from the Old Kingdom and were carved on the walls of the sarcophagus chambers of the pyramids at Saqqara. They were discovered in 1881, and their purpose was to promote the resurrection of the Pharaoh from the dead. Each utterance is separated from the others by dividing lines and thus represents a self-contained prayer. The following incantations are from the pyramids of Pepi I, a king in the Sixth Dynasty (ca. 2400 B.C.E.).

The Pharaoh Prays for Admittance to the Sky

Awake in peace, O Pure One, in peace!
Awake in peace, Horus-of-the-East, in peace!
Awake in peace, Soul-of-the-East, in peace!
Awake in peace, Horus-of-Lightland, in peace!
You lie down in the Night-bark,
You awake in the Day-bark,
For you are he who gazes on the gods,
There is no god who gazes on you!

O father of Pepi, take Pepi with you
Living, to you mother Nut!
Gates of sky, open for Pepi,
Gates of heaven, open for Pepi,
Pepi comes to you, make him live!
Command that this Pepi sit beside you,
Beside him who rises in lightland!
O father of Pepi, command to the goddess beside you
To make wide Pepi's seat at the stairway of heaven!

Poems from the Pyramid Texts are from Miriam Lichtheim, trans. and ed., *Ancient Egyptian Literature: A Book of Readings*, vol. 1 (Berkeley: University of California Press, 1973), pp. 44, 49–50. © 1973 The Regents of the University of California. Reprinted by permission.

Command the Living One, the son of Sothis,
To speak for this Pepi,
To establish for Pepi a seat in the sky!
Commend this Pepi to the Great Noble,
The beloved of Ptah, the son of Ptah,
To speak for this Pepi,
To make flourish his jar-stands on earth,
For Pepi is one with these four gods:
Imsety, Hapy, Duamutef, Kebhsenuf,
Who live by maat [truth],
Who lean on their staffs,
Who watch over Upper Egypt.

He flies, he flies from you men as do ducks,
He wrests his arms from you as a falcon,
He tears himself from you as a kite,
Pepi frees himself from the fetter of earth,
Pepi is released from bondage!

The Pharaoh Prays to the Sky Goddess

O Great One who became Sky,
You are strong, you are mighty,
You fill every place with your beauty,
The whole earth is beneath you, you possess it!
As you enfold earth and all things in your arms,
So have you taken this Pepi to you,
An indestructible star within you!

The Book of the Dead: Negative Confession

The Book of the Dead *is a collection of texts dating from the Middle and New Kingdoms that reflect a growing concern for the welfare of the dead and their search for eternal happiness. The Egyptians believed that upon death, one was judged by Osiris, god of the underworld, who determined one's fate on the basis of truth* (maat) *and moral purity. The "negative confession" that follows was part of the summation of one's life in the presence of Osiris. The emphasis is not on one's positive accomplishments in life, but rather on the unrighteous acts that were not committed—hence the term "negative confession." The following*

"The Book of the Dead: Negative Confession" is from E. A. Wallace Budge, trans., *The Book of the Dead According to the Theban Recension* (New York: E. P. Dutton, 1922), Ch. 125. Reprinted by permission of George Routledge and Sons, Ltd.

selection is from the tomb of Nu, an administrator of the Eighteenth Dynasty (1570–1085 B.C.E.).

Homage to thee, O Great God [Osiris], . . . I have come to thee, O my Lord, I have brought myself hither that I may behold thy beauties. . . . In truth I have come to thee, and I have brought maat to thee, and I have expelled wickedness for thee.

1. I have not done evil to mankind.
2. I have not oppressed the members of my family.
3. I have not wrought evil in the place of right and truth.
4. I have had no knowledge of worthless men.
7. I have not brought forward my name for exaltation to honors.
8. I have not ill-treated servants.
9. I have not belittled a god.
10. I have not defrauded the oppressed one of his property.
11. I have not done that which is an abomination unto the gods.
14. I have made no man to suffer hunger.
15. I have made no one to weep.
16. I have done no murder.
17. I have not given the order for murder to be done for me.
18. I have not inflicted pain upon mankind.
22. I have not committed fornication.
26. I have not encroached upon the fields of others.
29. I have not carried away the milk from the mouths of children.
30. I have not driven away the cattle which were upon their pastures.
38. I have not obstructed a god in his procession. I am pure! I am pure! I am pure! I am pure!

Hymn to the Aton
AKHENATON

Egyptian civilization was noted for its tradition, respect for authority, and unchanging cycles which gave unity and stability to the land for thousands of years. Yet one of the most radical changes in this pattern took place briefly during the reign of Amenhotep IV (1372–1355 B.C.E.). He changed the very course of Egyptian religion by eliminating the several gods and goddesses that were the basis for Egyptian polytheism. He replaced them with one god, a solar disk, whom he called Aton. In accordance with these new principles, Amenhotep IV ("Amon rests") changed his name to Akhenaton ("Aton is satisfied") and constructed a

"Hymn to the Aton" is from William Kelley Simpson, ed., *The Literature of Ancient Egypt* (New Haven: Yale University Press, 1972), pp. 290–295. Copyright © 1972 by Yale University Press. Reprinted by permission.

new capitol at Amarna. Systematically, the names of the old gods were erased from temple walls and public inscriptions. All worship was to be directed toward Aton, a universal deity. Thus Akhenaton sacrificed his own divinity to promote himself as the son and interpreter of Aton.

Akhenaton's monotheism has been hotly debated. Some regard it as a unique and creative approach to religion which even influenced later Hebrew monotheism; others see it as the development of earlier Egyptian thought with new elements included. In any event, Akhenaton's new religion was considered a heresy and did not survive his reign. The following prayer to Aton is the quintessential expression of Akhenaton's devotion to his universal god. Note the similarities between it and Psalm 104 of the Old Testament.

> You rise in perfection on the horizon of the sky,
> living [Aton], who started life.
> Whenever you are risen upon the eastern horizon
> you fill every land with your perfection.
> You are appealing, great, sparkling, high over every land;
> your rays hold together the lands as far as everything you
>   have made.
> Since you are Re, you reach as far as they do,
> and you curb them for your beloved son.
> Although you are far away, your rays are upon the land;
> you are in their faces, yet your departure is not observed.
>
> Whenever you set on the western horizon,
> the land is in darkness in the manner of death.
> They sleep in a bedroom with heads under the covers,
> and one eye does not see another.
> If all their possessions which are under their heads were
>   stolen,
> they would not know it.
> Every lion who comes out of his cave and all the serpents
>   bite,
> for darkness is a blanket.
> The land is silent now, because he who made them
> is at rest on his horizon.
>
> But when day breaks you are risen upon the horizon,
> and you shine as the [Aton] in the daytime.
> When you dispel darkness and you give forth your rays
> the two lands are in festival,
> alert and standing on their feet,
> now that you have raised them up.
> Their bodies are clean, and their clothes have been put
>   on;
> their arms are [lifted] in praise at your rising.

The entire land performs its works:
all the cattle are content with their fodder,
trees and plants grow,
birds fly up to their nests,
their wings [extended] in praise for your Ka.
All the kine prance on their feet;
everything which flies up and alights,
they live when you have risen for them.
The barges sail upstream and downstream too,
for every way is open at your rising.
The fishes in the river leap before your face
when your rays are in the sea.

You who have placed seed in woman
and have made sperm into man,
who feeds the son in the womb of his mother,
who quiets him with something to stop his
    crying;
you are the nurse in the womb,
giving breath to nourish all that has been begotten.
When he comes down from the womb to breathe
on the day he is born,
you open up his mouth [completely], and supply his
    needs.
When the fledgling in the egg speaks in the shell,
you give him air inside it to sustain him.
When you grant him his allotted time to break out from the
    egg,
he comes out from the egg to cry out at his fulfillment,
and he goes upon his legs when he has come forth from it.
How plentiful it is, what you have made,
although they are hidden from view,
sole god, without another beside you;
you created the earth as you wished,
when you were by yourself, [before]
mankind, all cattle and kine,
all beings on land, who fare upon their feet,
and all beings in the air, who fly with their wings.

The lands of Khor and Kush
and the land of Egypt:
you have set every man in his place,
you have allotted their needs,
every one of them according to his diet,
and his lifetime is counted out.
Tongues are separate in speech,

and their characters as well;
their skins are different,
for you have differentiated the foreigners.
In the underworld you have made a Nile
that you may bring it forth as you wish
to feed the populace,
since you made them for yourself, their utter master,
growing weary on their account, lord of every land.
For them the [Aton] of the daytime arises,
great in awesomeness.

All distant lands,
you have made them live,
for you have set a Nile in the sky
that it may descend for them
and make waves upon the mountains like the sea
to irrigate the fields in their towns.
How efficient are your designs,
Lord of eternity:
a Nile in the sky [meaning "rain"] for the foreigners
and all creatures that go upon their feet,
a Nile coming back from the underworld for Egypt.

Your rays give suck to every field:
when you rise they live,
and they grow for you.
You have made the seasons
to bring into being all you have made:
the Winter to cool them,
the Heat that you may be felt.
You have made a far-off heaven
in which to rise
in order to observe everything you have made.
Yet you are alone,
rising in your manifestations as the Living [Aton]:
appearing, glistening, being afar, coming close;
you make millions of transformations of yourself.
Towns, harbors, fields, roadways, waterways:
every eye beholds you upon them,
for you are the [Aton] of the daytime on the face of the
     earth.
When you go forth
every eye [is upon you].
You have created their sight
but not to see [only] the body . . .
which you have made.

You are my desire,
and there is no other who knows you
except for your son . . .
for you have apprised him of your designs and your power.
The earth came forth into existence by your hand,
and you made it.
When you rise, they live;
when you set, they die.
You are a lifespan in yourself;
one lives by you.
Eyes are upon your perfection until you set:
all work is put down when you rest in the west.

When [you] rise, [everything] grows
for the King and [for] everyone who hastens on foot,
because you have founded the land
and you have raised them for your son
who has come forth from your body,
the King of Upper and Lower Egypt, the one Living on
    Maat,
Lord of the Two Lands . . .
son of Re, the one Living on Maat, Master of Regalia,
[Akhenaton], the long lived,
and the Foremost Wife of the King, whom he loves,
the Mistress of the Two Lands, . . .
living and young, forever and ever.

Old Testament: Psalm 104

Bless Yahweh, my soul.
Yahweh my God, how great you are!
Clothed in majesty and glory,
wrapped in a robe of light!

You stretch the heavens out like a tent,
you build your palace on the waters above;
using the clouds as your chariot,
you advance on the wings of the wind;
you use the winds as messengers
and fiery flames as servants.

You fixed the earth on its foundations,
unshakable for ever and ever;
you wrapped it with the deep as with a robe,
the waters overtopping the mountains.

At your reproof the waters took to flight,
they fled at the sound of your thunder,
cascading over the mountains, into the valleys,
down to the reservoir you made for them;
you imposed the limits they must never cross again,
or they would once more flood the land.

You set springs gushing in ravines,
running down between the mountains,
supplying water for wild animals,
attracting the thirsty wild donkeys;
near there the birds of the air make their nests
and sing among the branches.

From your palace you water the uplands
until the ground has had all that your heavens have to offer;
you make fresh grass grow for cattle
and those plants made use of by man,
for them to get food from the soil:
wine to make them cheerful,
oil to make them happy,
bread to make them strong.

The trees of Yahweh get rain enough,
those cedars of Lebanon he planted;
here the little birds build their nest
and, on the highest branches, the stork has its home.
For with the goats there are the mountains,
in the crags rock-badgers hide.

You made the moon to tell the seasons,
the sun knows when to set:
you bring darkness on, night falls,
all the forest animals come out:
savage lions, roaring for their prey,
claiming their food from God.

The sun rises, they retire,
going back to lie down in their lairs,
and man goes to work, and to labour until dusk.
Yahweh, what variety you have created,

arranging everything so wisely!
Earth is completely full of things you have made:

among them vast expanse of ocean,
teeming with countless creatures,
creatures large and small,
with the ships going to and from
and Leviathan whom you made to amuse you.

All creatures depend on you
to feed them throughout the year;
you provide the food they eat,
with generous hand you satisfy their hunger,

You turn your face away, they suffer,
you stop their breath, they die
and revert to dust.
You give breath, fresh life begins,
you keep renewing the world.

Glory for ever to Yahweh!
May Yahweh find joy in what he creates,
at whose glance the earth trembles,
at whose touch the mountains smoke!

I mean to sing to Yahweh all my life,
I mean to play for my God as long as I live.
May these reflections of mine give him pleasure,
as much as Yahweh gives me!
May sinners vanish from the earth
and the wicked exist no more!

Bless Yahweh, my soul.

Hebrew Civilization

Origins, Oppression, and the Exodus of the Hebrews from Egypt

*The first few pages from Genesis in the Old Testament of the Bible contain some
of the most powerful and influential ideas in Western Civilization. Genesis explains the origins of the universe by one omnipotent and omniscient God, who
created human beings in his likeness, gave them dominion over nature, and*

endowed them with an inherent goodness. It is the story of the creation of woman, the origins of sin, and the fall from God's grace. This concept of monotheism and the ethical and social structure that derived from the development of these ideas were the primary contributions of the Hebrews to Western Civilization.

The story of the Hebrews in the Old Testament begins with the wandering patriarch Abraham, who led his family from Ur in Sumer around 1800 B.C.E. to the promised land of Canaan by about 1700 B.C.E. A group of Hebrews led by Joseph continued south to Egypt, where they were hospitably received by the Hyksos, a Semitic people like the Hebrews, who had conquered Egypt about 1710 B.C.E. Joseph, according to the Old Testament, actually ruled Egypt for a time. But by 1570 B.C.E., a resurgent Egypt had ended the Hyksos's control, and the Pharaohs enslaved the Hebrews and forced them to build new Egyptian cities. Shortly after 1300 B.C.E., Moses was directed by God to lead his people out of Egypt, across the Red Sea, and back to the promised land of Canaan.

The Creation of the World

In the beginning, God created heaven and earth. Now the earth was a formless void, there was darkness over the deep, with a divine wind sweeping over the waters.

God said, "Let there be light," and there was light. God saw that light was good, and God divided light from darkness. God called light "day," and darkness he called "night." Evening came and morning came: the first day.

God said, "Let there be a vault through the middle of the waters to divide the waters in two." And so it was. God made the vault, and it divided the waters under the vault from the waters above the vault. God called the vault "heaven." Evening came and morning came: the second day.

God said, "Let the waters under heaven come together into a single mass, and let dry land appear." And so it was. God called the dry land "earth" and the mass of waters "seas," and God saw that it was good.

God said, "Let the earth produce vegetation: seed-bearing plants, and fruit trees on earth, bearing fruit with their seed inside, each corresponding to its own seed-bearing fruit with their seed inside, each corresponding to its own species." And so it was. . . . God saw that it was good. Evening came and morning came: the third day.

God said, "Let there be lights in the vault of heaven to divide day from night, and let them indicate festivals, days and years. Let them be lights in the vault of heaven to shine on the earth." And so it was. God made the two great lights, the greater light to govern the day, the smaller light to govern the night, and the stars. . . . God saw that it was good. Evening came and morning came: the fourth day.

God said, "Let the waters be alive with a swarm of living creatures, and let birds wing their way above the earth across the vault of heaven." And so it was. God created great sea-monsters and all the creatures that glide and teem in the waters in their own species, and winged birds in their own species. God saw that it was good. God blessed them, saying, "Be fruitful, multiply, and fill the waters of the seas; and let the birds multiply on land." Evening came and morning came: the fifth day.

God said, "Let the earth produce every kind of living creature in its own species: cattle, creeping things and wild animals of all kinds." And so it was. . . . God saw that it was good.

God said, "Let us make man in our own image, in the likeness of ourselves, and let them be masters of the fish of the sea, the birds of heaven, the cattle, all the wild animals, and all the creatures that creep along the ground."

> God created man in the image of himself,
> in the image of God he created him,
> male and female he created them.

God blessed them, saying to them, "Be fruitful, multiply, fill the earth and subdue it. Be masters of the fish of the sea, the birds of heaven and all the living creatures that move on earth." God also said, "Look, to you I give all the seed-bearing plants everywhere on the surface of the earth, and all the trees with seed-bearing fruit; this will be your food. And to all the wild animals, all the birds of heaven and all the living creatures that creep along the ground, I give all the foliage of the plants as their food." And so it was. God saw all he had made, and indeed it was very good. Evening came and morning came: the sixth day.

Thus heaven and earth were completed with all their array. On the seventh day God had completed the work he had been doing. He rested on the seventh day after all the work he had undertaken. God blessed the seventh day and made it holy, because on that day he rested after all his work of creating.

Paradise and the Fall from Grace

At the time when Yahweh God made earth and heaven, there was as yet no wild bush on the earth nor had any wild plant yet sprung up, for Yahweh God had not sent rain on the earth, nor was there any man to till the soil. Instead, water flowed out of the ground and watered all the surface of the soil. Yahweh God shaped man from the soil of the ground and blew the breath of life into his nostrils, and man became a living being.

Yahweh God planted a garden in Eden, which is in the east, and there he put the man he had fashioned. From the soil, Yahweh God caused to grow every kind of tree, enticing to look at and good to eat, with the tree of life in the middle of the garden, and the tree of the knowledge of good and evil. . . .

Yahweh God took the man and settled him in the garden of Eden to cultivate and take care of it. Then Yahweh God gave the man this command, "You are free to eat of all the trees in the garden. But of the tree of the knowledge of good and evil you are not to eat; for, the day you eat of that, you are doomed to die."

Yahweh God said, "It is not right that the man should be alone. I shall make him a helper. . . ." Then Yahweh God made the man fall into a deep sleep. And, while he was asleep, he took one of his ribs and closed the flesh up again forthwith. Yahweh God fashioned the rib he had taken from the man into a woman, and brought her to the man. And the man said:

> This one at last is bone of my bones
> and flesh of my flesh!
> She is to be called Woman,
> because she was taken from Man.

This is why a man leaves his father and mother and becomes attached to his wife, and they become one flesh. Now, both of them were naked, the man and his wife, but they felt no shame before each other.

Now the snake was the most subtle of all the wild animals that Yahweh God had made. It asked the woman, "Did God really say you were not to eat from any of the trees in the garden?" The woman answered the snake, "We may eat the fruit of the trees in the garden. But of the fruit of the tree in the middle of the garden God said, 'You must not eat it, nor touch it, under pain of death.'" Then the snake said to the woman, "No! You will not die! God knows in fact that the day you eat it your eyes will be opened and you will be like gods, knowing good from evil." The woman saw that the tree was good to eat and pleasing to the eye and that it was enticing for the wisdom that it could give. So she took some of the fruit and ate it. She also gave some to her husband who was with her, and he ate it. Then the eyes of both of them were opened and they realized that they were naked. So they sewed fig-leaves to make themselves loin-cloths.

The man and his wife heard the sound of Yahweh God walking in the garden in the cool of the day, and they hid from Yahweh God among the trees of the garden. "Where are you?" he asked. . . . "Have you been eating from the tree I forbade you to eat?" The man replied, "It was the woman you put with me; she gave me some fruit from the tree, and I ate it." Then Yahweh God said to the woman, "Why did you do that?" The woman replied, "The snake tempted me and I ate." Then Yahweh God said to the snake, "Because you have done this,

> Accursed be you
> of all animals wild and tame!
> On your belly you will go
> and on dust you will feed
> as long as you live.
> I shall put enmity
> between you and the woman,
> and between your offspring and hers;
> it will bruise your head
> and you will strike its heel."

To the woman he said:

> "I shall give you intense pain in childbearing,
> you will give birth to your children in pain.
> Your yearning will be for your husband,
> and he will dominate you."

To the man he said, "Because you listened to the voice of your wife and ate from the tree of which I had forbidden you to eat,

> Accursed be the soil because of you!
> Painfully will you get your food from it
> as long as you live. . . .
> By the sweat of your face
> will you earn your food,
> until you return to the ground,
> as you were taken from it.
> For dust you are
> and to dust you shall return."

The man named his wife "Eve" because she was the mother of all those who live. Yahweh made tunics of skins for the man and his wife and clothed them. Then Yahweh God said, "Now that the man has become like one of us in knowing good from evil, he must not be allowed to reach out his hand and pick from the tree of life too, and eat and live forever!" So Yahweh God expelled him from the garden of Eden, to till the soil from which he had been taken. He banished the man, and in front of the garden of Eden he posted the great winged creatures and the fiery flashing sword to guard the way to the tree of life.

The Hebrew Bondage

Then there came to power in Egypt a new king who knew nothing of Joseph. "Look," he said to his subjects, "these people, the sons of Israel, have become so numerous and strong that they are a threat to us. We must be prudent and take steps against their increasing any further, or if war should break out, they might add to the number of our enemies. They might take arms against us and so escape out of the country." Accordingly they put slave-drivers over the Israelites to wear them down under heavy loads. In this way they built the store-cities of Pithom and Ramses for Pharaoh. But the more they were crushed, the more they increased and spread, and men came to dread the sons of Israel. The Egyptians forced the sons of Israel into slavery, and made their lives unbearable with hard labour, work with clay and brick, all kinds of work in the fields; they forced on them every kind of labour. . . .

The Burning Bush

During this long period the king of Egypt died. The sons of Israel, groaning in their slavery, cried out for help and from the depths of their slavery their cry came up to God. God heard their groaning and he called to mind his covenant with Abraham, Isaac and Jacob. God looked down upon the sons of Israel, and he knew. . . .

Moses was looking after the flock of Jethro, his father-in-law, priest of Midian. He led his flock to the far side of the wilderness and came to Horeb, the mountain of God. There the angel of Yahweh appeared to him in the shape of a flame of fire, coming from the middle of a bush. Moses looked; there was the bush blazing, but it was not being burnt up. "I must go and look at this strange sight," Moses said, "and see why the bush is not burnt." Now Yahweh saw him go forward to look, and God called to him from the middle of the bush. "Moses, Moses!" He said. "Here I am," he answered. "Come no nearer," He said. "Take off your shoes, for the place on which you stand is holy ground. I am the God of your father," He said, "the God of Abraham, the god of Isaac and the God of Jacob." At this Moses covered his face, afraid to look at God. . . .

"The Hebrew Bondage" is from Exodus 1, from *The Jerusalem Bible* by Alexander Jones, ed., p. 78. Copyright © 1966 by Darton, Longman & Todd, Ltd., and Doubleday, a division of Bantam, Doubleday, Dell Publishing Group, Inc. Reprinted by permission.

"The Burning Bush" is from Exodus 2–3, from *The Jerusalem Bible* by Alexander Jones, ed., p. 80. Copyright © 1966 by Darton, Longman & Todd, Ltd., and Doubleday, a division of Bantam, Doubleday, Dell Publishing Group, Inc. Reprinted by permission.

The Mission of Moses

God spoke to Moses and said to him, "I am Yahweh. To Abraham and Isaac and Jacob I appeared as El Shaddai; I did not make myself known to them by my name Yahweh. Also, I made my covenant with them to give them the land of Canaan, the land they lived in as strangers. And I have heard the groaning of the sons of Israel, enslaved by the Egyptians, and have remembered my covenant. Say this, then, to the sons of Israel, 'I am Yahweh.

I will free you of the burdens which the Egyptians lay on you. I will release you from slavery to them, and with my arm outstretched and my strokes of power I will deliver you. I will adopt you as my own people, and I will be your God. Then you shall know that it is I, Yahweh your God, who have freed you from the Egyptians' burdens. Then I will bring you to the land I swore that I would give to Abraham, and Isaac, and Jacob, and will give it to you for your own; I, Yahweh, will do this!'" Moses told this to the sons of Israel, but they would not listen to him, so crushed was their spirit and so cruel their slavery.

Yahweh then said to Moses, "Go to Pharaoh, king of Egypt, and tell him to let the sons of Israel leave his land." But Moses answered to Yahweh's face: "Look," said he "since the sons of Israel have not listened to me, why should Pharaoh listen to me, a man slow of speech?" Yahweh spoke to Moses and Aaron and ordered them to both go to Pharaoh, king of Egypt, and to bring the sons of Israel out of the land of Egypt.

The Departure of the Israelites

When Pharaoh had let the people go, God did not let them take the road to the land of the Philistines, although that was the nearest way. God thought that the prospect of fighting would make the people lose heart and turn back to Egypt. Instead, God led the people by the roundabout way of the wilderness to the Sea of Reeds [Red Sea]. . . .

Yahweh went before them, by day in the form of a pillar of cloud to show them the way, and by night in the form of a pillar of fire to give them light: thus they could continue their march by day and by night. The pillar of cloud never failed to go before the people during the day, nor the pillar of fire during the night. . . .

When Pharaoh, king of Egypt, was told that the people had made their escape, he and his courtiers changed their minds about the people. "What have we done," they said, "allowing Israel to leave our service?" So Pharaoh had his chariot harnessed and gathered his troops about him, taking six hundred of the best chariots and all the other chariots in Egypt, each manned by a picked team. Yahweh made Pharaoh, king of Egypt, stubborn, and he gave chase to the sons of Israel as they made their triumphant escape. So the Egyptians gave chase and came up with them where they lay encamped beside the sea—all the horses, the chariots of Pharaoh, his horsemen, his army—near Pi-hahiroth, facing Baalzephon. And as Pharaoh approached, the sons of Israel looked round—and there were the Egyptians in pursuit of them! The sons of Israel were terrified and cried out to Yahweh. To Moses they said, "Were there no graves in Egypt that you must lead us out to die in the wilderness? What good have you done us, bringing us out of Egypt? We spoke of this in Egypt, did we not? Leave us alone, we said, we would rather work for the Egyptians! Better to work of the Egyptians than die in the wilderness!" Moses answered the people, "Have no fear! Stand firm, and you will see what Yahweh will do to save you today: the Egyptians you see today, you will never see again. Yahweh will do the fighting for you: you have only to keep still."

Yahweh said to Moses, "Why do you cry to me so? Tell the sons of Israel to march on. For yourself, raise your staff and stretch out your hand over the sea and part it for the sons of Israel to walk through the sea on dry ground. I for my part will make the heart of the Egyptians so stubborn that they will follow them. So shall I win myself glory at the expense of Pharaoh, of all his army, his chariots, his horsemen. And when I have won glory for myself, at the expense of Pharaoh and his chariots and his army, the Egyptians will learn that I am Yahweh."

Then the angle of Yahweh, who marched at the front of the army of Israel, changed station and moved to their rear. The pillar of cloud changed station from the front to the rear of them, and remained there. It came between the camp of the Egyptians and the camp of Israel. The cloud was dark, and the night passed without the armies drawing any closer the whole night long. Moses stretched out his hand over the sea. Yahweh drove back the sea with a strong easterly wind all night, and he made dry land of the sea. The waters parted and the sons of Israel went on dry ground right into the sea, walls of water to right and to left of them. The Egyptians gave chase: after them they went, right into the sea, all Pharaoh's horses, his chariots, and his horsemen. . . . Yahweh said to Moses "that the waters may flow back on the Egyptians and their chariots and their horsemen." Moses stretched out his hand over the sea and, as day broke, the sea returned to its bed. The fleeing Egyptians marched right into it, and Yahweh overthrew the Egyptians in the very middle of the sea. The returning waters overwhelmed the chariots and the horsemen of Pharaoh's whole army, which had followed the Israelites into the sea; not a single one of them was left. But the sons of Israel had marched through the sea on dry ground, walls of water to right and to left of them. That day, Yahweh rescued Israel from the Egyptians, and Israel saw the Egyptians lying dead on the shore. Israel witnessed the great act that Yahweh had performed against the Egyptians, and the people venerated Yahweh; they put their faith in Yahweh and in Moses, his servant.

Covenant and Commandments

*After the Exodus of the Hebrews from Egypt, Yahweh established the nation of Is-
rael and through Moses made a covenant with his chosen people that he would
protect them in return for their obedience to his laws. The law code that God
handed down to Moses on Mt. Sinai is called the Decalogue or Ten Commandments and is absolute in nature. Other laws that are less absolute and generally
reflect the needs and values of Hebrew society are called the Covenant Code; they
are included after the Ten Commandments and were probably written centuries
later. Note the similarity between this Covenant Code and the laws of Hammurabi.*

The Ten Commandments

Three months after they came out of the land of Egypt . . . on that day the
sons of Israel came to the wilderness of Sinai. . . .

Moses then went up to God, and Yahweh called to him from the mountains,
saying, "Say this to the House of Jacob, declare this to the sons of Israel, 'You
yourselves have seen what I did with the Egyptians, how I carried you on eagle's
wings and brought you to myself. From this you know that now, if you obey my
voice and hold fast to my covenant, you of all the nations shall be my very own
for all the earth is mine. I will count you a kingdom of priests, a consecrated nation.' Those are the words you are to speak to the sons of Israel." . . .

Yahweh said to Moses, "Go to the people and tell them to prepare themselves today and tomorrow. Let them wash their clothing and hold themselves in readiness for the third day, because on the third day Yahweh will descend on the mountain of Sinai in the sight of all the people. You will mark
out the limits of the mountain and say, 'Take care not to go up the mountain
or to touch the foot of it. Whoever touches the mountain will be put to death.
No one must lay a hand on him: he must be stoned or shot down by arrow,
whether man or beast; he must not remain alive.' When the ram's horn
sounds a long blast, they are to go up the mountain." . . .

Now at daybreak on the third day there were peals of thunder on the
mountain and lightning flashes, a dense cloud, and a loud trumpet blast, and
inside the camp all the people trembled. Then Moses led the people out of
the camp to meet God; and they stood at the bottom of the mountain. The
mountain of Sinai was entirely wrapped in smoke, because Yahweh had descended on it in the form of fire. Like smoke from a furnace the smoke went
up, and the whole mountain shook violently. Louder and louder grew the
sound of the trumpet, Moses spoke, and God answered him with peals of

thunder. Yahweh came down on the mountain of Sinai, on the mountain top, and Yahweh called Moses to the top of the mountain; and Moses went up. . . .

Then God spoke all these words. He said, "I am Yahweh your God who brought you out of the land of Egypt, out of the house of slavery.

"You shall have no gods except me.

"You shall not make yourself a carved image or any likeness of anything in heaven or on earth beneath or in the waters under the earth; you shall not bow down to them or serve them. For I, Yahweh your God, am a jealous God and I punish the father's fault in the sons, the grandsons, and the great-grandsons of those who hate me; but I show kindness to thousands of those who love me and keep my commandments.

"You shall not utter the name of Yahweh your God to misuse it, for Yahweh will not leave unpunished the man who utters his name to misuse it.

"Remember the sabbath day and keep it holy. For six days you shall labour and do all your work, but the seventh day is a sabbath for Yahweh your God. You shall do no work that day, neither you nor your son nor your daughter nor your servants, men or women, nor your animals nor the stranger who lives with you. For in six days Yahweh made the heavens and the earth and the sea and all that these hold, but on the seventh day he rested; that is why Yahweh has blessed the sabbath day and made it sacred.

"Honour your father and your mother so that you may have a long life in the land that Yahweh your God has given to you.

"You shall not kill.

"You shall not commit adultery.

"You shall not steal.

"You shall not bear false witness against your neighbour.

"You shall not covet your neighbour's house. You shall not covet your neighbour's wife, or his servant, man or woman, or his ox, or his donkey, or anything that is his."

The Covenant Code

"This is the ruling you [Moses] are to lay before them: . . .

"Anyone who strikes a man and so causes his death, must die. If he has not lain in wait for him but God has delivered him into his hands, then I will appoint you a place where he may seek refuge. But should a man dare to kill his fellow by treacherous intent, you must take him even from my altar to be put to death.

"The Covenant Code" is from Exodus 21–22, 24, from *The Jerusalem Bible* by Alexander Jones, ed., pp. 104, 106, 108. Copyright © 1966 by Darton, Longman & Todd, Ltd., and Doubleday, a division of Bantam, Doubleday, Dell Publishing Group, Inc. Reprinted by permission.

"Anyone who strikes his father or mother must die. Anyone who abducts a man—whether he has sold him or is found in possession of him—must die. Anyone who curses father or mother must die.

"If men quarrel and one strikes the other a blow with stone or fist so that the man, though he does not die, must keep his bed, the one who struck the blow shall not be liable provided the other gets up and can go about, even with a stick. He must compensate him, however, for his enforced inactivity, and care for him until he is completely cured.

"If a man beats his slave, male or female, and the slave dies at his hands, he must pay the penalty. But should the slave survive for one or two days, he shall pay no penalty because the slave is his by right of purchase.

"If, when men come to blows, they hurt a woman who is pregnant and she suffers a miscarriage, though she does not die of it, the man responsible must pay the compensation demanded of him by the woman's master; he shall hand it over, after arbitration. But should she die, you shall give life for life, eye for eye, tooth for tooth, hand for hand, foot for foot, burn for burn, wound for wound, stroke for stroke. . . .

"You must not molest the stranger or oppress him, for you lived as strangers in the land of Egypt. You must not be harsh with the widow, or with the orphan; if you are harsh with them, they will surely cry out to me, and be sure I shall hear their cry; my anger will flare and I shall kill you with the sword, your own wives will be widows, your own children orphans.

"If you lend money to any of my people, to any poor man among you, you must not play the usurer with him: you must not demand interest from him.

"If you take another's cloak as a pledge, you must give it back to him before sunset. It is all the covering he has; it is the cloak he wraps his body in; what else would he sleep in? If he cries to me, I will listen, for I am full of pity. . . ."

Moses went and told the people all the commands of Yahweh and all the ordinances. In answer, all the people said with one voice, "We will observe all the commands that Yahweh has decreed." Moses put all the commands of Yahweh into writing.

The Hebrew Monarchy: The Wealth and Wisdom of Solomon

When the Hebrews settled in the land of Canaan (modern Israel) after the Exodus from Egypt in the early thirteenth century B.C.E., it soon became apparent that the loose confederacy of Hebrew tribes was ineffective when faced with enemies. Of special concern were the Philistines, who settled in the region about 1200 B.C.E., destroyed the Hebrew sanctuary at Shiloh about 1050 B.C.E., and carried off the Ark of the Covenant. In response to this, the Hebrew people demanded strong leadership and elected a king named Saul. He was not a particularly effective leader and died in battle with the Philistines. His successor was the famous David (1020–1000 B.C.E.) whose personal defeat of the Philistine Goliath led to security and domestic reform. David established the Hebrew capital at Jerusalem and equipped it with a central administration. At last, a united Israel was born.

David's progressive spirit was continued by his son Solomon (961–922 B.C.E.), who strengthened centralized control of the state by the king. His construction of the Temple and palace complex required frequent taxes and even oppressive forced labor. Still, Solomon developed a reputation for wisdom and fairness. It was only later in his reign that he incurred the wrath of God. The following selections from the Old Testament provide insight into Solomon's reign and character.

The Construction of the Temple

Hiram the king of Tyre sent an embassy to Solomon, having learnt that he had been anointed king in succession to his father and because Hiram had always been a friend of David. And Solomon sent this message to Hiram, "You are aware that David my father was unable to build a temple for the name of Yahweh, his God, because his enemies waged war on him from all sides, until Yahweh should put them under his control. But now Yahweh my God has given me rest on every side: not one enemy, no calamities. I therefore plan to build a temple for the name of Yahweh my God, just as Yahweh said to David my father, 'Your son whom I will place on your throne to succeed you shall be the man to build a temple for my name.' So now have cedars of Lebanon been cut down for me; my servants will work with your servants, and I will pay for the hire of your servants at whatever rate you fix.". . . When Hiram heard what Solomon had said, he was delighted. "Now blessed be Yahweh" he said "who has given David a wise son to rule over this great people!" . . .

King Solomon raised a levy throughout Israel for forced labour: the levy numbered thirty thousand men. He sent these to Lebanon in relays, ten thousand a month; they spent one month in Lebanon and two months at home. Adoram was in charge of the forced labour. Solomon also had seventy thousand porters and eighty thousand quarrymen in the mountains, as well as the administrators' officials who supervised the work, three thousand three hundred of them in charge of the men employed in the work. At the king's orders they quarried huge stones, special stones, for the laying of the temple foundations, dressed stones. Solomon's workmen and Hiram's workmen and the Giblites cut and assembled the wood and stone for the building of the Temple. In the four hundred and eightieth year after the Israelites came out of the land of Egypt, in the fourth year of Solomon's reign over Israel, . . . he began to build the Temple of Yahweh.

The Wisdom of Solomon

Then two prostitutes came to the king and stood before him. "If it please you, my lord," one of the women said, "this woman and I live in the same house, and while she was in the house I gave birth to a child. Now it happened on the third day after my delivery that this woman also gave birth to a child. We were alone together; there was no one else in the house with us; just the two of us in the house. Now one night this woman's son died; she overlaid him. And in the middle of the night she got up and took my son from beside me while your servant was asleep; she put him to her breast and put her own dead son to mine. When I got up to suckle my child, there he was, dead. But in the morning I looked at him carefully, and he was not the child I had borne at all." Then the other woman spoke, "That is not true! My son is the live one, yours is the dead one"; and the first retorted, "That is not true! Your son is the dead one, mine is the live one." And so they wrangled before the king. "This one says," the king observed 'My son is the one who is alive; your son is dead,' while the other says, 'That is not true! Your son is the dead one, mine is the live one.' "Bring me a sword," said the king; and a sword was brought into the king's presence. "Cut the living child in two," the king said, "and give half to one, and half to the other." At this the woman who was the mother of the living child addressed the king, for she burned with pity for her son. "If it please you, my lord," she said "let them give her the child; only do not let them think of killing it!" But the other said, "He shall belong to neither of us. Cut him up." Then the king gave his decision. "Give the child to the first woman," he said "and do not kill him. She is his mother." All Israel came to hear of the judgment the king had pronounced, and held the king in awe, recognizing that he possessed divine wisdom for dispensing justice.

Solomon's Decline

He had seven hundred wives of royal rank, and three hundred concubines. When Solomon grew old his wives swayed his heart to other gods; and his heart was not wholly with Yahweh his God as his father David's had been. Solomon became a follower of Astarte, the goddess of the Sidonians, and of Milcom, the Ammonite abomination. He did what was displeasing to Yahweh, and was not a wholehearted follower of Yahweh, as his father David had been. Then it was that Solomon built a high place for Chemosh the god of Moab on the mountain to the east of Jerusalem, and to Milcom the god of the

Ammonites. He did the same for all his foreign wives, who offered incense and sacrifice to their gods.

Yahweh was angry with Solomon because his heart had turned from Yahweh the God of Israel who had twice appeared to him and who had then forbidden him to follow other gods; but he did not carry out Yahweh's order. Yahweh therefore said to Solomon, "Since you behave like this and do not keep my covenant or the laws I laid down for you, I will most surely tear the kingdom away from you and give it to one of your servants. For your father David's sake, however, I will not do this during your lifetime, but will tear it out of your son's hands. Even so, I will not tear the whole kingdom from him. For the sake of my servant David, and for the sake of Jerusalem which I have chosen, I will leave your son one tribe."

The New Covenant of Jeremiah

Solomon's oppressive policies split the Hebrew nation into two parts after his death: Israel became the northern kingdom, and Judah formed in the south. Such division made the two kingdoms vulnerable to rising new empires. Israel fell to the Assyrians in 722 B.C.E. and Judah to the Chaldeans in 586 B.C.E., whereupon the Jews were removed from the land of Canaan in what was called the Babylonian Captivity. They were finally released when the Persian Cyrus the Great conquered the Chaldean empire and liberated Babylon in 539 B.C.E.

During the years 750–550 B.C.E., when the Hebrews were trying to survive in the face of foreign invasion, they were also struggling internally. A succession of prophets arose who claimed to speak for Yahweh and condemned social injustice and the people's general disregard for the covenant they had made with God under Moses. The most influential of these prophets was Jeremiah (626–586 B.C.E.). He not only decried the faithlessness of the people of Israel and warned of the wrath of God, but also offered a solution to the problem: a new covenant. God destroys, but he also builds anew. Of utmost importance was a new covenant within each individual (rather than with the nation as a whole) which would renew moral and spiritual commitment.

"Deep Within Them I Will Plant My Law"

The word that was addressed to Jeremiah by Yahweh, "Go and stand at the gate of the Temple of Yahweh and there proclaim this message. Say, 'Listen to the word of Yahweh, all you men of Judah who come in by these gates to worship Yahweh. Yahweh Sabaoth, the God of Israel, says this: Amend your behavior

"'Deep Within Them I Will Plant My Law'" is from Jeremiah 7, 31, from *The Jerusalem Bible* by Alexander Jones, ed., pp. 1264, 1304. Copyright © 1966 by Darton, Longman & Todd, Ltd., and Doubleday, a division of Bantam, Doubleday, Dell Publishing Group, Inc. Reprinted by permission.

and your actions and I will stay with you here in this place. Put no trust in delusive words like these: This is the sanctuary of Yahweh, the sanctuary of Yahweh, the sanctuary of Yahweh! But if you do amend your behavior and your actions, if you treat each other fairly, if you do not exploit the stranger, the orphan and the widow (if you do not shed innocent blood in this place), and if you do not follow alien gods, to your own ruin, then here in this place I will stay with you, in the land that long ago I gave to your fathers for ever. Yet here you are, trusting delusive words, to no purpose! Steal, would you, murder, commit adultery, perjure yourselves, burn incense to Baal, follow alien gods that you do not know?—and then come presenting yourselves in this Temple that bears my name, saying: Now we are safe—safe to go on committing all these abominations! Do you take this Temple that bears my name for a robbers' den? I, at any rate, am not blind—it is Yahweh who speaks. . . .

"'And now, since you have committed all these sins—it is Yahweh who speaks—and have refused to listen when I spoke so urgently, so persistently, or to answer when I called you, I will treat this Temple that bears my name, and in which you put your trust, and the place I have given to you and your ancestors, just as I treated Shiloh. I will drive you out of my sight, as I drove all your kinsmen, the entire race of Ephraim.'" . . . "See, the days are coming—it is Yahweh who speaks—when I am going to sow the seed of men and cattle on the House of Israel and on the House of Judah. And as I once watched them to tear up, to knock down, to overthrow, destroy and bring disaster, so now I shall watch over them to build and to plant. It is Yahweh who speaks. In those days people will no longer say: 'The fathers have eaten unripe grapes; the children's teeth are set on edge.' But each is to die for his own sin. Every man who eats unripe grapes is to have his own teeth set on edge.

"See, the days are coming—it is Yahweh who speaks—when I will make a new covenant with the House of Israel (and the House of Judah), but not a covenant like the one I made with their ancestors on the day I took them by the hand to bring them out of the land of Egypt. They broke that covenant of mine, so I had to show them who was master. It is Yahweh who speaks. No, this is the covenant I will make with the House of Israel when those days arrive—it is Yahweh who speaks. Deep within them I will plant my Law, writing it on their hearts. Then I will be their God and they shall be my people. There will be no further need for neighbour to try to teach neighbour, or brother to say to brother, 'Learn to know Yahweh!' No, they will all know me, the least no less than the greatest—it is Yahweh who speaks—since I will forgive their inequity and never call their sin to mind."

CHRONOLOGY: Civilization in the Ancient Near East: Mesopotamia, Egypt, and Israel (All dates are approximate)

3500 B.C.E. Bronze Age cultures develop in Mesopotamia, "the land between the rivers."

3200–2260 B.C.E. Old Kingdom in Egypt: strong pharaonic authority as reflected by the building of the pyramids.

3000 B.C.E. The Sumerians found the first "Western Civilization" in the southern portion of the Tigris and Euphrates River Valley: development of writing and agriculture.

2340 B.C.E. Sargon of Akkad, Semitic king, extends his empire over Sumer to the "cedar forests of Lebanon," on the west coast of the Mediterranean.

2052–1786 B.C.E. Middle Kingdom in Egypt: Pharaonic authority reestablished after civil war among nomarchs (regional governors).

2000 B.C.E. *The Epic of Gilgamesh*, a collection of stories about the Sumerian king of Uruk, is written. Hittites, who were among the first to use iron, appear in Anatolia.

1800–1700 B.C.E. Hebrew patriarch, Abraham, leaves Ur in Sumer and establishes himself in Canaan. Joseph continues to Egypt.

1792–1750 B.C.E. Reign of Hammurabi, Amorite (Babylonian) king who ruled from Babylonia and established order in the region through the fullest and best-preserved law code extant from Mesopotamia.

1575–1086 B.C.E. New Kingdom in Egypt: period of expansion and authority throughout the eastern Mediterranean. Led by conquerors, Thutmose III (1490–1436) and Ramses II (1301–1234), and the enigmatic Akhenaton (1367–1350), whose insistence on monotheism disrupts this traditional culture. King Tutankhamon dies ca. 1350 B.C.E.

1300 B.C.E. According to the Old Testament, Moses leads Hebrews out of Egypt, across the Red Sea, and back to Canaan.

1200 B.C.E. Destruction throughout Mediterranean. "Sea Peoples" attack Egypt, destroy Hittites, and disrupt Mycenaean Greek culture. Power vacuum filled by developing cultures of Phoenicians and Hebrews.

1000–922 B.C.E. Reigns of King David and King Solomon. Establishment of law and military presence.

722 B.C.E. Assyrian conquest of Israel (Northern Kingdom).

586 B.C.E. Destruction of Jerusalem; fall of Judah (Southern Kingdom); the Babylonian Captivity begins.

539 B.C.E.   Persians defeat Babylonians and end the Babylonian Captivity of Jews.

STUDY QUESTIONS

1. In the preface to the Code of Hammurabi, why does Hammurabi feel justified in setting forth this law code? What are some of the penalties? Do they seem too harsh to be fair? Why is a law code such as this a sign of progress in civilization?

2. What makes *The Epic of Gilgamesh* such an enduring story? Compare the two accounts of the Flood. Which account do you find more vivid or exciting? What are the reasons given for the Flood and what does it signify? Compare especially the roles of the deities. How does God of the Old Testament differ in manner and action from Enlil or Ea?

3. Kingship and authority are major themes in ancient Near Eastern civilization. What do the readings reveal as true indicators of the authority of the Egyptian Pharaoh?

4. Carefully read Howard Carter's account of the discovery of King Tut's tomb. What does it reveal about the process of exploration and discovery? Does it depend on luck or methodical preparation? What differentiates the treasure seeker and tomb robber from the archaeologist? Where is the "line of discretion" between the two?

5. Compare the selections from the *Pyramid Texts* and *The Book of the Dead*. When were they written and what were they expected to accomplish? Can you draw any conclusions from your analysis? What do your conclusions say about Egyptian religion? Explain the term "negative confession." What is the rationale behind this practice?

6. Compare Egyptian and Mesopotamian views of religion by analyzing the various selections on the nature of the gods, death, and the afterlife. What general conclusions can you draw? The geography of a region often influences the development of a civilization. In what ways did geography influence the religious outlooks of Mesopotamia and Egypt?

7. What was the Amarna "revolution" and why was it a radical change for Egyptians? What does the "Hymn to the Aton" reveal about Akhenaton's conception of the deity? Compare this with Psalm 104 from the Old Testament. What are the similarities? Can you make any conclusions?

8. After reading the selections from Genesis on the origin of the world, paradise, and the fall from grace, analyze why these have been so influential in Western Civilization. What do the Garden of Eden and the Tree of Life represent? What are the two stories about the creation of woman? What is the relative position of women to men at the biblical origin of life? How have these passages from Genesis been used to structure social attitudes and expectations throughout the centuries? Do they still have impact today?

9. What was Moses' mission as recorded in the Old Testament? Why is the Exodus from Egypt central to the Jewish experience? What does it say about Yahweh's relationship with the Hebrews? How does the "new covenant" of Jeremiah

differ from the original (as embodied in the Ten Commandments) established by Yahweh with Moses? Why the need for a new covenant? Be specific in your use of the primary sources.

10. Note the Hebrew concern for moral instructions and law. Compare the Covenant Code with the Code of Hammurabi. In what ways are they similar? Were the Mesopotamians, Egyptians, and Hebrews all concerned with living a good, moral life? What values were most appreciated?

11. How did the duties and responsibilities of a king differ among the Mesopotamians, Egyptians, and Hebrews? Compare especially Sargon, Hammurabi, Akhenaton, Ramses II, and Solomon.

PART II

THE GREEK WORLD

2

The Glory of Greece

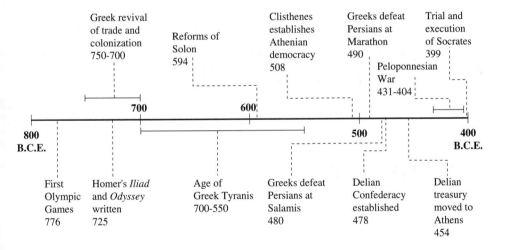

Greek revival of trade and colonization 750-700

Reforms of Solon 594

Clisthenes establishes Athenian democracy 508

Greeks defeat Persians at Marathon 490

Trial and execution of Socrates 399

Peloponnesian War 431-404

700

600

500

800 B.C.E.

400 B.C.E.

First Olympic Games 776

Homer's *Iliad* and *Odyssey* written 725

Age of Greek Tyrants 700-550

Greeks defeat Persians at Salamis 480

Delian Confederacy established 478

Delian treasury moved to Athens 454

Zeus spoke, and nodded with his darkish brows, and immortal locks fell forward from the lord's deathless head, and he made great Olympus tremble.

—Homer

You could not step twice in the same river, for other and yet other waters are ever flowing on.

—Heraclitus

Go and be happy, but remember whom you leave shackled by love.

—Sappho

Of all the wondrous things on earth, the greatest of these is man.

—Sophocles

Democracy is based on the conviction that man has the moral and intellectual capacity, as well as the inalienable right, to govern himself with reason and justice.

—Harry S Truman

Excessive freedom leads to anarchy, which in turn results in despotism, the most burdensome and most brutal slavery.

—Plato

In the strict sense of the term, a true democracy has never existed and never will exist.

—Jean-Jacques Rousseau

When the Athenians finally wanted not to give to society, but for society to give to them, when the freedom they wished for was freedom from responsibility, then Athens ceased to be free.

—Edward Gibbon

CHAPTER THEMES

- *Systems of Government:* What was the relationship between Homeric kings like Agamemnon and retainers like Achilles and Odysseus? Is aristocracy, or "rule by the best," a workable form of government? How would you define democracy in the classical sense of the term? Was Athens a democracy? Is democracy the best and most natural form of government for people?

- *Imperialism:* How did Athens gain and maintain its empire? Can a democracy possess an empire, or is this a moral contradiction?

- *Beliefs and Spirituality:* What role did the gods play in the imagination of the early Greeks? How sophisticated was the pantheon of Greek gods when compared with the monotheism of the Hebrews? What was the Greek view of the afterlife? How do the stories and legends regarding the Greek gods and their interaction with humans reflect the creativity of Greek culture?

- *Women in History:* How were women portrayed in early Greek society as viewed in the *Iliad* and *Odyssey* of Homer? Is this picture consistent with the view of women during the Golden Age of Greece in the fifth century B.C.E.? Did the Athenian democracy consider women political equals?

- ***Historical Change and Transition:***   The history of fifth-century Greece has generally been viewed as a great success story. Is success in war or government a necessary foundation for success in the arts? How essential is arrogance to the progress of civilization? Was Athens created and then destroyed by its hubris?

- ***The Big Picture:***   Do the great artistic and literary creations of civilization justify the means of obtaining them? Is there a political price to pay for cultural progress?

When people think of history, they often assume that it is the compilation of facts and dates that have happened in the past, which therefore play no relevant role in our contemporary lives. This is a common misapprehension fueled by sterile presentations in textbooks and numbing multiple-choice tests in school. Actually the word "history" is derived from a Greek root meaning "inquiry." The task of the historian is not to compile "facts," but rather to inquire into the records of past societies in hopes of establishing what actually happened and, more importantly, why it happened. The historian has often been likened to a detective, searching for clues, analyzing and interpreting evidence. It is a profession that is immediately relevant. For in the discussion of past societies, historians deal primarily with human beings, their hopes and fears, their ideas, their hostilities, their successes and failures. Always at issue is the question "Why?" History, therefore, is about interpretation. What constitutes a "fact"? Since history is often written by the victors, they can interpret without defiance and create belief through propaganda. The "truth" is often a casualty of such interpretation, and therein lies the value of assessment and reassessment of the past by professional historians. The road toward Truth is a difficult path, obscured by time, conflicting evidence, or governments with "ideological priorities." Every student must learn to evaluate the past and become his or her own historian. This is essential in creating the perspective necessary to evaluate one's own life and place in society.

In trying to establish just what happened in the past and why, historians focus on a wide variety of sources, most of which were not originally composed or constructed to serve as a window to the past: secret dispatches, letters, diary accounts, poems, newspaper articles, propaganda fliers, coins, pottery, and even wall graffiti can open a new world to the historian. One of the more uncertain and controversial historical sources is the evidence of legend and myth. The mythology of a culture—the stories of heroism, of deities, of moral instruction—often seems to reflect a fantasy world where reality is suspended and the pure joy of creativity is unleashed. But the legends of a culture not only tell us about the values of a people, they can also lead historians toward reconstruction of the past. This question of the appropriateness of legend in the reconstruction of the past is nowhere more evident than in the debate regarding the Trojan War and the Minoan and Mycenaean societies of Bronze Age Greece.

Can we accept the monumental narrative poems of the *Iliad* and the *Odyssey*, which deal with the legendary Troy and its fight to the death with the forces from mainland Greece about 1230 B.C.E., as valid historical sources, or must they be relegated to the world of fantasy? The skepticism is even more fundamental: Did their author, Homer, even exist? Was he one person or several, or simply the compiler of oral legends that had been handed down and amplified by several singers over the centuries? What can they tell us of the developing values and ideals of Greek society?

A second focus of this chapter will be on the greatness and moral contradictions apparent in classical Greek society during its Golden Age. The city-state of Athens has been widely admired for its contributions to Western Civilization during the fifth century B.C.E. This was a time of great intellectual energy, producing enduring works of art, architecture, philosophy, drama, and history. The confidence necessary to achieve such heights was granted early in the century when the Greek city-states united to repel two invasions by the mighty Persian empire. The Spartan military machine had proved its worth at the battle of Thermopylae, and the Athenian reputation for cleverness was established by Themistocles at the battle of Salamis in 480 B.C.E. On this note of triumph, the Golden Age of Athens began.

During the period from 480 to 430 B.C.E., leaders such as Pericles extolled the superiority of Athenian democratic government and the freedom essential to Athenian greatness. Yet, critics of the time pointed out the shortcomings of the democracy and of its leadership. At root, it might be argued that the greatness of Athenian civilization depended upon her "allies," or fellow members of the Delian Confederacy. This Confederacy was established in 478 B.C.E., after the Persian wars, to ensure that the Greeks would not be attacked by Persia again. Further, Greek cities on the coast of Asia Minor were to be freed and booty obtained from Persia to offset the costs of Confederate expeditions and past losses. Theoretically, Athens had no greater vote than any of her Confederates, but almost from the outset she held the keys to power, contributing both the administrators of the treasury on the island of Delos and the commanders of the military expeditions. By 466 B.C.E., after several Confederate victories, it became evident that Persia no longer posed a threat to the city-states of Greece or the islands in the Aegean Sea. Some members wished to secede (Naxos in 469, Thasos in 465 B.C.E.), but they were opposed and militarily crushed by Athens. Secession from the Confederacy would not be tolerated. In 454 B.C.E., the treasury was moved from the island of Delos to Athens. The patron goddess, Athena, supervised the protection of all tribute that came into Athens (called the "first fruits"). The great Athenian orator Pericles maintained the Athenian Empire (as the Delian Confederacy came to be called) partly to counter Spartan land power and managed it efficiently so as to produce revenues essential to the glorification of Athens. By 447 B.C.E., work on the Parthenon had begun, and several other building projects, artists, and sculptors would be financed by funds contributed by Athenian "allies."

Athens controlled its empire rigidly, maintaining order by imposing its own laws and customs on subject cities. Every four years, its subjects came to Athens to participate in the Panatheneia, a celebration honoring the patron goddess Athena. There they gathered to learn what their tax assessment would be for the next four years. The Athenians inscribed these assessments on a great monolith, located on the Acropolis, called the Tribute Lists. Such a blatant reminder of their subservience must have been difficult for the Athenian allies to bear.

From 431 to 404 B.C.E., the Spartans and Athenians entered into a great conflict that came to be called the Peloponnesian War. This war was born of Spartan distrust for the growing Athenian power and trade influence in areas heretofore controlled by Sparta and its allies. The two city-states, so different in outlook and political orientation, fought, as the historian Thucydides noted, the greatest war "in Greek history, affecting a large part of the non-Greek world, and I might also say, the whole of mankind."

In the end, Athens lost not only the physical struggle and its empire, but also the edge of confidence that had propelled its democracy and inspired its poets and statesmen. Perhaps the greatest indication of this loss was the execution of the philosopher Socrates. His penetrating questions demanded reflection on Athenian values and ideals. He considered himself a gadfly whose job it was to prod Athens to self-awareness by challenging the very foundation of its beliefs. Socrates was condemned to death in 399 B.C.E. on rather nebulous charges. His death was symbolic of the rigid defensiveness of a decaying democracy.

The historical problem at issue here involves the compatibility of democracy and empire. From a moral standpoint, should a state that espouses freedom for all of its citizens control an empire that is maintained by fear and force? Is it even possible for a democratic government to rule an empire effectively? Finally, do the beauty and cultural worth of the monuments of a civilization justify the means of obtaining them? In other words, what price civilization?

The World of Early Greece

The Trojan War: Homer's Iliad

The Trojan War stands as one of the most famous events in history. The poet Homer compiled the account of this epic confrontation between the Greeks (led by Agamemnon together with his greatest warrior, Achilles, and the "quick-witted" Odysseus) and the Trojans, whose warriors controlled the northwestern coast of modern Turkey. The Greeks had set out to avenge the abduction of the beautiful Helen, wife of their overlord, Menelaus, by the wily Paris, prince of Troy. The Greek gods also assumed a prominence in the conflict. They had their favorites among the mortals and intervened as their "human personalities" demanded. The story of the Iliad *and the destruction of Troy is a powerful classic of world literature.*

The story begins with Achilles' anger at Agamemnon's claim of the beautiful woman Briseis, who had been granted to Achilles as a prize. The action moves to Achilles' friend, Patroclus, who fights and dies at the hands of Troy's greatest warrior, Hector, while Achilles sulks in his camp. The last passage recounts the vengeance of Achilles as he fights Hector to the death.

Hateful to me as the gates of Hades is that man who hides one thing in his heart and speaks another.

—Homer

It would have been a far better thing for me to stand up to Achilles, and either kill him and come home alive or myself die gloriously in front of Troy.

—Homer

Friendship between us is impossible, and there will be no truce of any kind till one of us has fallen and glutted the stubborn god of battles with his blood. So summon any courage you may have.

—Homer

The Wrath of Achilles

HOMER

King Agamemnon took him up at once. "You are a great man, Prince Achilles, but do not imagine you can trick me into that. I am not going to be outwitted or cajoled by you. 'Give up the girl,' you say, hoping, I presume, to keep your own prize safe. Do you expect me tamely to sit by while I am robbed? No; if the army is prepared to give me a fresh prize, chosen to suit my taste and to make up for my loss, I have no more to say. If not, I shall come and help myself to your prize, or that of Aias; or I shall walk off with Odysseus's. And what an angry man I shall leave behind me! However, we can deal with all that later on. For the moment, let us run a black ship down into the friendly sea, give her a special crew, embark the animals for sacrifice, and put the girl herself, Chryseis of the lovely cheeks, on board. And let some Councillor of ours go as captain—Aias, Idomeneus, the excellent Odysseus, or yourself, my lord, the most redoubtable man we could choose—to offer the sacrifice and win us back Apollo's favor."

Achilles the great runner gave him a black look. "You shameless schemer," he cried, "always aiming at a profitable deal! How can you expect any of the

"The Wrath of Achilles" is from Homer, *The Iliad*, trans. E. V. Rieu (Baltimore, Md., and Harmondsworth, Middlesex: Penguin Books, 1950), pp. 26–29. Copyright © E. V. Rieu, 1950. Reprinted by permission.

men to give you loyal service when you send them on a raid or into battle? It was no quarrel with the Trojan spearmen that brought me here to fight. They have never done me any harm. They have never lifted cow or horse of mine, nor ravaged any crop that the deep soil of Phythia grows to feed her men; for the roaring seas and many a dark range of mountains lie between us. The truth is that we joined the expedition to please you; yes, you unconscionable cur, to get satisfaction from the Trojans for Menelaus and yourself—a fact which you utterly ignore. And now comes this threat from you of all people to rob me of my prize, my hard-earned prize, which was a tribute from the ranks. It is not as though I am ever given as much as you when the Achaeans sack some thriving city of the Trojans. The heat and burden of the fighting fall on me, but when it comes to dealing out the loot, it is you that take the lion's share, leaving me to return exhausted from the field with something of my own, however small. So now I shall go back to Phythia. That is the best thing I can do—to sail home in my beaked ships. I see no point in staying here to be insulted while I pile up wealth and luxuries for you."

"Take to your heels, by all means," Agamemnon King of men retorted, "if you feel the urge to go. I am not begging you to stay on my account. There are others with me who will treat me with respect, and the Counsellor Zeus is first among them. Moreover, of all the princes here, you are the most disloyal to myself. To you, sedition, violence and fighting are the breath of life. What if you are a great soldier—who made you so but God? Go home now with you ships and your men-at-arms and rule the Myrmidons. I have no use for you: your anger leaves me cold. But mark my words. In the same way as Phoebus Apollo is robbing me of Chryseis, whom I propose to send off in my ship with my own crew, I am going to pay a visit to your hut and take away the beautiful Briseis, your prize, Achilles, to let you know that I am more powerful than you, and to teach others not to bandy words with me and openly defy their King."

This cut Achilles to the quick. In his shaggy breast his heart was torn between two courses, whether to draw his sharp sword from his side, thrust his way through the crowd, and kill King Agamemnon, or to control himself and check the angry impulse. He was deep in this inward conflict, with his long sword half unsheathed, when Athena came down to him from heaven. . . . Athena stood behind him and seized him by his golden locks. No one but Achilles was aware of her; the rest saw nothing. He swung round in amazement, recognized Pallas Athena at once—so terrible was the brilliance of her eyes—and spoke out to her boldly: "And why have you come here, Daughter of aegis-bearing Zeus? Is it to witness the arrogance of my lord Agamemnon? I tell you bluntly—and I make no idle threats—that he stands to pay for this outrage with his life."

"I come from heaven," replied Athena of the Flashing Eyes, "in the hope of bringing you to your senses. . . . Come now, give up this strife and take your hand from your sword. Sting him with words instead, and tell him what you mean to do. Here is a prophecy for you—the day shall come when gifts three times as valuable as what you now have lost will be laid at your feet in

payment for this outrage. Hold your hand then, and be advised by us." . . .
With that he checked his great hand on the silver hilt and drove the long
sword back into its scabbard, in obedience to Athena. . . . Not that Achilles
was appeased. . . .

"Mark my words, for I am going to take a solemn oath. Look at this staff. . . .
By this I swear (and I could not choose a better token) that the day is coming
when the Achaeans one and all will miss me sorely, and you in your despair
will be powerless to help them as they fall in their hundreds to Hector, killer
of men. Then, you will tear your heart out in remorse for having treated the
best man in the expedition with contempt."

The Death of Patroclus

HOMER

When Achilles had drawn them all up, officers and men, in their proper
places, he made them a forceful speech. "Myrmidons," he said, "let none of
you forget what you have been threatening to do to the Trojans all the time I
kept you here beside your ships while I indulged my anger. There is not one
of you who did not abuse your prince. You called me a brute for keeping my
men idle here against their will. I was a sort of monster, brought up on bile
instead of mother's milk." . . .

"Well now, a bit of real work has come your way, just such a fight as you
have longed for. Go to it then, and fall on the Trojans like brave men." His
words filled every one of them with daring, and the ranks dressed closer
when they heard their prince. . . . But Achilles went off to his hut. . . . Then
he went to the middle of the forecourt to pray and looked up into the sky as
he poured out the wine, watched all the time by thunder-loving Zeus. "Lord
Zeus," he began, "you listened when I prayed to you before, and you showed
your regard for me by striking a mighty blow at the Achaean army. Grant me
another wish. I myself am going to stay among the ships, but I am sending my
comrade with many of the Myrmidons into the field. Bless him with victory . . .
and fill his heart with daring, so that Hector himself may find out whether my
squire can fight on his own, or whether his hands are invincible only when I
throw myself into the fray."

Zeus the Counsellor heard Achilles' prayer and granted him half of it but
not the rest. The Father agreed that Patroclus should chase the Trojans from
the ships, but not that he should come back safely from the battle. . . .

When Hector saw the great Patroclus creeping wounded from the field, he
made his way towards him through the ranks, and coming up, he struck him

"The Death of Patroclus" is from Homer, *The Iliad*, trans. E. V. Rieu (Baltimore, Md., and Harmondsworth, Middlesex: Penguin Books, 1950), pp. 297–299, 314–315. Copyright © E. V. Rieu,
1950. Reprinted by permission.

with a spear in the lower part of the belly, driving the bronze clean through. Patroclus fell with a thud; and the whole Achaean army was appalled. It was like the conquest of an indomitable wild-boar by a lion, after a battle fought in high fury up in the mountains over a little stream at which both wish to drink. The lion's strength prevails and his panting enemy is overcome. So, after killing many men himself, [Patroclus] fell to a short spear-cast from Hector, son of Priam, who now addressed him as his conqueror. "Patroclus," he said, "you thought you would sack my town, make Trojan women slaves, and ship them off to your own country. You were a fool. In their defence, Hector's fast horses were hastening into battle; and so was Hector himself, I, Hector, finest spearman of the war-loving Trojans, who stand between them and the day of slavery. So now the vultures here are going to eat you up. Poor wretch; even the strong arm of Achilles did not save you. I can imagine all he told you when he sent you out—and stayed behind. 'Patroclus, master of the Horse, don't let me see you back at the hollow ships, till you have torn the tunic on man-killing Hector's breast and soaked it with his blood.' That is what he must have said; and like a lunatic you took him at his word."

And what did Patroclus say to this? "Hector," he replied in a failing voice, "boast while you may. The victory is yours—a gift from Zeus the Son of Cronos and Apollo. They conquered me. . . . Already Destiny and Death are very close to you, death at the hands of Achilles the peerless son of Peleus."

Death cut Patroclus short and his disembodied soul took wing for the House of Hades, bewailing its lot and the youth and manhood that it left. But illustrious Hector spoke to him again, dead though he was. "Patroclus," he said, "why be so sure of an early end for me? Who knows? Achilles, son of Thetis of the Lovely Locks, may yet forestall me by ending his life with a blow from my spear."

The Death of Hector

HOMER

"Hector!" the old man called, stretching out his arms to him in piteous appeal. "I beg you, my dear son, not to stand up to that man alone and unsupported. You are courting defeat and death at his hands. He is far stronger than you, and he is savage. . . . So come inside the walls, my child, to be the savior of Troy and the Trojans; and do not throw away your own dear life to give a triumph to the son of Peleus. Have pity too on me, your poor father, who is still able to feel. Think of the hideous fate that Father Zeus has kept in store for my old age, the horrors I shall have to see before I die, the massacre

"The Death of Hector" is from Homer, *The Iliad*, trans. E. V. Rieu (Baltimore, Md., and Harmondsworth, Middlesex: Penguin Books, 1950), pp. 398–400, 403–408, 410. Copyright © E. V. Rieu, 1950. Reprinted by permission.

of my sons, my daughters mauled, their bedrooms pillaged, their babies dashed on the ground by the brutal enemy, and my sons' wives hauled away by foul Achaean hands. Last of all my turn will come to fall to the sharp bronze, and when someone's javelin or sword has laid me dead, I shall be torn to pieces by ravening dogs at my own street door. . . ."

Hector thought: "If I retire behind the gate and wall, Polydamnas will be the first to cast it in my teeth that, in this last night of disaster when the great Achilles came to life, I did not take his advice and order a withdrawal into the city, as I certainly ought to have done. As it is, having sacrificed the army to my own perversity, I could not face my countrymen and the Trojan ladies in their trailing gowns. I could not bear to hear some commoner say: 'Hector trusted in his own right arm and lost an army.' But it will be said, and then I shall know that it would have been a far better thing for me to stand up to Achilles, and either kill him and come home alive or myself die gloriously in front of Troy. . . ."

While Hector stood engrossed in this inward debate, Achilles drew near him, looking like the god of War in his flashing helmet, girt for battle. Over his right shoulder he brandished the formidable ashen spear of Pelion, and the bronze on his body glowed like a blazing fire or the rising sun. Hector looked up, saw him, and began to tremble. . . .

Great Hector of the flashing helmet spoke first: "My lord Achilles, I have been chased by you three times round the great city of Priam without daring to stop and let you come near. But now I am going to run away no longer. I have made up my mind to fight you man to man and kill you or be killed. But first let us make a bargain, you with your gods for witness, I with mine. . . . If Zeus allows me to endure, and I kill you, I undertake to do no outrage to your body that custom does not sanction. All I shall do, Achilles, is to strip you of your splendid armor. Then I will give up your corpse to the Achaeans. Will you do the same for me?"

Achilles of the nimble feet looked at him grimly and replied: "Hector, you must be mad to talk to me about a pact. Lions do not come to terms with men, nor does the wolf see eye to eye with the lamb—they are enemies to the end. It is the same with you and me. Friendship between us is impossible, and there will be no truce of any kind till one of us has fallen and glutted the stubborn god of battles with his blood. So summon any courage you may have. This is the time to show your spearmanship and daring. Not that anything is going to save you now, when Pallas Athena is waiting to fell you with my spear. This moment you are going to pay the full price for all you made me suffer when your lance mowed down my friends." . . .

Achilles saw that Hector's body was completely covered by the fine bronze amour he had taken from the great Patroclus when he killed him, except for an opening at the gullet where the collar bones lead over from the shoulders to the neck, the easiest place to kill a man. As Hector charged him, Prince Achilles drove at this spot with his lance; and the point went right through the tender flesh of Hector's neck, though the heavy bronze head did not cut his windpipe, and left him able to address his conqueror. . . .

Hector of the flashing helmet spoke to him once more at the point of death. "How well I know you and can read your mind!" he said. "Your heart is hard as iron. . . . Nevertheless, pause before you act, in case the angry gods remember how you treated me, when your turn comes and you are brought down. . . ."

Death cut Hector short and his disembodied soul took wing for the House of Hades, bewailing its lot and the youth and manhood that it left. But Prince Achilles spoke to him again though he was gone. "Die!" he said. "As for my own death, let it come when Zeus and the other deathless gods decide." . . .

The next thing that Achilles did was to subject the fallen prince to shameful outrage. He slit the tendons at the back of both his feet from heel to ankle, inserted leather straps, and made them fast to his chariot, leaving the head to drag. Then he lifted the famous armor into his chariot, got in himself, and with a touch of his whip started the horses, who flew off with a will. Dragged behind him, Hector raised a cloud of dust, his black locks streamed on either side, and dust fell thick upon his head, so comely once, which Zeus now let his enemies defile on his own native soil.

Thus Hector's head was tumbled in the dust. When his mother saw what they were doing to her son, she tore her hair, and plucking the bright veil from her head cast it away with a loud and bitter cry. His father groaned in anguish, the people round them took up the cry of grief, and the whole city gave itself up to despair. They could not have lamented louder if Ilium had been going up in flames, from its crowning citadel to its lowest street. . . .

Andromache, with palpitating heart, rushed out of the house like a mad woman, and her maidservants went with her. When they came to the wall, where the men had gathered in a crowd, she climbed up on the battlements, searched the plain, and saw them dragging her husband in front of the town—the powerful horses were hauling him along at an easy canter towards the Achaean ships. The world went black as night before Andromache's eyes. She lost her senses and fell backward to the ground. . . . As she lay there in a dead faint, her husband's sisters and his brothers' wives crowded around her and supported her between them. When at length she recovered and came to herself, she burst out sobbing and made her lament to the ladies of Troy.

"Alas, Hector; alas for me!" she cried. . . . "For you are on your way to Hades and the unknown world below, leaving me behind in misery, a widow in your house. And your son is no more than a baby, the son we conceived between us, we unhappy parents. You, Hector, now that you are dead, will be no joy to him, nor he to you. Even if he escapes the horrors of the Achaean war, nothing lies ahead of him but hardship and trouble. . . . And you, by the beaked ships, far from your parents, will be eaten by the worms when the dogs have had their fill. . . ."

Thus Andromache lamented through her tears, and the women joined in her lament.

Greek Values: The Odyssey *of Homer*

The Iliad *and the* Odyssey *were perhaps the most influential works in Greek history. Greek and Roman education was fundamentally concerned with the values expressed in these two works. Alexander the Great was even said to have slept with a copy of the* Iliad *under his pillow. And yet the* Odyssey *is very different in temperament and theme than the* Iliad. *The* Odyssey *speaks of homecoming, of love, longing, and revenge. It is the story of Odysseus, a great fighter for the Greeks at Troy whose inspired ploy of the Trojan horse resulted in the Greek victory over the Trojans. But in spite of his brilliance, or perhaps because of it, his homecoming was delayed for ten years as the gods conspired with monsters and witches to interrupt his life. His adventure with the one-eyed Cyclops and his dramatic visit to the underworld, where he meets the souls of Achilles and Agamemnon, are two of the most dramatic stories in literature. But Odysseus's return to his island of Ithaca, his introduction to his adult son, Telemachus, his vengeance on the suitors of his wife, Penelope, and their tearful recognition capture the brilliance of the poet history has called Homer.*

Tell me, Muse, of the man of many devices, who wandered far and wide after he had sacked Troy's sacred city, and saw the towns of many men and knew their mind.

—Homer

I will drink life to the lees: all times I have enjoyed greatly, have suffered greatly, both with those that love me, and alone. . . . I am become a name; for always roaming with a hungry heart much have I seen and known; cities of men and manners, climates, councils, governments. . . . and drunk delight of battle, with my peers, far on the ringing plains of windy Troy. I am a part of all that I have met.

—Alfred Lord Tennyson ("Ulysses")

The Adventure of the Cyclops

HOMER

"When [the Cyclops] had done with his business and finished all his jobs, he lit up the fire, spied us, and began asking questions.

" 'Strangers!' he said. 'And who may you be? Where do you hail from over the highways of the sea? Is yours a trading venture; or are you cruising the main on chance, like roving pirates, who risk their lives to ruin other people?'

"The Adventure of the Cyclops" is from Homer, *The Odyssey*, trans. E. V. Rieu (Baltimore, Md., and Harmondsworth, Middlesex: Penguin Books, 1946), pp. 146–150, 152–153. Copyright © E. V. Rieu, 1946. Reprinted by permission.

"Our hearts sank within us. The booming voice and the very sight of the monster filled us with panic. Still, I managed to find words to answer him.

"'We are Achaeans,' I said, 'on our way back from Troy, driven astray by contrary winds across a vast expanse of sea. Far from planning to come here, we meant to sail straight home; but we lost our bearings, as Zeus, I suppose, intended that we should. We are proud to belong to the forces of Agamemnon, Atreus' son, who by sacking the great city of Ilium [Troy] and destroying all its armies has made himself the most famous man in the world today. We, less fortunate, are visiting you here as suppliants, in the hope that you may give us friendly entertainment or even go further in your generosity. You know the laws of hospitality: I beseech you, good sir, to remember your duty to the gods. For we throw ourselves on your mercy; and Zeus is there to avenge the suppliant and the guest. He is the travellers' god; he guards their steps and he invites them with their rights.'

"So said I, and promptly he answered me out of his pitiless heart: 'Stranger, you must be a fool, or must have come from very far afield, to preach to me of fear or reverence for the gods. We Cyclopes care not a jot for Zeus with his aegis [shield], nor for the rest of the blessed gods, since we are much stronger than they. It would never occur to me to spare you or your men against my will for fear of trouble from Zeus. But tell me where you moored your good ship when you came. Was it somewhere up the coast, or near by? I should like to see her.'

"He was trying to get the better of me, but I knew enough of the world to see through him and I met him with deceit. 'As for my ship,' I answered, 'it was wrecked by the Earth-shaker Poseidon on the confines of your land. The wind had carried us onto a lee shore. He drove the ship up to a headland and hurtled it on the rocks. But I and my friends managed to escape with our lives.'

"To this the cruel brute made no reply. Instead, he jumped up, and reaching out towards my men, seized a couple and dashed their heads against the floor as though they had been puppies. Their brains ran out on the ground and soaked the earth. Limb by limb he tore them to pieces to make his meal, which he devoured like a mountain lion, never pausing till entrails and flesh, marrow and bones, were all consumed, while we could do nothing but weep and lift up our hands to Zeus in horror at the ghastly sight, paralysed by our sense of utter helplessness. When the Cyclops had filled his great belly with this meal of human flesh, which he washed down with unwatered milk, he stretched himself out for sleep among his flocks inside the cave. . . ."

"'Here Cyclops, have some wine to wash down that meal of human flesh, and find out for yourself what kind of vintage was stored away in our ship's hold. I brought it for you by way of an offering in the hope that you would be charitable and help me on my homeward way. But your savagery is more than we can bear. Cruel monster, how can you expect ever to have a visitor again from the world of men, after such deeds as you have done?'"

"The Cyclops took the wine and drank it up. And the delicious draught gave him such exquisite pleasure that he asked me for another bowlful. . . .

Three times I filled it up for him; and three times the fool drained the bowl to the dregs. At last, when the wine had fuddled his wits, I addressed him with disarming suavity.

"'Cyclops,' I said, 'you wish to know the name I bear. I'll tell it to you; and in return I should like to have the gift you promised me. My name is Nobody. That is what I am called by my mother and father and by all my friends.'

"The Cyclops answered me with a cruel jest. 'Of all his company I will eat Nobody last, and the rest before him. That shall be your gift.'

"He had hardly spoken before he toppled over and fell face upwards on the floor, where he lay with his great neck twisted to one side, conquered, as all men are, by sleep. His drunkenness made him vomit, and a stream of wine mixed with morsels of men's flesh poured from his throat. I went at once and thrust our pole deep under the ashes of the fire to make it hot, and meanwhile gave a word of encouragement to all my men, to make sure that no one should play the coward and leave me in the lurch. When the fierce glow from the olive stake warned me that it was about to catch alight in the flames, green as it was, I withdrew it from the fire and brought it over to the spot where my men were standing ready. Heaven now inspired them with a reckless courage. Seizing the olive pole, they drove its sharpened end into the Cyclops' eye, while I used my weight from above to twist it home, like a man boring a ship's timber with a drill which his mates below him twirl with a strap they hold at either end, so that it spins continuously. In much the same way we handled our pole with its red-hot point and twisted it in his eye till the blood boiled up round the burning wood. The fiery smoke from the blazing eyeball singed his lids and brow all round, and the very roots of his eye crackled in the heat. I was reminded of the loud hiss that comes from a great axe . . . when a smith plunges it into cold water—to temper it and give strength to the iron. That is how the Cyclops' eye hissed round the olive stake. He gave a dreadful shriek, which echoed round the rocky walls, and we backed away from him in terror, while he pulled the stake from his eye, streaming with blood. Then he hurled it away from him with frenzied hands and raised a great shout for the other Cyclopes who lived in neighboring caves along the windy heights. These, hearing his screams, came from every quarter, and gathering outside the cave asked him what ailed him:

"'What on earth is wrong with you, Polyphemus? Why must you disturb the peaceful night and spoil our sleep with all this shouting? Is a robber driving off your sheep, or is somebody trying by treachery or violence to kill you?'

"Out of the cave came Polyphemus' great voice in reply: 'O my friends, it's Nobody's treachery, no violence, that is doing me to death.'

"'Well then,' they answered, in a way that settled the matter, 'if nobody is assaulting you in your solitude, you must be sick. Sickness comes from almighty Zeus and cannot be helped. All you can do is to pray to your father, the Lord Poseidon.'

[The next morning, Odysseus and his men escaped from the Cyclops' cave by holding on to the underside of Polyphemus' sheep. The blinded Cyclops felt the top of each sheep as they left the cave, but did not detect any of Odysseus' men.]

"When we had put a little distance between ourselves and the courtyard of the cave, I first freed myself from under my ram and next untied my men from theirs. Then, quickly, though with many a backward look, we drove our long-legged sheep right down to the ship.... With a nod, [I made clear my will to each man], bidding them make haste to tumble all the fleecy sheep on board and put to sea. So in they jumped, ran to the benches, sorted themselves out, and plied the grey water with their oars.

"But before we were out of earshot, I let Polyphemus have a piece of my mind. 'Cyclops!' I called. 'So he was not such a weakling after all, the man whose friends you meant to overpower and eat in that snug cave of yours! And your crimes came home to roost, you brute, who have not even the decency to refrain from devouring your own guests. Now Zeus and all his fellow-gods have paid you out.'

"My taunts so exasperated the angry Cyclops that he tore the top off a great pinnacle of rock and hurled it at us. The rock fell just ahead of our blue-painted bows. As it plunged in, the water rose and the backwash, like a swell from the open sea, swept us landward and nearly drove us on the beach. ... After I roused my crew with urgent nods, ... they buckled to and rowed with a will ... and brought us across the water to twice our previous distance. ... My spirit was up, and in my rage I called to him once more:

"'Cyclops, if anyone ever asks you how you came by your unsightly blindness, tell him your eye was put out by Odysseus, Sacker of Cities, the son of Laertes, who lives in Ithaca.'"

Odysseus in the Underworld

HOMER

[I saw the soul of Agamemnon, which] burst into tears, stretching his arms out in my direction in his eagerness to reach me. But this he could not do, for all the strength and vigor had gone forever from those once supple limbs. Moved to compassion at the sight, I too gave way to tears and spoke to him from my heart:

"'Illustrious son of Atreus, Agamemnon, King of men, tell me what mortal stroke of fate it was that laid you low. Did Poseidon rouse the winds to fury and overwhelm your ships? Or did you fall to some hostile tribe on land as you were rounding up their cattle and their flocks or fighting with them for their town and women?'

"'Royal son of Laertes, Odysseus of the nimble wits,' he answered me at once, 'Poseidon did not wreck my ships; nor did I fall to any hostile tribe on land. It was Aegisthus who plotted my destruction and with my accursed wife

"Odysseus in the Underworld" is from Homer, *The Odyssey,* trans. E. V. Rieu (Baltimore, Md., and Harmondsworth, Middlesex: Penguin Books, 1946), pp. 182–184. Copyright © E. V. Rieu, 1946. Reprinted by permission.

put me to death. He invited me to the palace, he feasted me, and he killed me as a man fells an ox at its manger. That was my most miserable end. And all around me my companions were cut down in ruthless succession, like white-tusked swine slaughtered in the mansion of some great and wealthy lord, for a wedding, a club banquet, or a sumptuous public feast. You, Odysseus, have witnessed the deaths of many men in single combat or the thick of battle, but none with such horror as you would have felt had you seen us lying there by the wine-bowl and the laden tables in the hall, while the whole floor swam with our blood. Yet the most pitiable thing of all was the cry I heard from Cassandra, daughter of Priam, whom that foul traitress Clytemnestra [Agamemnon's wife] murdered at my side. As I lay on the ground, I raised my hands in a dying effort to grip Clytemnestra's sword. But the harlot turned her face aside, and had not even the grace, though I was on my way to Hades, to shut my eyes with her hands or to close my mouth. And so I say that for brutality and infamy there is no one to equal a woman who can contemplate such deeds. Who else could conceive so hideous a crime as her deliberate butchery of her husband and her lord? Indeed, I had looked forward to a rare welcome from my children and my servants when I reached home. But now, in the depth of her villainy, she has branded not herself alone but the whole of her sex and every honest woman for all time to come.'

"'Alas!' I exclaimed. 'All-seeing Zeus has indeed proved himself a relentless foe to the House of Atreus, and from the beginning he has worked his will through women's crooked ways. It was for Helen's sake that so many of us met our deaths, and it was Clytemnestra who hatched the plot against her absent lord.'

"'Let this be a lesson to you also,' replied Agamemnon. 'Never be too gentle even with your wife, nor show her all that is in your mind. Reveal a little of your counsel to her, but keep the rest of it to yourself. Not that your wife, Odysseus, will ever murder you. Icarius' daughter is far too sound in heart and brain for that. The wise Penelope! She was a young bride when we said goodbye to her on our way to the war. She had a baby son at her breast. And now, I suppose, he has begun to take his seat among the men. The lucky lad! His loving father will come home and see him, and he will kiss his father. That is how things should be. Whereas that wife of mine refused me even the satisfaction of setting eyes on my son. She could not wait so long before she killed his father. And now let me give you a piece of advice which I hope you will take to heart. Do not sail openly into port when you reach your home-country. Make a secret approach. Women, I tell you, are no longer to be trusted. . . .'

"Such was the solemn conversation that we two had as we stood there with our sorrows and the tears rolled down our cheeks. And now there came the souls of Peleus' son Achilles, of Patroclus, of the noble Antilochus, and of Aias. . . . It was the soul of Achilles, the great runner, who recognized me. In mournful, measured tones he greeted me by my titles, and went on: 'What next, Odysseus, dauntless heart? What greater exploit can you plan to cap your voyage here? How did you dare to come below to Hades' realm, where the dead live on without their wits as disembodied ghosts?'

"'Achilles,' I answered him, 'son of Peleus and flower of Achaean chivalry, I came to consult with Teiresias in the hope of finding out from him how I could reach my rocky Ithaca. For I have not managed to come near Achaea yet, nor set foot on my own island, but have been dogged by misfortune. How different from you, Achilles, the most fortunate man that ever was or will be! For in the old days when you were on earth, we Argives honored you as though you were a god; and now, down here, you are a mighty prince among the dead. For you, Achilles, Death should have lost his sting.'

"'My lord Odysseus,' he replied, 'spare me your praise of Death. Put me on earth again, and I would rather be a serf in the house of some landless man, with little enough for himself to live on, than king of all these dead men that have done with life.'"

The Return of Odysseus

HOMER

Amid all the Suitors' banter, the cool-headed Odysseus had poised the great bow and given it a final inspection. And now . . . he strung the great bow without effort or haste and with his right hand proved the string, which gave a lovely sound in answer like a swallow's note. The Suitors were confounded. The color faded from their cheeks; while to mark the signal moment there came a thunderclap from Zeus, and Odysseus' long-suffering heart leapt up for joy at this sign of favor from the son of Chronos. . . .

One arrow lay exposed on the table beside him, the rest, which the Achaean lords were soon to feel, being still inside their hollow quiver. He picked up this shaft, set it against the bridge of the bow, drew back the grooved end and the string together, all without rising from his stool, and aiming straight ahead he shot. Not a single axe did he miss. From the first axe, right through them all and out at the last, the arrow sped with its burden of bronze. Odysseus turned to his son.

"'Telemachus,' he said, 'the stranger sitting in your hall has not disgraced you. I scored no miss, nor made hard work of stringing the bow. My powers are unimpaired, and these gentlemen were mistaken when they scornfully rated them so low. . . .'

"As he finished, Odysseus gave a nod. Whereupon his son and heir, Prince Telemachus, slung on his sharp-edged sword and gripping his spear took his stand by the chair at his father's side, armed with resplendent bronze.

"The Return of Odysseus" is from Homer, *The Odyssey*, trans. E. V. Rieu (Baltimore, Md., and Harmondsworth, Middlesex: Penguin Books, 1946), pp. 326–329, 345–347. Copyright © E. V. Rieu, 1946. Reprinted by permission.

"Shedding his rags, the indomitable Odysseus leapt onto the great threshold with his bow and his full quiver, and poured out the winged arrows at his feet.

"'That match is played and won!' he shouted to the Suitors. 'Now for another target! No man has hit it yet; but with Apollo's help I'll try.' And with that he levelled a deadly shaft straight at Antinous.

"Antinous had just reached for his golden cup to take a draught of wine, and the rich, two-handled beaker was balanced in his hands. No thought of bloodshed had entered his head. For who could guess, there in that festive company, that one man, however powerful he might be, would bring calamity and death to him against such odds? Yet Odysseus shot his bolt and struck him in the throat. The point passed clean through the soft flesh of his neck. Dropping the cup as he was hit, he lurched over to one side. His life-blood gushed from his nostrils in a turbid jet. His foot lashed out and kicked the table from him; the food was scattered on the ground, and his bread and meat were smeared with gore. . . .

"The unconquerable Odysseus looked down on the Suitors with a scowl. 'You curs!' he cried. 'You never thought to see me back from Troy. So you ate me out of house and home; you raped my maids; you wooed my wife on the sly though I was alive—with no more fear of the gods in heaven than of the human vengeance that might come. I tell you, one and all, your doom is sealed.'

[*Odysseus and his son Telemachus then killed all of the suitors who were trapped in the Great Hall. After the battle, Odysseus met his wife, Penelope, for the first time in nineteen years. Penelope, who had resisted all overtures from the suitors, decided to confirm Odysseus's identity by subjecting him to a test.*]

"'What a strange creature!' Odysseus exclaimed. 'Heaven made you as you are, but for sheer obstinacy you put all the rest of your sex in the shade. No other wife could have steeled herself to keep as long out of the arms of a husband she had just got back after nineteen years of misadventure. Well, nurse, make a bed for me to sleep alone in. For my wife's heart is just about as hard as iron.'

"'You too are strange,' said the cautious Penelope. 'I am not being haughty or indifferent. I am not even unduly surprised. But I have too clear a picture of you in my mind as you were when you sailed from Ithaca in your long-oared ship. Come, Eurycleia, make him a comfortable bed outside the bedroom that he built so well himself. Place the big bed out there, and make it up with rugs and blankets, and with laundered sheets.'

"This was her way of putting her husband to the test. But Odysseus flared up at once and rounded on his loyal wife. 'Penelope,' he cried, 'you exasperate me! Who, if you please, has moved my bed elsewhere? Short of a miracle, it would be hard even for a skilled workman to shift it somewhere else, and the strongest young fellow alive would have a job to budge it. For a great secret went into the making of that complicated bed; and it was my work and mine alone. Inside the court there was a long-leaved olive tree, which had grown to full height with a stem as thick as a pillar. Round this I built my room of close-set stone-work, and when that was finished, I roofed it over thoroughly, and put in a solid, neatly fitted, double door. Next I lopped all the twigs off the olive, trimmed the stem from the root up, rounded it smoothly and carefully with my adze and trued it to the line, to make my bed-post. This I drilled through where necessary, and used as a basis for the bed itself, which I worked away at till that too was done, when I finished it off with an inlay of gold, silver, and ivory, and fixed a set of purple straps across the frame. There is our secret, and I have shown you that I know it. What I don't know, madam, is whether my bedstead stands where it did, or whether someone has cut the tree-trunk through and shifted it elsewhere.'

"Her knees began to tremble as she realized the complete fidelity of his description. All at once her heart melted. Bursting into tears she ran up to Odysseus, threw her arms round his neck and kissed his head. 'Odysseus,' she cried, 'do not be cross with me, you who were always the most reasonable of men. All our unhappiness is due to the gods, who couldn't bear to see us share the joys of youth and reach the threshold of old age together. But don't be angry with me now, or hurt because the moment when I saw you first I did not kiss you as I kiss you now. For I had always had the cold fear in my heart that somebody might come here and bewitch me with his talk. There are plenty of rogues who would seize such a chance. . . . But now all's well. You have faithfully described our token, the secret of our bed, which no one ever saw but you and I. . . . You have convinced your unbelieving wife.'

"Penelope's surrender melted Odysseus' heart, and he wept as he held his dear wife in his arms, so loyal and so true. Sweet moment too for her, sweet as the sight of land to sailors struggling in the sea. . . . If that is bliss, what bliss it was for her to see her husband once again! She kept her white arms round his neck and never quite let go. Dawn with her roses caught them at their tears."

Early Greek Philosophy

The Greeks were the originators of philosophy in the Western historical tradition. Philosophy means "love of wisdom," and in this the Greeks had no rivals in Western Civilization for originality of thought and beauty of expression. The Greek language is endowed with a formidable vocabulary that allows for an expressive discussion of abstract thoughts. This amazing civilization, which produced the likes of Plato and Aristotle, began its intellectual journey with Thales of Miletus (ca. 600 B.C.E.), who asked the simple question, "What are things made of?" The inspiration of the question alone reveals much about the inquiring nature of the Greeks, but its answer would lend Thales and other "monists" like Anaximenes to reduce the world to one primary element around which all others existed. For Thales, it was water; for Anaximenes, air. For others, like Pythagoras (ca. 550 B.C.E.), the world could best be explored through numerical ratios and resulting harmonies. Indeed, life itself, through the transmigration of the soul, was a cycle of rebirth.

Thales of Miletus: Water Is the Primary Element
ARISTOTLE

Some say that the earth rests on water. This in fact is the oldest view that has been transmitted to us, and they say that it was advanced by Thales of Miletus who thought that the earth rests because it can float like a log or something else of that sort (for none of these things can rest on air, but they can rest on water)—as though the same must not hold of the water supporting the earth as holds of the earth itself.

Most of the first philosophers thought that principles in the form of matter were the only principles of all things. For they say that the element and first principle of the things that exist is that from which they all are and from which they first come into being and into which they are finally destroyed, its substance remaining and its properties changing. . . . There must be some nature—either one or more than one—from which the other things come into being, it being preserved. But as to the number and form of this sort of principle, they do not all agree. Thales, the founder of this kind of philosophy, says that it is water (that is why he declares that the earth rests on water). He perhaps came to acquire this belief from seeing that the nourishment of everything is moist and that heat itself comes from this and lives by this (for that from which anything comes into being is its first principle)—he came to his belief both for this reason and because the seeds of everything have a moist nature, and water is the natural principle of moist things.

Anaximenes: "The First Principle Is Infinite Air"
HIPPOLYTUS

Anaximenes, son of Eurystratus, was also a Milesian. He said that the first principle is infinite air, from which what is coming into being and what has come into being and what will exist and gods and divinities come into being, while everything else comes into being from its offspring. The form of the air is this: when it is most uniform it is invisible, but it is made apparent by the hot and the cold and the moist and the moving. It is always in motion; for the things that change would not change if it were not in motion. For as it is condensed and rarefied it appears different: when it dissolves into a more rarefied condition it becomes fire; and winds, again, are condensed air, and cloud is produced from air by compression. Again, when it is more condensed it is water, when still further condensed it is earth, and when it is as dense as possible it is stones. Thus the most important factors in coming into being are opposites—hot and cold.

The earth is flat and rides on air; in the same way the sun and the moon and the other heavenly bodies, which are all fiery, ride the air because of their flatness. The heavenly bodies have come into being from earth, because mist rose from the earth and was rarefied and produced fire, and the heavenly bodies are composed of this fire when it is aloft. There are also some earthy substances in the region of the heavenly bodies which orbit with them. He says that the heavenly bodies move not under the earth, as others have supposed, but round the earth—just as a felt cap turns on the head. And the sun is hidden not because it goes under the earth but because of its greater distance from us. The heavenly bodies do not heat us because of their great distance.

Winds are generated when the air is condensed and driven along. As it collects together and is further thickened, clouds are generated and in this way it changes into water. Hail comes about when the water falling from the clouds solidifies, and snow when these same things solidify in a more watery form. Lightning occurs when the clouds are parted by the force of winds; for when they part a bright and fiery flash occurs. Rainbows are generated when the sun's rays fall on compacted air; earthquakes when the earth is considerably altered by heating and cooling.

These are the views of Anaximenes. He flourished in the first year of the fifty-eighth Olympiad [548/547 B.C.E.].

Pythagoras on the Transmigration of the Soul
DIODORUS

Pythagoras believed in metempsychosis [transmigration of the soul] and thought that eating meat was an abominable thing, saying that the souls of all animals enter different animals after death. He himself used to say that he remembered being, in Trojan times, Euphorbus, Panthus' son, who was killed by Menelaus. They say that once when he was staying at Argos he saw a shield from the spoils of Troy nailed up, and burst into tears. When the Argives asked him the reason for his emotion, he said that he himself had borne that shield at Troy when he was Euphorbus. They did not believe him and judged him to be mad, but he said he would provide a true sign that it was indeed the case; on the inside of the shield there had been inscribed in archaic lettering EUPHORBUS. Because of the extraordinary nature of his claim they all urged that the shield be taken down—and it turned out that on the inside the inscription was found.

"Pythagoras on the Transmigration of the Soul" is from Jonathan Barnes, *Early Greek Philosophy* (Baltimore, Md., and Harmondsworth, Middlesex: Penguin Books, 1969), p. 87. Copyright © Jonathan Barnes, 1987. Reprinted by permission.

Pythagoras on the Harmony of Numbers
ARISTOTLE

Since other things seemed to be like numbers in their entire nature, and numbers were the first of every nature, they assumed that the elements of numbers were the elements of all things, and that the whole heavens were harmony and number. And whatever characteristics in numbers and harmonies they could show were in agreement with the properties of the heavens and its parts and with its whole arrangement, these they collected and adapted; and if there chanced to be any gap anywhere, they eagerly sought that the whole system might be connected with these (stray phenomena). To give an example of my meaning: inasmuch as ten seemed to be the perfect number and to embrace the whole nature of numbers, they asserted that the number of bodies moving through the heavens were ten, and when only nine were visible, for the reason just stated they postulated the counter-earth, as the tenth. . . . [The Pythagoreans] certainly seem to consider number as the first principle, and as it were the matter in things and in their conditions and states; and the odd and the even are elements of number, and of these the former is limited, the latter unlimited, and unity is the product of both of them, for it is both odd and even, and number arises from unity, and the whole heaven, as has been said, is numbers.

Democracy and Empire: The Golden Age of Athens

The Greek Polis: Two Ways of Life

The City-State of Sparta: Reforms of Lycurgus
PLUTARCH

The city-state, or polis, evolved during the period 1200–500 B.C.E. and offered a unique organization for the Greeks. Each polis was independent in its particular form of government, provided for its own defensive arrangements, and conducted its own foreign policy. Thus one city-state might be a monarchy, another a democracy, and a third an oligarchy. One of the most fascinating city-states was Sparta. In the eighth century B.C.E., it had prospered in a rather open political

---

"Pythagoras on the Harmony of Numbers" is from Milton C. Nahm, *Selections from Early Greek Philosophy*, 4th ed. (New York: Appleton-Century-Crofts, 1964), p. 55. Copyright © 1964 by Meredith Publishing Company. Reprinted by permission.

"The Reforms of Lycurgus" is from Plutarch, Lycurgus, 9–12, in *Readings in Ancient History*, vol. 1, ed. William S. Davis (New York: Allyn and Bacon, 1912), pp. 104–105. Translation modernized by the editor.

and economic environment. But in the late seventh century, Sparta, under the leadership of Lycurgus, adopted a rigid military system that produced one of the most efficient and feared armies in antiquity. The Spartans enslaved some of the surrounding population (calling them helots) and used them to work the land while Spartan warriors honed their military skills. The following accounts describe the reforms of Lycurgus and the Spartan way of life. Though they never produced great literature or ideas, the Spartans were admired because they prevented chaos in their society.

Lycurgus commanded that all gold and silver coin should be called in, and that only a sort of money made of iron should be current, a great weight and quantity of which was but very little worth; so that to lay up twenty or thirty pounds there was required a pretty large closet, and, to remove it, nothing less than a yoke of oxen. With the distribution of this money, at once a number of vices were banished from Sparta; for who would rob such a coin? Who would unjustly detain or take by force, or accept as a bribe, a thing which it was not easy to hide, nor a credit to have, nor indeed of any use to cut in pieces?

In the next place, he declared an outlawry of all needless and superfluous arts; . . . merchants sent no shiploads into Spartan ports; no rhetoric master, no itinerant fortune teller, or gold or silversmith, engraver, or jeweler, set foot in a country which had no money; so that luxury, deprived little by little of that which fed and fomented it, wasted to nothing, and died away of itself. For the rich had no advantage here over the poor, as their wealth and abundance had no road to come abroad by, but were shut up at home doing nothing. And in this way they became excellent artists in common necessary things; bedsteads, chairs, and tables, and such life staple utensils in a family, were admirably well made there.

The Ordinances Against Luxury

The third and most masterly stroke of this great lawgiver, by which he struck a yet more effectual blow against luxury and the desire of riches, was the ordinance he made, that they should all eat in common, of the same bread and same meat, and of kinds that were specified, and should not spend their lives at home, laid on costly couches at splendid tables, delivering themselves up into the hands of their tradesmen and cooks, to fatten them in corners, like greedy brutes, and to ruin not their minds only, but their very bodies, which, enfeebled by indulgence and excess, would stand in need of long sleep, warm bathing, freedom from work, and, in a word, of as much care and attendance as if they were continually sick. . . . For the rich, being obliged to go to the same table with the poor, could not make use or enjoy their abundance, nor so much as please their vanity by looking at or displaying it. Nor were they allowed to take food at home first, and then attend the public tables, for every one had an eye upon those who did not eat and drink like the rest, and reproached them with being dainty and effeminate. . . .

Spartan Discipline

PLUTARCH

Nor was it in the power of the father to dispose of the child as he thought fit; he was obliged to carry it before certain officials at a place called Lesche; these were some of the elders of a tribe to which the child belonged; their business it was carefully to view the infant, and, if they found it strong and well formed, they gave order for its rearing, and allowed to it one of the nine thousand shares of land above mentioned for its maintenance, but if they found it puny and ill-shaped, ordered it to be taken to . . . a sort of chasm [and exposed to the elements]; as thinking it neither for the good of the child itself, nor for the public interest, that it should be brought up, if it did not, from the very outset, appear . . . healthy and vigorous. There was much care and art, too, used by the nurses; they had no swaddling bands; the children grew up free and unconstrained in limb and form, and not dainty and fanciful about their food; not afraid in the dark, or of being left alone; without any irritability or ill humor or crying. Upon this account, Spartan nurses were often . . . hired by people of other countries. . . .

Lycurgus would not have tutors brought out of the market for his young Spartans; nor was it lawful, indeed, for the father himself to raise the children after his own fancy; but as soon as they were seven years old they were to be enrolled in certain companies and classes, where they lived under the same order and discipline, doing their exercises and playing together. Of these, he who showed the most conduct and courage was made captain; they had their eyes always upon him, obeyed his order, and underwent patiently whatsoever punishment he inflicted; so that the whole course of their education was one continued exercise of a ready and perfect obedience. The old men, too, were spectators of their performances, and often raised quarrels and disputes among them, to have a good opportunity of finding out their different characters, and of seeing which would be valiant, which a coward, when they should come to more dangerous encounters. Reading and writing they gave them, just enough to serve their turn; their chief care was to make them good subjects, and to teach them to endure pain and conquer in battle. To this end, as they grew in years, their discipline was proportionably increased; their heads were close clipped, and they were accustomed to go barefoot, and for the most part to play naked.

The Second Stage of the Spartan Education

After they were twelve years old, they were no longer allowed to wear any undergarment; they had one coat to serve them a year; their bodies were hard and dry, with but little acquaintance of baths and unguents; these human indulgences they were allowed only on some few particular days in the year.

"Spartan Discipline" is from Plutarch, Lycurgus, 16–19, in *Readings in Ancient History*, vol. 1, ed. William S. Davis (New York: Allyn and Bacon, 1912), pp. 107–111. Translation modernized by the editor.

They lodged together in little bands upon beds made of the reeds which grew by the banks of the river, which they were to break off with their hands without a knife; if it were winter, they mingled some thistledown with their reeds, which it was thought had the property of giving warmth. . . . [Spartan youths were required to steal wood and herbs], which they did by creeping into the gardens, or conveying themselves cunningly and closely into the eating houses: if they were taken in the act, they were whipped without mercy, for thieving so poorly and awkwardly. They stole, too, all other meat they could lay their hands on, looking out and watching all opportunities, when people were asleep or more careless than usual. If they were caught, they were not only punished with whipping, but hunger, too, being reduced to their ordinary allowance, which was very slender, and so contrived on purpose, that they might set about to help themselves, and be forced to exercise their energy and ingenuity.

So seriously did the Spartan children go about their stealing, that a youth, having stolen a young fox and hid it under his coat, allowed it to tear out his very guts with its teeth and claws, and died upon the place, rather than let it be seen. What is practiced to this very day in Sparta is enough to gain credit to this story, for I myself have seen several of the youths endure whipping to death. . . .

They taught them, also, to speak in a natural and graceful manner, and to express much in few words. . . . Children in Sparta, by a habit of long silence, came to give just and wise answers; for, indeed, as loose and incontinent livers are seldom fathers of many children, so loose and incontinent talkers seldom originate many sensible words. When some Athenian laughed at their short swords, . . . King Agis answered him, "We find them long enough to reach our enemies"; and as their swords were short and sharp, so, it seems to me, were their sayings. They reach the point and arrest the attention of the hearers better than any other kind.

The City-State of Athens: Funeral Oration of Pericles (430 B.C.E.)

THUCYDIDES

The Athenian polis was, in most respects, the opposite of Sparta. In 510 B.C.E., under the leadership of Cleisthenes, Athens adopted a democratic system in which all citizens were expected to vote, serve in public office and offer themselves as jurors. Active participation in political affairs was demanded, and one who shunned such responsibility was called "idiotes," or "private person"; the word has come down to us as "idiot," with all its pejorative connotations.

"The Funeral Oration of Pericles" is from Thucydides, *The Peloponnesian War*, 2.35–2.45, trans. Rex Warner (Baltimore, Md., and Harmondsworth, Middlesex: Penguin Books, 1954), pp. 117–121. Copyright © Rex Warner, 1954, 1972. Reprinted by permission.

The leader of the Athenian democracy in the middle of the fifth century B.C.E. *was the great orator Pericles. After the first year of the Peloponnesian War (430 B.C.E.), Pericles spoke to the wives and parents of those who had died in the fighting in an attempt to justify their loss. This Funeral Oration that follows was recorded by the Athenian historian Thucydides; it is the quintessential expression of the structure and values of the Athenian democracy.*

"I have no wish to make a long speech on subjects familiar to you all: so I shall say nothing about the warlike deeds by which we acquired our power or the battles in which we or our fathers gallantly resisted our enemies, Greek or foreign. What I want to do is, in the first place, to discuss the spirit in which we faced our trials and also our constitution and the way of life which has made us great. After that I shall speak to praise of the dead, believing that this kind of speech is not inappropriate to the present occasion, and that this whole assembly, of citizens and foreigners, may listen to it with advantage.

"Let me say that our system of government does not copy the institutions of our neighbours. It is more the case of our being a model to others, than of our imitating anyone else. Our constitution is called a democracy because power is in the hands not of a minority but of the whole people. When it is a question of settling private disputes, everyone is equal before the law; when it is a question of putting one person before another in positions of public responsibility, what counts is not membership of a particular class, but the actual ability which the man possesses. No one, so long as he has it in him to be of service to the state, is kept in political obscurity because of poverty. And, just as our political life is free and open, so is our day-to-day life in our relations with each other. . . . We are free and tolerant in our private lives; but in public affairs we keep to the law. This is because it commands our deep respect.

"We give our obedience to those whom we put in positions of authority, and we obey the laws themselves, especially those which are for the protection of the oppressed, and those unwritten laws which it is an acknowledged shame to break.

"And here is another point. When our work is over, we are in a position to enjoy all kinds of recreation for our spirits. There are various kinds of contests and sacrifices regularly throughout the year; in our own homes we find a beauty and a good taste which delight us every day and which drive away our cares. Then the greatness of our city brings it about that all the good things from all over the world flow in to us, so that to us it seems just as natural to enjoy foreign goods as our own local products.

"Then there is a great difference between us and our opponents, in our attitude towards military security. Here are some examples: our city is open to the world, and we have no periodical deportations in order to prevent people observing or finding out secrets which might be of military advantage to the enemy. This is because we rely, not on secret weapons, but on our own real courage and loyalty. There is a difference, too, in our educational systems.

The Spartans, from their earliest boyhood, are submitted to the most laborious training in courage; we pass our lives without all these restrictions, and yet are just as ready to face the same dangers as they are.... There are certain advantages, I think, in our way of meeting danger voluntarily, with an easy mind, instead of with a laborious training, with natural rather than with state-induced courage. We do not have to spend our time practising to meet sufferings which are still in the future; and when they are actually upon us we show ourselves just as brave as these others who are always in strict training. This is one point in which, I think, our city deserves to be admired. There are also others:

"Our love of what is beautiful does not lead to extravagance; our love of the things of the mind does not make us soft. We regard wealth as something to be properly used, rather than as something to boast about. As for poverty, no one need be ashamed to admit it: the real shame is in not taking practical measures to escape from it. Here each individual is interested not only in his own affairs but in the affairs of the state as well: even those who are mostly occupied with their own business are extremely well-informed on general politics—this is a peculiarity of ours: we do not say that a man who takes no interest in politics is a man who minds his own business; we say that he has no business here at all. We Athenians, in our persons, take our decisions on policy or submit them to proper discussions: for we do not think that there is an incompatibility between words and deeds; the worst thing is to rush into action before the consequences have been properly debated. And this is another point where we differ from other people. We are capable at the same time of taking risks and of estimating them beforehand. Others are brave out of ignorance; and, when they stop to think, they begin to fear. But the man who can most truly be accounted brave is he who best knows the meaning of what is sweet in life and of what is terrible, and then goes out undeterred to meet what is to come.

"Again, in question of general good feeling there is a great contrast between us and most other people. We make friends by doing good to the more reliable, since we want to keep alive the gratitude of those who are in our debt by showing continued good will to them.... We are unique in this. When we do kindnesses to others, we do not do them out of any calculations of profit or loss: we do them without afterthought, relying on our free liberality. Taking everything together then, I declare that our city is an education to Greece, and I declare that in my opinion each single one of our citizens, in all the manifold aspects of life, is able to show himself the rightful lord and owner of his own person, and do this, moreover, with exceptional grace and exceptional versatility. And to show that this is no empty boasting for the present occasion, but real tangible fact, you have only to consider the power which our city possesses and which has been won by those very qualities which I have mentioned. Athens, alone of the states we know, comes to her testing time in a greatness that surpasses what was imagined of her. In her case, and in her case alone, no invading enemy is ashamed at being defeated,

The rocky plateau of the ancient Acropolis overlooks the city of Athens. The Parthenon (center), temple of the patron goddess Athena, was built with funds garnered from the Athenian Empire. What price civilization? (Nat Norman/Photo Researchers, Inc.)

and no subject can complain of being governed by people unfit for their responsibilities. Mighty indeed are the marks and monuments of our empire which we have left. Future ages will wonder at us, as the present age wonders at us now. . . . For our adventurous spirit has forced an entry into every sea and into every land; and everywhere we have left behind us everlasting memorials of good done to our friends or suffering inflicted on our enemies.

"This, then, is the kind of city for which these men, who could not bear the thought of losing her, nobly fought and nobly died. It is only natural that every one of us who survive them should be willing to undergo hardships in her service. And it was for this reason that I have spoken at such length about our city, because I wanted to make it clear that for us there is more at stake than there is for others who lack our advantages; also I wanted my words of praise for the dead to be set in the bright light of evidence. And now the most important of these words has been spoken. I have sung the praises of our city; but it was the courage and gallantry of these men, and of people like them, which made her splendid. Now would you find it true in the case of many of the Greeks, as it is true of them, that no words can do more than justice to their deeds.

"To me it seems that the consummation which has overtaken these men shows us the meaning of manliness in its first revelation and in its final proof. Some of them, no doubt, had their faults; but what we ought to remember first is their gallant conduct against the enemy in defence of their native land. They have blotted out evil with good, and done more service to the commonwealth than they ever did harm in their private lives. . . .

"So and such they were, these men—worthy of their city. We who remain behind may hope to be spared their fate, but must resolve to keep the same daring spirit against the foe. It is not simply a question of estimating the advantages in theory. I could tell you a long story (and you know it as well as I do) about what is to be gained by beating the enemy back. What I would prefer is that you should fix your eyes every day on the greatness of Athens as she really is, and should fall in love with her. When you realize her greatness, then reflect that what made her great was men with a spirit of adventure, men who knew their duty, men who were ashamed to fall below a certain standard. If they ever failed in an enterprise, they made up their minds that at any rate the city should not find their courage lacking to her, and they gave to her the best contribution they could. They gave her their lives, to her and to all of us, and for their own selves they won praises that never grow old, the most splendid of sepulchres—not the sepulchre in which their bodies are laid, but where their glory remains eternal in men's minds, always there on the right occasion to stir others to speech or to action. For famous men have the whole earth as their memorial: it is not only the inscriptions on their graves in their own country that mark them out; no, in foreign lands also, not in any visible form but in people's hearts, their memory abides and grows. It is for you to try to be like them. Make up your minds that happiness depends on being free, and freedom depends on being courageous. Let there be no relaxation in face of the perils of the war. The people who have most excuse for despising death are not the wretched and unfortunate, who have no hope of doing well for themselves, but those who run the risk of a complete reversal in their lives, and who would feel the difference most intensely, if things went wrong for them. Any intelligent man would find a humiliation caused by his own slackness more painful to bear than death, when death comes to him unperceived, in battle, and in the confidence of his patriotism."

A Critic of Democracy (425 B.C.E.)
THE "OLD OLIGARCH"

Although the Athenian democracy inspired idealism and admiration, it engendered controversy as well. Among the most revealing critics of the democratic system was an anonymous author called the "Old Oligarch." He wrote this treatise in about 425 B.C.E., and though exaggerated in places, it gives perhaps a more realistic assessment of the nature of Athenian democracy.

Now, as for the constitution of the Athenians, and the type or manner of constitution which they have chosen, I praise it not, in so far as the very choice involves the welfare of the baser folk as opposed to that of the better class. I repeat, I withhold my praise so far; but, given the fact that this is the type agreed upon, I propose to show that they set about its preservation in the right way. . . .

In the first place, in regard to what some people are puzzled to explain—the fact that everywhere greater consideration is shown to the base, to poor people and to common folk, than to persons of good quality—so far from being a matter of surprise, this, as can be shown, is the keystone of the preservation of the democracy. It is these people, this common folk, this worse element, whose prosperity, combined with the growth of their numbers, enhances the democracy. Whereas, a shifting of fortune to the advantage of the wealthy and the better classes implies the establishment on the part of the commons of a strong power in opposition to itself. In fact, all the world over, the cream of society is an opposition to the democracy. Naturally, since the smallest amount of intemperance and injustice, together with the highest scrupulousness in the pursuit of excellence, is to be found in the ranks of the better class, while within the ranks of the People will be found the greatest amount of ignorance, disorderliness, rascality—poverty acting as a stronger incentive to base conduct, not to speak of lack of education and

"A Critic of Democracy" is from Pseudo-Xenophon, *The Constitution of the Athenians*, trans. H. G. Dakyns, revised by E. G. Sihler, in *Hellenic Civilization: Records of Civilization Series* (New York: Columbia University Press, 1920), pp. 222–225, 231–232.

ignorance, traceable to the lack of means which afflicts the average of mankind.

The objection may be raised that it was a mistake to allow the universal right of speech and a seat in council. These should have been reserved for the cleverest, the flower of the community. But here, again, it will be found that they are acting with wise deliberation in granting to even the baser sort the right of speech, for supposing only the better people might speak, or sit in council, blessings would fall to the lot of those like themselves, but to the commons the reverse of blessings. Whereas now, any one who likes, any base fellow, may get up and discover something to the advantage of himself and his equals. . . .

The common people put a stop to citizens devoting their time to athletics and to the cultivation of music, disbelieving in the beauty of such training, and recognising the fact that these are things the cultivation of which is beyond its power. On the same principle, in the case of the choregia [director of the dramatic chorus], the management of athletics, and the command of ships, the fact is recognised that it is the rich man who trains the chorus, and the People from whom the chorus is trained; it is the rich man who is naval commander or superintendent of athletics, and the People that profits by their labours. In fact, what the People looks upon as its right is to pocket money. To sing and run and dance and man the vessels is well enough, but only in order that the people may be the gainer, while the rich are made poorer. And so in the courts of justice, justice is not more an object of concern to the jurymen than what touches personal advantage.

To speak next of the allies, and in reference to the point that emissaries from Athens come out, and, according to common opinion . . . vent their hatred upon the better sort of people, this is done on the principle that the ruler cannot help being hated by those whom he rules; but that if wealth and respectability are to wield power in the subject cities the empire of the Athenian People has but a short lease of existence. This explains why the better people are punished with infamy, robbed of their money, driven from their homes, and put to death, while the baser sort are promoted to honour. On the other hand, the better Athenians protect the better class in the allied cities. And why? Because they recognise that it is to the interest of their own class at all times to protect the best element in the cities. It may be urged that if it comes to strength and power the real strength of Athens lies in the capacity of her allies to contribute their money quota. But to the democratic mind it appears a higher advantage still for the individual Athenian to get hold of the wealth of the allies, leaving them only enough to live upon and to cultivate their estates, but powerless to harbour treacherous designs. . . .

I repeat that my position concerning the constitution of the Athenians is this: the type of constitution is not to my taste, but given that a democratic form of government has been agreed upon, they do seem to me to go the right way to preserve the democracy by the adoption of the particular type which I have set forth.

The Persian Wars and the Defense of Greece (490–480 B.C.E.)

The Spartans at Thermopylae (480 B.C.E.)

HERODOTUS

In 499 B.C.E., the Ionian city-state of Miletus rebelled against Persian rule and asked the Athenians for support. Athens not only aided the rebels, but marched inland and burned one of the Persian capitals at Sardis. Such impulsive aggression could not go unpunished, and Persia's King Darius launched an invasion against Athens in 490 B.C.E., which the Greeks heroically repulsed on the plains of Marathon. The Persian defeat at Marathon served only to anger and frustrate an empire now bent on revenge. The new king, Xerxes, decided to take no chances and formed a massive army of about 250,000 men; this force made its way by land and sea north across the Dardanelles and down into Greece itself. In the face of such power, many Greek city-states surrendered to the Persian horde. While the Athenians evacuated their city, a Spartan force of three hundred warriors and one of their kings (Leonidas) left to prevent a Persian invasion of Greece by making a stand in a pass called Thermopylae. A disgruntled Greek shepherd named Ephialtes told Xerxes of a way around the pass. The following selection by the Greek historian Herodotus recounts the Spartan heroism.

The barbarians under Xerxes began to draw near; and the Greeks under Leonidas, as they now went forth determined to die, advanced much farther than on previous days, until they reached the more open portion of the pass. Hitherto they had held their station within the wall, and from this had gone forth to fight at the point where the pass was the narrowest. Now they joined battle. . . . and carried a slaughter among the barbarians, who fell in heaps. Behind [the Persians] the captains of the squadrons, armed with whips, urged their men forward with continual blows. Many were thrust into the sea, and there perished; a still greater number were trampled to death by their own soldiers; no one heeded the dying. For the Greeks, reckless of their own safety and desperate, since they knew that, as the mountain had been crossed, their destruction was nigh at hand, exerted themselves with the most furious valor against the barbarians.

By this time the spears of the greatest number were all shivered, and with their swords they hewed down the ranks of the Persians; and here, as they strove, Leonidas [the Spartan king] fell fighting bravely, together with many other famous Spartans, whose names I have taken care to learn on account of their great worthiness, as indeed I have those of all the three hundred. There

"The Spartans at Thermopylae" is from Herodotus, *The Histories,* 7.223–228, trans. George Rawlinson, in *The History of Herodotus* (New York: E. P. Dutton, 1910), pp. 207–209. Translation modernized by the editor.

fell too at the same time very many famous Persians: among them, two brothers of Xerxes. . . .

And now there arose a fierce struggle between the Persians and the Spartans over the body of Leonidas, in which the Greeks four times drove back the enemy, and at last by their great bravery succeeded in bearing off the body. This combat was scarcely ended when the Persians with Ephialtes approached; and the Greeks, informed that they drew near, made a change in the manner of their fighting. Drawing back into the narrowest part of the pass, and retreating even behind the cross wall, they posted themselves upon a hillock, where they stood all drawn up together in one close body. The hillock whereof I speak is at the entrance of the pass, where the stone lion stands which was set up in honor of Leonidas. Here they defended themselves to the last, such as still had swords using them, and the others resisting with their hands and teeth; till the barbarians, who in part had pulled down the wall and attacked them in front, in part had gone round and now encircled them upon every side, overwhelmed and buried the remnant left beneath showers of missile weapons.

Thus nobly did the whole body of Spartans behave, but nevertheless one man is said to have distinguished himself above all the rest, . . . Dieneces the Spartan. A speech which he made before the Greeks engaged the Persians remains on record. One of the Trachinians told him, "Such was the number of the barbarians [Persians], that when they shot forth their arrows the sun would be darkened by their multitude." Dieneces, not at all frightened at these words, but making light of the Persian numbers, answered, "Our Trachinian friend brings us excellent tidings. If the Persians darken the sun, we shall have our battle in the shade." . . .

The slain were buried where they fell; and in their honor, not less in honor of those who died before Leonidas sent the allies away, an inscription was set up, which said. . . .

Go, stranger, and to Sparta tell
That here, obedient to her laws, we fell.

The Defense of Athens:
Inscriptional Evidence (480 B.C.E.)

After the massacre of the Spartans at Thermopylae, the Persians overran Athens and burned the city in revenge for the earlier destruction of their capital, Sardis. The Greek defense was led by an Athenian, Themistocles, who offered the following measures in preparation for the coming battle. The historical source below is a stone inscription found in 1958; its authenticity has been the subject of many scholarly debates.

"The Defense of Athens: Inscriptional Evidence" is from N. Lewis, ed., *Greek Historical Documents: The Fifth Century B.C.E.* (Toronto: A. M. Hakkert, 1971), pp. 4–5.

Gods. The council and assembly decree, on motion of Themistokles son of Neokles, of (the deme) Phrearrhoi: to deposit the city in the care of Athena protectress of Athens and all the other gods to guard and ward off the barbarian in behalf of the land; and that all the Athenians and the foreigners resident in Athens deposit their children and wives in Troizen under the protection of Pittheus the tutelary hero of the land, and deposit their aged and possessions in Salamis; and that the treasurers and priestesses remain on the acropolis to guard the property of the gods; and that all the other adult Athenians and foreigners embark on the two hundred prepared ships and, together with the Spartans, Corinthians, Aiginetans and the others willing to share the danger, ward off the barbarian for the sake of their own freedom and that of the rest of the Greeks; and that the generals, beginning tomorrow morning, appoint two hundred trierarchs [naval commanders]—one for each ship. . . . and that when all the divisions have been distributively constituted and allotted to the triremes, the council and the generals shall man fully all two hundred ships after offering a propitiatory sacrifice to Zeus all-powerful and Athena and Nike and Poseidon safe-guarder; and when the ships have been manned, with one hundred of them to lend aid at Artemision in Euboia, and with the other hundred of them to lie to wait around Salamis and the rest of Attika and guard the land [the inscription ends here].

The Battle of Salamis (480 B.C.E.)
AESCHYLUS

Through a clever trick, Themistocles lured the Persians into the narrow straits between the Greek shore and the island of Salamis. There, they were crushed in a surprise attack by the Athenian fleet. Xerxes, the Persian king, watched impotently from a nearby hill. This dramatic account of the battle is excerpted from the play The Persians *by Aeschylus.*

Persian Messenger: The Persians knew their error; fear gripped every man.
They were not fugitives who sang that terrifying
Paean, but Hellenes [Greeks] charging with courageous hearts
To battle. The loud trumpet flamed along their ranks.
At once their frothy oars moved with a single pulse,
Beating the salt waves to the bo'sons' chant; and soon
Their whole fleet hove clear into view; their right wing first,
In precise order, next their whole array came on,

And at that instant a great shout beat on our ears:
Forward, you sons of Hellas! Set your country free!
Set free your sons, your wives, tombs of your ancestors,
And temples of your gods. All is at stake: Now fight!
Then from our side in answer rose the manifold
Clamour of Persian voices; and the hour had come.

At once ship into ship battered its brazen beak.
A Hellene ship charged first, and chopped off the whole stern
Of a Phoenician galley. Then charge followed charge
On every side. At first by its huge impetus
Our [Persian] fleet withstood them. But soon, in that narrow space,
Our ships were jammed in hundreds; none could help another.
They rammed each other with their prows of bronze; and some
Were stripped of every oar. Meanwhile the enemy [Greeks]
Came round us in a ring and charged. Our vessels heeled
Over; the sea was hidden, carpeted with wrecks
And dead men; all the shores and reefs were full of dead. . . .

This depth of horror Xerxes saw, close to the sea
On a high hill he sat, where he could clearly watch
His whole force both by sea and land. He wailed aloud,
And tore his clothes, weeping; and instantly dismissed
His army, hastening them to a disordered flight.

Athenian Imperialism

From Confederacy to Empire
THUCYDIDES

By 479 B.C.E., the combined Greek armies had defeated the Persian forces, which returned home never to invade Greece again. Still, many of the Greek city-states thought it wise to establish an organization intended to protect against any future Persian invasion, to gain booty, and to liberate Greek city-states on the coast of Ionia still under Persian control. Toward this end, many Greek islands pledged their eternal unity to the cause, formed the Delian Confederacy, and contributed money or ships for use against the Persians. Although all members had the same voting weight, the Athenians initially led the organization by supplying the generals and controlling the treasury. Gradually, however, the Athenian allies became Athenian subjects. The historian Thucydides discusses this transition in the following selection.

"From Confederacy to Empire" is from Thucydides, *History of The Peloponnesian War*, 1.97, 1.99, in *A Source-Book of Ancient History*, ed. George W. Botsford (New York: Macmillan, 1912), pp. 177–178.

At first the allies were independent and deliberated in a common assembly under the leadership of Athens. But in the interval between the Persian and Peloponnesian wars, by their military success and by policy in dealing with the barbarian, with their own rebellious allies and with the Peloponnesians [Spartans] who came across their path from time to time, the Athenians made immense strides in power. . . .

The causes which led to the defection of the allies were of different kinds, the principal one being their neglect to pay the tribute or to furnish ships, and, in some cases, failure of military service. For the Athenians were exacting and oppressive, using coercive measures toward men who were neither willing nor accustomed to work hard. And for various reasons they soon began to prove less agreeable leaders than at first. They no longer fought upon an equality with the rest of the confederates, and they had no difficulty in reducing them when they revolted. Now the allies brought all this upon themselves; for the majority of them disliked military service and absence from home, and so they agreed to contribute a regular sum of money instead of ships. Whereby the Athenian navy was proportionately increased, while they themselves were always untrained and unprepared for war when they revolted.

Maintaining the Athenian Empire: Inscriptional Evidence

In 454 B.C.E. the Athenians moved the treasury of the Confederacy from the island of Delos to Athens itself. The patron goddess Athena was entrusted with protection of the funds and received an offering (one-sixtieth of the tribute) for her services. Pericles used Athena's "commission" to rebuild and beautify Athens; the Parthenon, for example, was begun in 447 B.C.E. The Persian empire was no longer a threat, and a peace treaty in 449 B.C.E. rendered the Confederacy obsolete. Still, Athens maintained allegiance and control of her empire by force. The inscription below concerns the Athenian collection of tribute and reflects the strict control that Athens held over her empire.

The council and the [Athenian] governors, as well as the visiting overseers, shall see to it that the tribute is collected each year and is brought to Athens. They shall issue seals to the cities, so that it will not be possible for those bringing the tribute to perpetuate fraud; the city shall write on a tablet the tribute that it is sending, mark it with the seal, and send it to Athens; those bringing it shall deliver the tablet in the council for verification when they deliver the tribute. . . . [The treasurers will] disclose to the Athenians the cities that have delivered the tribute in full and, separately, those falling short, if any. The Athenians shall choose four men to send to the cities to give

"Maintaining the Athenian Empire: Inscriptional Evidence" is from N. Lewis, ed., *Greek Historical Documents: The Fifth Century B.C.* (Toronto: A. M. Hakkert, 1971), pp. 13–14.

receipts for the tribute delivered, and to exact the undelivered tribute from those falling short: two men shall sail on swift triremes to the cities in the Islands and Ionia, and two to the cities in Hellespont and Thrace.

Greek Tragedy

Oedipus the King (430 B.C.E.)

SOPHOCLES

The greatness of Athenian civilization in the fifth century B.C.E. was evident in many ways. Not only was the city decorated with temples such as the Parthenon and other monuments on the Acropolis, but Athens was also glorified by the splendor of her intellectual accomplishment. During the century, three dramatists emerged who are comparable in quality to Shakespeare: Aeschylus, Sophocles, and Euripides. Aeschylus, a true patriot, wanted to be remembered only as having fought at the battle of Marathon. Sophocles, a commander in the Athenian navy, won first place in dramatic competition for his play about Oedipus, an unfortunate king of Thebes who unwittingly killed his father (Laius) and married his mother. Such sin, even if unintended and unperceived, cannot go unpunished by the gods: When the truth is revealed Jocasta (his mother/wife) commits suicide and Oedipus blinds himself. The Athenians loved the "no-win" situation, both for the problems it presented and for the moral choices it demanded. In the following selection, note the importance of self-discovery and truth, no matter the outcome.

Attendant: O you most honourable lords of the city of Thebes,
Weep for the things you shall hear, the things you must see,
If you are true sons and loyal to the house of Labdacus.
Not all the water of Ister, the waters of Phasis,
Can wash this dwelling clean of the foulness within,
Clean of the deliberate acts that soon shall be known,
Of all horrible acts most horrible, wilfully chosen.

Chorus: Already we have wept enough for the things we have known,
The things we have seen. What more will your story add?

Attendant: First, and in brief—Her Majesty is dead.

Chorus: Alas, poor soul: what brought her to this end?

Attendant: Her own hand did it. You that have not seen,
And shall not see, this worst, shall suffer the less.

"Oedipus the King" is from Sophocles, *Oedipus the King*, in *The Theban Plays*, trans. E. F. Watling (Baltimore, Md., and Harmondsworth, Middlesex: Penguin Books, 1947), pp. 59–61 (lines 1125–1318). Copyright © E. F. Watling, 1947. Reprinted by permission.

But I that saw, will remember, and will tell what I remember
Of her last agony.
    You saw her cross the threshold
In desperate passion. Straight to her bridal-bed
She hurried, fastening her fingers in her hair.
There in her chamber, the doors flung sharply to,
She cried aloud to Laius long since dead,
Remembering the son she bore long since, the son
By whom the sire was slain, the son to whom
The mother bore yet other children, fruit
Of luckless misbegetting, there she bewailed
The twice confounded issue of her wifehood—
Husband begotten of husband, child of child.
So much we heard. Her death was hidden from us.
Before we could set out her tragedy,
The King broke in with piercing cries, and all
Had eyes only for him. This way and that
He strode among us. 'A sword, a sword!' he cried;
'Where is that wife, no wife of mine—that soil
Where I was sown, and whence I reaped my harvest!'
While thus he raved, some demon guided him—
For none of us dare to speak—to where she was.
As if in answer to some leader's call
With wild hallooing cries he hurled himself
Upon the locked doors, bending by main force
The bolts out of their sockets—and stumbled in.
    We saw a knotted pendulum, a noose,
A strangled woman swinging before our eyes.
    The King saw too, and with heart rending groans
Untied the rope, and laid her on the ground.
But worse was yet to see. Her dress was pinned
With golden brooches, which the King snatched out
And thrust, from full arm's length, into his eyes—
Eyes that should see no longer his shame, his guilt,
No longer see those they should never have seen,
Nor see, unseeing, those he had longed to see,
Henceforth seeing nothing but night. . . . To this wild tune
He pierced his eyeballs time and time again,
Till bloody tears ran down his beard—not drops
But in full spate a whole cascade descending
In drenching cataracts of scarlet rain.
    Thus two have sinned; and on two heads, not one—
On man and wife—falls mingled punishment.
Their old long happiness of former times
Was happiness earned with justice; but to-day
Calamity, death, ruin, tears, and shame,
All ills that there are name for—all are here.

Antigone (441 B.C.E.)

SOPHOCLES

Sophocles continued the story of Oedipus in Antigone, *a play about Oedipus's tainted children. The play won first prize in the dramatic competition and again demonstrates the tragedy of those who are not guilty but are condemned by the misdeeds of others. In the following excerpt, Antigone and her sister Ismene must decide whether to bury the body of their brother, thus satisfying the laws of the gods, or to leave it unburied as the king (Creon) has decreed.*

Scene: Before the Palace at Thebes

Enter Ismene from the central door of the Palace. Antigone follows, anxious and urgent; she closes the door carefully, and comes to join her sister.

Antigone: O sister! Ismene dear, dear sister Ismene!
You know how heavy the hand of God is upon us;
How we who are left must suffer for our father, Oedipus.
There is no pain, no sorrow, no suffering, no dishonour
We have not shared together, you and I.
And now there is something more. Have you heard this order,
This latest order that the King has proclaimed to the city?
Have you heard how our dearest are being treated like enemies?

Ismene: I have heard nothing about any of those we love,
Neither good nor evil—not, I mean, since the death
Of our two brothers, both fallen in a day.
The Argive army, I hear, was withdrawn last night.
I know no more to make me sad or glad.

Antigone: I thought you did not. That's why I brought you
out here,
Where we shan't be heard, to tell you something alone.

Ismene: What is it, Antigone? Black news, I can see already.

Antigone: O Ismene, what do you think? Our two dear brothers. . . .
Creon has given funeral honours to one,
And not to the other; nothing but shame and ignominy.
Eteocles has been buried, they tell me, in state,
With all honourable observances due to the dead.
But Polynices, just as unhappily fallen—the order
Says he is not to be buried, not to be mourned;
To be left unburied, unwept, a feast of flesh

"Antigone" is from Sophocles, *Antigone,* in *The Theban Plays,* trans. E. F. Watling (Baltimore, Md., and Harmondsworth, Middlesex: Penguin Books, 1947), pp. 126–129, 135–136 (lines 1–112, 339–370, 1262–1353). Copyright © E. F. Watling, 1947. Reprinted by permission.

For keen-eyed carrion birds. The noble Creon!
It is against you and me he has made this order.
Yes, against me. And soon he will be here himself
To make it plain to those that have not heard it,
And to enforce it. This is not idle threat;
The punishment for disobedience is death by stoning.
So now you know. And now is the time to show
Whether or not you are worthy of your high blood.

Ismene: My poor Antigone, if this is really true,
What more can I do, or undo, to help you?

Antigone: Will you help me? Will you do something with me? Will
you?

Ismene: Help you do what, Antigone? What do you mean?

Antigone: Would you help me lift the body . . . you and me?

Ismene: You cannot mean . . . to bury him? Against the order?

Antigone: Is he not my brother, and yours, whether you like it
Or not? I shall never desert him, never.

Ismene: How could you dare, when Creon has expressly forbidden
it?

Antigone: He has no right to keep me from my own.

Ismene: O sister, sister, do you forget how our father
Perished in shame and misery, his awful sin
Self-proved, blinded by his own self-mutilation?
And then his mother, his wife—for she was both—
Destroyed herself in a noose of her own making.
And now our brothers, both in a single day
Fallen in an awful exaction of death for death.
Blood for blood, each slain by the other's hand.
Now we two left; and what will be the end of us,
If we transgress the law and defy our king?
O think, Antigone; we are women; it is not for us
To fight against men; our rulers are stronger than we,
And we must obey in this, or in worse than this.
May the dead forgive me, I can do no other
But as I am commanded; to do more is madness.

Antigone: No; then I will not ask for your help.
Nor would I thank you for it, if you gave it.
Go your own way; I will bury my brother;
And if I die for it, what happiness!
Convicted of reverence—I shall be content
To lie beside a brother whom I love.
We have only a little time to please the living,
But all eternity to love the dead.

There I shall lie for ever. Live, if you will;
Live, and defy the holiest laws of heaven.

Ismene: I do not defy them; but I cannot act
Against the State. I am not strong enough.

Antigone: Let that be your excuse, then. I will go
And heap a mound of earth over my brother.

Ismene: I fear for you, Antigone; I fear—

Antigone: You need not fear for me. Fear for yourself.

Ismene: At least be secret. Do not breathe a word.
I'll not betray your secret.

Antigone: Publish it
To all world! Else I shall hate you more.

Ismene: Your heart burns! Mine is frozen at the thought.

Antigone: I know my duty, where true duty lies.

Ismene: If you can do it; but you're bound to fail.

Antigone: When I have tried and failed, I shall have failed.

Ismene: No sense in starting on a hopeless task.

Antigone: Oh, I shall hate you if you talk like that!
And he will hate you, rightly. Leave me alone
With my own madness. There is no punishment
Can rob me of my honourable death.

Ismene: Go then, if you are determined, to your folly.
But remember that those who love you. . . . love you still.

[Condemned to death for defying the king and burying her brother, Antigone explains her actions]

Antigone: So to my grave,
My bridal-bower, my everlasting prison,
I go, to join those many of my kinsmen
Who dwell in the mansions of Persephone,
Last and unhappiest, before my time.
Yet I believe my father will be there
To welcome me, my mother greet me gladly,
And you, my brother, gladly see me come.
Each one of you my hands have laid to rest,
Pouring the due libations on your graves.
It was by this service to your dear body, Polynices,
I earned the punishment which now I suffer,
Though all good people know it was for your honour.
   O but I would not have done the forbidden thing
For any husband or for any son.

For why? I could have had another husband
And by him other sons, if one were lost;
But, father and mother lost, where would I get
Another brother? For thus preferring you,
My brother, Creon condemns me and hales me away,
Never a bride, never a mother, unfriended,
Condemned alive to solitary death.
What law of heaven have I transgressed? What god
Can save me now? What help or hope have I,
In whom devotion is deemed sacrilege?
If this is God's will, I shall learn my lesson
In death; but if my enemies are wrong,
I wish them no worse punishment than mine. . . .

[Antigone, thus condemned by Creon, commits suicide as does her intended husband, Haemon, son of Creon. In this passage, Creon realizes that he was blind to wisdom and that his laws have defied the gods and cost him the lives of his son and also his wife.]

Enter Creon with the body of Haemon.

Creon: The sin, the sin of the erring soul
Drives hard unto death.
Behold the slayer, the slain,
The father, the son.
O the curse of my stubborn will!
Son, newly cut off in the newness of youth,
Dead for my fault, not yours.

Chorus: Alas, too late you have seen the truth.

Creon: I learn in sorrow. Upon my head
God has delivered this heavy punishment,
Has struck me down in the ways of wickedness,
And trod my gladness under foot.
Such is the bitter affliction of mortal man.

Enter the Messenger from the palace.

Messenger: Sir, you have this and more than this to bear.
Within there's more to know, more to your pain.
Creon: What more? What pain can overtop this pain?

Messenger: She is dead—your wife, the mother of him that is dead—
The death-wound fresh in her heart. Alas, poor lady!

Creon: Insatiable Death, wilt thou destroy me yet?
What say you, teller of evil?
I am already dead,

And there is more?
Blood upon blood?
More death? My wife?

The central doors open, revealing the body of Eurydice.

Chorus: Look then, and see; nothing is hidden now.

Creon: O second horror!
What fate awaits me now?
My child here in my arms . . . and there, the other. . . .
The son . . . the mother. . . .

Messenger: There at the altar with the whetted knife
She stood, and as the darkness dimmed her eyes
Called on the dead, her elder son and this,
And with her dying breath cursed you, their slayer.

Creon: O horrible. . . .
Is there no sword for me,
To end this misery?

Messenger: Indeed you bear the burden of two deaths.
It was her dying word.

Creon: And her last act?

Messenger: Hearing her son was dead, with her own hand
she drove the sharp sword home into her heart.

Creon: There is no man can bear this guilt but I.
It is true, I killed him.
Lead me away, away. I live no longer.

Chorus: 'Twere best, if anything is best in evil times.
What's soonest done, is best, when all is ill.

Creon: Come, my last hour and fairest,
My only happiness . . . come soon.
Let me not see another day.
Away . . . away. . . .

Chorus: The future is not to be known; our present care
Is with the present; the rest is in other hands.

Creon: I ask no more than I have asked.

Chorus: Ask nothing.
What is to be, no mortal can escape.

Creon: I am nothing. I have no life.
Lead me away. . . .
That have killed unwittingly
My son, my wife.
I know not where I should turn,
Where look for help.

My hands have done amiss, my head is bowed
With fate too heavy for me.

Chorus: Of happiness the crown
And chiefest part
Is wisdom, and to hold
The gods in awe
This is the law
That, seeing the stricken heart
Of pride brought down,
We learn when we are old.

[The last excerpt from Antigone is the famous choral passage that expresses the Greek view of man.]

Chorus: Wonders are many on earth, and the greatest of these
Is man, who rides the ocean and takes his way
Through the deeps, through wind-swept valleys of perilous seas
      That surge and sway.
   He is master of ageless Earth, to his own will bending
The immortal mother of gods by the sweat of his brow,
As year succeeds year, with toil unending
      Of mule and plough.
   He is lord of all things living; birds of the air,
Beasts of the field, all creatures of sea and land
He taketh, cunning to capture and ensnare
            With sleight of hand;
   Hunting the savage beast from the upland rocks,
Taming the mountain monarch in his lair,
Teaching the wild horse and the roaming ox
            His yoke to bear.
   The use of language, the wind-swift motion of brain
He learnt; found out the laws of living together
In cities, building him shelter against the rain
            And wintry weather.
   There is nothing beyond his power. His subtlety
Meeteth all chance, all danger conquereth.
For every ill he hath found its remedy,
            Save only death.
   O wondrous subtlety of man, that draws
To good or evil ways! Great honour is given
And power to him who upholdeth his country's laws
            And the justice of heaven.
   But he that, too rashly daring, walks in sin
In solitary pride to his life's end.
At door of mine shall never enter in
            To call me friend.

The Peloponnesian War and the Decline of Athens (431–400 B.C.E.)

The Mytilenian Debate (427 B.C.E.)

THUCYDIDES

The Peloponnesian War (431–404 B.C.E.) was fought primarily over the threat that Athens posed to the security and economic well-being of Sparta and her allies. After the first two years of the war, Pericles died from a plague raging in Athens. With the loss of this far-sighted statesman, the democracy fell prey to more demagogic leaders who influenced people with effective oratory but whose policies were often extreme. The prime example of this extremist leadership was a man named Cleon, who succeeded Pericles in influence.

In 428 B.C.E., the city of Mytilene, located on the island of Lesbos and a subject of the Athenian empire, rebelled against its master. After the revolt was quelled, Cleon convinced the Athenian people to execute all the men of Mytilene and to sell the women and children into slavery. A ship was sent out immediately to implement the sentence of the democracy. The next day, says the historian Thucydides, there was a sudden change of feeling, and the Athenians reflected on the implications of their decision. The debate that ensued says much about the nature of Athenian democracy and imperialism. The first speaker is Cleon, who had originally proposed the harsh punishment.

I have remarked again and again that a democracy cannot manage an empire, but never more than now, when I see you regretting your condemnation of the Mytilenaeans. Having no fear or suspicion of one another in daily life, you deal with your allies upon the same principle, and you do not consider that whenever you yield to them out of pity or are misled by their specious tales, you are guilty of a weakness dangerous to yourselves, and receive no thanks from them. You should remember that your empire is a despotism exercised over unwilling subjects, who are always conspiring against you; they do not obey in return for any kindness which you do them to your own injury, but in so far as you are their masters; they have no love of you, but they are held down by force. Besides, what can be more detestable than to be perpetually changing your minds? . . . We should from the first have made no difference between the Mytilenaeans and the rest of our allies, and then their insolence would never have risen to such a height; for men naturally despise those who court them, but respect those who do not give way to them. . . . Reflect: if you impose the same penalty upon those of your allies who wilfully rebel and upon those who are [forced to rebellion] by the enemy, which of them will not revolt upon any pretext however trivial, seeing that, if he

"The Mytilenian Debate" is from Thucydides, *History of The Peloponnesian War*, 3.39–40; 3.46–49, trans. Benjamin Jowett, vol. 1, 2nd ed. (Oxford: The Clarendon Press, 1900), pp. 207, 210–212, 216–219. Translation modernized by the editor.

succeed, he will be free, and, if he fail, no irreparable evil will follow? We in the meantime shall have to risk our lives and our fortunes against every one in turn. When [we prove] conquerors, we shall recover only a ruined city, and, for the future, the revenues which are our strength will be lost to us. But if we fail, the number of our adversaries will be increased. And when we ought to be employed in repelling the enemies, . . . we shall be wasting time in fighting against our own allies.

Do not then hold out a hope, which eloquence can secure or money buy, that they are to be excused and that their error is to be deemed human and venial. Their attack was premeditated; they knew what they were doing. This was my original contention, and I still maintain that you should abide by your former decision, and not be misled either by pity, or by the charm of words, or by a too forgiving temper. There are no three things more destructive to your [imperial] power. Mercy should be reserved for the merciful, and not thrown away upon those who will have no compassion on us, and who must by the force of circumstances always be our enemies. . . . Be true then to yourselves, and recall as vividly as you can what you felt at the time; think how you would have given the world to crush your enemies, and now take your revenge. Do not be soft-hearted at the sight of their distress, but remember the danger which was once hanging over your heads. Punish them as they deserve, and prove by an example to your other allies that rebellion will be punished with death. If this is made quite clear to them, your attention will no longer be diverted from your enemies by wars against your own allies.

Such were the words of Cleon; and after him Diodotus the son of Eucrates, who in the previous assembly had been the chief opponent of the decree which condemned the Mytilenaeans, came forward again and spoke as follows: . . . We ought not to act hastily out of a mistaken reliance on the security which the penalty of death affords. Nor should we drive our rebellious subjects to despair; they must not think that there is no place for repentance, or that they may not at any moment give up their mistaken policy. Consider: at present, although a city may actually have revolted, when she becomes conscious of her weakness she will capitulate while still able to defray the cost of the war and to pay tribute for the future; but if we are too severe, will not the citizens make better preparations, and, when besieged, resist to the last, knowing that it is all the same whether they come to terms early or late? Shall not we ourselves suffer? For we shall waste our money by sitting down before a city which refuses to surrender; when the place is taken it will be a mere wreck, and we shall in future lose the revenues derived from it; and in these revenues lies our military strength. Do not then weigh offences with the severity of a judge, when you will only be injuring yourselves, but have an eye to the future; let the penalties which you impose on rebellious cities be moderate, and then their wealth will be undiminished and at your service. Do not hope to find a safeguard in the severity of your laws, but only in the vigilance of your administration. At present we do just the opposite; a free people under a strong government will always revolt in the hope of independence; and when we have put them down we think that they cannot be punished too severely. But instead of inflicting extreme penalties on free men who revolt, we should practice extreme vigilance before they revolt, and never allow such a thought to enter their minds. When however they have been once put down we ought to extenuate their crimes as much as possible. . . .

Be assured then that what I advise is for the best, and yielding neither to pity nor to leniency, for I am as unwilling as Cleon can be that you should be influenced by any such motives, but simply weighing the arguments which I have urged, accept my proposal: Pass sentence at your leisure on the [ring-leaders of the rebellion]; but leave the rest of the inhabitants where they are. This will be good policy for the future, and will strike present terror into your enemies. For wise counsel is really more formidable to an enemy than the severity of unreasoning violence.

Thus spoke Diodotus, and such were the proposals on either side which most nearly represented the opposing parties. In spite of the reaction, there was a struggle between the two opinions; the show of hands was very near, but the motion of Diodotus prevailed. The Athenians instantly despatched an-other trireme, hoping that, if the second could overtake the first, which had a start of about twenty-four hours, it might be in time to save the city. The Mytilenaean envoys provided wine and barley for the crew, and promised great rewards if they arrived first. And such was their energy that they continued rowing while they ate their barley. . . . and slept and rowed by turns. Fortunately no adverse wind sprang up, and, the first of the two ships sailing in no great hurry on her distasteful mission, and the second hastening as I have described, the one did indeed arrive sooner than the other, but not much sooner. [The commander] had read the decree and was about to put it into execution, when the second appeared and arrested the fate of the city.

So near was Mytilene to destruction.

The Melian Dialogue (416 B.C.E.)
THUCYDIDES

Although Mytilene escaped Athenian wrath after reevaluation by the democracy, the island of Melos was not so lucky. Melos, located off the southern tip of the Peloponnesus, was a Spartan colony. Even so, the Melians maintained a strict neutrality during the Peloponnesian War. Thucydides, the Athenian historian, wrote this contrived dialogue to demonstrate the brutal force used by Athens in maintaining her empire. The ideals expounded by Pericles in the Funeral Ora-

"The Melian Dialogue" is from Thucydides, *The History of The Peloponnesian War*, 5.84–116, trans. and ed. R. W. Livingstone (Oxford: The Clarendon Press, 1943), pp. 266–274. Reprinted by permission of Oxford University Press.

tion are thus balanced by power politics in which logic is no defense and might makes right. Melos was conquered by Athens in 416 B.C.E.

The next summer the Athenians made an expedition against the isle of Melos. The Melians are a colony of Sparta that would not submit to the Athenians like the other islanders, and at first remained neutral and took no part in the struggle, but afterwards, upon the Athenians using violence and plundering their territory, assumed an attitude of open hostility. The Athenian generals encamped in their territory with their army, and before doing any harm to their land sent envoys to negotiate. . . . The Athenian envoys then said:

Athenians: If you have met us in order to make surmises about the future, or for any other purpose than to look existing facts in the face and to discuss the safety of your city on this basis, we will break off the conversations; otherwise, we are ready to speak.

Melians: In our position it is natural and excusable to explore many ideas and arguments. But the problem that has brought us here is our security, so, if you think fit, let the discussion follow the line you propose.

Athenians: Then we will not make a long and unconvincing speech, full of fine phrases, to prove that our victory over Persia justifies our empire, or that we are now attacking you because you have wronged us, and we ask you not to expect to convince us by saying that you have not injured us, or that, though a colony of Sparta, you did not join her. . . .

Melians: As you ignore justice and have made self-interest the basis of discussion, we must take the same ground, and we say that in our opinion it is in your interest to maintain a principle which is for the good of all—that anyone in danger should have just and equitable treatment and any advantage, even if not strictly his due, which he can secure by persuasion. This is your interest as much as ours, for your fall would involve you in a crushing punishment that would be a lesson to the world.

Athenians: We have no apprehensions about the fate of our empire, if it did fall; those who rule other peoples, like the Spartans, are not formidable to a defeated enemy. Nor is it the Spartans with whom we are now contending: the danger is from subjects who of themselves may attack and conquer their rulers. But leave that danger to us to face. At the moment we shall say we are seeking the safety of your state; for we wish you to become our subjects with least trouble to ourselves, and we would like you to survive in our interests as well as your own.

Melians: It may be your interest to be our masters: how can it be ours to be your slaves?

Athenians: By submitting you would avoid a terrible fate, and we should gain by not destroying you.

Melians: Would you not agree to an arrangement under which we should keep out of the war, and be your friends instead of your enemies, but neutral?

Athenians: No: your hostility injures us less than your friendship. That, to our subjects, is an illusion of our weakness, while your hatred exhibits our power.

Melians: Is this the construction which your subjects put on it? Do they not distinguish between states in which you have no concern, and peoples who are most of them your colonies, and some conquered rebels?

Athenians: They think that one nation has as good rights as another, but that some survive because they are strong and we are afraid to attack them. So, apart from the addition of our empire, your subjection would give us security: the fact that you are islanders (and weaker than others) makes it more important that you should not get the better of the mistress of the sea.

Melians: But do you see no safety in our neutrality? Will you not make enemies of all neutral Powers when they see your conduct and reflect that some day you will attack them? Will not your action strengthen your existing opponents, and induce those who would otherwise never be your enemies to become so against their will?

Athenians: No. The mainland states, secure in their freedom, will be slow to take defensive measures against us, and we do not consider them so formidable as independent island powers like yourselves, or subjects already smarting under our yoke. These are most likely to take a thoughtless step and bring themselves and us into obvious danger.

Melians: Surely, then, if you are ready to risk so much to maintain your empire, and the enslaved peoples so much to escape from it, it would be criminal cowardice in us, who are still free, not to take any and every measure before submitting to slavery?

Athenians: No, if you reflect calmly: for this is not a competition in heroism between equals, where your honor is at stake, but a question of self-preservation to save you from a struggle with a far stronger Power.

Melians: Still, we know that in war fortune is more impartial than the disproportion in numbers might lead one to expect. If we submit at once, our position is desperate; if we fight, there is still a hope that we shall stand secure.

Athenians: Hope encourages men to take risks; men in a strong position may follow her without ruin, if not without loss. But when they stake all that they have to the last coin (for she is a spendthrift), she reveals her real self in the hour of failure, and when her nature is known she leaves them without means of self-protection. You are weak, your future hangs on a turn of the scales; avoid the mistake most men make, who might save themselves by human means, and then, when visible hopes desert them, in their extremity turn to the invisible—prophecies and oracles and all those things which delude men with hopes, to their destruction.

Melians: We too, you can be sure, realize the difficulty of struggling against your power and against Fortune if she is not impartial. Still we trust that Heaven will not allow us to be worsted by Fortune, for in this quarrel we are right and you are wrong. Besides, we expect the support of Sparta to supply the deficiencies in our strength, for she is bound to help us as her kinsmen, if for no other reason, and from a sense of honor. So our confidence is not entirely unreasonable.

Athenians: As for divine favor, we think that we can count on it as much as you, for neither our claims nor our actions are inconsistent with what men believe about Heaven or desire for themselves. We believe that Heaven, and we know that men, by a natural law, always rule where they are stronger. We did not make the law nor were we the first to act on it; we found it existing, and it will exist forever, after we are gone; and we know that you and anyone else as strong as we are would do as we do. As to your expectations from Sparta and your belief that she will help you from a sense of honor, we congratulate you on your innocence but we do not admire your folly. So far as they themselves and their natural traditions are concerned, the Spartans are a highly virtuous people; as for their behavior to others, much might be said, but we can put it shortly by saying that, most obviously of all people we know, they identify their interests with justice and the pleasantest course with honor. Such principles do not favor your present irrational hopes of deliverance.

Melians: That is the chief reason why we have confidence in them now; in their own interest they will not wish to betray their own colonists and so help their enemies and destroy the confidence that their friends in Greece feel in them.

Athenians: Apparently you do not realize that safety and self-interest go together, while the path of justice and honor is dangerous; and danger is a risk which the Spartans are little inclined to run. . . . Here experience may teach you like others, and you will learn that Athens has never abandoned a siege from fear of another foe. You said that you proposed to discuss the safety of your city, but we observe that in all your speeches you have never said a word on which any reasonable expectation of it could be founded. Your strength lies in deferred hopes; in comparison with the forces now arrayed against you, your resources are too small for any hope of success. You will show a great want of judgment if you do not come to a more reasonable decision after we have withdrawn. Surely you will not fall back on the idea of honor, which has been the ruin of so many when danger and disgrace were staring them in the face. How often, when men have seen the fate to which they were tending, have they been enslaved by a phrase and drawn by the power of this seductive word to fall of their own free will into irreparable disaster, bringing on themselves by their folly a greater dishonor than fortune could inflict! If you are wise, you will avoid that fate. The greatest of cities makes you a fair offer, to keep your own land and become her tributary ally: there is not dishonor in that. The choice between war and safety is given you; do not obstinately take the worse alternative. The most successful people are those who stand up to their equals, behave properly to their superiors, and treat their inferiors fairly. Think it over when we withdraw, and reflect once again that you will have only one country, and that its prosperity or ruin depends on one decision.

The Athenians then withdrew from the conference; and the Melians, left to themselves, came to a decision corresponding with what they had maintained in the discussion, and answered, "Our resolution, Athenians, is unaltered. We will not in a moment deprive of freedom a city by which the gods have preserved it until now, and in the help of men, that is, of the Spartans; and so we will try and save ourselves. Meanwhile we invite you to allow us to be friends to you and foes to neither party, and to retire from our country after making such a treaty as shall seem fit to us both.

Such was the answer of the Melians. The Athenians broke up the conference saying, "To judge from your decision, you are unique in regarding the future as more certain than the present and in allowing your wishes to convert the unseen into reality; and as you have staked most on, and trusted most in, the Spartans, your fortune, and your hopes, so will you be most completely deceived."

The Athenian envoys now returned to the army, and as the Melians showed no signs of yielding the generals at once began hostilities, and drew a line of circumvallation round the Melians . . . besieged the place. . . .

Summer was now over . . . and the siege was now pressed vigorously; there was some treachery in the town, and the Melians surrendered at discretion to the Athenians, who put to death all the grown men whom they took, and sold the women and children for slaves. . . .

The Trojan Women (415 B.C.E.)
EURIPIDES

One year after the destruction of Melos, the great Athenian dramatist Euripides reacted to the incident by composing The Trojan Women. *The subject of his play is the fate of the women of Troy after their husbands had been killed and their city destroyed by the Greek force in 1230 B.C.E. In the following passage, Andromache, wife of the valiant Trojan leader Hector, is informed of the fate proscribed for her young son. Note how her argument parallels that of "The Melian Dialogue."* The Trojan Women *failed to win a prize in the dramatic competition that year.*

"The Trojan Women" is from Euripides, *The Women of Troy*, in *The Bacchae and Other Plays*, trans. Philip Vellacott (Baltimore, Md., and Harmondsworth, Middlesex: Penguin Books, 1954), pp. 105–107 (lines 704–778). Copyright © Philip Vellacott, 1954. Reprinted by permission.

Talthybius: Andromache, widow of the bravest of the Trojans: do not hate me. It is with great reluctance that I have to convey to you the decision unanimously reached by the Greeks and their two generals, the sons of Pelops.

Andromache: What is this? Your words hint at the worst.

Talthybius: It was decided that your son—how can I say it?

Andromache: He is to have a different master from mine?

Talthybius: No Greek will ever be his master.

Andromache: What? Is he to be the one Trojan left behind in Troy?

Talthybius: My news is bad. It is hard to find words.

Andromache: Thank you for your sympathy. What have you to say?

Talthybius: You must know the worst: they mean to kill your son.

Andromache: Oh, gods! His sentence is worse than mine.

Talthybius: In a speech delivered before the whole assembly Odysseus carried his point—

Andromache [sobbing passionately]:   Oh, Oh! This is more than I can bear.

Talthybius: —that the son of so distinguished a father must not be allowed to attain manhood—

Andromache: May he hear the same sentence passed on his own son!

Talthybius: —but should be thrown down from the battlements of Troy. Now show yourself a sensible woman, and accept this decision. Don't cling to him, or imagine you have any chance of resisting: you have none. Bear what must be like a queen. There is no one who can help. You can see for yourself: your city and your husband are gone; you are in our hands. Shall we match our strength against one woman? We can. So I hope that you won't feel inclined to struggle, or to call down curses on the Greeks, or do anything that might lead to violent measures or resentment. If you say anything to anger the army, this child will die without rites of pity, without burial. If you are quiet, and accept the inevitable in a proper spirit, you will be allowed to lay your child in his grave, and you will find the Greeks more considerate to yourself.

Andromache: Darling child, precious beyond all price! You will die, killed by our enemies, leaving your mother to mourn. Your noble father's courage, which saved others, has condemned you; his spirit was a fatal inheritance. I thought, on that day when I entered Hector's house as a bride, on that ill-fated night, that my son would rule the teeming multitudes of the East—not die by a Greek ritual of murder.

Are you crying, little one? Do you understand? Why do you tug my hand, cling to my dress, nestling like a bird under its mother's wing? No Hector will rise from the grave and step forth to save you, gripping his glorious spear; none of your father's brothers, no army of Phrygians. You must leap from that horrible height, and fall, and break your neck, and give up your life, and be pitied by no one.

My baby, so young in my arms, and so dear! O the sweet smell of your skin! When you were newly born, how I wrapped you up and gave you my breast, and tended you day and night, and was worn out with weariness—all for nothing, for nothing! Now say good-bye to me for the last time; come close to your mother, wind your arms round my neck, and put your lips to mine.

O men of Hellas, inventors of cruelty unworthy of you! Why will you kill him? What has he done?—Helen, child of Hyndareus, you are no daughter of divine Majesty! You had many fathers, and I can name them: the Avenging Curse was one, Hate was the next, then Murder and Death and every evil that lives on earth! I will swear that Zeus never fathered you to ruin men's lives by tens of thousands through Asia and Hellas! My curse on you! With the shining glance of your beauty you have brought this rich and noble country to a shameful end.

Take him! Carry him away, throw him down, if your edict says 'Throw!' Feast on his flesh! God is destroying us! I have no power to save my child from death. Hide my miserable body, throw me on board! I go to my princely marriage, and leave behind me my dear child.

The Sicilian Disaster (413 B.C.E.)

THUCYDIDES

In 415 B.C.E., the Athenians embarked on a grand plan to capture the city of Syracuse on the island of Sicily; Athens intended to use it as a base against Sparta and her allies. The Spartans, therefore, aided Syracuse, and eventually the Athenian fleet was bottled up in the harbor and destroyed (413 B.C.E.). In this selection, Thucydides reflects on the fate of the Athenians and the meaning of the disaster.

Those who were imprisoned in the quarries were at the beginning of their captivity harshly treated by the Syracusans. There were great numbers of them, and they were crowded in a deep and narrow place. At first the sun by day was still scorching and suffocating, for they had no roof over their heads, while the autumn nights were cold, and the extreme of temperature engendered violent disorders. Being cramped for room they had to do everything on the same spot. The corpses of those who died from their wounds, exposure to heat and cold, and the like, lay heaped one upon another. The smells were intolerable; and they were at the same time afflicted by hunger and thirst. During eight months they were allowed only about half a pint of water and a pint of food a day. Every kind of misery which could befall a man in such a place befell them. This was the condition of all the captives for about

---

"The Sicilian Disaster" is from Thucydides, *The History of The Peloponnesian War*, 7.87–8.1, trans. Benjamin Jowett, vol. 2, 2nd ed. (Oxford: The Clarendon Press, 1900), pp. 333–336. Translation modernized by the editor.

ten weeks. At length the Syracusans sold them, with the exception of the Athenians and of any Sicilian or Italian Greeks who sided with them in the war. The whole number of the public prisoners is not accurately known, but they were not less than seven thousand.

Of all the Hellenic actions which took place in this war, or indeed, as I think, of all Hellenic actions which are on record, this was the greatest—the most glorious to the victors, the most ruinous to the vanquished; for they were utterly and at all points defeated, and their sufferings were prodigious. Fleet and army perished from the face of the earth; nothing was saved, and of the many who went forth few returned home.

Thus ended the Sicilian expedition.

The news was brought to Athens, but the Athenians could not believe that the armament had been so completely annihilated, although they had the positive assurances of the very soldiers who had escaped from the scene of action. At last they knew the truth; and then they were furious with the orators who had joined in promoting the expedition—as if they had not voted it themselves—and with the soothsayers, and prophets, and all who by the influence of religion had at the time inspired them with the belief that they would conquer Sicily. Whichever way they looked there was trouble; they were overwhelmed by their calamity, and were in fear and consternation unutterable. The citizens and the city were alike distressed; they had lost a host of cavalry and hoplites and the flower of their youth, and there were none to replace them. And when they saw an insufficient number of ships in their docks, and no crews to man them, nor money in the treasury, they despaired of survival. . . . Their enemies in Greece, whose resources were now doubled, would . . . set upon them with all their might both by sea and land, and would be assisted by their own rebellious allies. Still they determined, so far as their situation allowed, not to give way. . . . After the manner of a democracy, they were very disciplined while their fright lasted. . . .

Women and War: Lysistrata (411 B.C.E.)

ARISTOPHANES

Athens not only produced great tragedians such as Sophocles and Euripides, but also great comic dramatists as well. The brilliant playwright Aristophanes poked fun at the major personalities of the day (Socrates included) and influenced public opinion about the most divisive political issues. Aristophanes was born about 447 B.C.E. at a time when Athens was at the height of her power and influence.

"Women and War: Lysistrata" is from Aristophanes, *Lysistrata and Other Plays*, trans. Alan H. Sommerstein (New York, and Harmondsworth, Middlesex: Penguin Classics, 1973), pp. 200–202, 206–208. Copyright © Alan H. Sommerstein, 1973. Reproduced by permission of Penguin Books Ltd.

*He was often critical of the democracy and especially the prosecution of the Pelo-
ponnesian War. After the tragic destruction of Athenian forces at Syracuse in
413 B.C.E., and the impotent leadership in the years that followed, Aristophanes
contrived his own solution for the end of the war, which he presented in 411
B.C.E. in the play* Lysistrata: *The women of both Sparta and Athens would take
the initiative in stopping the war by withholding sex while their husbands were
on leave until the men came to their senses!*

*Of special note here is the presentation of women in Athenian society. Although
it is debated whether women were allowed to attend the theater (Plato gives evidence
that they did), in other ways their lives were extremely restricted. They were not allowed to leave their homes unescorted, could not vote, hold public office, own property, or even attend social gatherings in their own homes. They were essentially
bound to the will and decisions of their husbands or fathers. Perhaps the biggest joke
in Athens after the presentation of* Lysistrata *was that women could have conceived and organized such a bold and effective plan for ending the Peloponnesian
War. In this scene, the leader of the Athenian women, Lysistrata, and her compa-
triot, Stratyllis, confront the male Athenian leadership.*

Magistrate: Anyway, what business are war and peace of yours?

Lysistrata: I'll tell you.

Magistrate [restraining himself with difficulty]:   You'd better or else.

Lysistrata: I will if you'll listen and keep those hands of yours under control.

Magistrate: I can't—I'm too livid. . . . Say what you have to say.

Lysistrata: In the last war we were too modest to object to anything you men
did—and in any case you wouldn't let us say a word. But don't think we approved! We knew everything that was going on. Many times we'd hear at
home about some major blunder of yours, and then when you came home
we'd be burning inside but we'd have to put on a smile and ask what it was
you'd decided to inscribe in the pillar underneath the Peace Treaty. And
what did my husband always say?—'Shut up and mind your own business!'
And I did.

Stratyllis: I wouldn't have done!

Magistrate: He'd have given you one if you hadn't.

Lysistrata: Exactly—so I kept quiet. But sure enough, next thing we knew
you'd make an even sillier decision. And if I so much as said, 'Darling, why
are you carrying on with this silly policy?' he would glare at me and say, 'Back
to your weaving, woman, or you'll have a headache for a month. Go and attend to your work; let war be the care of the menfolk.'

Magistrate: Quite right too, by Zeus.

Lysistrata: Right? That we should not be allowed to make the least little sug-
gestion to you, no matter how much you mismanage the City's affairs? And
now, look, every time two people meet in the street, what do they say? 'Isn't

there a man in the country?' and the answer comes, 'Not one.' That's why we women got together and decided we were going to save Greece. What was the point of waiting any longer, we asked ourselves. Well now, we'll make a deal. You listen to us—and we'll talk sense, not like you used to—listen to us and keep quiet, as we've had to do up to now, and we'll clear up the mess you've made.

Magistrate: Insufferable effrontery! I will not stand for it!

Lysistrata [magisterially]:   Silence!

Magistrate: You, confound you, a woman with your face veiled, dare to order me to be silent! Gods, let me die! . . .

Leader: Disgraceful!—women venturing to prate
In public so about affairs of State!
They even (men could not be so naive)
The blandishments of Sparta's wolves believe!
The truth the veriest child could surely see:
This is a Monarchist Conspiracy.
I'll fight autocracy until the end:
My freedom I'll unswervingly defend. . . .
And from this place
I'll give this female one upon the face!
[He slaps Stratyllis hard on the cheek.]

Stratyllis [giving him a blow in return that sends him reeling]:
Don't trifle with us, rascals, or we'll show you
Such fisticuffs, your mothers will not know you!

Chorus of Women: My debt of love today
To the City I will pay,
And I'll pay it in the form of good advice;
For the City gave me honour
(Pallas blessing be upon her!),
And the things I've had from her deserve their price. . . .

Stratyllis: See why I think I have a debt to pay?
'But women can't talk politics,' you say.
Why not? What is it you insinuate?
That we contribute nothing to the State?
Why, we give more than you! See if I lie:
We cause men to be born, you make them die.
What's more, you've squandered all the gains of old;
And now, the taxes you yourselves assess
You do not pay. Who's got us in this mess?
Do you complain? Another grunt from you,
And you will feel the impact of this shoe! . . .

Leader: If once we let these women get the semblance of a start,
Before we know, they'll be adept at every manly art!

The Trial of Socrates (399 B.C.E.)

PLATO

The Peloponnesian War came to an end in 404 B.C.E. The Athenians suffered a humiliating defeat and were divested of their empire, military forces, and dignity. A Spartan occupation force assumed control of the city and replaced Athenian democracy with the reactionary rule of the Thirty Tyrants, vindictive Athenian citizens who used the months from 404 to 403 B.C.E. to settle scores with their former political enemies. Although a democracy was reinstituted, it no longer espoused the tolerance of ideas and freedom of speech which had been such a part of former Athenian glory. A true indicator of this decline was the trial of Socrates.

Socrates, a stonecutter by trade, had dutifully served the Athenian state in a political capacity and also as a soldier in war. He disliked the advances of popular teachers called "sophists" who claimed to be able to teach anything for a fee. Socrates instead claimed that he knew nothing and set about informally teaching people to question in the hope of finding wisdom. He considered himself the gadfly whose responsibility it was to prod the democracy continually in hopes that self-reflection might produce wise policy. His "services" were free of charge, and he became quite influential among the youth of Athens. In 399 B.C.E., he was accused by various Athenian leaders of not believing in the gods of the state and of corrupting the youth. His most famous pupil, Plato, watched the proceedings in the court and wrote an account of Socrates' defense, called the Apology; *an excerpt is presented below. In the end, Socrates was condemned to death and actually insisted on drinking the poisonous hemlock. In his martyrdom lay the destruction of Athenian ideals.*

This inquisition has led to my having many enemies of the worst and most dangerous kind, and has given occasion also to many injuries. . . .

There is another thing: young men of the richer classes, who have not much to do, come about me of their own accord; they like to hear the pretenders examined, and they often imitate me, and proceed to examine others; there are plenty of persons, as they quickly discover, who think they know something, but really know little or nothing; and then those who are examined by them instead of being angry with themselves are angry with me: This confounded Socrates, they say; this villainous misleader of youth!—and then if somebody asks them, Why, what evil does he practice or teach? they do not know, and cannot tell; but in order that they may not appear to be at a loss, they repeat the ready-made charges which are used against all philosophers about teaching things up in the clouds and under the earth, and having no gods, and making the worse appear the better cause; for they do not like to confess that their pretense of knowledge has been detected—which is the

"The Trial of Socrates" is from Plato, *Apology*, in *The Dialogues of Plato*, 3rd ed., trans. Benjamin Jowett (Oxford: The Clarendon Press, 1875). Translation modernized by the editor.

truth: and as they are numerous and ambitious and energetic, and are drawn up in battle array and have persuasive tongues, they have filled your ears with their loud and inveterate slanders. And this is the reason why my three accusers, Meletus and Anytus and Lycon, have set upon me. . . .

Some one will say: And are you not ashamed, Socrates, of a course of life which is likely to bring you to an untimely end? To him I may fairly answer: There you are mistaken: a man who is good for anything ought not to calculate the chance of living or dying; he ought only to consider whether in doing anything he is doing right or wrong—acting the part of a good man or of a bad. . . . And therefore if you let me go now, . . . if you say to me, Socrates, this time we will not mind Anytus, and you shall be let off, but upon one condition, that you are not to enquire and speculate in this way any more, and that if you are caught doing so again you shall die; if this was the condition on which you let me go, I should reply: Men of Athens, I honor and love you; but I shall obey God rather than you, and while I have life and strength I shall never cease from the practice and teaching of philosophy, exhorting anyone whom I meet and saying to him after my manner: You, my friend—a citizen of the great and mighty and wise city of Athens—are you not ashamed of heaping up the greatest amount of money and honor and reputation, and caring so little about wisdom and truth and the greatest improvements of the soul, which you never regard or heed at all? And if the person with whom I am arguing, says: Yes, but I do care; then I do not leave him or let him go at once; but I proceed to interrogate and examine and cross-examine him, and if I think that he has no virtue in him, but only says that he has, I reproach him with undervaluing the greater, and overvaluing the less. . . . This is my teaching, and if this is the doctrine which corrupts youth, I am a mischievous person. . . .

And now, Athenians, I am not going to argue for my own sake, as you may think, but for yours, that you may not sin against God by condemning me, who am his gift to you. For if you kill me you will not easily find a successor to me, who, if I may use such a ludicrous figure of speech, am a sort of gadfly, given to the state by God; and the state is a great and noble steed who is tardy in his motions owing to his very size, and requires to be stirred into life. I am that gadfly which God has attached to the state, and all day long and in all places am always fastening upon you, arousing and persuading and reproaching you. You will not easily find another like me, and therefore I would advise you to spare me. I dare say that you may feel out of temper (like a person who is suddenly awakened from sleep), and you think that you might easily strike me dead as Anytus advises, and then you would sleep on for the remainder of your lives, unless God in his care of you sent you another gadfly. . . .

And now, O men who have condemned me, I would give prophecy to you; for I am about to die, and in the hour of death men are gifted with prophetic power. And I prophecy to you who are my murderers, that immediately after my departure punishment far heavier than you have inflicted on me will surely await you. Me you have killed because you wanted to escape the accuser, and not to give an account of your lives. But that will not be as you suppose: far otherwise. For I say that there will be more accusers of you than there are now; accusers whom hitherto I have restrained: and as they are younger they will be more inconsiderate with you, and you will be more offended at them. If you think that by killing me you can prevent someone from censuring your evil lives, you are mistaken; that is not a way of escape which is either possible or honorable; the easiest and noblest way is not to be disabling others, but to be improving yourselves. This is the prophecy which I utter before my departure to the judges who have condemned me. . . .

Still I have a favor to ask of them. When my sons are grown up, I would ask you, O my friends, to punish them; and I would have you trouble them, as I have troubled you if they seem to care about riches, or anything, more than about virtue; or if they pretend to be something when they are really nothing—then reprove them, as I have reproved you, for not caring about that for which they ought to care, and thinking that they are something when they are really nothing. And if you do this, both I and my sons will have received justice at your hands.

The hour of departure has arrived, and we go on our ways—I to die, and you to live. Which is better God only knows.

CHRONOLOGY: The Glory of Greece

3000 B.C.E.	Beginning of Minoan civilization on Crete.
2000–1300 B.C.E.	Hittites leading power in Asia Minor.
1600–1400 B.C.E.	Great Age of Minoan civilization. Culture flourishes on Crete. Palace at Cnossus is complex and gives rise to legend concerning King Minos and his labyrinth, which contains the half-man, half-bull Minotaur. Minoans are a peaceful people who wrote in Linear A script.
1450 B.C.E.	Destruction of Cretan palaces, except Cnossus, by Mycenaean Greek invasion from the mainland. Eclipse of Minoan power.
1400–1200 B.C.E.	Great Age of Mycenaean civilization. Culture flourishes at Mycenae, Pylos, Thebes, and Athens on mainland Greece. Trade with Egypt and relations with Hittites.
1287 B.C.E.	Battle of Cadesh between Egypt (Ramses the Great) and the Hittite empire. Beginning of decline for both powers.
1230–1150 B.C.E.	Breakdown of settled conditions in the eastern Mediterranean and Greece.
1230–1220 B.C.E.	Trojan War between Mycenaean Greeks and Trojans recounted later (725 B.C.E.) by Homer in the epic poems, *The Iliad* and *The Odyssey*. Trojan War perhaps weakened Mycenaean Greeks and made them vulnerable to invasions about 1200 B.C.E.

1200 B.C.E.	Massive destruction throughout eastern Mediterranean. Mycenaean settlements destroyed on mainland Greece (Athens excepted). Linear B tablets burned and preserved in the fires that accompanied the destruction. Population flows east toward Asia Minor. Hittite civilization destroyed. Could this be the "Dorian invasion" of legend? Was this an internal revolution or a domestic civil war between rival cities?
1188 B.C.E.	Massive attack on Egypt repelled with great difficulty. Egyptian records on palace walls record invasions of "Sea Peoples" ("Peleset"). Could the "Sea Peoples" be Dorian invaders from north of Greece? Was the destruction of the Hittites and Egyptians the result of one invader who also destroyed the Mycenaean settlements, or several peoples on the move?
1100–750 B.C.E.	Greek "Dark Ages" or Middle Ages. Population on mainland is reduced, trade curtailed, and Greeks forget how to write. They survive in small geographically isolated communities which form the origins of the polis or city-state so important in fifth-century Greece.
776 B.C.E.	First Olympic games. Athletic competition develops between small developing Greek city-states. Greek chronology reckoned in four-year periods from this date called "olympiads."
750–700 B.C.E.	Greeks emerge from Dark Ages and begin process of trading and colonizing throughout the Mediterranean. Greek alphabet based on letters, not syllables, adapted by Greeks, probably from the Phoenician example, and writing develops. *The Iliad* and *The Odyssey*, epic poems passed down through the Dark Ages by oral tradition, compiled and composed, perhaps by a poet named Homer (ca. 725 B.C.E.).
650 B.C.E.	Sparta quells a rebellion of helots (Messenian slaves) and defeats Argos in a long war. Reforms of Lycurgus make Spartan state into a military academy and camp.
600–550 B.C.E.	Age of Tyrants. Because of difficult economic conditions, factional divisions within the ruling Greek aristocracies often resulted in the establishment of tyrants, strongmen who restructured society and oversaw public works and security within the polis.
600–500 B.C.E.	Development of early Greek philosophy. Thales of Miletus (ca. 600 B.C.E.) and Pythagoras (ca. 550 B.C.E.) search for the primary elements around which life revolves and the numerical relationships and harmonies within the universe.
594 B.C.E.	Reforms of Solon in Athens to relieve debt slavery.
546–510 B.C.E.	Athens under the control of the tyrant Pisistratus and his sons.

508–501 B.C.E.	Cleisthenes institutes democratic reforms in Athens.
499–494 B.C.E.	Greek cities on the coast of Persian territory (Ionia) rebel.
490 B.C.E.	Battle of Marathon. Athenians led by Miltiades defeat Persian forces sent by Darius.
480 B.C.E.	Persian forces under Xerxes invade Greece, overcome Spartan resistance at Thermopylae, and burn Athens before being defeated under the command of Themistocles at the Battle of Salamis.
478 B.C.E.	Delian Confederacy established among Aegean islands and cities in order to protect against future Persian attacks. Athens supplies the commanders and administers the treasury on the island of Delos.
454 B.C.E.	Treasury of the Delian Confederacy moved from Delos to Athens. Confederacy is transformed into the Athenian Empire.
449 B.C.E.	Peace of Callias established between Persia and Greek city-states.
447 B.C.E.	Parthenon begun with funds garnered from the Delian Confederacy's treasury in Athens.
441 B.C.E.	Antigone by Sophocles performed at Athens. Wins first prize in the competition. Climax of Athenian tragic drama.
431–404 B.C.E.	The Peloponnesian War pits Athens against Sparta for leadership of the Greek world. Pericles expounds on Athenian greatness in his funeral oration (430 B.C.E.). "The Mytilenian Debate" (427 B.C.E.) and "The Melian Dialogue" (416 B.C.E.) by Thucydides and *The Trojan Women* (415 B.C.E.) by Euripides emphasize the hypocrisy between the ideals of Athenian democracy and the brutalities of imperial rule.
399 B.C.E.	Trial and execution of Socrates, whose role as "gadfly" forced self-reflection upon the Athenian democracy.

STUDY QUESTIONS

1. After reading the selections from Homer's *Iliad* on the Trojan War, what can you say about the relationships between Agamemnon, leader of the Greek expedition, and his warriors such as Achilles? Was Agamemnon a strong king with absolute control over his men, or was he considered "first among equals"? What does this tell you about Mycenaean society?
2. What roles do the gods play in the selections from Homer's *Iliad*? What specific human characteristics do they exhibit, and how essential were they to the success or failure of each contesting army?

3. Compare the deaths of Patroclus and Hector. How did each die, and what does the manner in which they died tell you about the heroic values of this age? Why did both Patroclus and Hector have to fight? What human themes are present in these selections, and why has *The Iliad* been considered a classic of Western literature?

4. What human themes dominate *The Odyssey?* Note specific passages in the selections from *The Odyssey* that support your ideas. How are Odysseus's cleverness and wit demonstrated in the story of the Cyclops? What qualities in a warrior are most appreciated? Compare Odysseus and Achilles in this respect. What do we learn about the Greek view of death from Odysseus's visit to the underworld? How do you interpret Achilles' reply to Odysseus's statement, "For you, Achilles, Death should have lost its sting"?

5. In the excerpt in which Odysseus returns to Ithaca, why does he decide to kill all the suitors of Penelope? What informal law in Greek society have the suitors violated? How did the Cyclops, Polyphemus, violate this same law? How did Penelope "test" Odysseus before she would accept him as her true husband? Why is Homer's *Odyssey* considered a classic of Western literature?

6. How are women portrayed in Homer's *Iliad* and *Odyssey?* Compare the homecoming experience of Agamemnon and his wife Clytemnestra with that of Odysseus and Penelope. Note also the sorrows of Hector's wife, Andromache, as she saw the body of her husband dragged around the city of Troy by the victor Achilles. What messages about war and suffering is Homer trying to convey? Compare these scenes with the agony of Andromache after the Greeks enter Troy victoriously as portrayed by Euripides in the selection entitled, *The Trojan Women.*

7. What were the main ideas of Thales of Miletus? Why is his fundamental question about the composition of things in the world so expressive of the Greek spirit of inquiry? What were the contributions of Anaximenes and Pythagoras? Why has it been proposed that the Greeks invented philosophy?

8. How were the city-states of Athens and Sparta diametrically opposed? According to Pericles in his Funeral Oration, what qualities made Athens great? What was the basis of Spartan achievement?

9. Were the Persians justified in their invasions of Greece? In the accounts of the Persian Wars, what, for you, is the most memorable scene? In what ways did the Persian Wars benefit the Greeks?

10. In his Funeral Oration, how does Pericles justify Athenian imperialism? What benefits does Athens give her allies and what does she get in return? Is this equitable? Are there any weaknesses or defects in Pericles' arguments?

11. According to the Old Oligarch, what are the weaknesses of Athenian democracy and how does he view Athenian imperialism?

12. What does the decree on collection of Athenian tribute specify? What does this say about the Athenian empire?

13. Note the dramatic selections by Sophocles. What are some of his main ideas about justice, responsibility, and law? How do these ideas reflect a prosperous civilization?

14. What are the main issues argued by Cleon and Diodotus in "The Mytilenian Debate"? Is mercy an issue? What argument seems more persuasive if one wants to maintain an empire? Why?

15. In "The Melian Dialogue," what is the basic argument of the Athenians? of the Melians? Choose the most effective phrases from this source and explain why they are important and what they reveal about the nature of power and democracy. Is Thucydides a moralist? What is his view of human nature?

16. Do you think it is possible for a democracy to rule an empire, or is this a moral contradiction? Can you apply this question to the United States in a contemporary setting?

17. In what ways does the excerpt from *The Trojan Women* by Euripides parallel the arguments of "The Melian Dialogue"? Be specific in your answer. What is Euripides trying to say about power and innocence? What does the production of this play say about the nature of freedom in Athens?

18. Thucydides, the historian, maintained that one of the reasons Athens lost the Peloponnesian War was that it was guilty of "hubris," or going beyond the limits imposed by the gods. How does the Sicilian Disaster reflect this? Does this belief appear in Sophocles' plays as well? Be specific in your answer.

19. What can you discern from Aristophanes' *Lysistrata* about the treatment of women in Greek society? Note how critical the women are about how the war has been conducted. What was Aristophanes trying to do—criticize the state, or make light of the impotent status of women? Do you regard satire as a legitimate vehicle for reform?

20. How is Socrates critical of the Athenian leaders in his *Apology?* What does he say in particular about freedom and virtue? Why is the condemnation of Socrates symbolic of the failure of Athenian civilization?

3

The Age of
Alexander the Great

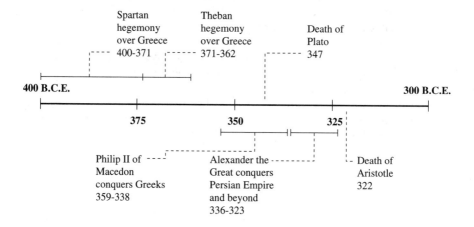

Liberty doesn't work as well in practice as it does in speeches.

—Will Rogers

There is no conflict between liberty and safety. We will have both or neither.

—Ramsey Clark

The best government is a benevolent tyranny tempered by an occasional assassination.

—Voltaire

Greatness lies not in being strong, but in the right use of strength.

—Henry Ward Beecher

The great are great only because we are on our knees.

—Pierre-Joseph Proudhon

CHAPTER THEMES

- *Systems of Government:* After the death of Alexander the Great, his empire broke down into smaller regions ruled by lesser kings who fought among themselves. Can a government which is based on a cult of personality endure once that personality dies? Do "power vacuums" result in desperate and inherently unstable governments? Therefore, is the transfer of power the most crucial and dangerous phase of politics?

- *Imperialism:* Alexander the Great expanded his empire beyond the known limits of the Greek world. By bringing Greek culture to the East, was Alexander a force for progress? Can imperialism be progressive?

- *Propaganda:* Who was Alexander the Great? To what extent were his exploits the stuff of legend, with little foundation in reality? How do we separate the myth from the man? Is the "Hero" in history simply a myth?

- *Women in History:* What were Plato's ideas regarding an ideal society ruled by "philosopher-kings"? What role was assigned to women in this ideal society, and how would children be reared in this Republic? What does this say about the role of women in Greek society?

- *Historical Change and Transition:* Had Alexander not lived, would history have been different? What if Alexander had turned west in his search for empire instead of east—how would history have been changed? How important is the influence of the individual on historical events? In what ways did civilization progress in spite of Alexander?

- *The Big Picture:* Should Alexander be called "the Great," or does greatness lie not in conquering but in consolidating and maintaining society? Were the Romans better role models in this regard than the Greeks?

In the fifth century B.C.E., the Greek city-state of Athens developed a society imbued with democratic ideals and creative inspiration. The century has become known as the Golden Age because Athenian contributions in art, philosophy, drama, and literature have been recognized as fundamental for the advancement of Western Civilization. The century closed, however, on a pessimistic note. The vast political and economic differences between Athens and Sparta drove the two city-states into the long and costly Peloponnesian War. At the war's conclusion in

404 B.C.E., Athenian power had been destroyed and with it the confidence and energy necessary for cultural leadership.

Sparta, as the victor in the war, was now thrust into a position of leadership over the Greeks. Yet it too had been weakened in the struggle and, in any event, was an insular polis that did not enjoy spending time away from the domestic affairs of its own territory. Spartan leadership (or "hegemony" as it was called) over the Greeks did not last long and was replaced in 371 B.C.E. by the dominant city-state of Thebes. Under the innovative military direction of a general named Epaminondas, the Thebans were able to assume hegemony until his death in 362 B.C.E. Although one polis wielded the greatest influence, others attempted to compete, asserting their own power and influence. In this spirit, Athens reestablished its democracy and even tried to regain its empire through alliance and conquest. Eventually, internal problems restricted its conduct of foreign affairs.

During the first half of the fourth century B.C.E., Greece in general and Athens in particular were in a state of domestic chaos. Nearly continuous warfare and political strife interfered with trade and thus contributed to economic dislocation and depression. A widening gulf developed between rich and poor, and this was reflected in political dissension and indecision. There was a genuine desire to return to the days of glory and honor when Athens commanded the respect of the world; yet there was much debate on how to regain such a position. Many eyes turned toward the Persians, whose defeat in 480 B.C.E. by Greek tenacity and ingenuity had ushered in the Golden Age. The Athenian orator Isocrates strongly advocated foreign conquest as the panacea for depression but also knew that the Greeks had to be unified in order to defeat Persian power. His solution was to support the leadership of the King of Macedon, Philip II. In this, Isocrates was opposed by perhaps the greatest orator of all, Demosthenes. Demosthenes firmly believed that accepting the leadership of Philip in such a cause was in fact accepting the end of Greek freedom. His speeches against Philip (called the "Philippics") are models of persuasive argument. Demosthenes influenced the democracy to resist the advances of Philip, but in 338 B.C.E. Athens was militarily defeated and made to join the League of Corinth in support of Macedon.

With Greece securely under his control, Philip could now afford to move ahead with his plans to invade Persia. But in 336 B.C.E., he was assassinated during a wedding feast. His twenty-year-old son Alexander, who had inherited his ambition for the conquest of Persia, assumed his position as King of Macedon. Alexander certainly capitalized on his father's plans and preparations, and his conquest of the Persian empire became the stuff of legends. It is difficult to decide which of his adventures are fact and which are fiction. His influence on the world around him and on the course of history has also been hotly debated. It is easy to degenerate into historical "what-ifs?" What if Alexander had not decided to conquer Persia, but had turned west instead toward the infant Roman civilization? What would have happened to Greece if Alexander had died early in the Persian campaign? Had he lived longer, would he still be called "the Great"? These questions are unanswerable, but his conquest of the world was a feat of amazing endurance and determination. It is important to ask the right questions of it in order to obtain meaningful answers.

The period after Alexander's death in 323 B.C.E. is called Hellenistic, or "Greeklike." The age of Greek political domination was past, and soon the Romans would conquer and control the region. Still, the Greeks of the fourth and third centuries continued to influence Western Civilization with the philosophies of Plato, Aristotle, and various schools of Stoics, Epicureans, and Cynics. The Greeks continued to dominate artistic style, education, and scholarship, providing tutors and oratorical instruction for the Mediterranean world. Scientific inquiry was one of the great advancements of the age, and urban planning can largely be traced to the Greeks of this period. In all, we see transition from the dying ideals of the Greeks to the more realistic and practical foundations of Roman civilization. This chapter will focus on the highlights of this important period.

Democracy and Disillusionment

The great philosopher Plato had grown into manhood during the Peloponnesian War in the late fifth century B.C.E. In the chaos and political dissension that accompanied the Athenian defeat, Plato watched as his mentor, Socrates, was falsely accused and then executed in 399 B.C.E. on charges of atheism and corrupting the youth. His disillusionment with democracy is reflected in the following passages from two of his dialogues. Plato distrusted the wisdom of majority rule and advocated instead the leadership of enlightened "philosopher-kings" who controlled rather than consulted the masses.

The Unenlightened Majority
PLATO

Socrates: And now, my friend, as you are already beginning to be a public character, and are admonishing and reproaching me for not being one, suppose that we ask a few questions of one another. Tell me, then Callicles, how about making any of the citizens better? Was there ever a man who was once vicious, or unjust, or intemperate, or foolish, and became by the help of Callicles good and noble? Was there ever such a man, whether citizen or stranger, slave or freeman? Tell me, Callicles, if a person were to ask these questions of you, what would you answer? Whom would you say that you had improved by your conversation? May there not be good deeds of this sort which were done by you as a private person, before you came forward in public? If you have any, will you mention them?

"The Unenlightened Majority" is from Plato, *Gorgias*, in *The Dialogues of Plato*, vol. III, trans. Benjamin Jowett (New York: Charles Scribner's Sons, 1911), pp. 106–108.

Callicles: You are pugnacious, Socrates.

Socrates: No, I ask you, not out of pugnacity, but because I really want to know in what way you think that affairs should be administered among us—whether, when you come to the administration of them, you have any other aim but the improvement of the citizens? Have we not already admitted many times over that this is the duty of a public man? No, we have surely agreed to that, for if you will not answer for yourself I must answer for you. But if this is what the good man ought to effect for the benefit of his own State, allow me to recall to you the names of those whom you were just now mentioning, Pericles, and Cimon, and Miltiades, and Themistocles [all leaders of Athens in the fifth century B.C.E.], and ask whether you still think that they were good citizens.

Callicles: I do.

Socrates: But if they were good, then clearly each of them must have made the citizens better instead of worse?

Callicles: Yes.

Socrates: And, therefore, when Pericles first began to speak in the assembly, the Athenians were not so good as when he spoke last?

Callicles: Very likely.

Socrates: No, my friend, "likely" is not the word; for if he was a good citizen, the inference is certain.

Callicles: And what difference does that make?

Socrates: None; only I should like further to know whether the Athenians are said to have been made better by Pericles, or, on the contrary, to have been corrupted by him; for I hear that he was the first who gave the people pay, and made them idle and cowardly, and encouraged them in the love of talk and of money.

Callicles: You heard that, Socrates, from [Spartan sympathizers].

Socrates: But what I am going to tell you now is not mere hearsay, but well known both to you and me: that at first, Pericles was glorious and his character unimpeached by any verdict of the Athenians—this was during the time when they were not so good—yet afterwards, when they had been made good and gentle by him, at the very end of his life, they convicted him of theft, and almost put him to death, clearly under the notion that he was a malefactor.

Callicles: Well, but how does that prove Pericles' badness?

Socrates: Why, surely you would say that he was but a bad manager of asses or horses or oxen, who had received them originally neither kicking nor butting nor biting him, and imparted to them all these savage tricks? Would he not be a bad manager of any animals who received them gentle, and made them fiercer than they were when he received them? What do you say to that?

Callicles: I will do you the favor of saying "yes."

Socrates: And will you also do me the favor of saying whether man is an animal?

Callicles: Certainly he is.

Socrates: And was not Pericles a shepherd of men?

Callicles: Yes.

Socrates: And if he was a good political shepherd, ought not the animals who were under him, as we were just now acknowledging, to have become more just, and not more unjust?

Callicles: Quite right.

Socrates: And are not just men gentle, as Homer says?—or are you of another mind?

Callicles: I agree.

Socrates: And yet he really did make them more savage than he received them, and their savageness was shown towards himself; and this was the last thing which he would have desired.

Callicles: Do you want me to agree with you?

Socrates: Yes, if I seem to you to speak the truth.

Callicles: I will admit what you say.

Socrates: And if they were more savage, must they not have been more unjust and inferior?

Callicles: Granted.

Socrates: Then upon this view, Pericles was not a good statesman?

Callicles: That is, upon your view.

Socrates: No, the view is yours, after what you have admitted. What do you say about Cimon again? Did not the very persons whom he was serving ostracize him, in order that they might not hear his voice for ten years? and they did just the same to Themistocles, adding the penalty of exile; and they voted that Miltiades, the hero of Marathon, should be thrown into the pit of death, and he was only saved by the chief Prytanis [public official]. And yet, if they had been really good men as you say, this would never have happened to them. For the good charioteers are not those who at first keep their place, and then, when they have broken-in their horses, and themselves become better charioteers, are thrown out—that is not the way either in charioteering or in any other sort of occupation. What do you think?

Callicles: I should think not.

Socrates: Well, and that proves the original assertion that no one has ever shown himself a good statesman in this State; and you admitted that this was true of our present statesmen, but not true of former ones, and you preferred them to the others; but they have turned out to be no better than our present ones. . . .

The Freedom of Democracy

PLATO

[And in a democracy, there is no necessity,] I said, for you to govern . . . even if you have the capacity, or to be governed, unless you like, or to go to war when the rest go to war, or to be at peace when others are at peace, unless you are so disposed—there being no necessity also . . . to hold office or . . . not hold office . . . if you have a fancy—is not this a way of life which for the moment is supremely delightful?

For the moment, yes.

And is not their humanity to the condemned in some cases quite charming? Have you not observed how, in a democracy, many persons, although they have been sentenced to death or exile, just stay where they are and walk about the world—the gentleman parades like a hero, and nobody sees or cares?

Yes, he replied, many and many a one.

See too, I said, the forgiving spirit of democracy, and the "don't care" about trifles, and the disregard which she shows of all the fine principles which we solemnly laid down at the foundations of the city—as when we said that, except in the case of some rarely gifted nature, there never will be a good man who has not from his childhood been used to play amid things of beauty and make of them a joy and a study—how grandly does she trample all these fine notions of ours, under her feet, never giving a thought to the pursuits which make a statesman, and promoting to honor any one who professes to be the people's friend.

Yes, she is of a noble spirit.

These and other kindred characteristics are proper to democracy, which is a charming form of government, full of variety and disorder, and dispensing a sort of equality to equals and unequals alike.

We know her well. . . .

Yes, I said, [a citizen in a democracy] lives from day to day indulging the appetite of the hour; and sometimes he is lapped in drink and strains of the flute; then he becomes a water-drinker, and tries to get thin; then he takes a turn at gymnastics; sometimes idling and neglecting everything, then once more living the life of a philosopher; often he is busy with politics, and starts to his feet and says and does whatever comes into his head; and, if he is emulous of any one who is a warrior, off he is in that direction, or of men of business, once more in that. His life has neither law nor order; and this distracted existence he terms joy and bliss and freedom; and so he goes on.

Yes, he replied, he is all liberty and equality.

Yes, I said; his life is motley and manifold and an epitome of the lives of many;—he answers to the State which we described as fair and spangled. And

"The Freedom of Democracy" is from Plato, *The Republic,* in *The Dialogues of Plato,* vol. II, trans. Benjamin Jowett (Boston: The Aldine Publishing Company, 1911), pp. 326–327, 332–333.

many a man and many a woman will take him for their pattern, and many a constitution and many an example of manners is contained in him.

Just so.

Let him then be set over against democracy; he may truly be called the democratic man.

The Rise of Macedon and the Fall of Greece

The First Philippic (351 B.C.E.)

DEMOSTHENES

In 359 B.C.E., Philip II became king of Macedon, an area just to the north of Greece. It had always been a backward and disunited region, but within two years Philip succeeded in organizing and training an aggressive and competent army. His intentions, however, were unknown to the Greeks. The great Athenian orator Demosthenes saw Philip's increasing participation in Greek affairs as alarming and dangerous. In the following speech against Philip, Demosthenes tried to rouse the democracy to action against a threat which few realized.

Men of Athens, nothing, if you are on your guard, is to be feared, nothing, if you are negligent, goes as you desire. . . . For all men will side with and respect those whom they see prepared and willing to take action. . . . If you will adopt this principle now . . . and if each citizen who can and ought to give his service to the state is ready to give it without excuse, the rich to contribute, the able-bodied to enlist; if, put bluntly, you will become your own masters and each cease expecting to do nothing himself while his neighbor does everything for him, then, God willing, you will recover your own, get back what has been frittered away, and turn the tables on Philip. Do not imagine that his power is ever-lasting like that of a god. There are those who hate and fear and envy him, men of Athens, even among those who now seem most friendly. We can assume that all the feelings that are in other men belong also to his adherents. But now they are all afraid, having no refuge because of your apathy and indolence, which I urge you to abandon at once. For you see, men of Athens, to what pitch of arrogance the man has advanced: he leaves you not even the choice of action or inaction, he threatens and uses outrageous language, he cannot rest content in possession of his conquests but continually widens their circle, and while we dally and delay, he throws this net around us.

When then, Athenians, when will you act as becomes you? What are you waiting for? When it is necessary? I suppose. And how should we regard what is

"The First Philippic" is from Demosthenes, *First Philippic*, 2–12, 38, 45, 50, in *Orations of Demosthenes*, trans. Charles R. Kennedy (New York: D. Appleton & Co., 1912).

happening now? Surely to free men the strongest necessity is the disgrace of their condition. Or tell me, do you like wailing about and asking one another, "Is there any news?" Could there be more startling news than that a Macedonian is subduing Athenians and directing the affairs of Greece? "Is Philip dead?" you ask. "No, but he is sick." What difference does it make? Should anything happen to this man, you will soon create a second Philip if that is the way you attend to affairs. For this Philip has grown great not so much by his own strength as by our negligence. . . . Shameful it is, men of Athens, to delude ourselves, and by putting off everything unpleasant to miss the time of action and be unable even to understand that skillful makers of war should not follow circumstances, but be in advance of them; for just as a general may be expected to lead his armies, so statesmen must guide circumstances if they are to carry out their policies and not be forced to follow at the heels of events. Yet you, men of Athens, with greater resources than any people—ships, infantry, cavalry, revenue—have never up to this day made proper use of them. . . .

One thing is clear: he will not stop, unless someone stops him. Are we to wait for this? Do you think all is well if you dispatch empty ships and the vague hope of some deliverer? Shall we not man the fleet? Shall we not sail with at least a part of our troops, now if never before? Shall we not make a landing on his coast? "Where, then, shall we land?" someone asks. The war itself, men of Athens, will uncover the weak parts of his empire, if we make the effort; but if we sit at home listening to the orators accuse and malign one another, no good can ever be achieved. I believe that wherever you send a force of our own citizens—or even partly ours—there Heaven will bless us and Fortune will aid our struggle. . . . Remember only that Philip is our enemy, that he has long been robbing and insulting us, that wherever we have expected aid from others we have found hostility, that the future depends on ourselves, and that unless we are willing to fight him there we shall perhaps be forced to fight here. . . . You need not speculate about the future except to assure yourselves that it will be disastrous unless you face the facts and are willing to do your duty.

Address to Philip (346 B.C.E.)

ISOCRATES

Although Philip had his enemies in Greece, he also had his supporters. Many viewed him as a positive force, as a pathway to greater Greek glory. Philip, it was argued, would finally unite the Greek city-states and lead them in the conquest of Persia. The most vocal advocate of this position was the orator Isocrates. The following excerpt from his "Address to Philip" sets forth his views that a strong man was necessary to stop domestic disputes and provide the leadership necessary to fulfill Greece's destiny.

"Address to Philip" is from Isocrates, *Philip*, 16, 30–31, 42, 72–75, 89, 152, in *Orations of Isocrates*, vol. I, trans. J. H. Freese (London: G. Bell & Sons, 1894).

I chose to address my discourse to you Philip, [because] . . . you were the possessor to a greater degree than any man in Hellas of wealth and power, the only two things in existence which can both persuade and compel—things which I think will also be required by the enterprise which I am going to propose. For my intention is to advise you to take the lead both in securing the harmony of Hellas and in conducting a campaign against the barbarians; and as persuasion is expedient in dealing with the Greeks, so force is useful in dealing with the barbarians. Such, then, is the general scope of discourse. . . .

I will now direct my remarks to the subject at hand. I say that, while neglecting none of your own interests, you ought to try to reconcile Argos, Sparta, Thebes, and our state; for if you are able to bring these together you will have no difficulty in uniting the others as well. . . . And you have a good opportunity, for . . . it is a good thing to appear as the benefactor of the leading states and at the same time to be furthering your own interests no less than theirs. . . . It is also beyond question that there is nothing which all men remember so well as benefits received in times of trouble. And you can see how they have been reduced to distress by war. . . .

While I admit that there is no one else who could reconcile these states, to you such an undertaking is not difficult. For I see that you have accomplished many things which others considered hopeless and beyond expectations, and that therefore it would not be strange if you alone should be able to effect this union. In fact, men of high aspirations and eminent position should not attempt enterprises which any ordinary man could carry out, but should confine themselves to those which no one could attempt except men of abilities and power like yours. . . .

I should be satisfied with what I have already said on this subject had I not omitted one point, not from forgetfulness, but from a certain unwillingness to mention it. However, I think I ought to disclose it now, for I am of the opinion that it is as much to your advantage to hear what I have to say concerning it as it is becoming to me to speak with an accustomed freedom.

I perceive that you are being slandered by those who are jealous of you and are accustomed to throw their own cities into confusion—men who regard the peace which is for the good of all as a war against their own selfish interests. Unconcerned about everything else, they speak of nothing but your power, asserting that its growth is not for the interests of Hellas but against them, and that you have been already for a long time plotting against us all, and that, while you pretend to be anxious to assist . . . you are in reality endeavoring to get the Peloponnesus into your power. . . . By talking such nonsense and pretending that they possess an accurate knowledge of affairs, and by predicting a speedy overthrow of the whole world, they persuade many. . . .

On these points no sensible man would venture to contradict me. And I think that it would occur to any others who should propose to advise in favor of the expedition to Asia to point out that all whose lot it has been to undertake war against the Persian kings have risen from obscurity to renown, from poverty to wealth, and from low estate to the ownership of many lands and cities. . . . When Fortune honorably leads the way, it is a disgrace to lag behind and show yourself unready to advance in whatever direction she wishes.

The League of Corinth: Loyalty Oath (338 B.C.E.)

By 338 B.C.E., it was apparent that Philip intended to conquer Greece whether for good or ill. Demosthenes managed to whip up an Athenian defense, but his efforts were too little and too late to compete with the military power of Macedon. The Greeks were defeated in the battle of Chaeronea (338 B.C.E.), and Philip then called representatives of the various city-states of Greece to a meeting at Corinth. Sparta alone refused to come, and Philip wisely did not demand its presence. The League of Corinth was founded to unite Greece and free all Greek states under the control of Persia. The League thus became the legal basis of Philip and Alexander's invasion of Persia. The following inscription is the loyalty oath that was required of all members of the League. Philip forged Greek unity by eliminating Greek independence. Macedonian garrisons maintained the loyalty of the Greeks.

I swear by Zeus, Earth, Sun, Poseidon, Athena, Ares, and all the gods and goddesses that I will keep the Peace, and I will not break the treaties with Philip of Macedon. I will not bear arms with hostile intent by land or by sea against those who keep the oaths, nor will I attack in war by any device or stratagem any city, fort, or harbor which belongs to any one who shares in the Peace. I will not oppose the kingship of Philip and his offspring nor those constitutions that were in effect in each city when it swore the oath of peace. I will not do anything against the oath, and will prevent anyone else from doing so as far as I can. If anyone does anything against the oath, I will aid in so far as possible those who have been wronged in the way they want me to. I will fight whoever transgresses the common peace in so far as it seems best to the common council and the leader's orders.

On the Crown (330 B.C.E.)
DEMOSTHENES

Eight years after Philip defeated the Greeks and enrolled them as members of the League of Corinth, the great Athenian orator Demosthenes delivered a speech defending his policy of resistance to the Macedonians. The speech, "On the Crown," has been viewed as a funeral oration on Greek freedom.

[If the defeat of the Greeks at the hands of Philip could have been foreseen,] not even then should the city have abandoned her policy [of opposition] if she had any regard for glory, or ancestry, or the future. As it is, she appears to have failed, a thing to which all men are liable if the gods so decide. But if Athens, claiming to be the leader of Greece, had abandoned her claim, she

---

"The League of Corinth: Loyalty Oath" is from John Wickersham and Gerald Verbrugghe, eds., *Greek Historical Documents: The Fourth Century B.C.* (Toronto: A. M. Hakkert, 1973), p. 106.

"On the Crown" is from Demosthenes, *On the Crown,* 198–200, 203–205, 208, in *Orations of Demosthenes,* trans. Charles R. Kennedy (New York: D. Appleton & Co., 1912).

would have incurred the charge of betraying all to Philip. Why, had we resigned without a struggle that which our ancestors had encountered every danger to win, who would not have spit upon you. . . . But it seems that to the Athenians of that day [5th century] such conduct would not have been national, or natural, or endurable; no one could at any period of time persuade the city to attain herself to the security of slavery to the powerful and unjust: through every age has she persevered in a perilous struggle for first place in honor and glory. And this you esteem so noble and consistent with your character that among your ancestors you honor most those who acted in such a spirit. . . . The Athenians of that day looked not for an orator or a general who would lead them to a pleasant servitude; they scorned to live if it could not be in freedom. Each of them considered that he was not born to his father or mother only, but also to his country. What is the difference? He who thinks himself born for his parents only is satisfied to wait for his fated and natural end; he who thinks himself born for his country as well will sooner die than see her in slavery, and he will regard the insults and indignities which must be borne in a city enslaved as more to be feared than death itself. . . . But never, never can you have done wrong, men of Athens, in undertaking the battle for the freedom and safety of all! I swear it by your ancestors— those who met the peril at Marathon, those who took the field at Plataea, those in the sea battles at Salamis and Artemisium, and many other brave men who repose in the public monuments, all of whom alike, as being worthy of the same honor, the country buried, not the successful and victorious alone! For the duty of brave men has been done by all; their fortune has been such as heaven assigned to each.

Alexander the Great

"Carve Out A Kingdom Worthy of Yourself!"
PLUTARCH

One of the most fascinating and controversial figures of history was Alexander III of Macedon. After Philip's assassination in 336 B.C.E., Alexander was elected to the kingship and continued with his father's plans to invade and conquer Persia. His exploits became legendary, and it is difficult to separate fact from fiction. The following selection recounts an early indication of Alexander's special abilities when he tamed a horse too wild for others to control.

Philonicus the Thessalian brought the horse Bucephalus to Philip, offering to sell him for thirteen talents; but when they went into the field to try him, they found him so very vicious and unmanageable, that he reared up when

---

"Carve Out a Kingdom Worthy of Yourself" is from Plutarch, *Life of Alexander*, 5, in *Readings in Ancient History*, vol. 1, ed. William S. Davis (Boston: Allyn and Bacon, 1912), pp. 301–302.

they endeavored to mount him, and would not so much as endure the voice of any of Philip's attendants. Upon which, as they were leading him away as wholly useless and intractable, Alexander, who stood by, said, "What an excellent horse do they lose, for want of skill and boldness to manage him!" Philip at first took no notice of what he said; but when he heard him repeat the same thing several times, and saw he was very frustrated to see the horse sent away, "Do you criticize," said Philip, "those who are older than yourself, as if you knew more, and were better able to manage him then they?" "I could manage this horse," replied Alexander, "better than others do." "And if you do not," said Philip, "what will you forfeit for your rashness?" "I will pay," answered Alexander, "the whole price of the horse." At this the whole company fell laughing; and as soon as the wager was settled among them, he immediately ran to the horse, and, taking hold of the bridle, turned him directly towards the sun, having, it seems, observed that he was disturbed at and afraid of the motion of his own shadow; then letting him go forward a little, still keeping the reins in his hand, and stroking him gently when he began to grow eager and fiery, . . . with one nimble leap, Alexander securely mounted him, and when he was seated, by little and little drew in the bridle, and curbed him without either striking or spurring him. Presently, when he found him free from all rebelliousness, and only impatient for the course, he let him go at full speed, inciting him now with a commanding voice, and urging him also with his heel. Philip and his friends looked on at first in silence and anxiety for the result, [but when he came] back rejoicing and triumphing for what he had performed, they all burst out into acclamations of applause; and his father, shedding tears, it is said, for joy, kissed him as he came down from his horse, and in his transport said, "O my son, carve out a kingdom equal to and worthy of yourself, for Macedonia is too small for you."

"Alexander Ran Him Through!"
PLUTARCH

When Alexander left for Persia, he took with him a potent military force, but also naturalists and historians to study the Persian environment and record his exploits. Alexander, like most of his compatriots, drank heavily and preferred his wine undiluted (as opposed to the Greek custom). The following account of the murder of his childhood friend Cleitus reveals much about Alexander's personality.

After the company had drunk a good deal somebody began to sing the verses of a man named Pranichus . . . which had been written to humiliate and make fun of some Macedonian commanders who had recently been defeated

"Alexander Ran Him Through" is from Plutarch, *Life of Alexander*, 50–52, in *The Age of Alexander*, trans. Ian Scott-Kilvert (Baltimore, Md., and Harmondsworth, Middlesex: Penguin Books, 1973), pp. 307–309. Copyright © Ian Scott-Kilvert, 1973. Reprinted by permission of the publisher.

by the barbarians. The older members of the party took offense at this and showed their resentment of both the poet and the singer, but Alexander and those sitting near him listened with obvious pleasure and told the man to continue. Thereupon Cleitus, who had already drunk too much and was rough and hot-tempered by nature, became angrier than ever and shouted that it was not right for Macedonians to be insulted in the presence of barbarians and enemies, even if they had met with misfortune, for they were better men than those who were laughing at them. Alexander retorted that if Cleitus was trying to disguise cowardice as misfortune, he must be pleading his own case. At this Cleitus sprang to his feet and shouted back, 'Yes, it was my cowardice that saved your life, you who call yourself the son of the gods, when you were turning your back to Spithridates' sword. And it is the blood of these Macedonians and their wounds which have made you so great that you disown your father Philip and claim to be the son of Ammon!'

These words made Alexander furious. 'You scum,' he cried out, 'do you think that you can keep on speaking of me like this, and stir up trouble among the Macedonians and not pay for it?' 'Oh, but we Macedonians do pay for it,' Cleitus retorted. 'Just think of the rewards we get for all our

A mosaic of Alexander the Great leading his Macedonian troops into battle. Alexander conquered but never consolidated his vast empire. *(Art Resource, N.Y.)*

efforts. It's the dead ones who are happy, because they never lived to see Macedonians being beaten with Median rods, or begging the Persians for an audience with our own king.' Cleitus blurted out all this impulsively, whereupon Alexander's friends jumped up and began to abuse him, while the older men tried to calm down both sides. . . . But Cleitus refused to take back anything and he challenged Alexander to speak out whatever he wished to say in front of the company, or else not invite to his table freeborn men who spoke their minds: it would be better for him to spend his time among barbarians and slaves, who would prostrate themselves before his white tunic and his Persian girdle. At this Alexander could no longer control his rage: he hurled one of the apples that lay on the table at Cleitus, hit him, and then looked around for his dagger. One of his bodyguards, Aristophanes, had already moved it out of harm's way, and the others crowded around him and begged him to be quiet. But Alexander leaped to his feet and shouted out in the Macedonian tongue for his bodyguard to turn out, a signal that this was an extreme emergency. . . . As Cleitus still refused to give way, . . . Alexander seized a spear from one of his guards, faced Cleitus as he was drawing aside the curtain of the doorway, and ran him through. With a roar of pain and a groan, Cleitus fell, and immediately the king's anger left him. When he came to himself and saw his friends standing around him speechless, he snatched the weapon out of the dead body and would have plunged it into his own throat if the guards had not forestalled him by seizing his hands and carrying him by force to his chamber.

There he spent the rest of the night and the whole of the following day sobbing in an agony of remorse. At last he lay exhausted by his grief, uttering deep groans but unable to speak a word, until his friends, alarmed at his silence, forced their way into his room. He paid no attention to what any of them said, except that when Aristander the diviner reminded him . . . that these events had long ago been ordained by fate, he seemed to accept this assurance.

The Leadership of Alexander

ARRIAN

Alexander's military abilities are beyond question, but it takes more than tactical knowledge to inspire and encourage a force to move thousands of miles away from their homeland in pursuit of the unknown. Finally, deep in India, Alexander's troops forced him to forget the "ends of the earth" and to return to Macedon. The journey home was difficult, and Alexander lost many men to the hardship of the desert. His leadership, as the following account reveals, was never in doubt.

"The Leadership of Alexander" is from Arrian, *Anabasis*, 6.26, in *The Campaigns of Alexander*, trans. Aubrey de Sélincourt (Baltimore, Md., and Harmondsworth, Middlesex: Penguin Books, 1958), pp. 338–339. Copyright © Aubrey de Sélincourt, 1958, 1971. Reprinted by permission of the publisher.

At this point in my story I must not leave unrecorded one of the finest things Alexander ever did. . . . The army was crossing a desert of sand; the sun was already blazing down upon them, but they were struggling on under the necessity of reaching water, which was still far away. Alexander, like everyone else, was tormented by thirst, but he was none the less marching on foot at the head of his men. It was all he could do to keep going, but he did so, and the result (as always) was that the men were the better able to endure their misery when they saw that it was equally shared. As they toiled on, a party of light infantry which had gone off looking for water found some—just a wretched little trickle collected in a shallow gully. They scooped up with difficulty what they could and hurried back, with their priceless treasure, to Alexander; then, just before they reached him, they tipped the water into a helmet and gave it to him. Alexander, with a word of thanks for the gift, took the helmet, and, in full view of his troops, poured the water on the ground. So extraordinary was the effect of this action that the water wasted by Alexander was as good as a drink for every man in the army. I cannot praise this act too highly; it was a proof, if anything was, not only of his power of endurance, but also of his genius for leadership.

Alexander and the Brotherhood of Man
PLUTARCH

Over the centuries the debate has raged as to why Alexander conquered the Persian Empire and beyond. Was he a megalomaniac whose sole purpose was to gratify himself by conquering others? Was he propelled by insatiable curiosity or lust for wealth? Or did Alexander have larger concerns? When he had his soldiers take Persian brides, was he trying, by intermingling blood and customs, to break the intellectual and physical confines of the Greek city-states and thus unite East and West? Or was the creation of his empire the result of impulse and chance? The following account by Plutarch addresses some of these questions.

Alexander did not follow Aristotle's advice to treat the Greeks as a leader, the barbarians as a master, cultivating the former as friends and kinsmen, and treating the latter as animals or plants. Had he done so his kingdom would have been filled with warfare, banishments and secret plots, but he regarded himself as divinely sent to mediate and govern the world. And those whom he failed to win over by persuasion he overpowered in arms, bringing them together from every land, combining, as it were in a loving cup, their lives,

"Alexander and the Brotherhood of Man" is from Plutarch, *DeAlexandri Magni Fortuna est Virtute, Oratio I.* Reprinted with permission of The Free Press, a Division of Simon & Schuster, Inc. from *Sources in Western Civilization: Ancient Greece*, pp. 199–200, translated and edited by Truesdell S. Brown. Copyright © 1965 by The Free Press.

customs, marriages and manner of living: he bade them all look on the inhabited world as their native land, on his camp as their citadel and protection, on good men as their kinsmen and evil doers as aliens, and not to distinguish Greek from barbarian by the . . . shield, or the sword, or the sleeved tunic but to associate Hellenism with virtue and barbarians with evil doing; and to regard their clothing, food, marriages and manners as common to all, blended together by their blood and their children.

. . . For he did not cross Asia like a robber, nor did he have it in mind to ravage and despoil it for the booty and loot presented by such an unheard-of stroke of fortune. . . . Instead he conducted himself as he did out of a desire to subject all the races in the world to one rule and one form of government, making all mankind a single people. Had not the divinity that sent Alexander recalled his soul so soon, there would have been a single law, as it were, watching over all mankind, and all men would have looked to one form of justice as their common source of light. But now, that portion of the world that never beheld Alexander has remained as if deprived of the sun.

The Thought of the Age

The Philosophy of Plato

Plato was one of the greatest philosophers in Western Civilization. His influence has been so decisive that one scholar remarked that all subsequent thought is but a series of footnotes to Plato. He was a student of Socrates and shared his view that universal truths exist and can be discovered. Plato went further by developing a system called the "Theory of Ideas," which defies simple explanation but rather requires a kind of immersion in thought to understand its tenets. Plato's doctrine is founded on the belief that there are two worlds, one we can readily see and experience with our senses, and the other unseen and eternal. All objects in the sensory world are imperfect and transitory; the only true and perfect things, the eternal Ideas, exist in the abstract realm. Man's task in life is to struggle toward the ideal realm, the world of thought and spirit, by pursuing reason and logic. In this way, Plato hoped to address the concerns of his day. For Plato, democracy had failed, misdirecting society into constant turmoil, war, doubt, and depression. He saw a need to look to a higher ideal, a realm that was secure and offered answers and organization in a chaotic world. As Plato noted in his work The Republic, *"Until philosophers are kings or the kings and rulers of this world have the spirit of philosophy, until political power and wisdom are united . . . states will never have rest from their evils, nor . . . will the human race."*

Allegory of the Cave

PLATO

The following passage from The Republic *explains Plato's Theory of Ideas. In the "Allegory of the Cave," he stresses the need to move away from the "shadows," which exist in the everyday realm of the senses, into the world of eternal truth and spiritual reality. Notice that Plato also believes that those who see the light, move toward it, and are thus freed from the captivity of the shadows, need to return in order to enlighten others; this is how civilization will progress.*

Behold! human beings living in an underground den, which has a mouth open toward the light and reaching all along the den; here they have been from their childhood, and have their legs and necks chained so that they cannot move, and can only see before them, being prevented by the chains from turning round their heads. Above and behind them a fire is blazing at a distance, and between the fire and the prisoners there is a raised way; and you will see, if you look, a low wall built along the way, like the screen which marionette players have in front of them, over which they show the puppets. And do you see men passing along the wall carrying all sorts of vessels, and statues and figures of animals made of wood and stone and various materials, which appear over the wall? Some of them are talking, others silent.

You have shown me a strange image, and they are strange prisoners.

Like ourselves, I replied; and they see only their own shadows, or the shadows of one another, which the fire throws on the opposite wall of the cave?

True, he said; how could they see anything but the shadows if they were never allowed to move their heads?

And of the objects which are being carried in like manner they would only see the shadows. And if they were able to converse with one another, would they not suppose that they were naming what was actually before them?

Very true.

And suppose further that the prison had an echo which came from the other side, would they not be sure to notice when one of the passersby spoke that the voice which they heard came from the passing shadows? To them the truth would be literally nothing but the shadows of the images.

And now look again, and see what will naturally follow if the prisoners are released and exonerated of their error. At first, when any of them is liberated and compelled suddenly to stand up and turn his neck around and walk and look toward the light, he will suffer sharp pains; the glare will distress him, and he will be unable to see the realities of which in his former state he had seen the shadows; and then conceive someone saying to him, that what he saw before was an illusion, but that now, when he is approaching nearer to

"Allegory of the Cave" is from Plato, *The Republic*, 7.514–7.521, in *The Dialogues of Plato*, vol. II, trans. Benjamin Jowett (Boston: The Aldine Publishing Company, 1911), pp. 265–274. Translation modernized by the editor.

being and his eye is turned toward more real existence, he has a clearer vision—what will be his reply? And you may further imagine that his instructor is pointing to the objects as they pass and requiring him to name them—will he not be perplexed? Will he not think that the shadows which he formerly saw are truer than the objects which are now shown him?

And if he is compelled to look straight at the light, will he not have a pain in his eyes which will make him turn away to take refuge in the objects of vision which he can see, and which he will conceive to be in reality clearer than the things which are now being shown to him?

And suppose once more, that he is reluctantly dragged up a steep and rugged ascent, and held fast until he is forced into the presence of the sun himself, is he not likely to be pained and irritated? When he approaches the light his eyes will be dazzled, and he will not be able to see anything at all of what are now called realities. He will require to grow accustomed to the sight of the upper world. And first he will see the shadows best, next the reflection of men and other objects in the water, and then the objects themselves; then he will gaze upon the light of the moon and the stars and the spangled heaven; and he will see the sky and the stars by night better than the sun or the light of the sun by day. Last of all he will be able to see the sun, and not mere reflections of him in the water, but he will see him in his own proper place, and not in another; and he will contemplate him as he is. He will then proceed to argue that this is he who gives the seasons and the years, and is the guardian of all that is in the visible world, and in a certain way the cause of all things which he and his fellows have accustomed to behold.

And when he remembered his old habitation, and the wisdom of the den and his fellow prisoners, do you not suppose that he would be happy about the change, and pity them? And if they were in the habit of conferring honors among themselves on those who were quickest to observe the passing shadows and to remark which of them went before, and which followed after, and which were together; and who were therefore best able to draw conclusions as to the future, do you think that he would care for such honors and glories or envy the possessors of them? Would he not say with Homer, "Better to be the poor servant of a poor master," and to endure anything, rather than think as they do and live after their manner?

Imagine once more such a one coming suddenly out of the sun to be replaced in his old situation; would he not be certain to have his eyes full of darkness? And if there were a contest, and he had to compete in measuring the shadows with the prisoners who had never moved out of the den, while his sight was still weak, and before his eyes had become steady (and the time which he needed to acquire this new habit of sight might be very considerable), would he not be ridiculous? Men would say of him that up he went and down he came without his eyes; and that it was better not even to think of ascending; and if anyone tried to loose another and lead him up to the light, let them only catch the offender, and they would put him to death.

This entire allegory, you may now append, dear Glaucon, to the previous argument; the prison-house is the world of sight, the light of the fire is the sun, and you will not misunderstand me if you interpret the journey upwards to be the ascent of the soul into the intellectual world according to my poor belief, which, at your desire, I have expressed—whether rightly or wrongly God knows. But, whether true or false, my opinion is that in the world of knowledge the idea of good appears last of all, and is seen only with an effort: and, when seen, is also inferred to the universal author of all things beautiful and right, parent of light, and of the lord of light in this visible world, and the immediate source of reason and truth in the intellectual; and that this is the power upon which he who would act rationally either in public or private life must have his eye fixed.

I agree, he said, as far as I am able to understand you.

Moreover, you must not wonder that those who attain to this beatific vision are unwilling to descend to human affairs; for their souls are ever hastening into the upper world where they desire to dwell; which desire of theirs is very natural, if our allegory may be trusted.

Yes, very natural. . . .

Then the business of us who are the founder of the State will be to compel the best minds to attain that knowledge which has been already declared by us to be the greatest of all—they must continue to ascend until they arrive at the good; but when they have ascended and seen enough we must not allow them to do as they do now.

What do you mean?

I mean that they remain in the upper world: but this must not be allowed; they must be made to descend again among the prisoners in the den, and partake of their labors and honors, whether they are worth having or not.

But is not this unjust? he said; ought we to give them an inferior life, when they might have a superior one?

You have forgotten, my friend, the intention of the legislator, who did not aim at making any one class in the State happy above the rest; the happiness was to be in the whole State, and he held the citizens together by persuasion and necessity, making them benefactors of the State, and therefore benefactors of one another; to this end he created them, not that they should please themselves, but they were to be his instruments in binding up the State.

True, he said, I had forgotten.

Observe, Glaucon, that there will be no injustice in compelling our philosophers to have a care and providence of others; we shall explain to them that in other States, men of their class are not obliged to share in the toils of politics: and this is reasonable, for they grow up at their own sweet will, and the government would rather not have them. Now the wild plant which owes culture to nobody, has nothing to pay for culture. But we have brought you into the world to be rulers of the hive, kings of yourselves and of the other citizens, and have educated you far better and more perfectly than they have been educated, and you are better able to share in the double duty. Wherefore each of you, when his turn comes, must go down to the general underground abode, and get the habit of seeing in the dark; for all is habit; and by accustoming yourselves you will see ten thousand times better than the dwellers in the den, and you will know what the images are, and of what they are images, because you have seen the beautiful and just and good in their truth. And thus the order of our State, and of yours, will be a reality, and not a dream only, as the order of States too often is, for in most of them men are fighting with one another about shadows and are distracted in the struggle for power, which in their eyes is a great good. Whereas the truth is that the State in which the rulers are most reluctant to govern is best and most quietly governed, and the State in which they are most willing, the worst.

Quite true, he replied.

And will our pupils, when they hear this, refuse to share in turn the toils of State, when they are allowed to spend the greater part of their time with one another in the heaven of ideas?

Impossible, he answered; for they are just men, and the commands which we impose upon them are just; there can be no doubt that every one of them will take office as a stern necessity, and not like our present ministers of State.

Yes, my friend, and there lies the point. You must contrive for your future rulers another and a better life than that of a ruler, and then you may have a well-ordered State; for only in the State which offers this, will they rule who are truly rich, not in silver and gold, but in virtue and wisdom, which are the true blessings of life. Whereas if they go to the administration of public affairs, poor and hungering after their own private advantage, thinking that hence they are to snatch the good of life, order there can never be; for they will be fighting about office, and the civil and domestic broils which thus arise will be the ruin of the rulers themselves and of the whole State.

Most true, he replied.

The Equality of Women in the State
PLATO

This passage presents Plato's thoughts concerning the role of women in his idealized Republic. *In it, he denounces some of the laws and traditions of Greek society that restricted the political rights and social access of females to such an extent that Greek women were mere trustees of their husbands and fathers. In Plato's* Republic, *however, women would not only vote, but would have access to positions of authority and responsibility, as magistrates and priests. The training of Guardians, who because of their character and intellect ruled the State, and the fitness of women for that position, is at issue in the following passage from* The Republic. *The questions that Plato addresses reflect our modern concern for equality of opportunity between men and women. But note how Plato extends the*

"The Equality of Women in the State" is from Plato, *The Republic*, in *The Dialogues of Plato*, vol. II, trans. Benjamin Jowett (New York: Scribner, Armstrong, and Co., 1874), pp. 280–283. Translation modernized by the editor.

argument at the end to a problematical level. At what point does true equality become socially unacceptable?

Socrates: Can you mention any pursuit of man in which the male sex does not have all qualities in a far higher degree than the female? Need I waste time in speaking of the art of weaving, and the management of pancakes and preserves, in which womankind does really appear to be great, and in which the superiority of the other sex is the most laughable thing in the world?

Glaucon: You are quite right, in maintaining the general inferiority of the female sex; at the same time many women are in many things superior to many men, though, speaking generally, what you say is true.

Socrates: And so, my friend, in the administration of a State neither a woman as a woman, nor a man as a man has any special function, but the gifts of nature are equally diffused in both sexes; all the pursuits of men are the pursuits of women also, and in all of them a woman is inferior to a man?

Glaucon: Very true.

Socrates: Then are we to impose all our enactments on men and none of them on women?

Glaucon: That will never do.

Socrates: One woman has a gift of healing, another not; one is a musician and another is not musician?

Glaucon: Very true.

Socrates: And one woman has ability in gymnastics and military exercises, while another is unwarlike and hates gymnastics?

Glaucon: Beyond question.

Socrates: And one woman is a philosopher, and another is an enemy of philosophy; one has spirit, and another is without spirit?

Glaucon: That is also true.

Socrates: Then one woman will have the temper of a guardian, and another not; for was not the selection of the male guardians determined by these sort of differences?

Glaucon: That is true.

Socrates: Then the woman has equally with the man the qualities which make a guardian; she differs only in degrees of strength?

Glaucon: That is obvious.

Socrates: And those who have such qualities are the women who are to be selected as the companions and colleagues of our guardians, and who will resemble them in ability and character?

Glaucon: Clearly.

Socrates: And being of the same nature with them, ought they not to have the same pursuits?

Glaucon: They ought.

Socrates: Then, as we were saying before, there is nothing unnatural in assigning music and gymnastics to the wives of the guardians. To that we come round again.

Glaucon: Yes, Socrates.

Socrates: The law which enacted this instead of being an impossibility or mere aspiration was agreeable to nature, and the contrary practice, which prevails at present, is in reality a violation of nature.

Glaucon: That appears to be true.

Socrates: There was, first, the possibility, and secondly, the advantage of such an arrangement, which has to be considered?

Glaucon: Yes.

Socrates: And the possibility has been allowed?

Glaucon: Yes.

Socrates: And the advantage has next to be acknowledged?

Glaucon: That is the next question.

Socrates: You would admit that the same education which makes a man a good guardian will make a woman a good guardian; for their original nature is the same?

Glaucon: Yes, Socrates. . . .

Socrates: Well, and may we not further say that the guardians are the best of our citizens?

Glaucon: By far the best.

Socrates: And will not these be the best women?

Glaucon: Yes, again I say the very best.

Socrates: And can there be anything better for the interests of the State than that the men and women of a State should be as good as possible?

Glaucon: There can be nothing better.

Socrates: And our course of music and gymnastics will accomplish this?

Glaucon: Certainly.

Socrates: Then we have made an enactment not only possible but in the highest degree advantageous to the State?

Glaucon: True.

Socrates: Then let the wives of our guardians strip, having virtue for their robes, and share in the toils of war and the defense of their country; only in the distribution of labor are the lighter tasks to be assigned to the women, as being the weaker vessels, but in other respects their duties are to be the same. And as for the man who laughs at naked women exercising in gymnastics for the sake of the highest good, his laughter is a fruit of unripe wisdom, which he gathers, and he himself is ignorant of what he is laughing at, or what he is about; for this is, and ever will be, the best of sayings, that the useful is virtuous and the hurtful is bad.

Glaucon: Very true.

Socrates: Here, then, is one difficulty in our law about women which we have escaped; the wave has not swallowed us up alive for enacting that the guardians of either sex should have all their pursuits in common; to the utility and possibility of this the argument is its own witness.

Glaucon: Yes, Socrates, that was a mighty wave which you have escaped.

Socrates: Yes, but a much greater wave is coming; you will not think much of this when you see the next.

Glaucon: Go on, let me see.

Socrates: The law, which is the sequel of this and of all that has preceded, is to this effect: "that the wives of these guardians are to be common, and their children also common, and no parent is to know his own child, nor any child his parent."

Glaucon: Yes, Socrates, that is a much greater wave than the other; and the utility as well as the possibility of such a law is far more doubtful.

Socrates: I do not think, Glaucon, that there can be any dispute about the very great utility of having wives and children in common—the possibility is quite another matter, and will be very much disputed.

Glaucon: Both would be disputed, hot and strong!

The Thought of Aristotle

Aristotle (384–322 B.C.E.) was another of the great philosophers of this era who would greatly influence thinkers in the Middle Ages. A student of Plato and tutor to Alexander the Great, Aristotle believed that ideal forms and truths existed but were not found in some abstract world apart from everyday life. In fact, one could discover Truth by observing sensory objects and then logically (through the process of induction) discerning their universal characteristics. Thus Aristotle was very practical and believed that all theories must be abandoned if they could not be observed to be true. Aristotle wrote widely on politics and ethics and is very contemporary in application. Note how many of the following ideas can be applied to our own world.

Against Communism

ARISTOTLE

Next let us consider what should be our arrangements about property; should the citizens of the perfect state have possessions in common or not?. . .

There is always a difficulty in men living together and having things in common, but especially in their having common property. . . . Property should be in a certain sense common, but, as a general rule, private. For when everyone has his separate interest, men will not complain of one another, and they will make more progress, because everyone will be attending to his own business. Yet among good men, and as regards use, "friends," as the proverb says, "will have all things common.". . . For although every human has his own property, some things he will place at the disposal of his friends, while of others he shares the use of them. . . .

Again, how immeasurably greater is the pleasure, when a man feels a thing to be his own! For love of self is a feeling implanted by nature and not given in vain, although selfishness is rightly condemned. This, however, is not mere love of self, but love of self in excess, like the miser's love of money; for all, or almost all, men love money, and other such objects in a measure. Furthermore, there is the greatest pleasure in doing a kindness or service to friends or guests or companions, which can only be done when a man has private property. These advantages are lost by the excessive unification of the state. . . . No one, when men have all things in common, will any longer set an example of liberality or do any liberal action; for liberality consists in the use a man makes of his own property.

Such [communistic] legislation may have a specious appearance of benevolence. Men readily listen to it, and are easily induced to believe that in some wonderful manner everybody will become everybody's friend, especially when someone is heard denouncing the evils now existing in states, suits about contracts, convictions for perjury, flatteries of rich men and the like, which are said to arise out of the possession of private property. These evils, however, are due to a very different cause—the wickedness of human nature. Indeed, we see that there is much more quarreling among those who have all things in common, though there are not many of them when compared with the vast numbers who have private property.

Again, we ought to reckon, not only the evils from which the citizens will be saved, but also the advantages which they will lose. . . . Unity there should be, both of the family and of the state, but in some respects only. For there is a point at which a state may attain such a degree of unity as to be no longer a state, or at which, without actually ceasing to exist, it will become an inferior state, like harmony passing into unison, or rhythm which has been reduced to a single foot. The state, as I was saying, is a plurality, which should be united and made into a community by education. . . .

"Against Communism" is from Aristotle, *Politics,* 2.5, in *The Politics of Aristotle,* trans. Benjamin Jowett (Oxford: Oxford University Press, 1905), pp. 62–64.

On Education

ARISTOTLE

No one will doubt that a lawgiver should direct his attention above all to the education of youth, or that the neglect of education does harm to states. The citizen should be molded to suit the form of government under which he lives. For each government has a peculiar character, which originally formed and which continues to preserve it. The character of democracy creates democracy, and the character of oligarchy creates oligarchy. The better the character, always the better the government.

Now for the exercise of any faculty or art a previous training and practice are required; clearly they are required for the exercise of virtue. And since the entire state has one end, manifestly education should be one and the same for all, and should be public and not private. It should not be as at present, when everyone looks after his own children separately, and gives them separate instruction of the sort he thinks best. The training in things of common interest should be the same for all. Neither must we suppose that any one of the citizens belongs to himself, for they all belong to the state, and are each of them a part of the state, and the care of each part is inseparable from the care of the whole. In this particular the Spartans are to be praised, for they take the greatest pains about their children, and make education the business of the state.

That education should be regulated by law and should be an affair of state is not to be denied; but what should be the character of this public education, and how young persons should be educated, are questions yet to be considered. For men are by no means agreed about the things to be taught, whether we aim at virtue or the best life. Neither is it clear whether education should be more concerned with intellectual or with moral virtue. Existing practice is perplexing; no one knows on what principle we should proceed. Should the useful in life, or should virtue, or should higher knowledge, be the aim of our training? All three opinions have been entertained. Again, about method there is no agreement; for different persons, starting with different ideas about the nature of virtue, naturally disagree about the practice of it.

Undoubtedly children should be taught those useful things that are really necessary, but not all useful things. For occupations are divided into liberal and illiberal, and to young children should be imparted only such kinds of knowledge as will be useful to them without vulgarizing them. Any occupation, art, or science, which makes the body or soul or mind of the free man less fit for the practice or exercise of virtue, is vulgar. Therefore we call those arts vulgar which tend to deform the body, and likewise all paid employments; they absorb and degrade the mind. . . .

The customary branches of an education are four, namely, (1) reading and writing, (2) gymnastic exercises, (3) music, to which is sometimes added (4) drawing. Of these, reading, writing, and drawing are regarded as useful for

"On Education" is from Aristotle, Politics, 8.1–8.3, in *The Politics of Aristotle*, trans. Benjamin Jowett (Oxford: Oxford University Press, 1905), pp. 300–303.

the purposes of life in a variety of ways, and gymnastic exercises are thought to infuse courage. As to music a question may be raised. In our own day most men cultivate it for pleasure, but originally it was included in education because nature herself, as has been often said, requires that we should be able, not only to work well, but to use our leisure well. For, as I must repeat once again, the prime end of all action is leisure. Both are necessary, but leisure is better than labor.

Hence now the question must be asked in good earnest, what ought we to do when at leisure? Clearly we ought not to be always amusing ourselves, for then amusement would be the end of life. . . .

Apparently then there are branches of learning and education which we should study solely with a view to the employment of leisure, and these are to be valued for their own sake; whereas the kinds of knowledge which are useful in business are necessary, and exist for the sake of other things. Therefore our fathers admitted music into education, not on the ground of either its necessity or its utility; for it is not necessary, nor even useful in the same way that reading and writing are useful in wealth getting, in the management of a household, in the acquisition of knowledge, and in political life. Nor is it, like drawing, useful for a more correct judgment of the works of artists, nor again, like gymnastics, does it give health and strength, for neither of these is to be gained from music. There is, however, a use of music for intellectual enjoyment in leisure, which seems indeed to have been the reason of its introduction into education. For music is one of the ways in which, it is thought, a freeman might pass his leisure. . . .

Evidently, then, there is a sort of education in which parents should train their sons, not because it is useful or necessary, but because it is liberal or noble.

Virtue and Moderation: The Doctrine of the Mean
ARISTOTLE

Aristotle's principle concern in his Ethics *is moral virtue, which might best be described as "good character." One obtains a good character by continually doing right acts until they become second nature. In defining "right action," Aristotle offers his Doctrine of the Mean, which serves as a guide toward achieving moral virtue and happiness. Right acts are those that lie between two extremes: courage, therefore, is the mean between the extremes of cowardice and rashness. Aristotle explains this in the following passage.*

It is not sufficient, however, merely to define virtue in general terms as a characteristic: we must also specify what kind of characteristic it is. It must, then, be remarked that every virtue or excellence (1) renders good the thing

"Virtue and Moderation: The Doctrine of the Mean" is from Aristotle, *Ethics,* 2.6. Reprinted with permission of Macmillan Publishing Company from Aristotle, *Nichomachean Ethics,* pp. 41–44, trans. Martin Oswald. Copyright © 1962 by Macmillan Publishing Company.

itself of which it is the excellence, and (2) causes it to perform its function well. For example, the excellence of the eye makes both the eye and its function good, for good sight is due to the excellence of the eye. Likewise, the excellence of a horse makes it both good as a horse and good at running, at carrying its rider, and at facing the enemy. Now, if this is true of all things, the virtue or excellence of man, too, will be characteristic which makes him a good man, and which causes him to perform his own function well. . . .

Of every continuous entity that is divisible into parts it is possible to take the larger, smaller, or equal either in relation to the entity itself, or in relation to us. The "equal" part is something median between excess and deficiency. By the median of an entity I understand a point equidistant from both extremes, and this point is one and the same for everybody. By the median relative to us I understand an amount neither too large nor too small, and this is neither one nor the same for everybody. To take an example . . . if ten pounds of food is much for a man to eat and two pounds little, it does not follow that the trainer will prescribe six pounds, for this may in turn be much or little for him to eat; it may be little for Mile [the wrestler] and much for someone who has just begun to take up athletics. The same applies to running and wrestling. Thus we see that an expert in any field avoids excess and deficiency, but seeks the median and chooses it—not the median of the object but the median relative to us.

If this, then, is the way in which every science perfects its work, by looking to the median and by bringing its work up to that point—and this is the reason why it is usually said of a successful piece of work that it is impossible to detract from it or to add to it, the implication being that excess and deficiency destroy success while the mean safeguards it (good craftsmen, we say, look toward this standard in the performance of their work)—and if virtue, like nature, is more precise and better than any art, we must conclude that virtue aims at the median. I am referring to moral virtue: for it is moral virtue that is concerned with emotions and actions, and it is in emotions and actions that excess, deficiency, and the median are found. Thus we can experience fear, confidence, desire, anger, pity, and generally any kind of pleasure and pain either too much or too little, and in either case not properly. But to experience all this at the right time, toward the right objects, toward the right people, for the right reason, and in the right manner—that is the median and the best course, the course that is a mark of virtue.

Similarly, excess, deficiency, and the median can also be found in actions. Now virtue is concerned with emotions and actions; and in emotions and actions excess and deficiency miss the mark, whereas the median is praised and constitutes success. . . .

We may thus conclude that virtue or excellence is a characteristic involving choice, and that it consists in observing the mean relative to us, a mean which is defined by a rational principle, such as a man of practical wisdom would use to determine it. It is the mean by reference to two vices: the one of excess and the other of deficiency. It is, moreover, a mean because some vices exceed and the others fall short of what is required in emotion and in action, whereas virtue finds and chooses the median.

The Status of Women

ARISTOTLE

He who thus considers things in their first growth and origin, whether a state or anything else, will obtain the clearest view of them. In the first place (1) there must be a union of those who cannot exist without each other; for example, of male and female, that the race may continue; and this is a union which is formed, not of deliberate purpose, but because, in common with other animals and with plants, mankind have a natural desire to leave behind them an image of themselves. And (2) there must be a union of natural ruler and subject, that both may be preserved. For he who can foresee with his mind is by nature intended to be lord and master, and he who can work with his body is a subject, and by nature a slave; hence master and slave have the same interest. . . .

Of household management we have seen that there are three parts—one is the rule of a master over slaves, which has been discussed already, another of a father, and the third of a husband. A husband and father rules over wife and children, both free, but the rule differs, the rule over his children being a royal, over his wife a constitutional rule. For although there may be exceptions to the order of nature, the male is by nature fitter for command than the female, just as the elder and full-grown is superior to the younger and more immature. . . .

Now it is obvious that the same principle applies generally, and therefore almost all things rule and are ruled according to nature. But the kind of rule differs; the freeman rules over the slave after another manner from that in which the male rules over the female, or the man over the child; although the parts of the soul are present in all of them, they are present in different degrees. For the slave has no deliberative faculty at all; the woman has, but it is without authority, and the child has, but it is immature. So it must necessarily be with the moral virtues also; all may be supposed to partake of them, but only in such manner and degree as is required by each for the fulfillment of his duty. . . . The courage of a man is shown in commanding, of a woman in obeying. . . . All classes must be deemed to have their special attributes; as the poet says of women, "Silence is a woman's glory," but this is not equally the glory of man. . . .

Epicureanism

Hellenistic philosophy (after 323 B.C.E.) was concerned with surviving in an insecure world where political and social chaos was fast becoming a normal standard of life. Many people found consolation in the Stoic philosophy, which was fatalistic and advocated adherence to duty and responsibility (see Chapter 6: "The Pax Romana and the Decline of Rome"). One of the most popular schools of Hellenistic

"The Status of Women" is from Aristotle, *Politics*, Bk. I, trans. Benjamin Jowett (Oxford: Clarendon Press, 1885), pp. 49–54.

thought was founded by Epicurus (342–270 B.C.E.). The Epicureans denied that there was any interference of gods in human affairs or any life after death. All things were composed of atoms, which eventually returned to the "void." For an Epicurean, pleasure was the key to life. The following selections are maxims of Epicurus himself.

Golden Maxims

EPICURUS

Pleasure is an original and natural good, but we do not choose every pleasure. Sometimes we avoid pleasures when a greater pain follows them; and many pains we consider preferable to pleasure when they lead eventually to a greater pleasure. Self-sufficiency is to be sought. Luxuries are hard to get, but natural things are easy and give us much pleasure.

When we say pleasure is the purpose of life, we do not mean the pleasures of the sensually self-indulgent, as some assert, but rather freedom from bodily pain and mental disturbance. The life of pleasure does not come from drinking or revels, or other sensual pleasures. It comes from sober thinking, the sensible investigation of what to choose and to avoid, and getting rid of ideas which agitate the soul. Common sense is our best guide. It tells us that we cannot live happily unless we live wisely, nobly, and justly without being happy. The virtues are inseparably linked with pleasure. For whom do you rate higher than the man who has correct beliefs about God, who has no fear of death, who has understood the purpose of Nature, who realizes that pain does not last long, and that Necessity, which some people consider the directing force of the world, is partly a matter of luck, and partly in our power?

• • •

Gods exist, but they are not as they are popularly thought to be. To destroy the gods as they are commonly thought to be is not impious; actually it is impious to have such distorted notions. The divine powers, blessed and incorruptible, neither are troubled themselves nor do they feel anger or gratitude toward men.

• • •

Accustom yourself to think that death means nothing to us. For what is good and bad is a matter of sensation, and death is an end of sensation. Grasping this principle makes human life pleasant, not by giving us any promise of immortality, but by freeing us from any desire for immortality. For there is nothing in life to be afraid of for a man who understands that he need not be afraid of its extinction. So death, usually regarded as the greatest of calamities, is actually nothing to us; for while we are, death is not, and when death is here, we are not. So death means nothing to either the living or the dead, for it has nothing to do with the living and the dead do not exist.

Skepticism

Pyrrhro of Elis developed another important Hellenistic philosophy called skepticism. The Skeptics delighted in pointing out the inadequacies of the various competing philosophies of the day. They thought that nothing could really be known because reality was distorted by appearances. Since nothing could be known, they consoled themselves by insisting that nothing mattered. Life thus consisted of adaptation and acceptance of the world as it was.

The Principles of Skepticism
SEXTUS EMPIRICUS

The originating cause of Skepticism is, we say, the hope of attaining quietude. Men of talent, who were perturbed by the contradictions in things and in doubt as to which of the alternatives they ought to accept, were led on to inquire what is true in things and what false, hoping by the settlement of this question to attain quietude. The main basic principle of the Skeptic system is that of opposing to every proposition an equal proposition; for we believe that as a consequence of this we end by ceasing to dogmatize. . . .

That the senses differ from one another is obvious. Thus, to the eye paintings seem to have recesses and projections, but not so to the touch. Honey, too, seems to some pleasant to the tongue but unpleasant to the eyes; so that it is impossible to say whether it is absolutely pleasant or unpleasant. The same is true of sweet oil, for it pleases the sense of smell but displeases the taste. . . . Rain water, too, is beneficial to the eyes but roughens the windpipe and lungs; as also does olive oil, though it mollifies the epidermis. The cramp fish, also, when applied to the extremities produces cramp, but it can be applied to the rest of the body without hurt. Consequently we are unable to say what is the real nature of each of these things, although it is possible to say what each thing at the moment appears to be. . . .

Seeing, then, that there is a controversy . . . regarding "the true," since some assert that something true exists, others that nothing true exists, it is im-

"The Principles of Skepticism" is reprinted by permission of the publishers and the Loeb Classical Library from Sextus Empiricus, *Outlines of Pyrrhonism,* trans. R. G. Bury, vol. 1 (Cambridge, Mass.: Harvard University Press, 1933), pp. 9, 45, 205, 213.

possible to decide the controversy, because the man who says that something true exists will not be believed without proof, on account of the controversy; and if he wishes to offer proof, he will be disbelieved if he acknowledges that his proof is false, whereas if he declares that his proof is true he becomes involved in circular reasoning and will be required to show proof of the real truth of his proof, and another proof of that proof, and so on ad infinitum. But it is impossible to prove an infinite series; and so it is impossible also to get to know that something true exists. . . .

And since the criterion of truth has appeared to be unattainable, it is no longer possible to make positive assertions either about those things which . . . seem to be evident or about those which are non-evident; . . . if we are forced to suspend judgment about the evident, how shall we dare to make pronouncements about the non-evident?

Hellenistic Science: Archimedes

Scientific inquiry and discovery were among the great successes of Hellenistic civilization. Of special significance in this regard was Archimedes (ca. 287–212 B.C.E.). His contributions to physics, mathematics, and engineering were great indeed. His famous boast on discovering the principle of the lever says much about his personality: "Give me a place to stand and I will move the earth!" In the following passage, Archimedes has offered his services as an inventor and engineer to Hiero, the leader of Syracuse. The Romans were invading the city and its defense had been the responsibility of Archimedes himself.

The Destruction of the Roman Fleet at Syracuse
PLUTARCH

Archimedes . . . wrote that with a given power he could move any given weight whatever, and, as if rejoicing in the strength of his demonstration, he is said to have declared that if he were given another world to stand upon, he could move this upon which we live. Hiero wondered at this, and begged him to put this theory into practice and show him something great moved by a small force. Archimedes took a three-masted ship, a transport in the king's navy, which had just been dragged up on land with great labor and many men; in this he placed her usual complement of men and cargo, and then sitting at some distance, without any trouble, by gently pulling with his hand the end of a system of pullies, he dragged it towards him with as smooth and even a motion as if it were passing over the sea. The king wondered greatly at this,

"The Destruction of the Roman Fleet at Syracuse" is from Plutarch, *Archimedes*, 14–17, trans. A. Stewart and G. Long (London: G. Bell and Sons, 1889).

and perceiving the value of his arts, prevailed upon Archimedes to construct for him a number of machines, some for the attack and some for the defense of a city, of which he himself did not make use, as he spent most of his life in unwarlike and literary leisure, but now these engines were ready for use in Syracuse, and the inventor also was present to direct their working.

So when the Romans attacked by sea and land at once, the Syracusans were first terrified and silent, dreading that nothing could resist such an armament. But Archimedes opened fire from his machines, throwing upon the land forces all manners of darts and great stones, with an incredible noise and violence, which no man could withstand; but those upon whom they fell were struck down in heaps, and their ranks thrown into confusion, while some of the ships were suddenly seized by iron hooks, and by a counter-balancing weight were drawn up and then plunged to the bottom. Others they caught by the irons like hands or claws suspended from cranes, and first pulled them up by their bow till they stood upright upon their sterns, and then cast down into the water, or by means of windlasses and tackles worked inside the city, dashed them against the cliffs and rocks at the base of the walls, with terrible destruction to their crews. Often was seen the fearful sight of a ship lifted out of the sea into the air, swaying and balancing about, until the men were all thrown out or overwhelmed with stones from slings, when the empty vessel would either be dashed against the fortifications or dropped into the sea by the claws being let go. . . . For most of the machines on the walls had been devised by Archimedes, and the Romans thought that they were fighting against gods and not men, as destruction fell upon them from invisible hands.

One cannot therefore disbelieve the stories which are told of Archimedes: how he seemed ever bewitched by the song of some indwelling siren of his own so as to forget to eat his food, and neglect his person, and how, when dragged forcibly to the baths and perfumers, he would draw geometrical figures with the ashes on the hearth, and when his body was anointed would trace lines on it with his finger, absolutely possessed and inspired by the joy he felt in his art. He discovered many beautiful problems, and is said to have begged his relatives and friends to place upon his tomb when he died a cylinder enclosing a sphere, and to write on it the proof of the ratio of the containing solid to the contained.

CHRONOLOGY: The Age of Alexander the Great

404–403 B.C.E.	End of the Peloponnesian War and rule of the Thirty Tyrants in Athens.
400–371 B.C.E.	Spartan hegemony over Greece. Second Athenian Confederation established (378 B.C.E.).
371–362 B.C.E.	Rise of Thebes under the leadership of Epaminondas. Theban hegemony over Greece.
347 B.C.E.	Death of Plato, whose philosophy reflects disillusionment with democracy and advocates the rule of enlightened philosopher-kings.
359–338 B.C.E.	Philip II becomes King of Macedon (359 B.C.E.) and seeks involvement in Greek affairs. Debate in Athens between supporters who want Philip's leadership (Isocrates) and those who believe him dangerous to Greek freedom (Demosthenes). League of Corinth established (338 B.C.E.) after Greek defeat at Chaeronea.
336–323 B.C.E.	Reign of Alexander III, the Great. Accedes to power after assassination of his father, Philip II. Alexander invades Persia (334 B.C.E.), defeats King Darius III, and reaches Indus Valley (327 B.C.E.). Dies of fever and his generals carve up the parts of his empire that did not fall away immediately. Transition to Hellenistic ("Greek-like") era.
322 B.C.E.	Death of Aristotle, student of Plato, teacher of Alexander.

STUDY QUESTIONS

1. What were some of Plato's ideas about democracy? Why did he feel this way? Do you think his assessment is correct?
2. What is Demosthenes' main message to the Athenians in the First Philippic? How does he view Philip and what does he want the Athenians to do about him? Be specific in your citation of evidence.
3. What does Isocrates advocate in his "Address to Philip"? Are his arguments persuasive? Do you regard him as a traitor to Athens or as a far-sighted statesman?
4. What specifically does the loyalty oath for the League of Corinth require of the Greek city-states? Is it abusive in its demands? In the final analysis, why did Athens lose its freedom? Was it inevitable? Who gave better advice for the welfare of Greece, Isocrates or Demosthenes?
5. After reading the sources on Alexander the Great, describe what kind of man he was. Be specific in your answer. Do you think his actions warrant the epithet "the Great"? Does "greatness" imply more than conquest? Is it more difficult to

conquer than it is to consolidate and rule territory? To what extent can an individual change the course of history?

6. Assess the motives of Alexander the Great. Did he conquer for personal glory, for the glory of Macedon and Greece, for vengeance against the Persians, or to better his father? What do you think of the "Brotherhood of Man" argument advocated by Plutarch? Was Alexander really trying to tie East and West together?

7. In Plato's "Allegory of the Cave," how do you interpret the fire, shadows, and prisoners? How does Plato express his Theory of Ideas in this allegory?

8. In what specific ways can Plato's view of women in his ideal Republic be considered progressive? Compare his proposal with the restricted status of women in Greek society. How does Plato extend the argument for equality at the end of the dialogue? Is true equality socially unacceptable? What is Aristotle's view of the function and status of women?

9. How does Aristotle's philosophy differ from that of Plato? Do you agree with his assessment of communism? His assessment of education? Define the "Doctrine of the Mean." Why is Aristotle called a "practical philosopher"?

10. Explain the nature of pleasure for an Epicurean philosopher. How would he define pleasure and what does it consist of? Do you consider Epicureanism to be a practical philosophy? Why or why not?

11. In what way can Skepticism be called a "defensive" philosophy? What are its basic tenets? For the Skeptic, what is true? What are the advantages to being a Skeptic? Are there any disadvantages?

12. Can we call the fourth century B.C.E. and Hellenistic period an age of decline? How does it show decline, and how does it show progress? Be specific in your answer.

PART III

THE ROMAN WORLD

4

Breakdown and Rebirth: The Crisis of the Roman Republic

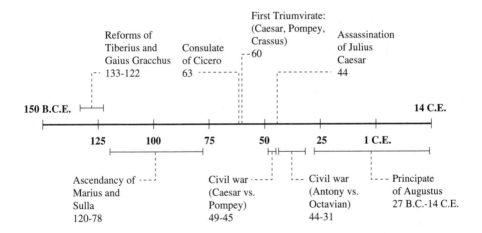

Men are much more attracted by immediate than by remote events; when they find things going well in the present, they are pleased, and think of nothing else.

—Niccolò Machiavelli, *The Prince*

Idealism is the noble toga that political gentlemen drape over their will to power.

—Aldous Huxley

No one with absolute power can be trusted to give it up even in part.

—Justice Louis D. Brandeis

CHAPTER THEMES

- *Systems of Government:* How would you define the concept of a republic, and how does it differ from a democracy? Is a republic a more practical and workable form of government than a democracy? Why did the Roman Republic fail?

- *Revolution:* How did the Gracchan revolution in economic and social reforms contribute to changes in Roman society? Did those changes ultimately result in the disintegration of the Roman Republic under the weight of military competition?

- *Imperialism:* How did success in the establishment of an empire by military force contribute to the prestige of generals and the decline of the Roman Republic? Does success in imperialism give greater credence to the voices of extremism?

- *Propaganda:* Some historians have maintained that Augustus's rule was based less on his control of the military machine than on his patronage of poets in the realm. How was his image enhanced by various forms of propaganda? In this regard, could you compare Augustus to Alexander the Great, or to Adolf Hitler or Joseph Stalin?

- *Historical Change and Transition:* How did Augustus fill the power vacuum left by the Roman civil war and maintain stability throughout the Roman world? Does history move in a cycle between chaos and stability? Why are some societies able to maintain stability longer than others? What are the sources of societal instability and chaos? Do these forces lead to repressive regimes which maintain domestic control at the expense of personal freedom?

- *The Big Picture:* Do all societies pass through a critical period of change that results in renewal or destruction? Must societies be challenged in order to survive and progress? Is this "challenge and response" theory of civilization applicable to one's personal life? Is a civilization, like a human being, a biological entity?

The rise and fall of the Roman Empire has been a topic of fascination and controversy for over fifteen hundred years. Even the Romans themselves were amazed at their history and understood that their accomplishments were unique and their legacy imposing. The story of Rome began, as legend has it, on April 21, 753 B.C.E., with the foundation of the city on the banks of the Tiber River in Italy. At first, Rome was a monarchy; various kings ruled until the last was overthrown and a republic created in 509 B.C.E. The succeeding years saw the establishment of an unwritten constitution and the promotion of domestic reforms to assure political equality for all citizens—a condition the Romans proudly achieved without violence.

Besides solving domestic concerns, the Romans came into contact with neighboring tribes. Primarily because of their military superiority, achieved by discipline and organization, the Romans were able to defeat adversaries and thus extend the boundaries of their city. By 270 B.C.E., Rome had expanded to the southern tip of Italy and succeeded in establishing contractual alliances with the peoples she defeated. The Romans were liberal in their settlements, allowing cities to keep their own governments, traditions, and laws, demanding only tribute and military support in return. The Italian alliance was strong and proved essential in the succeeding years.

The challenge to Roman authority, however, was not long in coming. In 264 B.C.E., the Carthaginians, who had established a commercial hegemony of sorts over the western Mediterranean, believed that the ascendant Rome threatened their control of the region. A series of Carthaginian (Punic) wars began that not only challenged the authority of Rome but also threatened her very existence. Perhaps the most dramatic episode in Roman history recounts the struggle against the great Carthaginian general Hannibal, from 218 to 202 B.C.E. In the end, Roman tenacity prevailed and Carthage was humbled. In 146 B.C.E., Rome finally decided to obliterate the Carthaginian presence altogether. The walls of Carthage were torn down, salt was sowed into the ground, and curses pronounced over the area. Rome had freed herself completely from physical and psychological threat; she was now at a crossroads in her development.

Although Rome seemed preeminent in the Mediterranean area by the middle of the second century B.C.E., other domestic problems were fast arising to threaten the state from within. The Romans had destroyed the Carthaginian menace largely by depending on an army composed of free farmers who had exchanged their hoes for swords. After the victory over Hannibal, many returned to find that his fifteen-year presence in Italy had destroyed their land. Rather than rebuild, which was expensive and a gamble in any event, many decided to sell their property to members of the senatorial aristocracy. The nobility thus increased their land holdings and created plantations called latifundia, which were farmed by the cheap slave labor abundant after the Punic wars. Since one had to own property to be in the army, many of the displaced veterans went to the city of Rome, hoping to find employment. A gulf widened between rich and poor that threatened the unity of the state.

In response to this, a tribune named Tiberius Gracchus proposed redistributing the senatorial estates. His murder by the nobility in 133 B.C.E. established a precedent for violence, which had never before played a role in Roman domestic politics. As violence and intimidation became acceptable tools of change, the state balanced on the brink of chaos. Soon generals such as Marius and Sulla, promising glory, booty, and land after service, offered men entrance into the army without property qualification. In this way, a new army became the focal point of power, an army composed of professional soldiers who owed their loyalty to their general rather than to the state. Under the direction of men such as Marcus Crassus, Pompey the Great, and Julius Caesar, the army became a tool for the achievement of glory and the defense of one's dignity. The Republic degenerated into civil war and dictatorship. With it died the ideals and character that had established equality among Roman citizens and had defeated the likes of Hannibal. When Rome emerged from the throes of civil war, she found peace and prosperity under the rule of Augustus. Still, his promotion of republican forms of government could not belie the autocracy that formed the basis of his rule. Citizens were made to feel free, however, and most were thus willing to trade the true liberty of a republic for the benefits of peace and security offered by Augustus's new "principate."

This chapter explores the fall of the Roman Republic and its transformation into the principate of Augustus. Of particular importance is the topic of freedom. What was the basis of Roman strength and achievement, and why did the state collapse under the weight of generals who fought in defense of their traditional ideas of dignity and liberty? What is the importance of recognizing appearance and reality in any government? If one feels free in a controlled state, is one truly free? The problem of appearance and reality is of great concern in modern democracies, where leaders are often elected or their policies implemented not on the basis of what is said but on how it is said. Media manipulation was as alive in Augustan Rome as it is in twentieth-century America. Perhaps the true genius of the Roman was his capacity for adaptation and transformation. Survival is often the result of such compromises.

The Senate and the Gracchan Reform Plan

The Growth of the Latifundia

APPIAN

After the Punic wars, the influx of cheap slave labor undermined the Roman soldier who often returned home to find his farmland neglected or destroyed and hence unworkable. There was great resentment of the latifundia system, as the following selection notes.

The wealthy, getting hold of the greater part of the undistributed lands, growing bold by lapse of time and thinking they would never be ousted, added to their original holdings the small farms of their poor neighbors. This they did partly by purchase, yet partly by force: and so they cultivated the vast tracts of land in lieu of mere private estates. To work them they used slaves as farm hands and herdsmen, lest free laborers should be forced to quit farm work for the army. The ownership of slaves brought huge profit from the

"The Growth of the Latifundia" is from Appian, *The Civil Wars*, 1.7–9, in *Readings in Ancient History*, vol. 2, ed. William S. Davis (Boston: Allyn and Bacon, 1913), pp. 104–105.

multitude of the children of the slaves, who increased because they were exempt from army service. Thus the magnates became marvelously rich, and the race of slaves multiplied through the land, while the free folk of Italy dwindled alike in numbers and power, ground down as they were by poverty, taxation, and constant service in the army. If any relaxation from these evils came, they passed their time in sheer idleness, for the land was in the clutches of the rich, who employed slaves as farm hands, not freemen.

The Murder of Tiberius Gracchus (133 B.C.E.)
PLUTARCH

In 133 B.C.E., a tribune named Tiberius Gracchus proposed a land redistribution plan designed to limit the amount of acreage any individual could hold. In this way, he hoped to salvage the free farmer. Members of the senatorial oligarchy were the first to resort to violence in the murder of Tiberius, thus ending a Roman tradition of peaceful domestic reform through compromise. Tiberius's brother, Gaius, who proposed further reforms ten years later, was also killed. This breakdown in political unity is noted by the critic Sallust in the last selection.

[Nasica, a senatorial leader, urged strong measures:] "Let every one who will defend the laws follow me." [Nasica,] then, casting the edge of his toga over his head, hastened to the Capitol; those who bore him company wrapped their togas also about their arms and forced their way after him. And as they were persons of the greatest authority in the city the common people did not venture to obstruct their passing, but were so eager to clear the way for them that they tumbled over one another in haste. The attendants they brought with them had furnished themselves with clubs and staves from their houses, and they themselves picked up the feet and other fragments of stools and chairs, which were broken by the hasty flight of the common people.

Thus armed, they made toward Tiberius, knocking down those whom they found in front of him, and those were soon wholly dispersed, and many of them slain. Tiberius tried to save himself by flight. As he was running, he was stopped by one who caught hold of him by the toga; but he threw it off, and fled in his undergarments only. And stumbling over those who before had been knocked down, as he was endeavoring to get up again, Publius Satureius, a tribune, one of his colleagues, was observed to give him the first fatal stroke, by hitting him upon the head with a foot of a stool. The second blow was claimed, as though it had been a deed to be proud of, by Lucius Rufus. And of the rest there fell over three hundred, killed by clubs and staves only, none by an iron weapon.

"The Murder of Tiberius Gracchus" is from Plutarch, *Life of Tiberius Gracchus,* 16–20, in *Readings in Ancient History,* vol. 2, ed. William S. Davis (Boston: Allyn and Bacon, 1913), pp. 108–109.

This, we are told, was the first sedition among the Romans, since the abrogation of kingly government, that ended in the effusion of blood. All former quarrels which were neither small nor about trivial matters, were always amicably settled, by mutual concessions on either side, the Senate yielding for fear of the commons, and the commons out of respect to the Senate. . . . But it is evident that this conspiracy was fomented against Tiberius, more out of the hatred and malice which the rich men had to his person, than for the reasons which they commonly pretended against him. In testimony of which, we may adduce the cruelty and unnatural insults with which they abused to his dead body. For they would not allow his own brother, though he earnestly begged the favor, to bury him in the night, but threw him, together with the other corpses, into the river.

The Breakdown of Roman Unity
SALLUST

Now the institution of parties and factions, with all their attendant evils, originated at Rome a few years before this as the result of peace and of an abundance of everything that mortals prize most highly. For before the destruction of Carthage the people and senate of Rome together governed the Republic peacefully and with moderation. There was not strife among the citizens either for glory or for power; fear of the enemy preserved the good morals of the state. But when the minds of the people were relieved of that dread, wantonness and arrogance naturally arose, vices which are fostered by prosperity. Thus the peace for which they had longed in time of adversity, after they gained it proved to be more cruel and bitter than adversity itself. For the nobles began to abuse their position and the people their liberty, and every man for himself robbed, pillaged, and plundered. Thus the community was split into two parties, and between these the state was torn to pieces. . . .

For example, when Tiberius and Gaius Gracchus, whose forefathers had added greatly to the power of the Republic in the Punic and other wars, began to assert the freedom of the commons and expose the crimes of the oligarchs, the nobility, who were guilty, were therefore panic stricken. They accordingly opposed the acts of the Gracchi. . . . And first Tiberius, then a few years later Gaius, who had followed in his brother's footsteps, were slain with the sword, although one was a tribune and the other a commissioner for founding colonies. . . . It must be admitted that the Gracchi were so eager for victory that they had not shown a sufficiently moderate spirit. . . .

The nobles then abused their victory to gratify their passions; they put many men out of the way by the sword or by banishment, and thus rendered

"The Breakdown of Roman Unity" is reprinted by permission of the publishers and the Loeb Classical Library from Sallust, *The War with Jugurtha*, 41–42, trans. J. C. Rolfe (Cambridge, Mass.: Harvard University Press, 1921), pp. 223, 225, 227.

themselves for the future rather dreaded than powerful. It is the spirit which has commonly ruined great nations, when one party desires to triumph over another by any and every means and to avenge itself on the vanquished with excessive cruelty. But if I should attempt to speak of the strife of parties and of the general character of the state in detail or according to the importance of the theme, time would fail me sooner than material.

The Ascendency of the Generals (100–45 B.C.E.)

The Wrath of Sulla (82 B.C.E.)

By the opening of the first century B.C.E., Roman armies were no longer recruited from the free land-holding farmers, but rather from those displaced veterans and unemployed who had migrated to Rome. A successful general named Marius offered them employment in the army without the requirement of property ownership. Marius thus created a professional army of soldiers who were promised land, booty, and glory; in return, they gave loyalty to their general. Competition for commands against important foreign enemies became intense and sometimes resulted in civil war. The following selection recounts the vengeance of the general Sulla against Marius's troops in 82 B.C.E. Blood-letting was becoming epidemic in its proportions.

"Absolute Tyranny"
APPIAN

Sulla himself called the Roman people together in an assembly and made them a speech, vaunting his own exploits and making other menacing statements in order to inspire terror. He finished by saying that he would bring about a change which would be beneficial to the people if they would obey him, but of his enemies he would spare none, but would visit them with the utmost severity. He would take vengeance by strong measures on . . . everybody . . . who had committed any hostile act . . . [against] him. . . . After saying this, he forthwith proscribed about forty senators and 1,600 equites. He seems to have been the first to make such a formal list of those whom he condemned to death, to offer prizes to assassins and rewards to informers, and to threaten with punishment those who concealed the proscribed. Shortly after-

---

"'Absolute Tyranny'" is reprinted by permission of the publishers and the Loeb Classical Library from Appian, *The Civil Wars*, 1.11.95–12.103, trans. Horace White (Cambridge Mass.: Harvard University Press, 1913), pp. 175, 177, 183, 185.

ward he added the names of other senators to the proscription. Some of these, taken unawares, were killed where they were caught, in their homes, in the streets, or in the temples. Others were hurled through mid-air and thrown at Sulla's feet. Others were dragged through the city and trampled on, none of the spectators daring to utter a word of remonstrance against these horrors. Banishment was inflicted upon some, and confiscation upon others. Spies were searching everywhere for those who had fled from the city, and those whom they caught they killed. . . .

Thus Sulla became king, or tyrant, a de facto—not elected but holding power by force and violence. . . . There had been autocratic rule before—that of the dictators—but it was limited to short periods; under Sulla it first became unlimited, and so an absolute tyranny. But this much was added for propriety's sake, that they chose him dictator for the enactment of such laws as he himself might deem best and for the settlement of the commonwealth. . . .

Marcus Licinius Crassus

> *One of Sulla's commanders, Marcus Crassus, became known in antiquity as the richest man in Rome. He argued that one could not be considered wealthy unless one could maintain an army at personal expense. Wealth became a major factor in achieving political influence in the late Republic, and Crassus was a master at bribery. His methods of gaining his fortune are recounted below.*

The Richest Man in Rome
PLUTARCH

People [said] that the many virtues of Crassus were darkened by the one vice of avarice, and indeed he seemed to have no other but that; for it, being the most predominant, obscured others to which he was inclined. For when Sulla seized the city, and exposed to sale the goods of those that he had caused to be slain, accounting them booty and spoils, and, indeed, calling them so too, and was desirous of making as many, and as eminent men as he could, partakers in the crime, Crassus never was the man that refused to accept, or give money for them.

Moreover, observing how extremely subject the city was to fire, and to the falling down of houses, by reason of their height and their standing so near together, he bought slaves that were builders and architects, and when he had collected these to the number of more than five hundred, he made it his practice to buy houses that were on fire, and those in the neighborhood

---

"The Richest Man in Rome" is from Plutarch, *Life of Crassus*, 2–3, in *Readings in Ancient History,* vol. 2, ed. William S. Davis (Boston: Allyn and Bacon, 1913), pp. 127–128.

which, in the immediate danger and uncertainty, the proprietors were willing to part with for little or nothing; so that the greatest part of Rome, at one time or other, came into his hands.

Yet though he had so many workmen, he never built anything but his own house, and used to say that those that were addicted to building would undo themselves soon enough without the help of other enemies. And though he had many silver mines, and much valuable land, and laborers to work in it, yet all this was nothing in comparison to his slaves, such a number and variety did he possess of excellent readers, amanuenses, silversmiths, stewards, and table waiters. . . .

Pompey the Great

A major figure of the first century B.C.E., Pompey was considered by many to be the greatest general of his age. He earned a reputation for efficiency: when given the two-year assignment to rid the Mediterranean of pirates, a problem that had gone unsolved for decades, Pompey accomplished the feat in three months. Some of his other victories are recorded in the first selection. He was accorded a magnificent triumph over Rome's persistent enemy, Mithradates, in 61 B.C.E., similar to the one described in the second excerpt.

A Glorious Record
PLINY

But it concerns the glory of the Roman Empire, and not that of one man, to mention in this place all the records of the victories of Pompey the Great and all his triumphs, which equal the brilliance of the exploits not only of Alexander the Great but even almost of Hercules. . . . After the recovery of Sicily, . . . and after the conquest of the whole of Africa and its reduction under our sway and the acquirement . . . of the title of the Great, he rode back in a triumphal chariot. . . . Subsequently he was dispatched to the whole of the seas and then to the far East, and he brought back titles without limit for his country. . . . Consequently he bestowed . . . honors on the city in the shrine of Minerva that he was dedicating out of the proceeds of the spoils of war: "Gnaeus Pompeius Magnus, commander-in-chief, having completed a thirty years' war, routed, scattered, slain, or received the surrender of 12,183,000 people, sunk or taken 846 ships, received the capitulation of 1,538 towns and forts, subdued . . . lands . . . to the Red Sea, duly dedicates his offering vowed to Minerva."

"A Glorious Record" is reprinted by permission of the publishers and the Loeb Classical Library from Pliny, *Natural History*, 7.26, trans. H. Rackham (Cambridge, Mass.: Harvard University Press, 1941), pp. 567, 569, 571.

This is his summary of his exploits in the East. But the announcement of the triumphal procession that he led . . . was as follows: "After having rescued the seacoast from pirates and restored to the Roman people the command of the sea, he celebrated a triumph over Asia, Pontus, Armenia, Paphlagonia, Cappadocia, Cilicia, Syria, the Scythians, Jews and Albanians, Iberia, the Island of Crete, the Bastarnians, and, in addition to these, over King Mithridates and Tigranes."

The crowning pinnacle of this glorious record was (as he himself declared in assembly when discoursing on his achievements) to have found Asia the remotest of the provinces and then to have made her a central dominion of his country. If anybody on the other side desires to review in similar manner the achievements of Caesar, who showed himself greater than Pompey, he must assuredly roll off the entire world, and this it will be agreed is a task without limit.

A Roman Triumph

ZONARAS

Now the celebration of a military victory which they call a triumph was somewhat as follows. When any great success worthy of a triumph had been gained, the general was immediately saluted as imperator by the soldiers. . . . On arriving home he would assemble the senate and ask to have the triumph voted him. And if he obtained a vote from the senate and from the people, his title of imperator was confirmed. . . .

Arrayed in the triumphal dress and wearing armlets, with a laurel crown upon his head, and holding a branch in his right hand, he called together the people. After praising collectively the troops who had served with him, and some of them individually, he presented them with money and honored them also with decorations. Upon some he bestowed armlets and spears without the iron; to others he gave crowns, sometimes of gold, sometimes of silver, bearing the name of each man and the representation of his particular feat. . . . And these rewards were not only given to men singly, as the result of individual deeds of prowess, but were also bestowed upon whole companies and legions. A large part of the spoils also was assigned to the soldiers who had taken part in the campaign; but some victors have distributed the spoils even among the entire populace and have devoted them toward the expenses of the festival or turned them over to the treasury. . . .

After these ceremonies the triumphant general would mount his chariot. Now this chariot did not resemble one used in games or in war, but was fashioned in the shape of a round tower. And he would not be alone in the chariot, but if he had children or relatives, he would make the girls and the infant male

"A Roman Triumph" is reprinted by permission of the publishers and the Loeb Classical Library from Zonaras, *Dio's Roman History*, vol. 1, 7.21, trans. Earnest Cary (Cambridge, Mass.: Harvard University Press, 1914), pp. 193, 195, 197, 199, 201.

children get up beside him in it and place the older ones upon the horses. . . . If there were many of them, they would accompany the procession on chargers, riding along beside the victor. . . . Thus arrayed, they entered the city, having at the head of the procession the spoils and trophies and figures representing the captured forts, cities, mountains, rivers, lakes, and seas—everything, in fact, that they had taken. If one day did not suffice for the exhibition of these things in procession, the celebration was held during a second and a third day. When these adjuncts had gone on their way, the victorious general arrived at the Roman Forum, and after commanding that some of the captives be led to prison and put to death, he rode up to the Capitol. There he performed certain rites and made offerings and dined in the porticoes up there, after which he departed homeward towards evenings, accompanied by flutes and pipes. Such were the triumphs in [Republican] times.

Cicero and the Conspiracy of Catiline (63 B.C.E.)

Another major figure of the late Republic was Marcus Tullius Cicero. Cicero came from a family of little social distinction, and his rise to the consulship was the result of his oratorical skill. Cicero's greatest moment occurred when he discovered a plot to overthrow the government, led by a dissolute politician named Catiline. In the first excerpt, the scene is set by the Roman moralist Sallust. In the second, Cicero himself comments on his victory in a speech delivered before the senate.

Catiline Plots Revolt
SALLUST

After Sulla had recovered the government by force of arms, everybody became robbers and plunderers. Some set their hearts on houses, some on lands. His victorious troops knew no restraint, no moderation, but inflicted on the citizens disgraceful and inhumane outrages.

When wealth was once counted an honor, and glory, authority, and power attended it, virtue lost her influence, poverty was thought a disgrace, and a life of innocence was regarded as a life of mere ill nature. From the influence of riches, accordingly, luxury, avarice, pride came to prevail among the youth. They grew at once rapacious and prodigal. They undervalued what was their own; they had no modesty and continence; they lost all distinction between sacred and profane, and threw off all consideration and self-restraint.

In so populous and corrupt a city [as Rome] Catiline easily kept about him, as a bodyguard, crowds of the lawless and desperate. All the shameless

"Catiline Plots Revolt" is from Sallust, *The Conspiracy of Catiline*, 11–16, in *Readings in Ancient History*, vol. 2, ed. William S. Davis (Boston: Allyn and Bacon, 1913), pp. 136–138.

libertines and profligate rascals were his associates and intimate friends,—the men who had squandered their paternal estates by gaming, luxury, sensuality, and all too who had plunged heavily into debt to buy immunity for crimes; all assassins or sacrilegious persons from every quarter, convicted, or dreading conviction for their misdeeds; all likewise, for whom their tongue or hand won a livelihood by perjury or bloodshed; all, in short, whom wickedness, poverty, or a guilty conscience goaded were friends to Catiline.

The young men [his close companions] . . . he enticed by various methods into evil practice. From among them he furnished false witnesses and forgers of signatures; and he taught them all to regard with equal unconcern property and danger. At length when he had stripped them of all character and shame he led them to other and greater iniquities. When there was no ready motive for crime, he nevertheless stirred them up to murder quite inoffensive persons, just as if they had injured him, lest their hand or heart should grow stale for want of employment.

Trusting to such confederates and comrades, . . . Catiline accordingly formed the design of overthrowing the government.

"The Enemy Is Within"
CICERO

At length, O Romans, we have dismissed from the city, or have driven out or, when he was departing of his own accord, we have pursued with words, Lucius Catiline, mad with audacity, breathing wickedness, impiously planning mischief to his country, threatening fire and sword to you and to this city. He is gone, he has departed, he has disappeared, he has rushed out. No injury will now be prepared against these walls within the walls themselves by that monster and prodigy of wickedness. And we have without controversy defeated him, the sole general of this domestic war. For now that danger will no longer hover about our sides; we shall not be afraid in the campus, in the forum, in the senate house—, ay and within our private walls. He was moved from his place when he was driven from the city. Now we shall openly carry on a regular war with an enemy without hinderance.

Beyond all question we ruin the man; we have defeated him splendidly when we have driven him from secret treachery into open warfare. But that he has not taken with him his sword red with blood as he intended—that he has left us alive—that we wrested the weapon from his hands—that he has left the citizens safe and the city standing, what great and overwhelming grief must you think that his is to him! Now he lies prostrate, O Romans, and feels himself stricken down and abject, and often casts back his eyes towards this city, which he mourns over as snatched from his jaws, but which seems to me to rejoice at having vomited forth such a pest and cast it out of doors. . . .

"'The Enemy Is Within'" is from Cicero, *Catilinarian Oration*, in *Select Orations of Cicero*, ed. C. D. Yonge (New York: Harper and Brothers, 1860), pp. 15–21.

But I am confident that some fate is hanging over these men [the conspira-
tors] and that the punishment long since due to their iniquity and worthless-
ness and wickedness and lust is either visibly at hand or at least rapidly approaching. And if my consulship shall have removed, since it can not cure
them, it will have added not some brief span but many ages of existence to the
Republic. For there is no nation for us to fear—no king who can make war on
the Roman people. All foreign affairs are tranquilized, both by land and sea, by
the valor of one man. Domestic war alone remains. The only plots against us are
within our own walls—the danger is within—the enemy is within. We must war
with luxury, with madness, with wickedness. For this war, O citizens, I offer myself as the general. I take on myself the enmity of profligate men. What can be
cured I will cure by whatever means it may be possible. What must be cut away,
I will not allow to spread to the ruin of the Republic.

The Civil War (49–45 B.C.E.)

*The most famous Roman of them all, Julius Caesar, had a difficult time achiev-
ing the kind of military glory or wealth needed to compete with Pompey and Crassus. When he finally got a major command in Gaul (58 B.C.E.), he conquered
and consolidated the area, gaining wealth and the loyalty of his troops. After
first cooperating with Pompey and Crassus, Caesar realized he would have to
fight a senatorial aristocracy that distrusted him and championed Pompey. The
first selection recounts Caesar's famous decision to cross the Rubicon River, thus
beginning the civil war. Cicero, a supporter of Pompey and the senate, also gives
his perspective in letters written in the midst of this crisis.*

"The Die Is Cast": Caesar Crosses the Rubicon
SUETONIUS

When the news came to Ravenna, where Caesar was staying that [his compromise plan] had been utterly rejected, ... he immediately sent forward some
troops, yet secretly, to prevent any suspicion of his plan. ... Coming up with
his troops on the banks of the Rubicon, which was the frontier of his
province, he halted for a while, and revolving in his mind the importance of
the step he meditated, he turned to those about him, saying: "Still we can retreat! But once we pass this little bridge,—nothing is left but to fight it out
with arms!". ... Caesar cried out, "Let us go when the omens of the Gods and
the crimes of our enemies summon us! THE DIE IS NOW CAST!" Accordingly he
marched his army over the river.

"'The Die is Cast': Caesar Crosses the Rubicon" is from Suetonius, Life of Caesar, 31–33, in *Readings in Ancient History*, vol. 2, ed. William S. Davis (Boston: Allyn and Bacon, 1913), pp. 149–150.

"We Must Trust to the Mercy of the Storm"

CICERO

Menturnea, January 22, 49 B.C.E.

It is civil war, though it has not sprung from division among our citizens but from the daring of one abandoned citizen. He is strong in military forces, he attracts adherents by hopes and promises, he covets the whole universe. Rome is delivered to him stripped of defenders, stocked with supplies: one may fear anything from one who regards her temples and her homes not as his native land but as his loot. What he will do, and how he will do it, in the absence of senate and magistrates, I do not know. He will be unable even to pretend constitutional methods. But where can our party raise its head, or when?... We depend entirely upon two legions that were kept here by a trick and are practically disloyal. For so far the draft has found unwilling recruits, disinclined to fight. But the time of compromise is past. The future is obscure. We, or our leaders, have brought things to such a pass that, having put to sea without a rudder, we must trust to the mercy of the storm.

Formiae, February 8 or 9, 49 B.C.E.

I see there is not a foot of ground in Italy which is not in Caesar's power. I have no news of Pompey, and I imagine he will be captured unless he has taken to the sea. . . . What can I do? In what land or on what sea can I follow a man when I don't know where he is? Shall I then surrender to Caesar? Suppose I could surrender with safety, as many advise, could I do so with honor? By no means. . . . The problem is insoluble.

Formiae, March 1, 49 B.C.E.

I depend entirely on news from Brundisium. If Caesar has caught up with our friend Pompey, there is some slight hope of peace: but if Pompey has crossed the sea, we must look for war and massacre. Do you see the kind of man into whose hands the state has fallen? What foresight, what energy, what readiness! Upon my word, if he refrain from murder and rapine he will be the darling of those who dreaded him most. The people of the country towns and the farmers talk to me a great deal. They care for nothing at all but their lands, their little homesteads, and their tiny fortunes. And see how public opinion has changed: they fear the man they once trusted [Pompey] and adore the man they once dreaded [Caesar]. It pains me to think of the mistakes and wrongs of ours that are responsible for this reaction.

'We Must Trust to the Mercy of the Storm'" is reprinted by permission of the publishers and the Loeb Classical Library from Cicero, *Letter to Atticus*, 7.13, 7.22, 8.13, trans. E. O. Winstead (Cambridge, Mass.: Harvard University Press, 1913), pp. 61, 63, 89, 161, 163.

The Fall of the Roman Republic (44–31 B.C.E.)

DICTATORSHIP AND ASSASSINATION

Caesar managed to defeat Pompey in a major battle at Pharsalus in 48 B.C.E. Pompey fled to Egypt, where he was murdered on orders of the young pharaoh who thereby hoped to ingratiate himself with Caesar. When Caesar arrived in Egypt, he mourned Pompey as a noble warrior and former son-in-law. Caesar was able, in the next years, to defeat the rest of Pompey's supporters, and he arrived in Rome amidst acclamations of joy from the people. But a faction of about sixty senators saw in Caesar's reforms and imperial manner the makings of a king. They planned his murder and assassinated him on March 15, 44 B.C.E. The following selections describe these events.

Caesar's Reforms

SUETONIUS

Turning his attention to the reorganization of the state, [Caesar] reformed the calendar, which the pontiffs had long since so disordered, by neglecting to order the necessary intercalations, that the harvest festivals did not come in summer nor those of the vintage in the autumn. He adjusted the year to the sun's course by making it consist of 365 days, abolishing the intercalary month and adding one day every fourth year. . . .

He filled the vacancies in the senate, enrolled additional patricians, and increased the number of praetors, aediles, and quaestors as well as of minor officials. . . .He shared the elections with the people on this basis: that except in the case of the consulship, half of the magistrates should be appointed by the people's choice while the rest should be those whom he personally had nominated. . . . He then reduced the number of those who received grain at public expense from 320,000 to 150,000. . . . He conferred citizenship on all who practiced medicine at Rome, and on all teachers of the liberal arts, to make them more desirous of living in the city and to induce others to resort to it.

As to debts, he disappointed those who looked for their cancellation, which was often agitated, but finally decreed that the debtors should satisfy their creditors according to a valuation of their possessions at the price which they paid for them before the Civil War—an arrangement which wiped out about a fourth part of their indebtedness. He dissolved all associations, except those on ancient foundation. He increased the penalties for crimes. . . .

"Caesar's Reforms" is reprinted by permission of the publishers and the Loeb Classical Library from Suetonius, *Life of Caesar*, vol. 1, 37–38, 40–44, trans. J. C. Rolfe (Cambridge, Mass.: Harvard University Press, 1913), pp. 55, 57, 59, 61, 63.

Julius Caesar. "He allowed honors to be bestowed on him which were too great for mortal man."—Suetonius. *(Roman coin Aureus with head of Julius Caesar. Obverse. Struck by Trajan, 107 c.e. Museum of Fine Arts, Boston)*

He administered justice with the utmost conscientiousness and strictness. Those convicted of extortion he even expelled from the senatorial order. . . . In particular he enforced the law against extravagance. . . .

In particular, for the beautification and convenience of the city, as well as for guarding and extending the bounds of the empire, he formed more projects and more extensive ones every day: first of all, to raise a temple to Mars, greater than any in existence, filling up and leveling the pool in which he had exhibited the sea fight, and to build a theater of vast size over by the Tarpeian Rock; to reduce the civil law to fixed limits, and of the vast . . . mass of statutes to include only the best and most essential in a limited number of volumes; to open to the public the greatest possible libraries of Greek and Latin books, assigning to Marcus Varro the charge of procuring and classifying them; to drain the Pomptine Marshes; to let out the water from Lake Fucinus; to make a highway from the Adriatic across the summit of the Apennines to the Tiber; to cut a canal through the Isthmus of Corinth; to check the Dacians, who had poured into Pontus and Thrace; then to make war on the Parthians by way of Lesser Armenia, but not to risk a battle with them until he had first tested their mettle. All these enterprises and plans were cut short by his death.

Abuse of Power

SUETONIUS

Yet after all, his other actions and words so turn the scale, that it is thought that he abused his power and was justly slain. For not only did he accept excessive honors, such as an uninterrupted consulship, the dictatorship for life,

"Abuse of Power" is reprinted by permission of the publishers and the Loeb Classical Library from Suetonius, *Life of Caesar,* vol. 1, 76–78, trans. J. C. Rolfe (Cambridge, Mass.: Harvard University Press, 1913), pp. 99, 101, 103.

and the censorship of public morals, as well as the forename Imperator, the surname of Father of his Country, a statue among those of the kings, and a raised couch in the orchestra; but he also allowed honors to be bestowed on him which were too great for mortal man: a golden throne in the House and on the judgment seat; a chariot and litter in the procession at the circus; temples, altars, and statues beside those of the gods; a special priest, . . . and the calling of one of the months by his name. In fact, there were no honors which he did not receive or confer at pleasure. . . .

No less arrogant were his public utterances: . . . that the Republic was nothing, a mere name without body or form; that Sulla did not know his A.B.C.'s when he laid down his dictatorship; that men ought now to be more circumspect in addressing him, and to regard his word as law. . . .

But it was the following action that roused deadly hatred against him. When the Senate approached him in a body with many highly honorary decrees, he received them before the temple of Venus Genetrix without rising. Some think that when he attempted to get up, he was held back by Cornelius Balbus; others, that he made no such move at all, but on the contrary frowned angrily on Gaius Trebatius when he suggested that he should rise. And this action of his seemed the more intolerable, because when he himself in one of his triumphal processions rode past the benches of the tribunes, he was so incensed because a member of the college, Pontius Aquila by name, did not rise, that he cried: "Come then, Aquila, take back the Republic from me, you mighty tribune"; and for several days he would not make a promise to anyone without adding, "That is, if Pontius Aquila will allow me."

The Assassination of Julius Caesar (44 B.C.E.)

PLUTARCH

Antony, Caesar's faithful friend and a man of great physical strength, was detained outside the building by Brutus Albinus, who deliberately engaged him in a long conversation. When Caesar entered, the senate rose in his honor. Some of Brutus' accomplices stood behind his chair while others went to meet him, pretending to support the petition of Tullius Cimber for the recall of his brother from exile. They kept up their entreaties until he came to his chair. When he was seated he rejected their request, but they continued more and more urgently until he began to grow angry. Cimber then grasped his toga with both hands and pulled it off his neck, which was the signal for the attack. Casca struck the first blow, stabbing Caesar in the neck with his dagger. But the wound was not mortal or even dangerous, probably because at the beginning of so bold an action he was very nervous. Caesar therefore was able to turn around and grasp the dagger and hold on to it. At the same

"The Assassination of Julius Caesar" is from Plutarch, *Life of Caesar,* 66, trans. John and William Langhorne (New York: Harper and Brothers, 1872).

This silver coin depicts Brutus, one of Julius Caesar's assassins. Coins were often used as propaganda vehicles to inform and to gain popular support. *(Roger-Viollet/Liaison Agency, Inc.)*

time they both cried out, Caesar in Latin, "Casca, you villain! What does this mean!" and Casca in Greek to his brother, "Brother, help!"

After such a beginning, those who were unaware of the conspiracy were so astonished and horrified that they could neither run away or assist Caesar, nor could they even utter a word. But all the conspirators now drew their daggers and hemmed Caesar in on every side. Whichever way he turned he met with blows and saw nothing but cold steel gleaming in his face. Like some wild beast attacked by hunters, he found every hand lifted against him, for they had agreed that all must share in this sacrifice and flesh themselves with his blood. For this reason Brutus also gave him a stab in the groin. Some say that Caesar resisted all the others, shifting his body to escape the blows and calling for help, but when he saw Brutus' drawn dagger he covered his head with his toga and sank to the ground. Either by chance or because he was pushed by his murderers, he fell against the pedestal of Pompey's statue and drenched it with his blood. So Pompey himself seemed to preside over this act of vengeance, treading his enemy under his feet and enjoying his agonies. Those agonies were great, for they say he received twenty-three wounds. And many of the conspirators wounded each other as they aimed their blows at him.

The Murder of Cicero

Whether Caesar intended to establish a monarchy or not will remain a subject of controversy among historians. But his death unleashed the forces of violence and chaos as the state once again endured civil wars, first against Caesar's assassins, then between Caesar's trusted commander Mark Antony and his nephew and heir Gaius Octavian. Cicero, ever the republican, harshly criticized Antony in several orations and paid for it with his life.

"Antony's Greatest and Bitterest Enemy"
APPIAN

Cicero, who had held supreme power after Caesar's death as much as a public speaker could, was proscribed together with his son, his brother, his brother's son and all his household, faction, and friends. He fled in a small boat, but as he could not endure the seasickness he landed and went to a country place of his own . . . near Caieta, a town of Italy, and here he remained quiet. . . . Many soldiers were hurrying around in squads, inquiring if Cicero had been seen anywhere. Some people, moved by good will and pity, said that he had already put to sea. But a shoemaker . . . who had been a most bitter enemy of Cicero, pointed out the path to Laena, the centurion, who was pursuing with a small force.

Thereupon the slaves, thinking that more soldiers were coming, were terror-stricken and Laena, although he had once been saved by Cicero when under trial, drew [Cicero's] head out of the litter and cut it off, striking it three times, or rather sawing it off because of his inexperience. He also cut off the hand with which Cicero had written the speeches against Antony as tyrant, which he had entitled Philippics in imitation of Demosthenes. Then some of the soldiers hastened on horseback and others by ship to bring the good news quickly to Antony. The latter was sitting in front of the tribunal in the Forum when Laena, a long distance off, showed him the head and hand by lifting them up and shaking them. Antony was delighted beyond measure. He crowned the centurion and gave him 25,000 Attic drachmas in addition to the stipulated reward, for killing the man who had been his greatest and bitterest enemy. The head and hand of Cicero were suspended for a long time from the Rostra in the Forum where formerly he had been accustomed to make public speeches, and more people came together to behold this spectacle than had previously come to listen to him. It is said that even at his meals Antony placed Cicero's head before his table, until he became satiated with the horrible sight. Thus was Cicero, a man famous for his eloquence and one who had rendered the greatest service to his country when he held the office of consul, slain and insulted after his death.

Cleopatra

One of the most fascinating personalities of this period was Cleopatra, Queen of Egypt. She had bewitched Caesar when he arrived in Egypt on the trail of Pompey, and he brought her back to Rome. Mark Antony saw her there and, after Caesar's assassination, became romantically involved with her. As the first

"'Antony's Greatest and Bitterest Enemy'" is reprinted by permission of the publishers and the Loeb Classical Library from Appian, *The Civil Wars*, vol. 4, 4.4.19–20, trans. Horace White (Cambridge, Mass.: Harvard University Press, 1913), pp. 171, 173, 175.

excerpt indicates, her beauty and ability were renowned; Antony fell under her spell. She fought with him at Actium in 31 B.C.E. against the forces of Octavian and, after their defeat, both committed suicide in Egypt. Years later, the poet Horace, writing in support of Octavian, gave an assessment of her, as recounted in the second excerpt.

Cleopatra's Influence over Mark Antony
PLUTARCH

On her arrival, Antony sent to invite her to supper. She thought it fitter he should come to her; so, willing to show his good humor and courtesy, he complied, and went. He found the preparations to receive him magnificent beyond expression. . . .

For her actual beauty, it is said, was not in itself so remarkable that none could be compared with her, or that no one could see her without being struck by it, but the contact of her presence, if you lived with her, was irresistible; the attraction of her person, joining with the charm of her conversation, and the character that attended all she said or did, was something bewitching. It was a pleasure merely to hear the sound of her voice, with which, like an instrument of many strings, she could pass from one language to another; so that there were few of the barbarian nations that she answered by an interpreter; to most of them she spoke herself.

"She Was No Weak-Kneed Woman"
HORACE

Now for a drinking spree, now for a loose-footed
light fantastic, now is the time to pay
    our debt to the gods, my friends,
        and spread a spectacular banquet.

Before today, to bring the Caecuban from
family storerooms was wrong, while the crazy
    queen was still scheming with her
        sickly eunuchs, her pack of perverts,

"Cleopatra's Influence over Mark Antony" is from Plutarch, *Life of Antony,* 15–19, in *Readings in Ancient History,* vol. 2, ed. William S. Davis (Boston: Allyn and Bacon, 1913), pp. 163–164.

"'She Was No Weak-Kneed Woman'" is from Horace, *Odes,* 1.37, in *The Odes and Epodes of Horace,* trans. Joseph P. Clancy (Chicago: University of Chicago Press, 1960), pp. 70–71. © 1960 by the University of Chicago. Reprinted by permission of the publisher.

to send the Capitol crashing and bury
the empire: wild were her dreams of doing
    whatever she wished, the best
        luck was her liquor. She sobered up

when her ships caught fire, scarcely one unscathed,
and delusions of mind nursed on Egypt's wine
    were cured by Caesar [Octavian] with the facts
        of fear, his navy close as she fled

from Italy, like a hawk going after
a gentle dove, or a swift hunter tracking
    a hare over snow-covered fields
        in Thessaly: chains awaited this

damnable monster. But a heroine's death
was her goal: she showed no female shivers
    at the sight of a sword, and her
        fast-sailing fleet sought no secret harbors.

Her courage was great: she looked on her fallen
palace, a smile still on her face, and boldly
    played with venomous serpents,
        her flesh drinking their bitter poison,

so highly she dared, her mind set on her death.
Not for her the enemy ship, the crownless
    voyage, her role in the grand
        parade: she was no weak-kneed woman.

The Establishment of the Augustan Principate

By 27 B.C.E., Antony was dead and Octavian, by virtue of his military support, controlled the entire Roman Empire. At this point, he went to the senate and proclaimed that he had restored the Republic. Upon request of the senators, he decided to assume the advisory position of princeps or "first citizen" and the honorary title of "Augustus." The Republic was to function as it had in the past, with voting in the assemblies, election of magistrates, and traditional freedom. But as long as Augustus controlled the army, his "advice" could not be safely ignored. His system of government, called the principate, lasted in the same basic form until 180 C.E. The following accounts describe the powers of the princeps (or emperor, as he was also called). Note especially the cynicism of the historian Tacitus, who saw through the facade of republicanism and decried the loss of liberty.

The Powers and Authority of the Emperor

DIO CASSIUS

In this way the power of both people and senate passed entirely into the hands of Augustus, and from this time there was, strictly speaking, a monarchy; for monarchy would be the truest name for it. . . . Now, the Romans so detested the title "monarch" that they called their emperors neither dictators nor kings nor anything of this sort. Yet, since the final authority for government devolves upon them. . . . In order to preserve the appearance of having this authority not through their power but by virtue of the laws, the emperors have taken themselves all the offices (including the titles) which under the Republic possessed great power with the consent of the people. . . . Thus, they very often become consuls . . . instead of the . . . "king" or "dictator." These latter titles they have never assumed since they fell out of use in the constitution but the actuality of those offices is secured to them. . . . By virtue of the titles named, they secure the right to make levies, collect funds, declare war, make peace, and rule foreigners and citizens alike everywhere and always. . . .

Thus by virtue of these Republican titles they have clothed themselves with all the powers of the government, so that they actually possess all the prerogatives of kings without the usual title. For the appellation "Caesar" or "Augustus" confers upon them no actual power but merely shows in the one case that they are the successors of their family line, and in the other the splendour of their rank. The name "Father" perhaps gives them a certain authority over us all—the authority which fathers once had over their children; yet it did not signify this at first, but betokened honor and served as an admonition both to them to love their subjects as they would their children, and to their subjects to revere them as they would their fathers. . . .

Augustus did not enact all laws on his sole responsibility, but some of them he brought before the popular assembly in advance, in order that, if any features caused displeasure, he might learn it in time and correct them; for he encouraged everybody whatsoever to give him advice, in case anyone could think of any improvement in them, and he accorded them great freedom of speech; and he actually changed some provisions. Most important of all, he took as advisors . . . the consuls, . . . one of each of the other kinds of officials, and fifteen men chosen by lot from the remainder of the senatorial body, so that it was his custom to communicate proposed legislation after a fashion through these to all the other senators. For although he brought some matters before the whole senate, he generally followed this course, considering it better to take under preliminary advisement in a leisurely fashion most matters, and especially the most important ones, in consultation with a few; and sometimes he even sat with these men in trials. The senate as a body, it is true, continued to sit in judgment as before, and in certain cases transacted

"The Powers and Authority of the Emperor" is reprinted by permission of the publishers and the Loeb Classical Library from Dio Cassius, *Roman History*, vol. 6, 53.17.1–18, 53.3.21, trans. Earnest Cary (Cambridge, Mass.: Harvard University Press, 1917), pp. 235, 237, 241, 243, 249, 251.

business with embassies and envoys from both peoples and kings; and the people and the plebs, moreover, continued to come together for the election; but nothing was actually done that did not please Caesar. At any rate, in the case of those who were to hold office, he himself selected and nominated some; and though he left the election of others in the hands of the people and the plebs, in accordance with the ancient practice, yet he took care that no persons should hold office who were unfit or elected as the result of factious combinations or bribery.

The Transition from Republic to Principate

TACITUS

Augustus won over the soldiers with gifts, the populace with cheap [grain], and all men with the sweets of repose, and so grew greater by degrees, while he concentrated in himself the functions of the Senate, the magistrates, and the laws. He was wholly unopposed, for the boldest spirits had fallen in battle, or in the proscription, while the remaining nobles, the readier they were to be slaves, were raised the higher by wealth and promotion, so that, aggrandised by revolution, they preferred the safety of the present to the dangerous past. Nor did the provinces dislike that condition of affairs, for they distrusted the government of the Senate and the people, because of the rivalries between the leading men and the rapacity of the officials. . . . At home all was tranquil, and there were magistrates with the same titles; there was a younger generation, sprung up since the victory of Actium, and even many of the older men had been born during the civil wars. How few were left who had seen the Republic.

Thus the State had been revolutionized, and there was not a vestige left of the old sound morality. Stripped of equality, all looked up to the commands of a sovereign without the least apprehension for the present, while Augustus in the vigour of life, could maintain his own position, that of his house, and the general tranquility.

Res Gestae: The Accomplishments of Augustus

AUGUSTUS

The following document was written by Augustus himself in 14 C.E., the year of his death. Although it is largely factual and therefore important as a historical source, it is nevertheless a subjective political document that summarizes his career as he wanted it remembered.

"The Transition from Republic to Principate" is from Tacitus, *Annals*, 1.2–4, trans. Alfred Church and William Brodribb (New York: Macmillan and Co., 1891).

"Res Gestae: The Accomplishments of Augustus" is from *Res Gestae Divi Augusti*, in *Roman Civilization, Sourcebook II: The Empire*, ed. N. Lewis and M. Reinhold (New York: Columbia University Press, 1955), pp. 9–11, 13–14, 16–19. Copyright © 1955. Reprinted by permission.

This statue of Augustus depicts the emperor as a majestic and authoritative leader. Augustus brought stability to a Roman world racked by civil war and chaos. But was his freedom only a state of mind? *(Vatican Museums/Alinari/Art Resource, N.Y.)*

Below is a copy of the accomplishments of the deified Augustus by which he brought the whole world under the empire of the Roman people, and of the moneys expended by him on the state and the Roman people, as inscribed on two bronze pillars set up in Rome.

1. At the age of nineteen, on my own initiative and at my own expense, I raised an army by means of which I liberated the Republic, which was oppressed by the tyranny of a faction. For which reason the senate, with honorific decrees, made me a member of its order in the consulship of Gaius Pansa and Aulus Hirtius, giving me at the same time consular rank in voting, and granted me the imperium [right of command]. It ordered me as propraetor, together with consuls, to see to it that the state suffered no harm. Moreover, in the same year, when both consuls had fallen in the war, the people elected me consul and a triumvir for the settlement of the commonwealth.

2. Those who assassinated my father I drove into exile, avenging their crime by due process of law; and afterwards when they waged war against the state, I conquered them twice on the battlefield.

3. I waged many wars throughout the whole by land and by sea, both civil and foreign, and when victorious I spared all citizens who sought pardon. Foreign peoples who could safely be pardoned I preferred to spare rather than to extirpate. About 500,000 Roman citizens were under military oath to me. Of these, when their terms of service were ended, I settled in colonies or sent back to their own municipalities a little more than 300,000, and to all these I allotted lands or granted money as rewards for military service. . . .

4. Twice I celebrated ovations, three times curule triumphs, and I was acclaimed imperator twenty-one times. When the senate decreed additional triumphs to me, I declined them on four occasions. I deposited in the Capitol laurel wreaths . . . after fulfilling the vows which I had made in each war. For successes achieved on land and on sea by me or through my legates under my auspices the senate decreed fifty-five times that thanksgiving be offered to the immortal gods. Moreover, the number of days on which, by decree of the senate, such thanksgiving was offered, was 890. In my triumphs there were led before my chariot nine kings or children of kings. At the same time I wrote this document, I had been consul thirteen times, and I was in the thirty-seventh year of my tribunician power.

5. The dictatorship offered to me in the consulship of Marcus Marcellus and Lucius Arruntius by the people and by the senate, both in my absence and in my presence, I refused to accept. In the midst of a critical scarcity of grain I did not decline the supervision of the grain supply, which I so administered that within a few days I freed the whole people from the imminent panic and danger by my expenditures and efforts. The consulship, too, which was offered to me at that time as an annual office for life, I refused to accept. . . . I refused to accept any office offered me which was contrary to the traditions of our ancestors.

13. The temple of Janus Quirinus, which our ancestors desired to be closed whenever peace with victory was secured by sea and by land throughout the entire empire of the Roman people, and which before I was born is recorded to have been closed only twice since the founding of the city, was during my principate three times ordered by the senate to be closed.

15. To the Roman plebs I paid 300 sesterces apiece in accordance with the will of my father; and in my fifth consulship I gave each 400 sesterces in my own name out of the spoils of war; and a second time in my tenth consulship I paid out of my own patrimony a largess of 400 sesterces to every individual; in my eleventh consulship I made twelve distributions of food out of grain purchased at my own expense; and in the twelfth year of my tribunician power for the third time I gave 400 sesterces to every individual. These largesses of mine reached never less than 250,000 persons. In the eighteenth year of my tribunician power and my twelfth consulship I gave sixty denarii to each of 320,000 persons of the urban plebs. And in my fifth consulship I gave out of the spoils of war 1,000 sesterces apiece to my soldiers settled in colonies. This largess on the occasion of my triumph was received by about 120,000 persons in the colonies. In my thirteenth consulship I gave sixty denarii apiece to those of the plebs who at that time were receiving public grain; the number involved was a little more than 200,000 persons.

22. I have a gladiatorial show three times in my own name, and five times in the names of my sons or grandsons; at these shows about 10,000 fought. Twice I presented to the people in my own name an exhibition of athletes invited from all parts of the world, and a third time in the name of my grandson. I presented games in my own name four times, and in addition twenty-three times in the place of other magistrates. . . . Twenty-six times I provided for the people, in my own name or in the names of my sons or grandsons, hunting spectacles of African wild beasts in the circus or in the Forum or in the amphitheaters; in these exhibitions about 3,500 animals were killed.

26. I extended the frontiers of all the provinces of the Roman people on whose boundaries were peoples not subject to our empire. . . . I added Egypt to the empire of the Roman people.

28. I established colonies of soldiers in Africa, Sicily, Macedonia, in both Spanish provinces, in Achaea, Asia, Syria, Narbonese Gaul, and Pisidia. Italy, moreover, has twenty-eight colonies established by me, which in my lifetime have grown to be famous and populous.

29. A number of military standards lost by other generals I recovered, after conquering the enemy, from Spain, Gaul, and the Dalmations. The Parthians I compelled to restore to me the spoils and standards of three Roman armies and to seek the friendship of the Roman people as suppliants. The standards, moreover, I deposited in the inner shrine of the temple of Mars Ultor.

34. In my sixth and seventh consulships, after I had put an end to the civil wars, having attained supreme power by universal consent, I transferred the state from my own power to the control of the Roman senate and people. For this service of mine I received the title of Augustus by decree of the senate,

and the doorposts of my house were publicly decked with laurels, the civic crown was affixed over my doorway, and a golden shield was set up in the Julian senate house, which, as the inscription of this shield testifies, the Roman senate and people gave me in recognition of my valor, clemency, justice, and devotion. After that time I excelled all in authority, but I possessed no more power than the others who were my colleagues in each magistracy.

35. When I held my thirteenth consulship, the senate, the equestrian order, and the entire Roman people gave me the title of "father of the country" and decreed that this title should be inscribed in the vestibule of my house, in the Julian senate house, and in the Augustan Forum on the pedestal of the chariot which was set up in my honor by decree of the senate. At the time I wrote this document I was in my seventy-sixth year.

Propaganda for the New Order

Propaganda is an important component of the success of any new government or regime. It has been asserted that if people are told things often enough, they will believe them. One of the great accomplishments of the Augustan principate was the establishment and maintenance of a period of peace and stability that lasted for over two hundred years. It was during the Pax Romana, or the Roman Peace, as it was called, that Roman roads, aqueducts, and baths were built, the provinces of the empire flourished, the Roman legal system developed, and Christianity grew. Augustus cultivated his poets well; in turn, they celebrated the new order. He is remembered particularly through their efforts, as the following selections indicate.

The Peace of Augustus

HORACE

Phoebus, as I was about to celebrate
battles and cities conquered, twanged on the lyre,
    warning me not to hoist a small sail
        on the Tuscan sea. Your era, Caesar [Augustus],

has brought plentiful harvests back to the fields,
and restored to our shrine of Jove the banners
    torn from the high and mighty poles
        of the Parthians, and closed Janus' temple,

"The Peace of Augustus" is from Horace, Odes, 4.15, in *The Odes and Epodes of Horace,* trans. Joseph P. Clancy (Chicago: University of Chicago Press, 1960), pp. 186–187. Copyright © 1960 by the University of Chicago. Reprinted by permission of the publisher.

This depiction of Augustus and his family is from the Altar of Peace, constructed in 9 B.C.E. to commemorate his new secure world order. The presentation of family as a stabilizing element was a primary topic of Augustan propaganda. His own family caused him no end of concern and difficulty. *(Perry M. Rogers)*

for no war was on, and imposed restrictions
on the freedom that wandered beyond proper
    boundaries, and expelled wrongdoing,
        and recalled the ancestral way of life

by which the Latin name of the power of
Italy grew, and the fame of the empire
    and its majesty stretched from the sun's
        western bed to the place of his rising.

While the state is in Caesar's [Augustus'] charge, no civil
madness, no disturbance shall drive away peace,
    nor shall hatred, that forges its swords
        and transforms poor towns into enemies.

Nor shall those who drink the Danube's deep waters
break the Julian laws, nor shall the Getae,
    the Seres, the faithless Parthians,
        nor those born near the river Tanais.

All of us, on working days and holy days,
among the gifts of laughter-loving Bacchus,
accompanied by wives and children,
    will first, as is proper, pray to the gods,

then, in the way of our fathers, to the sound
of Lydian flutes we will hymn our heroes
and their noble achievements and Troy,
    Anchises, and kind Venus' descendants.

"To Spare the Conquered and Crush the Proud"
VIRGIL

Now then, I shall describe the future glory that is to attend the Trojan people, the descendants from the Italian people that await you, illustrious souls destined to succeed to our name, and I shall unfold to you your fate. . . . Romulus, son of Mars . . . do you see how a double plume stands on his helmet, and how his father marks him out even now by his distinctive badge as one of the gods? Yes, my son, it is under his auspices that glorious Rome will extend her empire to the ends of the earth and her heroism to the sky, and will encircle together her seven hills with a wall, fortunate in her brood of heroes. . . . Now turn your eyes here, behold this stock, your Romans. Here is Caesar and the whole progeny of Iulus, destined to come under the great vault of the sky. This, this is he, the man you have heard promised to you so often, Augustus Caesar, son of a god, who will once again establish the Golden Age. . . .

Those souls, now, which you see equally agleam in armor, harmonious now and as long as they are confined in darkness, alas! How great a war will they wage against each other if they reach the light of day, what battles, what carnage will ensue, the father-in-law descending from the ramparts of the Alps . . . the son-in-law arrayed against him with the forces of the east! [This is an allusion to the civil war between Pompey and Julius Caesar.] Do not, do not, my children, cherish such wars of your country; and do you first, you who derive your descent from the gods, do you forbear, cast the weapons from your hands, my descendant. . . .

Others, doubtless, will mould lifelike bronze with greater delicacy, will win from marble the look of life, will plead cases better, chart the motions of the sky with the rod and foretell the risings of the stars. You, O Roman, remember to rule the nations with might. This will be your genius—to impose the way of peace, to spare the conquered and crush the proud.

CHRONOLOGY: Breakdown and Rebirth: The Crisis of the Roman Republic

149–146 B.C.E.   Rome destroys Carthage in Third Punic War and Corinth in 146 B.C.E. Rome extends its control over the Mediterranean world.

133 B.C.E.   The tribune, Tiberius Gracchus, proposes redistributing senatorial estates among Roman people. He is killed during an ensuing riot. Breakdown of Roman unity begins.

120–78 B.C.E.   Ascendancy of the generals, Marius and Sulla. Roman armies become more loyal to individual generals than to the state.

78–50 B.C.E.   Competition for position and influence among Pompey, Crassus, and Caesar.

63 B.C.E.   Cicero becomes consul and thwarts Catilinarian Conspiracy.

60 B.C.E.   Political alliance known as the First Triumvirate established between Caesar, Pompey, and Crassus.

49–45 B.C.E.   Civil war between senatorial supporters under Pompey, and Caesar's popular faction. Pompey is murdered in Egypt, Caesar defeats Pompey's supporters and controls Roman world.

44 B.C.E.   Assassination of Julius Caesar by Brutus, Cassius, and other Republicans, who decry Caesar's despotism.

44 B.C.E.–31 B.C.E.   Competition for power between Octavian, Caesar's heir, and Mark Antony, Caesar's friend and general. Cicero murdered by Antony's men.

31 B.C.E.   Octavian destroys Cleopatra's fleet at Actium, and Mark Antony commits suicide. Octavian in control of the Roman world.

27 B.C.E.–14 C.E.   Octavian "restores" the Roman Republic and assumes the title Augustus. Government is a republic in form, but a despotism in fact.

STUDY QUESTIONS

1. Violence seems to be a key to understanding the fall of the Roman Republic and the establishment of the Augustan principate. Use this "key" to analyze the primary sources. How and why was violence employed? When you consider all the primary sources, why did the Romans, who had a long tradition of moderation, succumb to violence? Is violence symptomatic of the decline of a civilization?
2. What role did armies play in the decline of the Republic and the transformation to the Augustan principate? What was the essential problem with the loyalty of the armies during this period?
3. Compare the great personalities of the age. What qualities did they possess in common? What abilities were unique to each?

4. Why was Julius Caesar assassinated? Did his actions appear to you to be tyranni-cal? After his assassination, his murderers made no plans, thinking that the Re-public, once freed of the dictator, would be restored automatically. Why is this considered a naïve idea? Should the conspirators also have killed Mark Antony? Why or why not?

5. Cicero seems like such an unusual individual during this period. How did he dif-fer from his rivals such as Pompey, Crassus, and Mark Antony? How did Cicero achieve power, and why was he killed? What do his career and death tell you about the nature of power in the late Republic?

6. What options for ruling the state did Octavian have after he defeated Antony? What was his political solution to the collapse of the Roman Republic? What are Tacitus's specific criticisms of the Augustan system?

7. Analyze "The Accomplishments of Augustus." Note the specific vocabulary in section 1. Which words have the greatest impact and why? What is Augustus trying to tell you in this document? Are there any phrases throughout that are designed to show Augustus in a good light but mask the truth? Note specifi-cally section 34 in this regard.

8. Read the quote by Machiavelli at the beginning of this chapter. Do you agree with it? What role does propaganda have in the success of a new government?

9. In section 34 of "The Accomplishments of Augustus," Augustus says, "I excelled all in authority, but I possessed no more power than others who were my col-leagues in each magistracy." The authority of the emperor was the basis for the success of the Augustan principate. What is the difference between "power" and "authority"? Can you relate this concept to the presidency of the United States? Does the success of our president depend on his power or his authority?

10. The Augustan system of government has often been regarded as a "sham," a deception that made the people feel they had control of their government when in fact they did not. Is freedom most importantly a thing of the mind? If the institutions of government are controlled yet *appear* to be free, and if you *feel* that you are free, are you free? How important is it to be *truly* free? Can you comment on this question using contemporary examples from the world around you?

5

Caesar and Christ

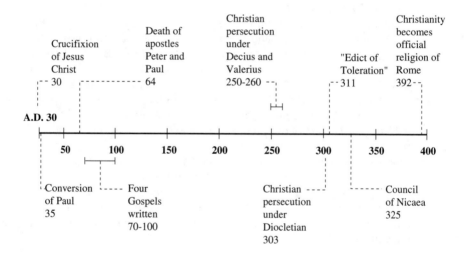

Christianity, above all, has given a clear-cut answer to the demands of the human soul.

—Alexis Carrel

The blood of martyrs is the seed of the Church.

—Tertullian

The tyrant dies and his rule ends, the martyr dies and his rule begins.

—Søren Kierkegaard

So urgent . . . is the necessity of believing, that the fall of any system of mythology will probably be succeeded by the introduction of some other mode of superstition.

—Edward Gibbon

CHAPTER THEMES

- ***Beliefs and Spirituality:***   What are the basic tenets of the Christian religion? How did they differ from the values and beliefs of Roman state religion, other mystery cults, and paganism in general?

- ***Church/State Relationships:***   Why did the Romans, who easily tolerated so many other religious cults, find the Christian religious movement so dangerous? Why were Christians persecuted? Can one serve both Caesar and Christ at the same time with equal devotion?

- ***Historical Change and Transition:***   How did Christianity survive persecution and become the official religion of the Roman Empire by the fourth century C.E.? Was persecution essential to the victory of Christianity? In what ways did Christianity change the civilization of Rome? How did Christianity provide the foundation for medieval civilization?

- ***The Big Picture:***   To what extent does any society depend on a religious base? Does religion contribute to political and social stability or instability? How important is mythology to the character and success of a civilization?

The Roman Empire in the first and second centuries C.E. was a model of administrative excellence. Aqueducts, sewers, and public baths contributed to the cleanliness and convenience of city dwellers, and a vast highway network linked the provinces to the city of Rome. Although a few incompetent emperors and a major civil war threatened the political stability of the state, the government of the principate, which Augustus had established, functioned well. The frontiers of the empire were, for the most part, well defended, and the Roman peace (*Pax Romana*) ensured the maintenance of Western Civilization. As the great eighteenth-century historian Edward Gibbon remarked, "The empire of Rome comprehended the fairest part of the earth, and the most civilized portion of mankind."

One aspect of civilization that stabilized Roman society was religion. The Romans had traditionally considered religion an important part of the prosperity of the state. They had established an intricate system of worship that employed nature gods, pagan deities syncretized from the Greeks, and a priesthood that saw to it the state enjoyed a close relationship with the gods by divining the future through the reading of animal entrails and the interpretation of omens. The state religion during the first century C.E. also came to include the worship of the emperor. Sacrifices to his health, however, were primarily patriotic in nature and did not demand or even encourage the emotional involvement of the people. For such satisfaction, many turned to the consoling logic of philosophy or the emotional excitement of oriental mystery cults.

During the period of the Republic, the Roman state had come into contact with several religious cults, such as those worshiping Isis, Cybele, Mithras, and Dionysus, and had tolerated them so long as they did not disturb the peace or break Roman law. In fact, the cults provided an emotional outlet that the Roman state religion did not supply. Roman toleration of foreign customs and religions had helped maintain the empire. The Jews, for example, were respected by the Romans and even accorded special protection and tax exemption. This toleration ended when the Jews, objecting to the Roman presence in their land, revolted in 66 C.E. The Romans methodically crushed the rebellion four years later, by overrunning the Jewish fortification at Masada.

As a result, the Temple at Jerusalem was destroyed, and the Jews were required to pay taxes directly to the Romans. The lesson was clear: Religion would be tolerated so long as it did not serve as a basis for political action—especially rebellion.

The growth of Christianity from an obscure Jewish sect to the official religion of the Roman Empire during the first through fourth centuries is one of the most fascinating dramas in history. But success for Christianity did not come easily. In addition to facing competition from religious cults and philosophies, Christianity labored under misunderstandings fostered by anti-Christian propaganda. The Roman state was concerned not only with what was described as a morally dissolute religion, but perhaps most of all with the threat Christianity posed to the political stability of the state. Christians refused to worship the emperor (merely a token of political allegiance), and their talk of a "messiah" and a "kingdom" connoted political unrest and agitation. Rome tried to punish and even eradicate the religion in sporadic persecutions (Nero in 64, Decius in 250, Diocletian and Galerius from 303 to 311), but Roman policy was often confused and ambivalent. By 311, Christianity was tolerated and later endorsed by the Emperor Constantine. By the end of the fourth century, Christianity had become the official religion of the Roman Empire.

In this chapter, we shall look closely at the relationship between Christianity and the Roman state. The theme of religious versus secular authority is fundamentally important in Western Civilization. Which is more powerful? Which legacy is more enduring? To what extent does a society need a religious base, and how does religion contribute to political and social stability or instability? These issues are all essential to our understanding of civilization; they play a particularly important role in the history of Rome.

Roman State Religion and the Mystery Cults

The Roman government was very strict in its own adherence to the state religion. Certain priesthoods even offered formulaic prayers to the gods for the safety and security of the state. In some ways, this practice resembled a legal contract that provided a sacrifice in return for a service. Since the Romans did not worship living beings, a sacrifice for the health of the emperor did not demonstrate much more than political loyalty. Such practices were devoid of emotion or personal commitment, so many turned for solace to the Eastern mystery cults. As the following selections reveal, the popularity and frenzied ritual of the various cults demonstrated the need for such an outlet, and they alerted Rome to its responsibility for keeping an orderly society.

Formulaic Prayers

Formalism of the State Religion

PLINY

To slaughter a sacrificial victim without a prayer does not seem to be of any avail or to constitute due consultation of the gods. In addition, there is one formula for obtaining favorable omens, another for averting evil, another for praising the gods. And we see that the highest magistrates employ formula in their prayers, that not a single word may be omitted or said out of its proper place, that someone dictates from writing [the formula to the magistrate], and another is assigned as watcher to listen carefully, and a third is placed in charge of ordering that ceremonial silence be maintained, while a flutist plays to prevent any other words from being heard. There are memorable instances on record of the times when unlucky portents impeded and spoiled [the ceremony], and when there was a mistake in the prayer....

Sacrifices for the Emperor Nero

In the same consulship, on October 13, Lucius Salvius Otho Titianus, master of the college, performed the following sacrifices in the name of the Arval Brethren in the Capitol in behalf of the rule of Nero Claudius Caesar Augus-

"Formalism of the State Religion" is from Pliny, *Natural History*, 28.3.10–12, in *Roman Civilization, Sourcebook II: The Empire*, ed. N. Lewis and M. Reinhold, p. 552. Copyright © 1955 by Columbia University Press. Reprinted by permission of the publisher.

"Sacrifices for the Emperor Nero" is from N. Lewis and M. Reinhold, eds. *Roman Civilization, Sourcebook II: The Empire*, p. 554. Copyright © 1955 by Columbia University Press. Reprinted by permission of the publisher.

tus Germanicus: to Jupiter, an ox; to Juno, a cow; to Minerva, a cow; to Public Felicity, a cow; to the genius of the emperor, a bull; to the deified Augustus, an ox; to the deified Augusta, a cow; to the deified Claudius, an ox. . . .

The Imperial Cult
The Deification of Augustus
DIO CASSIUS

[The senate] declared Augustus immortal, assigned to him a college of priests and sacred rites, and made Livia [his wife], who was already called Julia and Augusta, his priestess; . . . On her part, she bestowed a million sesterces upon a certain Numerius Atticus, a senator and ex-praetor, because he swore that he had seen Augustus ascending to heaven in the manner of the traditions concerning Proculus and Romulus. A shrine voted by the senate and built by Livia and Tiberius was erected to him in Rome, and others in many different places, some of the communities building them voluntarily and others unwillingly. Also the house at Nola where he passed away was made a precinct sacred to him. While his shrine in Rome was being erected, they placed a golden image of him on a couch in the temple of Mars and to this they paid all the honors that they were afterwards to give his statue. Other honors voted him were that his image should not be borne in anybody's funeral procession, that the consuls should celebrate his birthday with games like those in honor of Mars, and that the tribunes of the plebs, since they were sacrosanct, should manage these Augustan Games. These officials conducted everything in the customary manner. . . .

The Mystery Cults
Invasion of the Eastern Cults
MINUCIUS FELIX

Hence it is that throughout wide empires, provinces, and towns, we see each people having its own individual rites and worshipping the local gods—the Eleusinians Ceres, the Phrygians the Great Mother, the Epidaurians Aesculapius, the Chaldaeans Baal, the Syrians Astarte, the Taurians Diana, the

"The Deification of Augustus" is reprinted by permission of the publishers and the Loeb Classical Library from Dio Cassius, *Roman History,* 56.46, trans. Earnest Cary (Cambridge, Mass.: Harvard University Press, 1924), vol. 7, pp. 105–107.

"Invasion of the Eastern Cults" is reprinted by permission of the publishers and the Loeb Classical Library from Minucius Felix, *Octavius,* 6, 23.1, trans. Gerold H. Rendall (Cambridge, Mass.: Harvard University Press, 1931), pp. 327, 329, 381, 383.

Gauls Mercury, the Romans one and all. Thus it is that their power and authority have embraced the circuit of the whole world, and have advanced the bounds of the Empire beyond the paths of the sun and the confines of ocean; while they practice in the field god-fearing valor, make strong their city with awe of sacred rites, with chaste virgins, with many a priestly dignity and title. . . . In captured fortresses, even in the first flush of victory, they reverence the conquered deities. Everywhere they entertain the gods and adopt them as their own; they raise altars even to the unknown deities, and to the spirits of the dead. Thus is it that they adopt the sacred rites of all nations, and withal have earned dominion. . . .

Consider the sacred rites of the mysteries; you will find tragic deaths, dooms, funerals, mourning and lamentations of woebegone gods. Isis, with her Dog-head and shaven priests, mourning, bewailing, and searching for her lost son; her miserable votaries beating their breasts and mimicking the sorrows of the unhappy mother; then, when the stripling is found, Isis rejoices, her priests jump for joy, the Dog-head glories in his discovery; and, year by year, they cease not to lose what they find or to find what they lose. Is it not absurd either to mourn your object of worship, or to worship your object of mourning? Yet these old Egyptian rites have now found their way to Rome, so that you may play the fool to the swallow and sistrum of Isis, the scattered limbs and the empty tomb of your Serapis or Osiris.

Orgiastic Frenzy
APULEIUS

They appeared garbed in various colors, misshapen, their faces smeared with foul paint and their eyes painted with oil, wearing turbans, saffron-colored vestments, and garments of fine linen and silk; and some wore white tunics painted with purple stripes in all directions like little spears, girt with belts, their feet shod with yellow shoes. . . . Then with their arms naked up to their shoulders, holding up huge swords and axes, they shout and dance a frenzied dance, aroused by the sound of the pipe. After we had passed not a few cottages, we came to the villa of a certain rich property owner, where as soon as they entered they let forth with discordant howlings and darted about in a frenzied way. And for a long time they would bend their heads down, twist their necks with supple movements, and whirl their hanging hair in a circle. And sometimes they would take to biting their own flesh, and finally each one cut his arms with the two-edged sword he was carrying, while one of them, who was more frenzied, panting rapidly from the depths of his heart, as though he were filled with the divine spirit of deity, feigned he was smitten with madness. . . . He began to speak with

"Orgiastic Frenzy" is from Apuleius, *The Golden Ass*, 8.27–28, in *Roman Civilization, Sourcebook II: The Empire*, ed. N. Lewis and M. Reinhold, pp. 578–579. Copyright © 1955 by Columbia University Press. Reprinted by permission of the publisher.

a noisy prophecy, inventing a lie, assailing and accusing himself, alleging that he had perpetrated some wrong against the rules of the holy religion, and demanding just punishment at his own hands for the noxious crime. And finally, seizing a whip, a special accoutrement of these effeminate men . . . he scourged himself. . . . You might see the ground wet and defiled with the effeminate blood from the cutting of the swords and the blows of the scourges. . . . But when at length they were weary, or at least satisfied with lacerating themselves, they put a stop to this bloody business. . . .

The Message of Jesus

The New Testament of the Bible records the life of Jesus in four Gospels (Matthew, Mark, Luke, and John), the Acts of the Apostles, twenty-one Epistles (didactic letters), and the Book of Revelation. The New Testament is the primary source for the teaching of Jesus, who was crucified by the Romans about 30 C.E. The following excerpts relate some of the more pacifistic Christian beliefs regarding love, sympathy, forgiveness, and the nature of the Kingdom of God.

The Baptism of Jesus

At that time Jesus went from Galilee to the Jordan, and came to John to be baptized by him. But John tried to make him change his mind. "I ought to be baptized by you," John said, "yet you come to me!" But Jesus answered him, "Let it be this way for now. For in this way we shall do all that God requires." So John agreed.

As soon as Jesus was baptized, he came up out of the water. Then heaven was opened to him, and he saw the Spirit of God coming down like a dove and lighting on him. And then a voice said from heaven, "This is my own dear Son, with whom I am well pleased.". . .

From that time Jesus began to preach his message: "Turn away from your sins! The Kingdom of heaven is near!"

The Sermon on the Mount

Jesus went all over Galilee, teaching in their meeting houses, preaching the Good News of the Kingdom, and healing people from every kind of disease and sickness. The news about him spread through the whole country of Syria,

"The Baptism of Jesus" is from Matthew 3:13–17, 4:17, from the *Good News New Testament, The New Testament in Today's English Version*, 4th ed. (1976). Copyright © American Bible Society 1966, 1971, 1976. Reprinted by permission. All subsequent references to the New Testament are reprinted from this translation.

"The Sermon on the Mount" is from Matthew 4:23–25; 5:1–25, 5:38–48, 6:5–15.

so that people brought him all those who were sick with all kinds of diseases, and afflicted with all sorts of troubles: people with demons, and epileptics and paralytics—Jesus healed them all. Great crowds followed him from Galilee and the Ten Towns, from Jerusalem, Judea, and the land on the other side of the Jordan.

Jesus saw the crowds and went up a hill, where he sat down. His disciples gathered around him, and he began to teach them:

"Happy are those who know they are spiritually poor:
the Kingdom of heaven belongs to them!
"Happy are those who mourn:
God will comfort them!
"Happy are the meek:
they will receive what God has promised!
"Happy are those whose greatest desire is to do what
God requires:
God will satisfy them fully!
"Happy are those who show mercy to others:
God will show mercy to them!
"Happy are the pure in heart:
they will see God!
"Happy are those who work for peace among men:
God will call them his sons!
"Happy are those who will suffer persecution because they
do what God requires:
the Kingdom of heaven belongs to them!

"Happy are you when men insult you and mistreat you and tell all kinds of evil lies against you because you are my followers. Rejoice and be glad, because a great reward is kept for you in heaven. This is how men mistreated the prophets who lived before you.

"You are like salt for the earth. If the salt loses its taste, there is no way to make it salty again. It has become worthless, and so it is thrown away where people walk on it.

"You are like the light for the world. A city built on a high hill cannot be hid. Nobody lights a lamp to put it under a bowl; instead he puts it on the lamp-stand, where it gives light for everyone in the house. In the same way your light must shine before people, so that they will see the good things you do and give praise to your Father in heaven.

"Do not think that I have come to do away with the Law of Moses and the teaching of the prophets. I have not come to do away with them, but to give them real meaning. Remember this! As long as heaven and earth last, the least point or the smallest detail of the Law will not be done away with—not until the end of all things. Therefore, whoever breaks even the smallest of the commandments, and teaches others to do the same, will be least in the Kingdom of heaven. On the other hand, whoever obeys the Law, and teaches others to do the same, will be great in the Kingdom of heaven. I tell you, then, you will be able to enter the Kingdom of heaven only if your standard of life is far above the standard of the teachers of the Law and the Pharisees.

"You have heard that men were told in the past, 'Do not murder; anyone who commits murder will be brought before the judge.' But now I tell you: whoever is angry with his brother will be brought before the judge; whoever calls his brother 'You good-for-nothing!' will be brought before the Council; and whoever calls his brother a worthless fool will be in danger of going to the fire of hell. So if you are about to offer your gift to God at the altar and there you remember that your brother has something against you, leave your gift there in front of the altar and go at once to make peace with your brother; then come back and offer your gift to God. . . .

"You have heard that it was said, 'An eye for an eye, and a tooth for a tooth.' But now I tell you: do not take revenge on someone who does you wrong. If anyone slaps you on the right cheek, let him slap your left cheek too. And if someone takes you to court to sue you for your shirt, let him have your coat as well. And if one of the occupation troops forces you to carry his pack one mile, carry it another mile. When someone asks you for something, give it to him; when someone wants to borrow something, lend it to him.

"You have heard that it was said, 'Love your friends, hate your enemies.' But now I tell you: love your enemies, and pray for those who mistreat you, so that you will become the sons of your Father in heaven. For he makes his sun to shine on bad and good people alike, and gives rain to those who do right and those who do wrong. Why should you expect God to reward you, if you love only the people who love you? Even the tax collectors do that! And if you speak only to your friends, have you done anything out of the ordinary? Even the pagans do that! You must be perfect—just as your Father in heaven is perfect. . . .

"And when you pray, do not be like the hypocrites! They love to stand up and pray in the meeting houses and on the street corners so that everybody will see them. Remember this! They have already been paid in full. But when you pray, go to your room and close the door, and pray to your Father who is unseen. And your Father, who sees what you do in private, will reward you.

"In your prayers do not use a lot of words, as the pagans do, who think that God will hear them because of their long prayers. Do not be like them; God is your Father and he already knows what you need before you ask him. This is the way you should pray:

> Our Father in heaven:
> May your name be kept holy,
> May your Kingdom come,
> May your will be done on earth as it is in heaven.
> Give us today the food we need;
> Forgive us what we owe you as we forgive what others owe us;
> Do not bring us to hard testing, but keep us safe from Evil. . . .

For if you forgive others the wrongs they have done you, your Father in heaven will forgive you. But if you do not forgive others, then your Father in heaven will not forgive the wrongs you have done."

The Good Samaritan

Then a certain teacher of the Law came up and tried to trap him. "Teacher," he asked, "what must I do to receive eternal life?" Jesus answered him, "What do the scriptures say? How do you interpret them?" The man answered: "'You must love the Lord your God with all your heart, and with all your soul, and with all your strength, and with all your mind'; and, 'You must love your neighbor as yourself.'" "Your answer is correct," replied Jesus; "do this and you will live."

But the teacher of the Law wanted to put himself in the right, so he asked Jesus, "Who is my neighbor?" Jesus answered: "A certain man was going down from Jerusalem to Jericho, when robbers attacked him, stripped him and beat him up, leaving him half dead. It so happened that a priest was going down that road; when he saw the man he walked on by, on the other side. In the same way a Levite also came there, went over and looked at the man, and then walked on by, on the other side. But a certain Samaritan who was travelling that way came upon him, and when he saw the man his heart was filled with pity. He went over to him, poured oil and wine on his wounds and bandaged them; then he put the man on his own animal and took him to an inn, where he took care of him. The next day he took out two silver coins and gave them to the innkeeper. 'Take care of him,' he told the innkeeper, 'and when I come back this way I will pay you back whatever you spend on him.'" And Jesus concluded, "Which one of these three seems to you to have been a neighbor to the man attacked by the robbers?" The teacher of the Law answered, "The one who was kind to him." Jesus replied, "You go, then, and do the same."

The Mission of Jesus

One of the more difficult regions of the empire for the Roman government to manage was the province of Judea. Encompassing the Jewish homeland, it was a continual hotbed of disagreement and dissatisfaction. The career of a Roman administrator might easily be placed in jeopardy if he failed to maintain peace. Although much of this dissent was in response to Roman occupation of the area, various Jewish sects also competed among themselves for influence in the region. Thus, the appearance of a young, popular leader who was proclaimed by some as "King of the Jews" and who himself claimed to be the long-awaited Messiah, gave pause to both the Jewish hierarchy and Roman authorities. The following selections from Matthew reveal Jesus' own conception of his mission.

"The Good Samaritan" is from Luke 10:25–37.

Instructions to the Twelve Disciples

Jesus called his twelve disciples together and gave them power to drive out the evil spirits and to heal every disease and every sickness. These are the names of the twelve apostles: first, Simon (called Peter) and his brother Andrew; James and his brother John, the sons of Zebedee; Philip and Bartholomew; Thomas and Matthew, the tax collector; James, the son of Alphaeus, and Thaddaeus; Simon the patriot, and Judas Iscariot, who betrayed Jesus.

Jesus sent these twelve men out with the following instructions: "Do not go to any Gentile territory or any Samaritan towns. Go, instead, to the lost sheep of the people of Israel. Go and preach, 'The Kingdom of heaven is near!' Heal the sick, raise the dead, make the lepers clean, drive out demons. You have received without paying, so give without being paid; do not carry a beggar's bag for the trip, or an extra shirt, or shoes, or a walking stick. A worker should be given what he needs.

"When you come to a town or village, go in and look for someone who is willing to welcome you, and stay with him until you leave that place. When you go into a house say, 'Peace be with you.' If the people in that house welcome you, let your greeting of peace remain; but if they do not welcome you, then take back your greeting. And if some home or town will not welcome you or listen to you, then leave that place and shake the dust off your feet. Remember this! On the Judgment Day God will show more mercy to the people of Sodom and Gomorrah than to the people of that town!

"Listen! I am sending you just like sheep to a pack of wolves. You must be as cautious as snakes and as gentle as doves. Watch out, for there will be men who will arrest you and take you to court, and they will whip you in their meeting houses. You will be brought to trial before rulers and kings for my sake, to tell the Good News to them and to the Gentiles. When they bring you to trial, do not worry about what you are going to say or how you will say it; when the time comes, you will be given what you will say. For the words you speak will not be yours; they will come from the Spirit of your Father speaking in you.

"Men will hand over their own brothers to be put to death, and fathers will do the same to their children; children will turn against their parents and have them put to death. Everyone will hate you, because of me. But the person who holds out to the end will be saved. And when they persecute you in one town, run away to another one. I tell you, you will not finish your work in all the towns of Israel before the Son of Man comes. . . .

"Do not think that I have come to bring peace to the world; no, I did not come to bring peace, but a sword. I came to set sons against their fathers, daughters against their mothers, daughters-in-law against their mothers-in-law; a man's worst enemies will be the members of his own family.

"Instructions to the Twelve Disciples" is from Matthew 10:1–42.

"Whoever loves his father or mother more than me is not worthy of me; whoever loves his son or daughter more than me is not worthy of me. Whoever does not take up his cross and follow in my steps is not worthy of me. Whoever tries to gain his own life will lose it: whoever loses his life for my sake will gain it.

"Whoever welcomes you, welcomes me; and whoever welcomes me, welcomes the one who sent me. Whoever welcomes God's messenger because he is God's messenger will share in his reward; and whoever welcomes a truly good man, because he is that, will share in his reward. And remember this! Whoever gives even a drink of cold water to one of the least of these my followers, because he is my follower, will certainly receive his reward.". . .

Peter: The Rock

Jesus went to the territory near the town of Caesarea Phillipi, where he asked his disciples, "Who do men say the Son of Man is?" "Some say John the Baptist," they answered. "Others say Elijah, while others say Jeremiah or some other prophet." "What about you?" he asked them. "Who do you say I am?" Simon Peter answered, "You are the Messiah, the Son of the living God." "Simon, son of John, you are happy indeed!" answered Jesus. "For this truth did not come to you from any human being, it was given to you directly by my Father in heaven. And so I tell you: you are a rock, Peter, and on this rock I will build my church. Not even death will ever be able to overcome it. I will give you the keys of the Kingdom of heaven: what you prohibit on earth will be prohibited in heaven; what you permit on earth will be permitted in heaven." Then Jesus ordered his disciples that they were not to tell anyone that he was the Messiah.

Suffering, Persecution, and the Son of Man

From that time on Jesus began to say plainly to his disciples: "I must go to Jerusalem and suffer much from the elders, the chief priests, and the teachers of the Law. I will be put to death, and on the third day I will be raised to life." Peter took him aside and began to rebuke him. "God forbid it, Lord!" he said. "This must never happen to you!" Jesus turned around and said to Peter: "Get away from me, Satan! You are an obstacle in my way, for these thoughts of yours are men's thoughts, not God's!"

Then Jesus said to his disciples: "If anyone wants to come with me, he must forget himself, carry his cross, and follow me. For the man who wants to save his own life will lose it; but the man who loses his life for my sake will find it. Will a man gain anything if he wins the whole world but loses his life? Of

"Peter: Rock" is from Matthew 16:13–18.
"Suffering, Persecution, and the Son of Man" is from Matthew 16:21–28, 24:3–14, 29.

course not! There is nothing a man can give to regain his life. For the Son of Man is about to come in the glory of his Father with his angels, and then he will repay everyone according to his deeds. Remember this! There are some here who will not die until they have seen the Son of Man come as King.". . . .

As Jesus sat on the Mount of Olives, the disciples came to him in private. "Tell us when all this will be," they asked, "and what will happen to show that it is the time for your coming and the end of the age."

Jesus answered: "Watch out, and do not let anyone fool you. Because many men will come in my name, saying, 'I am the Messiah!' and fool many people. You are going to hear the noise of battles close by and the news of battles far away; but, listen, do not be troubled. Such things must happen, but they do not mean that the end has come. One country will fight another country, one kingdom will attack another kingdom. There will be famines and earthquakes, everywhere. All these things are like the first pains of childbirth.

"Then men will arrest you and hand you over to be punished, and you will be put to death. All mankind will hate you because of me. Many will give up their faith at that time; they will betray each other and hate each other. Then many false prophets will appear and fool many people. Such will be the spread of evil that many people's love will grow cold. But the person who holds out to the end will be saved. And this Good News about the Kingdom will be preached throughout all the world, for a witness to all mankind—and then will come the end. . . .

"Soon after the trouble of those days the sun will grow dark, the moon will no longer shine, the stars will fall from heaven, and the powers in space will be driven from their course. Then the sign of the Son of Man will appear in the sky; then all the tribes of earth will weep, and they will see the Son of Man coming on the clouds of heaven with power and great glory. The great trumpet will sound, and he will send out his angels to the four corners of the earth, and they will gather his chosen people from one end of the world to the other. . . ."

The Final Judgment

"When the Son of Man comes as King, and all the angels with him, he will sit on his royal throne, and all the earth's people will be gathered before him. Then he will divide them into two groups, just as a shepherd separates the sheep from the goats: he will put the sheep at his right and the goats at his left. Then the King will say to the people on his right: 'You who are blessed by my Father: come! Come and receive the kingdom which has been prepared for you ever since the creation of the world. I was hungry and you fed me, thirsty and you gave me drink; I was a stranger and you received me in your homes, naked and you clothed me; I was sick and you took care of me, in prison and you visited me.' The righteous will then answer him: 'When, Lord,

"The Final Judgment" is from Matthew 25:31–46.

did we ever see you hungry and feed you, or thirsty and give you drink? When did we ever see you a stranger and welcome you in our home, or naked and clothe you? When do we ever see you sick or in prison, and visit you?' The King will answer back, 'I tell you, indeed, whenever you did this for one of these poorest brothers of mine, you did it for me!'

"Then he will say to those on his left: 'Away from me, you who are under God's curse! Away to the eternal fire which has been prepared for the Devil and his angels! I was hungry but you would not feed me, thirsty but you would not give me drink; I was a stranger but you would not welcome me in your homes, naked but you would not clothe me; I was sick and in prison but you would not take care of me.' Then they will answer him: 'When, Lord, did we ever see you hungry, or thirsty, or a stranger, or naked, or sick, or in prison, and we would not help you?' The King will answer them back, 'I tell you, indeed, whenever you refused to help one of these poor ones, you refused to help me.' These, then, will be sent off to eternal punishment; the righteous will go to eternal life."

The Work of Paul

Paul of Tarsus (ca.10–65 C.E.) was a Hellenized Jew who had once persecuted Christians before his conversion. He was instrumental in establishing fundamental doctrines and in spreading the teachings of Jesus throughout the Roman Empire, seeking converts among Jews and Gentiles alike on faith, love, and the Resurrection of Christ.

Paul's Answer to the Intellectuals

Christ did not send me to baptize. He sent me to tell the Good News, and to tell it without using the language of men's wisdom, for that would rob Christ's death on the cross of all its power.

For the message about Christ's death on the cross is nonsense to those who are being lost; but for us who are being saved, it is God's power. For the scripture says,

I will destroy the wisdom of the wise,

I will set aside the understanding of the scholars.

So then, where does that leave the wise men? Or the scholars? Or the skillful debaters of this world? God has shown that this world's wisdom is foolishness!

For God in his wisdom made it impossible for men to know him by means of their own wisdom. Instead, God decided to save those who believe, by means of the "foolish" message we preach. Jews want miracles for proof, and

"Paul's Answer to the Intellectuals" is from 1 Corinthians 1:17–2:8.

Greeks look for wisdom. As for us, we proclaim Christ on the cross, a message that is offensive to the Jews and nonsense to the Gentiles, but for those whom God has called, both Jews and Gentiles, this message is Christ, who is the power of God and the wisdom of God. For what seems to be God's foolishness is wiser than men's wisdom, and what seems to be God's weakness is stronger than men's strength.

Now remember what you were, brothers, when God called you. Few of you were wise, or powerful, or of high social status, from the human point of view. God purposely chose what the world considers nonsense in order to put wise men to shame, and what the world considers weak in order to put powerful men to shame. He chose what the world looks down on, and despises, and thinks is nothing, in order to destroy what the world thinks is important. . . .

When I came to you, my brothers, to preach God's secret truth to you, I did not use long words and great learning. For I made up my mind to forget everything while I was with you except Jesus Christ, and especially his death on the cross. So when I came to you I was weak and trembled all over with fear, and my speech and message were not delivered with skillful words of human wisdom, but with convincing proof of the power of God's Spirit. Your faith, then, does not rest on man's wisdom, but on God's power.

Yet I do speak wisdom to those who are spiritually mature. But it is not the wisdom that belongs to this world, or to the powers that rule this world—powers which are losing their power. The wisdom I speak is God's secret wisdom, hidden from men, which God had already chosen for our glory, even before the world was made. None of the rulers of this world knew this wisdom. If they had known it, they would not have nailed the Lord of glory to the cross.

On Faith

For it is through faith that all of you are God's sons in union with Christ Jesus. For all who are baptized into union with Christ have taken upon themselves the qualities of Christ himself. So there is no difference between Jews and Gentiles, between slaves and free men, between men and women: you are all one in union with Christ Jesus. If you belong to Christ, then you are the descendants of Abraham, and will receive what God has promised.

The Resurrection of Christ

And now I want to remind you, brother, of the Good News which I preached to you, which you received, and on which your faith stands firm. That is the gospel, the message that I preached to you. You are saved by the gospel if you hold firmly to it—unless it was for nothing that you believed.

"On Faith" is from Galatians 3:26–29.
"The Resurrection of Christ" is from 1 Corinthians 15:1–22, 31–32, 35–39, 42–55.

I passed on to you what I received, which is of the greatest importance: that Christ died for our sins, as written in the Scriptures; that he was buried and raised to life on the third day, as written in the Scriptures; that he appeared to Peter, and then to all twelve apostles. Then he appeared to more than five hundred of his followers at once, most of whom are still alive, although some have died. Then he appeared to James, and then to all the apostles.

Last of all he appeared also to me—even though I am like one who was born in a most unusual way. For I am the least of all the apostles—I do not even deserve to be called an apostle, because I persecuted God's church. But by God's grace I am what I am, and the grace that he gave me was not without effect. On the contrary, I have worked harder than all the other apostles, although it was not really my own doing, but God's grace working with me. So then, whether it came from me or from them, this is what we all preach, this is what you believe.

Now, since our message is that Christ has been raised from death, how can some of you say that the dead will not be raised to life? If that is true, it means that Christ was not raised; and if Christ has not been raised from death, then we have nothing to preach, and you have nothing to believe. More than that, we are shown to be lying against God, because we said of him that he raised Christ from death—but if the dead are not raised, neither has Christ been raised. And if Christ has not been raised, then your faith is a delusion and you are still lost in your sins. It would also mean that the believers in Christ who have died are lost. If our hope in Christ is good for this life only, and no more, then we deserve more pity than anyone else in all the world.

But the truth is that Christ has been raised from death, as the guarantee that those who sleep in death will also be raised. For just as death came by means of a man, in the same way the rising from death comes by means of a man. For just as all men die because of their union to Adam, in the same way all will be raised to life because of their union to Christ. . . .

Brothers, I face death every day! The pride I have in you in our life in Christ Jesus our Lord makes me declare this. If I have fought "wild beasts" here in Ephesus, as it were, simply from human motives, what have I gained? As the saying goes, "Let us eat and drink, for tomorrow we will die"—if the dead are not raised to life. . . .

Someone will ask, "How can the dead be raised to life? What kind of body will they have?" You fool! When you plant a seed in the ground it does not sprout to life unless it dies. And what you plant in the ground is a bare seed, perhaps a grain of wheat, or of some other kind, not the full-bodied plant that will grow up. God provided that seed with the body he wishes; he gives each seed its own proper body. . . .

This is how it will be when the dead are raised to life. When the body is buried it is mortal; when raised, it will be immortal. When buried, it is ugly and weak; when raised, it will be beautiful and strong. When buried, it is a physical body; when raised, it will be a spiritual body. There is, of course, a physical body, so there is bound to be a spiritual body. For the scripture says: "The first man, Adam, was created a living being"; but the last Adam is the lifegiving Spirit. It is not the spiritual that comes first, but the physical, and then the spiritual. The first Adam was made of the dust of the earth; the second Adam came from heaven. Those who belong to the earth are like the one who was made of earth; those who are of heaven are like the one who came from heaven. Just as we wear the likeness of the men made of earth, so we will wear the likeness of the Man from heaven.

This is what I mean, brothers: what is made of flesh and blood cannot share in God's Kingdom, and what is mortal cannot possess immortality.

Listen to this secret: we shall not all die, but in an instant we shall all be changed, as quickly as the blinking of an eye, when the last trumpet sounds. For when it sounds, the dead will be raised immortal beings, and we shall all be changed. For what is mortal must clothe itself with what is immortal: what will die must clothe itself with what cannot die. So when what is mortal has been clothed with what is immortal, and when what will die has been clothed with what cannot die, then the scripture will come true: "Death is destroyed: victory is complete!"

"Where, O Death, is your victory?

Where, O Death, is your power to hurt?"

On Love

I may be able to speak the languages of men and even of angels, but if I have not love, my speech is no more than a noisy gong or a clanging bell. I may have the gift of inspired preaching; I may have all knowledge and understand all secrets; I may have all the faith needed to move mountains—but if I have not love, I am nothing. I may give away everything I have, and even give up my body to be burned—but if I have not love, it does me no good.

Love is patient and kind; love is not jealous, or conceited, or proud; love is not ill-mannered, or selfish, or irritable; love does not keep a record of wrongs; love is not happy with evil, but is happy with the truth. Love never gives up: its faith, hope, and patience never fail.

Love is eternal. There are inspired messages, but they are temporary; there are gifts of speaking, but they will cease; there is knowledge, but it will pass. For our gifts of knowledge and of inspired messages are only partial; but when what is perfect comes, then what is partial disappears.

When I was a child, my speech, feelings, and thinking were all those of a child; now that I am a man, I have no more use for childish ways. What we see now is like the dim image in a mirror; then we shall see face to face. What I know now is only partial; then it will be complete, as complete as God's knowledge of me.

Meanwhile these three remain: faith, hope, and love; and the greatest of these is love.

"On Love" is from 1 Corinthians 13:1–13.

Conflict and the Development of the Christian Church

Roman Imperial Policy

The Persecution Under Nero (64 C.E.)

TACITUS

At the beginning of their movement, Christians had difficulty achieving an iden-
tity distinct from the Jews. But by the middle of the first century C.E., they had
begun to spread Jesus' beliefs into the provinces. Christianity was not immedi-
ately popular, and many despised the missionaries for their zealous conversion
methods. Paul himself had difficulty appealing to the Athenians in 51 C.E. The
first recorded persecution of Christians took place in 64 C.E. when the emperor
Nero blamed a destructive fire in Rome on them in order to deflect suspicion from
himself. It was in this persecution, confined to the city of Rome, that Saint Peter
and Saint Paul were killed.

All human efforts, all the lavish gifts of the emperor, and the propitiations
of the gods, did not banish the sinister belief that the fire was the result of
an order. Consequently, to get rid of the report, Nero fastened the guilt
and inflicted the most exquisite tortures on a class hated for their abominations, called Christians by the populace. Christus, from whom the name had
its origin, suffered the death penalty during the reign of Tiberius at the
hands of one of our procurators, Pontius Pilate, and a most mischievous superstition, thus checked for the moment, again broke out not only in
Judea, the first source of the evil, but even in Rome, where all things
hideous and shameful from every part of the world find their centre and become popular. Accordingly, an arrest was first made of all who pleaded
guilty; then, upon their information, an immense multitude was convicted,
not so much of the crime of firing the city, as of hatred against mankind.
Mockery of every sort was added to their deaths. Covered with the skins of
beasts, they were torn by dogs and perished, or were nailed to crosses, or
were doomed to the flames and burnt, to serve as a nightly illumination,
when daylight had expired. . . . Even for criminals who deserved extreme
and exemplary punishment, there arose a feeling of compassion; for it was
not, as it seemed, for the public good, but to glut one man's cruelty that
they were being destroyed.

"The Persecution Under Nero" is from Tacitus, *Annals*, 15.44, trans. Alfred Church and
William Brodribb (New York: Macmillan, 1891).

The Correspondence Between Trajan and Pliny

The emperor Trajan (d. 117) enjoyed a reputation as a strong leader whose military conquests added to the empire and whose administrative talents helped secure it. The following selection is a letter from the Roman governor of Bithynia, Pliny the Younger. A friend of Trajan's, Pliny was anxious about maintaining the peace in his province and confused about official policy toward the Christians. Trajan's famous reply is also included.

Letter of Pliny the Younger to Trajan

It is my custom, my Lord, to refer to you all things concerning which I am in doubt. For who can better guide my indecision or enlighten my ignorance?

I have never taken part in the trials of Christians; hence I do not know for what crime or to what extent it is customary to punish or investigate. I have been in no little doubt as to whether any consideration should be given to age, or should the treatment of the young differ from that of the old; whether pardon is granted in case of repentance, or should a man who was once a Christian gain nothing by having ceased to be one; whether the name itself without the proof of crimes, or only the crimes associated with the name, are to be punished.

Meanwhile I have followed this procedure in the case of those who have been brought before me as Christians. I asked them whether they were Christians; those who confessed I questioned a second and a third time, threatening them with punishment; those who persisted I ordered executed. For I did not doubt that, whatever it was that they had confessed, their stubbornness and inflexible obstinacy ought certainly to be punished. There were others of similar madness; but because they were Roman citizens, I signed an order sending them to Rome.

Soon, the crime spreading, as is usual when attention is called to it, more cases arose. An anonymous accusation, containing many names, was presented. Those who denied that they were or had been Christian, ought, I thought, to be dismissed since they repeated after me a prayer to your image; . . . besides, they cursed Christ, one of which things they say those who are really Christians cannot be compelled to do. Others, accused by the informer, said that they were Christians and afterwards denied it; in fact, they had been but had ceased to be, some many years ago, some even twenty years before. They all worshipped your image and the statues of the gods; and cursed Christ. They maintained that the substance of their fault or error had been that on a fixed day they were accustomed to come together before daylight and sing by turns a hymn to Christ as though he were a god, and to bind themselves by oath, not for some crime, nor

"The Correspondence Between Trajan and Pliny" is from Pliny the Younger, *Letters*, 10.96–97, in *Translations and Reprints from the Original Sources of European History*, vol. 4, no. 1, ed. D. C. Munro and Edith Bramhall (Philadelphia, 1898).

to commit robbery, theft, or adultery, nor to betray a trust. . . . After this it was customary to disperse and to come together again to partake of food of an ordinary and harmless kind. Even this they ceased to do after the publication of my edict in which, according to your orders, I had forbidden associations. Hence I believe it the more necessary to examine two female slaves, who were called deaconesses, in order to find out what was true, and to do it by torture. I found nothing but a vicious, extravagant superstition.

Consequently, I postponed the examination and hastened to consult you. For it seemed to me that the subject would justify consultation, especially on account of the number of those involved. For many of all ages, of every rank, and even of both sexes are and will be endangered. The infection of this superstition has not only spread to the cities but also to the villages and country districts. But it seems possible to check it and cure it. It is plain enough that the temples, which had been almost deserted, have begun to be frequented again, that the sacred rites, which had been neglected for a long time, have begun to be restored, and that food for sacrifice, for which until now there was scarcely a purchaser, is sold. From this it is easy to imagine that a multitude of people can be reclaimed if repentance is permitted.

Trajan's Reply

You have followed the correct procedure, my dear Pliny, in conducting the cases of those who were accused before you as Christians, for no general rule can be laid down as a set form. They are not to be sought out; if they are brought before you and convicted, they ought to be punished, with the proviso that whoever denies that he is a Christian and proves it by worshipping our gods, even though he may have been under suspicion in the past, shall obtain pardon on repentance. In no case should attention be paid to anonymous charges, for they afford a bad precedent and are not worthy of our age.

The Persecution Under Diocletian (305 C.E.)
LACTANTIUS

Diocletian was an important emperor who in 285 C.E. instituted reforms that were crucial to the survival of the empire. Still, he persecuted Christians with a zeal not seen since that of the emperor Decius in 250 C.E. This was the last empire-wide persecution, but also the severest and most sustained, lasting from 303 to 311.

On the following day an edict was published providing that men of that religion should be deprived of all honors and rank; that they should be subjected to tor-

"The Persecution Under Diocletian" is from Lactantius, *On the Deaths of the Persecutors,* 12–14, in *Roman Civilization, Sourcebook II: The Empire,* ed. N. Lewis and M. Reinhold, pp. 598–599. Copyright © 1955 by Columbia University Press. Reprinted by permission of the publisher.

ture, from whatever rank and station they might come; that every legal action should be pressed against them, but they themselves were not to have the right to sue for any wrong or for adultery or theft; and finally, that they should be accorded no freedom and no voice. A certain person, although it was wrong, yet with great courage ripped down this edict and tore it up. . . . Brought to judgment at once, he was not only tortured but was burned in the legal manner, and displaying admirable endurance was finally consumed by the flames.

But Galerius [Diocletian's colleague] was not satisfied with the terms of the edict and sought another way to influence Diocletian. For to drive him to a determination to employ an excess of cruelty in persecution, he employed private agents to set the palace on fire; and when some part of it had gone up in flames, the Christians were accused as public enemies, and tremendous prejudice flared up against the very name of Christian as the palace burned. It was said that the Christians had plotted in concert with the eunuchs to destroy the princes, and that the two emperors had almost been burned alive in their own palace. But Diocletian, who always wanted to appear shrewd and intelligent, suspected nothing of the deception; inflamed with anger, he began immediately to torture all his domestics.

Anti-Christian Propaganda

MINUCIUS FELIX

In the confusion surrounding the Christian movement, many pagans were willing to believe whatever they heard about the religion. The following selection is by a Roman lawyer named Minucius Felix around 250 C.E. Note the emphasis on threatening political terms such as "faction" and "conspiracy."

Is it not deplorable that a faction . . . of abandoned, hopeless outlaws makes attacks against the gods? They gather together ignorant persons from the lowest dregs, and credulous women, easily deceived as their sex is, and organize a rabble of unholy conspirators, leagued together in nocturnal associations and by ritual fasts and barbarous foods not for the purpose of some sacred rite but for the sake of sacrilege—a secret tribe that shuns the light, silent in public but talkative in secret places. They despise the temples as if they were tombs, they spit upon the gods, they ridicule our sacred rites. Pitiable themselves, they pity . . . our priests; half-naked themselves, they despise offices and official robes. What amazing folly! What incredible arrogance! They despise present tortures yet dread uncertain future ones; while they fear to die after death, they have no fear of it in the meantime; deceptive hope soothes away their terror with the solace of a life to come.

"Anti-Christian Propaganda" is from Minucius Felix, *Octavius*, 8.3–12.6, in *Roman Civilization, Sourcebook II: The Empire*, ed. N. Lewis and M. Reinhold, pp. 584–585. Copyright © 1955 by Columbia University Press. Reprinted by permission of the publisher.

Already . . . decay of morals spreads from day to day throughout the entire world, and the loathsome shrines of this impious conspiracy multiply. This plot must be completely rooted out and execrated. They recognize one another by secret signs and tokens; they love one another before they are acquainted. Everywhere a kind of religion of lust is also associated with them, and they call themselves promiscuously brothers and sisters, so that ordinary fornication, through the medium of a sacred name, becomes incest. And thus their vain and mad superstition glories in crimes. And for themselves, if there were not a basis of truth, knowing rumor would not tell of gross and unspeakable abominations. I hear that in some absurd conviction or other they consecrate and worship the head of an ass, the most repulsive of beasts—a religion worthy of the morals that begot it. Others say that they reverence the private parts of their director and high priest, and adore them as if belonging to a parent. Whether this is false I know not, but suspicion naturally attaches to secret and nocturnal rites. To say that a man put to death for a crime and the lethal wooden cross are objects of their veneration is to assign altars suitable for abandoned and impious men, the kind of worship they deserve. What is told of the initiation of neophytes is as detestable as it is notorious. An infant covered with a blanket to deceive the unsuspecting is set before the one to be initiated in the rites. The neophyte is induced to strike what seem to be harmless blows on the surface of the blanket, and this infant is killed by his random and unsuspecting blows. Its blood—oh, shocking!—they greedily lap up; the limbs they eagerly distribute; and by this victim they league themselves, and by this complicity in crime they pledge themselves to mutual silence. . . . Their form of banqueting is notorious; everywhere all talk of it. . . . On an appointed day they assemble at a feast with all their children, sisters, and mothers, people of both sexes and every age. There, after much feasting, when the banquet has become heated and intoxication has inflamed the drunken passions of incestuous lust, a dog which has been tied to a lamp is incited to rush and leap forward after a morsel thrown beyond the range of the cord by which it was tied. The telltale light is upset and extinguished, and in the shameless dark they exchange embraces indiscriminately, and all, if not actually, yet by complicity are equally involved in incest. . . .

A Christian Defense

TERTULLIAN

In response to pagan misconception, Christian apologists like Tertullian (c. 160–230 c.e.) sought to clarify and defend the Christian position.

"A Christian Defense" is from Sister Emily Joseph Daly, C.S.J., trans. *Tertullian: Apologetical Works, and Minucius Felix, Octavius* (New York: Fathers of the Church, 1950), vol. X: *Fathers of the Church* (Washington, D.C.: The Catholic University of America Press), pp. 7–8, 10–12, 15–16, 25, 35, 85–86, 88, 102. Reprinted by permission of the publisher.

Magistrates of the Roman Empire, seated as you are before the eyes of all, in al-most the highest position in the state to pronounce judgment: if you are not to conduct an open and public examination and inquiry as to what the real truth is with regard to the Christians; if, in this case alone your authority fears or blushes to conduct a public investigation with the diligence demanded by jus-tice; if, finally—as happened lately in the private courts—hatred of this group has been aroused to the extent that it actually blocks their defense, then let the truth reach your ears by the private and quiet avenue of literature.

Truth makes no appeal on her own behalf, because she does not wonder at her present condition. She knows that she plays the role of an alien on earth, that among strangers she readily discovers enemies, but she has her origin, abode, hope, recompense, and honor in heaven. Meanwhile, there is one thing for which she strives: That she be not condemned without a hearing. . . .

This, then, is the first grievance we lodge against you, the injustice of the hatred you have for the name of Christian. The motive which appears to ex-cuse this injustice is precisely that which both aggravates and convicts it; namely, ignorance. For, what is more unjust than that men should hate what they do not know, even though the matter itself deserves hatred? Only when one knows whether a thing deserves hatred does it deserve it. But, when there is no knowledge of what is deserved, how is the justice of hatred defensible? Men remain in ignorance as long as they hate, and they hate unjustly as long as they remain in ignorance.

The proof of their ignorance, which condemns while it excuses their injus-tice, is this: In the case of all who formerly indulged in hatred [of Christian-ity] because of their ignorance of the nature of what they hated, their hatred comes to an end as soon as their ignorance ceases. . . .

If then, it is decided that we are the most wicked of men, why do you treat us so differently from those who are on a par with us, that is, from all other criminals? . . . Christians alone are permitted to say nothing that would clear their name, vindicate the truth, and aid the judge to come to a fair decision. One thing only is what they wait for; this is the only thing necessary to arouse public hatred: the confession of the name of Christian, not an investigation of the charge. Yet, suppose you are trying any other criminal. If he confesses to the crime of murder, sacrilege, incest, or treason—to particularize the in-dictments hurled against us—you are not satisfied to pass sentence immedi-ately; you weigh the attendant circumstances, the character of the deed, the number of times it was committed, the time, the place, the witnesses, and the partners-in-crime. In our case there is nothing of this sort. No matter what false charge is made against us, we must be made to confess it; for example, how many murdered babies one has devoured, how many deeds of incest one has committed under cover of darkness, what cooks and what dogs were on hand. Oh, what glory for that governor who should have discovered someone who had already consumed a hundred infants! . . .

Now that I have set down these remarks as a preface, as it were, to stigma-tize the injustice of the public hatred against us, I shall take the stand to

The Coliseum in Rome, where hundreds of Christians were sporadically sacrificed to the lions as condemned reprobates during the imperial era in the first through fourth centuries c.e. "If the weather will not change, if there is an earthquake, a famine, a plague—straightway the cry is heard: 'Toss the Christians to the lions!'"—Tertullian. *(Perry M. Rogers)*

defend our innocence. Not only shall I refute the charges which are brought against us, but I shall even hurl them back upon those who make them, so that men may thereby know that [they will find among Christians what they are aware of in themselves]; and that, at the same time, they may blush when, as utter reprobates, they accuse—I do not say the most righteous of men—but, as they themselves would have it, their equals. We shall reply to each charge individually; to those which we are said to commit in secret and to those which we are found to be committing before the eyes of all—charges on the basis of which we are held to be criminals, deceivers, reprobates, and objects of ridicule. . . .

We are spoken of as utter reprobates and are accused of having sworn to murder babies and to eat them and of committing adulterous acts after the repast. Dogs, you say, the pimps of darkness, overturn candles and procure license for our impious lusts. We are always spoken of in this way, yet you take no pains to bring into the light the charges which for so long a time have been made against us. Now, either bring them into the light, if you believe them, or stop believing them, inasmuch as you have not brought them to the light! . . .

"You do not worship the gods," you say, "and you do not offer sacrifice for the emperors." It follows that we do not offer sacrifices for others for the same reason that we do not do it even for ourselves—it follows immediately from our not worshipping the gods. Consequently, we are considered guilty of sacrilege and treason. This is the chief accusation against us—in fact, it is the whole case—and it certainly deserves investigation, unless presumption and injustice dictate the decision, the one despairing of the truth, the other refusing it. We cease worshipping your gods when we find out that they are nonexistent.

For, in our case, we pray for the welfare of the emperors to the eternal God, the true God, the living God, whom even the emperors themselves prefer to have propitious to them before all other gods. They know who has given them power; they know—for they are men—who has given them life; they feel that He is the only God in whose power alone they are, commencing with whom they are second, after whom they stand first, who is before all and above all gods. . . . Looking up to Him, we Christians—with hands extended, because they are harmless, with head bare because we are not ashamed, without a prayer leader because we pray from the heart—constantly beseech Him on behalf of all emperors. We ask for them long life, undisturbed power, security at home, brave armies, a faithful Senate, an upright people, a peaceful world, and everything for which a man or a Caesar prays. . . .

There is also another, even greater obligation for us to pray for the emperors; yes, even for the continuance of the empire in general and for Roman interests. We realize that the tremendous force which is hanging over the whole world, and the very end of the world with its threat of dreadful afflictions, is arrested for a time by the continued existence of the Roman Empire. This event we have no desire to experience, and, in praying that it may be deferred, we favor the continuance of Rome. . . .

On the other hand, those men deserve the name of a secret society who band together in hatred of good and virtuous men, who cry out for the blood of the innocent, at the same time offering as a justification of their hatred the idle plea that they consider that the Christians are the cause of every public calamity and every misfortune of the people. If the Tiber rises as high as the city walls, if the Nile does not rise to the fields, if the weather will not change, if there is an earthquake, a famine, a plague—straightway the cry is heard: "Toss the Christians to the lion!" So many of them for just one beast?

The Early Church Fathers

The defense of Christianity in the face of anti-Christian propaganda and persecution by Roman officials during the second century was an important component in defining Christian doctrine. But the process of selecting or rejecting ideas that were competing within a fluid intellectual environment became an even more crucial mission for the eventual success of Christianity.

The main struggle of early Christian apologists was against Gnosticism, a religious movement that existed before Christianity and sought to dissolve distinctions among competing religions and fuse them into a broad abstract vision of God as Spirit. Since Jesus, in the Christian conception of the Trinity, was viewed at once as pure God, pure man, and pure Spirit, the early Christian fathers focused on defending this Trinitarian relationship. In addition, they sought to preserve the unity of Christianity by deciding just how a Christian lived within the world, and by defining the nature of an ecumenical church that served as the authority for the teaching of Christian doctrine.

The first selection is by Origen (ca. 185–254), who was a brilliant visionary of the unity of Christian theology. He was an original thinker and a great teacher whose allegorical and subjective interpretation of Scripture was both controversial and influential in the development of Christian thought. The second excerpt is from Saint Cyprian (ca. 200–258), who was the first African bishop to be martyred. He stressed the doctrine that Christians cannot exist in the world apart from the one and only Christian church.

First Principles of the Early Church (225 C.E.)

ORIGEN

All who believe and are convinced that grace and truth came by Jesus Christ, and who know Christ to be the truth, . . . derive the knowledge which calls men to lead a good and blessed life from no other source but the very words and teachings of Christ. . . .

Many of those, however, who profess to believe in Christ, hold conflicting opinions not only on small and trivial questions, but also on some that are great and important; on the nature, for instance, of God or of the Lord Jesus Christ or of the Holy Spirit, and in addition on the natures of those created beings, the dominions and the holy powers. In view of this it seems necessary first to lay down a definite line and unmistakable rule in regard to each of these, and to postpone the inquiry into other matters until afterwards. . . .

The kinds of doctrines which are believed in plain terms through the apostolic teaching are the following:

First, that God is one, who created and set in order all things, and who, when nothing existed, caused the universe to be. He is God from the first creation and foundation of the world, the God of all righteous men . . .

"First Principles of the Early Church" is from Origen, *First Principles*, trans. by G.W. Butterworth (London: Society for Promoting Christian Knowledge, 1916), pp. 1–6.

Then again: Christ Jesus, he who came to earth, was begotten of the Father before every created thing. And after he had ministered to the Father in the foundation of all things, for "all things were made through him," in these last times he emptied himself and was made man, was made flesh, although he was God: and being made man, he still remained what he was, namely God. He took to himself a body like our body, differing in this alone that it was born of a virgin and of the Holy Spirit. And this Jesus Christ was born and suffered in truth and not merely in appearance, and truly died our common death. Moreover, he truly rose from the dead, and after the resurrection companied with his disciples and was then taken up into heaven.

Then again, the apostles delivered this doctrine, that the Holy Spirit united in honor and dignity with the Father and Son. In regard to him it is not yet clearly known whether he is to be thought of as begotten or unbegotten, or as being himself also a son of God or not; but these are matters which we must investigate to the best of our power from holy scripture, inquiring with wisdom and diligence. . . .

Next after this the apostles taught that the soul, having a substance and life of its own, will be rewarded according to its deserts after its departure from this world; for it will either obtain an inheritance of eternal life and blessedness, if its deeds shall warrant this, or it must be given over to eternal fire and torments, if the guilt of its crimes shall so determine. . . .

Further, in regard to the devil and his angels and the opposing spiritual powers, the Church teaching lays it down that these beings exist, but what they are or how they exist it has not explained very clearly. Among most Christians, however, the following opinion is held, that this devil was formerly an angel, but became an apostate and persuaded as many angels as he could to fall away with him; and these are even now called his angels.

The Church teaching also included the doctrine that this world was made and began to exist at a definite time and that by reason of its corruptible nature it must suffer dissolution. But what existed before this world, or what will exist after it, has not yet been made known openly to the many, for no clear statement on the point is set forth in the Church teaching. . . .

This also is contained in the Church teaching, that there exist certain angels of God and good powers, who minister to him in bringing about the salvation of men; but when these were created, and what they are like, or how they exist, is not very clearly defined. And as for the sun, moon and stars, the tradition does not clearly say whether they are living beings or without life.

Everyone therefore who is desirous of constructing out of the foregoing a connected body of doctrine must use points like these as elementary and foundation principles, in accordance with the commandment which says, "Enlighten yourselves with the light of knowledge." Thus by clear and cogent argument he will discover the truth about each particular point and so will produce, as we have said, a single body of doctrine, with the aid of such illustrations and declarations as he shall find in the Holy Scriptures and of such conclusions as he shall ascertain to follow logically from them when rightly understood.

On the Unity of the Church (251 C.E.)

SAINT CYPRIAN OF CARTHAGE

Our Lord solemnly warns us: "You are the salt of the earth," and bids us in our love of good to be not only simple but prudent as well. Accordingly, dearest brethren, what else ought we to do but be on our guard and watch vigilantly, in order to know the snares of our crafty foe and to avoid them? Otherwise, after putting on Christ who is the Wisdom of God the Father, we may be found to have failed in wisdom for the care of our souls. It is not persecution alone that we ought to fear, nor those forces that in open warfare range abroad to overthrow and defeat the servants of God. It is easy enough to be on one's guard when the danger is obvious; one can stir up one's courage for the fight when the Enemy shows himself in his true colors. There is more need to fear and beware of the Enemy when he creeps up secretly, when he beguiles us by a show of peace and steals forward by those hidden approaches which have earned him the name of the "Serpent." Such is ever his craft: lurking in the dark, he ensnares men by trickery. . . .

Can any one then be so criminal and faithless, so mad in his passion for quarreling, as to believe it possible that the oneness of God, the garment of the Lord, the Church of Christ should be divided, or dare to divide it himself? Christ admonishes and teaches us in His Gospel: "And they shall be one flock and one shepherd." And does anyone think that in any one place there can be more than one shepherd or more than one flock? The Apostle Paul, too, commends this same oneness when he begs and exhorts us: "I beseech you, brethren, by the name of Our Lord Jesus Christ, that you all speak the same thing and that there be no schisms among you; but that you be knit together, having the same mind and the same judgment." . . . In God's house, in the Church of Christ do those of one mind dwell, there they abide in concord and simplicity.

That is also the reason why the Holy Spirit comes in the form of a dove: it is a simple joyous creature, not bitter with gall, not biting savagely, without vicious tearing claws; it loves to dwell with humankind, it keeps to one house for assembling; when they mate they hatch their young together; when they fly anywhere they keep their formation; . . . in all things they fulfill the law of unanimity. The same is the simplicity of the Church which we need to learn; this is the charity we must acquire, that we may imitate the doves in our love for the brethren, and rival lambs and sheep in their meekness and gentleness. . . .

Let no one think that good men can leave the Church; it is not the grain that the wind carries away, nor the solidly rooted tree that the storm blows down: it is the empty chaff that is swept away by the storm, the weakling trees that are overturned by the blast of the whirlwind. On these men fall the curse and the rod of John the Apostle when he says: "They went out from us, but they were not of us. For if they had been of us, they would have stayed with us."

"On the Unity of the Church" is from St. Cyprian, *The Lapsed and The Unity of the Catholic Church*, trans. by Maurice Bevenot, S.J. in *Ancient Christian Writers*, XXV (Westminster, Maryland: The Newman Press, 1957), pp. 43, 66–67.

Heresies have often arisen and still arise because of this, that disgruntled minds will quarrel, or disloyal trouble-makers will not keep the unity. But these things the Lord allows and endures, leaving man's freedom unimpaired, so that when our minds and hearts are tested by the touchstone of truth, the unswerving faith of those who are approved may appear in the clearest light.

The City of God

SAINT AUGUSTINE

One of the most important voices of early Christianity was that of Saint Augustine. He was born in North Africa in 354 C.E. and lived, by his own admission, a rather dissolute life until his conversion to Christianity in 386 at age thirty-two. He became a priest in 391 and Bishop of Hippo in 396. Three years later, Augustine wrote the Confessions, *an account of his life and conversion to Christianity. His greatest work,* The City of God, *was written as a consequence of the sack of Rome in 410 by Alaric the Visigoth. In it, Augustine answered pagan charges that this catastrophe was the result of the anger of the old gods against Christianity. In the following excerpt, Augustine explores the relationship between the City of Man and the City of God. His towering intellect maintained a close connection with classical intellectual traditions and provided continuity for Western and Eastern Christianity during a difficult and chaotic time.*

But the families which do not live by faith seek their peace in the earthly advantages of this life; while the families which live by faith look for those eternal blessings which are promised, and use as pilgrims such advantages of time and of earth as do not fascinate and divert them from God. . . . The earthly city, which does not live by faith, seeks an earthly peace, and the end it proposes, in the well-ordered concord of civic obedience and rule, is the combination of men's wills to attain the things which are helpful to this life. The heavenly city, or rather the part of it which sojourns on earth and lives by faith, makes use of this peace only because it must, until this mortal condition which necessitates it shall pass away. Consequently, so long as it lives like a captive and a stranger in the earthly city, though it has already received the promise of redemption, . . . [it has no difficulty obeying] the laws of the earthly city, whereby the things necessary for the maintenance of this mortal life are administered; and thus, as this life is common to both cities, so there is a harmony between them in regard to what belongs to it. . . .

This heavenly city, then, while it sojourns on earth, calls citizens out of all nations, and gathers together a society of pilgrims of all languages, not caring

"The City of God" is from Augustine, *The City of God,* trans. M. Dods (Buffalo, N.Y.: The Christian Literature Co., 1887), pp. 412–413.

about diversities in the manners, laws, and institutions whereby earthly peace is secured and maintained, but recognizing that, however various these are, they all tend to one and the same end of earthly peace. It therefore is so far from re-scinding and abolishing these diversities, that it even preserves and adopts them, so long only as no hindrance to the worship of the one supreme and true God is thus introduced. Even the heavenly city, therefore, while in its state of pilgrimage, avails itself of the peace of earth, and, so far as it can without injur-ing faith and godliness, desires and maintains a common agreement among men regarding the acquisition of the necessities of life, and makes this earthly peace bear upon the peace of the reasonable creatures, consisting as it does in the perfectly ordered and harmonious enjoyment of God and of one another in God. When we shall have reached that peace, this mortal life shall give place to one that is eternal, and our body shall be no more this animal body which by its corruption weights down the soul, but a spiritual body feeling no want.

The Triumph of Christianity

On decree of the emperor Galerius in 311 c.e., Christianity proceeded from a per-secuted to a tolerated sect. The emperor Constantine next raised Christianity to a favored position but still continued to erect pagan temples and was not formally baptized until on his deathbed in 337. After an unsuccessful attempt to revive paganism under the emperor Julian the Apostate in 360, Christianity finally be-came the official religion of the Roman Empire under Theodosius the Great in 392. The following selections trace this successful rise.

The Edict of Toleration (311 C.E.)
EUSEBIUS

In view of our most gentle clemency and considering our consistent practice whereby we are wont to grant pardon to all men, we have thought fit in this case, too, to extend immediate indulgence, to wit: that they may be Christians once more and that they may reconstitute their places of assembly, on condi-tion that they do nothing contrary to public order. In another letter, more-over, we shall indicate to governors of provinces what rules they are to ob-serve. Wherefore, in accordance with this indulgence of ours, they are bound to implore their own god for our safety, for that of the state, and for their own, so that on every side the state may be rendered secure and they may be able to live tranquilly in their own homes.

The Edict of Milan (313 C.E.)
EUSEBIUS

When I, Constantine Augustus, and I, Licinius Augustus, met under happy auspices in Milan and had under discussion all matters that concerned the public advantage and security, among other measures that we saw would benefit most men we considered that first of all regulations should be drawn up to secure respect for divinity, to wit: to grant both to the Christians and to all men unrestricted right to follow the form of worship each desired, to the end that whatever divinity thereby on the heavenly seat may be favorably disposed and propitious to us and all those placed under our authority. Accordingly, with salutary and most upright reasoning, we resolved on adopting this policy, namely that we should consider that no one whatsoever should be denied freedom to devote himself either to the cult of the Christians or to such religion as he deems best suited for himself, so that the highest divinity, to whose worship we pay allegiance with free minds, may grant us in all things his wonted favor and benevolence.

The Theodosian Code: Prohibition of Pagan Worship (392 C.E.)

Emperors Theodosius and Valentinian, Augustuses: To Isidorus, Praetorian Prefect:

We prohibit all persons of criminal pagan mind from the accursed immolation of victims, from damnable sacrifices, and from all other such practices that are prohibited by the authority of the more ancient sanctions. We command that all their . . . temples and shrines, if even now any remain entire, shall be destroyed by the command of the magistrates, and shall be purified by the erection of the sign of the venerable Christian religion. All men shall know that if it should appear, by suitable proof before a competent judge, that any person has mocked this law, he shall be punished with death.

The Authority of the Papacy

In the Early Middle Ages from about 500 to 1000, the church struggled to maintain unity and purity of doctrine against the threat of heresy and the contending authority of the Byzantine emperor, who exercised secular control over the Christian church in the East. The authority of the pope (technically, the bishop of Rome) as universal leader of Christianity was established in the Western church by Matthew 16:18: "And I say to you, that you are Peter, and upon this rock I will build my church; and the gates of hell shall not prevail against it. And I will give to you the keys to the Kingdom of Heaven." According to the pope's interpretation of this verse, which was disputed by the patriarchs of the East, Rome was the center of Christianity, and he was the successor to Saint Peter, the Vicar of Christ and the direct authority for the will of God. The Petrine theory is explained in the first selection by Pope Leo I (440–461).

The second reading is an oath from an English bishop named Boniface. His commitment to the doctrine of papal supremacy expresses the ideal of devotion.

The Petrine Theory

POPE LEO I

Col. 628. Our Lord Jesus Christ, the Saviour of the world, caused his truth to be promulgated through the apostles. And while this duty was placed on all the apostles, the Lord made St. Peter the head of them all, that from him as from their head his gifts should flow out into all the body. So that if anyone separates himself from St. Peter he should know that he has no share in the divine blessing.

Col. 995. Constantinople has its own glory and by the mercy of God has become the seat of the empire. But secular matters are based on one thing, ecclesiastical matters on another. For nothing will stand which is not built on the rock [Peter] which the Lord laid in the foundation. . . .

Col. 1031. You will learn with what reverence the bishop of Rome treats the rules and canons of the church if you read my letters by which I resisted the ambition of the patriarch of Constantinople, and you will see also that I am the guardian of the catholic faith and of the decrees of the church fathers.

Col. 615. . . . We have the care of all the churches, and the Lord, who made Peter the prince of the apostles, holds us responsible for it.

Col. 881. . . . It is reasonable and just that the holy Roman church, through St. Peter, the prince of the apostles, is the head of all the churches of the whole world.

Col. 147. . . . In my humble person he [Peter] should be seen and honored who has the care over all the shepherds and the sheep committed to him, and whose dignity is not lacking in me, his heir, although I am unworthy.

"The Petrine Theory" is from Oliver Thatcher and Edgar McNeal, eds., *A Source Book of Medieval History* (New York: Charles Scribner's Sons, 1905), pp. 85–86.

Loyalty to the Pope: Oath to Gregory II (723 c.e.)
BISHOP BONIFACE

I, Boniface, by the grace of God bishop, promise thee, St. Peter, prince of the apostles, and thy vicar, blessed pope Gregory, and his successors, through the Father, Son, and Holy Spirit, the inseparable Trinity, . . . that I will hold the holy Catholic faith in all its purity, and by the help of God I will remain in unity with it, without which there is no salvation. I will in no way consent to anyone who acts against the unity of the church, but, as I have said, I will preserve the purity of my faith and give my support to thee [St. Peter] and to thy church, to which God has given the power of binding and loosing, and to thy vicar, and to his successors. And if I find out that any bishops are acting contrary to the ancient rules of the holy fathers, I will have no communion or association with them, but I will restrain them as far as I can. But if I cannot restrain them I will report it at once to my lord the pope. And if I shall ever in any way, by any deceit, or under any pretext, act contrary to this my promise, I shall be found guilty in the day of judgment, and shall suffer the punishment. . . . This text of my oath, I, Boniface, unworthy bishop, have written with my own hand, and have placed it over the most holy body of St. Peter; before God as my witness and judge, I have taken this oath, which also I promise to keep.

CHRONOLOGY: Caesar and Christ

4 B.C.E.–30 C.E.	Life span of Jesus of Nazareth. According to the New Testament, Jesus preached a message of love, charity, and humility. He was crucified in Judaea by Roman procurator, Pontius Pilate, after incurring the enmity of Jewish religious leaders.
35	Conversion of Paul of Tarsus to Christianity. Born Saul, he was a Roman citizen and Hellenized Jew who persecuted Christians until his own conversion.
64–65	Roman emperor, Nero, blames the destructive fire in Rome on the Christians in order to deflect suspicion from himself. Both Paul and the apostle Peter were killed in the succeeding persecution.
70–100	Four Gospel accounts of Jesus' early life written (Matthew, Mark, Luke, John).
ca. 117	Emperor Trajan's advice to Pliny: "Do not seek the Christians out."

Loyalty to the Pope: Oath to Gregory II" is from Oliver Thatcher and Edgar McNeal, eds., *A Source Book of Medieval History* (New York: Charles Scribner's Sons, 1905), pp. 93–95.

ca. 120	First non-Christian mention of Christians in Tacitus's *Annals*.
250–260	Major persecution of Christians under the emperors Decius (249–251) and Valerius (253–260).
303	Empire-wide persecution of Christians under the emperor Diocletian begins.
311	Emperor Galerius issues the "Edict of Toleration."
312	Battle of the Milvian Bridge and the conversion of the emperor Constantine.
325	Headed by Constantine, the Council of Nicaea resolves division of Christianity. Declares Arianism a heresy. Orthodox position: Jesus is both fully human and fully divine.
392	Theodosian Code established. Christianity becomes official religion of the Roman Empire. Pagan worship prohibited.
396	St. Augustine, author of *The City of God*, becomes Bishop of Hippo.
440–461	Reign of Pope Leo I who promulgated the Petrine theory which argued that Rome was the center of Christianity and he was the successor to Saint Peter, the Vicar of Christ and the direct authority for the will of God.

STUDY QUESTIONS

1. Characterize the Roman state religion. What are the advantages of such a structured approach to religion? Why were the mystery cults so popular, and why did Rome tolerate them?
2. Note the deification of Augustus. Why was it important for the emperors to promote the imperial cult?
3. What is Jesus' basic message and mission? Discuss this with specific examples. Do you see anything in his message that might be considered politically threatening to the Roman state? Consider, in particular, the vocabulary.
4. What were Paul's contributions to the message of Jesus? How did the *Pax Romana* contribute to the success of missionaries like Paul who were spreading the word of Christ?
5. What was Roman policy on Christianity? Why was Rome concerned about the Christians? How did Christians threaten the Roman state, and why were they persecuted? Why were Christians finally tolerated by Constantine and Theodosius?
6. According to Tertullian, what are the main reasons for persecution of the Christians? Is Tertullian fair in his assessment of the Roman position and actions? Why or why not?

7. Analyze the Roman propaganda directed against the Christians. In your opinion, what makes it effective or ineffective propaganda? Does Tertullian do a good job of defending the Christian position against such misstatements?

8. In the selection, "First Principles of the Early Church," Origen seems concerned that the Holy Scriptures be "rightly understood." In this early statement of doctrine, which issues are Origen clear about, and which are unclear in the church teaching? Origen seeks the "light of Knowledge" in producing a "single body of doctrine." Why was it important for the early church to do this? What does Saint Cyprian have to say about the importance of the unity of the church? Who is the "Enemy" and why can't "good men" leave the church?

9. Do you believe Christianity threatened Roman imperial rule? If you had been an emperor during this period and were trying to maintain stability in the empire, what would your policy toward the Christians have been?

10. Explain the Petrine Theory and analyze its purpose. In the excerpt by Leo I, the pope is viewed as the shepherd and the Christian community as the sheep committed to him. Compare this with Saint Cyprian's view that Christians should "rival lambs and sheep in their meekness and gentleness." Why was the image of this relationship important to the structure of early Christianity? How does Bishop Boniface in his oath to Pope Gregory II exemplify Christian obedience and humility?

6

The *Pax Romana* and the Decline of Rome

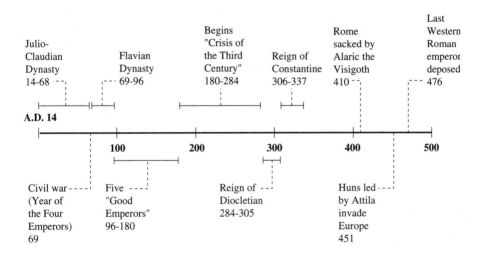

Julio-Claudian Dynasty 14-68

Flavian Dynasty 69-96

Begins "Crisis of the Third Century" 180-284

Reign of Constantine 306-337

Rome sacked by Alaric the Visigoth 410

Last Western Roman emperor deposed 476

A.D. 14

100   200   300   400   500

Civil war (Year of the Four Emperors) 69

Five "Good Emperors" 96-180

Reign of Diocletian 284-305

Huns led by Attila invade Europe 451

But you, Roman, must remember that you have to guide nations by your authority, for this is to be your skill, to graft tradition onto peace, to show mercy to the conquered, and to wage war until the haughty are brought low.

—Virgil, *Aeneid*

As yourselves, your empires fall. And every kingdom hath a grave.

—William Hobbington

We can destroy ourselves by cynicism and disillusionment just as effectively as by bombs.

—Kenneth Clark

Civilization is a stream with banks. The stream is sometimes filled with blood from people killing, stealing, shouting and doing things historians usually record, while on the banks, unnoticed, people build homes, make love, raise children, sing songs, [and] write poetry. . . . The history of civilization is the story of what happened on the banks.

—Will and Ariel Durant

CHAPTER THEMES

- ***Systems of Government:*** The system of government instituted by Augustus, called the "principate," functioned as a complex blend of power and authority. How well did his successors as emperors of Rome maintain his system of rule? Is freedom most importantly a thing of the mind? If the institutions of government are controlled, yet *appear* to be free, and if you feel that you are free, are you free?

- ***Imperialism:*** How did the Romans control their empire? Were they efficient rulers who were respected by their subjects? Is imperialism which results in political and social stability necessarily a bad thing?

- ***Historical Change and Transition:*** What were the components of Roman decline? Did the Romans make specific mistakes, or is decline a natural and inevitable fate of each society? How much can a society change and adapt before it loses the elements that gave it purpose and success?

- ***The Big Picture:*** Is each civilization biological in nature, and does it have a "life span" like human beings? What are the most important remnants of one civilization that form the seeds of the succeeding civilization?

The Roman Republic had once been hailed as a progressive society of balance and restraint, where freedom was guaranteed by law and defended with the blood of those committed to such ideals. Yet during the first century B.C.E., the Republic was destroyed, a victim of extremist political factions, domestic dissension, and violence. Roman armies, which had once silenced foreign foes, became the preserve of generals who were committed more to their personal advancement than to the security of the state. The Republic died amid the clash of civil war, and in its place flourished a "restored republic," the principate of Augustus.

The Augustan principate was designed to establish and maintain peace and harmony in the state. The institutions of the Republic were retained; people voted in the assemblies, senators vied for office and discussed issues in much the

This contemporary view of the Roman Forum from the Palatine hill, which contained the palaces of the emperors, can now only hint at the majesty of the great capital of the Roman Empire and the busy "emporium of the world." (*Perry M. Rogers*)

same way as they had done for years. Augustus, in his role as princeps (first citizen), merely advised the senate on issues that he thought were important for the welfare of the empire. But since the army was loyal to him and represented the true power in the state, Augustus's opinions and suggestions assumed the greatest importance. Yet Augustus maintained a political equilibrium by stressing his authority, not his blatant military power. He respected the dignity of the senators and their need to feel as if they actually controlled the government; in return, they generally supported his political solutions to the chaos of the Roman Republic. And although some senators grumbled and decried this facade of freedom, nevertheless the system worked for over two hundred years. Those succeeding emperors who played the game well, respected the dignity of the senate, and maintained control of the army usually survived and prospered. Those who did not, like the emperors Caligula and Domitian, were assassinated.

Since the Augustan system of government brought political security to the state, the Roman Empire flourished in peace, a universal peace known as the *Pax Romana.* It was during this time that the city of Rome served as the emporium of the world. All roads indeed ended sooner or later in the center of the magnificent city, whose population swelled to a million inhabitants. To hail from the provinces of the empire and to see Rome for the first time must have been a numbing experience. The theaters, baths, sewers, aqueducts, and monuments provided services and entertainment on a magnificent scale. And the spectacle was even more impressive in the Coliseum, where gladiators fought, or in the Circus Maximus, where over 250,000 people could thrill to the chariot races.

Outside the city, a road system was built that connected the provinces of the empire and unified Europe as never before. The provincials were allowed to retain their own customs, languages, and religions; all Rome demanded in return were taxes and peace. It is testament to the loyalty and satisfaction of provincial subjects that Rome maintained the security of her enormous empire with only about 350,000 soldiers.

Still, perhaps the greatest failure in Western Civilization was Rome's inability to sustain her hegemony. Confronted with political, social, and economic dislocation in the third century c.e., Rome struggled to survive. External pressures by Germanic tribes also took their toll on an increasingly overburdened army which no longer reflected the efficiency and tenacity of the famous Roman legions. The Roman Empire declined gradually, losing its unity and organization by the fifth century c.e. The eternal question is: why?

This chapter will evaluate the Roman Empire during its era of strength and its period of decline. This is a particularly relevant chapter because many have compared Roman society to American society. Some have thus viewed Roman civilization as a laboratory in which we might see the seeds of our own destruction. But what are the components of greatness and decline? And can we ascertain our position along the way? Rome has many lessons to offer that continue to make its history important and meaningful.

—◦⟨⟩ ⟨⟩◦—

Strength and Success (14–180 C.E.)

Political and Military Control

The Augustan system of government generally functioned well during the first century C.E., *outlasting bad emperors and a brief civil war, and prospering especially during the reigns of Tiberius, Claudius, and Vespasian. Rome's greatest achievement during this period was the establishment of peace throughout the empire, which was maintained by an efficient and dedicated army.*

The Blessings of Imperial Rule:
Peace and Prosperity
PLUTARCH

The greatest blessings that cities can enjoy are peace, prosperity, populousness, and concord. As far as peace is concerned the people have no need of political activity, for all war, both Greek and foreign, has been banished and has disappeared from among us. Of liberty the people enjoy as much as our rulers allot them, and perhaps more would not be better. A bounteous productiveness of soil; a mild, temperate climate; wives bearing children . . . and security for the offspring—these are the things that the wise man will ask for his fellow citizens in his prayers to the gods.

"To Rome": An Oration
AELIUS ARISTEIDES

Extensive and sizable as the Empire is, perfect policing does much more than territorial boundaries to make it great. . . . Like a well-swept and fenced-in front yard . . . the whole world speaks in unison, more distinctly than a chorus; and so well does it harmonize under this director-in-chief that it joins in praying this Empire may last for all time. All everywhere are ruled equally. The mountain people are lowlier in their submissiveness than the inhabitants of the most exposed plains. The owners and occupants of rich plains are your peasants. Continent and island are no longer separate. Like one continuous country and one people, all the world quietly obeys. Everything is carried out by command or nod, and it is simpler than touching a string. If a need arises, the thing has only to be decided on, and it is done. The governors assigned to cities and provinces govern their various subjects; but among themselves and in relation to one another, all of them alike are governed . . . [by] the supreme governor, the chief executive [the emperor]. They are convinced that he knows what they are doing better than they know it themselves. They fear and respect him more than any slave could fear his master standing over him personally and giving orders. None of them are so proud that they can sit still if they so much as hear his name. They leap up, praise him, bow, and utter a double prayer—to the gods on behalf of him, and to him on their own behalf. If they felt the slightest doubt about their subjects' lawsuits, public or private, or whether petitions should be granted, they immediately send to him and ask what to do, and they wait for a signal from him, as a chorus from its director. No need for him to wear himself out making the rounds of the whole Empire, or to be in one place after another adjusting the affairs of each people whenever he sets foot in their country. Instead, he can very easily sit and manage the whole world by letters, which are practically no sooner written than delivered, as if flown by birds. . . . The constitution is a universal democracy under the one man that can rule and govern best.

The Imperial Army

FLAVIUS JOSEPHUS

If one goes on to study the organization of [the Roman] army as a whole, it will be seen that this vast empire of theirs has come to them as the prize of valor, and not as a gift of fortune. For they do not wait for the outbreak of war, nor do they sit with folded hands in peacetime only to put them in motion in the hour of need. On the contrary, as though they had been born with weapons in hand, they never have a truce from training, never wait for the emergencies to arise. Moreover, their peacetime maneuvers are no less strenuous than veritable warfare; each soldier daily throws all his energy into his drill, as though he were in action. Hence that perfect ease with which they sustain the shock of battle. . . .

The Romans never lay themselves open to a surprise attack; for, whatever hostile territory they may invade, they engage in no battle until they have fortified their camp. . . . Thus an improvised city, as it were, springs up, with its market place, its artisan quarter, its judgment seats, where officers adjudicate

"The Imperial Army" is reprinted by permission of the publishers and the Loeb Classical Library from Josephus, *The Jewish War*, 3.5.71–107, trans. H. St. J. Thackery (Cambridge, Mass.: Harvard University Press, 1927), pp. 597, 599, 601, 603, 605.

The Pont du Gard, perhaps the most majestic of all Roman ruins, was an aqueduct that carried water through southern France. The provinces were thus served by Roman engineering genius. *(Perry M. Rogers)*

any differences which may arise. The outer wall and all the installations within are completed more quickly than thought, so numerous and skilled are the workmen. . . .

Once entrenched, the soldiers take up their quarters in their tents by companies, quietly and in good order. All their fatigue duties are performed with the same discipline, the same regard for security: the procuring of wood, of food supplies, and water, as required—each company having its allotted task. The hour for supper and breakfast is not left to individual discretion; all take their meals together. The hours for sleep, sentinel duty, and rising are announced by the sound of trumpets; nothing is done without a word of command. At daybreak the rank and file report to their respective centurions, the centurions go to salute the tribunes, the tribunes with all the officers then wait on the commander-in-chief, and he gives them according to custom the watchword and other orders to be communicated to the lower ranks. The same precision is maintained on the battlefield; the troops wheel smartly round in the requisite direction, and, whether advancing to the attack or retreating, all move as a unit.

When the camp is to be broken up, the trumpet sounds a first call; at that none remain idle; instantly, at this signal, they strike the tents and make all ready for departure. The trumpets sound a second call to prepare the march; at once they pile their baggage on the mules and other beasts of burden, and stand ready to start. . . . They then set fire to the encampment, both because they can easily construct another . . . and to prevent the enemy from ever making use of it. A third time the trumpets give a similar signal for departure, to hasten the movements of stragglers, whatever the reason for their delay, and to ensure that none is out of his place in the ranks. Then the herald, standing on the right of the commander, inquires in their native tongue whether they are ready for war. Three times they loudly and lustily shout in reply, "We are ready," some even anticipating the question; and worked up to a kind of martial frenzy, they raise their right arms in the air along with the shout. . . .

The infantry are armed with cuirasses and helmets and carry a sword on either side; that on the left is far the longer of the two, the dagger on the right being no longer than a span. The picked infantry, forming the general's guard, carry a spear and round shield, the regiments of the line a javelin and oblong shield; the equipment of the latter includes, further, a saw, a basket, a pick, and an axe, not to mention a strap, a bill-hook, a chain, and three days' rations, so that an infantry man is almost as heavily laden as a pack mule. . . .

By their military exercises the Romans instill into their soldiers fortitude not only of body but also of soul; fear, too, plays its part in their training. For they have laws which punish with death not merely desertion but even a slight neglect of duty; and their generals are held in even greater awe than the laws. For the high honors with which they reward the brave prevent the offenders whom they punish from regarding themselves as treated cruelly.

This perfect discipline with regard to their generals makes the army an ornament of peacetime, and in battle welds the whole into a single body; so compact are their ranks, so alert their movements in wheeling, so quick their ears for orders, their eyes for signals, their hands for tasks. Prompt as they consequently ever are in action, none are slower than they in succumbing to suffering, and never have they been known in any predicament to be beaten by numbers, by ruses, by difficulties of terrain, or even by fortune; for victory is more certain for them than fortune.

Rome and Its Provinces

The security afforded by the Pax Romana *allowed the empire to prosper economically, as the following excerpts show. Although Rome was the political center of this vibrant empire, she was supported economically by goods and metals that flowed from her provinces. Roman roads facilitated the commerce that made cities like Alexandria thriving centers.*

Alexandria: Crossroads of the World
DIO CHRYSOSTOM

[Alexandria] is admittedly ranked second [to Rome] among all cities beneath the sun. For not only does the mighty land of Egypt constitute the framework of your city—or, more accurately, its appanage—but the peculiar nature of the river [Nile], when compared with all others, defies description with regard to both its marvelous habits and its usefulness; and furthermore, not only have you a monopoly of the shipping of the entire Mediterranean by reason of the beauty of your harbors, the magnitude of your fleet, and the abundance and the marketing of the products of every land, but also the outer waters that lie beyond are in your grasp, both the Red Sea and the Indian Ocean, whose name was rarely heard in former days. The result is that the trade, not merely of islands, ports, a few straits and isthmuses, but of practically the whole world is yours. For Alexandria is situated, as it were, at the crossroads of the whole world, of even the most remote nations thereof, as if it were a market serving a single city, a market which brings together into one place all manner of men, displaying them to one another and, as far as possible, making them a kindred people. . . . For I behold among you, not merely Greeks and Italians and people from neighboring Syria, Libya, Cilicia, not merely Ethiopians and Arabs from more distant regions, but even Bactrians and Scythians and Persians and a few Indians.

Pliny the Younger: Imperial Patronage

Essential to the welfare of provincial communities was imperial support from Rome itself. We have a rare opportunity to view the affairs of one province in particular. The governor of Bithynia (near the Black Sea) was a man named Pliny the Younger. His letters to the emperor Trajan, about 112 c.e., depict a close relationship that resulted in improvements for the province. Note, however, Trajan's reluctance to support an organized group of firemen. The emperor was wary of the potential force for organized rebellion masked by such a seemingly innocent facade.

Pliny to Trajan: The people of Prusa, Sire, have a public bath in a neglected and dilapidated state. They wish—with your kind permission—to restore it; but I think a new one ought to be built, and I reckon you can safely comply with their wishes.

"Alexandria: Crossroads of the World" is reprinted by permission of the publishers and the Loeb Classical Library from Dio Chrysostom, *Discourses*, 32.36, 40, trans. H. Lamar Crosby (Cambridge, Mass.: Harvard University Press, 1940), pp. 205, 207, 211.

"Pliny the Younger: Imperial Patronage" is from Pliny the Younger, *Letters*, 10.25 ff., in *Readings in Ancient History*, vol. 2, ed. William S. Davis (Boston: Allyn and Bacon, 1913), pp. 215–217.

Trajan to Pliny: If the building of a new bath will not cripple the finances of Prusa, we can indulge their wishes; only it must be understood that no new taxes are to be raised to meet the cost, and that their contributions for necessary expenses shall not show any falling off.

Pliny to Trajan: A desolating fire broke out in Nicomedia, and destroyed a number of private houses, and two public buildings—the almshouse and the temple of Isis—although a road ran between them. The fire was allowed to spread farther than necessary, first owing to the violent wind; second, to the laziness of the citizens, it being generally agreed they stood idly by without moving, and simply watched the conflagration. Besides there was not a single public fire engine or bucket in the place, and not one solitary appliance for mastering a fire. However, these will be provided upon orders I have already given. But, Sire, I would have you consider whether you think a fire company of about 150 men ought not to be formed? I will take care that no one who is not a genuine fireman shall be admitted. . . . Again there would be no trouble in keeping an eye on so small a body.

Trajan to Pliny: You have formed the idea of a possible fire company at Nicomedia on the model of various others already existing; but remember that the province of Bithnia, and especially city states like Nicomedia, are the prey of factions. Give them the name we may, and however good be the reasons for organization, such associations will soon degenerate into [dangerous] secret societies. It is better policy to provide fire apparatus, and to encourage property holders to make use of them, and if need comes, press the crowd which collects into the same service.

Pliny to Trajan: Sire, the people of Nicomedia spent 3,229,000 sesterces upon an aqueduct, which was left in an unfinished state, and I may say in ruin, and they also levied taxes to the extent of 2,000,000 sesterces for a second one. This, too, has been abandoned, and to get a water supply those who have wasted these vast sums must go to a new expense. I have visited a splendid clear spring, from which it seems to me the supply ought to be brought to the town [and have formed a scheme that seems practicable].

Trajan to Pliny: Steps must certainly be taken to provide Nicomedia with a water supply; and I have full confidence you will undertake the duty with all due care. But I profess it is also part of your diligent duty to find out who is to blame for the waste of such sums of money by the people of Nicomedia on their aqueducts, and whether or not there has been any serving of private interests in this beginning and then abandoning of [public] works. See that you bring to my knowledge whatever you find out.

The Realities of Roman Rule

Imperial patronage and good will was dependent on the maintenance of peace in the provinces. The Roman army was an efficient fighting machine that had the responsibility not only to protect the empire from external invasion, but also to quell any internal disturbance. Successful governors were not heavy-handed when they brought stability to a region, but sought ways to win the loyalty of the inhabitants, as the following selection indicates. Agricola, a successful general, has just assumed his responsibilities as governor of Britain in 78 C.E.

Techniques of Roman Control
TACITUS

Agricola, by the repression of ... abuses in his very first year of office, restored to peace its good name. ... When ... summer came, assembling his forces, he continually showed himself in the ranks, praised good discipline, and kept the stragglers in order. He would himself choose the position of the camp, himself explore the estuaries and forests. Meanwhile he would allow the enemy no rest, laying waste his territory with sudden incursions, and, having sufficiently alarmed him, would then by [clemency] display the allurements of peace. In consequence, many states, which up to that time had been independent, gave hostages, and laid aside their animosities; garrisons and forts were established among them with a skill and diligence with which no newly-acquired part of Britain had before been treated.

The following winter passed without disturbance. ... Agricola gave private encouragement and public aid to the building of temples, courts of justice and dwelling-houses, praising the energetic, and reproving the indolent. Thus honourable rivalry took the place of compulsion. He likewise provided a liberal education for the sons of the chiefs. ... Hence, too, a liking sprang up for our style of dress, and the "toga" became fashionable. Step by step [the Britons] were led to things which dispose to vice, the lounge, the bath, the elegant banquet. All this in their ignorance, they called civilization, when it was but a part of their servitude.

Submission and Safety
TACITUS

Although Rome was generally a benign master, there were rebellions, especially on the part of the Jews, whose revolt from 66 to 70 C.E. ended with the methodical elimination of the rebels at Masada and the consequent destruction of the Temple at Jerusalem. The following excerpt relates the aftermath of a rebellion of the Gauls in 70 C.E. The Roman commander bluntly and realistically sums up the

"Techniques of Roman Control" is from Tacitus, *Agricola*, 20–21, trans. Alfred Church and William Brodribb (New York: Macmillan, 1877).

"Submission and Safety" is from Tacitus, *Histories*, 4.73–74, trans. Alfred Church and William Brodribb (New York: Macmillan, 1894).

imperial policy of submission and safety and the advantages to be obtained through cooperation.

"Gaul always had its petty kingdoms and intestine wars, till you submitted to our authority. We, though so often provoked, have used the right of conquest to burden you only with the cost of maintaining peace. For the tranquility of nations cannot be preserved without armies; armies cannot exist without pay; pay cannot be furnished without tribute; all else is common between us. You often command our legions. You rule these and other provinces. There is no privilege, no exclusion. From worthy Emperors you derive equal advantage, though you dwell so far away, while cruel rulers are most formidable to their neighbors. Endure the passions and rapacity of your masters, just as you bear barren seasons and excessive rains and other natural evils. There will be vices as long as there are men. But they are not perpetual, and they are compensated by the occurrence of better things. . . . Should the Romans be driven out (which God forbid) what can result but wars between all these nations? By the prosperity and order of eight hundred years has this fabric of empire

Spoils from the destruction of the Temple of Jerusalem. Roman troops ended the stubborn resistance of the Jews in 70 c.e. and brought back many of the Jewish artifacts to be displayed in Titus's great triumph through the city of Rome. Submission and safety were other alternatives for provincials. *(Alinari/Art Resource, N.Y.)*

been consolidated, nor can it be overthrown without destroying those who overthrow it. Yours will be the worst peril, for you have gold and wealth, and these are the chief incentives to war. Give therefore your love and respect to the cause of peace, and to that capital in which we, conquerors and conquered, claim an equal right. Let the lessons of fortune in both its forms teach you not to prefer rebellion and ruin to submission and safety." With words to this effect he quieted and encouraged his audience, who feared harsher treatment.

"They Make a Desolation and Call It Peace"
TACITUS

These famous words were written by Tacitus, a senator and later critic of Rome. The following selection is a speech that Tacitus attributes to the Caledonian chieftain Galgacus, just before his defeat at the hands of Roman armies. His sentiments balance the view of Rome as the protector of freedom. Not everyone believed it.

Whenever I consider the origin of this war and the necessities of our position, I have a sure confidence that this day, and this union of yours, will be the beginning of freedom to the whole of Britain. . . . Now, however, the furthest limits of Britain are thrown open, and the unknown always passes for the marvelous. But there are no tribes beyond us, nothing indeed but waves and rocks, and the yet more terrible Romans, from whose oppression escape is vainly sought by obedience and submission. Robbers of the world, having by their universal plunder exhausted the land, they rifle the deep. If the enemy be rich, they are rapacious; if he be poor, they lust for dominion; neither the east nor the west has been able to satisfy them. Alone among men they covet with equal eagerness poverty and riches. To robbery, slaughter, plunder, they give the lying name of empire; they make a desolation and call it "peace."

"All Roads Lead to Rome"

The city of Rome was the vibrant center of this extensive empire. It provided services and entertainment to a teeming population of about one million inhabitants from all over the world. The following excerpts reveal the advantages and disadvantages of city life.

"'They Make a Desolation and Call It Peace'" is from Tacitus, *Agricola,* 29–30, trans. Alfred Church and William Brodribb (New York: Macmillan, 1877).

The Glory of the City
STRABO

[The Romans] paved the roads, cut through hills, and filled up valleys, so that the merchandise may be conveyed by carriage from the ports. The sewers, arched over with hewn stones, are large enough in parts for actual hay wagons to pass through, while so plentiful is the supply of water from the aqueducts, that rivers may be said to flow through the city and the sewers, and almost every house is furnished with water pipes and copious fountains.

We may remark that the ancients [of Republican times] bestowed little attention upon the beautifying of Rome. But their successors, and especially those of our own day, have at the same time embellished the city with numerous and splendid objects. Pompey, the Divine Caesar [i.e., Julius Caesar], and Augustus, with his children, friends, wife, and sister have surpassed all others in their zeal and munificence in these decorations. The greater number of these may be seen in the Campus Martius which to the beauties of nature

A view of the Arch of Titus and the magnificent Roman Coliseum beyond. Each successive building "caused you speedily to forget that which you have seen before. Such then is Rome!"—Strabo. *(Perry M. Rogers)*

"The Glory of the City" is from Strabo, *Geography,* 5.3.8, in *Readings in Ancient History,* vol. 2, ed. William S. Davis (Boston: Allyn and Bacon, 1913), pp. 179–181.

adds those of art. The size of the plain is remarkable, allowing chariot races and the equestrian sports without hindrance, and multitudes [here] exercise themselves with ball games, in the Circus, and on the wrestling grounds. . . . The summit of the hills beyond the Tiber, extending from its banks with panoramic effect, present a spectacle which the eye abandons with regret.

Near to this plain is another surrounded with columns, sacred groves, three theaters, an amphitheater, and superb temples, each close to the other, and so splendid that it would seem idle to describe the rest of the city after it. For this cause the Romans esteeming it the most sacred place, have erected funeral monuments there to the illustrious persons of either sex. The most remarkable of these is that called the "Mausoleum" [the tomb of Augustus] which consists of a mound of earth raised upon a high foundation of white marble, situated near the river, and covered on the top with evergreen shrubs. Upon the summit is a bronze statue of Augustus Caesar, and beneath the mound are the funeral urns of himself, his relatives, and his friends. Behind is a large grove containing charming promenades. . . . If then you proceed to visit the ancient Forum, which is equally filled with basilicas, porticoes, and temples, you will there behold the Capitol, the Palatine, and the noble works that adorn them, and the piazza of Livia [Augustus' Empress],—each successive work causing you speedily to forget that which you have seen before. Such then is Rome!

The Dark Side of Rome

JUVENAL

I cannot bear, Romans, a Greek Rome; and yet, how small a portion of our dregs is from Greece! Long since, Syrian Orontes [a river] has flowed into the Tiber, and has brought with it its language and manners. . . . The coming of the Greek has brought us a Jack-of-all-trades—grammarian, rhetorician, geometrician, painter, wrestling manager, prophet, rope-walker, physician, magician; he knows everything. Bid the hungry Greekling go to heaven, he will go. . . . The poor among the Romans ought to have emigrated in a body long ago. Not easily do those emerge from obscurity whose noble qualities are cramped by domestic poverty. But at Rome the attempt is still harder for them; a great price must be paid for a wretched lodging, a great price for slaves' keep, a great price for a modest little dinner. A man is ashamed to dine off earthenware. . . . Here splendour of dress is carried beyond people's means; here something more than is enough is occasionally borrowed from another man's strongbox. This vice is common to all of us; here all of us live in a state of pretentious poverty. In a word, in Rome everything costs money. . . .

Many a sick man dies here from want of sleep, the sickness itself having been produced by undigested food clinging to the fevered stomach. For what

"The Dark Side of Rome" is from Juvenal, *Satires*, 3, trans. J. D. Lewis (London: Trubner, 1873).

rented lodgings allow of sleep? It takes great wealth to sleep in the city. Hence the origin of the disease. The passage of carriages in the narrow winding streets, and the abuse of the drivers of the blocked teams would rob even [the heaviest sleepers] of sleep.

If a social duty calls him, the rich man will be carried through the yielding crowd and will speed over their heads on his huge Liburnian litter bearers; he will read on his way, or write, or even sleep inside, for a litter with closed windows induces sleep. Yet he will arrive before us. We in our hurry are impeded by the wave in front, while the multitude which follows us presses on our back in dense array; one strikes me with his elbow, another with a hard pole, one knocks a beam against my head, another a wine jar. My legs are sticky with mud; before long I am trodden on all sides by large feet, and the hobnails of a soldier stick into my toe. . . .

Observe now the different and varied dangers of the night. What a height it is to the lofty roofs, from which a tile brains you, and how often cracked and broken utensils fall from windows—with what a weight they mark and damage the pavement when they strike it! You may well be accounted remiss and improvident about sudden accidents if you go out to supper without making a will. There are just so many fatal chances as there are wakeful windows open at night when you are passing by. Hope, then, and carry this pitiable prayer about with you, that they may be content merely to empty broad wash basins over you.

The Magnificence of the Baths

LUCIAN

The building suits the magnitude of the site, accords well with the accepted idea of such an establishment, and shows regard for the principles of lighting. The entrance is high, with a flight of broad steps of which the tread is greater than the pitch, to make them easy to ascend. On entering, one is received into a public hall of good size, with ample accommodation for servants and attendants. On the left are the lounging rooms, also of just the right sort for a bath, attractive, brightly lighted retreats. Then, besides them, a hall, larger than need be for the purposes of a bath, but necessary for the reception of richer persons. Next, . . . locker rooms to undress in, on each side, with a very high and brilliantly lighted hall between them, in which are three swimming pools of cold water; it is finished in Laconian marble, and has two statues of white marble in the ancient style. . . .

"The Magnificence of the Baths" is reprinted by permission of the publishers and the Loeb Classical Library from Lucian, *Hippias,* trans. A. M. Harmon, vol. 1 (Cambridge, Mass.: Harvard University Press, 1913), pp. 39, 41, 43.

On leaving this hall, you come into another which is slightly warmed instead of meeting you at once with fierce heat; it is oblong, and has an apse on each side. Next to it, on the right, is a very bright hall, nicely fitted up for massage, which has on each side an entrance decorated with Phrygian marble, and receives those who come in from the exercising floor. Then near this is another hall, the most beautiful in the world, in which one can stand or sit with comfort, linger without danger, and stroll about with profit. It also is resplendent with Phrygian marble clear to the roof. Next comes the hot corridor, faced with Numidian marble. The hall beyond it is very beautiful, full of abundant light and aglow with color like that of purple hangings. It contains three hot tubs.

When you have bathed, you need not go back through the same rooms, but can go directly to the cold room through a slightly warmed chamber. Everywhere there is copious illumination and full indoor daylight. . . . Why should I go on to tell you of the exercising floor and of the cloak rooms? . . . Moreover, it is beautified with all other marks of thoughtfulness—with two toilets, many exits, and two devices for telling time, a water clock that makes a bellowing sound and a sundial.

The Bathing Establishment
SENECA

I live over a bathing establishment. Picture to yourself now the assortment of voices, the sound of which is enough to sicken one. When the stronger fellows are exercising and swinging heavy leaden weights in their hands, when they are working hard or pretending to be working hard, I hear their groans; and whenever they release their pent-up breath, I hear their hissing and jarring breathing. When I have to do with a lazy fellow who is content with a cheap rubdown, I hear the slap of the hand pummeling his shoulders, changing its sound according as the hand is laid flat or curved. If now a professional ball player comes along and begins to keep score, I am done for. Add to this the arrest of a brawler or a thief, and the fellow who always likes to hear his own voice in the bath, and those who jump into the pool with a mighty splash as they strike the water. In addition to those whose voices are, if nothing else, natural, imagine the hair plucker keeping up a constant chatter in his thin and strident voice, to attract more attention, and never silent except when he is plucking armpits and making the customer yell instead of yelling himself. It disgusts me to enumerate the varied cries of the sausage dealer and confectioner and of all the peddlers of the cook shops, hawking their wares, each with his own peculiar intonation.

"Bread and Circuses"
FRONTO

The emperors were very careful not to neglect the basic needs of the inhabitants of Rome. Since an idle population was prone to boredom and rioting, the emperors promoted building programs that not only increased the glory of the city but also employed the masses. A sizable number of citizens were on the grain dole, a welfare program, that offered free grain for those who could not afford to buy it. It was therefore essential that grain ships arrived from Egypt on a regular basis, for a hungry populace was also prone to disturbance. Finally, the people demanded entertainment, and Rome responded with gladiatorial games in the Coliseum and chariot races in the Circus Maximus. The Circus was especially popular and could hold 250,000 people at one time—a quarter of the population of Rome! "Bread and Circuses" were the essential ingredients of harmony in the great city.

It was the height of political wisdom for the emperor not to neglect even actors and the other performers of the stage, the circus, and the arena, since he knew that the Roman people is held fast by two things above all, the grain supply and the shows, that the success of the government depends on amusements as much as on serious things. Neglect of serious matters entails the greater detriment, of amusements the greater unpopularity. The money largesses are less eagerly desired than the shows; the largesses appease only the grain-doled plebs singly and individually, while the shows keep the whole population happy.

Gladiatorial Combat
SENECA

By chance I attended a mid-day exhibition, expecting some fun, wit, and relaxation—an exhibition at which men's eyes have respite from the slaughter of their fellow-men. But it was quite the reverse. The previous combats were the essence of compassion; but now all the trifling is put aside and it is pure

"'Bread and Circuses'" is from Fronto, *Elements of History,* 17, in *Roman Civilization, Sourcebook II: The Empire,* ed. N. Lewis and M. Reinhold (New York: Columbia University Press, 1955), pp. 229–230. Copyright © 1955 by Columbia University Press. Reprinted by permission of the publisher.

"Gladiatorial Combat" is reprinted by permission of the publishers and the Loeb Classical Library from Seneca, *Moral Epistles,* 7.3–5, trans. Richard Gummere, vol. 1 (Cambridge, Mass.: Harvard University Press, 1917), pp. 31, 33.

murder. The men have no defensive armour. They are exposed to blows at all points, and no one ever strikes in vain. . . . In the morning they throw men to the lions and the bears; at noon, they throw them to the spectators. The spectators demand that the slayer shall face the man who is to slay him in his turn; and they always reserve the latest conqueror for another butchering. The outcome of every fight is death, and the means are fire and sword. This sort of thing goes on while the arena is empty. You may retort: "But he was a highway robber; he killed a man!" And what of it? Granted that, as a murderer, he deserved this punishment, what crime have you committed, poor fellow, that you should deserve to sit and see this show? In the morning they cried "Kill him! Lash him! Burn him! Why does he meet the sword in so cowardly a way? Why does he strike so feebly? Why doesn't he die game? Whip him to meet his wounds! Let them receive blow for blow, with chests bare and exposed to the stroke!" And when the games stop for the intermission, they announce: "A little throat-cutting in the meantime, so that there may still be something going on!"

Social and Intellectual Aspects of the *Pax Romana*

The Rural Life of a Roman Aristocrat

City life had its excitement and advantages, but many of the rich preferred the seclusion of their country estates, especially during the summer months. Pliny the Younger, a Roman aristocrat, offered the following glimpse into life in the country.

"Charming Privacy"
PLINY THE YOUNGER

In the morning Spurinna keeps his couch; at the second hour he calls for his shoes and walks three miles, exercising mind as well as body. If he has friends with him, the time is passed in conversation on the noblest themes, otherwise a book is read aloud, and sometimes this is done even when his friends are present, but never in such a way as to bore them. Then he sits down, and there is more talk for preference; afterward he enters his carriage, taking with him either his wife . . . or one of his friends, a distinction I recently enjoyed. How delightful, how charming that privacy is! What glimpses of old times one gets! What noble deeds and noble men he tells you of! What

"'Charming Privacy'" is from Pliny the Younger, Letters, 3.1, in *Readings in Ancient History*, vol. 2, ed. William S. Davis (Boston: Allyn and Bacon, 1913), pp. 241–242.

lessons you drink in! Yet at the same time, he blends his learning with modesty, that he never seems to be playing the schoolmaster.

After riding seven miles he walks another mile, then resumes his seat, or betakes himself to his room and his pen; for he composes, both in Latin and Greek, the most scholarly lyrics. They have a wonderful grace, wonderful sweetness and wonderful humor, and the chastity of the writer enhances its charm. When he is told that the bathing hour has come, . . . he takes a walk naked in the sun, if there is no wind. Then he plays at ball for a long spell, throwing himself heartily into the game, for it is by means of this kind of active exercise that he battles with old age.

After his bath he lies down and waits a little while before taking food, listening in the meantime to the reading of some light and pleasant book. All this time his friends are at perfect liberty to imitate his example or do anything else they prefer. Then dinner is served, the table being as bright as it is modest, and the silver plain and old-fashioned: he has also some Corinthian vases in use, for which he has a taste but not a mania. The dinner is often relieved by actors of comedy, so that the pleasures of the table may have a seasoning of letters. Even in the summer the meal lasts well into the night, but no one finds it long, for it has kept up with such good humor and charm. The consequence is that, though he has passed his seventy-seventh year, his hearing and eyesight are as good as ever, his body is still active and alert, and the only symptom of his age is his wisdom.

This is the sort of life that I [Pliny] have vowed and determined to forestall, and I shall enter upon it with zest, as soon as my age justifies me in beating a retreat.

Slavery in the Roman Empire

Rome was a slave-holding society; it had obtained thousands of slaves during the Republic as spoils of conquest. Despite the decrease in war captives during the Pax Romana, *there was still a thriving slave trade. The philosopher and politician Seneca commented, "On one occasion, a proposal was made by the senate to distinguish slaves from freemen by their dress; it then became apparent how great would be the impending danger if our slaves began to count our number." Slaves generally led a life of toil without many benefits; a slave in the mines might last a couple of years. Still, domestic service was often pleasant, and educated slaves from Greece became trusted tutors or accountants. Although the Romans feared slave rebellions, they passed legislation designed to regulate the treatment of slaves. In fact, Romans generally respected their slaves and often granted manumission. When a slave became a freedman, he gained in social stature and, with knowledge of a trade, could even make a fortune (as did Trimalchio in the selection below) or control the strings of political power; the emperors were often supported (or dominated in the case of the emperor Claudius) by their freedmen. The following excerpts discuss the nature of slavery in the Roman Empire.*

A Slave Rebellion
PLINY THE YOUNGER

Gaius Plinius to his dear Acilius, greeting.

Here is the terrible story, deserving of much more than a letter, of how Larcius Macedo, a man of praetorian rank, was treated by his slaves. To be sure, he was a haughty and cruel master, who remembered too little—or rather, only too well—that his own father was once a slave.

He was bathing at his villa near Formiae. Suddenly slaves surrounded him, one seized him by the throat, another struck him in the face, another pommeled him on the chest, the stomach, and even, shocking to relate, on the private parts; and when they thought he was lifeless they threw him onto the hot floor, to see if he was alive. He, either unconscious or pretending to be, lay stretched out and motionless, giving the impression that death was complete. Then, finally, they carried him out as if he had fainted with the heat. Faithful slaves received him, and his concubines rushed up, wailing and shrieking. So, aroused by their noise and refreshed by the cool air, he opened his eyes and moved his body to show, since it was now safe, that he was alive. Slaves fled in all directions, but most of them were apprehended, and a search is going on for the rest. He himself was with difficulty kept alive a few days, and did not die without the consolation of revenge.

The Proper Treatment of Slaves
SENECA

The proverb is current: "As many enemies as you have slaves." They are not enemies when we acquire them; we make them enemies. I shall pass over the other cruel and inhuman conduct toward them; for we maltreat them, not as if they were men, but as if they were beasts of burden. When we recline at a banquet, one slave mops up the disgorged food, another crouches beneath the table and gathers up the leftovers of the tipsy guests. Another carves the priceless game birds; with unerring strokes and skilled hand he cuts choice morsels along the breast and rump. . . . Another, who serves the wine, must dress like a woman and wrestle with his advancing years; he cannot get away from his boyhood, but is dragged back to it; and though he has already acquired a soldier's figure, he is kept beardless by having his hair smoothed away or plucked out by the roots, and he must remain awake throughout the night, dividing his time between his master's drunkenness and his lust—in

"A Slave Rebellion" is from Pliny the Younger, *Letters*, 3.14, in *Roman Civilization, Sourcebook II: The Empire*, ed. N. Lewis and M. Reinhold, p. 266. Copyright © 1955 by Columbia University Press. Reprinted by permission of the publisher.

"The Proper Treatment of Slaves" is reprinted by permission of the publishers and the Loeb Classical Library from Seneca, *Moral Epistles*, 47, trans. Richard M. Gummere, vol. 1 (Cambridge, Mass.: Harvard University Press, 1917), pp. 303, 305, 307, 311.

the bedchamber he must be a man, at the feast a boy. Another, whose duty it is to put a valuation on the guests, must stick to his task, poor fellow, and watch to see whose flattery and whose immodesty, whether appetite or of language, is to get them an invitation for tomorrow. . . .

Kindly remember that he whom you call your slave sprang from the same stock, is smiled upon by the same skies, and like yourself breathes, lives, and dies. It is just as possible for you to see in him a freeborn man as for him to see in you a slave. . . . I do not wish to involve myself in too large a question and discuss the treatment of slaves, toward whom we Romans are excessively haughty, cruel, and insulting. But this is my advice in a nutshell: Treat those below you as you would be treated by those above you. And as often as you reflect how much power you have over a slave, remember that your master has just as much power over you. "But I have no master," you say. You are still young, perhaps you will have one. . . .

You should therefore not be deterred by these finicky persons from showing yourself to your slave as an affable person and not proudly superior to them. They ought to respect you rather than fear you. . . . He who respects also loves, and love and fear do not mix.

Legislation Against the Abuse of Slaves
GAIUS

At the present time neither Roman citizens nor any other persons who are under the rule of the Roman people are permitted to treat their slaves with excessive and baseless cruelty. For, by enactment of the Emperor Antoninus, a man who kills his own slave without cause is ordered to be held just as liable as one who kills another's slave. And even excessive severity of masters is restrained by enactment of the same emperor. For, when consulted by certain governors of provinces about those slaves who seek asylum in temples of the gods or at statues of the emperors, he ordained that if the cruelty of the masters is found to be intolerable they are to be compelled to sell their slaves.

Trimalchio: A Wealthy Freedman
PETRONIUS

Come, my friends, make yourselves at home. I too was once just like you, but by my ability I've reached my present position. What makes man is the heart, the rest is all trash. "I buy well, and I sell well;" others have different ideas. I

"Legislation Against the Abuse of Slaves" is from Gaius, *Institutes,* 1.53, in *Roman Civilization, Sourcebook II: The Empire,* ed. N. Lewis and M. Reinhold, p. 269. Copyright © 1955 by Columbia University Press. Reprinted by permission of the publisher.

"Trimalchio: A Wealthy Freedman" is from Petronius, *Satyricon,* 65.8–67.6, in *Petronii Cena Trimanchionis,* trans. W. D. Lowe (Cambridge, England: Cambridge University Press, 1905).

am ready to burst with good luck. . . . My good management brought me to my present good fortune. I was only as big as the candlestick here when I came from Asia, in fact I used to measure myself by it every day and I smeared my lips with the lamp oil to get a hairy face quicker. Still for fourteen years I was my master's favorite. And where's the disgrace in doing what one's master tells one? All the same I managed to get into my mistress' good graces, too (you know what I mean: I hold my tongue, as I am not one to boast).

But by heaven's help I became master in the house, and then I took in my fool of a lord. To be brief, he made me co-heir with the emperor to his property, and I got a senator's fortune. But no one is ever satisfied, and I wanted to go into business. To cut it short, I built five ships, I loaded them with a cargo of wine—it was worth its weight in gold at that time—and I sent it to Rome. You would have thought I had ordered my bad luck: every ship was wrecked; it's a fact, no story. . . . Do you think I failed? No, I swear the loss only whetted my appetite as if nothing had happened. I built more ships, larger, better, and luckier ones, and everybody called me a courageous man—you know, a great ship shows great strength. I loaded them with wine again, bacon fat, beans, perfume, and slaves. . . . On one voyage I cleared around 10,000,000 sesterces. I immediately bought back all the estates that had belonged to my patron. I built a mansion, I bought up young slaves to sell, and beasts of burden: everything I touched grew like a honeycomb.

Once I was worth more than my whole native town put together, I quit the game: I retired from business and started lending money, financing freedmen. . . . I'll have done well enough in my lifetime. Meantime, with Mercury watching over me, I built this residence. As you know, it was a cottage; now it's fit for a god. It's got four dining rooms, twenty bedrooms, two marble colonnades, and the upstairs apartments, my own bedroom where I sleep, . . . an excellent porter's lodge, and enough guest rooms for all my guests. . . . And there are lots of other things, which I'll show you presently. Believe me, have a penny, you're worth a penny; have something, you'll be treated like something. And so your friend, once a mere worm, is now a king.

The Life and Death of the City of Pompeii

One of the most famous incidents in antiquity was the eruption of the volcano Vesuvius on August 24, 79 C.E. The accompanying earthquakes destroyed several villages and the cities of Herculaneum and Pompeii. Both these cities have yielded magnificent ruins that were well preserved because they were buried under rich volcanic ash. In Pompeii, once a thriving port city of about 25,000 people, we can glimpse life as it was just before the tragedy occurred. The graffiti that adorned the walls of the city give testimony to a vibrant political life and a "service-oriented" community that catered to traders and sailors. A rare eyewitness account of the destruction of the city, given by Pliny the Younger, follows.

Wall Inscriptions

His neighbors urge you to elect Lucius Statius Receptus duovir with judicial power; he is worthy. Aemilius Celer, a neighbor, wrote this. May you take sick if you maliciously erase this!

The petty thieves support the election of Vatia as aedile.

I ask you to elect Marcus Cerrinius Vatia to the aedileship. All the late drinkers support him.

I ask you to elect Aulus Vettius Firmus aedile. He is worthy of the city. I ask you to elect him, ballplayers. Elect him!

Here slept Vibius Restitutus all by himself, his heart filled with lust for his Urbana.

I wonder, O wall, that you may not have fallen in ruins from supporting the stupidities of so many scribblers!

The Destruction of Pompeii (79 C.E.)
PLINY THE YOUNGER

My uncle was stationed at Misenum in active command of the fleet. On 24 August, in the early afternoon, my mother drew his attention to a cloud of unusual size and appearance. He had been out in the sun, had taken a cold bath, and lunched while lying down, and was then working at his books. He called for his shoes and climbed up to a place which would give him the best view of the phenomenon. It was not clear at that distance from which mountain the cloud was rising (it was afterwards known to be Vesuvius); its general appearance can best be expressed as being like a pine rather than any other tree, for it rose to a great height on a sort of trunk and then split off into branches, I imagine because it was thrust upwards by the first blast and then left unsupported as the pressure subsided, or else it was borne down by its own weight so that it spread out and gradually dispersed. Sometimes it looked white, sometimes blotched and dirty, according to the amount of soil and ashes it carried with it. My uncle's scholarly acumen saw at once that it was important enough for a closer inspection, and he ordered a fast boat to be made ready, telling me I could come with him if I wished. I replied that I preferred to go on with my studies, and as it happened he had himself given me some writing to do.

As he was leaving the house he was handed a message from Rectina, wife of Tascius, whose house was at the foot of the mountain, so that escape was impossible except by boat. She was terrified by the danger threatening her

"Wall Inscriptions" is from William S. Davis, ed., *Readings in Ancient History*, vol. 2 (Boston: Allyn and Bacon, 1913), pp. 262–263.

"The Destruction of Pompeii" is reprinted by permission of the publishers and the Loeb Classical Library from Pliny the Younger, *Letters*, 6.16, 6.20, trans. Betty Radice, vol. 1 (Cambridge, Mass.: Harvard University Press, 1969), pp. 427, 429, 431, 433, 439, 441, 443, 445, 447.

The ruins of Pompeii, a prosperous port city that was completely destroyed by the eruption of Vesuvius in 79 C.E. The remarkably well-preserved ruins tell historians much about life in the small cities of the Roman Empire. *(Corbis)*

and implored him to rescue her from her fate. He changed his plans, and what he had begun in a spirit of inquiry he completed as a hero. He gave orders for the warships to be launched and went on board himself with the intention of bringing help to many more people besides Rectina, for this lovely stretch of coast was thickly populated. He hurried to the place which everyone else was hastily leaving, steering his course straight for the danger zone. He was entirely fearless, describing each new movement and phase of the portent to be noted down exactly as he observed them. Ashes were already falling, hotter and thicker as the ships drew near, followed by bits of pumice and blackened stones, charred and cracked by the flames: then suddenly they were in shallow water, and the shore was blocked by the debris from the mountain. For a moment my uncle wondered whether to turn back, but when the helmsman advised this he refused, telling him that Fortune stood by the courageous. . . . This wind was of course full in my uncle's favour, and he was able to help his ship in. He embraced his terrified friend, cheered and encouraged him, and thinking he could calm his fears by showing his own composure. . . .

Meanwhile on Mount Vesuvius broad sheets of fire and leaping flames blazed at several points, their bright glare emphasized by the darkness of night. . . . The buildings were now shaking with violent shocks, and seemed to be swaying to and fro as if they were torn from their foundations . . . there was the danger of falling pumice-stones, even though these were light and porous. . . . As a protection against falling objects they put pillows on their heads tied down with cloths.

Elsewhere there was daylight by this time, but they were still in darkness, blacker and denser than any night that ever was, which they relieved by lighting torches and various kinds of lamp. My uncle decided to go down to the shore and investigate on the spot the possibility of any escape by sea, but he found the waves were still wild and dangerous. A sheet was spread on the ground for him to lie down, and he repeatedly asked for cold water to drink. Then the flames and smell of sulphur which gave warning of the approaching fire drove the others to take flight and roused him to stand up. He stood leaning on two slaves and then suddenly collapsed, I imagine because the dense fumes choked his breathing by blocking his windpipe which was constitutionally weak and narrow and often inflamed. When daylight returned on the 26th—two days after the last day he had seen—his body was found intact and uninjured, still fully clothed and looking more like sleep than death.

• • •

So the letter which you asked me to write on my uncle's death has made you eager to hear about the terrors and also the hazards I had to face when left at Misenum, for I broke off at the beginning of this part of my story. . . .

After my uncle's departure I spent the rest of the day with my books, as this was my reason for staying behind. Then I took a bath, dined, and then dozed fitfully for a while. For several days past there had been earth tremors which were not particularly alarming because they are frequent in Campania: but that night the shocks were so violent that everything felt as if it were not only shaken but overturned. My mother hurried into my room and found me already getting up to wake her if she were still asleep. We sat down in the forecourt of the house, between the buildings and the sea close by. . . .

By now it was dawn, but the light was still dim and faint. The buildings round us were already tottering, and the open space we were in was too small for us not to be in real and imminent danger if the house collapsed. This finally decided us to leave the town. We were followed by a panic-stricken mob of people wanting to act on someone else's decision in preference to their own (an element in fear which is like prudence), who hurried us on our way by pressing hard behind in a dense crowd. Once beyond the buildings we stopped, and there we had some extraordinary experiences which thoroughly alarmed us. The carriages we had ordered to be brought out began to run in different directions though the ground was quite level, and would not remain stationary even when wedged with stones. We also saw the sea sucked away and apparently forced back by the earthquake: at any rate it receded from the shore so that quantities of sea creatures were left stranded on dry sand. On the landward side a fearful black cloud was rent by forked and quivering

bursts of flame, and parted to reveal great tongues of fire, like flashes of light-
ening magnified in size.

At this point my uncle's friend from Spain spoke up still more urgently: "If
your . . . uncle is still alive, he will want you both to be saved; if he is dead, he
would want you to survive him—so why put off your escape?" We replied that
we would not think of considering our own safety as long as we were uncertain of his. Without waiting any longer, our friend rushed off and hurried out
of danger as fast as he could.

Soon afterwards the cloud sank down to earth and covered the sea; it had
already blotted out Capri and hidden the promontory of Misenum from
sight. Then my mother implored, entreated, and commanded me to escape,
whereas she was old and slow and could die in peace so long as she had not
been the cause of my death too. I told her I refused to save myself without
her, and grasping her hand forced her to quicken her pace. She gave in reluctantly, blaming herself for delaying me. Ashes were already falling, not as
yet very thickly. I looked round: a dense black cloud was coming up behind
us, spreading over the earth like a flood. "Let us leave the road while we can
still see," I said, "or we shall be knocked down and trampled underfoot in the
dark by the crowd behind." We had scarcely sat down to rest when darkness
fell, not the dark of a moonless or cloudy night, but as if the lamp had been
put out in a closed room. You could hear the shrieks of women, the wailing of
infants, and the shouting of men; some were calling their parents, others
their children or their wives, trying to recognize them by their voices. People
bewailed their own fate or that of their relatives, and there were some who
prayed for death in their terror of dying. Many besought the aid of the gods,
but still more imagined there were no gods left and that the universe was
plunged into eternal darkness for evermore. . . . A gleam of light returned,
but we took this to be a warning of the approaching flames rather than daylight. However, the flames remained some distance off; then darkness came
on once more and ashes began to fall again, this time in heavy showers. We
rose from time to time and shook them off, otherwise we should have been
buried and crushed beneath their weight. I could boast that not a groan or
cry of fear escaped me in these perils, had I not derived some poor consolation in my mortal lot from the belief that the whole world was dying with me
and I with it.

At last the darkness thinned and dispersed into smoke or cloud; then
there was genuine daylight, and the sun actually shone out, but yellowish as it
is during an eclipse. We were terrified to see everything changed, buried
deep in ashes like snowdrifts. We returned to Misenum where we attended to
our physical needs as best we could, and then spent an anxious night alter-
nating between hope and fear. Fear predominated, for the earthquakes went
on, and several hysterical individuals made their own and other people's
calamities seem ludicrous in comparison with their frightful predictions. But
even then, in spite of the dangers we had been through and were still expecting, my mother and I had still no intention of leaving until we had news of
my uncle.

The Stoic Philosophy

The Romans were never known for their contributions to abstract thought and did not produce a unique philosophy. Still, they borrowed well and adapted ideas that complemented their values. For the Roman, duty and organization were particularly important; consequently, the Stoic philosophy, which had originated in Greece in the third century B.C.E., *was especially popular among the aristocracy. According to Stoic tenets, a divine plan ordered the universe, so whatever lot or occupation fell to one in life should be accepted and coped with appropriately. Restraint and moderation characterized the ideal Stoic, and he advocated tolerance as an essential component of the "brotherhood of man." To a Stoic who felt that his honor was somehow compromised, suicide was an acceptable and dutiful way of preserving his dignity. The following selections come from the writings of three Stoics of diverse backgrounds. Epictetus was the slave of a rich freedman; Seneca was tutor to the emperor Nero and finally committed suicide at his command in 66* C.E; *Marcus Aurelius became emperor in 161* C.E., *an occupation he did not seek, but dutifully executed.*

Epictetus

I must die: if instantly, I will die instantly; if in a short time, I will dine first; and when the hour comes, then I will die. How? As becomes one who restores what is not his own.

Do not you know that both sickness and death must overtake us? At what employment? The husbandman at his plough; the sailor on his voyage. At what employment would you be taken? For my own part, I would be found engaged in nothing but in the regulation of my own Will; how to render it undisturbed, unrestrained, uncompelled, free. I would be found studying this, that I may be able to say to God, "Have I transgressed Thy commands? Have I perverted the powers, the senses, the instincts, which Thou hast given me? Have I ever accused Thee, or censured Thy dispensations? I have been sick, because it was Thy pleasure, like others; but I willingly. I have been poor, it being Thy will; but with joy. I have not been in power, because it was not Thy will; and power I have never desired. Hast Thou ever seen me saddened because of this? Have I not always approached Thee with a cheerful countenance; prepared to execute Thy commands and the indications of Thy will? Is it Thy pleasure that I should depart from this assembly? I depart. I give Thee all thanks that Thou hast thought me worthy to have a share in it with Thee; to behold Thy works, and to join with Thee in comprehending Thy administration." Let death overtake me while I am thinking, while I am writing, while I am reading such things as these.

"Epictetus" is from T. W. Higginson, ed., *The Works of Epictetus* (Boston: Little, Brown, 1886).

Seneca

What is the principal thing in human life? . . . To raise the soul above the threats and promises of fortune; to consider nothing as worth hoping for. For what does fortune possess worth setting your heart upon? . . . What is the principal thing? To be able to endure adversity with a joyful heart; to bear whatever occurs just as if it were the very thing you desired to have happen to you. For you would have felt it your duty to desire it, had you known that all things happen by divine decree. Tears, complaints, lamentations are rebellion [against divine order]. . . .

What is the principal thing? To have life on the very lips, ready to issue when summoned. This makes a man free, not by right of Roman citizenship but by right of nature. He is, moreover, the true freeman who has escaped from bondage to self; that slavery is constant and unavoidable—it presses us day and night alike, without pause, without respite. To be a slave to self is the most grievous kind of slavery; yet its fetters may easily be struck off, if you will cease to make large demands upon yourself, if you will cease to seek a personal reward for your services, and if you will set before your eyes your nature and your age, even though it be the bloom of youth; if you will say to yourself, "Why do I rave, and pant, and sweat? Why do I ply the earth? Why do I haunt the Forum? Man needs but little, and that not for long."

Marcus Aurelius

1. He who acts unjustly acts impiously. For since the universal nature has made rational animals for the sake of one another to help one another according to their deserts, but in no way to injure one another, he who transgresses her will, is clearly guilty of impiety towards the highest divinity. And he too who lies is guilty of impiety to the same divinity; for there is a universal nature of things that are; and things that are have a relation to all things that come into existence. . . .

2. It would be a man's happiest lot to depart from mankind without having had any taste of lying and hypocrisy and luxury and pride. However, to breathe out one's life when a man has had enough of these things is the next best voyage, as the saying goes. . . .

3. Do not despise death, but be well content with it, since this too is one of those things which nature wills. For such as it is to be young and to grow old, and to increase and to reach maturity, and to have teeth and beard and grey hairs, and to beget, and to be pregnant and to bring forth, and all the other natural operations which the seasons of thy life bring, such also is dissolution.

"Seneca" is from Seneca, *Natural Questions*, 3. Preface, 10–17, trans. J. Clarke (London, 1910).

"Marcus Aurelius" is from Marcus Aurelius, *Meditations*, trans. George Long (London: The Chesterfield Library, 1862), pp. 241–242, 253.

This, then, is consistent with the character of a reflecting man, to be neither careless nor impatient nor contemptuous with respect to death, but to wait for it as one of the operations of nature. . . .

4. Wipe out imagination: check desire: extinguish appetite: keep the ruling faculty in its own power.

Failure and Decline (180–500 C.E.)

Political Dislocation

The Roman Empire generally prospered during the first and second centuries C.E. During the third century, however, the empire gradually fell prey to problems that had existed to some extent in preceding years, but had never reached crisis proportions. One of the main problems was a lack of leadership. Rome had survived bad emperors before, but during the fifty years from 235 to 285 C.E., there were twenty-two emperors and only one died a natural death in his bed. The rest fell victim to assassination or violent death on the battlefield. The following excerpt describes the political chaos upon the death of the emperor Pertinax in 193 C.E. The empire was sold to the highest bidder by the emperor's personal troops, the Praetorian Guard. The "winner," Didius Julianus, ruled for three months before he himself was killed by these same Praetorian Guardsmen.

"Empire for Sale" (193 C.E.)
DIO CASSIUS

Didius Julianus, at once an insatiate money getter and a wanton spendthrift, who was always eager for revolution, and hence had been exiled by Commodus to his native city of Milan, now, when he heard of the death of Pertinax, hastily made his way to the [Praetorian] camp and, standing at the gates of the enclosure, made bids to the soldiers for the rule over the Romans. Then ensued a most disgraceful business and one unworthy of Rome. For, just as if it had been in some market or auction room, both the city and its entire Empire were auctioned off. The sellers were the ones who had slain their emperor, and the would-be buyers were Sulpicianus and Julianus, who vied to outbid each other, one from the inside, the other from outside. They gradually raised their bids up to 20,000 sesterces per soldier. Some of the soldiers

"'Empire for Sale'" is reprinted by permission of the publishers and the Loeb Classical Library from Dio Cassius, *Roman History,* 74.11.2–6, trans. Earnest Cary, vol. 9 (Cambridge, Mass.: Harvard University Press, 1927), pp. 143, 145.

would carry word to Julianus, "Sulpicianus offers so much; how much more do you bid?" And to Sulpicianus in turn, "Julianus promises so much; how much do you raise him?" Sulpicianus would have won the day, being inside and being prefect of the city and also the first to name the figure of 20,000, had not Julianus raised his bid no longer by a small amount but by 5,000 at one time, shouting it in a loud voice and also indicating the amount with his fingers. So the soldiers, captivated by this extravagant bid . . . received Julianus inside and declared him emperor.

Economic Dislocation

The empire was saved for a time through the efforts of the emperor Diocletian (284–305). Diocletian developed a system of providing for peaceful succession and more efficient rule of the empire. He divided it into four prefectures, each with a leader responsible for the administration and security of his region. The system worked while Diocletian was in power but fell victim to ambitious generals once Diocletian retired.

One problem that Diocletian never solved was economic dislocation. As the first excerpt indicates, there was a general distrust of coinage issued by emperors whose short reigns did not inspire confidence in the value of money. Diocletian tried to control inflation by setting a maximum price that could be paid for goods. Note the penalty for transgressing the system.

Distrust of Imperial Coinage (260 c.e.)

From Aurelius Ptolemacus, . . . strategus [governor] of the Oxyrhynchite nome [in Egypt]. Whereas the public officials have assembled and have accused the bankers of the exchange banks of having closed them because of their unwillingness to accept the divine coin of the emperors, it has become necessary to issue an order to all owners of the banks to open them and to accept and exchange all coin except the absolutely spurious and counterfeit—and not alone to them but to those who engage in business transactions of any kind whatever—knowing full well that if they disobey this order they will experience the penalties already ordained for them in the past by His Majesty the Prefect. Signed by me. Year 1, Hathyr 28.

"Distrust of Imperial Coinage" is reprinted by permission of the publishers and the Loeb Classical Library from *Oxyrhynchus Papyrus,* no. 1411, trans. A. S. Hunt, vol. 2 (Cambridge, Mass.: Harvard University Press, 1932), pp. 127, 129.

Price Controls

Aroused justly and rightfully by all the facts set forth above, and in response to the needs of mankind itself, which appears to be praying for release, we have decided that maximum prices of articles for sale must be established. We have not set down fixed prices, for we do not deem it just to do this, since many provinces occasionally enjoy the good fortune of welcome low prices and the privilege, as it were, of prosperity. Thus, when the pressure of high prices appears anywhere—may the gods avert such a calamity!—avarice . . . will be checked by the limits fixed in our statute and by the restraining curbs of the law.

It is our pleasure, therefore, that the prices listed in the subjoined schedule be held in observance in the whole of our Empire. And every person shall take note that the liberty to exceed them at will has been ended, but that the blessing of low prices has in no way been impaired in those places where supplies actually abound. . . . Moreover, this universal edict will serve as a necessary check upon buyers and sellers whose practice it is to visit ports and other provinces. For when they too know that in the pinch of scarcity there is no possibility of exceeding the prices fixed for commodities, they will take into account in their calculations at the time of sale the localities, the transportation costs, and all other factors. In this way they will make apparent the justice of our decision that those who transport merchandise may not sell at higher prices anywhere.

It is agreed that even in the time of our ancestors it was the practice in passing laws to restrain offenses by prescribing a penalty. For rarely is a situation beneficial to humanity accepted spontaneously; experience teaches that fear is the most effective regulator and guide for the performance of duty. Therefore it is our pleasure that anyone who resists the measures of this statute shall be subject to a capital [death] penalty for daring to do so. And let no one consider the statute harsh, since there is at hand a ready protection from danger in the observance of moderation. . . . We therefore exhort the loyalty of all, so that a regulation instituted for the public good may be observed with willing obedience and due scruple, especially as it is seen that by a statute of this kind provision has been made, not for single municipalities and peoples and provinces but for the whole world. . . .

Barbarian Invasions

The most distressing and ultimately ruinous cause for the fall of the empire was the constant influx of Germanic invaders. Rome had been able to cope with Germanic incursions during the first and second centuries by either defeating them militarily or by allowing them to fight with Roman troops as confederates. In the latter circumstance, Germans were often "Romanized," learning the Latin

"Price Controls" is from E. Graser, trans., "Edict on Maximum Prices," as contained in T. Frank, ed., *Economic Survey of Ancient Rome*, V (Baltimore: Johns Hopkins University Press, 1940), pp. 314–317. Copyright © 1940 by The Johns Hopkins University Press. Reprinted by permission of the publisher.

A contemporary view of the ruins of the Roman Forum from the Temple of Saturn: "As yourselves, your empires fall. And every kingdom hath a grave."—William Hobbington *(Perry M. Rogers)*

language and respecting Roman traditions. Perhaps because of perceptions of Roman weakness, or in response to pressures from other nomadic eastern peoples (such as the Huns), in the mid-second and third centuries the Germanic tribes moved more aggressively into the empire, often overwhelming Roman armies that were hampered by a lack of political and military direction. The first selection is by Tacitus, who describes the values and lifestyle of the Germanic "barbarians" in the second century. By the fifth century, the empire had been overrun. Jerome, a Christian writer in the East, described the scene in the western provinces.

The Germanic Tribes

TACITUS

I agree in the opinion that the Germans have never been inter-married with other nations; but to be a race pure, unmixed, and stamped with a distinct character. Hence a family likeness pervades the whole, though they are so

"The Germanic Tribes" is from Tacitus, *Germania*, 4–20, in *Readings in Ancient History*, vol. 1, ed. William S. Davis (Boston: Allyn and Bacon, 1913), pp. 313–314.

numerous:—eyes stern and blue; ruddy hair; large bodies, powerful in sudden exertions, but impatient of toil and labor, least of all capable of sustaining thirst and heat. Cold and hunger they are accustomed by their climate and soil to endure. . . . Swords or broad lances are seldom used; but they generally carry a spear . . . which has an iron blade, short and narrow, but so sharp and manageable that, as occasion requires, they use it either for close or distant fighting. Few are provided with armor and . . . helmets though all have shields.

Their line of battle is drawn in wedges. To give ground, provided they rally again, is considered rather as a prudent strategem than cowardice. . . . The greatest disgrace that can befall them is to have abandoned their shields. A person branded with this ignominy cannot join in their religious rites, or enter their assemblies; so that many, after escaping from battle, have ended their infamy by suicide. In election of kings they have regard to birth; in that of generals to valor. Their kings have not an absolute or unlimited power, and their generals command less through the force of authority than of example. If they are daring, adventurous, and conspicuous in action, they procure obedience from the admiration they inspire. It is a principal incentive to their courage that their squadrons and battalions are not formed by men fortuitously collected, but by the assemblage of families and clans. Their pledges are also near at hand; they have within hearing the yells of the women, and the cries of their children. . . .

On affairs of small moment the chiefs consult. On those of greater importance, the whole community, yet with the circumstance that what is referred to the decision of the people is first maturely discussed by the chiefs. At their assemblies, they all sit down armed. Silence is proclaimed by the priests. Then the king, or chief, or such others as are conspicuous for age, birth, military renown, or eloquence are heard; and gain attention rather from their ability to persuade, than their authority to command. If a proposal displeases, the assembly reject it by an inarticulate murmur; if it prove agreeable, they clash their javelins; for the most honorable expression of assent among them is from the sound of arms.

News of the Attacks

JEROME

Innumerable and most ferocious people have overrun the whole of Gaul. The entire area bounded by the Alps, the Pyrenees, the ocean and the Rhine is occupied by the Quadi, Vandals, Carmatians, Alanni, Gepides, Saxons, Burgundians, Alammani—oh weep for the empire—and the hostile Pannonians.

. . . Mainz, once a noble city, is captured and razed, and thousands have been massacred in the church. Worms has succumbed to a long siege. Rheims, the impregnable, Amiens, Artois . . . Tours, Nimes and Strasburg are in the hands of the Germans. The provinces of Aquitane, . . . of Lyons and Narbonne are completely occupied and devastated either by the sword from without or famine within. I cannot mention Toulouse without tears, for until now it has been spared, due to the merits of its saintly bishop Exuperus. The Spaniards tremble, expecting daily the invasion and recalling the horrors Spaniards suffer in continual anticipation.

Who would believe that Rome, victor over all the world, would fall, that she would be to her people both the womb and the tomb. Once all the East, Egypt and Africa acknowledged her sway and were counted among her men servants and her maid servants. Who would believe that holy Bethlehem would receive as beggars, nobles, both men and women, once abounding in riches? Where we cannot help we mourn and mingle with theirs our tears. . . . There is not an hour, not even a moment, when we are not occupied with crowds of refugees, when the peace of the monastery is not invaded by a horde of guests so that we shall either have to shut the gates or neglect the Scriptures for which the gates were opened. Consequently I have to snatch furtively the hours of the night, which now with winter approaching are growing longer, and try to dictate by candle light and thus . . . relieve a mind distraught. I am not boasting of our hospitality, as some may suspect, but simply explaining to you the delay.

Decline and Christianity

One of the more famous theories for the decline of the Roman Empire belongs to Edward Gibbon, the celebrated eighteenth-century historian. His work The Decline and Fall of the Roman Empire *has proved an authoritative analysis of the end. After a Biblical warning of Rome's fated collapse, Gibbon's famous theory is presented.*

A Biblical Warning: The Book of Revelation

After this I saw another angel coming down out of heaven. He had great authority, and his splendor brightened the whole earth. He cried out in a loud voice, "She has fallen! Great Babylon [Rome] has fallen! She is now haunted by demons and unclean spirits; all kinds of filthy and hateful birds live in her.

For she gave her wine to all peoples and made them drink it—the strong wine of her immoral lust. The kings of the earth committed immorality with her, and the businessmen of the world grew rich from her unrestrained lust."

> Then I heard another voice from heaven, saying,
> "Come out, my people! Come out from her!
>   You must not take part in her sins;
>   you must not share her punishment!
> For her sins are piled up as high as heaven,
>   and God remembers her wicked ways.
> Treat her exactly as she has treated you;
>   pay her back twice as much as she has done.
> Fill her cup with a drink twice as strong
>   as the drink she prepared for you.
> Give her as much suffering and grief
>   as the glory and luxury she gave herself.
> For she keeps telling herself:
> 'Here I sit, a queen!
>   I am no widow,
>   I will never know grief!'
> Because of this her plagues will all strike
>   her in one day,
>   disease, grief, and famine.
> And she will be burned with fire,
>   because the Lord God, who judges her,
>   is mighty."

The kings of the earth who shared her immorality and lust will cry and weep over the city when they see the smoke of her burning. They stand a long way off, because they are afraid of her suffering, and say, "How terrible! How awful! This great and mighty city Babylon! In just one hour you have been punished!"

The businessmen of the earth also cry and mourn for her, because no one buys their goods any longer; no one buys their gold, silver, precious stones, and pearls; their goods of linen, purple cloth, silk, and scarlet; all kinds of rare woods, and all kinds of objects made of ivory and of expensive wood, of bronze, iron, and marble; and cinnamon, spice, incense, myrrh, and frankincense; wine and oil, flour and wheat, cattle and sheep, horses and carriages, slaves and even men's souls. The businessmen say to her, "All the good things you longed to own have disappeared, and all your wealth and glamour are gone, and you will never find them again!" The businessmen, who became rich from doing business in that city, will stand a long way off, because they are afraid of her suffering. They will cry and mourn, and say, "How terrible! How awful scarlet, and cover herself with gold ornaments, precious stones, and pearls! And in one hour she has lost all this wealth!"

All the ship captains and passengers, the sailors and all others who earn their living on the sea, stood a long way off, and cried out as they saw the smoke of her burning, "There never has been another city like the great city!" They threw dust on their heads, they cried and mourned, saying, "How terrible! How awful for the great city! She is the city where all who have ships sailing the seas became rich on her wealth! And in one hour she has lost everything!"

Be glad, heaven, because of her destruction! Be glad, God's people, and the apostles and prophets! Because God has judged her for what she did to you!

Then a mighty angel picked up a stone the size of a large millstone and threw it into the sea, saying, "This is how the great city Babylon will be thrown down with violence, and will never be seen again. . . ."

The Theory of Edward Gibbon

As the happiness of a future life is the great object of religion, we may hear, without surprise or scandal, that the introduction, or at least the abuse, of Christianity had some influence on the decline and fall of the Roman empire. The clergy successfully preached the doctrines of patience and pusillanimity; the active virtues of society were discouraged; and the last remains of the military spirit were buried in the cloister; a large portion of public and private wealth was consecrated to the specious demands of charity and devotion; and the soldiers' pay was lavished on the useless multitudes of both sexes, who could only plead the merits of abstinence and chastity. Faith, zeal, curiosity, and the more earthly passions of malice and ambition kindled the flame of theological discord; the church, and even the state, were distracted by religious factions, whose conflicts were sometimes bloody, and always implacable; the attention of the emperors was diverted from camps to [church] synods; the Roman world was oppressed by a new species of tyranny; and the persecuted sects became the secret enemies of their country. Yet party-spirit, however pernicious or absurd, is a principle of union as well as of dissension. The bishops, from eighteen hundred pulpits, inculcated the duty of passive obedience to a lawful and orthodox sovereign; their communion of distant churches; and the benevolent temper of the gospel was strengthened, though confined by the spiritual alliance of the Catholics. The sacred indolence of the monks was devoutly embraced by a servile and effeminate age; but, if superstition had not afforded a decent retreat, the same vices would have tempted the unworthy Romans to desert, from baser motives, the standard of the republic. Religious precepts are easily obeyed, which indulge and sanctify the natural inclinations of their votaries; but the pure and genuine influence of Christianity may be traced in its beneficial though imperfect, effects on the Barbarian proselytes of the North. If the decline of the Roman empire was hastened by the conversion of [the Emperor] Constantine, his victorious religion broke the violence of the fall, and mollified the ferocious temper of the conquerors.

"The Theory of Edward Gibbon" is from Edward Gibbon, *The History of the Decline and Fall of the Roman Empire*, vol. 4, ed. J. B. Bury (London, 1901), pp. 162–163.

The Lessons of Rome

The decline of Roman civilization presents an appropriate occasion for reflection on the lessons that can be learned from the experience. The following modern historians offer some ideas.

The Barbarization of Civilization
M. I. ROSTOVTZEFF

None of the existing theories fully explains the problem of the decay of ancient civilization, if we can apply the word "decay" to the complex phenomenon which I have endeavoured to describe. Each of them, however, has contributed much to the clearing of the ground, and has helped us to perceive that the main phenomenon which underlies the process of decline is the gradual absorption of the educated classes by the masses and the consequent simplification of all the functions of political, social, economic, and intellectual life, which we call the barbarization of the ancient world.

The evolution of the ancient world has a lesson and a warning for us. Our civilization will not last unless it be a civilization not of one class, but of the masses. The Oriental civilizations were more stable and lasting than the Greco-Roman, because, being chiefly based on religion, they were nearer to the masses. Another lesson is that violent attempts at levelling have never helped to uplift the masses. They have destroyed the upper classes, and resulted in accelerating the process of barbarization. But the ultimate problem remains like a ghost, ever present and unlaid: Is it possible to extend a higher civilization to the lower classes without debasing its standard and diluting its quality to the vanishing point? Is not every civilization bound to decay as soon as it begins to penetrate the masses?

An Equitable Distribution of Wealth
F. W. WALBANK

In one way or another our own society has incorporated within its texture all that matters of classical culture and the culture of still earlier civilizations. The decline and fall of Rome was real enough, a genuine decay springing from a complex of causes that are only too painfully clear. Yet, for all that, it was the route along which humanity passed, through the long apparent stagnation of feudalism to that fresh burst of progress, which created the modern world. And now, having advanced, not indeed along that straight upward line of which we spoke in an earlier chapter, but by the time-honoured method of one step backwards, two steps forwards, we find ourselves once more standing at the crossroads and turning with Gibbon to read anew the lesson of the decline of Rome.

"This awful revolution," he wrote, "may be usefully applied to the instruction of the present age." What then are the alternatives which it indicates for us? They are not in doubt. One choice that confronts us is to plan the resources of our society for the whole of our peoples, whether black or white; to rid ourselves of the menace of underconsumption, that incubus which we share with the Roman Empire; to effect a more equitable distribution of wealth; and to give full scope for the employment of the new technical forces man already controls. This is a new path along which antiquity cannot light us, because it never trod that way. The alternative is to ignore the lesson which history offers, to follow in the footsteps of the ancient world (which never solved this problem because it could not), to plan—or fail to plan—for the few, for underconsumption at home, for a scramble after markets abroad, and so eventually for further, deadlier wars and ultimate ruin.

That this ruin might, like the ruin of Rome, give rise to new social developments, leading in the fullness of time to some future society, which would in turn be presented with the same problem, is little consolation to us if we fail now. But because we have the choice, where the ancients had none, let us be more charitable as we contemplate their downfall and the inexorable chain of cause and effect, as it operated throughout the whole of the social structure of antiquity. Let us avoid taking sides hastily, either with the Emperors, who were salvaging at a heavy price the remnants of civilization in the only way open to them, or with their utopian enemies who, from altruistic or selfish motives, fought to extort an individual freedom which society could not grant. Instead of solacing ourselves with the passing of moral judgments on those who are now long since dead, we shall do better to be quite sure that we know why ancient society declined to an inevitable end; and, having learnt the lesson of that "awful revolution," we may reserve our passions and our energies for the more immediate task of helping to right what is wrong in our own civilization.

CHRONOLOGY: The *Pax Romana* and the Decline of Rome

27 B.C.–14 C.E.	The principate of Augustus. Augustus "restores" the Roman Republic yet controls it as emperor through his authority and military power.
C.E. 14–68	Julio-Claudian Dynasty (Tiberius, Caligula, Claudius, Nero).
66–70	Jewish rebellion crushed by Titus after siege at Masada. Temple destroyed. A final rebellion led by Simon Bar-Kochba brutally suppressed in 135.
69	Year of the Four Emperors. Civil war results in suicide of Nero and power struggle eventually won by Vespasian.
69–96	Flavian Dynasty (Vespasian, Titus, Domitian). Eruption of Vesuvius and destruction of Pompeii and Herculaneum (79).
96–180	The five "Good Emperors" (Nerva, Trajan, Hadrian, Antoninus Pius, Marcus Aurelius) expand the Roman Empire and preside over the *Pax Romana.* Succession is based on an adoptive principle of choosing a leader who will maintain the efficiency and stability of the state. Breaks down with succession of Commodus (180–193).
180–284	Decline of Roman leadership ("Barrack emperors"), economic crisis, and Germanic invasions cause the "Crisis of the Third Century."
284–305	Reign of Diocletian. Establishment of Dominate. Tetrarchy designed to provide a secure succession by dividing the Roman Empire among four emperors.
306–337	Rule of Constantine. Economic reforms postpone Roman collapse. Dedication of Constantinople as new capital of the empire (330).
379–395	Rule of Theodosius, the last emperor to control both the eastern and western halves of the Roman Empire. Christianity becomes the official state religion.
410	Rome invaded by Visigoths under Alaric.
413–426	St. Augustine writes *The City of God.*
450	Anglo-Saxon invasion of Britain.
451–453	Huns invade Europe led by Attila, "Scourge of God."
455	Vandals overrun Rome.
476	Barbarian Odoacer deposes last Western Roman emperor, Romulus Augustulus.
489–493	Theodoric establishes Ostrogothic Kingdom in Italy.

STUDY QUESTIONS

1. Note carefully the opening document ("The Powers of the Emperor"). What were the specific rights of an emperor? Do they sound reasonable and necessary for efficient rule? Or are they arbitrary and prone to abuse? Was the emperor truly a "first citizen," or was he an autocratic monarch?

2. Was the relationship of Rome to its provinces generally a good one? If so, what made the Romans good rulers? What were some of the specific criticisms of Roman rule? On balance, would you have liked living as a provincial under Roman control?

3. Discuss some of the benefits and drawbacks of life in imperial Rome. Do you consider the Romans barbaric because they often enjoyed such sports as chariot racing or gladiatorial combat? Can you think of any modern parallels to such activity in our own society?

4. Why do you think that Romans held slaves? Did they treat their slaves well? Was there any social mobility in the Roman Empire? What does this say about the relative freedom of Roman society?

5. In your opinion, what is the most memorable part of Pliny's description of the destruction of Pompeii? What do the wall inscriptions tell you about life in the city?

6. Pick out specific passages from the selections on Stoicism that reflect the tenets of that philosophy as described in the section introduction. Why can this be considered a philosophy compatible with Roman values?

7. What were some of the main reasons for the decline of the Roman Empire? Be specific in your analysis of the primary sources presented in the section "Failure and Decline." In your opinion, which is the most important factor for the decline of a civilization and why?

8. What is Gibbon's theory on Roman decline? Do you regard it as valid? Why or why not? What do you think of the "barbarization" theory of M. I. Rostovtzeff? How would you define "underconsumption," as mentioned by F. W. Walbank?

9. It has been said that Americans are very much like Romans in outlook and response as a society. Do you agree? What do you think is the most valuable lesson to be gained from observing the decline of the Roman Empire?

10. The process of decline has fascinated humanity for centuries. Are civilizations biological in nature? Are they born and do they grow, mature, age, and die, as do other living entities? Does each civilization progress and transfer its benefits to the developing successor civilization? Are there any warning signs for decline, and can a civilization reverse the process once it has been started? Does technology have anything to do with decline? As we get more advanced technologically, does this speed up the process of decline? Compare Roman and American societies in this regard.

PART IV

THE MEDIEVAL WORLD

7

The Sword of Faith: Western Civilization During the Middle Ages

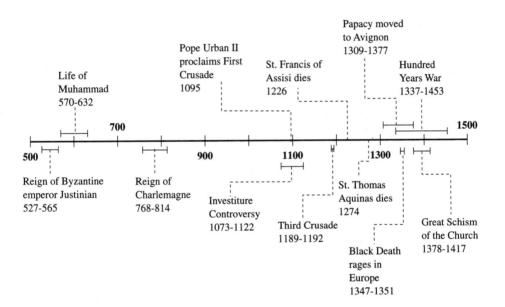

Papacy moved
to Avignon
1309-1377

Pope Urban II
proclaims First
Crusade
1095

St. Francis of
Assisi dies
1226

Hundred
Years War
1337-1453

Life of
Muhammad
570-632

700

1500

500

900

1100

1300

Reign of Byzantine
emperor Justinian
527-565

Reign of
Charlemagne
768-814

Investiture
Controversy
1073-1122

Third Crusade
1189-1192

St. Thomas
Aquinas dies
1274

Black Death
rages in
Europe
1347-1351

Great Schism
of the Church
1378-1417

Understanding is the reward of faith. Therefore, do not seek to understand that you may believe, but believe that you may understand.

—St. Augustine

If the work of God could be comprehended by reason, it would no longer be wonderful.

—Pope Gregory I

There are two ways to slide through life: to believe everything or to doubt everything; both ways save us from thinking.

—Alfred Korzybski

To believe in God is impossible—not to believe in Him is absurd.

—Voltaire

To raise society to a higher level is the chief business of the Church. To overcome evil with good is the genius of Christianity.

—A. P. Gouthrey

Man is great only when he is kneeling.

—Pope Pius XII

CHAPTER THEMES

- **Beliefs and Spirituality:** How did the establishment of the Christian church and the development of the papacy structure Christian beliefs, thus providing a spiritual foundation for the Middle Ages? How was devotion, whether Christian or Islamic, an encompassing theme for the period? Why did the church decline in the Late Middle Ages?

- **Church/State Relationships:** Was medieval society primarily spiritual or secular in nature? In the confrontation between church and state, which authority was dominant, and which legacy more enduring? How did the papacy decline and lose influence in the face of royal control?

- **Imperialism:** Some historians have considered the Crusades to be examples of a great "religious enterprise." To what extent were the Crusades about religion and to what extent about the assertion of blatant military imperialism and lust for conquest?

- **Women in History:** What were the social and political positions of women during the Middle Ages? Was the Middle Ages a period of relative freedom for women, and to what extent was this based on the popular worship of the Virgin Mary? Were women really placed on pedestals, and did the medieval concept of chivalry enhance their positions? Did the Islamic view of women differ?

- **Historical Change and Transition:** In what ways did medieval civilization represent a change from the civilizations of the ancient world and the Renaissance yet to come? Can we speak of progress in the Middle Ages, or was the entire period a "Dark Age"?

- **The Big Picture:** To what extent can religion serve as a progressive and stabilizing force in society? Do people need religion? How can it be manipulated by the state in order to control a population? Are popes in essence the same as kings?

Some historians have argued that one of the greatest disasters in history was the failure of Rome to maintain her civilization. The internal economic and social decay of the third and fourth centuries, and the weakened military and political structure of the empire, paved the way for the barbarization of the realm by an uncontrolled influx of Germanic invaders. Western Europe was subjected to an era of chaos and disaster, marked by brutish force and devoid of the moderation that maintains civilized existence; by the fifth century, darkness had descended upon Europe. As the noted art historian Sir Kenneth Clark said, "In so far as we are the heirs of Greece and Rome, we got through by the skin of our teeth."

The period between the collapse of Roman civilization in the fifth century and the revival of classical learning in the Renaissance of the fifteenth century is called the Middle Ages or the medieval world. Renaissance man viewed his own era as one of light and progress, of renewed hope, where the emphasis centered no longer on God but on humanity. It was a secular era that condemned the chanting of prayers as mindless and viewed the collection of holy relics as absurd; it saw these practices as contradictory to the freedom of a new society focused on creativity. The Middle Ages were viewed with regret and scorn. Petrarch, a poet of the fourteenth century, lamented that "the Muse of History has been dead for a thousand years." When Rome fell, the Dark Ages settled over western Europe and civilization retreated—and then remained static.

This view of the Middle Ages was accepted and remained popular until perhaps the nineteenth century, when a more detached and less advocative scholarship began to assess critically the contributions and limitations of the medieval world. Perhaps the Middle Ages seemed so foreign because it was generally an age of faith, in contrast to the secular and rational emphasis of the modern world. The Christian church had been born during the height of Roman civilization and developed by drawing from Roman organization, making accommodation and enduring occasional persecution. Christianity survived and triumphed eventually as the official religion of the Roman Empire because of the broad appeal of its doctrine, its committed membership, and its superior organization. While the facade of Roman civilization gradually crumbled, the spiritual substructure of Christianity kept the Latin language, architectural styles, and other Roman cultural benefits alive. This was not easy given the dislocation that Europe experienced from about 500 to 1000 C.E. This period (called the Early Middle Ages) was indeed a difficult time. It was an era of transition, when leaders such as Charlemagne in Europe and Justinian in the eastern Byzantine empire were reestablishing political control. Waves of Viking invasions, starting around 850, led to major changes in social and political organization as peasants sought protection and nobles raised armies. Feudalism, which originated in late Roman times, became a complex, yet workable system of establishing authority and ordering society.

This period of disruption ended by 1100 as the Viking invasions dwindled in intensity and frequency. No longer was European civilization struggling to survive; anxiety gave way to confidence and confirmation that God held sway over the world. The years from about 1000 to 1300 (called the High Middle Ages) represent the acme of medieval civilization. During this era, universities were established and the great cathedrals were built as testaments of faith and devotion to God. This Christian devotion bordered on fanaticism as thousands marched off to the glory of the Crusades, hoping to achieve divine victory against the Muslims. The issue of authority was also brought more fully into question as popes and kings contended for ultimate supremacy in the earthly realm.

The conflict between religious and secular authority is one of the fundamental themes of Western Civilization. Because of the diversity of human needs ranging from physical security to emotional support, establishing and maintaining order and harmony in a city or state is a complex and difficult task. It might be argued that two basic spheres of leadership exist in human affairs: the secular sphere, including matters of government, law, and domestic harmony, as well as defense and foreign affairs; and the spiritual sphere, generally, but not exclusively, attending to less tangible and more abstract human concerns. Questions of deity, creation, ethics, life, death, and afterlife are the concerns of religious leadership. In order for one person or a small group of people to rule effectively, he (they) not only must control the apparatus of physical coercion in the state (military, police, etc.), but must also be recognized as head, or at least protector, of the people's religion. Thus the pharaohs of Egypt were revered as divine beings; in ancient Rome, the emperors bore the title Pontifex Maximus and served as head of the state religion, often to be deified after death. In modern totalitarian autocracies, control of party and state must be balanced by control of the state church or suppression of religion. Such is the essence of despotic authority.

We should therefore not be surprised to find that in the Middle Ages many kings and popes aspired to both secular and religious power. Both claimed supremacy over the other and based their positions on the evidence of scripture and logical argument. A king might well argue that the very survival of the church depended on his military strength; as defender of the faith, his will should prevail. On the other hand, the pope's position as successor to Saint Peter and representative of God on earth commanded the respect of all. For he was entrusted with the "Keys of Heaven," and there could be no exception to the ultimate authority of God.

The Late Middle Ages spanned the years from about 1300 to 1450 and was a time of stress as the church became more divided and declined in stature. The fourteenth century in particular saw the bloody Hundred Years' War between France and England, which was itself interrupted by perhaps the most destructive force yet encountered in Western Civilization—Black Death. The bubonic plague killed nearly half the population of Europe and contributed to massive economic and social change. It was this era of crisis that gave way to the ideals and attitudes of the Renaissance. The transition was made possible by a new human-centered energy, much as the transition from the ancient world was effected by energy sustained through devotion to God. But it should be remembered that the transition between the Middle Ages and the Renaissance was not abrupt, but gradual. We must resist the simplistic assumption that the medieval world was an "age of faith," rooted in mundane abstractions, and that the Renaissance was an "age of light," where man had thrown off the shackles of religion. In truth, such a gross distortion has little foundation in the historical evidence of the period.

It is difficult to assess the Middle Ages as a whole because there are so many different aspects to consider. However, one dominant theme is devotion. Devotion to God was a foundation of the medieval world; the ascetic principles and dutiful prayers of the monks had great purpose in maintaining a proper relationship with the Creator. Popular devotion was also evident in the construction of magnificent cathedrals like Notre Dame, Chartres, and Canterbury. Generations of construction workers labored to make their local cathedral impressive in the eyes of God. They were followed by generations of pilgrims who journeyed long distances simply to pray and offer gifts to an enshrined saint. The devotion of a vassal to his lord also proved to be the foundation of political organization, and the abstract devotion of a knight to chivalric ideals provided purpose and direction in life. The relationship of chaos and unity is another major theme. Much of the history of this period involves attempts to achieve unity by restraining the forces that contributed to chaos. In this respect, the conflicts between the representatives of church and state, as well as the Viking invasions and the Black Death, were primary threats to the unity of medieval civilization. They were countered by movements that organized and directed energy such as the Crusades or the cult of the Virgin Mary (to whom so many cathedrals were dedicated), or by the security of the feudal relationship. In so many other ways, the Middle Ages was an era of economic and technological progress—progress that flowed from a spiritual base.

This chapter is divided into three distinct sections, which can be studied individually or compared for analytic purposes; they are bound together by the theme of progress. The historical sources contained in this chapter reflect the problems and chaos of the medieval world and offer insight into the conditions and ideas that are truly representative of this important era.

SECTION I: THE EARLY MIDDLE AGES (500–1000)

Byzantine Civilization

The Emperor Justinian (527–565)

As the Western Roman Empire succumbed to Germanic invaders in the fourth and fifth centuries C.E., *power shifted from Rome, which was at constant risk, to the city of Byzantium. The emperor Constantine the Great began the rebuilding of Byzantium in 324 and renamed the city Constantinople in 330. Its well-defended and critical location on the lucrative eastern trade routes at the entrance to the Black Sea augured a dynamic future. Greek culture dominated the region, and this eastern successor to the glory of Rome became known as the Byzantine Empire. Between 324 and its demise in 1453, the Byzantine Empire provided an important link between the Eastern and Western cultures of the former Roman Empire.*

One of the most famous and arguably the most influential rulers of this empire was Justinian. He and his brilliant wife, Theodora, ruled from 527 to 565 with the official policy of "one God, one empire, one religion." To this end Justinian sought to reestablish Byzantine control over the former Roman Empire in the West through an ambitious and partially successful policy of conquest and consolidation. Justinian also collated and revised or codified Roman law, which was perhaps the most enduring legacy of his reign.

The first selections are from the "poison pen" of Procopius, Justinian's court historian. In his Secret History, *Procopius paints a tabloid view of the degenerate characters of Justinian and his infamous wife, Theodora. She in fact was the daughter of a bear trainer in the circus who rose to the heights of power. Whether one believes the portrait of Procopius or not, Theodora must have been a remarkable woman whose influence and character shone through when Justinian was faced with the Nika riots in 532.*

The last selection comes from the Digest of Roman Law *and highlights Justinian's achievements in maintaining an empire bound together by law.*

The Secret History of Justinian and Theodora
PROCOPIUS

The Depravity of Theodora

[On her rise to power], Theodora joined the actors in all the business of the theater and played a regular part in their stage performances, making herself

---

the butt of their ribald buffoonery. She was extremely clever and had a biting wit, and quickly became popular as a result. There was not a particle of modesty in the little hussy, and no one ever saw her taken aback; she complied with the most outrageous demands without the slightest hesitation, and she was the sort of girl who if somebody walloped her . . . would make a jest of it and roar with laughter; and she would throw off her clothes and exhibit naked to all and sundry those regions, both in front and behind, which the rules of decency require to be kept veiled and hidden from masculine eyes.

She used to tease her lovers by keeping them waiting, and by constantly playing about with novel methods of intercourse she could always bring the lascivious to her feet; so far from waiting to be invited by anyone she encountered, she herself by cracking dirty jokes and wiggling her hips suggestively would invite all who came her way, especially if they were still in their teens. Never was anyone so completely given up to unlimited self-indulgence. Often she would go to a bring-your-own-food dinner-party with ten young men or more, all at the peak of their physical powers and with fornication as their chief object in life, and would lie with all her fellow-diners in turn the whole night long: when she had reduced them all to a state of exhaustion she would go to their menials, as many as thirty on occasions, and copulate with every one of them; but not even so could she satisfy her lust. . . .

Such then was the birth and upbringing of this woman, the subject of common talk among women of the streets and among people of every kind. But when she arrived back in Byzantium Justinian conceived an overpowering passion for her. At first he consorted with her only as a mistress, though he did promote her to Patrician rank. This at once enabled Theodora to possess herself of immense influence and of very considerable wealth. For as so often happens to men consumed with passion, it seemed in Justinian's eyes the most delightful thing in the world to lavish all his favors and all his wealth upon the object of his passion. And the whole State became fuel for this passion. With Theodora to help him he impoverished the people far more than before, not only in the capital but in every part of the Empire. As both had long been supporters of the Blue Faction [chariot race fans in the Hippodrome], they gave the members of this faction immense powers over State affairs. It was a very long time before the evil was mitigated to any great extent. . . .

The Demon Justinian

Some of those who were in the Emperor's company late at night, conversing with him (evidently in the Palace)—men of the highest possible character—thought that they saw a strange demonic form in his place. One of them declared that he more than once rose suddenly from the imperial throne and walked round and round the room; for he was not in the habit of remaining seated for long. And Justinian's head would momentarily disappear, while the rest of his body seemed to continue making these long circuits. The watcher himself, thinking that something had gone seriously wrong with his eyesight, stood for a long time distressed and quite at a loss. But later the head returned to the body, and he thought that what a moment before had been lacking was, contrary to expectation, filling out again. A second man said that he stood by the Emperor's side as he sat, and saw his face suddenly transformed to a shapeless lump of flesh: neither eyebrows nor eyes were in their normal position, and it showed no other distinguishing feature at all; gradually, however, he saw the face return to its usual shape. I did not myself witness the events I am describing, but I heard about them from men who insist that they saw them at the time.

The Nika Riot (532)

PROCOPIUS

An insurrection broke out unexpectedly in Byzantium among the populace, and, contrary to expectation, it proved to be a very serious affair, and ended in great harm to the people and to the senate. . . . In every city the population has been divided for a long time past into the Blue and the Green factions; but within comparatively recent times it has come about that, for the sake of these names and the seats which the rival factions occupy in watching the games, they spend their money and abandon their bodies to the most cruel tortures, and even do not think it unworthy to die a most shameful death. And they fight against their opponents knowing not for what end they imperil themselves, but knowing well that, even if they overcome their enemy in the fight, the conclusion of the matter for them will be to be carried off straightway to the prison, and finally, after suffering extreme torture, to be destroyed. So there grows up in them against their fellow men a hostility which has no cause, and at no time does it cease or disappear. . . .

At this time the officers of the city administration in Byzantium were leading away to death some of the rioters. But the members of the two factions, conspiring together and declaring a truce with each other, seized the prisoners and then straightway entered the prison and released all those who were in confinement there, whether they had been condemned on a charge of stirring up sedition, or for any other unlawful act. And all the attendants in the service of the city government were killed indiscriminately; meanwhile, all of the citizens who were sane-minded were fleeing to the opposite mainland, and fire was applied to the city as if it had fallen under the hand of an enemy. . . . During this time the emperor and his consort with a few members of the senate shut themselves up in the palace and remained quietly there. Now the watchword which the populace passed around to one another was Nika [Victory], and the insurrection has been called by this name up to the present time. . . .

Now the emperor Justinian and his court were deliberating as to whether it would be better for them if they remained or if they took to flight in the ships. And many opinions were expressed favoring either course. And the Empress Theodora also spoke to the following effect: "As to the belief that a woman ought

"The Nika Riot" is reprinted by permission of the publishers and the Loeb Classical Library from Procopius, *History of the Wars,* trans. H. B. Dewing (Cambridge, Mass.: Harvard University Press, 1914), pp. 219–239.

not to be daring among men or to assert herself boldly among those who are holding back from fear, I consider that the present crisis most certainly [demands that we] settle the issue immediately. . . . My opinion then is that the present time, above all others, is inopportune for flight, even though it brings safety. For while it is impossible for a man who has seen the light not only to die, for one who has been an emperor, it is unendurable to be a fugitive. May I never be separated from this purple [the color of royalty], and may I not live that day on which those who meet me shall not address me as empress. If, now, it is your wish to save yourself, O Emperor, there is no difficulty. For we have much money, and there is the sea, here the boats. However, consider whether it will not come about after you have been saved that you would gladly exchange that safety for death. As for myself, I approve a certain ancient saying that royalty is a good burial-shroud." When the queen had spoken this, all were filled with boldness, and, turning their thoughts towards resistance, they began to consider how they might be able to defend themselves if any hostile force could come against them.

The Digest of Roman Law

Regarding the Lex Aquila

If a slave were to die as the result of an assault and without any contributory factor like neglect on the part of his owner or lack of professional skill in a doctor, an action may properly be brought for killing him wrongfully.

One night a shopkeeper had placed a lantern above his display counter which adjoined the footpath, but some passerby took it down and carried it off. The shopkeeper pursued him, calling for his lantern, and caught hold of him; but in order to escape from his grasp the thief began to hit the shopkeeper with the whip that he was carrying, on which there was a spike. From this encounter a real brawl developed in which the shopkeeper put out the eye of the lantern-stealer and he asked my opinion as to whether he had inflicted wrongful damage, bearing in mind that he had been hit with the whip first. My opinion was that unless he had poked out the eye intentionally he would not appear to have incurred liability, as the damage was really the lantern-stealer's own fault for hitting him first with the whip; on the other hand, if he had not been provoked by the beating, but had started the brawl when trying to snatch back his lantern, the shop-keeper would appear to be accountable for the loss of the eye.

Some mules were pulling two loaded carts up the Capitol Hill. The front cart had tipped up, so the drivers were trying to lift the back to make it easier for the mules to pull it up the hill, but suddenly it started to roll backwards. The muleteers, seeing that they would be caught between the two carts, leapt out of its path and it rolled back and struck the rear cart, which careered down the hill and ran over someone's slave boy. The owner of the boy asked me whom he should sue. I replied that it all depended on the facts of the case.

"The Digest of Roman Law" is from *The Digest of Roman Law,* trans. C. F. Kolbert (New York and Harmondsworth, Middlesex: Penguin Books, 1979), pp. 99–100. Copyright © C. F. Kolbert, 1979. Reprinted by permission.

If the drivers who were holding up the front cart had got out of its way of their own accord and that had been the reason why the mules could not take the weight of the cart and had been pulled back by it, in my opinion no action could be brought against the owner of the mules. The boy's owner should rather sue the men who had been holding up the cart; for damage is no less wrongful when someone voluntarily lets go of something in such circumstances and it hits someone else. For example, if a man failed to restrain an ass that he was driving he would be liable for any damage that he caused, just as if he threw a missile or anything else from his hand. But if the accident that we are considering had occurred because the mules had shied at something and the drivers had left the cart for fear of being crushed, no action would lie against them; but in such a case action should be brought against the owner of the mules. On the other hand, if neither the mules nor the drivers were at fault, as for example if the mules just could not take the weight, or if in trying to do so they had slipped and fallen and the cart had then rolled down the hill because the men could not hold it when it tipped up, there would be no liability on the owner or on the drivers. It is quite clear, furthermore, that however the accident happened, no action could be brought against the owner of the mules pulling the cart behind, for they fell back down the hill not through any fault of theirs, but because they were struck by the cart in front.

Byzantine Spiritual Foundations

The religious history of the Byzantine Empire is particularly interesting, owing to the relatively unrestricted and speculative intellectual heritage of the Greek East. A free flow of ideas had always been a feature of Greek philosophy, and the Christian churches in the eastern Mediterranean had been absorbed in this tradition. The patriarchs of Constantinople, Alexandria, Antioch, and Jerusalem were especially influential and competitive. Many doctrinal differences arose between the pope in Rome and these eastern patriarchs over such issues as the nature of the Trinity and the worship of religious icons (representation of saints and other religious artifacts), not to mention whether papal authority held primacy for Byzantine Christians. Eventually these matters led to a split in the Christian church in 1054, with the establishment of Eastern Orthodox Christianity and Roman Catholic Christianity. The churches still remain split, though Pope John Paul II has renewed the call for unity.

Byzantine emperors had a long tradition of involvement with religious affairs. In fact, the term "Caesaro-papism" describes this melding of political power and religious authority in the person of the emperor. The first selection discusses the concern over the appearance of a dangerous heresy in the late third century, which threatened the unity of the early Christian church. Arius was an Egyptian priest who argued that Jesus was the Son of God and since sons always existed after fathers, then Jesus could not be both the Son of God and God at the same time. Jesus was a created being and therefore not eternal, nor made of the same substance (homoousion) as the Father. Arius believed that Jesus was made of similar substance (homoiousion), but was primarily human. Constantine himself called the Council of Nicaea in 325 to settle the dispute and therein was formed the Nicene Creed, which settled the matter and provided a precedent for secular influence within the Eastern churches.

Heresy: The Threat of Arianism
EUSEBIUS

In this manner the emperor [Constantine], like a powerful herald of God, [wrote] to all the provinces, at the same time warning his subjects against superstitious error, and encouraging them in the pursuit of true godliness. But in the midst of his joyful anticipations of the success of this measure, he received tidings of a most serious disturbance which had invaded the peace of the Church. This intelligence he heard with deep concern, and at once endeavored to devise a remedy for the evil. The origin of this disturbance may be thus described.

The people of God were in a truly flourishing state, and abounding in the practice of good works. No terror from without assailed them, but a bright and most profound peace, through the favor of God, encompassed his Church on every side. Meantime, however, the spirit of envy was watching to destroy our blessings, which at first crept in unperceived, but soon revelled in the midst of the assemblies of the saints. At length it reached the bishops themselves, and arrayed them in angry hostility against each other, on pretense of a jealous regard for the doctrines of Divine truth. Hence it was that a mighty fire was kindled as it were from a little spark, and which, originating in the first instance in the Alexandrian church, overspread the whole of Egypt and Libya, . . . and eventually extended its ravages to the other provinces and cities of the empire; so that not only the prelates of the churches might be seen encountering each other in the strife of words, but the people themselves were completely divided, some adhering to one faction and others to another. So notorious did the scandal of these proceedings become, that the sacred matters of inspired teaching were exposed to the most shameful ridicule in the very theaters of the unbelievers. . . .

The Nicene Creed (325)
EUSEBIUS

[In accordance with the Emperor Constantine's instructions,] the bishops drew up this formula of faith:

"Heresy: The Threat of Arianism" is from Eusebius, *The Life of the Blessed Emperor Constantine*, in *A Select Library of Nicene and Post-Nicene Fathers of the Christian Church*, vol. I, trans. Ernest C. Richardson (New York: The Christian Literature Company, 1890), pp. 515–516.

"The Nicene Creed" is from Eusebius, *The Life of the Blessed Emperor Constantine*, in *A Select Library of Nicene and Post-Nicene Fathers of the Christian Church*, vol. I, trans. Ernest C. Richardson (New York: The Christian Literature Company, 1890), pp. 515–518.

'We believe in one God, the Father Almighty, Maker of all things visible and invisible: and in one Lord Jesus Christ, the Son of God, the only-begotten of the Father, that is of the substance of the Father; God of God, Light of light, true God of true God; begotten not made, consubstantial with the Father; by whom all things were made both which are in heaven and on earth; who for the sake of us men, and on account of our salvation, descended, became incarnate, was made man, suffered and rose again on the third day; he ascended into the heavens and will come to judge the living and the dead. We believe also in the Holy Spirit. But those who say "There was a time when he was not," or "He did not exist before he was begotten," or "He was made of nothing," or assert that "He is of other substance or essence than the Father," or that the Son of God is created, or mutable, or susceptible of change, the Catholic and apostolic Church of God rejects. . . .

'Consequently [Christ] is no creature like those which were made by him, but is of a substance far excelling any creature; which substance the Divine Oracles teach was begotten of the Father by such a mode of generation as cannot be explained nor even conceived by any creature. Thus also the declaration that "the Son is consubstantial [homoousios] with the Father" having been discussed, it was agreed that this must not be understood in a corporeal sense, or in any way analogous to mortal creatures; inasmuch as it is neither by division of substance, nor by any change of the Father's substance and power, since the underived nature of the Father is inconsistent with all these things. That he is consubstantial with the Father then simply implies, that the Son of God has no resemblance to created things, but is in every respect like the Father only who begat him; and that he is of no other substance or essence but of the Father. . . . Accordingly, since no divinely inspired Scripture contains the expression, "of things which do not exist" and "there was a time when he was not," and such other phrases as are therein subjoined, it seemed unwarrantable to utter and teach them.'

Iconoclasm and Orthodoxy:
The Second Council of Nicaea (787)

Another primary religious dispute within Eastern Christianity was the tradition of worshiping images of Christ, the Virgin, and the saints. Although this was acceptable practice in Western churches, in 726 the Byzantine emperor Leo IV abolished the cult of images by imperial edict. This was called "iconoclasm," and it is a primary example of Caesaro-papism. In 787, however, the empress Irene, who served as regent to her young son, reestablished the veneration of images at the

---

"Iconoclasm and Orthodoxy" is from Joseph G. Ayer, Jr., ed. *A Source Book for Ancient Church History* (New York: Charles Scribner's Sons, 1913), pp. 696–697.

Second Council of Nicaea, as the following source indicates. This policy remained under dispute for centuries.

We, therefore, following the royal pathway and the divinely inspired authority of our holy Fathers and the traditions of the Catholic Church for, as we all know, the Holy Spirit dwells in her, define with all certitude and accuracy, that just as the figure of the precious and life-giving cross, so also the venerable and holy images, as well in painting and mosaic, as of other fit materials, should be set forth in the holy churches of God. . . . For by so much the more frequently as they are seen in artistic representation, by so much the more readily are men lifted up to the memory of their prototypes, and to a longing after them; and to these should be given due salutation and honorable reverence, not indeed that true worship which pertains alone to the divine nature; but to these, as to the figure of the precious and life-giving cross, and to the book of the Gospels and to other holy objects, incense and lights may be offered according to ancient pious custom. For the honor which is paid to the image passes on to that which the image represents, and he who shows reverence to the image shows reverence to the subject represented in it.

Those, therefore, who dare to think or teach otherwise, or as wicked heretics dare to spurn the traditions of the Church and to invent some novelty, or else to reject some of those things which the Church hath received, to wit, the book of the Gospels, or the image of the cross, or the pictorial icons, or the holy relics of a martyr, or to devise anything subversive of the lawful traditions of the Catholic Church, or to turn to common uses the sacred vessels and the venerable monasteries, if they be bishops or clerics we command that they be deposed [and] be cut off from communion.

A Western Attitude Toward the Byzantine Greeks (1147)
ODO OF DEUIL

One of the primary obstacles to the eventual success of the Crusades was the lack of trust and cooperation between the Roman Catholic Church in the West and the Greek Orthodox Church in the East. These two Christian churches had separated in 1054 over doctrinal differences, and this rift fueled a political and economic competition between Western forces and those of the Byzantine emperor. The following selection notes Western disgust for the Byzantine Greeks at the beginning of the Second Crusade.

"A Western Attitude Toward the Byzantine Greeks" is from Odo of Deuil, *De Profectione Ludovici VII,* ed. and trans. Virginia G. Berry, p. 57. Copyright © 1948 by Columbia University Press. Reprinted by permission of the publisher.

We know other heresies of theirs, both concerning their treatment of the Eucharist and concerning the procession of the Holy Ghost, but none of these matters would mar our page if not pertinent to our subject. Actually, it was for these reasons that the Greeks had incurred the hatred of our men, for their error had become known even among the lay people. Because of this they were judged not to be Christians, and the Franks considered killing them a matter of no importance and hence could with more difficulty be restrained from pillage and plundering.

And then the Greeks degenerated entirely... putting aside all manly vigor, both of words and of spirit, they lightly swore whatever they thought would please us, but they neither kept faith with us nor maintained respect for themselves. In general they really have the opinion that anything which is done for the holy empire [that is, Byzantium] cannot be considered perjury.

Islamic Civilization

The Religious Tenets of the Qur'an

The rise of Islamic civilization is a story of faith and confrontation amidst societies in political and cultural transition. The basic ideas of the Islamic worldview derived from a single prophetic revelation of the prophet Muhammad in the Qur'an: *"There is but one God and his prophet is Muhammad." It is a simple revelation that has formed the basis of one of the world's most influential religions.*

Muhammad (ca. 570–632) was an orphan who had worked on a caravan before marrying a wealthy widow. He was a man of great spiritual depth who had become troubled about the idolatry, worldliness, and lack of social conscience that plagued his society. Muhammad's discontent with this moral status quo and his searching nature positioned him to found a new religion that would address the needs of his particular Arabic community. On repeated occasions, he felt himself called by God (Allah) to "rise and warn" his fellow Arabs about their moral vacuousness. God's word had been delivered through other prophets prior to Muhammad, including Abraham, Moses, and Jesus. But the final revelation of God's work, the recitation (qur'an), was given to Muhammad by the messenger angel Gabriel. The message was clear: The Prophet Muhammad was to warn Arabs of God's displeasure with idolatrous worship and injustices to the weak and sick, the poor, widows, orphans, and women. God spoke of a judgment day when believers would enjoy the pleasures of paradise and nonbelievers would be cast into eternal hellfire, to be damned forever. God forgives the penitent and rewards those who respect his law and offer proper gratitude. Through submission (islam) to God's will, one becomes submissive (muslim) in worship and morality. A fervent monotheism is essential to the acceptance of the religion of Islam. Only humans have been given the choice either to obey or to reject the one true God.

At first Muhammad's revelations and strict demands invited opposition and even persecution in the city of Mecca, but his reputation as a moral leader increased and he was accepted in the city of Medina. This emigration (hegira) *from Mecca to Medina in 622 became the starting point for year one of the Islamic calendar, signifying the creation of the Islamic community* (umma).

Devotion to Islam is based on five basic principles or "pillars": (1) the acceptance of one God, Allah, and Muhammad as his prophet; (2) recitation of prayers five times a day toward Mecca after ritual purification before worship; (3) daytime fasting and abstinence from sexual relations from sunrise to sunset for one month a year; (4) payment of a tithe to support poor and unfortunate Muslims; and (5) a pilgrimage to Mecca at least once in a lifetime (hajj), *if one is able. The moral codes of Islam help define the religion: allegiance to the Islamic community, abstention from alcohol and pork, and modesty in personal affairs.*

After Muhammad's death in 632, the Islamic community struggled to maintain its unity since Muhammad had not named a successor. The success of Islam in organizing itself and in promoting the religion not only throughout Arab lands but beyond to Europe and the East is one of the great dramas of history. The influence of Islam on our contemporary world is formidable indeed, and it is important to understand the spiritual foundations of this impressive religion.

The following excerpts are primarily from the Qur'an *and provide insight into some of the most important aspects of Islam.*

The Heritage of Islam

In the Name of Allah, the Compassionate, the Merciful

This Book is not to be doubted. It is a guide for the righteous, who have faith in the unseen and are steadfast in prayer; who bestow in charity a part of what We have given them; who trust what has been revealed to you and to others before you, and firmly believe in the life to come. These are rightly guided by their Lord; these shall surely triumph.

As for the unbelievers, it is the same whether or not you forewarn them; they will not have faith. God has set a seal upon their hearts and ears; their sight is dimmed and grievous punishment awaits them. . . .

To Moses We gave the Scriptures and after him We sent other apostles. We gave Jesus the son of Mary veritable signs and strengthened him with the Holy Spirit. Will you then scorn each apostle whose message does not suit your fancies, charging some with imposture and slaying others? They say: 'Our hearts are sealed.' But God has cursed them for their unbelief. They have but little faith.

And now that a Book confirming their own has come to them from God, they deny it, although they know it to be the truth and have long prayed for help against the unbelievers. God's curse be upon the infidels! Evil is that for which they have bartered away their soul. To deny God's own revelation, grudging the He should reveal His bounty to whom He chooses from among His servants! They have incurred God's most inexorable wrath. An ignominious punishment awaits the unbelievers. . . .

Many among the People of the Book [Jews and Christians] wish, through envy, to lead you back to unbelief, now that you have embraced the Faith and the truth has been made plain to them. Forgive them and bear with them until God makes known His will. God has power over all things.

Attend to your prayers and render the alms levy. Whatever good you do shall be rewarded by God. God is watching all your actions.

They declare: 'None shall enter Paradise but Jews and Christians.' Such are their wishful fancies. Say: 'Let us have your proof, if what you say be true.' Indeed, those that surrender themselves to God and do good works shall be rewarded by their Lord: they shall have nothing to fear or to regret.

The Jews say the Christians are misguided, and the Christians say it is the Jews who are misguided. Yet they both read the Scriptures. And the ignorant say the same of both. God will judge their disputes on the Day of Resurrection. . . .

They say: 'Accept the Jewish or the Christian faith and you shall be rightly guided.'

Say: 'By no means! We believe in the faith of Abraham, the upright one. He was no idolater.'

Say: 'We believe in God and that which is revealed to us; in what was revealed to Abraham, Ishmael, Isaac, Jacob, and the tribes; to Moses and Jesus and the other prophets by their Lord. We make no distinction among any of them, and to God we have surrendered ourselves.'

If they accept your faith, they shall be rightly guided; if they reject it, they shall surely be in schism. Against them God is your all-sufficient defender. He bears all and knows all. . . .

Believers, eat of the wholesome things with which We have provided you and give thanks to God, if it is Him you worship.

He has forbidden you carrion, blood, and the flesh of swine; also any flesh that is consecrated other than in the name of God. But whoever is compelled through necessity, intending neither to sin nor to transgress, shall incur no guilt. God is forgiving and merciful. . . .

Righteousness does not consist in whether you face towards the East or the West. The righteous man is he who believes in God and the Last Day, in the angels and the Book and the prophets; who, though he loves it dearly, gives away his wealth to kinsfolk, to orphans, to the destitute, to the traveller in need and to beggars, and for the redemption of captives; who attends to his prayers and renders the alms levy; who is true to his promises and steadfast in trial and adversity and in times of war. Such are the true believers; such are the God-fearing. . . .

Fight for the sake of God those that fight against you, but do not attack them first. God does not love the aggressors.

Slay them wherever you find them. Drive them out of the places from which they drove you. Idolatry is more grievous than bloodshed. But do not fight them within the precincts of the holy Mosque unless they attack you there; if they attack you put them to the sword. Thus shall the unbelievers be rewarded: but if they mend their ways, know that God is forgiving and merciful. Fight against them until idolatry is no more and God's religion reigns supreme. But if they desist, fight none except the evil-doers. . . .

Give generously for the cause of God and do not with your own hands cast yourselves into destruction. Be charitable; God loves the charitable.

Make pilgrimage and visit the Sacred House [in Mecca] for His sake. If you cannot, send such offerings as you can afford and do not shave your heads until the offerings have reached their destination. But if any of you is ill or suffers from an ailment of the head, he must pay a ransom either by fasting or by almsgiving or by offering a sacrifice. . . .

When the sky is rent asunder; when the stars scatter and the oceans roll together; when the graves are hurled about; each soul shall know what it has done and what it has failed to do.

O man! What evil has enticed you from your gracious Lord who created you, gave you an upright form, and proportioned you? In whatever shape He willed He could have molded you. Yet you deny the Last Judgement. Surely there are guardians watching over you, noble recorders who know of all your actions.

The righteous will surely dwell in bliss. But the wicked shall burn in Hell upon the Judgement-day: nor shall they ever escape from it.

Would that you knew what the Day of Judgement is! Oh, would that you knew what the Day of Judgement is! It is the day when every soul will stand alone and God will reign supreme.

The *Qur'an* on Women

In the Name of Allah, the Compassionate, the Merciful

Men, have fear of your Lord, who created you from a single soul. From that soul He created its mate, and through them He bestrewed the earth with countless men and women.

Fear God, in whose name you plead with one another, and honor the mothers who bore you. God is ever watching you.

Give orphans the property which belongs to them. Do not exchange their valuables for worthless things or cheat them of their possessions; for this would surely be a great sin. If you fear that you cannot treat orphan [girls] with fairness, then you may marry other women who seem good to you: two, three, or four of them. But if you fear that you cannot maintain equality among them, marry one only or any slave-girls you may own. This will make it easier for you to avoid injustice.

"The *Qur'an* on Women" is from *The Koran,* trans. N. J. Dawood (New York and Harmondsworth, Middlesex: Penguin Books, 1990), pp. 60–62, 64, 74. Copyright © N. J. Dawood, 1993. Reprinted by permission.

Give women their dowry as a free gift; but if they choose to make over to you a part of it, you may regard it as lawfully yours. . . .

God has thus enjoined you concerning your children: A male shall inherit twice as much as a female. If there be more than two girls, they shall have two-thirds of the inheritance; but if there be one only, she shall inherit the half. Parents shall inherit a sixth each, if the deceased have a child; but if he leaves no child and his parents be his heirs, his mother shall have a third. If he has brothers, his mother shall have a sixth after payment of any legacy he may have bequeathed or any debt he may have owed.

You may wonder whether your parents or your children are more beneficial to you. But this is the law of God; God is all-knowing and wise. . . .

If any of your women commit fornication, call in four witnesses from among yourselves against them; if they testify to their guilt confine them to their houses till death overtakes them or till God finds another way for them. . . .

Men have authority over women because God has made the one superior to the other, and because they spend their wealth to maintain them. Good women are obedient. They guard their unseen parts because God has guarded them. As for those from whom you fear disobedience, admonish them and send them to beds apart and beat them. Then if they obey you, take no further action against them. God is high, supreme. . . .

If a woman fears ill-treatment or desertion on the part of her husband, it shall be no offence for them to seek a mutual agreement, for agreement is best. . . . Try as you may, you cannot treat all your wives impartially. Do not set yourself altogether against any of them, leaving her, as it were in suspense. If you do what is right and guard yourselves against evil, you will find God forgiving and merciful. If they separate, God will compensate both out of His own abundance: God is munificent and wise.

The Love of Allah

AL-GHAZZALI

The love of God is the highest of all topics, and is the final aim to which we have been tending hitherto. We have spoken of spiritual dangers as they hinder the love of God in a man's heart, and we have spoken of various good qualities as being the necessary preliminaries to it. Human perfection resides in this, that the love of God should conquer a man's heart and possess it wholly, and even if it does not possess it wholly it should predominate in the heart over the love of all other things. Nevertheless, rightly to understand the love of God is so difficult a matter that one sect of theologians have

"The Love of Allah" is from Al-Ghazzali, *The Alchemy of Happiness*, trans. Claud Field, *The Wisdom of the East Series* (London: John Murray Publishers Ltd., 1910), pp. 51–54.

altogether denied that man can love a Being who is not of his own species, and they have defined the love of God as consisting merely in obedience. Those who hold such views do not know what real religion is.

All Muslims are agreed that the love of God is a duty. God says concerning the believers, "He loves them and they love Him," and the Prophet [Muhammad] said, "Till a man loves God and His Prophet more than anything else he has not the right faith. . . . "

When we apply this principle to the love of God we shall find that He alone is really worthy of our love, and that, if any one loves Him not, it is because he does not know Him. Whatever we love in any one we love because it is a reflection of Him. It is for this reason that we love Muhammad, because he is the Prophet and the Beloved of God, and the love of learned and pious men is really the love of God. We shall see this more clearly if we consider what are the causes which excite love.

The first cause is this, that man loves himself and the perfection of his own nature. This leads him directly to the love of God, for man's very existence and man's attributes are nothing else but the gift of God, but for whose grace and kindness man would never have emerged from behind the curtain of non-existence into the visible world. Man's preservation and eventual attainment to perfection are also entirely dependent upon the grace of God. It would indeed be a wonder, if one should take refuge from the heat of the sun under the shadow of a tree and not be grateful to the tree, without which there would be no shadow at all. Precisely in the same way, were it not for God, man would have no existence nor attributes at all; wherefore, then, should he not love God, unless he be ignorant of Him? Doubtless fools cannot love Him, for the love of Him springs directly from the knowledge of Him, and whence should a fool have knowledge?

Islamic Science and Mathematics

The Islamic community during the Middle Ages and beyond was not simply concerned with matters of faith and obedience to doctrine. As Muslim armies covered North Africa and the Middle East, even venturing into Europe, they carried with them some of the great advancements of Islamic civilization. Muslim learning was embraced in such academic centers as Córdoba, Spain, where Jewish scholars were central in establishing a conduit of knowledge to the West by translating Arabic science and medical texts into Spanish and Latin. Many of these ideas in astronomy, medicine, advanced mathematics, law, literature, poetry, philosophy, and history fell on deaf ears in the West because of the fear of doctrinal contamination. Indeed, for Western Christians, the followers of Allah were the "Infidel," to be feared and opposed through Crusades to recapture the Holy Land for the glory of a Christian God.

The following selections attest to the framework of learning and inquiry that was a most impressive benefit of Islamic civilization.

On the Separation of Mathematics and Religion
AL-GHAZZALI

Mathematics comprises the knowledge of calculation, geometry, and cosmography: it has no connection with the religious sciences, and proves nothing for or against religion; it rests on a foundation of proofs which, once known and understood, cannot be refuted. Mathematics tend, however, to produce two bad results.

The first is this: Whoever studies this science admires the subtlety and clearness of its proofs. His confidence in philosophy increases, and he thinks that all its departments are capable of the same clearness and solidity of proof as mathematics. But when he hears people speak on the unbelief and impiety of mathematicians, of their professed disregard for the Divine Law, which is notorious, it is true that, out of regard for authority, he echoes these accusations, but he says to himself at the same time that, if there was truth in religion, it would not have escaped those who have displayed so much keenness of intellect in the study of mathematics.

Next, when he becomes aware of the unbelief and rejection of religion on the part of these learned men, he concludes that to reject religion is reasonable. How many of such men gone astray I have met whose sole argument was that just mentioned. . . .

It is therefore a great injury to religion to suppose that the defence of Islam involves the condemnation of the exact sciences. The religious law contains nothing which approves them or condemns them, and in their turn they make no attack on religion. The words of the Prophet, "The sun and the moon are two signs of the power of God; they are not eclipsed for the birth or the death of any one; when you see these signs take refuge in prayer and invoke the name of God"—these words, I say, do not in any way condemn the astronomical calculations which define the orbits of these two bodies, their conjunction and opposition according to particular laws.

On the Causes of Small-Pox
AL-RAZI

Although [scholars] have certainly made some mention of the treatment of the Small-Pox (but without much accuracy and distinctness), yet there is not one of them who has mentioned the cause of the existence of the disease, and how it comes to pass that hardly any one escapes it, or who has disposed

"On the Separation of Mathematics and Religion" is from Al-Ghazzali, *The Confession of Al-Ghazzali*, trans. Claud Field, The Wisdom of the East Series (London: John Murray Publishers Ltd., 1908), pp. 33–34.

"On the Causes of Small-Pox" is from Abu Bekr Muhammad Ibn Zacariya Al-Razi, *A Treatise on Small-Pox and Measles*, trans. William A. Greenhill (London, 1848), pp. 28–31.

the modes of treatment in their right places. And for this reason I . . . have mentioned whatever is necessary for the treatment of this disease, and have arranged and carefully disposed everything in its right place, by GOD's permission. . . .

I say then that every man, from the time of his birth until he arrives at old age, is continually tending to dryness; and for this reason the blood of children and infants is much moister than the blood of young men, and still more so than that of old men. . . . Now the Small-Pox arises when the blood putrefies and ferments, so that the superfluous vapors are thrown out of it, and it is changed from the blood of infants, which is like must, into the blood of young men, which is like wine perfectly ripened: and the Small-Pox itself may be compared to the fermentation and the hissing noise which takes place in must at that time. And this is the reason why children, especially males, rarely escape being seized with this disease, because it is impossible to prevent the blood's changing from this state into its second state. . . .

As to young men, whereas their blood is already passed into the second state, its maturation is established, and the superfluous particles of moisture which necessarily cause putrefaction are now exhaled; hence it follows that this disease only happens to a few individuals among them, that is, to those whose vascular system abounds with too much moisture, or is corrupt in quality with a violent inflammation. . . .

And as for old men, the Small-Pox seldom happens to them, except in pestilential, putrid, and malignant constitutions of the air, in which this disease is chiefly prevalent. For a putrid air, which has an undue proportion of heat and moisture, and also an inflamed air, promotes the eruption of this disease. . . .

The Dawn of the European Middle Ages

Early Germanic Society

Laws of the Salian Franks

The Romans greatly respected the Germanic peoples who lived beyond the Rhine river. In his work, Germania, *the Roman historian Tacitus described them as "noble savages," who possessed a simple, but effective justice system based on relative equity, and a code of valor that reflected a war-like spirit. The Romans grew to admire their enemies even as Roman institutions broke down amid the*

"Laws of the Salian Franks" is from E.F. Henderson, ed., *Select Historical Documents of the Middle Ages* (London: George Bell and sons, 1892), pp. 180–185.

onslaught of Germanic invasions during the third century. The transformation of Western Civilization in the Early Middle Ages owed much to the mingling of Roman and Germanic traditions. The following law codes help us understand the structure of early Germanic society.

Title XIII: Concerning Rape Committed by Freemen.

1. If three men carry off a free born girl, they shall be compelled to pay 30 shillings.
2. If there are more than three, each one shall pay 5 shillings.
3. Those who shall have been present with boats shall be sentenced to three shillings.
4. But those who commit rape shall be compelled to pay 2500 denars, which make 63 shillings.

Title XVII: Concerning Wounds.

1. If any one have wished to kill another person, and the blow have missed, he on whom it was proved shall be sentenced to 2500 denars, which make 63 shillings.

If any person have wished to strike another with a poisoned arrow, and the arrow have glanced aside, and it shall be proved on him: he shall be sentenced to 2500 denars, which make 63 shillings.

If any person strike another on the head so that the brain appears, and the three bones which lie above the brain shall project, he shall be sentenced to 1200 denars, which make 30 shillings.

But if it shall have been between the ribs or in the stomach, so that the wound appears and reaches to the entrails, he shall be sentenced to 1200 denars—which make 30 shillings—besides five shillings for the physician's pay.

Title XXIV: Concerning the Killing of Little Children and Women.

If any one has slain a boy under 10 years—up to the end of the tenth—and it shall have been proved on him, he shall be sentenced to 24,000 denars, which make 600 shillings.

If any one has hit a free woman who is pregnant, and she dies, he shall be sentenced to 28,000 denars, which makes 700 shillings.

If any one has killed a free woman after she has begun bearing children, he shall be sentenced to 24,000 denars, which make 600 shillings.

After she can have no more children, he who kills her shall be sentenced to 8,000 denars, which make 200 shillings.

Title XXX: Concerning Insults.

If any one, man or woman, shall have called a woman harlot, and shall not have been able to prove it, he shall be sentenced to 1800 denars, which make 45 shillings.

If any person shall have called another "fox," he shall be sentenced to 3 shillings.

If any man shall have called another "hare," he shall be sentenced to 3 shillings.

Title XLI: Concerning the Murder of Freemen.

If any one shall have killed a free Frank, or a barbarian living under the Salic law, and it have been proved on him, he shall be sentenced to 8,000 denars.

But if he shall have thrown him into a well or into the water, or shall have covered him with branches or anything else, to conceal him, he shall be sentenced to 24,000 denars, which make 600 shillings.

But if any one has slain a man who is in the service of the king, he shall be sentenced to 24,000 denars, which make 600 shillings.

Beowulf: The Germanic Hero

Epic poetry has been used throughout history to transmit cultural traditions from one generation to another, initially without the aid of writing. Oral narratives like the Sumerian epic of Gilgamesh or Homer's Iliad *and* Odyssey *tell of legends and the glorious deeds of national ancestors. Because many of these heroic stories were at some time written down, they allow historians to understand the values and motivation of past societies.*

Beginning in the third century, Germanic tribes wandered throughout the western Roman Empire, contributing to its political disintegration and establishing new traditions upon the Roman foundation. Out of these Germanic wanderings came a rich oral tradition that included most importantly the epic adventures of Beowulf, written in Old English in the eighth century.

In the following excerpt, the Anglo-Saxon king Beowulf (Lord of the Geats) fights to the death with the fire-breathing monster, Grendel, who guards a great treasure-trove.

The king of the Geats roared a furious challenge. He shouted until his voice penetrated the cavern and his battle-cry thundered under the grey rock. The guardian of the treasure-hoard [Grendel] bristled with rage when it recognized the voice of a man. There was no time for appeasement. The monster's

"Beowulf: The Germanic Hero" is from *Beowulf,* trans. David Wright (New York and Harmondsworth, Middlesex: Penguin Books, 1957), pp. 87–91, 101. Copyright © David Wright, 1957. Reprinted by permission.

scorching breath spurted ahead of it, out of the rock, while earth reverberated. The hero, facing the barrow, swung his shield to meet the enemy; upon which the reptile was spurred to take the offensive. Already the king had drawn his sharp ancestral sword. But each of the adversaries was in awe of the other. The prince resolutely stood his ground in the shelter of his great shield while the Worm gathered its coils together. Bent like a bow, the flaming monster hurtled towards him and rushed upon its fate. But the king's shield gave protection to life and limb for a shorter time than he had hoped. For the first time Beowulf had to fight without success, because fate refused to grant it to him. Raising his hand, the lord of the Geats struck the glittering monster with his sword, but the blade bounded off the scales and scarcely bit, just when the king had most need. The blow infuriated the guardian of the barrow. It spat a blast of glistering fire which leapt hither and thither. The king could boast of no advantage now that his naked blade had failed him in battle, as no good sword should do. It was no easy thing for Beowulf to make up his mind to quit this world and take up his lodging in some other whether he liked it or not. But this is the way in which everyone has to die.

Soon the antagonists joined battle once more. The Dragon had taken fresh heart and found its second wind, while the king, hedged round with fire, suffered agony. His comrades-in-arms, who were sons of princes, utterly failed to support him in strength like good fighting-men, but fled into a wood to save their lives. Yet one among them was pricked by conscience. To a right-thinking man, blood must always be thicker than water.

His name was Wiglaf son of Weohstan, a well-liked Swedish prince of the house of Aelfhere. Wiglaf could see that the king, in spite of his armour, was in distress from the flames. . . . In bitterness of heart Wiglaf reminded his comrades of their duty. "I can remember a time when we used to accept to whom we swore that if ever he fell into straits like these we would make some return for our fighting-gear—these swords and helmets. That is why he gave me valuable gifts, and you as well. He thought that we were brave spearmen and daring soldiers. . . . Let us go forward to our king's assistance. . . ." Then he dived into the perilous smoke, bearing arms to the king's help and crying . . . : "Brave prince, renowned for feats of arms, defend your life with all your might—I am coming to your help!"

At these words the Worm angrily emerged once more in swirls of sparkling flame, to take the field against its enemies, the human beings which it hated. Wiglaf's shield was burnt to the boss by a cataract of fire, while his corselet gave him no protection. The lad slipped quickly behind his kinsman's shield as soon as the flames had burnt his own to cinders.

But the king was still mindful of his fame and struck so hard with his sword that, driven by the impetus, it struck square in the Dragon's head. Yet Beowulf's patterned sword, Naegling, failed him. It shattered to splinters. Never had it been his luck that a sword should be of use to him during a fight. His hand, they say, was so strong that the force of his blows overtaxed any weapon. Even when he carried one which was hardened in battle he was no better off.

The flame-spitting Dragon screwed up its courage for a third attack. When it saw its chance it set savagely upon the hero, catching him around the neck with lacerating fangs. A torrent of gore gushed out, and Beowulf was spattered with his own life-blood. . . .

Collecting his wits, the king pulled out a razor-sharp dagger which he wore at his corselet, and ripped open the belly of the Worm. Together the kinsmen killed their adversary. That is how a man should act in a right corner! It was Beowulf's crowning hour of triumph, his last feat of arms, and the end of his life's work.

For the wound which the Dragon had just inflicted upon him began to burn and swell. Beowulf soon discovered that mortal poison was working in his breast and had bitten deep into his entrails. . . . In spite of his pitiful wound, Beowulf began to speak. He knew well enough that his span of life and term of happiness on earth was over, his sum of days wholly spent, and death very close.

"I now would wish to hand over my armour to a son of mine, were it my luck to have had an heir of my body to come after me. I have reigned over this people for half a century, and there was not a king of any neighbouring nation who dared to attack me with an army or to threaten me with war. The destiny allotted to me on earth I endured; what was mine I defended well. I did not pick quarrels nor swear false oaths. Though wounded to death, I can rejoice in all these things; because when the life quits my body God cannot accuse me of the murder of my kin. . . . "

The people of the Geats prepared for Beowulf, as he had asked of them, a splendid pyre hung about with helmets, shields, and shining corselets. Then, mourning, the soldiers laid their loved and illustrious prince in the midst. Upon the hill the men-at-arms lit a gigantic funeral fire. . . . Then twelve chieftains, all sons of princes, rode round the barrow lamenting their loss, speaking of their king, reciting an elegy, and acclaiming the hero. They praised his manhood and extolled his heroic deeds. It is right that men should pay homage to their king with words, and cherish him in their hearts, when he has taken leave of the body. So the Geats who had shared his hall mourned the death of their lord, and said that of all kings he was the gentlest and most gracious of men, the kindest to his people and the most desirous of renown.

The Figure of Charlemagne

Biographical writing constitutes a considerable part of medieval literature, but much of it cannot be relied upon for accuracy. Medieval biographers who wrote about the lives of saints or kings often exaggerated their accomplishments for the sake of providing solid examples of moral living. A major exception to this practice was Einhard, a secretary and public works administrator at Charlemagne's court. Although his biography has some inaccuracies, nevertheless it is regarded as a trustworthy account of the life and deeds of Charlemagne, ruler of the Frankish empire from 768 to 814.

The Moderate and Progressive King

EINHARD

Charles was large and strong, and of lofty stature, though not excessively tall. The upper part of his head was round, his eyes very large and animated, nose a little long, hair auburn, and face laughing and merry. His appearance was always stately and dignified, whether he was standing or sitting, although his neck was thick and somewhat short and his abdomen rather prominent. The symmetry of the rest of his body concealed these defects. His gait was firm, his whole carriage manly, and his voice clear, but not so strong as his size led one to expect. His health was excellent, except during the four years preceding his death, when he was subject to frequent fevers; toward the end of his life he limped a little with one foot. Even in his later years he lived rather according to his own inclinations than the advice of physicians; the latter indeed he very much disliked, because they wanted him to give up roasts, to which he was accustomed, and to eat boiled meat instead. In accordance with national custom, he took frequent exercise on horseback and in the chase, in which sports scarcely any people in the world can equal the Franks. He enjoyed the vapors from natural warm springs, and often indulged in swimming, in which he was so skillful that none could surpass him; and hence it was that he built his palace at Aix-la-Chapelle, and lived there constantly during his later years. . . .

Charles was temperate in eating, and especially so in drinking, for he abhorred drunkenness in anybody, much more in himself and those of his household; but he could not easily abstain from food, and often complained that fasts injured his health. He gave entertainments but rarely, only on great feast-days, and then to large numbers of people. His meals consisted ordinarily of four courses not counting the roast, which his huntsmen were accustomed to bring in on the spit; he was more fond of this than of any other dish. While at table, he listened to reading or music. The subjects of the readings were the stories and deeds of olden time. He was fond, too, of St. Augustine's books, and especially of the one entitled *The City of God*. He was so moderate in the use of wine and all sorts of drink that he rarely allowed himself more than three cups in the course of a meal. . . .

Charles had the gift of ready and fluent speech, and could express whatever he had to say with the utmost clearness. He was not satisfied with ability to use his native language merely, but gave attention to the study of foreign ones, and in particular was such a master of Latin that he could speak it as well as his native tongue; but he could understand Greek better than he could speak it. He was so eloquent, indeed, that he might have been taken for a teacher of oratory. He most zealously cherished the liberal arts, held

"The Moderate and Progressive King" is from Frederick Ogg, ed., *A Source Book of Medieval History* (New York: American Book Company, 1907), pp. 109–114.

those who taught them in great esteem, and conferred great honors upon them. He took lessons in grammar of the deacon Peter of Pisa, at that time an aged man. Another deacon, Albin of Britain, surnamed Alcuin, a man of Saxon birth, who was the greatest scholar of the day, was his teacher in other branches of learning. The king spent much time and labor with him studying rhetoric, dialectic, and especially astronomy. He learned to make calculations, and used to investigate with much curiosity and intelligence the motions of the heavenly bodies. He also tried to write, and used to keep tablets and blanks in bed under his pillow, that at leisure hours he might accustom his hand to form the letters; however, as he began his efforts late in life, and not at the proper time, they met with little success.

He cherished with the greatest fervor and devotion the principles of the Christian religion, which had been instilled into him from infancy. Hence it was that he built the beautiful basilica at Aix-la-Chapelle, which he adorned with gold and silver and lamps, and with rails and doors of solid brass. He had the columns and marbles for this structure brought from Rome and Ravenna, for he could not find such as were suitable elsewhere. He was a constant worshipper at this church as long as his health permitted, going morning and evening, even after nightfall, besides attending mass. He took care that all the services there conducted should be held in the best possible manner, very often warning the sextons not to let any improper or unclean thing be brought into the building, or remain in it. He provided it with a number of sacred vessels of gold and silver, and with such a quantity of clerical robes that not even the door-keepers, who filled the humblest office in the church, were obliged to wear their everyday clothes when in the performance of their duties. He took great pains to improve the church reading and singing, for he was well skilled in both, although he neither read in public nor sang, except in a low tone and with others.

He was very active in aiding the poor, and in that open generosity which the Greeks call alms; so much so, indeed, that he not only made a point of giving in his own country and his own kingdom, but when he discovered that there were Christians living in poverty in Syria, Egypt, and Africa, at Jerusalem, Alexandria, and Carthage, he had compassion on their wants, and used to send money over the seas to them. The reason that he earnestly strove to make friends with the kings beyond seas was that he might get help and relief to the Christians living under their rule. He cared for the Church of St. Peter the Apostle at Rome above all other holy and sacred places, and heaped high its treasury with a vast wealth of gold, silver, and precious stones. He sent great and countless gifts to the popes; and throughout his whole reign the wish that he had nearest his heart was to reestablish the ancient authority of the city of Rome under his care and by his influence, and to defend and protect the Church of St. Peter, and to beautify and enrich it out of his own store above all other churches. Nevertheless, although he held it in such veneration, only four times did he repair to Rome to pay his vows and make his supplications during the whole forty-seven years that he reigned.

The Imperial Coronation:
"By the Will of God" (800)

THE ANNALS OF LORSCH

The coronation of Charlemagne by Pope Leo III in 800 has been regarded by some historians as a pivotal event in the Middle Ages. Charlemagne's title was upgraded from king to Emperor of the Franks. This afforded him greater prestige and recognition from the Byzantine and Islamic worlds, but it did not grant him new subjects, greater wealth, or more territory. By 800 Charlemagne had already established control over much of western Europe, and that was probably the extent of his ambition. Still, the coronation has been viewed as the informal establishment of the Holy Roman Empire, the successor to ancient Roman greatness.

The coronation is also controversial in that it is one of the first important instances of the church's assertion of supremacy over secular forces. By crowning Charlemagne in the name of God, did the pope assume a tacit control over him?

And because the name of emperor had now ceased among the Greeks, . . . it seemed both to Leo the pope himself, and to all the holy fathers who were present in the council, as well as to the rest of the Christian people, that they ought to take to be emperor Charles, king of the Franks, who held Rome herself, where the Caesars had always been sat, and all the other regions which he ruled through Italy and Gaul and Germany; and inasmuch as God had given all these lands into his hand, it seemed right that with the help of God, and at the prayer of the whole Christian people, he should have the name of emperor also. King Charles did not wish to refuse the pope's offer, but submitting himself with all humility to God, and at the prayer of the priests, and of the whole Christian people, on the day of the nativity of our Lord Jesus Christ, he took on himself the name of emperor, being consecrated by the Pope Leo. . . . For this also was done by the will of God . . . that the heathen might not mock the Christians if the name of emperor should have ceased among them.

Administration of the Frankish Empire

The greatness of a ruler has often been determined not just by how much territory he conquered, but by how well he maintained it. The administration of an empire as vast as Charlemagne's depended on efficient servants of the king. The selections below testify to Charlemagne's organization and efficient rule. The Missi Dominici *were members of the church and nobility who traveled throughout the realm administering justice by acting as an appellate court; it was an attempt to inject the presence of the king directly into the law and affairs of the realm. Notice the detail of the military summons as Charlemagne demanded the men and arms*

"The Imperial Coronation: 'By the Will of God' " is from Frederick Ogg, ed., *A Source Book of Medieval History* (New York: American Book Company, 1907), pp. 132–133.

pledged legally by feudal contract from the Abbot Fulrad. The last selection is a general accounting for taxation purposes.

The Missi Dominici (802)

Concerning the embassy sent out by the lord emperor. Therefore, the most serene and most Christian lord emperor Charles has chosen from his nobles the wisest and most prudent men, both archbishops and some of the other bishops also, and venerable abbots and pious laymen, and has sent them throughout his whole kingdom, and through them by all the following chapters has allowed men to live in accordance with the correct law. Moreover, where anything which is not right and just has been enacted in the law, he has ordered them to inquire into this most diligently and to inform him of it; he desires, God granting, to reform it. And let no one, through his cleverness or astuteness, dare to oppose or thwart the written law, as many would like to do, or the judicial sentence passed upon him, or to do injury to the churches of God or the poor or the widows or the wards or any Christian. But all shall live entirely in accordance with God's precept, justly and under a just rule, and each one shall be admonished to live in harmony with his fellows in his business or profession; the canonical clergy ought to observe in every respect a canonical life without seeking base gain, nuns ought to keep diligent watch over their lives, laymen and the secular clergy ought rightly to observe their laws without malicious fraud, and all ought to live in mutual charity and perfect peace.

A Military Summons (804–811)

CHARLEMAGNE

In the name of the Father, Son and Holy Ghost. Charles, most serene, August, crowned by God, great pacific Emperor, and also, by God's mercy, King of the Franks and Lombards, to Abbot Fulrad.

Be it known to you that we have decided to hold our general assembly this year in the eastern part of Saxony, on the river Bode, at the place which is called Strassfurt. Therefore, we have commanded you to come to the aforesaid place, with all your men well armed and prepared, on the fifteenth day before the Kalends of July, that is, seven days before the festival of St. John the Baptist. Come, accordingly, so equipped with your men to the aforesaid place that thence you may be able to go well prepared in any direction whither our summons shall direct; that is, with arms and gear also, and other equipment for war in food and clothing. So that each horseman shall have a

"The Missi Dominici" is from Dana Munro, ed., *Translations and Reprints from the Original Sources of European History,* vol. 6, pt. 5 (Philadelphia: University of Pennsylvania, 1899), p. 16.

"A Military Summons" is from Dana Munro, ed., *Translations and Reprints from the Original Sources of European History,* vol. 6, pt. 5 (Philadelphia: University of Pennsylvania, 1899), pp. 11–12.

shield, lance, sword, dagger, bow and quivers with arrows; and in your carts utensils of various kinds, that is, axes, planes, augers, boards, spades, iron shovels, and other utensils which are necessary in an army. In the carts also supplies of food for three months, dating from the time of assembly, arms and clothing for a half-year. And we command this in general, that you cause it to be observed that you proceed peacefully to the aforesaid place, through whatever part of our realm your journey shall take you, that is, that you presume to take nothing except fodder, wood and water; and let the men of each one of your vassals march along with the carts and horsemen, and let the leader always be with them until they reach the aforesaid place, so that the absence of a lord may not give an opportunity to his men of doing evil.

Send your gifts, which you ought to present to us at our assembly in the middle of the month of May, to the place where we then shall be; if perchance your journey shall so shape itself that on your march you are able in person to present these gifts of yours to us, we greatly desire it. See that you show no negligence in the future if you desire to have our favor.

The Carolingian Renaissance

Charlemagne's involvement in his empire went beyond its administrative regulation. He believed that learning was an essential aspect of life and established palace schools run by great scholars such as Alcuin of York. In these schools, members of the nobility were taught to read and write. In practical terms, this contributed to greater communication and a more efficient administration of the empire. In spiritual terms, the Bible and other Christian writings were now open to study and revision; accuracy was demanded by the emperor. The following selections are from letters written by Charlemagne to the clergy of his realm. They are clear statements of his educational policy.

Education and the Scriptures
CHARLEMAGNE

Charles, by the grace of God, King of the Franks and Lombards and Patrician of the Romans, to Abbot Baugulf and to all the congregation, also to the faithful committed to you, we have directed a loving greeting by our ambassadors in the name of omnipotent God.

We, together with our faithful, have considered it to be useful that the bishoprics and monasteries entrusted by the favor of Christ to our control, . . . ought to be zealous in teaching those who by the gift of God are able to learn, . . . so that those who desire to please God by living rightly should not neglect to please him

"Education and the Scriptures" is from Dana Munro, ed., *Translations and Reprints from the Original Sources of European History*, vol. 6, pt. 5 (Philadelphia: University of Pennsylvania, 1899), pp. 12–14.

by speaking correctly. . . . For although correct conduct may be better than knowledge, nevertheless knowledge precedes conduct. Therefore, each one ought to study what he desires to accomplish, so that so much the more fully the mind may know what ought to be done, as the tongue hastens in the praises of omnipotent God without the hindrances of errors. . . . For when in the years just passed letters were often written to us from several monasteries in which it was stated that the brethren who dwelt there offered up in our behalf sacred and pious prayers, we have recognized in most of these letters both correct thoughts and uncouth expressions; because what pious devotion dictated faithfully to the mind, the tongue, uneducated on account of the neglect of study, was not able to express in the letter without error. . . . And we all know well that, although errors of speech are dangerous, far more dangerous are errors of the understanding. Therefore, we exhort you not only not to neglect the study of letters, but also with most humble mind, pleasing to God, to study earnestly in order that you may be able more easily and more correctly to penetrate the mysteries of the divine Scriptures. . . . And may this be done with a zeal as great as the earnestness with which we command it. For we desire you to be, as it is fitting that soldiers of the church should be, devout in mind, learned in discourse, chaste in conduct and eloquent in speech, so that whosoever shall seek to see you out of reverence for God, or on account of your reputation for holy conduct, just as he is edified by your appearance, may also be instructed by your wisdom, which he has learned from your reading or singing, and may go away joyfully giving thanks to omnipotent God. Do not neglect, therefore, if you wish to have our favor, to send copies of this letter to all your fellow-bishops and to all the monasteries . . . farewell.

Carolingian Scholarship (790)
CHARLEMAGNE

Charles, by the aid of God king of the Franks and Lombards and patricius of the Romans, to the clergy of his realm. . . . Now since we are very desirous that the condition of our churches should constantly improve, we are endeavoring by diligent study to restore the knowledge of letters which has been almost lost through the negligence of our ancestors, and by our example we are encouraging those who are able to do so to engage in the study of the liberal arts. In this undertaking we have already, with the aid of God, corrected all the books of the Old and New Testament, whose texts had been corrupted through the ignorance of copyists. . . . Finally, since we have found that many of the lessons to be read in the nightly service have been badly compiled and that the texts of these readings are full of mistakes, and the names of their authors omitted, and since we could not bear to listen to such gross errors in the sacred lessons, we have diligently studied how the character of these readings might be improved. Accordingly we have commanded Paul the Deacon,

"Carolingian Scholarship" is from Oliver Thatcher and Edgar McNeal, eds., *A Source Book of Medieval History* (New York: Charles Scribner's Sons, 1905), pp. 56–57.

our beloved subject, to undertake this work; that is, to go through the writings of the fathers carefully, and to make selections of the most helpful things from them and put them together into a book, as one gathers occasional flowers from a broad meadow to make a bouquet. And he, wishing to obey us, has read through the treatises and sermons of the various catholic fathers and has picked out the best things. These selections he has copied clearly without mistakes and has arranged in two volumes, providing readings suitable for every feast day throughout the whole year. We have tested the texts of all these readings by our own knowledge, and now authorize these volumes and commend them to all of you to be read in the churches of Christ.

Feudalism

The Viking Onslaught (850–1050)

One of the most haunting of medieval images is the prow of a Viking ship. As the ship glided down the rivers of Europe, people understood that death and destruction would follow in its wake. The word "Viking" means warrior; it is a general appellation for the Swedes, Danes, and Norwegians who left Scandinavia in the ninth century, looking for booty and adventure. The sleek, open ships of the Northmen, as the Vikings were also called, hugged the coasts of Europe and Russia, sailed down the rivers, and survived passage of the open Atlantic to found settlements in North America. The navigational techniques of the Vikings and their establishment of trade routes to the Black Sea are reminders that they were important contributors to positive aspects of Western Civilization. But for the medieval family, their presence inspired fear and desperation. "The Annals of Xanten" which follow were originally the work of several ninth-century monks. These fragments chronicle the destruction brought by the Vikings and underscore the decline of the Carolingian dynasty; the successors to Charlemagne simply could not protect against the ravages of constant invasion. The second selection is by Abbo, a monk in Paris, who witnessed the siege of his city.

The Annals of Xanten (845–854)

According to their custom the Northmen plundered Eastern and Western Frisia and burned the town of Dordrecht, with two other villages, before the eyes of Lothaire [Charlemagne's grandson], who was then in the castle of Nimwegen, but could not punish the crime. The Northmen, with their boats filled with immense booty, including both men and goods, returned to their own country.

"The Annals of Xanten" is from J. H. Robinson, ed., *Readings in European History*, vol. 1 (Boston: Ginn and Company, 1904), pp. 158–162.

At this same time, as no one can mention or hear without great sadness, the mother of all churches, the basilica of the apostle Peter, was taken and plundered by the Moors, or Saracens, who had already occupied the region of Beneventum. The Saracens, moreover, slaughtered all the Christians whom they found outside the walls of Rome, either within or without this church. They also carried men and women away as prisoners. They tore down, among many others, the altar of the blessed Peter, and their crimes from day to day bring sorrow to Christians. Pope Sergius departed life this year.

After the death of Sergius no mention of the apostolic see has come in any way to our ears. Rabanus [Maurus], master and abbot of Fulda, was solemnly chosen archbishop as the successor of Bishop Otger, who died. Moreover the Northmen here and there plundered the Christians and engaged in a battle with the counts Sigir and Liuthar. They continued up the Rhine as far as Dordrecht, and nine miles farther to Megingard, when they turned back, having taken their booty.

While King Louis [Charlemagne's son] was ill his army of Bavaria took its way against the Bohemians. Many of these were killed and the remainder withdrew, much humiliated, into their own country. The heathen from the North wrought havoc in Christendom as usual and grew greater in strength; but it is revolting to say more of this matter.

On January 1st of that season, . . . towards evening, a great deal of thunder was heard and a mighty flash of lightning seen; and an overflow of water afflicted the human race during this winter. In the following summer an all too great heat of the sun burned the earth. Leo, pope of the apostolic see, an extraordinary man, built a fortification round the church of St. Peter the apostle. The Moors, however, devastated here and there the coast towns in Italy. . . .

The Normans inflicted much harm in Frisia and about the Rhine. A mighty army of them collected by the river Elbe against the Saxons, and some of the Saxon towns were besieged, others burned, and most terribly did they oppress the Christians. A meeting of our kings took place on the Maas. The steel of the heathen glistened; excessive heat; a famine followed. There was not fodder enough for the animals. . . .

The Siege of Paris (806)

ABBO

The Northmen came to Paris with 700 sailing ships, not counting those of smaller size which were commonly called barques. At one stretch the Seine was lined with the vessels for more than two leagues, so that one might ask in astonishment in what cavern the river had been swallowed up, since it was not to be seen. The second day after the fleet of the Northmen arrived under the

"The Siege of Paris" is from Frederick Ogg, ed., *A Source Book of Medieval History* (New York: American Book Company, 1907), pp. 168–171.

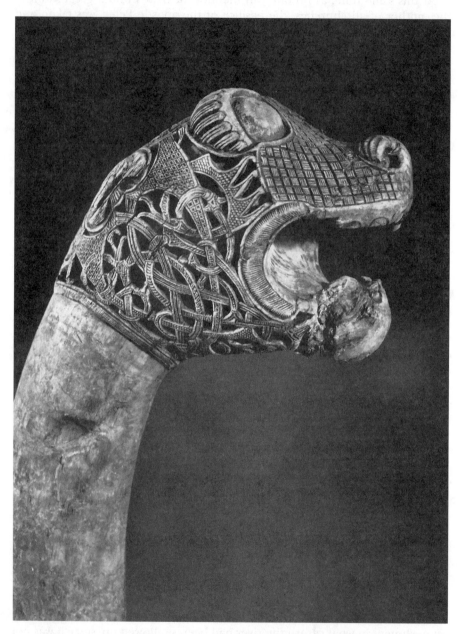

The headpost of a Viking ship. Graceful and flowing, nevertheless, the appearance of this prow often signaled danger to the inhabitants of Europe. *(Universitetets Oldsaksamling, Oslo)*

walls of the city, Siegfred, who was . . . in command of the expedition, came
to the dwelling of the illustrious bishop. He bowed his head and said:
"Gauzelin, have compassion on yourself and on your flock. We beseech you
to listen to us, in order that you may escape death. Allow us only the freedom
of the city. We will do no harm and we will see to it that whatever belongs either to you or to Odo shall be strictly respected." Count Odo, who later became king, was then the defender of the city. The bishop replied to Siegfred,
"Paris has been entrusted to us by the Emperor Charles, who, after God, king
and lord of the powerful, rules over almost all the world. He has put it in our
care, not at all that the kingdom may be ruined by our misconduct, but that
he may keep it and be assured of its peace. If, like us, you had been given the
duty of defending these walls, and if you should have done that which you ask
us to do, what treatment do you think you would deserve?" Siegfred replied:
"I should deserve that my head be cut off and thrown to the dogs. Nevertheless, if you do not listen to my demand, on the morrow our war machines will
destroy you with poisoned arrows. You will be the prey of famine and of pestilence and these evils will renew themselves perpetually every year." So saying,
he departed and gathered together his comrades.

In the morning the Northmen, boarding their ships, approached the
tower and attacked it. They shook it with their engines and stormed it with arrows. The city resounded with clamor, the people were aroused, the bridges
trembled. All came together to defend the tower. There Odo, his brother
Robert, and the Count Ragenar distinguished themselves for bravery; likewise
the courageous Abbot Ebolus, the nephew of the bishop. A keen arrow
wounded the prelate, while at his side the warrior Frederick was struck by a
sword. Frederick died, but the old man, thanks to God, survived. There perished many Franks; after receiving wounds they were deprived of life. At last
the enemy withdrew, carrying off their dead. . . . At sunrise the Danes . . .
once more . . . engaged the Christians in violent combat. On every side arrows sped and blood flowed. With the arrows mingled the stones hurled by
slings and war-machines; the air was filled with them. The tower which had
been rebuilt during the night groaned under the strokes of the darts, the city
shook with the struggle, the people ran hither and thither, the bells jangled.
The warriors rushed together to defend the tottering tower and to repel the
fierce assault. . . . The redoubtable Odo who never experienced defeat continually revived the spirits of the worn-out defenders. He ran along the ramparts and hurled back the enemy. On those who were secreting themselves so
as to undermine the tower he poured oil, wax, and pitch, which, being mixed
and heated, burned the Danes and tore off their scalps. Some of them died;
others threw themselves into the river to escape the awful substance. . . .

Now came the Emperor Charles, surrounded by soldiers of all nations,
even as the sky is adorned with resplendent stars. A great throng, speaking
many languages, accompanied him. He established his camp at the foot of
the heights of Montmartre, near the tower. He allowed the Northmen to
have the country of Sens to plunder; and in the spring he gave them 700

pounds of silver on condition that by the month of March they leave France for their own kingdom. Then Charles returned, destined to an early death.

The Feudal Relationship

Feudalism in its more refined form was born of the chaos caused by the Viking invasions, internal disputes, and poor leadership which together contributed to the destruction of Charlemagne's empire. As central authority (in the person of the king) collapsed, there evolved rather naturally a system of decentralized rule in which the most important nobles of the realm (lords) *protected their own regional holdings by contracting with lesser nobles* (vassals) *who fought for them. This involved an expression of* homage, *in which the vassal promised* fealty *(loyalty) to the lord. In return, he was usually granted a* fief *(parcel of land) from which he derived an income and, depending on the size of his land holdings, some measure of prestige. The vassal, in turn, might have other vassals pledged to himself in a hierarchy of support. This process was called* subinfeudation *and became quite complex since vassals could contract with several lords at once. In that case, one's ultimate fealty belonged to the original or most important noble, called the* liege lord.

Feudalism, then, is the political, military, and legal relationship between a lord and a vassal. It had existed rather informally since the later Roman Empire, but became more sophisticated and widespread during the ninth century as the Viking invasions demanded some form of defense. The lords provided the leadership, the vassals composed the army, and the people sought the protection of such regional strong-men. In return for this protection, the free peasant often gave up his land and labored on the fief of a noble for a specified amount of time. The peasant thus became a serf *and was responsible for the production and upkeep of the lord's manor. The social, economic, and legal relationship between a serf and a member of the fighting nobility for whom he worked is called* manorialism. *The following selections represent various aspects of medieval feudalism.*

Homage

The man should put his hands together as a sign of humility, and place them between the two hands of his lord as a token that he vows everything to him and promises faith to him; and the lord should receive him and promise to keep faith with him. Then the man should say: "Sir, I enter your homage and faith and become your man by mouth and hands [i.e., by taking the oath and placing his hands between those of the lord], and I swear and promise to keep faith, and loyalty to you against all others, and to guard your rights with all my strength."

"Homage" is from Oliver Thatcher and Edgar McNeal, eds., *A Source Book of Medieval History* (New York: Charles Scribner's Sons, 1905), p. 363.

Feudal Obligations (1020)
BISHOP FULBERT OF CHARTRES

To William most glorious duke of the Aquitanians, bishop Fulbert the favor of his prayers.

Asked to write something concerning the form of fealty, I have noted briefly for you on the authority of the books the things which follow. He who swears fealty to his lord ought always to have these six things in memory: what is harmless, safe, honorable, useful, easy, practicable. Harmless, that is to say that he should not be injurious to his lord in his body; safe, that he should not be injurious to him in his secrets or in the defences through which he is able to be secure; honorable, that he should not be injurious to him in his justice or in other matters that pertain to his honor; useful, that he should not be injurious to him in his possessions. . . .

However, that the faithful vassal should avoid these injuries is proper, but not for this does he deserve his holding; for it is not sufficient to abstain from evil, unless what is good is done also. It remains therefore, that in the same six things mentioned above he should faithfully counsel and aid his lord, if he wishes to be looked upon as worthy of his benefice and to be safe concerning the fealty which he has sworn.

The lord also ought to act toward his faithful vassal reciprocally in all these things. And if he does not do this he will be justly considered guilty of bad faith. . . .

I would have written to you at greater length, if I had not been occupied with many other things, including the rebuilding of our city and church which was lately entirely consumed in a great fire; from which loss though we could not for a while be diverted, yet by the hope of the comfort of God and of you we breathe again.

Legal Rules for Military Service
KING LOUIS IX

The baron and all vassals of the king are bound to appear before him when he shall summon them, and to serve him at their own expense for forty days and forty nights, with as many knights as each one owes; and he is able to extract from them these services when he wishes and when he has need of them. And if the king wishes to keep them more than forty days at their own expense, they are not bound to remain if they do not wish it. And if the king

"Feudal Obligations" is from Edward P. Cheyney, ed., *Translations and Reprints from the Original Sources of European History*, vol. 4, pt. 3 (Philadelphia: University of Pennsylvania, 1897), pp. 23–24.

"Legal Rules for Military Service" is from Edward P. Cheyney, ed., *Translations and Reprints from the Original Sources of European History*, vol. 4, pt. 3 (Philadelphia: University of Pennsylvania, 1897), p. 30.

wishes to keep them at his expense for the defence of the realm, they are bound to remain. And if the king wishes to lead them outside of the kingdom, they need not go unless they wish to, for they have already served their forty days and forty nights.

Liege Homage

I, John of Toul, make known that I am the liege man of the lady Beatrice, countess of Troyes, and of her son, Theobald, count of Champagne, against every creature, living or dead, save my allegiance to lord Enjorand of Coucy, lord John of Arcis, and the count of Grandpre. If it should happen that the count of Grandpre should be at war with the countess and count of Champagne on his own quarrel, I will aid the count of Grandpre in my own person, and will send to the count and countess of Champagne the knights whose service I owe to them for the fief which I hold of them. But if the count of Grandpre shall make war on the countess and the count of Champagne on behalf of his friends and not in his own quarrel, I will aid in my own person the countess and count of Champagne, and will send one knight to the count of Grandpre for the service which I owe him for the fief which I hold of him, but I will not go myself into the territory of the count of Grandpre to make war on him.

Restraint of Feudal Violence:
The Truce of God (1063)

Feudalism was a system of governance that dealt well with crisis and chaos. When invaders approached, the lord called his vassals into service (levy) and the enemy was engaged. Feudalism and manorialism regularized life and afforded security in an otherwise insecure age. Therefore, these systems were maintained even during times of peace. But vassals were trained to fight and became restless when they were not "employed." Disputes between lords broke out frequently and often resulted in bloodshed and the destruction of property. Tournaments, where knights (vassals) could display their manly prowess in a somewhat controlled atmosphere, were developed to channel the destructive energy of these nobles. In this respect, the laws of chivalry and the Crusades kept regional peace and directed hostility away from Europe and toward the infidel Muslims in the Holy Land. The church went further, attacking the problem of aggression by

---

"Liege Homage" is from Oliver Thatcher and Edgar McNeal, eds., *A Source Book of Medieval History* (New York: Charles Scribner's Sons, 1905), pp. 364–365.

"Restraint of Feudal Violence: The Truce of God" is from Oliver Thatcher and Edgar McNeal, eds., *A Source Book of Medieval History* (New York: Charles Scribner's Sons, 1905), pp. 417–418.

establishing laws of conduct since called "The Truce of God." Note the church's acceptance of trial by ordeal and what it entailed.

Drogo, bishop of Terouanne, and count Baldwin [of Hainault] have established this peace with the cooperation of the clergy and people of the land.

Dearest brothers in the Lord, these are the conditions which you must observe during the time of the peace which is commonly called the truce of God, and which begins with sunset on Wednesday and lasts until sunrise on Monday.

1. During those four days and five nights no man or woman shall assault, wound, or slay another, or attack, seize, or destroy a castle, burg, or villa, by craft or by violence.
2. If anyone violates this peace and disobeys these commands of ours, he shall be exiled for thirty years as a penance, and before he leaves the bishopric he shall make compensation for the injury which he committed. Otherwise he shall be excommunicated by the Lord God and excluded from all Christian fellowship.
3. All who associate with him in any way, who give him advice or aid, or converse with him, unless it be to advise him to do penance and to leave the bishopric, shall be under excommunication until they have made satisfaction.
4. If any violator of the peace shall fall sick and die before he completes his penance, no Christian shall visit him or move his body from the place where it lay, or receive any of his possessions.
5. In addition, brethren, you should observe the peace in regard to lands and animals and all things that can be possessed. If anyone takes from another an animal, a coin, or a garment, during the days of the truce, he shall be excommunicated unless he makes satisfaction. . . .
6. During the days of the peace, no one shall make a hostile expedition on horseback, except when summoned by the count; and all who go with the count shall take for their support only as much as is necessary for themselves and their horses.
7. All merchants and other men who pass through your territory from other lands shall have peace from you.
8. You shall also keep this peace every day of the week from the beginning of Advent to the octave of Epiphany and from the beginning of Lent to the octave of Easter, and from the feast of Rogations [the Monday before Ascension Day] to the octave of Pentecost.
9. We command all priests on feast days and Sundays to pray for all who keep the peace, and to curse all who violate it or support its violators.
10. If anyone has been accused of violating the peace and denies the charge, he shall take the communion and undergo the ordeal of hot iron. If he is found guilty, he shall do penance within the bishopric for seven years.

Ordeal of Hot Iron

After the accusation has been lawfully made, and three days have been passed in fasting and prayer, the priest, clad in his sacred vestments with the exception of his outside garment, shall take with a tongs the iron placed before the altar; and, singing the hymn of three youths, namely, "Bless him all his works," he shall bear it to the fire, and shall say this prayer over the place where fire is to carry out the judgment: "Bless, O Lord God, this place, that there may be for us in it sanctity, chastity, virtue and victory, and sanctimony, humility, goodness, gentleness and plenitude of law, and obedience to God the Father and the Son and the Holy Ghost."—After this, the iron shall be placed in the fire and shall be sprinkled with holy water; and while it is heating, he shall celebrate mass. But when the priest shall have taken the Eucharist, he shall adjure the man who is to be tried . . . and shall cause him to take the communion.—Then the priest shall sprinkle holy water above the iron and shall say: "The blessing of God the Father, the Son, and the Holy Ghost descend upon this iron for the discerning of the right judgment of God." And straightway the accused shall carry the iron to a distance of nine feet. Finally his hand shall be covered under seal for three days, and if festering blood be found in the track of the iron, he shall be judged guilty. But if, however, he shall go forth uninjured, praise shall be rendered to God.

SECTION II:
THE HIGH MIDDLE AGES
(1000–1300)

The Medieval Church in Ascendancy

The Crusades: "It is the Will of God!"

The Speech of Pope Urban II at Clermont (1095)

ROBERT THE MONK

The first expedition to free the Holy Land from the control of the Infidel Muslim was launched in 1095 at the Council of Clermont. Pope Urban II presided and in a rousing speech excited the crowd with this impassioned plea for action. Although we are not sure about the accuracy of the text (we have five contemporary

---

"Ordeal of Hot Iron" is from Ernest F. Henderson, ed., *Select Historical Documents of the Middle Ages* (London: George Bell and Sons, 1896), pp. 314–315.

"The Speech of Pope Urban II at Clermont" is from Oliver Thatcher and Edgar McNeal, eds., *A Source Book of Medieval History* (New York: Charles Scribner's Sons, 1905), pp. 518–520.

versions), the following account by Robert the Monk is credible and clearly illustrates Urban's justification for the First Crusade as well as his popular appeal.

In 1095 a great council was held in Auvergne, in the city of Clermont. Pope Urban II, accompanied by cardinals and bishops, presided over it. It was made famous by the presence of many bishops and princes from France and Germany. After the council had attended to ecclesiastical matters, the pope went out into a public square, because no house was able to hold the people, and addressed them in a very persuasive speech, as follows: "O race of the Franks, O people who live beyond the mountains [the Alps], O people loved and chosen of God, as is clear from your many deeds, distinguished over all other nations by the situation of your land, your catholic faith, and your regard for the holy church, we have a special message and exhortation for you. For we wish you to know what a grave matter has brought us to your country. The sad news has come from Jerusalem and Constantinople that the people of Persia, an accursed and foreign race, enemies of God, a generation that set not their heart aright, and whose spirit was not steadfast with God [Ps. 78:8], have invaded the lands of those Christians and devastated them with the sword, rapine, and fire. Some of the Christians they have carried away as slaves, others they have put to death. The churches they have either destroyed or turned into mosques. They desecrate and overthrow the altars. They circumcise the Christians and pour the blood from the circumcision on the altars or in the baptismal fonts. Some they kill in a horrible way by cutting open the abdomen, taking out a part of the entrails and tying them to a stake; they then beat them and compel them to walk until all their entrails are drawn out and they fall to the ground. Some they use as targets for their arrows. They compel some to stretch out their necks and then they try to see whether they can cut off their heads with one stroke of the sword. It is better to say nothing of their horrible treatment of the women. They have taken from the Greek empire a tract of land so large that it takes more than two months to walk through it. Whose duty is it to avenge this and recover that land, if not yours? For to you more than to other nations the Lord has given the military spirit, courage, agile bodies, and the bravery to strike down those who resist you. Let your minds be stirred to bravery by the deeds of your forefathers, and by the efficiency and greatness of [Charlemagne], and of Ludwig his son, and of the other kings who have destroyed Turkish kingdoms, and established Christianity in their lands. You should be moved especially by the holy grave of our Lord and Saviour which is now held by unclean peoples, and by the holy places which are treated with dishonor and irreverently befouled with their uncleanness.

"O bravest of knights, descendants of unconquered ancestors, do not be weaker than they, but remember their courage. If you are kept back by your love for your children, relatives and wives, remember what the Lord says in the Gospel: 'He that loveth father or mother more than me is not worthy of me' [Matt. 10:37]; 'and everyone that hath forsaken houses, or brothers, or sisters, or father, or mother, or wife, or children, or lands for my name's sake, shall receive a hundredfold and shall inherit everlasting life' [Matt. 19:29]. Let no possessions keep you back, no solicitude for your property. Your land is shut in on all sides by the sea and mountains, and is too thickly populated. There is not much wealth here, and the soil scarcely yields enough to support you. On this account you kill and devour each other, and carry on war and mutually destroy each other. Let your hatred and quarrels cease, your civil wars come to an end, and all your dissensions stop. Set out on the road to the holy sepulchre, take the land from that wicked people, and make it your own. . . . This land our Saviour made illustrious by his birth, beautiful with his life, and sacred with his suffering; he redeemed it with his death and glorified it with his tomb. This royal city is now held captive by her enemies, and made pagan by those who know not God. She asks and longs to be liberated and does not cease to beg you to come to her aid. She asks aid especially from you because, as I have said, God has given more of the military spirit to you than to other nations. Set out on this journey and you will obtain the remission of your sins and be sure of the incorrigible glory of the kingdom of heaven."

When Pope Urban had said this and much more of the same sort, all who were present were moved to cry out with one accord, "It is the will of God, it is the will of God!" When the pope heard this he raised his eyes to heaven and gave thanks to God, and, commanding silence with a gesture of his hand, he said: "My dear brethren, today there is fulfilled in you that which the Lord says in the Gospel, 'Where two or three are gathered in my name, there am I in the midst' [Matt. 18:20]. For unless the Lord God had been in your minds you would not all have said the same thing. For although you spoke with many voices, nevertheless it was one and the same thing that made you speak. So I say unto you, God, who put those words into your hearts, has caused you to utter them. Therefore let these words be your battle cry, because God caused you to speak them. Whenever you meet the enemy in battle, you shall all cry out, 'It is the will of God! It is the will of God!'"

The Fall of Jerusalem (1099)

The Crusaders who set out at the behest of Pope Urban II in 1096 were quite successful in defeating Muslim armies, capturing territory along the pilgrimage route into Syria, and maintaining it with defensive castles established at Edessa and Antioch. Their ultimate goal, however, was Jerusalem, a city sacred to Christian, Jew, and Muslim alike. Its bloody fall to the Christian forces in 1099 is described in the following account known as the Gesta Francorum.

"The Fall of Jerusalem" is from Rosalind Hill, ed., *Gesta Francorum* (London: Oxford University Press, 1962), pp. 89–92. Reprinted by permission of Oxford University Press.

During this siege, we suffered so badly from thirst that we sewed up the skins of oxen and buffaloes, and we used to carry water in them for the distance of nearly six miles. We drank the water from these vessels, although it stank, and what with foul water and barley bread we suffered great distress and affliction every day, for the Saracens used to lie in wait for our men by every spring and pool, where they killed them and cut them to pieces; moreover they used to carry off the beasts into their caves and secret places in the rocks.

Our leaders then decided to attack the city with engines, so that we might enter it and worship at our Savior's Sepulchre. They made two wooden siege-towers and various other mechanical devices. Duke Godfrey filled his siege-tower with machines, and so did Count Raymond, but they had to get the timber from far afield. When the Saracens saw our men making these machines, they built up the city wall and its towers by night, so they were exceedingly strong. When, however, our leaders saw which was the weakest spot in the city's defenses, they had a machine and a siege-tower transported round to the eastern side one Saturday night. They set up these engines at dawn, and spent Sunday, Monday and Tuesday in preparing the siege-tower and fitting

The Siege of Antioch (1098). During the First Crusade, Godfrey of Bouillion led his Christian forces against the "infidel" Muslims. Jerusalem fell to the Crusaders, but permanent political control was never achieved. *(Bridgeman/The Bridgeman Art Library International)*

it out, while the count of St. Gilles was getting his engine ready on the southern side. All this time we were suffering so badly from the shortage of water that for one penny a man could not buy sufficient to quench his thirst.

On Wednesday and Thursday we launched a fierce attack upon the city, both by day and by night, from all sides, but before we attacked, our bishops and priests preached to us, and told us to go in procession round Jerusalem to the Glory of God, and to pray and give alms and fast, as faithful men should do. On Friday at dawn we attacked the city from all sides but could achieve nothing, so that we were all astounded and very much afraid, yet, when that hour came when our Lord Jesus Christ deigned to suffer for us upon the cross, our Knights were fighting bravely on the siege-tower, led by Duke Godfrey and Count Eustace his brother. At that moment one of our knights, called Lethold, succeeded in getting on to the wall. As soon as he reached it, all the defenders fled along the walls and through the city, and our men went after them, killing them and cutting them down as far as Solomon's Temple, where there was such a massacre that our men were wading up to their ankles in enemy blood.

Count Raymond was bringing up his army and a siege-tower from the south to the neighborhood of the wall, but . . . when he heard that the Franks were in the city he said to his men, Why are you so slow? Look! All the other Franks are in the city already! Then the amir who held David's Tower surrendered to the count, and opened for him the gate where the pilgrims used to pay their taxes, so our men entered the city, chasing the Saracens and killing them up to Solomon's Temple, where they took refuge and fought hard against our men for the whole day, so that all the temple was streaming with their blood. At last, when the pagans were defeated, our men took many prisoners, both men and women, in the temple. They killed whom they chose, and whom they chose they saved alive. On the roof of the Temple of Solomon were crowded great numbers of pagans of both sexes. . . .

After this our men rushed round the whole city, seizing gold and silver, horses and mules, and houses full of all sorts of goods, and they all came rejoicing and weeping from excess of gladness to worship at the Sepulchre of our Saviour Jesus, and there they fulfilled their vows to him. Next morning they went cautiously up on to the Temple roof and attacked the Saracens, both men and women, cutting off their heads with drawn swords. Some of the Saracens threw themselves down headlong from the temple. . . . Our leaders then took counsel and ordered that every man should give alms and pray that God would choose for himself whomsoever he wished, to rule over the other and to govern the city. They also commanded that all the Saracen corpses should be thrown outside the city because of the fearful stench, for almost the whole city was full of their dead bodies. So the surviving Saracens dragged the dead ones out in front of the gates, and piled them up in mounds as big as houses. No-one has ever seen or heard of such a slaughter of pagans, for they were burned on pyres like pyramids, and no-one save God alone knows how many there were. . . .

An Islamic Perspective of the Crusades
USAMAH IBN-MUNQIDH

It has been said that history is often written through the eyes of the conquerors. And although one cannot speak of a "winner" or "loser" in the Crusades because of the complexities of the issues, it is true that there were distinct Christian and Islamic perspectives. Usamah Ibn-Munqidh, an Arab who lived through most of the twelfth century, was a keen observer of the Crusaders. The following accounts give a particularly interesting view of the Christians, their customs, and Muslim confidence in the protection of Allah.

My uncle had advised my father to get me to go to Apamea at the head of such competent troops as were with me at Schaizar, and to stir them up, together with the Arabs, to make a raid and lay waste the cultivated fields of Apamea. Our forces had been increased by a number of Arabs.

A few days after my uncle's departure, the herald called us to arms. I came accompanied by a small party, at most twenty horsemen. . . . We reached the valley of Bohemund, separated from the plunderers and Arabs who were scattered over the fields, and saw a considerable body of Franks coming towards us. That very night they had been reinforced by sixty knights and sixty foot-soldiers. We were driven from the valley and pursued. Finally we succeeded in catching up with those of our men who were busy destroying the crops.

The Franks gave vent to a piercing war-cry. I scorned death, thinking that everyone there was exposed to it as much as I was. At the head of the Franks appeared a knight who had thrown down his coat-of-mail, unburdening himself in order to be able to overtake us. I hurled myself on him and struck him full in the chest. His body fell a good way from his saddle. Then I rushed at their knights, who were coming up in single file. They retreated. And yet I had no experience of fighting, for this was my first battle. I was mounted on a horse as swift as a bird; I dashed in pursuit of them to strike a blow within their ranks, without feeling the least fear of them.

In the rear of the Franks was a knight on a black horse, large as a camel, wearing a coat of mail and the full armor of war. I was afraid of this horseman, lest he should draw me further ahead in order to get an opportunity to turn back and attack me. All of a sudden I saw him spur his horse, and as the horse began to wave its tail, I knew that it was already exhausted. So I hurled myself on the knight, struck him, and my lance pierced his body, coming out almost a cubit in front of him. The lightness of my body, the violence of the blow and the speed of my horse tumbled me out of my saddle. I got into it

"An Islamic Perspective of the Crusades" is from G. R. Potter, trans., *The Autobiography of Ousama* (1095–1188) (London: George Routledge and Sons, 1929), pp. 51–54.

again, pulled out my lance, quite convinced that I had killed the Frank, and collected my comrades. They were all safe and sound. . . .

[Returning to the camp, I said to my father]: "My lord, that was indeed my first fight. But the moment I saw that the Franks were in contact with our men, then I felt that death would be an easy matter for me. So I turned back to the Franks, either to be killed or to protect all of us." My father (may Allah have mercy upon him!) quoted the following verse as illustrating my case: "The coward flees to save his head; the brave man defends even those who are nothing to him."

My uncle (may Allah have mercy upon him!) returned a few days later. . . . He at once sent a messenger to me, asking me to appear before him at the usual time. He received me, having by his side one of the Franks. "This knight," he said, "has come from Apamea and wants to see the soldier who struck the knight Philip, for the Franks are amazed at the blow which he received which pierced his coat of mail in two places at the edge and yet the knight's life was saved." "What!" I exclaimed, "is it possible that he was saved?" The Frankish knight answered, "The stroke was blunted against the skin of his hips." I said, "A miracle of Destiny! Fate is an impregnable fortress! I could never have imagined that the knight could survive such a blow."

This is my opinion: It is indispensable for anyone who wants to give a blow with a lance to press his hand and his fore-arm against his side on the lance, and let his horse guide itself as best it can at the moment at which he strikes. For if a man moves his hand or his lance, or bends his hand to guide his lance, the blow leaves no trace and does no damage.

The Protection of Allah

USAMAH IBN-MUNQIDH

I saw a proof of the goodness of Allah and of his splendid protection when the Franks (the curse of Allah upon them!) encamped against us with knights and foot-soldiers. We were separated from one another by the Orontes River, whose waters were so swollen that the Franks could not reach us and we were prevented from reaching them. They pitched their tents on the mountain, while some took up their position in the gardens in their neighborhood, set their horses free in the meadows and went to sleep. Some young foot-soldiers from Schaizar took off their clothes, took their swords, swam towards these sleepers and killed several of them. Then a number of our enemies rushed at our companions, who took to the water and returned, while the Frankish army rushed down the mountain on horseback like a

"The Protection of Allah" is from G. R. Potter, trans., *The Autobiography of Ousama* (1095–1188) (London: George Routledge and Sons, 1929), pp. 123–124.

flood. Near them there was a mosque, the mosque of Abou'l-Madjd ibn Soumayya, in which there was a man named Hasan az-Zahid (the ascetic), who lived on a flat roof and used to retire to the mosque to pray. He was dressed in black woollen clothes. We saw him, but we had no means of reaching him. The Franks came, got down at the gate of the mosque and went towards him, while we said, "Power and might belong to Allah alone! The Franks will kill him." But he, by Allah, neither stopped praying nor moved from his position. The Franks stopped, turned away, remounted their horses and rode off, while he remained motionless in the same place, continuing to pray. We did not doubt that Allah (glory be to him!) had blinded the Franks with regard to him and had hidden him from their sight. Glory to the Almighty, the Merciful!

The Franks: "Superior in Courage, But Nothing Else"

USAMAH IBN-MUNQIDH

Glory be to Allah, the creator and author of all things! Anyone who is acquainted with what concerns the Franks can only glorify and sanctify Allah the All-Powerful; for he has seen in them animals who are superior in courage and in zeal for fighting but in nothing else, just as beasts are superior in strength and aggressiveness.

I will report some Frankish characteristics and my surprise as to their intelligence. . . .

Among the curiosities of medicine among the Franks, I will tell how the governor of Al-Mounaitira wrote to my uncle to ask him to send him a doctor who would look after some urgent cases. My uncle chose a Christian doctor named Thabit (?). He remained absent only ten days and then returned to us. There was a general exclamation: "How rapidly you have cured your patients!" Thabit replied: "They brought before me a knight with an abscess which had formed in his leg and a woman who was wasting away with a consumptive fever. I applied a little plaster to the knight; his abscess opened and took a turn for the better; the woman I forbade certain food and improved her condition." It was at this point that a Frankish doctor came up and said: "This man is incapable of curing them." Then, turning to the knight, he asked, "Which do you prefer, to live with one leg or die with two?" "I would rather live with one leg," the knight answered. "Bring a stalwart knight," said the Frankish doctor, "and a sharp hatchet." Knight and hatchet soon appeared. I was present at the scene. The doctor stretched the patient's leg on a

"The Franks: 'Superior Courage, But Nothing Else'" is from G. R. Potter, trans., *The Autobiography of Ousama* (1095–1188) (London: George Routledge and Sons, 1929), pp. 172–175, 181–182.

block of wood and then said to the knight, "Strike off his leg with the hatchet; take it off at one blow." Under my eyes the knight aimed a violent blow at it without cutting through the leg. He aimed another blow at the unfortunate man, as a result of which his marrow came from his leg and the knight died instantly. As for the woman, the doctor examined her and said, "She is a woman in whose head there is a devil who has taken possession of her. Shave off her hair!" His prescription was carried out, and like her fellows, she began once again to eat garlic and mustard. Her consumption became worse. The doctor then said, "It is because the devil has entered her head." Taking a razor, the doctor cut open her head in the shape of a cross and scraped away the skin in the centre so deeply that her very bones were showing. He then rubbed the head with salt. In her turn, the woman died instantly. After having asked them whether my services were still required and obtained an answer in the negative, I came back, having learnt to know what I had formerly been ignorant of about their medicine.

At Neapolis, I was once present at a curious sight. They brought in two men for trial by battle, the cause being the following. Some Mohammedan brigands had raided some property in the neighborhood of Neapolis. A farmer was suspected of having guided the brigands to this spot. The farmer took flight but soon returned, the king having had his children imprisoned. "Treat me with equity," said the accursed, "and allow me to fight with him who has named me as the person who brought the brigands into the village." The king then said to the lord who had received the village as a fief: "Send for his opponent." The lord returned to his village, picked out a blacksmith who was working there, and said to him, "You must go and fight a duel." For the owner of the fief was primarily anxious to see that none of his labourers got himself killed, for fear his crops should suffer.

I saw this blacksmith. He was a strong young man, but one who, walking or sitting, was always wanting something to drink. As for the other, the challenger to single combat, he was an old man of great courage, who snapped his fingers as a token of defiance and prepared for the fight without perturbation. The sheriff [and] governor of the town appeared, gave each of the two fighters a cudgel and shield and made the crowd form a ring round them.

The fight started. The old man forced the blacksmith backwards, throwing him on to the edge of the crowd, and then returned to the middle of the ring. The exchange of blows was so violent that the rivals, who remained standing, seemed to make up one pillar of blood.

The fight continued, while the sheriff urged them to force a conclusion. "Quicker," he shouted to them. The blacksmith profited by his experience at wielding a hammer. When the old man was exhausted, the blacksmith aimed a blow at him which overthrew him, making the cudgel, which he was holding in his hand, fall behind him. The blacksmith crouched over the old man so as to put his fingers into eyes, but he could not reach them because of the streams of blood which were flowing from them; he got up and struck his head so violently with his cudgel that he finished him off.

At once they put a rope round the neck of the corpse, which they took away and hung on a gibbet. The lord who had chosen the blacksmith gave him a considerable piece of property, made him get on a horse with his followers, took him off and went away. See from this example what law and judicial proceedings mean among the Franks (the curse of Allah upon them!).

The Investiture Controversy (1075–1122)

From about 1050 to 1300, a series of German popes, who had been influenced by the monastic reform movements of the tenth and early eleventh centuries, sought to purge the church of major abuses. Two of the most important abuses that had led to moral debasement of the clergy and the withdrawal of laymen from the organized church were simony (the purchase of church offices through money or illicit obligations) and the marriage or concubinage of clergy. The particular issue, however, that touched off a period of strained church-state relations was that of investiture.

A long-established practice allowed lay magnates such as feudal lords, kings, and, most importantly, Holy Roman Emperors to govern their territory with the help of bishops and archbishops. The prelates were generally educated, loyal, able administrators who provided a necessary link between the noble or king and his dependents. The kings chose and rewarded the prelates, and by the eleventh century also "invested" them with ring and staff, the symbols of episcopal power, sometimes with words "Receive thy church." The recent reform movement of the internal affairs of the church naturally lent itself to a redefinition of the church's position on lay magnates. The reformers came to challenge this practice of "lay investiture," arguing that the choice and investment of prelates was rightly a spiritual matter. In so doing, they challenged the basis of effective rule and royal authority.

The controversy came to a head when a young monk named Hildebrand succeeded to the papacy amid popular acclamation. He had established a reputation as an ardent and respected reformer and took the name Gregory VII (1073–1085). His main antagonist was the aggressive Holy Roman Emperor, Henry IV (1056–1106). The two soon quarreled over the issue of investiture, and Gregory did not hesitate to use his "spiritual sword," which included the extreme penalty of excommunication from the sacraments of the church and, as a result, eternal damnation in Hell. In the succeeding test of wills, the supremacy of church or state was hotly disputed. In a spiritual age, does the abstract control over one's soul demand more respect and allegiance than the tangible military power of the secular leader? The investiture dispute was but one incident among several between church and state that were vigorously pursued at the time. The contest for primacy continued until the fourteenth century, when events like the transfer of the papacy from Rome to Avignon (Babylonian Captivity) and the division of the church (Great Schism) led to a crisis in spiritual leadership. And yet, this basic controversy continues in the modern world whenever prayer in school is discussed and the concept of separation between church and state is debated. The investiture controversy makes us aware of the historical roots of this problem.

Decree on Lay Investiture (1075)

POPE GREGORY VII

Even before Gregory became Pope in 1073, friction had existed between the papacy and the Holy Roman Emperor, Henry IV. Gregory's predecessor, Alexander II, had rebuked Henry for, among other things, tolerating simony at his court. Although Henry later proved to be a most formidable and intransigent opponent, he readily accepted Gregory's election to the papacy because his authority was threatened by a rebellion in Saxony and he therefore was in no position to risk offending the new pope.

In 1074, Gregory held a council at Rome that reiterated the church's stand against simony and clerical marriage. The fundamental decree prohibiting lay investiture was first promulgated in February 1075, but the text has not survived. Included below are later enactments of 1078 and 1080. The substance of the original text was probably much the same.

Inasmuch as we have learned that, contrary to the establishments of the holy fathers, the investiture with churches is, in many places, performed by lay persons; and that from this cause many disturbances arise in the church by which the Christian religion is trodden under foot; we decree that no one of the clergy shall receive the investiture with a bishopric or abbey or church from the hand of an emperor or king or of any lay person, male or female. But if he shall presume to do so he shall clearly know that such investiture is bereft of apostolic authority, and that he himself shall be under excommunication until fitting satisfaction shall have been rendered.

Following the statutes of the holy fathers, . . . we now decree and confirm: that, if any one henceforth shall receive a bishopric or abbey from the hand of any lay person, he shall by no means be considered as among the number of bishops or abbots; nor shall any hearing be granted him as bishop or abbot. Moreover we further deny to him the favor of St. Peter and the entry of the church, until, coming to his senses, he shall desert the place that he has taken by the crime of ambition as well as by that of disobedience—which is the sin of idolatry.

Likewise if any emperor, king, duke, margrave, count, or any one at all of the secular powers or persons, shall presume to perform the investiture of the secular powers or persons, shall presume to perform the investiture with bishoprics or with any ecclesiastical dignity—he shall know that he is bound by the bonds of the same condemnation. And, moreover, unless he come to his senses and relinquish to the church her own prerogative, he shall feel, in this present life, the divine displeasure as well with regard to his body as to his other belongings: in order that at the coming of the Lord, his soul may be saved.

"Decree on Lay Investiture" is from E. G. Henderson, ed., *Select Historical Documents of the Middle Ages* (London: George Bell and Sons, 1896), pp. 365–366.

Dictatus Papae (1075)

POPE GREGORY VII

In March 1075, a month after Gregory issued his decree against lay investiture, the pope's official Register included a document known as the Dictatus Papae. *Peculiar and controversial, it contained the first explicit claim that a pope could depose an emperor. Not only was Gregory VII interested in moral reform, but he also believed strongly in papal authority and primacy, as the following selection reveals.*

1. That the Roman Church was founded by God alone.
2. That the Roman bishop [pope] alone is properly called universal.
3. That he alone has the power to depose bishops and reinstate them.
4. That we should not even stay in the same house with those who are excommunicated by him.
5. That the Pope is the only person whose feet are kissed by all princes.
6. That he has the power to depose emperors.
7. That no general synod may be called without his consent.
8. That no action of a synod, and no book, may be considered canonical without his authority.
9. That his decree can be annulled by no one, and that he alone may annul the decrees of any one.
10. That he can be judged by no man.
11. That the Roman Church has never erred, nor ever, by the testimony of Scripture, shall err, to all eternity.
12. That no one can be considered Catholic who does not agree with the Roman Church.
13. That he [the Pope] has the power to absolve the subjects of unjust rulers from their oath of fidelity.

The Excommunication of Emperor Henry IV (February, 1076)

POPE GREGORY VII

Gregory's decree against lay investiture and the Dictatus Papae *that declared papal primacy were both promulgated early in 1075. They did not deter Henry from supporting his own candidate for the bishopric of Milan against the pope's choice. This led to a brisk and inflammatory correspondence between the two.*

"Dictatus Papae" is from Frederick Ogg, ed., *A Source Book of Medieval History* (New York: American Book Company, 1907), pp. 262–264.

"The Excommunication of Emperor Henry IV" is from Oliver Thatcher and Edgar McNeal, eds., *A Source Book of Medieval History* (New York: Charles Scribner's Sons, 1905), pp. 155–156.

Henry deposed Gregory as pope, and Gregory countered by deposing Henry as Holy Roman Emperor. In addition, Gregory excommunicated Henry from the church, which had political as well as religious implications: Henry's nobles were thereby freed from their oaths of allegiance to him.

St Peter, prince of the apostles, incline your ear to me, I beseech thee, and hear me, thy servant, whom you have nourished from my infancy and have delivered from my enemies that hate me for my fidelity to thee . . . It is not by my efforts, but by thy grace, that I am set to rule over the Christian world which was specially entrusted to thee by Christ. It is by thy grace and as thy representative that God had given to me the power to bind and to loose in heaven and earth. Confident of my integrity and authority, I now declare in the name of omnipotent god, the Father, son, and Holy spirit, that Henry, son of the emperor Henry, is deprived of his kingdom of Germany and Italy; I do this by thy authority and in defense of the honor of thy church, because he has rebelled against it. He who attempts to destroy the honor of the church should be deprived of such honor as he may have held. He has re-fused to obey as a Christian should, he has not returned to God from whom he had wandered, he has had dealings with excommunicated persons, he has done many iniquities, he has despised the warnings which I sent to him for his salvation, he has cut himself off from thy church, and has attempted to rend it asunder; therefore, by thy authority, I place him under the curse. It is in thy name that I curse him, that all people may know that thou art Peter, and upon thy rock the son of the living God has built his church, and the gates of hell shall not prevail against it.

"Go To Canossa!": Henry's Penance (January 28, 1077)
POPE GREGORY VII

In joining battle with Gregory, Henry had misjudged his opponent. Although most of the German bishops (whom Henry had appointed) supported him, his no-bles, already restless, took the opportunity to rebel against their excommunicated king. Under such pressure, Henry promised to respect the pope and finally hum-bled himself before Gregory at the papal retreat high in the mountains at Canossa. There, Gregory granted him absolution, as recorded in a letter to the German nobles dated January 28, 1077. Henry's oath at Canossa follows.

In the meantime we learned that the king was approaching. Now before he entered Italy he had sent to us and had offered to make complete satisfaction

"'Go To Canossa!': Henry's Penance" is from Oliver Thatcher and Edgar McNeal, eds., *A Source Book of Medieval History* (New York: Charles Scribner's Sons, 1905), pp. 158–159.

for his fault, promising to reform and henceforth to obey us in all things, provided we would give him our absolution and blessing. We hesitated for some time, taking occasion in the course of the negotiations to reprove him sharply for his former sins. Finally, he came in person to Canossa, where we were staying, bringing with him only a small retinue and manifesting no hostile intentions. Once arrived, he presented himself at the gate of the castle, barefoot and clad only in wretched woollen garments, beseeching us with tears to grant him absolution and forgiveness. This he continued to do for three days, until all those about us were moved to compassion at his plight and interceded for him with tears and prayers. Indeed, they marveled at our hardness of heart, some even complaining that our action savored rather of heartless tyranny than of chastening severity. At length his persistent declarations of repentance and the supplications of all who were there with us overcame our reluctance, and we removed the excommunication from him and received him again into the bosom of the holy mother church. . . . Now that this arrangement has been reached to the common advantage of the church and the empire, we purpose coming to visit you in your own land [Germany] as soon as possible. For, as you will perceive from the conditions stated in the oath, the matter is not to be regarded as settled until we have held consultation with you. Therefore we urge your action. We have not bound ourself to anything, except that we assured the king that he might depend upon us to aid him in everything that looked to his salvation and honor.

Oath at Canossa (January 1077)
EMPEROR HENRY IV

I, Henry, king, promise to satisfy the grievances which my archbishops, bishops, dukes, counts, and other princes of Germany or their followers may have against me, within the time set by pope Gregory and in accordance with his conditions. If I am prevented by any sufficient cause from doing this within that time, I will do it as soon after that as I may. Further, if pope Gregory shall desire to visit Germany or any other land, on his journey thither, his sojourn there, and his return thence, he shall not be molested or placed in danger of captivity by me or by anyone whom I can control. This shall apply to his escort and retinue and to all who come and go in his service. Moreover, I will never enter into any plan for hindering or molesting him, but will aid him in good faith and to the best of my ability if anyone else opposes him.

[After Henry's oath in 1077, he attempted to reestablish authority among his nobles in Germany who had in the meantime supported a rival named Rudolf. After three years of civil war, Gregory finally decided to support Rudolf and for a second time deposed and excommunicated Henry. Gregory's attempt at "king-making" was badly timed. Henry's

"Oath at Canossa" is from Oliver Thatcher and Edgar McNeal, eds., *A Source Book of Medieval History* (New York: Charles Scribner's Sons, 1905), p. 160.

*influence was growing, and in December 1080 he defeated and killed Rudolf. Henry's mo-
mentum could not be halted and he soon denounced Gregory and invaded Italy, finally
occupying Rome in 1084 and besieging the pope in the fortress of Saint Angelo. Although
Gregory was rescued by his allies, he died in 1085, convinced that he had failed in all his
endeavors. For the rest of his reign, Henry was harassed by rebellious German nobles. He
never succeeded in establishing the strong, stable monarchy that his father had enjoyed.
His own son was leading a rebellion against him when Henry died in 1106.*

*A solution to the lay investiture problem was not to be found between Gregory VII
and Henry IV. Not until 1122 in the Concordat of Worms did Pope Calixtus II and
Henry V arrive at a compromise: The church would nominate and elect prelates and
then invest them with the ring and staff, symbol of spiritual authority. The emperor
thus formally renounced his power to so invest prelates. In exchange, the pope recognized the emperor's right to be present during the election of prelates, and in a disputed
election the emperor's decision was final. The emperor was also allowed to invest a
prelate with the "regalia" of his office (lands, worldly goods, and privileges).*

*With the Concordat of Worms, the investiture struggle had ended in a workable com-
promise, though it did not satisfy extremists in either camp. The dispute may have been
resolved, but the struggle between church and state, empire and papacy was to be renewed with even greater violence in the thirteenth and fourteenth centuries.]*

Innocent III and the Papal Supremacy

*The figure of Innocent III (1198–1216) dominated the medieval papacy. He firmly
believed that his position as Vicar of Christ and successor to the apostle Peter accorded him primacy in spiritual and secular affairs. In the eleventh century, Pope
Gregory VII had also exercised his authority by excommunicating the Holy Roman
Emperor, who was in defiance of his sanctions regarding lay investiture. But in the
end, Gregory had conceded to the threats of blatant military force. The power of God,
and especially the penalties that God might impose through his representative, the
pope, were not of this earth and could not compete with the immediate terror a king
might inflict. Still, this did not deter Innocent, who defied and dominated the kings
of Europe. The following accounts demonstrate his thought and action.*

The Sun and the Moon (1198)
POPE INNOCENT III

Innocent III to Acerbius, prior, and to the other clergy in Tuscany. As God,
the creator of the Universe, set two great lights in the firmament of heaven,
the greater light to rule the day, and the lesser light to rule the night [Gen.

"The Sun and the Moon" is from Oliver Thatcher and Edgar McNeal, eds., *A Source Book of Medieval History* (New York: Charles Scribner's Sons, 1905), p. 208.

1:15, 16], so He set two great dignities in the firmament of the universal church, . . . the greater to rule the day, that is, souls, and the lesser to rule the night, that is, bodies. These dignities are the papal authority and the royal power. And just as the moon gets her light from the sun, and is inferior to the sun in quality, quantity, position, effect, so the royal power gets the splendor of its dignity from the papal authority. . . .

The Punishment of Heretics (1198)
POPE INNOCENT III

The little boat of St. Peter is beaten by many storms and tossed about upon the sea, but it grieves us most of all that, against the orthodox faith, there are now arising more unrestrainedly and with more injurious results than ever before, ministers of diabolical error who are ensnaring the souls of the simple and ruining them. With their superstitions and false inventions they are perverting the meaning of the Holy Scriptures and trying to destroy the unity of the catholic church. Since we have learned from you [Archbishop of Auch] and others that this pestilential error is growing in Gascony and in the neighboring territories, we wish you and your fellow bishops to resist it with all your might, because it is to be feared that it will spread and that by its contagion the minds of the faithful will be corrupted. And therefore by this present apostolical writing we give you a strict command that, by whatever means you can, you destroy all these heresies and expel from your diocese all who are polluted with them. You shall exercise the rigor of the ecclesiastical power against them and all those who have made themselves suspected by associating with them. They may not appeal from your judgments, and if necessary, you may cause the princes and people to suppress them with the sword.

Innocent Chooses the Holy Roman Emperor (1201)
POPE INNOCENT III

In the name of the Father, Son, and Holy Spirit.

It is the business of the pope to look after the interests of the Roman empire, since the empire derives its origin and its final authority from the papacy; its origin, because it was originally transferred from Greece by and for the sake of the papacy, the pope making the transfer in order that the church might be better protected; its final authority, because the emperor is raised to his position by the pope who blesses him, crowns him, and invests him with

"The Punishment of Heretics" is from Oliver Thatcher and Edgar McNeal, eds., *A Source Book of Medieval History* (New York: Charles Scribner's Sons, 1905), pp. 209–210.

"Innocent Chooses the Holy Roman Emperor" is from Oliver Thatcher and Edgar McNeal, eds., *A Source Book of Medieval History* (New York: Charles Scribner's Sons, 1905), pp. 220, 226.

the empire. . . . [After an extended discussion on the matter, Innocent continues:] On the foregoing grounds, then, we decide that the youth [Frederick] should not at present be given the empire; we utterly reject Phillip [Frederick's uncle] for his manifest unfitness, and we order his usurpation to be resisted by all. As to the rest, we have commanded our legate to persuade the princes either to choose some suitable person or to refer the matter to us for final decision. If they cannot come to a decision, since we have waited long, have frequently urged them to agree, have instructed them as to our desires by letters and legates [we shall take the matter into our own hands]. . . . But since the affair will not brook delay, and since Otto is not only himself devoted to the church but comes from devout ancestors on both sides . . . therefore we decree that he [Otto] ought to be accepted and supported as king, and ought to be given the crown of the empire, after the rights of the Roman church have been secured.

Innocent Gains Control of England (1213)
KING JOHN I

In 1207, King John of England refused to accept Innocent's choice for Archbishop of Canterbury and defied the pope by selecting his own candidate and extorting money from the church. Innocent responded by excommunicating John and placing all of England under interdict. Finally, when it appeared that the king of France was preparing an invasion of England under Innocent's direction, John gave way—in style. Not only did he have to repay the money he had taken from the church, but he was forced to surrender his realm to the pope, who returned it as a fief. In essence, John was now a vassal of his feudal lord, the pope. The humiliating decree, given here, demonstrates the extent of Innocent's domination. The second selection shows Innocent protecting his interests by supporting John against his barons. This rebuke came after the barons had forced John to sign the Magna Carta in 1215.

John, by the grace of God king of England, lord of Ireland, duke of Normandy and Aquitaine, earl of Anjou, to all the faithful in Christ who shall inspect this present charter, greeting. We will it to be known by all of you . . . that we, having offended God and our mother the holy Church in many things, and being on that account known to need the Divine mercy, and unable to make any worthy offering for the performance of due satisfaction to God and the church, unless we humble ourselves and our realms . . . under no compulsion of force or of fear, but of our good and free will, and by the common consent of our barons, offer and freely grant to God and His holy

"Innocent Gains Control of England" is from Henry Gee, ed., *Documents Illustrative of English Church History* (London: Macmillan, 1910), pp. 75–76.

apostles Peter and Paul, and the holy Roman Church, our mother, and to our lord the Pope Innocent and his catholic successors, the whole realm of England and the whole realm of Ireland with all their rights and appurtenances, for the remission of our sins and those of all our race; . . . and from now receiving back and holding these, as a feudal dependent, from God and the Roman Church, . . . do and swear fealty for them to . . . our lord the Pope Innocent and his catholic successors and the Roman Church, according to the form written below, and will do liege homage to the same lord the Pope in his presence if we shall be able to be present before him; binding our successors and heirs by our wife, for ever, that in like manner to the supreme pontiff for the time being, and to the Roman Church, they should pay fealty and acknowledge homage without contradiction. . . . Let this charter of obligation . . . remain in force for ever.

Innocent Protects His Realm (1216)

POPE INNOCENT III

Innocent, etc., to his beloved sons, the magnates and barons of England, greeting and apostolic benediction.

We are gravely troubled to learn that a quarrel has arisen between our most beloved son, John, king of England, and some of you, about certain questions that have recently been raised. Unless wise counsel prevails and diligent measures are taken to end this quarrel, it will cause injury. It is currently reported that you have rashly made conspiracies and confederacies against him, and that you have insolently, rebelliously, presumptuously, and with arms in your hands, said things to him, which, if they had to be said, should have been said humbly and submissively. We utterly condemn your conduct in these matters. You must no longer try, by such means, to hinder the king in his good plans. By our apostolic authority we hereby dissolve all conspiracies and confederacies that have been made since the quarrel between the crown and the church began, and forbid them under threat of excommunication. We order you to endeavor by clear proofs of humility and devotion to placate your king and to win his favor by rendering him those customary services which you and your ancestors have paid to him and his predecessors. And in the future, if you wish to make a request of him, you shall do it, not insolently, but humbly and reverently, without offending his royal honor; and thus you will more readily obtain what you wish. We ask and beseech the king in the Lord and command him, in order to obtain forgiveness of his sins, to treat you leniently, and graciously to grant you just petitions. And thus you yourselves may rejoice to know that he has changed for

"Innocent Protects His Realm" is from Oliver Thatcher and Edgar McNeal, eds., *A Source Book of Medieval History* (New York: Charles Scribner's Sons, 1905), pp. 219–220.

the better, and on this account you and your heirs may serve him and his successors more promptly and devotedly. We ask, and, by this apostolic writing, command you to bear yourselves in such a way that England may obtain the peace she so earnestly longs for, and that you may deserve our aid and support in your times of trouble.

Medieval Monasticism

Monasticism arose in Egypt and western Asia and was practiced by monks who were true hermits. Their life was one of ascetic denial and personal devotion to God. As the movement spread to the West in the middle of the fourth century and became more popular, the monks began to live together in houses. Although they preserved as much of their personal isolation as possible, it became necessary to formulate rules of conduct. These rules, however, were not severe or even binding in most cases; monks did not even have to take a vow to remain in the monastery. The reforms of Saint Benedict were designed to remedy this problem and other abuses that permeated the monastic life. Benedict moved away from the hermetic emphasis of the East in favor of a common experience among the brothers in the order. His strict rule was popularized by Pope Gregory I (himself a Benedictine) and became the basis for all reforms in monasticism for several centuries. The following excerpts provide a glimpse into this structured life of contemplation and isolation from the world.

The Rule of Saint Benedict (530)

Ch. 1. The kinds of monks: There are four kinds of monks. The first kind is that of the cenobites, those who live in a monastery according to a rule, and under the government of an abbot. The second is that of the anchorites, or hermits, who have learned how to conduct the war against the devil by their long service in the monastery and their association with many brothers, and so, being well trained, have separated themselves from the troop, in order to wage single combat, being able with the aid of God to carry on the fight alone against the sins of the flesh. The third kind (and a most abominable kind it is) is that of the sarabites, who have not been tested and proved by obedience to the rule and by the teaching of experience, as gold is tried in the furnace, and so are soft and pliable like a base metal; who in assuming the tonsure are false to God, because they still serve the world in their lives. They do not congregate in the master's fold, but dwell apart without a shepherd, by twos and threes, or even alone. Their law is their own desires, since they call that holy which they like, and that unlawful which they do not like. The fourth kind is

---

"The Rule of Saint Benedict" is from Oliver Thatcher and Edgar McNeal, eds., *A Source Book of Medieval History* (New York: Charles Scribner's Sons, 1905), pp. 434–438, 440–442, 445–447, 454, 457, 459, 461–462, 467–468, 471–474.

composed of those who are called gyrovagi (wanderers), who spend their whole lives wandering about through different regions and living three or four days at a time in the cells of different monks. They are always wandering about and never remain long in one place, and they are governed by their own appetites and desires. They are in every way worse than the sarabites. But it is better to pass over in silence than to mention their manner of life. Let us, therefore, leaving these aside, proceed, with the aid of God, to the consideration of the cenobites, the highest type of monks.

Ch. 2. *The qualities necessary for an abbot:* The abbot who is worthy to rule over a monastery ought always to bear in mind by what name he is called and to justify by his life his title of superior. For he represents Christ in the monastery, receiving his name from the saving of the apostle: "Ye have received the Spirit of adoption, whereby we cry, Abba, Father" [Rom. 8:15]. Therefore the abbot should not teach or command anything contrary to the precepts of the Lord, but his commands and his teaching should be in accord with divine justice. He should always bear in mind that both his teaching and the obedience of his disciples will be inquired into the dread Day of Judgment. For the abbot should know that the shepherd will have to bear the blame if the Master finds anything wrong with the flock. Only in case the shepherd has displayed all diligence and care in correcting the fault of a restive and disobedient flock will he be freed from blame at the judgment of God. . . . Then shall the punishment fall upon the flock who scorned his care and it shall be the punishment of death. The abbot ought to follow two methods in governing his disciples: teaching the commandments of the Lord to the apt disciples by his words, and to the obdurate and the simple by his deeds. And when he teaches his disciples that certain things are wrong, he should demonstrate it in his own life by not doing those things. . . . Let there be no distinction of persons in the monastery. Let the abbot not love one more than another, unless it be one who excels in good works and in obedience. The freeman is not to be preferred to the one who comes into the monastery out of servitude, unless there be some other good reason. . . . For whether slave or free, we are all one in Christ. . . . Therefore, the abbot should have the same love toward all and should subject all to the same discipline according to their respective merits. . . . That is, he should suit his [disciplinary] methods to the occasion, using either threats or compliments, showing himself either a hard master or a loving father, according to the needs of the case. Thus he should reprove harshly the obdurate and the disobedient, the meek, and the gentle he should exhort to grow in grace. We advise also that he rebuke and punish those who neglect and scorn his teaching. . . .

The abbot should always remember his office and his title, and should realize that as much is intrusted to him, so also much will be required from him. Let him realize how difficult and arduous a task he has undertaken, to rule the hearts and care for the morals of many persons, who require, one encouragements, another threats, and another persuasion. Let him so adapt his methods to the disposition and intelligence of each one that he may not only preserve the flock committed to him entire and free from harm, but may even rejoice in its increase. . . .

Ch. 3. Taking counsel with the brethren: Whenever important matters come up in the monastery, the abbot should call together the whole congregation [that is, all the monks], and tell them what is under consideration. After hearing the advice of the brothers, he should reflect upon it and then do what seems best to him. . . .

Ch. 5. Obedience: The first grade of humility is obedience without delay, which is becoming to those who hold nothing dearer than Christ. So, when one of the monks receives a command from a superior, he should obey it immediately, as if it came from God himself, being impelled thereto by the holy service he has professed and by the fear of hell and the desire of eternal life. . . .

Ch. 6. Silence: . . . It is the business of the master to speak and instruct, and that of the disciples to hearken and be silent. And if the disciple must ask anything of his superior, let him ask it reverently and humbly, lest he seem to speak more than is becoming. Filthy and foolish talking and jesting we condemn utterly, and forbid the disciple ever to open his mouth to utter such words.

Ch. 7. Humility: . . . The sixth step of humility is this, that the monk should be contented with any lowly or hard condition in which he may be placed, and should always look upon himself as an unworthy laborer, not fitted to do what is intrusted to him. . . . The seventh step of humility is this, that he should not only say, but should really believe in his heart that he is the lowest and most worthless of all men. . . . The eighth step of humility is this, that the monk should follow in everything the common rule of the monastery and the examples of his superiors. . . .

The twelfth step of humility is this, that the monk should always be humble and lowly, not only in his heart, but in his bearing as well. Wherever he may be, in divine service, in the oratory, in the garden, on the road, in the fields, whether sitting, walking, or standing, he should always keep his head bowed and his eyes upon the ground. He should always be meditating upon his sins and thinking of the dread day of judgment, saying to himself as did that publican of whom the gospel speaks: "Lord, I am not worthy, I a sinner, so much as to lift mine eyes up to heaven" [Luke 18:13]; and again with the prophet: "I am bowed down and humbled everywhere" [Ps. 119:107]. . . .

Ch. 8. Divine worship at night [vigils]: During the winter; that is, from the first of November to Easter, the monks should rise at the eighth hour of the night; a reasonable arrangement, since by that time the monks will have rested a little more than half the night and will have digested their food. Those brothers who failed in the psalms or the readings shall spend the rest of the time after vigils in pious meditation. From Easter to the first of November [morning prayers] shall begin immediately after daybreak, allowing the brothers a little time for attending to the necessities of nature. . . .

Ch. 22. How the monks should sleep: The monks shall sleep separately in individual beds, and the abbot shall assign them their beds according to their conduct. If possible all the monks shall sleep in the same dormitory, but if their number is too large to admit of this, they are to be divided into tens or twenties and placed under the control of some of the older monks. A candle shall be kept burning in the dormitory all night until daybreak. The monks shall go to bed clothed and girt with girdles and cords, but shall not have their knives at their sides, lest in their dreams they injure one of the sleepers. They should be always in readiness, rising immediately upon the signal and hastening to the service, but appearing there gravely and modestly. The beds of the younger brothers should not be placed together, but should be scattered among those of the older monks. When the brothers arise they should gently exhort one another to hasten to the service, so that the sleepy ones may have no excuse for coming late. . . .

Ch. 33. *Monks should not have personal property:* The sin of owning private property should be entirely eradicated from the monastery. No one shall presume to give or receive anything except by the order of the abbot; no one shall possess anything of his own, books, paper, pens, or anything else; for monks are not to own even their own bodies and wills to be used at their own desire, but are to look to the father [abbot] of the monastery for everything. So they shall have nothing that has not been given or allowed to them by the abbot; all things are to be had in common according to the command of the Scriptures, and no one shall consider anything as his own property. If anyone has been found guilty of this most grievous sin, he shall be admonished for the first and second offence, and then if he does not mend his ways he shall be punished.

Ch. 38. *The weekly reader:* There should always be reading during the common meal, but it shall not be left to chance, so that anyone may take up the book and read. On Sunday one of the brothers shall be appointed to read during the following week. . . . At the common meal, the strictest silence shall be kept, that no whispering or speaking may be heard except the voice of the reader. The brethren shall mutually wait upon one another by passing the articles of food and drink, so that no one shall have to ask for anything; but if this is necessary, it shall be done by a sign rather than by words, if possible. In order to avoid too much talking no one shall interrupt the reader with a question about the reading or in any other way, unless perchance the prior may wish to say something in the way of explanation. . . .

Ch. 39. *The amount of food:* Two cooked dishes, served either at the sixth or the ninth hour, should be sufficient for the daily sustenance. We allow two because of differences in taste, so that those who do not eat one may satisfy their hunger with the other, but two shall suffice for all the brothers, unless it is possible to obtain fruit or fresh vegetables, which may be served as a third. . . . In the case of those who engage in heavy labor, the abbot may at his discretion increase the allowance of food, but he should not allow the monks to indulge their appetites by eating or drinking too much. For no vice is more inconsistent with the Christian character. . . .

Ch. 48. *The daily labor of the monks:* Idleness is the great enemy of the soul, therefore the monks should always be occupied, either in manual labor or in holy reading. . . . When the ninth hour sounds they shall cease from labor and be ready for the service at the second bell. After dinner they shall spend the time in reading the lessons and the psalms. During Lent the time from daybreak to the third hour shall be devoted to reading, and then they shall work at their appointed tasks until the tenth hour. At the beginning of Lent each of the monks shall be given a book from the library of the monastery which he shall read entirely through. One or two of the older monks shall be appointed to go about through the monastery during the hours set apart for reading, to see that none of the monks are idling away the time, instead of reading, and so not only wasting their own time but perhaps disturbing others as well. . . . Sunday is to be spent by all the brothers in holy reading, except by such as have regular duties assigned to them for that day. And if any brother is negligent or lazy, refusing or being unable profitably to read or meditate at the time assigned for that, let him be made to work, so that he shall at any rate not be idle. . . .

Ch. 58. The way in which new members are to be received: Entrance into the monastery should not be made too easy. . . . So when anyone applies at the monastery, asking to be accepted as a monk, he should first be proved by every test. He shall be made to wait outside four or five days, continually knocking at the door and begging to be admitted; and then he shall be taken in as a guest and allowed to stay in the guest chamber a few days. If he satisfies these preliminary tests, he shall then be made to serve a novitiate of at least one year, during which he shall be placed under the charge of one of the older and wiser brothers, who shall examine him and prove, by every possible means, his sincerity, his zeal, his obedience, and his ability to endure shame. And he shall be told in the plainest manner all the hardships and difficulties of the life which he has chosen. If he promises never to leave the monastery the rule shall be read to him after the first two months of his novitiate, and again at the end of six more months, and finally, four months later, at the end of his year. Each time he shall be told that this is the guide which he must follow as a monk, the reader saying to him at the end of the reading: "This is the law under which you have expressed a desire to live; if you are able to obey it, enter; if not, depart in peace." Thus he shall have been given every chance for mature deliberation and every opportunity to refuse the yoke of service. But if he still persists in asserting his eagerness to enter and his willingness to obey the rule and the commands of his superior, he shall then be received into the congregation, with the understanding that from that day forth he shall never be permitted to draw back from the service or to leave the monastery. . . .

The Vow of a Monk

I hereby renounce my parents, my brothers and relatives, my friends, my possessions and my property, and the vain and empty glory and pleasure of this world. I also renounce my own will, for the will of God. I accept all the hardships of the monastic life, and take the vows of purity, chastity, and poverty, in the hope of heaven; and I promise to remain a monk in this monastery all the days of my life.

"The Vow of a Monk" is from Oliver Thatcher and Edgar McNeal, eds., *A Source Book of Medieval History* (New York: Charles Scribner's Sons, 1905), p. 486.

A Description of the Abbey of Clairvaux
WILLIAM OF ST. THIERRY

The most important individual in the monastic reform movement of the twelfth century was Saint Bernard of Clairvaux (1091–1153). He was a particularly effective speaker and was influential in reinvigorating Europe with a sense of purpose and commitment. At the request of the pope, Bernard preached in support of the Second Crusade. But it was as a monastic reformer that Saint Bernard is best known. His foundation of the monastery at Clairvaux in 1115, which is described in the following excerpt from his contemporary biographer, William of St. Thierry, gave respect and energy to the growing Cistercian order.

At the first glance as you entered Clairvaux by descending the hill you could see that it was a temple of God; and the still, silent valley bespoke, in the modest simplicity of its buildings, the unfeigned humility of Christ's poor. Moreover, in the valley full of men, where no one was permitted to be idle, where one and all were occupied with their allotted tasks, a silence deep as that of night prevailed. The sounds of labor, or the chants of the brethren in the choral service, were the only exceptions. The orderliness of this silence, and the report that went forth concerning it, struck such a reverence even into secular persons that they dreaded breaking it . . . even by proper remarks. The solitude, also, of the place—between dense forests in a narrow gorge of neighboring hills—in a certain sense recalled the cave of our father St. Benedict [the compiler of the rules to which the monastery adhered], so that while they strove to imitate his life, they also had some similarity to him in their habitation and loneliness. . . .

Although the monastery is situated in a valley, it has its foundations on the holy hills, whose gates the Lord loveth more than all of the dwellings of Jacob. Glorious things are spoken of it, because the glorious and wonderful God therein worketh great marvels. There the insane recover their reason, and although their outward man is worn away, inwardly they are born again. There the proud are humbled, the rich are made poor, and the poor have the Gospel preached to them, and the darkness of sinners is changed into light. A large multitude of blessed poor from the ends of the earth have there assembled, yet have they one heart and one mind; justly, therefore, do all who dwell there rejoice with no empty joy. They have the certain hope of perennial joy, of their ascension heavenward already commenced. . . .

For my part, the more attentively I watch them day by day, the more do I believe that they are perfect followers of Christ in all things. When they pray and speak to God in spirit and in truth, by their friendly and quiet speech to Him, as well as by their humbleness of demeanor, they are plainly seen to be God's companions and friends. When, on the other hand, they openly praise

"A Description of the Abbey of Clairvaux" is from Frederic Ogg, ed., *A Source Book of Medieval History* (New York: American Book Company, 1907), pp. 258–260.

God with psalms, how pure and fervent are their minds, is shown by their posture of body in holy fear and reverence, while by their careful pronunciation and modulation of the psalms, is shown how sweet to their lips are the words of God—sweeter than honey to their mouths. As I watch them, therefore, singing without fatigue from before midnight to the dawn of day, with only a brief interval, they appear a little less than the angels, but much more than men. . . .

As regards their manual labor, so patiently and placidly, with such quiet countenances, in such sweet and holy order, do they perform all things, that although they exercise themselves at many works, they never seem moved or burdened in anything, whatever the labor may be. . . . Many of them, I hear, are bishops and earls, and many illustrious through their birth or knowledge; but now, by God's grace, all distinction of persons being dead among them, the greater any one thought himself in the world, the more in this flock does he regard himself as less than the least. I see them in the garden with hoes, in the meadows with forks or rakes, in the fields with scythes, in the forest with axes. To judge from their outward appearance, their tools, their bad and disordered clothes, they appear a race of fools, without speech or sense. But a true thought in my mind tells me that their life in Christ is hidden in the heavens. . . .

The Canticle of Brother Sun (1225)
SAINT FRANCIS OF ASSISI

One of the most remarkable figures in the world of the medieval church was Saint Francis. Born in 1181 to a wealthy merchant in the little town of Assisi, Saint Francis eventually rejected his prescribed role as heir to the family business, gave his belongings to the poor, and became a barefoot preacher. He quickly gained adherents by advocating a simple rule of poverty and complete service to God. His order received the approval of Pope Innocent III in 1209. He died in 1226 and was canonized in 1228. He was buried in the basilica San Francesco in Assisi, an ironic turn, since Saint Francis had always preached the virtues of poverty and simplicity.

The Franciscans were not a monastic order, but rather considered their business to be within the world. They were called friars, or brothers, and combined the asceticism and simplicity of a regular order of monks with the popular contact that was the preserve of the secular order of priests. With a foot in both worlds of the church and a dedication to poverty and simplicity, the Franciscans were a kind of hybrid, both reviled and admired by competing forces within the church.

Saint Francis's great love of nature and the purity of his devotion to God are distilled in perhaps the most articulate and sensitive of his poems, "The Canticle of Brother Sun." He began it in 1225, during his last illness amid intense physical suffering, and added the final verses about Sister Death shortly before his own death. The "Canticle," for all the depth of feeling it evokes about nature and the creatures he cared so much about, is an earnest prayer and hymn of praise to God.

Most high, all-powerful, all good, Lord!
　　All praise is yours, all glory, all honour
　　And all blessing.
To you, alone, Most High, do they belong.
　　No mortal lips are worthy
　　To pronounce your name.
All praise be yours, my Lord, through all that you have made,
　　And first my lord Brother Sun,
　　Who brings the day; and light you give to us through him.
How beautiful is he, how radiant in all his splendour!
　　Of you, Most High, he bears the likeness.
All praise be yours, my Lord, through Sister Moon and Stars;
　　In the heavens you have made them, bright
　　And precious and fair.
All praise be yours, my Lord, through Brothers Wind and Air,
　　And fair and stormy, all the weather's moods,
　　By which you cherish all that you have made.
All praise be yours, my Lord, through Sister Water,
　　So useful, lowly, precious and pure.
All praise be yours, my Lord, through Brother Fire,
　　Through whom you brighten up the night.
　　How beautiful is he, how gay! Full of power and strength.
All praise be yours, my Lord, through Sister Earth, our mother,
　　Who feeds us in her sovereignty and produces
　　Various fruits with coloured flowers and herbs.
All praise be yours, my Lord, through those who grant pardon
　　For love of you; through those who endure
　　Sickness and trial.
Happy those who endure in peace,
　　By you, Most High, they will be crowned.
All praise be yours, my Lord, through Sister Death,
　　From whom no mortal can escape.
Woe to those who die in mortal sin!
　　Happy those She finds doing your will!
　　The second death can do no harm to them.
Praise and bless my Lord, and give him thanks,
　　And serve him with great humility.

The Great Cathedrals

Perhaps the quintessential expression of faith and devotion in the medieval world was the cathedral. It served as the seat of a bishop or archbishop and provided a spiritual focal point that helped to unify society. Within its walls, the Christian "flock" learned what was expected from them in a society dependent upon obedience and structure. The chants and stained glass windows directed people toward right action and salvation through simple messages. The popular devotion to God can best be seen in the construction of these magnificent cathedrals; hundreds of people, often in small villages, labored for generations to contribute to the glory of God in some tangible way. By the middle of the twelfth century, a new architectural style, called "Gothic," had evolved; it produced cathedrals that soared higher than ever before and were filled with light. Many of these Gothic cathedrals (Chartres is an important example) were dedicated to the Virgin Mary, whose popularity contributed much to chivalric ideals. The following passages provide a sense of the importance of the cathedral to medieval life.

Faith and the Construction of the Cathedrals (1145)

ABBOT HAIMON OF SAINT-PIERRE-SUR-DIVES

Who has ever seen!—Who has ever heard tell, in times past, that powerful princes of the world, that men brought up in honor and in wealth, that nobles, men and women, have bent their proud and haughty necks to the harness of carts, and that, like beasts of burden, they have dragged to the abode of Christ these wagons, loaded with wines, grains, oil, stone, wood, and all that is necessary for the wants of life, or for the construction of the church? But while they draw these burdens, there is one thing admirable to observe; . . . they march in such silence that not a murmur is heard. . . . When they halt on the road, nothing is heard but the confession of sins, and pure and suppliant prayer to God to obtain pardon. At the voice of the priests who exhort their hearts to peace, they forget all hatred, discord is thrown far aside, debts are remitted, the unity of hearts is established. . . . There one sees the priests who preside over each wagon exhort every one to penitence, to confession of faults, to the resolution of better life! There one sees old people, young people, little children, calling on the Lord with a suppliant voice, and uttering to Him, from the depth of the heart, sobs and signs with words of glory and praise! After the people, warned by the sound of trumpets and the sight of banners, have resumed their road, the march is made with such ease that no obstacle can retard it. . . .

"Faith and the Construction of the Cathedrals" is from Henry Adams, *Mont Saint-Michel and Chartres* (Boston, 1904).

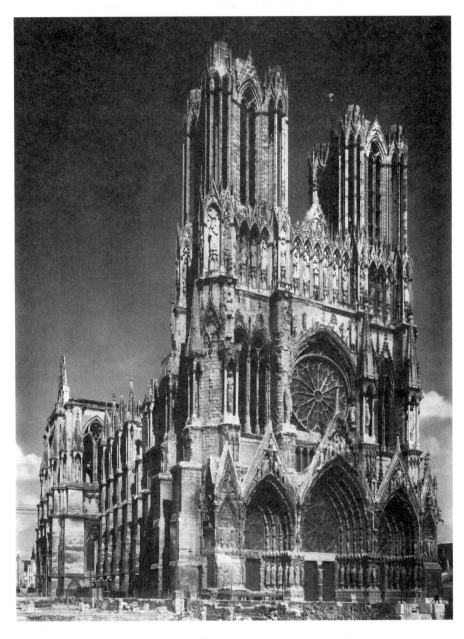

The cathedral at Reims, where the kings of France were crowned, is a good example of the beauty and majesty of Gothic architecture. Medieval civilization flowed from a spiritual base. *(Foto Marburg/Art Resource, N.Y.)*

The Power of the Virgin Mary (1275)

I found one more instance of the loving kindness of the glorious Virgin in an ancient sermon. A certain poor woman loved the Blessed Virgin and decorated her image with roses and lillies and other flowers that she could find. It happened that her son was arrested and hanged. The woman, in the bitterness of her soul, went to the Blessed Virgin and pleaded with her to bring back her son. Seeing that her son had not been restored as quickly as she had wished, she said: "Is this then the price of devotion to you, that you do not help me in my time of need?" Then, as though maddened by her extreme grief, she said: "If you do not restore my son, I will take away your Son." And, as she reached out her hand to remove the image of the little Babe, behold! her son stood beside her and seized her cloak and cried, "What are you doing, mother? Have you gone mad? Behold, the Mother of God has restored me to you." So the mother rejoiced at the recovery of her son.

An Inventory of Saintly Relics in Canterbury Cathedral (1346)

A piece of the Lord's sign of the Cross, of His lance, and His column. Of the manna which rained from Heaven. Of the stone whereon Christ's blood was spilt. Item, another little cross of silvered wood, containing pieces of the Lord's sepulcher and of St. Margaret's veil. Of the Lord's cradle in a certain copper reliquary.

Given by the Lord Dean [Bocheux]. In certain crystal vessel, portions of the stone tablets whereon God wrote the law for Moses with his finger. Item, in the same vessel, of the stone whereupon St. James crossed the sea. . . .

Of St. Mary. Of the hairs of St. Mary; item, of her robe; item, a shallow ivory box without any ornament save only a knob of copper, which box contains some of the flower which the Blessed Virgin held before her Son, and of the window through which the Angel Gabriel entered when he saluted her. . . .

Of the Martyrs. Of the tunic of St. Thomas of Canterbury, Archbishop and Martyr; of his hair shirt, of his dust, of his hairs. . . . Again of his hairs, of the blanket that covered him, of his woolen shirt. . . . Item, of the blood of the same St. Thomas of Canterbury. Item, the staff of the aforesaid St. Thomas the Martyr, Archbishop of Canterbury.

"The Power of the Virgin Mary" is from A. G. Little, ed., *Liber Exemplorum* (Aberdeen, 1908), p. 3. Translation modernized by the editor.

"An Inventory of Saintly Relics in Canterbury Cathedral" is from G. G. Coulton, ed., *Life in the Middle Ages*, vol. 1. (Cambridge: Cambridge University Press, 1928–1930), p. 52. Reprinted with the permission of Cambridge University Press.

Mind and Society in the Middle Ages

The World of Thought

Political Theory:
The Responsibilities of Kingship (1159)

JOHN OF SALISBURY

John of Salisbury was a trained logician who served as advisor to the Archbishop of Canterbury, Thomas Becket. Becket became famous for his defiance of King Henry II—defiance that resulted in his murder and subsequent martyrdom. John dedicated his Statesman's Book *to Becket in 1159; it was a compendium of political theory that he had acquired from the Bible, classical texts, and his own observation of political affairs. Note the emphasis on the respective responsibilities of the secular and spiritual spheres.*

The prince stands on a pinnacle which is exalted and made splendid with all the great and high privileges which he deems necessary for himself. And rightly so, because nothing is more advantageous to the people than that the needs of the prince should be fully satisfied; since it is impossible that his will should be found opposed to justice. Therefore, according to the usual definition, the prince is the public power, and a kind of likeness on earth of the divine majesty. Beyond doubt a large share of the divine power is shown to be in princes by the fact that at their nod men bow their necks and for the most part offer up their heads to the axe to be struck off, and, as by a divine impulse, the prince is feared by each of those over whom he is set as an object of fear. And this I do not think could be, except as a result of the will of God. For all power is from the Lord God, and has been with Him always, and is from everlasting. The power which the prince has is therefore from God, for the power of God is never lost, nor severed from Him, but He merely exercises it through a subordinate hand, making all things teach His mercy or justice. "Who, therefore, resists the ruling power, resists the ordinance of God," in Whose hand is the authority of conferring that power, and when He so desires, or withdrawing it again, or diminishing it. . . .

Princes should not deem that it detracts from their princely dignity to believe that the enactments of their own justice are not to be preferred to the justice of God, whose justice is an everlasting justice, and His law is equity. . . . No prince accordingly is the minister of the common interest and the bond-servant of equity, and he bears the public person in the sense that he punishes the wrongs and injuries of all, and all crimes, with even-handed

"Political Theory: The Responsibilities of Kingship" is from John Dickinson, trans., *The Statesman's Book of John of Salisbury* (New York: Alfred A. Knopf, 1927), pp. 3–4, 6–9, 65. Reprinted by permission of Prentice Hall.

equity. His rod and staff also, administered with wise moderation, restore irregularities and false departures to the straight path of equity, so that deservedly may the Spirit congratulate the power of the prince with the words, "Thy rod and thy staff, they have comforted me." His shield, too, is strong, but it is a shield for the protection of the weak, and one which wards off powerfully the darts of the wicked from the innocent. Those who derive the greatest advantage from his performance of the duties of his office are those who can do least for themselves, and his power is chiefly exercised against those who desire to do harm. Therefore not without reason he bears a sword, wherewith he sheds blood blamelessly, without becoming thereby a man of blood, and frequently puts men to death without incurring the name of guilt of homicide. . . .

This sword, then, the prince receives from the hand of the Church, although she herself has no sword of blood at all. Nevertheless she has this sword, but she uses it by the hand of the prince, upon whom she confers the power of bodily coercion, retaining to herself authority over spiritual things in the person of the pontiffs. The prince is, then, as it were, a minister of the priestly power, and one who exercises that side of the sacred offices which seems unworthy of the hands of the priesthood. For every office existing under, and concerned with the execution of, the sacred laws is really a religious office, but that is inferior which consists in punishing crimes, and which therefore seems to be typified in the person of the hangman. . . .

The place of the head in the body of the commonwealth is filled by the prince, who is subject only to God and to those who exercise His office and represent Him on earth, even as in the human body the head is quickened and governed by the soul. . . .

The Existence of God

SAINT THOMAS AQUINAS

The twelfth century was truly remarkable for its intellectual focus and development of thought. The new commitment to learning was reflected in a system of argument and study called Scholasticism. Scholars edited and commented on ancient writers, methodically arguing for the acceptance or rejection of such philosophers as Aristotle and Plato. No longer was it enough simply to accept the existence of God without a rational argument of proof. Saint Thomas Aquinas (1225–1274) is generally regarded as the most insightful and important philosopher of the Middle Ages. The following excerpts from his Summa Theologica *demonstrate the structure of Scholastic argument and relate his conclusions on*

"The Existence of God" is from *Summa Theologica*, trans. A. C. Pegis, in *Basic Writings of Saint Thomas Aquinas*, vol. 1 (New York: Random House, 1945), pp. 21–24. Reprinted by permission of the Estate of Anton Pegis.

the existence of God. Saint Bernard's passage on the love of God reflects the argument of faith.

Third Article: Whether God exists?

Objection 1: It seems that God does not exist; because if one of two contraries be infinite, the other would be altogether destroyed. But the name God means that He is infinite goodness. If, therefore, God existed, there would be no evil discoverable; but there is evil in the world. Therefore God does not exist.

Objection 2: Further, it is superfluous to suppose that what can be accounted for by a few principles has been produced by many. But it seems that everything we see in the world can be accounted for by other principles, supposing God did not exist. For all natural things can be reduced to one principle, which is human reason, or will. Therefore there is no need to suppose God's existence.

I Answer That: The existence of God can be proved in [three] ways: The first and more manifest way is the argument from motion. It is certain, and evident to our senses, that in the world some things are in motion. . . . [Now], whatever is moved must be moved by another. If that by which it is moved be itself moved, then this also must needs be moved by another, and that by another again. But this cannot go on to infinity, because then there would be no first mover, and, consequently, no other mover, seeing that subsequent movers move only inasmuch as they are moved by the first mover; as the staff moves only because it is moved by the hand. Therefore it is necessary to arrive at a first mover, moved by no other; and this everyone understands to be God.

The second way is from the nature of efficient cause. In the world of sensible things we find there is an order of efficient causes. There is no case known (neither is it, indeed, possible) in which a thing is found to be the efficient cause of itself; for so it would be prior to itself, which is impossible. Now in efficient causes it is not possible to go on to infinity, because in all efficient causes following in order, the first is the cause of the intermediate cause and the intermediate is the cause of the ultimate cause, whether the intermediate cause be several, or one only. Now to take away the cause is to take away the effect. Therefore, if there be no first cause among efficient causes, there will be no ultimate, nor any intermediate, cause. . . . Therefore it is necessary to admit a first efficient cause, to which everyone gives the name of God.

The [last] way is taken from the governance of the world. We see that things which lack knowledge, such as natural bodies, act for an end, and this is evident from their acting always, or nearly always, in the same way, so as to obtain the best result. Hence it is plain that they achieve their end, not fortuitously, but designedly. Now whatever lacks knowledge cannot move towards an end, unless it be directed by some being endowed with knowledge and intelligence; as the arrow is directed by the archer. Therefore some intelligent being exists by whom all natural things are directed to their end; and this being we call God.

The Love of God

SAINT BERNARD OF CLAIRVAUX

You would hear from me, then, why and how God is to be loved? I answer: The cause of loving God is God; the manner is to love without measure. Is this enough? Yes, perhaps, for the wise. But I am debtor to the unwise as well; where enough is said for the wise, we must comply with the others also. Therefore I will not refuse to repeat it, more fully rather than more deeply, for the sake of the slower in apprehension. I may say that God is to be loved for His own sake for a double reason: because nothing can be loved more justly, nothing more fruitfully. . . . Assuredly I find no other worthy cause of loving Him, save Himself. . . .

The Dialectical Method: *Sic et Non*

PETER ABELARD

One of the greatest minds of the Middle Ages belonged to Peter Abelard. He was a renowned scholar and teacher whose method of inquiring into spiritual issues often created formidable enemies (among them, Saint Bernard of Clairvaux). Abelard's method of applying critical thought to the interpretation of sacred texts is best revealed in his famous work Sic et Non *(Yes and No). Abelard would pose a problem and then cite arguments, supported by the most revered church fathers, that the statement was true. He then produced another series of logical and well-supported arguments that proved it false. Abelard did not want to reconcile the conflicting views, but by this dialectical process he hoped to "sharpen the minds" of his students. The pathway to Truth had to be critically examined. The following excerpts demonstrate his method and are good examples of Scholastic argument.*

Inasmuch as among the multitudinous words of the saints there are some which . . . not only [differ] but actually [contradict one another], we are not to judge lightly of these saints who themselves will judge the world. . . . If there are divine mysteries which we cannot understand in the spirit in which they were written, better to reserve judgment than to define rashly. We are not to rely on apocryphal writings and we must be sure that we have the correct text on the canonical. For example, Matthew and John say that Jesus was crucified at the sixth hour, but Mark at the third. This is an error of transcription in Mark. We are to observe because he carelessly incorporated the work of someone else, as Augustine confessed he had done with reference to Origen. We must bear in mind the diversity of situation in which particular sayings were uttered. In case of

"The Love of God" is from E. G. Gardner, trans., *On the Love of God* (London: J. M. Dent and Sons, 1916), p. 27. Reprinted by permission of the publisher.

"The Dialectical Method: *Sic et Non*" is from Roland Bainton, ed., *The Medieval Church* (Princeton, N.J.: D. Van Nostrand, 1962), pp. 129–130. Reprinted by permission of Wadsworth Publishing Company.

controversy between the saints, which cannot be resolved by reason, we should hold to that opinion which has the most ancient and powerful authority. And if sometimes the fathers were in error we should attribute this not to duplicity but ignorance, and if sometimes they were absurd, we are to assume that the text is faulty, the interpreter in error or simply that we do not understand.

Therefore it has seemed to us fitting to collect from the holy fathers apparently contradictory passages that tender readers may be incited to make inquiry after the truth. . . . By doubting we come to inquire, and by inquiry we arrive at the truth. . . . We are including nothing from the Apocrypha and nothing from the writings of Augustine which he later retracted.

Example XXXII. That God may do all things and that He may not.

Chrysostom said that God is called almighty because it is impossible to find anything that is impossible for Him. Nevertheless He cannot lie, or be deceived, He cannot be ignorant. He cannot have a beginning or an end.

He cannot forget the past, be involved in the present or be ignorant of the future. Finally, He cannot deny Himself. Augustine said there are some things God can do as to His power, but not as to His justice. Being himself justice He cannot commit injustice. He is omnipotent in the sense that He can do what He wants. But He cannot die, He cannot change and He cannot be deceived.

Example XI. That the divine persons differ from each other and that they do not.

Athanasius said there is one person of the Father, one of the Son and one of the Holy Spirit. The Father is not made, created or begotten. The son comes solely from the Father. He is not made or created but He is begotten. The spirit proceeds from the Father and the Son. He is not begotten or created but proceeding. But Pope Leo I said, "In the divine Trinity nothing is dissimilar, nothing unequal."

The Medieval Woman

Whether Woman Was Fittingly Made from the Rib of Man?

SAINT THOMAS AQUINAS

Throughout most of the Middle Ages, women were portrayed in a negative light, completely subservient to men, as temptresses to the will of God, banished from the halls of government and the fields of battle, and confined to the bed and nursery. But the twelfth century saw a renaissance of sorts in the position of women. The popularity of the Virgin Mary soared, and cathedrals were dedicated in her name. Women such as Eleanor of Aquitaine, the empress Matilda, Blanche of

"Whether Woman Was Fittingly Made from the Rib of Man?" is from *The Fathers of the English Dominican Province*, trans., *The Summa Theologica of St. Thomas Aquinas* (London: Burns, Oates & Washbourne, 1920), Part 1, Question 92.

Castile, and Marie de France assumed an unprecedented influence in the affairs of state. This resurgence did not continue much beyond the century, but important precedents had been set.

The following selections are from the Summa Theologica *of Saint Thomas Aquinas. Although he subscribed to the rigid Aristotelian concept of woman as the "misbegotten male," and thus reflected the church's conservatism, he also was willing to concede a certain dignity (albeit minor) regarding woman's creation and participation in baptism.*

Objection 1: It would seem that woman should not have been formed from the rib of man. For the rib was much smaller than the woman's body. Now from a smaller thing a larger thing can be made only, either by addition . . . or by [thinning out], because, as Augustine says: A body cannot increase in bulk except by [thinning out]. But the woman's body is not [thinner] than man's, at least not in the proportion of a rib to Eve's body. Therefore Eve was not formed from a rib of Adam.

Objection 2: Further, in those things which were first created there was nothing superfluous. Therefore a rib of Adam belonged to the integrity of his body. So if a rib was removed, his body remained imperfect; which is unreasonable to suppose.

Objection 3: Further, a rib cannot be removed from man without pain. But there was no pain before sin. Therefore, it was not right for a rib to be taken from the man, that Eve might be made from it.

On the contrary, It is written (Genesis, 2.22): God built the rib, which He took from Adam, into a woman.

I answer that: It was right for the woman to be made from a rib of man. First, to signify the social union of man and woman, for the woman should neither use authority over man, and so she was not made from his head; nor was it right for her to be subject to man's contempt as his slave, and so she was not made from his feet. [She was made from the rib of man by Divine Power], for the sacramental signification; for from the side of Christ sleeping on the Cross the Sacraments flowed—namely blood and water—on which the Church was established.

Whether a Woman Can Baptize?

SAINT THOMAS AQUINAS

Objection 1: It seems that a woman cannot baptize. For we read in the acts of the Council of Carthage: However learned and holy a woman may be, she must not presume to teach men in the church, or to baptize. But in no case is a woman allowed to teach in church, according to I Cor. 14. 35: It is a shame

"Whether a Woman Can Baptize?" is from The Fathers of the English Dominican Province, trans., *The Summa Theologica of St. Thomas Aquinas* (London: Burns, Oates & Washbourne, 1920), Part 3, Question 67.

for a woman to speak in the church. Therefore it seems that neither is a woman in any circumstances permitted to baptize.

Objection 2: Further, to baptize belongs to those having authority; wherefore baptism should be conferred by priests having charge of souls. But women are not qualified for this; according to I Tim. 2. 12: I suffer not a woman to teach, nor to use authority over man, but to be subject to him. Therefore a woman cannot baptize.

On the contrary, Pope Urban II says: . . . baptism is valid when, in cases of necessity, a woman baptizes a child in the name of the Trinity. . . .

But since the head of the woman is the man, and the head of . . . man, is Christ (I Cor. 11.3), a woman should not baptize if a man be available for the purpose; just as neither should a layman in the presence of a cleric, nor a cleric in the presence of a priest. . . .

In carnal generation male and female co-operate according to the power of their proper nature; wherefore the female cannot be the active, but only the passive, principle of generation. But in spiritual generation, they do not act, either of them, by their proper power, but only instrumentally by the power of Christ. Consequently, on the same grounds either man or woman can baptize in a case of urgency.

The Tragedy of Abelard and Heloise

The great logician, teacher, and scholar Peter Abelard (Sic et Non) *became legendary for his tragic love affair with a student named Heloise. He had attained an enviable yet controversial reputation among scholars and churchmen. But his life changed drastically when he met Heloise and the two fell passionately in love. Abelard relates the saga in his autobiography,* A Story of Calamities.

There was in Paris at the time a young girl named Heloise, the niece of Fulbert, one of the canons, and so much loved by him that he had done everything in his power to advance her education in letters. In looks she did not rank lowest, while in the extent of her learning she stood supreme. A gift for letters is so rare in women that it added greatly to her charm and had won her renown throughout the realm. I considered all the usual attractions for a lover and decided she was the one to bring to my bed, confident that I should have an easy success; for at that time I had youth and exceptional good looks as well as my great reputation to recommend me, and feared no rebuff from any woman I might choose to honour with my love. Knowing the girl's knowledge and love of letters I thought she would be all the more ready to consent, and that even when separated we could enjoy each other's presence by exchange of written messages in which we could speak more openly than in person, and so need never lack the pleasures of conversation.

All on fire with desire for this girl I sought an opportunity of getting to know her through private daily meetings and so more easily winning her over; and with this end in view I came to an arrangement with her uncle, with the help of some of his friends, whereby he should take me into his house, which was very near my school, for whatever sum he liked to ask. As a pretext I said that my household cares were hindering my studies and the expense was more than I could afford. Fulbert dearly loved money, and was moreover always ambitious to further his niece's education in letters, two weaknesses which made it easy for me to gain his consent and obtain my desire: he was all eagerness for my money and confident that his niece would profit from my teaching. This led him to make an urgent request which furthered my love and fell in with my wishes more than I had dared to hope; he gave me complete charge over the girl, so that I could devote all the leisure time left me by my school to teaching her by day and night, and if I found her idle I was to punish her severely. I was amazed by his simplicity—if he had entrusted a tender lamb to a ravening wolf it would not have surprised me more. . . .

Need I say more? We were united, first under one roof, then in heart; and so with our lessons as a pretext we abandoned ourselves entirely to love. Her studies allowed us to withdraw in private, as love desired, and then with our books open before us, more words of love than of our reading passed between us, and more kissing than teaching. My hands strayed oftener to her bosom than to the pages; love drew our eyes to look on each other more than reading kept them on our texts. . . . In short, our desires left no stage of love-making untried, and if love could devise something new, we welcomed it. We entered on each joy the more eagerly for our previous inexperience, and were the less easily stated.

Now the more I was taken up with these pleasures, the less time I could give to philosophy and the less attention I paid to my school. It was utterly boring for me to have to go to the school, and equally wearisome to remain there and to spend my days on study when my nights were sleepless with love-making. As my interest and concentration flagged, my lectures lacked all inspiration and were merely repetitive; I could do no more than repeat what had been said long ago, and when inspiration did come to me, it was for writing love-songs, not the secrets of philosophy. . . .

[After several months had passed, Heloise's uncle found out about her affair with Abelard. He separated the lovers, but they continued to meet and Heloise became pregnant. Abelard secretly married her and arranged that she remain in a convent for safety after the baby was born. Abelard continues the story:]

At this news her uncle and his friends and relatives imagined that I had tricked them, and had found an easy way of ridding myself of Heloise by making her a nun. Wild with indignation they plotted against me, and one night as I slept peacefully in an inner room in my lodgings, they bribed one of my servants to admit them and there took cruel vengeance on me of such appalling barbarity as to shock the whole world; they cut off the parts of my body whereby I had committed the wrong of which they complained. Then they fled, but the two who could be caught were blinded and mutilated as I had been, one of them being the servant who had been led by greed while in my service to betray his master.

Next morning the whole city gathered before my house, and the scene of horror and amazement, mingled with lamentations, cries and groans which exasperated and distressed me, is difficult, no, impossible, to describe. In particular, the clerks and, most of all, my pupils tormented me with their unbearable weeping and wailing until I suffered more from their sympathy than from the pain of my wound, and felt the misery of my mutilation less than my shame and humiliation. All sorts of thoughts filled my mind—how brightly my reputation had shone, and now how easily in an evil moment it had been dimmed or rather completely blotted out; how just a judgment of God had struck me in the parts of my body with which I had sinned. . . . What road could I take now? How could I show my face in public, to be pointed at by every finger, derided by every tongue, a monstrous spectacle to all I met? . . .

I admit that it was shame and confusion in my remorse and misery rather than any devout wish for conversion which brought me to seek shelter in a monastery cloister. Heloise had already agreed to take the veil in obedience to my wishes and entered a convent. So we both put on the religious habit, I in the Abbey of St. Denis, and she in the Convent of Argenteuil which I spoke of before. There were many people, I remember, who in pity for her youth tried to dissuade her from submitting to the yoke of monastic rule as a penance too hard to bear, but all in vain; she broke out as best she could through her tears and sobs into Cornelia's famous lament:

O noble husband,
Too great for me to wed, was it my fate
To bend that lofty head? What prompted me
To marry you and bring about your fall?
Now claim your due, and see me gladly pay. . . .

[Though they never saw one another again, Abelard and Heloise continued to correspond for years. Some letters discussed academic and spiritual subjects, while others reflected on their tragic love. Through it all, the letters reveal that the couple overcame self-pity and found acceptance of a changed, but everlasting, relationship.]

Chivalric Ideals: The Function of Knighthood
JOHN OF SALISBURY

The High Middle Ages saw the transition from a rather crude and barbaric nobility to one controlled by ideals of right action and proper conduct. Knights were expected to comport themselves with dignity and spiritual devotion, especially in the presence of ladies. Knighthood became a rigorous trial, and tales of the "quest" for the Holy Grail or the mystical unicorn became popular. The following account of John of Salisbury presents the ideal of knighthood.

"Chivalric Ideals: The Function of Knighthood" is from Frederick Ogg, ed., *A Source Book of Medieval History* (New York: American Book Company, 1907), p. 401.

Noblewomen watching a tournament. This painting reflects chivalric ideals of the knight and his lady. In fact, these mock battles served a useful purpose in providing a semi-controlled outlet for the aggression of the nobility. *(Corbis)*

But what is the office of the duly ordained soldiery? To defend the Church, to assail infidelity, to venerate the priesthood, to protect the poor from injuries, to pacify the province, to pour out their blood for their brothers (as the formula of their oath instructs them), and, if need be, to lay down their lives. The praises of God are in their throat, and two-edged swords are in their hands to execute punishment on the nations and rebuke upon the peoples, and to bind their kings in chains and their nobles in links of iron. But to what end? To the end that they may serve madness, vanity, avarice, or their own private self-will? By no means. Rather to the end that they may execute the judgment that is committed to them to execute; wherein each follows not his own will but the deliberate decision of God, the angels, and men, in accordance with equity and the public utility.... For soldiers that do these things are "saints", and are the more loyal to their prince in proportion as they more zealously keep the faith of God; and they advance the more successfully the honour of their own valour as they seek the more faithfully in all things the glory of their God.

To His Love Afar

JAUFRE RUDEL

The chivalric ideal of the High Middle Ages enhanced the position of women in medieval society. With the popularity of the Virgin Mary in the twelfth and thirteenth centuries, women were viewed less as temptresses who encouraged sinful thoughts and acts and more as respected individuals, worthy of love and adoration. Knights fought for the honor of their Lady, whom they set on a pedestal and worshiped from afar. The first poem reflects this idealistic detachment. Yet some women were becoming less inhibited about their feelings, and "love from afar" was not necessarily preferred—at least not for the Countess de Dia!

When the days lengthen in the month of May,
Well pleased am I to hear the birds
    Sing far away.
And when from that place I am gone,
I hang my head and make dull moan,
Since she my heart is set upon
    Is far away.

So far, that song of birds, flower o'the thorn,
Please me no more than winter morn,
    With ice and sleet.
Ah, would I were a pilgrim over sea,
With staff and scrip and cloak to cover me,
That some day I might kneel me on one knee
    Before her feet.

Most sad, most joyous shall I go away,
Let me have seen her for a single day,
    My love afar.
I shall not see her, for her land and mine
Are sundered, and the ways are hard to find,
So many ways, and I shall lose my way,
    So wills it God.

"To His Love Afar" is from Helen Wadell, trans., *The Wandering Scholars,* 7th ed. (London: Constable Publishers, 1934), pp. 205–206. Reprinted by permission of the publisher.

Yet shall I know no other love but hers,
And if not hers, no other love at all.
　　　She hath surpassed all.
So fair she is, so noble, I would be
A captive with the hosts of paynimrie
In a far land, if so be upon me
　　　Her eyes might fall.

God, who hath made all things in earth that are,
That made my love, and set her thus afar,
　　　Grant me this grace,
That I may some day come within a room,
Or in some garden gloom
　　　Look on her face.

It will not be, for at my birth they said
That one had set this doom upon my head,
　　　—God curse him among men!—
That I should love, and not till I be dead,
　　　Be loved again.

A Distressed Lover
THE COUNTESS DE DIA

I've lately been in great distress
over a knight who once was mine,
and I want it known for all eternity
how I loved him to excess.
Now I see I've been betrayed
because I wouldn't sleep with him;
night and day my mind won't rest
to think of the mistake I made.

How I wish just once I could caress
that chevalier with my bare arms,
for he would be in ecstasy
if I'd just let him lean his head against my breast.
I'm sure I'm happier with him
than Blancaflor with Floris.
My heart and love I offer him,
my mind, my eyes, my life.

　　"A Distressed Lover" is from Meg Bogin, trans., *The Women Troubadours* (New York: Padding-ton Press, 1976), p. 89.

Handsome friend, charming and kind
when shall I have you in my power?
If only I could lie beside you for an hour
and embrace you lovingly—
know this, that I'd give almost anything
to have you in my husband's place,
but only under the condition
that you swear to do my bidding.

SECTION III:
THE LATE MIDDLE AGES
(1300–1450)

The Waning of the Medieval Church

The Fall of Pope Boniface VIII

The struggle for supremacy between church and state, which had stirred such dissension in the eleventh and twelfth centuries, seemed settled by the strong leadership of Pope Innocent III in the early thirteenth century. Innocent simply dominated the secular world without a moment of hesitation. But conditions had changed by the late thirteenth century. The forceful kings of England and France were constantly in need of money and began levying taxes against the clergy of their realms. Boniface VIII (1294–1303), in the papal bull (decree) Clericis Laicos, *viewed this as an encroachment upon the liberty of the church.*

The second selection, Unam Sanctam, *was another decree wherein Boniface promulgated the famous "Doctrine of the Two Swords," designed to promote the unity of Christianity and the supremacy of the pope. This policy eventually failed, as Boniface was attacked, captured, and humiliated by agents of the French king, Philip IV; Boniface died soon after. The days of papal supremacy were over.*

Clericis Laicos (1298)
POPE BONIFACE VIII

It is said that in times past laymen practiced great violence against the clergy, and our experience clearly shows that they are doing so at present, since they are not content to keep within the limits prescribed for them, but strive to do that which is prohibited and illegal. And they pay no attention to the fact that

"Clericis Laicos" is from Oliver Thatcher and Edgar McNeal, eds., *A Source Book of Medieval History* (New York: Charles Scribner's Sons, 1905), pp. 311–313.

they are forbidden to exercise authority over the clergy and ecclesiastical persons and their possessions. But they are laying heavy burdens on bishops, churches, and clergy, both regular and secular, by taxing them, levying contributions on them, and extorting the half, or the tenth, or the twentieth, or some other part of their income and possessions. They are striving in many ways to reduce the clergy to servitude and to subject them to their own sway. And we grieve to say it, but some bishops and clergy, fearing where they should not, and seeking a temporary peace, and fearing more to offend man than God, submit, improvidently rather than rashly, to these abuses [and pay the sums demanded], without receiving the papal permission. Wishing to prevent these evils . . . by our apostolic authority, we decree that if any bishops or clergy, regular or secular, of any grade, condition, or rank, shall pay, or promise, or consent to pay laymen any contributions, or taxes, or the tenth, or the twentieth, or the hundredth, or any other part of their income or of their possessions, or of their value, real or estimated, under the name of aid, or loan, or subvention, or subsidy, or gift, or under any other name or pretext, without the permission of the pope, they shall, by the very act, incur the sentence of excommunication. And we also decree that emperors, kings, princes, dukes, counts, barons, [etc.] . . . who shall impose, demand, or receive such taxes, or shall seize . . . the property of churches or of the taxes, or shall seize . . . the property of churches or of the clergy . . . shall . . . incur the sentence of excommunication. We also put under the interdict all communities which shall be culpable in such matters. And under the threat of deposition we strictly command all bishops and clergy, in accordance with their oath of obedience, not to submit to such taxes without the express permission of the pope. . . . From this sentence of excommunication and interdict no one can be absolved except in the moment of death, without the authority and special permission of the pope. . . .

Unam Sanctam (1302)

POPE BONIFACE VIII

The true faith compels us to believe that there is one holy catholic apostolic church, and this we firmly believe and plainly confess. And outside of her there is no salvation or remission of sins. . . . In this church there is "one Lord, one faith, one baptism" [Eph. 4:5]. . . . Therefore there is one body of the one and only church, and one head, not two heads, as if the church were a monster. And this head is Christ and his vicar, Peter and his successor. . . . If therefore Greeks or anyone else say that they are not subject to Peter and his successors, they thereby necessarily confess that they are not of the sheep of Christ. For the Lord says in the Gospel of John, that there is one fold and only one shepherd [John 10:16]. By the words of the gospel we are taught that the two swords, namely,

"*Unam Sanctam*" is from Oliver Thatcher and Edgar McNeal, eds., *A Source Book of Medieval History* (New York: Charles Scribner's Sons, 1905), pp. 314–317.

the spiritual authority and the temporal are in the power of the church. . . .
Both swords, . . . the spiritual and the temporal, are in the power of the church.
The former is to be used by the church, the latter for the church; the one by the
hand of the priest, the other by the hand of kings and knights, but at the command and permission of the priest. Moreover, it is necessary for one sword to be
under the other, and the temporal authority to be subjected to the spiritual; for
the apostle says, "For there is no power but of God: and the powers that are ordained of God" [Rom. 13:1]; but they would not be ordained [i.e., arranged or
set in order] unless one were subjected to the other, and, as it were, the lower
made the higher by the other. . . . And we must necessarily admit that the spiritual power surpasses any earthly power in dignity and honor, because spiritual
things surpass temporal things. We clearly see that this is true from the paying
of tithes, from the benediction, from the sanctification, from the receiving of
the power, and from the governing of these things. For the truth itself declares
that the spiritual power must establish the temporal power and pass judgment
on it if it is not good. Thus the prophecy of Jeremiah concerning the church
and the ecclesiastical power is fulfilled: "See, I have this day set thee over the nations and over the kingdoms, to root out, and to pull down, and to destroy, and
to throw down, to build, and to plant" [Jer. 1:10]. Therefore if the temporal
power errs, it will be judged by the spiritual power, and if the lower spiritual
power errs, it will be judged by its superior. But if the highest spiritual power
errs, it can not be judged by men, but by God alone. For the apostle says: "But
he that is spiritual judgeth all things, yet he himself is judged of no man" [1 Cor.
2:15]. Now this authority, although it is given to man and exercised through
man, is not human, but divine. For it was given by the word of the Lord to Peter,
and the rock was made firm to him and his successors, in Christ himself, whom
he had confessed. For the Lord said to Peter: "Whatsoever thou shalt bind on
earth shall be bound in heaven: and whatsoever thou shalt loose on earth shall
be loosed in heaven" [Matt. 16:19]. Therefore, whosoever resisteth this power
thus ordained of God, resisteth the ordinance of God [Rom. 13:2]. . . . We
therefore declare, say, and affirm that submission on the part of every man to
the bishop of Rome is altogether necessary for his salvation.

The Argument Against Papal Supremacy:
Defensor Pacis (1324)
MARSILIUS OF PADUA

Marsilius of Padua was a canon of the church in Padua; he wrote Defensor
Pacis *(Defender of the Peace) in 1324. It is a political treatise that was heavily
influenced by the ideas of Aristotle. Marsilius firmly believed that all authority was generated from the whole body of citizens. Contrary to the arguments of*

"Defensor Pacis" is from Oliver Thatcher and Edgar McNeal, eds., *A Source Book of Medieval History* (New York: Charles Scribner's Sons, 1905), pp. 318–321.

Boniface VIII, Marsilius believed that a council of Christian prelates had the right to control the church, which existed merely to serve the spiritual needs of citizenry. In this, he foreshadowed some of the arguments employed in the conciliar movement later in the century. The following selections are conclusions from this treatise.

2. The general council of Christians or its majority alone has the authority to define doubtful passages of the divine law, and to determine those that are to be regarded as articles of the Christian faith, belief in which is essential to salvation; and no partial council or single person of any position has the authority to decide these questions.
3. The gospels teach that no temporal punishment or penalty should be used to compel observance of divine commandments.
5. No mortal has the right to dispense with the commands or prohibitions of the [New Testament]. . . .
7. Decretals and decrees of the bishop of Rome, or of any other bishops or body of bishops, have no power to coerce anyone by secular penalties or punishments. . . .
10. The election of any prince or other official, especially one who has the coercive power, is determined solely by the expressed will of the [citizens].
11. There can be only one supreme ruling power in a state or kingdom.
14. No bishop or priest has coercive authority or jurisdiction over any layman or clergyman, even if he is a heretic.
16. No bishop or priest or body of bishops or priests has the authority to excommunicate anyone or to interdict the performance of divine services. . . .
17. All bishops derive their authority in equal measure immediately from Christ, and it cannot be proved from the divine law that one bishop should be over or under another, in temporal or spiritual matters.
22. The prince who rules by the authority of the laws of Christians, has the right to determine the number of churches and temples, and the number of priests, deacons, and other clergy who shall serve in them.
30. The prince alone, acting in accordance with the laws of the [people], has the authority to condemn heretics, delinquents, and all others who should endure temporal punishment, to inflict bodily punishment upon them, and to exact fines from them.

The Babylonian Captivity (1309–1377)

One of the great spiritual crises of the Late Middle Ages was known as the "Babylonian Captivity." From 1309 to 1377, the popes resided not in Rome, but in southern France, in the town of Avignon. They established a papal palace there,

and the city became the haunt of pleasure seekers who were indulged by the luxu-
riant and corrupt papacy. This period of self-imposed exile from the spiritual seat
of the papal power in Rome irreparably damaged the church. One of the greatest
critics of this situation was the humanist Petrarch, who grew up in Avignon and
wrote this letter between 1340 and 1353, just before he moved to Rome.

On the Abuses of Avignon

PETRARCH

Now I am living in France, in the Babylon of the West. The sun in its travels sees nothing more hideous than this place on the shores of the wild Rhone, which suggests the hellish streams of Cocytus and Acheron. Here reign the successors of the poor fishermen of Galilee: they have strangely forgotten their origin. I am astounded as I recall their predecessors, to see these men loaded with gold and clad in purple, boasting of the spoils of princes and nations; to see luxurious palaces and heights crowned with fortifications, instead of a boat turned downwards for shelter.

We no longer find the simple nets which were once used to gain a frugal sustenance from the lake of Galilee, and with which, having labored all night and caught nothing, they took, at daybreak, a multitude of fishes, in the name of Jesus. One is stupified nowadays to hear the lying tongues, and to see worthless parchments turned by a leaden seal into nets which are used, in Christ's name, but by the arts of [the Devil], to catch hordes of unwary Christians. These fish, too, are dressed and laid on the burning coals of anxiety before they fill the insatiable [mouth] of their captors.

Instead of holy solitude we find a criminal host and crowds of the most infamous satellites; instead of soberness, licentious banquets; instead of pious pilgrimages, preternatural and foul sloth; instead of the bare feet of the apostle, the snowy coursers of brigands fly past us, the horses decked in gold and fed on gold, soon to be shod with gold, if the Lord does not check this slavish luxury. . . .

Here I am, at a more advanced age, back in the haunts of my childhood, dragged again by fate among the disagreeable surroundings of my early days, when I thought I was freed from them. I have been so depressed and overcome that the heaviness of my soul has passed into bodily afflictions, so that I am really ill and can only give voice to sighs and groans. . . . Sweet water cannot come from a bitter source. Nature has ordered that the sighs of an oppressed heart shall be distasteful, and the words of an injured soul harsh.

"On the Abuses of Avignon" is from James H. Robinson, ed., *Readings in European History*, vol. 1 (Boston: Ginn and Company, 1904), pp. 502–504.

The Conciliar Movement

The Great Schism: The Cardinals Revolt (1378)

*In 1378, Pope Gregory XI died and the cardinals elected Bartholomew, arch-
bishop of Bari, to replace him as Urban VI. But when it became evident that the
new pope was going to move the papal seat back to Rome, the French cardinals
became upset and elected a second pope, Clement VII, who remained in Avignon.
This was the beginning of the "Great Schism," or division, of the church. The
unity of Christendom collapsed as each pope excommunicated the other and drew
support from different European states. In the following manifesto, the French
cardinals explain the reasoning behind their action.*

After the apostolic seat was made vacant by the death of our lord, pope Gregory
XI, who died in March, we assembled in conclave for the election of a pope, as
is the law and custom, in the papal palace, in which Gregory had died. . . . Officials of the city with a great multitude of the people, for the most part armed
and called together for this purpose by the ringing of bells, surrounded the
palace in a threatening manner and even entered it and almost filled it. To the
terror caused by their presence they added threats that unless we should at
once elect a Roman or an Italian they would kill us. They gave us no time to deliberate but compelled us unwillingly, through violence and fear, to elect an
Italian without delay. In order to escape the danger which threatened us from
such a mob, we elected Bartholomew, archbishop of Bari, thinking that he
would have enough conscience not to accept the election, since every one knew
that it was made under such wicked threats. But he was unmindful of his own
salvation and burning with ambition, and so, to the great scandal of the clergy
and of the Christian people, and contrary to the laws of the church, he accepted
this election which was offered him although not all the cardinals were present
at the election, and it was extorted from us by the threats and demands of the
officials and people of the city. And although such an election is null and void,
and the danger for the people still threatened us, he was enthroned and
crowned, and called himself pope and apostolic. But according to the holy fathers and to the law of the church, he should be called apostate, anathema, Antichrist, and the mocker and destroyer of Christianity. . . .

The Council of Pisa (1409)

*With the development of the schism, the church found itself in an unprecedented
and dangerous position. There was no legal machinery to end the schism, and
the Holy Roman Emperor decided not to end it by force. Confronted with this*

"The Great Schism: The Cardinals Revolt" is from Oliver Thatcher and Edgar McNeal, eds., *A
Source Book of Medieval History* (New York: Charles Scribner's Sons, 1905), pp. 325–326.
"The Council of Pisa" is from Oliver Thatcher and Edgar McNeal, eds., *A Source Book of Me-
dieval History* (New York: Charles Scribner's Sons, 1905), pp. 327–328.

stalemate, some church scholars suggested that a council of influential prelates be called to discuss the situation and recommend a solution. The conciliar movement, as it was called, presented several problems for the papacy. Since the fifth century, the pope, as heir to Saint Peter and Vicar of Christ, had assumed authority for all theological and administrative decisions concerning the fate of the Christian church in the west. Must he now bend to the authority of a group of "overseers" who could issue decrees and dictate orders that the pope would have to obey? Indeed, many doubted that a council of the church could be called by anyone but the pope and that the council would have the authority to decide between two papal claimants. The council was finally called by the cardinals in 1409. Their statement is presented below.

This holy and general council, representing the universal church, decrees and declares that the united college of cardinals was empowered to call the council, and that the power to call such a council belongs of right to the aforesaid holy college of cardinals, especially now when there is a detestable schism. The council further declared that this holy council, representing the universal church, caused both claimants of the papal throne to be cited in the gates and doors of the churches of Pisa to come and hear the final decision [in the matter of the schism] pronounced, or to give a good and sufficient reason why such sentence should not be rendered.

The Continuance and Authority of Councils (1417)

In its final decree, the Council of Pisa deposed both popes and elected a new one; but neither of the existing popes accepted this decision, so for a time there were three claimants to the papal throne. Another church council was called at Constance (1414–1417) to rectify the situation. This council succeeded in establishing one head of the church, and the schism ended. The conciliar movement thus gained prestige and authority. Many wanted a regular convocation of councils, as the following excerpt indicates.

A good way to till the field of the Lord is to hold general councils frequently, because by them the briers, thorns, and thistles of heresies, errors, and schisms are rooted out, abuses reformed, and the way of the Lord made more fruitful. But if general councils are not held, all these evils spread and flourish. We therefore decree by this perpetual edict that general councils shall be held as follows: The first one shall be held five years after the close of this council, the second one seven years after the close of the first, and forever thereafter one shall be held every ten years. One month before the close of

"The Continuance and Authority of Councils" is from Oliver Thatcher and Edgar McNeal, eds., *A Source Book of Medieval History* (New York: Charles Scribner's Sons, 1905), pp. 331–332.

each council the pope, with the approval and consent of the council, shall fix the place for holding the next council. If the pope fails to name the place the council must do so.

The Papal Bull, *Execrabilis:* Condemnation of the Councils (1459)
POPE PIUS II

The conciliar theorists maintained that a general council of the church repre-sented the whole church and not particular interests. As such, it was the highest spiritual authority, to which even the pope had to submit. Still, councils after Constance were not nearly as productive. Nationalistic rivalries among prelates condemned the conciliar movement to tortuous bickering and inaction. The popes successfully resisted attempts to change the administration of the church or to in-stitute popular reforms. In 1459, Pope Pius II condemned all attempts at concil-iar domination.

The execrable and hitherto unknown abuse has grown up in our day, that certain persons, imbued with the spirit of rebellion, and not from a desire to secure a better judgment, but to escape the punishment of some offence which they have committed, presume to appeal from the pope to a future council, in spite of the fact that the pope is the vicar of Jesus Christ and to him, in the person of St. Peter, the following was said: "Feed my sheep" [John 21:16] and "Whatsoever thou shalt bind on earth shall be bound in heaven" [Matt. 16:18]. Wishing therefore to expel this pestiferous poison from the church of Christ and to care for the salvation of the flock entrusted to us, and to remove every cause of offence from the fold of our Saviour, with the advice and consent of our brothers, the cardinals of the holy Roman church, and of all the prelates, and of those who have been trained in the canon and civil law, who are at our court, and with our own sure knowledge, we condemn all such appeals and prohibit them as erroneous and detestable.

"The Papal Bull, *Execrabilis:* Condemnation of the Councils" is from Oliver Thatcher and Edgar McNeal, eds., *A Source Book of Medieval History* (New York: Charles Scribner's Sons, 1905), p. 332.

Disease and History:
The Black Death

Behold, a pale horse; and his name that sat on him was Death.

—Revelation 6:8

There is a Reaper whose name is Death,
And, with his sickle keen,
He reaps the bearded grain at a breath,
And the flowers that grow between.

—Henry Wadsworth Longfellow

We all labour against our own cure, for death is the cure of all diseases.

—Thomas Browne

Ring around the rosie,
Pocket full of posies,
Ashes, Ashes,
We all fall down. . . .

—Children's rhyme

The Black Death Arrives

In October 1347, a Genoese fleet docked in Sicily at the port of Messina. The entire crew was either dead or dying, afflicted with a disease that clung, as the chronicler noted, "to their very bones." The ship had arrived from the Black Sea region and was filled with grain for ready distribution. Also aboard were the omnipresent rats, Black rats, infested with fleas that, in turn, harbored the Yersinia pestis *bacillus. Before the fleet could be quarantined, the rats had run down the ropes and into the city. Over the next four years, the scene would be repeated again and again. The Black Death had arrived.*

The mere words "Black Death" have an ominous ring about them. They dredge up images of rotting corpses, broken families, and despair. The people of Europe were devastated by a disease they did not understand nor were prepared to suffer. It was an epidemic of such magnitude that one-third to one-half of the population of Europe was killed. In a recent study by the Rand Corporation, the Black Death ranked as one of the three greatest catastrophes in the history of the world. It did much more than eliminate people; it altered the very foundation of medieval life and jeopardized the unity of Western Civilization.

The Black Death is a general term for a combination of bubonic, pneumonic, and septicemic plague strains. All three raged in the epidemic of 1347–1351. By far the most common was the bubonic variety. These bacteria are usually transmitted by the bite of an infected flea; the disease has an incubation period of about six days. The victim has symptoms of high fever (103–105° F), sweating, chills, rapid pulse, and swelling of the lymph nodes, especially in the groin or armpit. Hemorrhaging then occurs under the skin, producing blackish blotches called buboes, from which the bubonic plague derives its name. This hemorrhaging produces a kind of intoxication of the nervous system that is perhaps responsible for the delusions and psychological disorders that accompany infection. Bubonic plague is the least virulent of the three strains, but nevertheless results in the death of 50–60 percent of its victims. Pneumonic plague is more lethal (killing 95–100 percent) and more easily transmitted since it is based in the lungs and is spread by simple coughing. Like bubonic plague, septicemic plague usually depends on transference by an insect and is the most virulent strain of all. A rash forms within hours and death occurs in a day. This type of plague is nearly always fatal.

But it is not enough to talk only of the pathology of the strain. Diseases exist in an environment, and conditions may not be conducive to the survival of the bacterium or the transmitting agent. Cold, for example, limits the flea's activity, and humidity of less than 70 percent kills it. Therefore, plague outbreaks were restricted to the summer and early fall. Another important factor in the sweeping devastation of the plague must have been the general health of the population of Europe. From the tenth to the mid-twelfth century, Europe's population increased 300 percent, to about eighty million people—higher than it had been for a thousand years. This was generally the result of improved agricultural techniques and inventions, as well as the greater security of society. But by the late twelfth century, the climate was changing: Europe was growing colder and wetter. The 1290s were an extremely rainy decade; seedlings died and fertile topsoil was washed away. The growing population soon outstripped food production capabilities, and in certain regions of Europe between 10 and 25 percent of the inhabitants died. Thus the Black Death arrived close on the heels of famine.

Many were in no condition to resist such a virulent disease. To the people who lived in the mid-fourteenth century, the Black Death was an incomprehensible agent of destruction. No one was safe, neither peasant nor aristocrat, priest nor king. In such a spiritual age, many believed that God was rendering His judgment upon humanity, or that a great cosmic struggle between the forces of Good and Evil was taking place, with the Devil emerging victorious. It was evident to all that Europe was in the throes of change by forces that could not be understood, moving toward a future that could not be guaranteed.

The Plague in France

JEAN DE VENETTE

Jean de Venette was a Carmelite friar in Paris. He came from peasant stock, yet became a master of theology at the University of Paris. His chronicle of the period is highly respected by historians and provides much valuable information on the political and religious life of the fourteenth century. His account of the Black Death reflects an intimate understanding of its devastation.

In 1348 C.E., the people of France and of almost the whole world were struck by a blow other than war. For in addition to the famine which I described in the beginning and to the wars which I described in the course of this narrative, pestilence and its attendant tribulations appeared again in various parts of the world. In the month of August, 1348, after Vespers when the sun was beginning to set, a big and very bright star appeared above Paris, toward the west. It did not seem, as stars usually do, to be very high above our hemisphere but rather very near. As the sun set and night came on, this star did not seem to me or to many other friars who were watching it to move from one place. At length, when night had come, this big star, to the amazement of all of us who were watching, broke into many different rays and, as it shed these rays over Paris toward the east, totally disappeared and was completely annihilated. Whether it was a comet or not, whether it was composed of airy exhalations and was finally resolved into vapor, I leave to the decision of astronomers. It is, however, possible that it was a presage of the amazing pestilence to come, which, in fact, followed very shortly in Paris and throughout France and elsewhere, as I shall tell. All this year and the next, the mortality of men and women, of the young even more than of the old, in Paris and in the kingdom of France, and also, it is said, in other parts of the world, was so great that it was almost impossible to bury the dead. People lay ill little more than two or three days and died suddenly. . . . He who was well one day was dead the next and being carried to his grave. Swellings appeared suddenly in the armpit or in the groin—in many cases both—and they were infallible signs of death. This sickness or pestilence was called an epidemic by the doctors. Nothing like the great numbers who died in the years 1348 and 1349 had been heard of or seen or read of in times past. This plague and disease came from . . . association and contagion, for if a well man visited the sick he only rarely evaded the risk of death. Wherefore in many towns timid priests withdrew, leaving the exercise of their ministry to such of the religious as were more daring. In many places not two out of twenty remained alive. So high was the mortality at the Hotel-Dieu in Paris that for a long time, more than five hundred dead were carried daily with great devotion in carts to the cemetery of the Holy Innocents in Paris for burial. A very great number of the saintly

"The Plague in France" is from Richard A. Newhall, ed., Jean Birdsall, trans., *The Chronicle of Jean de Venette* (New York: Columbia University Press, 1953), pp. 48–51. Copyright © 1953 Columbia University Press. Reprinted by permission of the author.

sisters of the Hotel-Dieu who, not fearing to die, nursed the sick in all sweetness and humility, rest in peace with Christ, as we may piously believe.

This plague, it is said, began among the unbelievers, came to Italy, and then crossing the Alps reached Avignon, where it attacked several cardinals and took from them their whole household. Then it spread, unforeseen, to France, through Gascony and Spain, little by little, from town to town, from village to village, from house to house, and finally from person to person. It even crossed over to Germany, though it was not so bad there as with us. During the epidemic, God of His accustomed goodness deigned to grant this grace, that however suddenly men died, almost all awaited death joyfully. Nor was there anyone who died without confessing his sins and receiving the holy viaticum. To the even greater benefit of the dying, Pope Clement VI through their confessors mercifully gave and granted absolution from penalty to the dying in many cities and fortified towns. Men died the more willingly for this and left many inheritances and temporal goods to churches and monastic orders, for in many cases they had seen their close heirs and children die before them.

Some said that this pestilence was caused by infection of the air and waters, since there was at this time no famine nor lack of food supplies, but on

Death taking printers and a bookseller. *(Corbis)*

the contrary great abundance. As a result of this theory of infected water and air as the source of the plague, the Jews were suddenly and violently charged with infecting wells and water and corrupting the air. The whole world rose up against them cruelly on this account. In Germany and other parts of the world where Jews lived, they were massacred and slaughtered by Christians, and many thousands were burned everywhere, indiscriminately. The unshaken . . . constancy of the men and their wives was remarkable. For mothers hurled their children first into the fire that they might not be baptized and then leaped in after them to burn with their husbands and children. It is said that many bad Christians were found who in a like manner put poison into wells. But in truth, such poisonings, granted that they actually were perpetrated, could not have caused so great a plague nor have infected so many people. There were other causes; for example, the will of God and the corrupt humors and evil inherent in air and earth. Perhaps the poisonings, if they actually took place in some localities, re-enforced these causes. The plague lasted in France for the greater part of the years 1348 and 1349 and then ceased. Many country villages and many houses in good towns remained empty and deserted. Many houses, including some splendid dwellings, very soon fell into ruins. Even in Paris several houses were thus ruined, though fewer here than elsewhere.

After the cessation of the epidemic, pestilence, or plague, the men and women who survived married each other. There was no sterility among the men, but on the contrary fertility beyond the ordinary. Pregnant women were seen on every side. Many twins were born and even three children at once. But the most surprising fact is that children born after the plague, when they became of an age for teeth, had only twenty or twenty-two teeth, though before that time men commonly had thirty-two in their upper and lower jaws together. What this diminution in the number of teeth signified I wonder greatly, unless it be a new era resulting from the destruction of one human generation by the plague and its replacement by another. But woe is me! The world was not changed for the better but for the worse by this renewal of population. For men were more avaricious and grasping than before, even though they had far greater possessions. They were more covetous and disturbed each other more frequently with suits, brawls, disputes, and pleas. Nor by the mortality resulting from this terrible plague inflicted by God was peace between kings and lords established. On the contrary, the enemies of the king of France and of the Church were stronger and wickeder than before and stirred up wars on sea and on land. Greater evils than before [spread] everywhere in the world. And this fact was very remarkable. Although there was an abundance of all goods, yet everything was twice as dear, whether it were utensils, [food], or merchandise, hired helpers or peasants and serfs, except for some hereditary domains which remained abundantly stocked with everything. Charity began to cool, and iniquity with ignorance and sin to abound, for few could be found in the good towns and castles who knew how or were willing to instruct children in the rudiments of grammar.

The Plague in Siena: An Italian Chronicle
AGNOLO DI TURA

Agnolo di Tura del Grasso produced a chronicle of events from 1300 to 1351 that was solidly based on observation and the consultation of public records. His personal contact with the plague makes his account particularly interesting.

The mortality began in Siena in May (1348). It was a cruel and horrible thing; and I do not know where to begin to tell of the cruelty and the pitiless ways. It seemed to almost everyone that one became stupified by seeing the pain. And it is impossible for the human tongue to recount the awful thing. Indeed one who did not see such horribleness can be called blessed. And the victims died almost immediately. They would swell beneath their armpits and in their groins, and fall over dead while talking. Father abandoned child, wife husband, one brother another; for this illness seemed to strike through the breath and sight. And so they died. And none could be found to bury the dead for money or friendship. Members of a household brought their dead to a ditch as best they could, without priest, without divine offices. Nor did the death bell sound. And in many places in Siena great pits were dug and piled deep with the multitude of dead. And they died by the hundreds both day and night, and all were thrown in those ditches and covered over with earth. And as soon as those ditches were filled more were dug.

And I, Agnolo di Tura, called the Fat, buried my five children with my own hands. And there were also those who were so sparsely covered with earth that the dogs dragged them forth and devoured many bodies throughout the city. There was no one who wept for any death, for all awaited death. And so many died that all believed that it was the end of the world. And no medicine or any other defense availed. And the lords selected three citizens who received a thousand gold florins from the commune of Siena that they were to spend on the poor sick and to bury the poor dead. And it was all so horrible that I, the writer, cannot think of it and so will not continue. This situation continued until September, and it would take too long to write of it. And it is found that at this time there died in Siena 36,000 persons twenty years of age or less, and the aged and other people (died), to a total of 52,000 in all in Siena. And in the suburbs of Siena 28,000 persons died; so that in all it is found that in the city and suburbs of Siena 80,000 persons died. Thus at this time Siena and its suburbs had more than 30,000 men, and there remained in Siena (alone) less than 10,000 men. And those that survived were like persons distraught and almost without feeling. And many walls and other things were abandoned, and all the mines of silver and gold and copper that existed in Sienese territory were abandoned as is seen; for in the countryside ... many more people died, many lands and villages were abandoned, and no one remained there. I will not write of the cruelty that there was in the countryside, of the wolves and wild beasts that ate the poorly buried corpses, and of other cruelties that would be too painful to those who read of them. ...

The city of Siena seemed almost uninhabited for almost no one was found in the city. And then, when the pestilence abated, all who survived gave themselves over to pleasures: monks, priests, nuns, and lay men and women all enjoyed themselves, and none worried about spending and gambling. And everyone thought himself rich because he had escaped and regained the world, and no one knew how to allow himself to do nothing. ...

At this time in Siena the great and noble project of enlarging the cathedral of Siena that had been begun a few years earlier was abandoned. ...

After the pestilence the Sienese appointed two judges and three non-Sienese notaries whose task it was to handle the wills that had been made at that time. And so they searched them out and found them. ...

1349. After the great pestilence of the past year each person lived according to his own caprice, and everyone tended to seek pleasure in eating and drinking, hunting, catching birds and gaming. And all money had fallen into the hands of nouveaux riches.

"A Most Terrible Plague"

GIOVANNI BOCCACCIO

Giovanni Boccaccio is best known as a humanist of the Italian Renaissance. The following excerpt is from his most famous work, The Decameron. *Written during the plague years between 1348 and 1353, it is a collection of stories told intimately between friends while they passed the time away from Florence in the solitude and safety of the country. It begins with a detailed description of the pestilence. Over two-thirds of the population of Florence died of the plague.*

In the year then of our Lord 1348, there happened at Florence, the finest city in all Italy, a most terrible plague; which, whether owing to the influence of the planets, or that it was sent from God as a just punishment for our sins, had broken out some years before in the Levant, and after passing from place to place, and making incredible havoc all the way, had now reached the west. There, in spite of all the means that art and human foresight could suggest, such as keeping the city clear from filth, the exclusion of all suspected persons, and the publication of copious instructions for the preservation of

---

"'A Most Terrible Plague'" is from Giovanni Boccaccio, *The Decameron*, in *Stories of Boccaccio*, trans. John Payne (London: Bibliophilist Library, 1903), pp. 1–6.

The "Danse Macabre" was a common art motif in the fourteenth century. Death seemed to mock the living and the "grim reaper" took his toll indiscriminately. *(Woodcut by Mich. Wohlgemuth, 1493. Corbis)*

health; and notwithstanding manifold supplications offered to God in processions and otherwise, it began to show itself in the spring of the aforesaid year, in a sad and wonderful manner. Unlike what had been seen in the east, where bleeding from the nose is the fatal prognostic, here there appeared certain tumours in the groin or under the armpits, some as big as a small apple, others as an egg; and afterwards purple spots in most parts of the body; in some cases large and but few in number, in others smaller and more numerous—both sorts the usual messengers of death. To the cure of this malady, neither medical knowledge nor the power of drugs was of any effect; whether because the disease was in its own nature mortal, or that the physicians (the number of whom, taking quacks and women pretenders into the account, was grown very great) could form no just idea of the cause, nor consequently devise a true method of cure; whichever was the reason, few escaped; but nearly all died the third day from the first appearance of the symptoms, some sooner, some later, without any fever or accessory symptoms. What gave the more virulence to this plague, was that, by being communicated from the sick to the healthy, it spread daily, like fire when it comes in contact with large masses of combustibles. Nor was it caught only by conversing with, or coming near the sick, but even by touching their clothes, or anything that they had before touched. . . .

These facts, and others of the like sort, occasioned various fears and devices amongst those who survived, all tending to the same uncharitable and cruel end; which was, to avoid the sick, and every thing that had been near them, expecting by that means to save themselves. And some holding it best to live temperately, and to avoid excesses of all kinds, made parties, and shut themselves up from the rest of the world; eating and drinking moderately of the best, and diverting themselves with music, and such other entertainments as they might have within doors; never listening to anything from without, to make them uneasy. Others maintained free living to be a better preservative, and would baulk no passion or appetite they wished to gratify, drinking and revelling incessantly from tavern to tavern, or in private houses (which were frequently found deserted by the owners, and therefore common to every one), yet strenuously avoiding, with all this brutal indulgence, to come near the infected. And such, at that time, was the public distress, that the laws, human and divine, were no more regarded; for the officers, to put them in force, being either dead, sick, or in want of persons to assist them, every one did just as he pleased. A third sort of people chose a method between these two: not confining themselves to rules of diet like the former, and yet avoiding the intemperance of the latter; but eating and drinking what their appetites required, they walked everywhere with [fragrances and nose-coverings], for the whole atmosphere seemed to them tainted with the stench of dead bodies, arising partly from the distemper itself, and partly from the fermenting of the medicines within them. Others with less humanity, but . . . with more security from danger, decided that the only remedy for the pestilence was to avoid it: persuaded, therefore, of this, and taking care for themselves only, men and women in great numbers left the city, their houses, relations, and effects, and fled into the country; as if the wrath of God had been restrained to visit those only within the walls of the city. . . .

I pass over the little regard that citizens and relations showed to each other; for their terror was such, that a brother even fled from his brother, a wife from her husband, and, what is more uncommon, a parent from his own child. Hence numbers that fell sick could have no help but what the charity of friends, who were very few, or the avarice of servants supplied; and even these were scarce and at extravagant wages, and so little used to the business that they were fit only to reach what was called for, and observe when their employer died; and this desire of getting money often cost them their lives. . . .

It fared no better with the adjacent country, for . . . you might see the poor distressed labourers, with their families, without either the aid of physicians, or help of servants, languishing on the highways, in the fields, and in their own houses, and dying rather like cattle than human creatures. The consequence was that, growing dissolute in their manners like the citizens, and careless of everything, as supposing every day to be their last, their thoughts were not so much employed how to improve, as how to use their substance for their present support.

What can I say more, if I return to the city, unless that such was the cruelty of Heaven, and perhaps of men, that between March and July following, according to authentic reckonings, upwards of a hundred thousand souls perished in the city only; whereas, before that calamity, it was not supposed to have contained so many inhabitants. What magnificent dwellings, what noble palaces were then depopulated to the last inhabitant! What families became extinct! What riches and vast possessions were left, and no known heir to inherit them! What numbers of both sexes, in the prime and vigour of youth . . . breakfasted in the morning with their living friends, and supped at night with their departed friends in the other world!

Effects of the Plague

Human populations are resilient enough to recover from an isolated epidemic, but pandemic plague gave impetus to the great permanent changes in the Late Middle Ages.

Historians can document some of the changes explicitly; other changes were more ephemeral and are subject to varying opinion. The depopulation of the cities, where the plague hit hardest, caused a crisis in trade and economic exchange. Production of goods was often curtailed with the death of skilled artisans, and those who replaced them offered work of inferior quality. The medieval church grew wealthier from the accumulation of property of those who willed it as a last token of faith before they died. But the church also had difficulty explaining the pestilence and was hard-pressed to defend against the argument that God was taking vengeance for the sins of humanity. The papacy itself was battered by criticism and charges of corruption that were proved daily during its residence in Avignon from 1303 to 1377. What the church gained in wealth, it lost in prestige. The plague also affected the political relationship between church and state that had been under dispute since the eleventh century. The question of whether the secular or spiritual realm had greater authority on earth had already been answered by the mid-fourteenth century, since popes no longer challenged the military might of kings. But this status was confirmed by the results of the Black Death. The traditional containers of monarchical power were the nobility and the clergy. Both groups depended on the strength that numbers and unity gave them in their struggles with the king. The plague reduced their numbers, thus allowing kings to secure their realms more easily.

Perhaps the greatest changes, however, were in the fabric of society. On a personal level, the plague destroyed patterns of life that contributed to social stability. Familial ties were shattered as people refused to care for their relatives out of fear of contracting the disease themselves. Whole families were destroyed; we can truly speak of "lost generations." Survivors were often left in psychological and moral crisis.

The Situation in Rochester (1349)
DENE OF ROCHESTER

The clergy struggled to maintain its authority and credibility during the plague. In the following selections, note the desperation the clergy felt in not being able to handle the crisis.

In this pestilence scarce one-third of the population remained alive. Then, also, there was so great scarcity and rarity of priests that parish churches remained altogether unserved, and beneficed parsons had turned aside from the care of their benefices for fear of death, not knowing where they might dwell. . . . Many chaplains and hired parish priests would not serve without excessive pay. The Bishop of Rochester (by a mandate of June 27, 1349, to the Archdeacon of Rochester), commanded these to serve at the same salaries, under pain of suspension and interdict. Moreover, many beneficed clergy, seeing that the number of their parishioners had been so diminished by the plague that they could not live upon such oblations as were left, deserted their benefices.

The Fate of Dutiful Friars (1361)
FRIAR MICHAEL OF PIAZZA

So did the plague increase at Messina [Sicily] that many sought to confess their sins to the priests and make their last testament, and the priests and judges and notaries refused to go to their houses; and if any of them did enter the sick men's houses for testamentary or other business, sudden death came unavoidably upon them. But the friars, who were willing (Franciscans and Dominicans and of other Orders) to enter the houses of the sick, and who confessed them of their sins, and who gave them penance according to the will [of God to satisfy] divine justice, were so infected with this deadly plague that scarce any of them remained in their cells. What shall I say more? The corpses lay abandoned in their own houses; no priest or son or father or kinsman dared to enter, but they gave rich fees to hirelings to bear the corpses to burial. . . .

"The Situation in Rochester" is from G. G. Coulton, *The Black Death* (London: Ernest Benn Limited, 1929), p. 47. Reprinted by permission of A&C Black Limited.

"The Fate of Dutiful Friars" is from G. G. Coulton, *The Black Death* (London: Ernest Benn Limited, 1929), p. 52. Reprinted by permission of A&C Black Limited.

"God's Hand Was Unstrung"

MATTEO VILLANI

Matteo Villani was the brother of Giovanni Villani, the first great chronicler of Florence. Giovanni had described the beginnings of the plague before he himself died of it. Matteo continued his brother's work and devoted two chapters to the effects of the plague. He himself succumbed to the disease in 1363. The confused reactions to the plague were often either to lead a very temperate life in hopes that God would approve and lift his ban against humanity or conversely to enjoy life to the utmost before Death knocked on the door. Villani describes the scene in Florence.

Those few discreet folk who remained alive expected many things, all of which, by reasons of the corruption of sin, failed among mankind, whose minds followed marvellously in the contrary direction. They believed that those whom God's grace had saved from death, having beheld the destruction of their neighbors, and having heard the same tidings from all the nations of the world, would become better-conditioned, humble, virtuous, and Catholic; that they would guard themselves from iniquity and sins, and would be full of love and charity one towards another. But no sooner had the plague ceased than we saw the contrary; for, since men were few, and since, by hereditary succession, they abounded in earthly goods, they forgot the past as though it had never been, and gave themselves up to a more shameful and disordered life than they had led before. For, mouldering in ease, they dissolutely abandoned themselves to the sin of gluttony, with feasts and taverns and delight of delicate foods; and again to games of hazard and to unbridled lechery, inventing strange and unaccustomed fashions and indecent manners in their garments, and changing all their household stuff into new forms. And the common folk, both men and women, by reason of the abundance and superfluity that they found, would no longer labour at their accustomed trades, but demanded the dearest and most delicate foods for their sustenance; and they married at their will, while children and common women clad themselves in all the fair and costly garments of the ladies dead by that horrible death. Thus, almost the whole city, without any restraint whatsoever, rushed into disorderliness of life; and in other cities or provinces of the world things were the same or worse. Therefore, according to such tidings as we could hear, there was no part of the world wherein men restrained themselves to live in temperance, when once they had escaped from the fury of the Lord; for now they thought that God's hand was unstrung. . . . Again, men dreamed of wealth and abundance in garments and in all other things . . . beyond meat and drink; yet, in fact, things turned out widely different; for most [luxury] commodities were more costly, by twice or more, than before the plague. And the price of labour, and the work of

"'God's Hand Was Unstrung'" is from G. G. Coulton, *The Black Death* (London: Ernest Benn Limited, 1929), pp. 66–68. Reprinted by permission of A&C Black Limited.

all trades and crafts, rose in disorderly fashion beyond the double. Lawsuits and disputes and quarrels and riots arose everywhere among citizens in every land, by reason of legacies and successions; the law-courts of our own city of Florence were long filled with such [cases], to our great expense and unwanted discomfort. Wars and . . . scandals arose throughout the world, contrary to men's expectation.

The Significance of the Black Death

Some historians have viewed the plague with an element of fatalism. The population had exceeded the capacity of food production, so the population had to be reduced. Black Death, as horrible as it appeared, was better than the agony of slow starvation—a trend that was evident in the 1320s. Yet these are arguments of hindsight; they would not have consoled plague victims. For them, the Day of Judgment had arrived, with all its attendant fears and psychological terror.

Historian Robert Gottfried has noted that the key to understanding the Late Middle Ages as the transition between the medieval world and the modern world is "man's helplessness before nature." The medieval physician, confronted with the specter of overwhelming death and despair, realized his ignorance. This realization was a factor that gave impetus to the Renaissance, to a philosophy of inquiry and an emphasis on the faculties of man without strict reliance on faith in God. To what extent, then, does the progress of Western Civilization depend on death and destruction?

Europe's Environmental Crisis
ROBERT S. GOTTFRIED

From the mid-thirteenth century to the end of the fifteenth century, Europe and much of the Middle East, North Africa, and Asia suffered the most severe environmental crisis in history. Biological and climatic determinants influenced virtually every aspect of human life, and did so to a greater degree than at any time since the beginning of civilization. The most horrific of these determinants was plague. Governed by cycles of insect and rodent ecology, plague epidemics recurred throughout the Late Middle Ages, touching man when conditions were right among fleas and rats for transfer of plague. Perhaps the key to understanding the fourteenth and fifteenth centuries, the watershed between medieval and modern civilizations, is man's helplessness before nature.

Some of the changes that the environmental crisis brought benefitted society. Most survivors became richer. Western European peasants were, for the most part, freed from their customary bonds, and Europeans in general were spared the relentless pauperization that unbridled population growth caused in other areas of the Old World. But the beneficial aspects of such disasters ought not to be over-stated. Many, indeed most, of these advantages are apparent only through hindsight, and were not evident to late medieval people. Survivors of a famine or an epidemic might benefit in the long run from a rise in per capita income or a few extravagant purchases or lavish feasts. More important, an attack of plague or the onslaught of some other disaster was a shocking, horrifying, and painful experience. The day of judgment, a terrifying prospect even for the most faithful, loomed omnipresent. Disaster and depopulation brought no good to those whose lives ended prematurely, and no sense of comfort, security, or well-being to those who survived but lived in bereavement and fear of the next attack.

For these reasons and others, the environmental crisis brought to the people of the later Middle Ages a violent, anxious, and skewed perspective on life. It brought to a crescendo the moral crisis which began in the thirteenth century. A principal characteristic of medieval society was its sense of community. People, at least in theory, shared a spiritual and material life and worked together for a common good. Property was never owned, but held of a higher authority, ultimately God. Society, theorists have noted, was structured and hierarchic, clearly divided between haves and have-nots. But earthly life was considered ephemeral. What counted was the eternal life of the spirit, God's salvation, and the Kingdom of Heaven. This helps to explain the continuing popularity of monasticism. Life in the monastery approximated on earth the ideal community of heaven more closely than any other form of existence.

Naturally, such idyllic notions of community were never put entirely into practice, not even in monasteries. And beginning around 1100, many members of society—for example, merchants with profits on their minds or peasants with too little food in their bellies—found other ideals more to their liking than those of the community, either monastic or secular. But it took recurrent pestilence, severe famine, and protracted foul weather to shake profoundly the old corporate world of the High Middle Ages, and eventually to shatter its ideals. Many aspects of this medieval corporation would linger through the nineteenth century. But its demise, beginning around 1300, was accompanied by a growing emphasis on individualism, one of the most important characteristics that scholars regard as typically modern. Plague, in general, and the Black Death, in particular, caused enormous upheaval— "the world turned upside down," as a popular poem put it. It engendered a new society with new attitudes, layers and bonds of authority, sources of wealth, and, most important, new ideas. There are few historical epochs as fluid as the Late Middle Ages. . . .

Christians stood in awe of nature, but tried to understand and work with it. "Nature, the vicar of almighty Lord," was to be mastered. Surely this idea was the motivation for Europe's great clockmakers and explorers. And it was the inspiration, too, of many of the doctors who practiced medicine after the Black Death. Older, ineffective methods and traditional authorities were cast away. New ideas, tools, and techniques were put into practice, and if they did not work, still newer ideas were tried. In the fourteenth and fifteenth centuries, the seeds of empirical, experimental science, perhaps the most distinctive characteristic of modern Western Civilization, were sown.

The impact of the Black Death, the greatest ecological upheaval, has been compared to that of the two world wars of the twentieth century. To a degree this is true. But the Black Death, compounded as it was by subsequent epidemics . . . wrought even more essential change. Civilizations are the result of complex combinations of institutional, cultural, material, and environmental characteristics. When these underpinnings are removed, the civilizations collapse. The environmental crisis of the Late Middle Ages caused existing social and political systems to stagnate or to regress. Deep-rooted moral, philosophical, and religious convictions were tested and found wanting. Generally, traditional standards seemed no longer to apply. The effects of this natural and human disaster changed Europe profoundly, perhaps more so than any other series of events. For this reason, alone, the Black Death should be ranked as the greatest biological-environmental event in history, and one of the major turning points of Western Civilization.

CHRONOLOGY: The Sword of Faith: Western Civilization During the Middle Ages

527–565	Reign of Justinian in Constantinople. Reconquest of North Africa and Italy, codification of Roman law, and building of the church, Hagia Sophia.
530	Monastic rule of Saint Benedict established in the West. Emphasis on a common experience among monks, rather than the heremitic emphasis in the eastern Mediterranean.
570–632	Life of Muhammad, who—according to the Qur'an (650)—received revelations from the angel Gabriel, attacked idolatry in Mecca, was driven out in 622 (Hegira), and established himself at Medina, where he began the spread of Islam.
732	Charles Martel ("The Hammer") defeats Muslims at Poitiers.
751	Pepin the Short, formerly Mayor of the Palace under the Merovingian Dynasty, becomes King of the Franks. Establishes Carolingian Dynasty and serves as papal protector.
768–814	Reign of Charlemagne, King of the Franks. Defeats Lombards in northern Italy (774) and establishes empire throughout modern-day France, parts of Germany and eastern Europe, Italy, and northern Spain. Charlemagne crowned emperor by

Pope Leo III (800). Establishment of Carolingian Renaissance under the direction of Alcuin of York.

814–840   Louis the Pious succeeds Charlemagne as emperor.

843   Treaty of Verdun partitions Carolingian Empire among sons of Louis the Pious. Disagreement and chaos follow.

910   Foundation of the monastery of Cluny with its strict emphasis on the rule of Saint Benedict. Cluny provides basis for general reform of the church.

962   Saxons under Otto II succeed Carolingians in Germany.

987   Capetian dynasty succeeds Carolingians in France.

1066   Norman invasion of Britain by William the Conqueror results in victory over Anglo-Saxon king, Harold Godwinson.

1075–1122   Investiture Controversy between Pope Gregory VII and Holy Roman Emperor Henry IV, which carried on to their successors. Resolution in the Concordat of Worms: Church would elect prelates and invest them with spiritual authority, emperor invests prelate with secular lands, goods, and privileges.

1091–1153   Saint Bernard founds monastery at Clairvaux (1115) and leads monastic reform movement throughout Europe.

1095   At the Council of Clermont, Pope Urban II calls for a crusade to free the Holy Land from Muslim control.

1099   Jerusalem falls to the Crusaders. Forty-five years of Western rule begins in the Holy Land.

1154–1189   Reign of King Henry II of England and his wife Eleanor of Aquitaine. Henry's difficult Archbishop of Canterbury, Thomas Becket, murdered (1170) and subsequently canonized.

1182–1226   Life of Saint Francis of Assisi, founder of the Franciscan order of Friars.

1189–1192   Third Crusade, which was attended by King Richard III of England, King Philip Augustus of France, and Holy Roman Emperor, Frederick Barbarossa, fails to recover Holy Land from Muslims.

1198–1216   Papacy of Innocent III, the most powerful and influential medieval pope.

1215   Magna Carta signed by King John of England. Rights of Englishmen established.

1225–1274   Life of Saint Thomas Aquinas, generally regarded as the most insightful and important medieval philosopher.

1337–1453	Hundred Years' War between France and England rages intermittently for 116 years over disputed claims to the French throne.
1346	English victory at Crécy.
1347–1351	Black Death first strikes in Sicily and moves north throughout Europe. Successive but less devastating plagues occur into the next century. Giovanni Boccaccio writes *The Decameron*.
1381	John Ball and Wat Tyler lead the English Peasant Revolt in protest over new taxes, tolls, and reduced wages. Short-lived and brutally crushed by aristocrats, it leaves the country divided for years. Black Death returns.
1415	English victory at Agincourt under the leadership of King Henry V.
1429	Joan of Arc leads French to victory at Orléans. She is executed as a heretic in 1431.

STUDY QUESTIONS

Section I: The Early Middle Ages (500–1000)

1. After reading the selections on the Byzantine rulers Justinian and Theodora, what kind of people do you think they were? Why has Procopius's portrait of them become the dominant, popular characterization? What insights into their characters and reign do the selections on the Nika riots and the Digest of Roman Law offer?

2. Why was the Arian heresy such a threat to the religious unity of Christianity? How did the Nicene Creed solve the controversy? How would you interpret the statement that Jesus was "begotten not made"? What was the emperor Constantine's role in the Council of Nicaea, and how does this reflect the principles of Caesaro-papism?

3. What are the basic tenets of Islam as noted in the selections from the *Qur'an* and from Al-Ghazzali on "The Love of Allah"? Was Muhammad, like Jesus, considered to be divine in nature? How do you interpret the phrase "Fight for the sake of God those that fight against you, but do not attack them first. God does not love the aggressors"? The next statement reads: "Slay them wherever you find them. Drive them out of places from which they drove you." Do you find these ideas to be contradictory? Why or why not? How are women viewed by the Qur'an? Do women have legal rights? Do they assume equal status with men?

4. What do the selections on mathematics and the scientific description of smallpox tell you about Islamic values? According to Al-Ghazzali, should mathematics and religion be separated? Why or why not?

5. According to the "Laws of the Salian Franks," how was Germanic society structured? What was the relative value of a freeman, a woman or a child? What does this tell you about Germanic society?

6. In the Anglo-Saxon epic, *Beowulf*, what values are important to this society as represented by the hero Beowulf? Apart from his ability in combat, why was he considered a great king? Why did Beowulf have to die? How would you describe his burial?

7. In what ways does Charlemagne's administration of his empire reflect authority and structure? What was the "Carolingian Renaissance," and what do these aspects of Charlemagne's rule say about life in the Dark Ages? According to the sources, why did Charlemagne demand attention to reading and writing? Was the church at risk when more people could read the Bible and other Christian literature? Why?

8. Carefully read the account of Charlemagne's coronation from the Annals of Lorsch. According to this source, why did the pope crown Charlemagne, and what benefits did Charlemagne derive from this action? What was the intention of the pope? Does Charlemagne appear to be a respectful and obedient son of the church?

9. How was Paris saved from the devastation of the Northmen? Would you call this a victory for the Franks? What does this accommodation say about the strength of the Franks and the security of western Europe?

10. Define feudalism. What conditions contributed to the rise of this system? Be specific in citing appropriate sources. How does homage differ from liege homage? What were some of the obligations of a vassal to his lord? Construct a sequence of contemporary events in the United States that could result in the imposition of feudal government. How realistic a proposal is this? Could it happen?

11. What was the purpose of the Truce of God? What in particular were some of the penalties for breaking the peace? Describe the "ordeal of hot iron." Why did the church sanction such a trial?

Section II: The High Middle Ages (1000–1300)

12. Carefully read the Clermont speech of Urban II. What specific reasons are given for the necessity of a Crusade to the Holy Land? How does he justify a military expedition in which bloodshed could be expected?

13. Who was Usamah Ibn-Monqidh and what was his general impression of the western Crusades? What theme seems to dominate his accounts of his contact with Europeans?

14. Both Emperor Henry IV and Pope Gregory VII opposed each other with actions as well as with words. What weapons did the pope have at his disposal to combat the emperor and, in turn, the emperor to combat the pope? What were the weaknesses and strengths of each arsenal?

15. From the evidence at hand, analyze the personalities of Gregory and Henry. Were these men similar in temperament? Why were Henry and Gregory unable to reach an agreement along the lines of the later Concordat of Worms?

16. From your study of the Investiture Controversy, which is the stronger power, that of the church or that of the state? By their very nature, must they oppose

each other? Is complete separation of church and state a solution to the problem of supremacy? Do you see any modern ramifications to this problem?

17. What was Innocent III's view of the relationship between pope and emperor? In this regard, discuss the passage on "The Sun and the Moon." What evidence can you give that Innocent III was a strong pope? Do you regard him as unreasonable in his actions against heretics, in his treatment of King John, or later in his defiance of the English barons? Carefully read the passage in which Innocent chooses the Holy Roman Emperor. What is his solution to the problem: who "wins" in the end and why?

18. What is monasticism and what medieval values does it represent? Why was the monastic movement so popular? Which of the rules of Saint Benedict impress you most and why? Compared to other lifestyles in the Middle Ages, was it hard being a monk?

19. Some regard the great cathedrals as the quintessential expression of medieval attitudes. Others would argue that the castle (or manor) better represents the medieval mentality. Which would you choose and why? What is a relic? Why were they so important to the medieval mind?

20. According to John of Salisbury, what are the responsibilities of a king? From whom does he derive his power, and why should he be respected? What is his relationship to the church? How can the king serve both the public interest and God?

21. What is Saint Thomas Aquinas's essential argument for the existence of God? Does it sound logical to you? Is it persuasive, or can you find defects in the proof? Is Saint Bernard's argument more satisfying?

22. Peter Abelard summed up his attitude in this way: "By doubting, we come to inquire, by inquiring, we come to the truth." Saint Anselm said, "I believe in order that I may understand." What is the essential difference between the two statements? Do you believe that Abelard was seeking to undermine faith in God? What is the "truth" he sought?

23. According to the readings, how did Saint Thomas Aquinas view women? Is his logic regarding the creation of women and their participation in baptism impeccable? In what ways does he evince a conservative and rather typical medieval view of woman, and in what ways is he more liberal in his attitude?

24. Explain the concept of chivalry. What were the most important functions of knighthood? Why was it important to provide an ideal for knights? Analyze the love poems by Jaufre Rudel and the Countess de Dia. What is their basic theme, and what do they say about the positions of women in the High Middle Ages?

25. Why was the love between Abelard and Heloise so tragic? It is interesting that both Abelard and Heloise retreated to monastic orders after their crisis. Why do you think they did this? What does this action say about the medieval church?

Section III: The Waning of the Middle Ages (1300–1450)

26. Carefully read the papal decrees "Clericis Laicos" and "Unam Sanctam." What concepts was Boniface VIII trying to promote? Is he persuasive in the logic of his

argument? What does the "Doctrine of the Two Swords" entail? What do those who defy the decrees risk? Why would a king be willing to risk such a penalty?

27. Discuss the ideas of Marsilius of Padua. In what ways do they specifically threaten the authority of the pope? How do they run counter to the ideas of Boniface VIII in "Unam Sanctam"?

28. Explain the significance of the Babylonian Captivity and the Great Schism to Western Christianity. Who was responsible for starting the schism? How did the church justify the authority of the councils?

29. What common actions or occurrences do the various accounts of the Black Death identify? Is there a theme that pervades the material? Which account or passage makes the greatest impression on you, and why?

30. In what ways were the interests of both church and state affected by the Black Death? Religion is often considered a stabilizing force in society. How was faith a casualty of this disease? How did the plague disrupt the balance between religious and secular forces that helped resolve the standoff between church and state?

31. What is Robert Gottfried's specific interpretation of the plague? Do you agree with it? For civilization to progress, must it encounter destruction and devastation at some time? Does it need the "challenge of recovery" to propel it to a more advanced stage?

32. What is the role of disease in history? How potent is disease as a force for historical change? How fatalistic are you? Must there be a plague or a war every so often for civilization to survive and for the world's population to remain in proper balance? Why do people spend so much time trying to prevent disease or war if it is a natural way of assuring the overall survival of humanity? Discuss the moral implications of this statement with reference to overpopulation in India, Mexico, or China. Is it time for another uncontrollable disease to strike humanity?

PART V

TRANSITIONS TO THE MODERN WORLD

8

The Age of the Renaissance

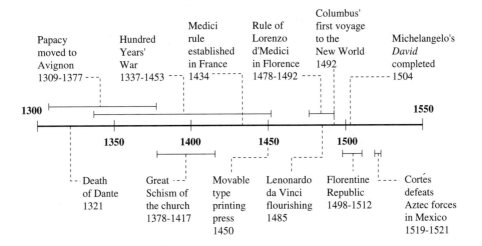

Papacy moved to Avignon 1309-1377

Hundred Years' War 1337-1453

Medici rule established in France 1434

Rule of Lorenzo d'Medici in Florence 1478-1492

Columbus' first voyage to the New World 1492

Michelangelo's *David* completed 1504

1300

1350

1400

1450

1500

1550

Death of Dante 1321

Great Schism of the church 1378-1417

Movable type printing press 1450

Lenonardo da Vinci flourishing 1485

Florentine Republic 1498-1512

Cortes defeats Aztec forces in Mexico 1519-1521

Learning is the only thing the mind never exhausts, never fears and never regrets.

—Leonardo da Vinci

What a piece of work is man, how noble in reason, how infinite in faculty; in form and moving, how express and admirable, in action how like an angel, in apprehension how like a god: a beauty of the world, the paragon of animals!

—William Shakespeare, *Hamlet*

Apart from man, no being wonders at his own existence.

—Arthur Schopenhauer

Man is the measure of all things.

—Protagoras

Man—a creature made at the end of the week's work when God was tired.

—Mark Twain

CHAPTER THEMES

- *Systems of Government:* How did the Medici family control Florence? Was their influence based on their "power" or on their "authority"? How could this be compared to the rule of the Roman emperor Augustus? Could the government of Savonarola legitimately be described as a theocracy?

- *Imperialism:* The Renaissance was a period of personal discovery and artistic creativity. It was also a period of brutal conquest of the Americas. Must exploration result in exploitation?

- *Women in History:* The Renaissance was a period in which conventional social, religious, and political structures were being challenged. Did women benefit from this new climate?

- *Church/State Relationships:* Could the Renaissance papacy be described as primarily secular and not spiritual? Had the Christian church during the Renaissance become essentially another secular institution in order to compete with European monarchs? Were the Renaissance popes secular rulers?

- *Beliefs and Spirituality:* What were the fundamental tenets of humanism, and why were they considered radical, especially to the church?

- *Historical Change and Transition:* The Renaissance has been seen as a period of transition between the "static" Middle Ages and the "vibrant" modern world. Is this a reasonable interpretation? How was progress measured during the Renaissance, and what drawbacks were evident? What debt does our contemporary world owe to the Renaissance?

- *The Big Picture:* Why was the Renaissance period so creative? Is artistic and cultural creativity best served by political and religious stability, or is the progress of civilization best served by the energy that chaos promotes?

The Late Middle Ages, from about 1300 to 1450, was a time of great struggle and calamity in western Europe. The fabric of medieval civilization was gradually torn apart by a plentitude of simultaneous catastrophes that oppressed the spirit and augured the decline of an age of faith.

The great political debacle of the period was the Hundred Years' War, which began in 1337 over English claims to the French throne and did not end until 1453. Though battles were fought only intermittently during this period, the war sapped the economic resources of the developing nation-states and directed the energy of Europe onto a path of self-destruction. No longer were Europeans united in some foreign crusade against the enemies of God; they now tore each other apart in rather mindless confusion. But wars are made by people, and at least they have some foreknowledge of the destruction that inevitably ensues. No one, however, could have predicted the devastating effects of the Black Death. From 1347 to 1351, it raged throughout Europe, destroying one-third to one-half of the population. Apart from the physical agony of the disease, the mental terror of an unseen, unknown enemy was enough to divert the energy of life into a dance of death. No one was exempt from the potential of its destruction. God seemed to forsake his flock, and the church was hard-pressed to explain or prevail against the "grim reaper." But the church's credibility as the instrument of God had already been called into question by corruption and disunity. In 1309, the papacy was transferred from its traditional seat in Rome to the city of Avignon, France. This "Babylonian Captivity," as it was called, deprived the papacy of authority and contributed to its loss of respect as prelates became known for their licentiousness and corruption. In 1378, the papacy was transferred back to Rome. But political maneuvering resulted in a "schism" that split Western Christianity into two camps, led by two popes, one in Rome and one in Avignon. This spiritual calamity was finally resolved by a series of councils of the church that were empowered to pass judgments on the papacy itself. In effect, they declared their superiority over the pope in spiritual affairs. The reformist zeal of these councils, however, did little but underscore the need for widespread change in the church. The papacy continued to degenerate: Pope Alexander VI fathered several children and Pope Julius II, bedecked in full armor, led papal armies against the French.

These political, social, and spiritual calamities sapped the energy of medieval civilization and destroyed the spiritual foundation which had inspired people to build the cathedrals and to resist the barbarism that came close on the heels of Rome's decline. The focus of Western Civilization was shifting from a dutiful devotion to God to an emphasis on the worth and importance of humanity. This transformation was centered, at the outset, in Italy, and began during the calamitous fourteenth century. By 1450, the Renaissance was in full bloom.

The term renaissance means "rebirth"; it was coined by scholars in the fifteenth and sixteenth centuries who felt a new inspiration. They viewed the medieval world as one of mindless chanting and uncreative introspection. According to Renaissance man, the preceding centuries were "Middle Ages" between the brilliance of the ancient Greeks and Romans and the reflection of that light in the culture of fifteenth-century Italy. The Middle Ages became synonymous with the "Dark Ages." For the scholars of the Renaissance, the hope of Western Civilization lay in a cultivation of the classical works of antiquity. The masters of thought and erudition were figures like Cicero, Aristotle, Plato, Virgil, and Thucydides. They became models and authorities for argument, insight, and eloquence. No longer was it enough to be able to read Cicero: One was now expected to imitate his Latin style. A cult of the classics developed as people admired the ancient monuments of Roman civilization and sought copies of the ancient texts. The Renaissance movement was primarily a scholarly pursuit of the ideals and values of classical civilization.

Chief among those values was the emphasis on man; this led to the movement known as humanism. The Renaissance emphasized the most positive aspects of humanity. Rational thought and creative instinct were prized. Man was composed of two natures: the brutal force of the animal and some of the divine qualities of God. Most important, he had the free will to pursue his own path. The course of his life was determined not by God, but by his own ambition, talent, or deceit. The glory of humanity was portrayed in the poetry and astoundingly rich art of the period. The names of Leonardo, Raphael, and Michelangelo evoke mastery of technique and perfection of style. But perhaps the most transparent assessment of reality was made by Niccolò Machiavelli. For him, power and control were the watchwords of existence. This was man, stripped of his embellishment and conscious of the political realities of life. *The Prince* was Machiavelli's manual on practical survival in a chaotic age. Glory could also be attained by strong, competent rule.

Machiavelli made people aware of the realities of power politics, and in doing so he was fulfilling a need in society. For Italy was not a united kingdom, but rather a disjointed chaotic grouping of city-states, led variously by despots, oligarchs, and republicans. It is a curious paradox that societal chaos seems to breed creativity; Michelangelo painted the Sistine Chapel while Rome was in peril of being taken by French armies. The relationship between chaos and creativity is a question worth pursuing, for it precedes discussion of a wider issue: the progress of civilization. Why was the Renaissance such a creative period, artistically, technologically, and politically? Is creativity truly an ingredient of progress, or is the progress of civilization best served by solid administration and continuity, as we found during the height of the Roman Empire? This chapter will investigate some of the ideas and attitudes that influenced European Renaissance society and beyond.

Criticism of the Renaissance Papacy

During the fifteenth and sixteenth centuries, the papacy degenerated greatly as popes became involved in the political disputes between various Italian city-states. The papal states were established around the area of Rome and were defended and enlarged especially by Pope Alexander VI (1492–1503) and Pope Julius II (1503–1513). Alexander's son, Cesare Borgia, was one of the most infamous and unscrupulous adventurers of the time. Julius II preferred not to fight by proxy, but went into battle himself against the French. The following excerpts testify to the widespread criticism of the papacy during the period. The first is by the cleric Nicholas Clamanges, from his work The Downfall of the Church; *the second is an anonymous warning about the future. Indeed, it would not be long before Martin Luther broke from the church and began the Reformation movement.*

The Vices of the Church

NICHOLAS CLAMANGES

After the great increase of worldly goods, the virtues of our ancestors being quite neglected, boundless avarice and blind ambition invaded the hearts of the churchmen. As a result they were carried away by the glory of their position and the extent of their power, and soon gave way to the degrading effects of luxury. Three most exacting and troublesome masters had now to be satisfied. Luxury demands sundry gratifications,—wine, sleep, banquets, music, debasing sports, courtesans, and the like. Display requires fine houses, castles, towers, palaces, rich and varied furniture, expensive clothes, horses, servants, and the pomp of luxury. Lastly is Avarice, which carefully brings together vast treasures to supply the demands of the above-mentioned vices or, if these are otherwise provided for, to gratify the eye by the vain contemplation of the coins themselves.

So insatiable are these lords, and so imperious are their demands, that the Golden Age of Saturn, which we hear of in stories, should it now return, would hardly suffice to ensure the requirements. Since it is impossible, however rich the bishop and ample his revenue, to satisfy these rapacious harpies with that alone, he must cast about for other sources of income.

For carrying on these exactions and gathering the gains into the [coffers] ... the popes annoint their collectors in every province,—those, namely, whom they know to be most skillful in extracting money, owing to peculiar energy, diligence, or harshness of temper, those, in short, who will neither spare nor except but would squeeze gold from a stone. To these the popes grant, moreover, the power of anathematizing any one, even prelates, and of expelling from the communion of the faithful every one who does not, within a fixed period, satisfy their demands for money. What ills these collectors have caused, and the extent to which poor churches and people have been oppressed, are questions best omitted, as we could never hope to do the matter justice. . . .

"The Vices of the Church" is from James H. Robinson, ed., *Readings in European History*, vol. 1 (Boston: Ginn and Company, 1904), pp. 508–510.

[Excommunication and interdict] were resorted to in the rarest instances by the fathers, and then only for the most horrible of crimes: for by these penalties a man is separated from the companionship of the faithful and turned over to Satan. But nowadays these inflictions are so fallen in esteem that they are used for the lightest offense, often for no offense at all, so that they no longer bring terror but are objects of contempt.

To the same cause is to be ascribed the ruin of numerous churches and monasteries and the leveling to the ground, in so many places, of sacred edifices, while the money which was formerly used for their restoration is exhausted in paying these taxes. But it even happens, as some well known, that holy relics in not a few churches—crosses, chalices, feretories and other precious articles—go to make up this tribute.

Who does not know how many abbots and other prelates, when they come to die, are, if they prove obnoxious to the papal body on account of their poverty, refused a dignified funeral, and even denied burial, except perchance in some field or garden, or other profane spot, where they are secretly disposed of. Priests, as we all see, are forced, by reason of their scanty means of support, to desert their parishes and their benefices, and in their hunger, seek bread where they may, performing profane services for laymen. Some rich and hitherto prosperous churches have, indeed, been able to support this burden, but all are now exhausted and can no longer bear to be cheated of their revenue.

The Wealth of the Church (1480)

It is as clear as day that by means of smooth and crafty words the clergy have deprived us of our rightful possessions. For they blinded the eyes of our forefathers, and persuaded them to buy the kingdom of heaven with their lands and possessions. If you priests give the poor and the chosen children of God their paternal inheritance, which before God you owe them, God will perhaps grant you such grace that you will know yourselves. But so long as you spend your money on your dear harlots and profligates, instead of upon the children of God, you may be sure that God will reward you according to your merits. For you have angered and overburdened all the people of the empire. The time is coming when your possessions will be seized and divided as if they were the possessions of an enemy. As you have oppressed the people, they will rise up against you so that you will not know where to find a place to stay.

"The Wealth of the Church" is from Oliver Thatcher and Edgar McNeal, eds., *A Source Book for Medieval History* (New York: Charles Scribner's Sons, 1905), p. 336.

The Humanist Movement

A Tribute to Petrarch (1436)

LEONARDO BRUNI

One of the founders of the humanist movement in the fourteenth century was the great luminary Petrarch (1304–1374). His poetry made him famous, and his devotion to the Latin language, and especially to the Roman orator Cicero, inspired others to follow his lead. Another great figure of the early Renaissance was Leonardo Bruni, who is most famous as one of the "civic humanists." These were scholars who not only devoted themselves to the classics, but also felt a responsibility to be involved in their respective cities and states. Bruni himself served as chancellor of Florence. In the following selections, he eulogizes Petrarch and offers his ideas about the importance of education in a letter to an aspiring young scholar. Both sources reflect the interests and attitudes of Renaissance humanists.

The Latin language, in all its perfection and greatness, flourished most vigorously in the time of Cicero, for its first state was not polished or refined or subtle, but, mounting little by little to perfection, it reached its highest summit in the time of Cicero. After his age it began to sink and to descend, as until that time it had risen, and many years had not passed before it experienced a great decline and diminution. . . .

Francesco Petrarch was the first who had such grace of talent, and who recognized and restored to light the ancient elegance of style which was lost and dead, and although in him it was not perfect, nevertheless by himself he saw and opened the way to this perfection, by recovering the works of Cicero, by enjoying them, by understanding them, and by adapting himself as much as he could, and he learned the way to that most elegant and perfect fluency. Certainly he did enough merely by showing the way to those who came after him. Thus, devoted to these studies and manifesting his talent even as a youth, Petrarch was much honoured and renowned, and was asked by the pope to act as secretary of his court, but he never consented or sought his own gain. . . .

He had in his studies a singular gift, that he was highly skilled in both prose and poetry, and in both forms he wrote a great many works. His prose was graceful and flowery, his poetry was refined and full and very lofty. And his grace in both forms of writing has existed in few or in none except him, because it seems that nature inclines either toward the one or the other and man is wont to dedicate himself to that one in which he excels by nature. Hence it happened that Virgil, who was most excellent in poetry, accomplished nothing

"A Tribute to Petrarch" is from "Petrarca and the Art of Poetry" by Leonardo Bruni, trans. Mary Martin McLaughlin, from *The Portable Renaissance Reader,* edited by James Bruce Ross and Mary Martin McLaughlin, pp. 127–130. Copyright 1953 by The Viking Press, Inc. Copyright renewed © 1981 by Viking Penguin Inc. Reprinted by permission of Viking Penguin Inc.

in prose, or wrote nothing: and Cicero, who was the greatest master of style in prose, achieved nothing in poetry. We see the same thing in other poets and orators, that they won high praise in one of these forms of writing, but none of them, that I remember having read about, in both. Petrarch alone excelled by his singular gift in both forms of writing, and he composed many works in prose and poetry, which there is no need to enumerate since they are well known.

A Humanist Education

LEONARDO BRUNI

Your recent letter gave me the greatest pleasure. For it demonstrated both the excellence of your spirit and your vigorous and intelligent schooling, the product of study and diligence. Considering your age and the penetration of that letter, it is clear to me that your maturity appears admirable and plainly beyond your years. Nor do I doubt, unless you should be untrue to yourself, that you will become a most distinguished man. Therefore, I beg you, take care, add a little every day and gather things in: remember that these studies promise you enormous prizes in both the conduct of your life and for the fame and glory of your name. These two, believe me, are the way to those ample riches which have never yet been lacking to famous and accomplished men, if only the will was present. You have an excellent teacher whose diligence and energy you should imitate. Devote yourself to two kinds of study. In the first place, acquire a knowledge of letters, not the common run of it, but the more searching and profound kind in which I very much want you to shine. Secondly, acquaint yourself with what pertains to life and manners—those things that are called humane studies because they are perfect and adorn man. In this kind of study your knowledge should be wide, varied, and taken from every sort of experience, leaving out nothing that might seem to contribute to the conduct of your life, to honor, and to fame. I shall advise you to read authors who can help you not only by their matter but also by the splendor of their style and their skill in writing; that is to say, the works of Cicero and of any who may possibly approach his level. If you will listen to me, you will thoroughly explore the fundamental and systematic treatment of those matters in Aristotle; as for beauty of expression, a rounded style, and all the wealth of words and speech, skill in these things you, if I may so put it, borrow from Cicero. For I would wish an outstanding man to be both abundantly learned and capable of giving elegant expression to his learning. However, no one can hope to achieve this without reading a lot, learning a lot, and taking a lot away from everywhere. Thus one must not only learn from

"A Humanist Education" is reprinted with permission of Macmillan Publishing Company from *Renaissance and Reformation, 1300–1648*, ed. G. R. Elton, pp. 52–53. © Macmillan Publishing Company 1963.

the scholars (which is the foundation of all study) but must also get instruction from poets, orators and historians, so that one's style may become eloquent, elegant, and never crude in substance. . . . If you do obtain that excellence which I expect of you, what riches will compare with the rewards of these studies?

Oration on the Dignity of Man (1486)

PICO DELLA MIRANDOLA

Perhaps the supreme statement of the Renaissance idolization of man is an extended essay by Pico della Mirandola, a linguist and philosopher who lived from 1463 to 1494. Note Pico's conception of man's relationship to God in this excerpt from the Oration on the Dignity of Man.

At last it seems to me I have come to understand why man is the most fortunate of creatures and consequently worthy of all admiration and what precisely is that rank which is his lot in the universal chain of Being—a rank to be envied not only by brutes but even by the stars and by minds beyond this world. It is a matter past faith and a wondrous one. Why should it not be? For it is on this very account that man is rightly called and judged a great miracle and wonderful creature indeed. . . . God the Father, the supreme Architect, had already built this cosmic home we behold, the most sacred temple of His godhead, by the laws of His mysterious wisdom. The region above the heavens He had adorned with Intelligences, the heavenly spheres He had quickened with eternal souls, and the . . . filthy parts of the lower world He had filled with a multitude of animals of every kind. But, when the work was finished, the Craftsman kept wishing that there were someone to ponder the plan of so great a work, to love its beauty, and to wonder at its vastness. Therefore, when everything was done . . . He finally took thought concerning the creation of man. But there was not among His archetypes that from which He could fashion a new offspring, nor was there in His treasure houses anything which He might bestow on His new son as an inheritance, nor was there in the seats of all the world a place where the latter might sit to contemplate the universe. All was now complete; all things had been assigned to the highest, the middle, and the lowest orders. But in its final creation it was not the part of the Father's power to fail as though exhausted. It was not the part of His wisdom to waver in a needful matter through poverty of counsel. It was not the part of His kindly love that he who was to praise God's divine generosity in regard to others should be compelled to condemn it in regard to himself. At last the best of artisans ordained that the creature to whom He

"Oration on the Dignity of Man" is from E. Cassirer, P. O. Kristeller, and J. H. Randall, Jr., eds., *The Renaissance Philosophy of Man* (Chicago: University of Chicago Press, 1948), pp. 223–225. Copyright 1948 by The University of Chicago. Reprinted by permission of the publisher.

had been able to give nothing proper to himself should have joint possession of what ever had been peculiar to each of the different kinds of being. He therefore took man as a creature of indeterminate nature and, assigning him a place in the middle of the world, addressed him thus: . . . "The nature of all other beings is limited and constrained within the bounds of laws prescribed by Us. Thou, constrained by no limits, in accordance with thine own free will, in whose hand We have placed thee, shalt ordain for thyself the limits of thy nature. We have set thee at the world's center that thou mayest from thence more easily observe whatever is in the world. We have made thee neither of heaven nor of earth, neither mortal nor immortal, so that with freedom of choice and with honor, as though the maker and molder of thyself, thou mayest fashion thyself in whatever shape thou shalt prefer. Thou shalt have the power to degenerate into the lower forms of life, which are brutish. Thou shalt have the power, out of thy soul's judgment, to be reborn into the higher forms, which are divine." O supreme generosity of God the Father, O highest and most marvelous felicity of man! To him it is granted to have whatever he chooses, to be whatever he wills.

The Soul of Man (1474)

MARSILIO FICINO

The ideas of the Greek philosopher Plato were revived during the Renaissance by Neoplatonists who applied his theory on transmigration of the soul to Christian concepts of resurrection. The leading exponent of this philosophy was Marsilio Ficino. Some of his ideas on God and man follow.

Man is really the vicar of God, since he inhabits and cultivates all elements and is present on earth without being absent from the ether. He uses not only the elements, but also all the animals which belong to the elements, the animals of the earth, of the water, and of the air, for food, convenience, and pleasure, and the higher celestial beings for knowledge and the miracles of magic. Not only does he make use of the animals, he also rules them. It is true, with the weapons received from nature some animals may at times attack man or escape his control. But with the weapons he has invented himself man avoids the attacks of wild animals, puts them to flight and tames them. Who has ever seen any human beings kept under the control of animals, in such a way as we see everywhere herds of both wild and domesticated animals obeying men throughout their lives? Man not only rules the animals by force, he also governs, keeps and teaches them. Universal providence belongs to

"The Soul of Man" is from Josephine L. Burroughs, trans., "Marsilio Ficino's Platonic Theology," *Journal of the History of Ideas* 5 (1944), pp. 234–236. Reprinted by permission of the *Journal of the History of Ideas*.

God, who is the universal cause. Hence man who provides generally for all things, both living and lifeless, is a kind of god. Certainly he is the god of the animals, for he makes use of them all, and instructs many of them. It is also obvious that he is the god of the elements for he inhabits and cultivates all of them. Finally, he is the god of all materials for he handles, changes and shapes all of them. He who governs the body in so many and so important ways, and is the vicar of the immortal God, he is no doubt immortal. . . .

Individual animals are hardly capable of taking care of themselves or their young. Man alone abounds in such a perfection that he first rules himself, something that no animals do, and thereafter rules the family, administers the state, governs nations and rules the whole world. . . .

We have shown that our soul in all its acts is trying with all its power to attain the first gift of God, that is, the possession of all truth and all goodness. Does it also seek His second attribute? Does not the soul try to become everything just as God is everything? It does in a wonderful way; for the soul lives the life of a plant when it serves the body in feeding it; the life of an animal, when it flatters the senses; the life of a man, when it deliberates through reason on human affairs; the life of the heroes, when it investigates natural things; . . . the life of the angels, when it enquires into the divine mysteries; the life of God, when it does everything for God's sake. Every man's soul experiences all these things in itself in some way, although souls do it in different ways, and thus the human species strives to become all things by living the lives of all things. . . . Man is a great miracle, a living creature worthy of reverence and adoration, for he . . . transforms himself into God as if he were God himself.

The Political Life of Florence

The Rule of Cosimo d'Medici

VESPASIANO

Florence was perhaps the city most representative of Renaissance activity and inspiration. This was the home of the statesman Leonardo Bruni, the sculptor Michelangelo, the political scientist Machiavelli, and the greatest literary figure of the age, Dante. But during this era, Florence truly belonged to one family—the Medici. They were led by Cosimo d'Medici, who developed the family's financial interests, and they eventually became the bankers of the papacy. Cosimo and his son Lorenzo (the Magnificent) wrote poetry, discussed philosophy, and heavily patronized the great artists of Florence. They were truly humanists in their own right. Although Florence was ostensibly a republic, it was in fact dominated by

---

"The Rule of Cosimo d'Medici" is from Vespasiano da Bisticci, Lives of Illustrious Men of the XV Century, trans. W. George and E. Waters (London: Routledge and Kegan Paul, Ltd., 1926), pp. 213, 217, 222–224.

the Medici family. In their reign, they applied a valuable lesson of "controlled freedom" from the Roman emperor Augustus. In many ways, Florence owed her greatness to their efforts. The portrait of Cosimo below is by the Renaissance biographer Vespasiano.

Cosimo di Giovanni dé Medici was of most honourable descent, a very prominent citizen and one of great weight in the republic. . . .

He had a knowledge of Latin which would scarcely have been looked for in one occupying the station of a leading citizen engrossed with affairs. He was grave in temperament, prone to associate with men of high station who disliked frivolity, and averse from all buffoons and actors and those who spent time unprofitably. He had a great liking for men of letters and sought their society. . . . His natural bent was to discuss matters of importance; and, although at this time the city was full of men of distinction, his worth was recognised on account of his praiseworthy qualities, and he began to find employment in affairs of every kind. By his twenty-fifth year he had gained great reputation in the city. . . . Cosimo and his party took every step to strengthen their own position. . . . Cosimo found that he must be careful to keep their support by temporising and making believe that [they would] enjoy power equal to his own. Meantime he kept concealed the source of his influence in the city as well as he could. . . .

I once heard Cosimo say that the great mistake of his life was that he did not begin to spend his wealth ten years earlier; because, knowing well the disposition of his fellow-citizens, he was sure that, in the lapse of fifty years, no memory would remain of his personality or of his house save the few fabrics he might have built. He went on, 'I know that after my death my children will be in worse case than those of any other Florentine who has died for many years past; moreover, I know I shall not wear the crown of laurel more than any other citizen.' He spake thus because he knew the difficulty of ruling a state as he had ruled Florence, through the opposition of influential citizens who rated themselves his equals in former times. He acted privately with the greatest discretion in order to safeguard himself, and whenever he sought to attain an object he contrived to let it appear that the matter had been set in motion by some one other than himself and thus he escaped envy and unpopularity. His manner was admirable; he never spoke ill of anyone, and it angered him greatly to hear slander spoken by others. He was kind and patient to all who sought speech with him: he was more a man of deeds than of words: he always performed what he promised, and when this had been done he sent to let the petitioner know that his wishes had been granted. His replies were brief and sometimes obscure, so that they might be made to bear a double sense. . . .

So great was his knowledge of all things, that he could find some matter of discussion with men of all sorts, he would talk literature with a man of letters and theology with a theologian, being well versed therein through his natural liking, and for the reading of the Holy Scripture. With philosophy it was just the same. . . . He took kindly notice of all musicians, and delighted greatly in their art. He had dealings with painters and sculptors and had in his house works of diverse masters. He was especially inclined towards sculpture and showed great favour to all worthy craftsmen, being a good friend to Donatello and all sculptors and painters; and because in his time the sculptors found scanty employment, Cosimo, in order that Donatello's chisel might not be idle, commissioned him to make the pulpits of bronze in St. Lorenzo and the doors of the sacristy. He ordered the bank to pay every week enough money to Donatello for his work and for that of his four assistants. . . . He had a good knowledge of architecture, as may be seen from the buildings he left, none of which were built without consulting him; moreover, all those who were about to build would go to him for advice.

"This Will Be Your Final Destruction" (1494)

GIROLAMO SAVONAROLA

In 1492, Lorenzo the Magnificent died and his brother Piero was unable to maintain the family dominance over political affairs in Florence. In 1494, Piero was expelled from the city; the resulting power vacuum was filled by Girolamo Savonarola, the prior of the Dominican convent of San Marco. His preaching against the tyranny of the Medici had a hypnotic effect on the Florentines. His message was directed as well against the corruption of the papacy, and he was soon excommunicated. Nonetheless, he mesmerized Florence for four years. The following excerpt is from a sermon he delivered right after the Medici were overthrown; it was the beginning of Savonarola's own domination. By 1498, the Florentines had become hostile toward Savonarola's restrictive theocracy; he was executed and his body burned at the stake—with the pope's blessing.

Oh, Florence, I cannot tell you everything I feel, for you could not bear it for the present. Oh, if I could tell you all, you would see that I am like a new vessel full of mist that is sealed up, with a seal on every word to prevent it from issuing forth! Many secrets are sealed up there which cannot be told because you would not believe them! Oh, Florence, if you have still been unable to believe, at least believe now; and if you have believed, believe more than ever little man full of sin! God has wished you to see and to know my incapacity so that you may see and realize so much the better that it is He and not I who does all. . . . You know that in these past years while I have preached to you, when everything seemed to be at peace and Florence was so quiet, I predicted to you that you would see much evil and many tribulations; and you did not believe it because you saw no sign of it. Now you have seen it, and you

"'This Will Be Your Final Destruction'" is from William J. Bouwsma, trans., in *Major Crises in Western Civilization*, vol. 1 (New York: Harcourt Brace and World, 1965), pp. 165–167. Translated from Mario Ferrara, ed., *Prediche e Scritti Commentati e Collegati da un Racconto Biografico. L'influenza del Savonarola Sulla Letteratura e L'arte del Quattrocento. Bibliografia Ragionata* (Florence: Casa Editrice Leo S. Olschki, 1952), pp. 156–166. Reprinted by permission of Casa Editrice Olschki.

see that they have begun, and you see the beginning of what I told you, and you cannot deny it. Therefore, you must now believe so much the more what I will tell you, since you have seen what was said in the past begin and be verified. And if, then, I predicted evil and you have seen it, now when I speak of good you must believe, because a prophet does not always predict evil. Listen,

After ruling Florence as a theocracy, the Dominican friar Girolamo Savonarola was executed and burned at the stake in the town square. Florence went through many subtle political transformations, at one time a republic, at another an enlightened despotism under the Medici. *(Alinari/Art Resource, N.Y.)*

Florence, this morning to what I am telling you. Hear what God has inspired in me. I trust only in Christ in what I am telling you; and I would fail if I wished to do good to you by myself.

In the first place, I tell you, do those things I have told you to do before: namely, that each one should confess and be purified of his sins, and that all should attend to the common good of the city. And if you will do this, your city will be glorious, because in this way it will be reformed both spiritually and temporally; and from you will come the reformation of all Italy, and Florence will become more rich and more powerful than she has ever been, and she will extend her empire into many places. But if you will not do this that I tell you . . . this will be your final destruction. . . . I have told you before that God wishes to renew his Church; do not doubt that he will renew it with the sword of tribulation, and soon. . . .

Above all you must take care lest anyone make himself head and dominate others in the city. Such men are deprived of God's grace and of his special providence, and they are generally the worst men, lacking in understanding and faithless. . . . Above all such men have no true friendship with anyone; they do not confide in anyone. True and joyous friendship is necessary in human affairs and conserves you in virtue; but such men have no good virtue, nor do they contract true friendship. They always hate good men and . . . employ only wicked and evil people. . . . Furthermore, their rule cannot be long and durable because all the people, even if they do not show it, hate their tyranny. A people under a tyrant is like a body of water compressed and held back by force, which, when it finds a little hole to escape, bursts forth impetuously and ruinously. . . . Have a care, therefore, that such men do not take control in your city, and attend to the common good. And how this should be done I will tell you, as God will inspire me.

I have told you, during the last few days, that when the natural agent wishes to do a thing, it must give every consideration to the form of that thing; therefore, I tell you that you must select a good form for your new government, and above all no one must think of making himself head if you wish to live in liberty. . . .

Precepts of Power

NICCOLÒ MACHIAVELLI

Over the centuries, the name of Machiavelli has become synonymous with evil. The adjective "Machiavellian" still evokes images of deceit and political back-stabbing. Machiavelli's ideas were condemned by the church as immoral and inspired by Satan himself. In reality, Niccolò Machiavelli (1469–1527) was a loyal citizen of Florence who had been schooled in the classics and had chosen a career in public service. He disliked the rule of the Medici and was a great advocate of republicanism. After Savonarola's fall from power in 1498, his theocracy was replaced by a true republic, led by elected officials of the people. Machiavelli became ambassador to France, and this duty served as a laboratory for the science of politics where he could observe men and governments in action. The Florentine republic was successful until 1512, when a Spanish mercenary army defeated Machiavelli's personally trained Florentine militia. They reinstalled Medici rule, and Machiavelli was tortured on the rack and thrown into prison for a time. He retired to the country and wrote a little book entitled The Prince. *In it, Machiavelli gives the wisdom of his experience in politics. It is a manual of power: how to obtain it, maintain it, and lose it. In his analysis, Machiavelli is brutally realistic about the nature of human beings and the world of power politics: Learn the rules and you may survive and prosper. In the political chaos of Renaissance Italy, where alliances shifted frequently and distrust prevailed, such a guide proved useful and popular. Some of Machiavelli's most important ideas from* The Prince *are excerpted below.*

On Those Who Hae Become Princes by Crime

It is to be noted that in taking a state its conqueror should weigh all the harmful things he must do and do them all at once so as not to have to repeat them every day, and in not repeating them to be able to make men feel secure and to win them over with the benefits he bestows upon them. Anyone who does otherwise, either out of timidity or because of poor advice, is always obliged to keep his knife in his hand; nor can he ever count upon his subjects, who, because of their fresh and continual injuries, cannot feel secure with him. Injuries, therefore, should be inflicted all at the same time, for the less they are tasted, the less they offend; and benefits should be distributed a bit at a time in order that they may be savored fully. And a prince should, above all, live with his subjects in such a way that no unforseen event, either good or bad, may make him alter his course; for when emergencies arise in adverse conditions, you are not in time to resort to cruelty, and what good you do will help you little, since it will be judged a forced measure and you will earn from it no thanks whatsoever.

On Cruelty and Mercy

A prince must be cautious in believing and in acting, nor should he be afraid of his own shadow; and he should proceed in such a manner, tempered by prudence and humanity, so that too much trust may not render him imprudent nor too much distrust render him intolerable.

From this arises an argument: whether it is better to be loved than to be feared, or the contrary. I reply that one should like to be both one and the other; but since it is difficult to join them together, it is much safer to be feared than to be loved when one of the two must be lacking. For one can generally say that about men: that they are ungrateful, fickle, simulators and deceivers, avoiders of danger, greedy for gain; and while you work for their good they are completely yours, offering you their blood, their property, their lives, and their sons, as I said earlier, when danger is far away; but when it comes nearer to you they turn away. And that prince who bases his power entirely on their words, finding himself stripped of other preparations, comes to ruin; for friendships that are acquired by a price and not by greatness and nobility of character are purchased but are not owned, and at the proper moment they cannot be spent. And men are less hesitant about harming someone who makes himself loved than one who makes himself feared because love is held together by a chain of obligation which, since men are a sorry lot, is broken on every occasion in which their own self-interest is concerned; but fear is held together by a dread of punishment which will never abandon you.

A prince must nevertheless make himself feared in such a manner that he will avoid hatred, even if he does not acquire love; since to be feared and not hated can very well be combined; and this will always be so when he keeps his hands off the property and the women of his citizens and his subjects. And if he must take someone's life, he should do so when there is proper justification and manifest cause; but, above all, he should avoid the property of others; for men forget more quickly the death of their father than the loss of their patrimony. Moreover, the reasons for seizing their property are never lacking; and he who begins to live by stealing always finds a reason for taking what belongs to others; on the contrary, reasons for taking a life are rarer and disappear sooner. . . . I conclude, therefore, returning to the problem of being feared and loved, that since men love at their own pleasure and fear at the pleasure of the prince, a wise prince should build his foundation upon that which belongs to him, and not upon that which belongs to others: he must strive only to avoid hatred, as has been said.

How a Prince Should Keep His Word

How praiseworthy it is for a prince to keep his word and to live by integrity and not by deceit everyone knows; nevertheless, one sees from the experience of our times that the princes who have accomplished great deeds are those who have cared little for keeping their promises and who have known how to manipulate the minds of men by shrewdness; and in the end they have surpassed those who laid their foundations upon honesty.

You must, therefore, know that there are two means of fighting: one according to the laws, the other with force; the first way is proper to man, the second to beasts; but because the first, in many cases, is not sufficient, it becomes necessary to have recourse to the second. Therefore, a prince must know how to use wisely the natures of the beast and the man. . . .

Since, then, a prince must know how to make good use of the nature of the beast, he should choose from among the beasts the fox and the lion; for the lion cannot defend itself from traps and the fox cannot protect itself from wolves. It is therefore necessary to be a fox in order to recognize the

Niccolò Machiavelli: "Let a prince therefore act to seize and to maintain the state; his methods will always be judged honorable and will be praised by all; for ordinary people are always deceived by appearances and by the outcome of a thing; and in the world there is nothing but ordinary people." *(Alinari/Art Resource, N.Y.)*

traps and a lion in order to frighten the wolves. Those who play only the part of the lion do not understand matters. A wise ruler, therefore, cannot and should not keep his word when such an observance of faith would be to his disadvantage and when the reasons which made him promise are removed. And if men were all good, this rule would not be good; but since men are a sorry lot and will not keep their promises to you, you likewise need not keep yours to them. A prince never lacks legitimate reasons to break his promises. Of this one could cite an endless number of modern examples to show how many pacts, how many promises have been made null and void because of the infidelity of princes; and he who has known best how to use the fox has come to a better end. But it is necessary to know how to disguise this nature well and to be a great hypocrite and a liar: and men are so simpleminded and so controlled by their present necessities that one who deceives will always find another who will allow himself to be deceived. . . .

A prince, therefore, must be very careful never to let anything slip from his lips which is not full of the five qualities mentioned above: he should appear, upon seeing and hearing him, to be all mercy, all faithfulness, all integrity, all kindness, all religion. And there is nothing more necessary than to seem to possess this last quality. And men in general judge more by their eyes than their hands; for everyone can see but few can feel. Everyone sees what you seem to be, few perceive what you are, and those few do not dare to contradict the opinion of the many who have the majesty of the state to defend them; and in the actions of all men, and especially of princes, where there is no impartial arbiter, one must consider the final result. Let a prince therefore act to seize and to maintain the state; his methods will always be judged honorable and will be praised by all; for ordinary people are always deceived by appearances and by the outcome of a thing; and in the world there is nothing but ordinary people. . . .

Renaissance Arts and Manners

On Art and Artists

Scholarship and Art: Leon Battista Alberti
GIORGIO VASARI

Leon Battista Alberti (1404–1472) was a brilliant humanist who came closer than anyone before Leonardo to being a "universal man." He was not only a man of letters, but an artist and architect as well. His ideas on the important connection between art and scholarship are described below by the great Renaissance biographer Giorgio Vasari.

The knowledge of letters and the study of the sciences are without doubt of the utmost value of all, and offer the most important advantages to every artist who takes pleasure therein; but most of all they are serviceable to sculptors, painters, and architects, for whom they prepare the path to various inventions in all the works executed by them; and be the natural qualities of a man what they may, his judgment can never be brought to perfection if he be

"Scholarship and Art: Leon Battista Alberti" is from *Lives of Seventy of the Most Eminent Painters, Sculptors and Architects,* trans. E. H. and E. W. Blashfield (New York: Charles Scribner's Sons, 1896), pp. 49–61.

deprived of the advantages resulting from the accompaniment of learning. . . . Since theory, when separated from practice, is, for the most part, found to avail very little; but when theory and practice chance to be happily united in the same person, nothing can be more suitable to the life and vocation of artists, as well because art is rendered much richer and more perfect by the aid of science, as because the councils and writings of learned artists have, in themselves, a greater efficacy, and obtain a higher degree of credit, than can be accorded to the words or works of those who know nothing beyond the simple process they use, and which they put in practice, well or ill, as it may chance.

Now that all this is true is seen clearly in the instance of Leon Battista Alberti, who having given his attention to the study of Latin as well as to that of architecture, perspective, and painting, has left behind him books, written in such a manner, that no artist of later times has been able to surpass him in his style and other qualities as an author, while there have been numbers, much more distinguished than himself in the practice of art, although it is very generally supposed (such is the force of his writings, and so extensive has been their influence on the pens and words of the learned, his contemporaries and others), that he was, in fact, superior to all those who have, on the contrary, greatly surpassed him in their works. We are thus taught, by experience, that, in so far as regards name and fame, the written word is that which, of all things has the most effectual force, the most vivid life, and the longest duration; for books make their way to all places, and everywhere they obtain the credence of men, provided they be truthful and written in the spirit of candor. We are therefore, not to be surprised if we find the renowned Leon Battista to be better known by his writings than by the works of his hand.

The Development of Art (1550)

GIORGIO VASARI

Giorgio Vasari was a talented painter, but he is best known for his biographies of Renaissance artists. In this selection, he sets his contemporary scene by comparing it artistically with past ages.

We find, then, that the art of sculpture was zealously cultivated by the Greeks, among whom many excellent sculptors appeared: Phidias, Praxiteles and Polycletus. . . . Painting was in like manner honoured, and those who practised it successfully were rewarded and among the ancient Greeks and

"The Development of Art" is from Giorgio Vasari, *Lives of the Most Eminent Painters, Sculptors and Architects*, trans. J. Foster (London: H. G. Bohn, 1850), pp. 20–22.

Romans; this is proved by their according the rights of citizenship, and the most exalted dignities, to such as attained high distinction in these arts. . . .

I suggested above that the origin of these arts was Nature itself—the first image or model, the most beautiful fabric of the world—and the master, the divine light infused into us by special grace, and which has made us not only superior to all other animals, but has exalted us, if it be permitted so to speak, to the similitude of God Himself. . . .

But as fortune, when she has raised either persons or things to the summit of her wheel, very frequently casts them to the lowest point, whether in repentance or for her sport, so it chanced that, after these things, the barbarous nations of the world arose, in [different] places, in rebellion against the Romans. . . . There ensued, in no long time, not only the decline of that great empire, but the utter ruin of the whole and more especially of Rome herself, when all the best artists, sculptors, painters, and architects, were in like manner totally ruined, being submerged and buried, together with the arts themselves, beneath the miserable slaughters and ruins of that much renowned city. . . .

But infinitely more ruinous than all other enemies to the arts above named, was the fervent zeal of the new Christian religion, which, after long and sanguinary combats, had finally overcome and annihilated the ancient creeds of the pagan world, by the frequency of miracles exhibited, and by the earnest sincerity of the means adopted; and ardently devoted, with all diligence, to the [elimination] of error, nay, to the removal of even the slightest temptation to heresy, it not only destroyed all the wondrous statues, paintings, sculptures, mosaics, and other ornaments of the false pagan deities, but at the same time extinguished the very memory, in casting down the honours, of numberless excellent ancients, to whom statues and other monuments had been erected, in public places, for their virtues, by the most virtuous times of antiquity. No, more than this, to build the churches of the Christian faith, this zeal not only destroyed the most renowned temples of the heathens, but, for the richer ornament of St. Peter's, and in addition to the many spoils previously bestowed on that building, the tomb of Adrian, now called the castle of St. Angelo, was deprived of its marble columns, to employ them for this church, many other buildings being in like manner despoiled, and which we now see wholly devastated. And although the Christian religion did not effect this from hatred to these works of art, but solely for the purpose of abasing and bringing into contempt the gods of the Gentiles, yet the result of this too ardent zeal did not fail to bring such total ruin over the noble arts, that their very form and existence was lost. . . .

The overwhelming flood of evils by which unhappy Italy had been submerged and devastated, had not only destroyed whatever could properly be called buildings, but, a still more deplorable consequence, had totally exterminated the artists themselves, when, by the will of God, in the year 1240, Giovanni Cimabue, of the noble family of that name, was born, in the city of Florence, to give the first light to the art of painting. . . .

The Notebooks of a Universal Man
LEONARDO DA VINCI

The Renaissance produced several outstanding artists, scholars, and statesmen, but no one seemed to imprint this creative age as did Leonardo da Vinci (1452–1519). Leonardo was a painter of great talent. He was especially innovative in his naturalistic backgrounds, his perfection of the techniques of perspective and geometric arrangement of figures, and the subtle treatment of light and shade. But Leonardo never really considered himself to be primarily a painter. His curiosity for the world around him was too great. He wanted to "learn the causes of things." Toward that end, he observed and made notes in a book for future reference and was constantly inventing machines that he believed would have military value; his sketches of helicopters, tanks, and submarines were far beyond the realities of his times. Leonardo's notebooks give fascinating insight into the workings of his fertile mind. Some of his comments on birds, flight, sketching, and painting are offered below.

The Observation of Birds and Thoughts of Flight

The thrushes and other small birds are able to make headway against the course of the wind, because they fly in spurts; that is they take a long course below the wind, by dropping in a slanting direction towards the ground, with their wings half closed, and they open the wings and catch the wind in them with their reverse movement, and so rise to a height; and then they drop again in the same way.

Remember that your bird should have no other model than the bat, because its membranes serve as an armor or rather as a means of binding together the pieces of its armor, that is the framework of the wings.

And if you take as your pattern the wings of feathered birds, these are more powerful in structure of bone and sinew because they are penetrable, that is to say the feathers are separated from one another and the air passes through them. But the bat is aided by its membrane which binds the whole together and is not penetrated by the air.

Of whether birds when continually descending without beating their wings will proceed a greater distance in one sustained curve, or by frequently making some reflex movement; and whether when they wish to pass in flight from one spot to another they will go more quickly by making impetuous, headlong movements, and then rising up with reflex movement and again making a fresh descent, and so continuing.—To speak of this subject you must . . . in the first book explain the nature of the resistance of

"The Notebooks of a Universal Man" is from Edward McCurdy, ed., *Leonardo Da Vinci Notebooks* (New York: Empire State Book Co., 1922), pp. 150–153, 188–189, 197–199.

The Flight of Birds. This page from the notebooks of Leonardo da Vinci demonstrates his precise powers of observation. Specific wing positions of the bird in flight were meticulously recorded and analyzed. *(Giraudon, Art Resource, N.Y.)*

the air, in the second the anatomy of the bird and of its wings, in the third the method of working of the wings in their various movements, in the fourth the power of the wings and of the tail, at such time as the wings are not being moved and the wind is favourable, to serve as a guide in different movements.

Dissect the bat, study it carefully, and on this model construct the machine.

There is as much pressure exerted by a substance against the air as by the air against the substance. Observe how the beating of its wings against the air suffices to bear up the weight of the eagle in the highly rarefied air which borders on the fiery element! Observe also how the air moving over the sea, beaten back by the bellying sails, causes the heavily laden ship to glide onwards! So that by adducing and expounding the reasons of these things you may able to realise that man when he has great wings attached to him, by exerting his strength against the resistance of the air and conquering it, is enabled to subdue it and to raise himself upon it.

The Importance of Sketching

When you have thoroughly learnt perspective, and have fixed in your memory all the various parts and forms of things, you should often amuse yourself when you take a walk for recreation, in watching and taking note of the attitudes and actions of men as they talk and dispute, or laugh or come to blows one with another, both their actions and those of the bystanders who either intervene or stand looking on at these things; noting these down with rapid strokes in this way, in a little pocket-book, which you ought always to carry with you. And let this be tinted paper, so that it may not be rubbed out; but you should change the old for a new one, for these are not things to be rubbed out but preserved with the utmost diligence; for there is such an infinite number of forms and actions of things that the memory is incapable of preserving them, and therefore you should keep those [sketches] as your patterns and teachers.

The Way to Paint a Battle

Show first the smoke of the artillery mingled in the air with the dust stirred up by the movement of the horses and of the combatants. . . . The smoke which is mingled with the dust-laden air will as it rises to a certain height have more and more the appearance of a dark cloud, at the summit of which the smoke will be more distinctly visible than the dust. The smoke will assume a bluish tinge, and the dust will keep its natural colour. From the side whence the light comes this mixture of air and smoke and dust will seem far brighter than on the opposite side.

As for the combatants, the more they are in the midst of this turmoil the less they will be visible, and the less will be the contrast between their lights and shadows. You should give a ruddy glow to the faces and the figures and the air around them, and to the gunners and those near to them, and this glow should grow fainter as it is further away from its cause. The figures which are between you and the light, if far away, will appear dark against a light background, and the nearer their limbs are to the ground the less will they be visible, for there the dust is greater and thicker. And if you make horses galloping away from the throng make little clouds of dust as far distant one from another as is the space between the strides made by the horse, and that cloud which is further away from the horse should be the least visible, for it should be high and spread out and thin, while that which is nearer should be more conspicuous and smaller and more compact.

Let the air be full of arrows going in various directions, some mounting upwards, others falling, others flying horizontally, and let the balls shot from the guns have a train of smoke following their course. Show the figures in the foreground covered with dust on their hair and eyebrows and such other level parts as afford the dust a space to lodge.

Make the conquerors running, with their hair and other things streaming in the wind, and with brows bent down; and they should be thrusting forward opposite limbs, that is, if a man advances the right foot the left arm should also come forward. If you represent any one fallen you should show the mark where he has been dragged through the dust, which has become changed to bloodstained mire, and round about in the half-liquid earth you should show the marks of the tramping of men and horses who have passed over it. Make a horse dragging the dead body of his master, and leaving behind him in the dust and mud the track of where the body was dragged along.

Make the beaten and conquered pallid, with brows raised and knit together, and let the skin above the brows be all full of lines of pain; at the sides of the nose show the furrows going in an arch from the nostrils and ending where the eye begins, and show the dilation of the nostrils which is the cause of these lines; and let the lips be arched displaying the upper row of teeth, and let the teeth be parted after the manner of such as cry in lamentation. Show some one using his hand as a shield for his terrified eyes, turning the palm of it towards the enemy, and having the other resting on the ground to support the weight of his body; let others be crying out with their mouths wide open, and fleeing away. Put all sorts of arms lying between the feet of the combatants, such as broken shields, lances, broken swords, and other things like these. Make the dead, some half buried in dust, others with the dust all mingled with the oozing blood and changing into crimson mud; and let the line of the blood be discerned by its colour, flowing in a sinuous stream from the corpse of the dust. Show others in the death agony grinding their teeth and rolling their eyes, with clenched fists grinding against their bodies, and with legs distorted . . . but see that there is no level spot of ground that is not trampled over with blood.

Images of Renaissance Women and Men

With the growing emphasis on diplomacy and contact with ambassadors of other states during the Renaissance, rules of etiquette were established. The new age demanded that knights become gentlemen and that the relationship between the sexes be redefined. Baldassare Castiglione provided the instruction in his Book of the Courtier.

Book of the Courtier (1518)

BALDASSARE CASTIGLIONE

I wish, then, that this Courtier of ours should be nobly born and of gentle race; because it is far less unseemly for one of ignoble birth to fail in worthy deeds, than for one of noble birth, who, if he strays from the path of his predecessors, stains his family name, and not only fails to achieve but loses what has been achieved already; for noble birth is like a bright lamp that manifests and makes visible good and evil deeds, and kindles and stimulates to virtue both by fear of shame and by hope of praise. . . .

But to come to some details, I am of the opinion that the principal and true profession of the Courtier ought to be that of arms; which I would have him follow actively above all else, and be known among others as bold and strong, and loyal to whomsoever he serves. And he will win a reputation for these good qualities by exercising them at all times and in all places, since one may never fail in this without severest censure. And just as among women, their fair fame once sullied never recovers its first lustre, so the reputation of a gentleman who bears arms, if once it be in the least tarnished with cowardice or other disgrace, remains forever infamous before the world and full of ignominy. Therefore the more our Courtier excels in this art, the more he will be worthy of praise; and yet I do not deem essential in him that perfect knowledge of things and those other qualities that befit a commander; since this would be too wide a sea, let us be content, as we have said, with perfect loyalty and unconquered courage, and that he be always seen to possess them. . . .

Therefore let the man we are seeking, be very bold, stern, and always among the first, where the enemy are to be seen; and in every other place, gentle, modest, reserved, above all things avoiding ostentation and that impudent self-praise by which men ever excite hatred and disgust in all who bear them. . . .

Then coming to the bodily frame, I say it is enough if this be neither extremely short nor tall, for both of these conditions excite a certain contemptuous surprise, and men of either sort are gazed upon in much the same way

"Book of the Courtier" is from Baldassare Castiglione, *Book of the Courtier,* trans. Leonard Opdycke (New York: Horace Liveright, 1903), pp. 22, 25–26, 28–31.

that we gaze on monsters. Yet if we must offend in one of the two extremes, it is preferable to fall a little short of the just measure of height than to exceed it, for besides often being dull of intellect, men thus huge of body are also unfit for every exercise of agility, which thing I should much wish in the Courtier. And so I would have him well built and shapely of limb, and would have him show strength and lightness and suppleness, and know all bodily exercises that befit a man of war: I think the first should be to handle every sort of weapon well on foot and on horse, to understand the advantages of each, and especially to be familiar with those weapons that are ordinarily used among gentlemen; for besides the use of them in war, where such subtlety in contrivance is perhaps not needful, there frequently arise differences between one gentleman and another, which afterwards result in duels often fought with such weapons as happen at the moment to be within reach: thus knowledge of this kind is a very safe thing. . . .

It is fitting also to know how to swim, to leap, to run, to throw stones, for besides the use that may be made of this in war, a man often has occasion to show what he can do in such matters; whence good esteem is to be won, especially with the multitude, who must be taken into account withal. Another admirable exercise, and one very befitting a man at court, is the game of tennis, in which are well shown the disposition of the body, the quickness and suppleness of every member, and all those qualities that are seen in nearly every other exercise. Nor less highly do I esteem vaulting on horse, which although it be fatiguing and difficult, makes a man very light and dexterous more than any other thing; and besides its utility, if this lightness is accompanied by grace, it is to my thinking a finer show than any of the others.

On the Nature and Purpose of Women and Men
BALDASSARE CASTIGLIONE

'Now you said that Nature's intention is always to produce the most perfect things, and therefore she would if possible always produce men, and that women are the result of some mistake or defect rather than of intention. But I can only say that I deny this completely. You cannot possible argue that Nature does not intend to produce the women without whom the human race cannot be preserved, which is something that Nature desires above everything else. For by means of the union of male and female, she produces children, who then return the benefits received in childhood by supporting their parents when they are old; then they renew them when they themselves have children. . . . In this way Nature, as if moving in a circle, fills out eternity and confers immortality on mortals. And since woman is as necessary to this process as man, I do not see how it can be that one is more the fruit of mere chance than the other. It is certainly true that Nature always intends to produce the most perfect things, and therefore always intends to produce the species man, though not male rather than female; and indeed, if Nature always produced males this would be imperfection: for just as there results from body and soul a composite nobler than its parts, namely man himself, so from the union of male and female there results a composite that preserves the human species, and without which its parts would perish. Thus male and female always go naturally together, and one cannot exist without the other. . . .'

Then signor Gaspare said: 'I do not wish us to go into such subtleties because these ladies would not understand them; and though I were to refute you with excellent arguments, they would still think that I was wrong, or pretend to at least; and they would at once give a verdict in their own favor. However, since we have made a beginning, I shall say only that, as you know, it is the opinion of very learned men that man is as the form and woman as the matter, and therefore just as form is more perfect than matter, and indeed it gives it its being, so man is far more perfect than woman. . . .'

The Magnifico Guiliano at once replied: 'The poor creatures do not wish to become men in order to make themselves more perfect but to gain their freedom and shake off the tyranny that men have imposed on them by their one-sided authority. Besides, the analogy you give of matter and form is not always applicable; for woman is not perfected by man in the way that matter is perfected by form. . . . Woman does not receive her being from man but rather perfects him just as she is perfected by him, and thus both join together for the purpose of procreation which neither can ensure alone. Moreover, I shall attribute woman's enduring love for the man with whom she has first been, and man's detestation for the first woman he possesses, . . . but to the resolution and constancy of women and the inconstancy of men. And for this, there are natural reasons: for because of its hot nature, the male sex possesses the qualities of lightness, movement and inconstancy, whereas from its coldness, the female sex derives its steadfast gravity and calm and is therefore more susceptible.'

Women and Witchcraft: "All Wickedness Is But Little to the Wickedness of a Woman"

Although the Renaissance period is generally described as an era of creativity and enlightened energy, there certainly existed intolerant attitudes as well. During the sixteenth century, the church established an organization that was designed to maintain purity of doctrine and authority over the faithful. The Inquisition, as it came to be called, was administered by Dominican friars, whose responsibilities had always involved the explanation of doctrine to those who had

---

"'All Wickedness Is But Little to the Wickedness of a Woman'" is from *Malleus Maleficiarum*, trans. M. Summers (London: John Rodker, 1920), pp. 43–44.

strayed from the path. Now they actively sought out those whose deeds and ideas seemed to contradict established Catholic doctrine. The Inquisition became a vehicle for reform through coercion, with allegiance being obtained through argument, intimidation, and torture if necessary.

Of special concern in the struggle against Satan was the perceived prevalence of witches. Men were accused of employing "black magic" as well, but women, especially elderly women, were often targeted as agents of the Devil. In the following excerpt from a manual entitled The Hammer of Witches *(1486), two Dominican friars establish the connection between women and witchcraft. Their explanation reveals a common attitude toward women during this era.*

Others again have propounded other reasons why there are more superstitious women found than men. And the first is, that they are more credulous; and since the chief aim of the devil is to corrupt faith, therefore he rather attacks them. . . . The second reason is that women are naturally more impressionable, and more ready to receive the influence of a disembodied spirit; and that when they use this quality well they are very good, but when they use it ill they are very evil.

The third reason is that they have slippery tongues, and are unable to conceal from their fellow-women those things which by evil arts they know, and, since they are weak, they find an easy and secret manner of vindicating themselves by witchcraft. . . . All wickedness is but little to the wickedness of a woman. And to this may be added that, as they are very impressionable, they act accordingly.

There are also others who bring forward yet other reasons, of which preachers should be very careful how they make use. For it is true that in the Old Testament the Scriptures have much that is evil to say about women, and this because of the first temptress, Eve, and her imitators. . . . But because in these times this perfidy is more often found in women than in men, as we learn by actual experience, if anyone is curious as to the reason, we may add to what has already been said the following: that since they are feebler both in mind and body, it is not surprising that they should come more under the spell of witchcraft.

CHRONOLOGY: The Age of the Renaissance

1265–1321	Life of poet Dante Alighieri (*Divine Comedy*).
1294–1303	Pope Boniface VIII boldly reasserts church's claim to temporal power in Clericis Laicos (1298) and Unam Sanctam (1302). Boniface attacked, captured, and beaten by agents of the French king, Philip IV (1303).
1309–1377	"Babylonian Captivity": Residency of popes transferred to Avignon, France.

1304–1374	Life of poet and papal critic, Petrarch, who is considered to be the "Father of Humanism."
1337–1453	Hundred Years' War rages intermittantly between England and France over English claims to the French throne.
1374–1444	Life of Leonardo Bruni, scholar and Chancellor of Florence, who gave definition to the humanist movement.
1378–1417	Great Schism, or division, between supporters of the popes in Rome and those who again reside in Avignon. Dispute has political ramifications as countries develop military alliances based on support of Rome or Avignon. Issue finally resolved by councils of the church.
1415	Execution of Czech reformer John Huss for heresy. After a decade of belligerent protests, the Hussites win significant religious reforms in Bohemia.
1434	Medici rule of Florence established by Cosimo d'Medici, banker to the popes, and patron of the arts.
1435–1455	Technology invented for movable type printing press by Johannes Gutenberg.
1452–1519	Life of Leonardo da Vinci, artist, scientist, and inventor.
1463–1494	Life of Pico della Mirandola, whose *Oration on the Dignity of Man* (1486) is the quintessential expression of humanism.
1478–1492	Florence ruled by Lorenzo d'Medici, called "The Magnificent." Florence at height of political and artistic influence.
1492	Columbus's first voyage to the eastern Bahamas in search of a route to India.
1492–1503	Corrupt papacy of Alexander VI.
1494–1498	Florence controlled by Dominican friar Girolamo Savonarola. He is excommunicated after a series of sermons condemning the pope. Savonarola welcomes French invasion of Charles VIII, but loses confidence of Florentines and is executed.
1498–1512	Florence survives as a true republic. Niccolò Machiavelli organizes the Florentine militia, which is defeated by Spanish mercenary forces (1512). Machiavelli looks toward a strong, practical rule and writes *The Prince* (1513).
1501–1504	Michelangelo's statue of David completed.
1503–1513	Papacy of Julius II, "Warrior Pope" and patron of the arts (commissions Michelangelo's painting of the Sistine Chapel, among other works).

| 1510–1511 | Raphael's School of Athens completed. |
| 1519–1521 | Hernando Cortés lands on the coast of Mexico and brutally defeats Aztec forces. |

STUDY QUESTIONS

1. How would you define "humanism"? Give examples of its most important tenets from the many sources offered in the section entitled "The Humanist Movement." According to Pico della Mirandola, what is man's relationship to God? The humanists were criticized by the church for their secular interest at the expense of devotion to God. Do you agree with this criticism? Were the humanists disrespectful of God and irreligious? Note especially Marsilio Ficino on this point. In his opinion, what is man's position with respect to God?

2. What is the essence of Savonarola's message in his sermon to the Florentines? Why is his oratorical technique so persuasive? In this regard, analyze his words and images. What makes a demagogue like Savonarola so attractive? Why did people follow him?

3. Niccolò Machiavelli has been called "the disciple of the Devil." After reading the excerpts from *The Prince,* why do you think this view has prevailed? Is it better for a prince to be loved or feared? Why kill all enemies or potential enemies when you come into power through crime? Interpret the phrase "the ends justify the means." How does Machiavelli's view of human nature compare with that of other Renaissance humanists? Do you see Machiavelli as moral, immoral, or amoral? Why did he write *The Prince?*

4. Why does Giorgio Vasari have such a low opinion of medieval art? What is wrong with it? Would you call him irreligious? Why or why not? Does his argument sound reasonable?

5. Why has Leonardo da Vinci been called a "universal man"? After reading the selections from his sketchbook, what impressions do you have of him? In answering this, make specific reference to passages in the sources. Leonardo was an illegitimate child and was very pleased with that fact. Why was illegitimacy beneficial for the aspiring Renaissance man?

6. Politically, the Renaissance in Italy was an insecure, chaotic period, with shifting alliances and numerous invasions. Amid all this disunity, an intense cultural creativity was reflected in the art and music of the period. Do you think that chaos is a prerequisite for creativity or at least a contributor to creative energy? Or are great art, literature, and music best fostered in an atmosphere of relative calm and security? Relate this question specifically to the Renaissance, but also give contemporary examples when possible.

7. What was a courtier, and what did Castiglione require of him? Why do you think Castiglione's book was so popular? What values of Renaissance society does it promote? According to Castiglione, what should be the relationship between women and men? Compare this discussion with the excerpts on

witchcraft. Why were women considered more superstitious and susceptible to the spell of Satan?

8. In 1929, the British author Virginia Woolf commented in her book *A Room of One's Own* that "women have served all these centuries as looking-glasses possessing the magic and delicious power of reflecting the figure of man at twice its natural size." How would you compare this idea to Castiglione's view that "woman does not receive her being from man, but rather perfects him just as she is perfected by him." Do you agree that the relationship between men and women is symbiotic or have women been held in lesser esteem throughout the centuries because they have been expected to enhance the image of men? How modern is Castiglione in his thinking?

9

The Reformation Era

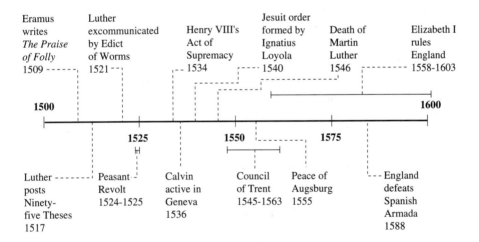

Eramus writes *The Praise of Folly* 1509

Luther excommunicated by Edict of Worms 1521

Henry VIII's Act of Supremacy 1534

Jesuit order formed by Ignatius Loyola 1540

Death of Martin Luther 1546

Elizabeth I rules England 1558-1603

1500

1600

1525

1550

1575

Luther posts Ninety-five Theses 1517

Peasant Revolt 1524-1525

Calvin active in Geneva 1536

Council of Trent 1545-1563

Peace of Augsburg 1555

England defeats Spanish Armada 1588

I am more afraid of my own heart than of the pope and all his cardinals. I have within me the great pope—Self.

—Martin Luther

Whatever your heart clings to and confides in, that is really your God.

—Martin Luther

All religions must be tolerated for every man must get to heaven his own way.

—Frederick the Great

CHAPTER THEMES

- ***Beliefs and Spirituality:*** Why did the Reformation occur? What led Martin Luther to challenge the belief system of the church? To what extent can faith and personal commitment to a religion change the course of history? Is faith a more powerful force than any army?

- ***Revolution:*** Was the Protestant Reformation a spiritual revolution, which consequently altered the political and economic institutions of Europe? Or was it a spiritually based reform movement that sought limited change in religious matters? Was Luther a revolutionary who was just as influential as Robespierre, Napoleon, or Lenin?

- ***Church/State Relationships:*** How did secular rulers benefit from the division of Christianity during the Reformation era? Which monarchs became "defenders of the church" and which aided the Reformers? Why? How did King Henry VIII of England solve the competition between church and state? Were his actions based on a sincere spirituality or on pure political expediency?

- ***Historical Change and Transition:*** Would the Protestant Reformation have occurred without Martin Luther? To what extent can an individual change the course of history? Was the printing press more essential to the success of this transitional movement than was Luther?

- ***The Big Picture:*** Was the Protestant Reformation ultimately the best thing that could have happened to the Christian church in the West? Do you expect another splinter movement in the contemporary Catholic Church, and if so what would be the ramifications?

During the Middle Ages, the church was the focal point of society. One's life was inextricably bound to the dictates of religion from the baptism that followed birth to the last rites that accompanied death. But by the sixteenth century, the omnipotence of the church, both in a spiritual sense and in the political realm, had been called into question. The church had lost much of the authority that had allowed it, in the eleventh through the thirteenth centuries, to claim superiority in the ongoing struggle between church and state. Crises such as the Babylonian Captivity (1309–1377) and the Great Schism (1378–1417) had strained the loyalty of the faithful and devastated the unity of the church for over a century. By the middle of the fifteenth century, the papacy was occupied with finding new sources of income that would help it fend off political challenges to its territory and increase its influence in the secular realm. The Renaissance papacy became infamous in its corruption and succumbed to the sensual delights of the world, as well as to the more traditional abuses of simony (the selling of church offices) and pluralism (allowing an individual to hold more than one position). Pope Julius II (1503–1513) was a glaring example of the age as, bedecked in armor, he personally led his armies into battle.

These actions resulted in a plentitude of criticism from within the church and especially from Christian humanists such as Desiderius Erasmus. Perhaps the most controversial practice of the church was the sale of indulgences. An indulgence was a piece of paper, signed by the pope, that remitted punishment in Purgatory due to sin. It was based on the theory that all humans are by nature sinful and after death will have to undergo a purgation of sin before being allowed to enter the Kingdom of Heaven. The pope, however, controlled an infinite "treasury of grace" that could be dispensed to mortals, thus removing the taint of sin and freeing the soul from Purgatory. By the late fifteenth century, the remission of sin was extended to both the living and the dead, and one could therefore liberate the soul of a relative "trapped" in Purgatory by purchasing an indulgence. The sale of indulgences became a routine affair of peddling forgiveness of purgatorial punishment, and the papacy came to rely on it as a necessary source of income. In 1507, Pope Julius II issued a plenary indulgence in order to obtain funds for the construction of Saint Peter's Basilica in Rome. Leo X renewed the indulgence in 1513, and subcommissioners actively began selling to the faithful. It was in response to this sale that a young monk named Martin Luther protested and nailed his *Ninety-five Theses* to the door of the Wittenberg church.

It is important to note that although Luther called into question the sale of indulgences, the main issue was salvation. Salvation, he reasoned, was cheap indeed if it could be purchased. Luther was tortured by the demands of God for perfection and worried that his own righteousness was insufficient for salvation in the sight of God. The church taught that in addition to winning grace through faith, one could also merit God's grace through good works or the remission of sin by indulgence. In fact, the purchase of an indulgence was considered a good work. But to Luther's mind, salvation required more, much more, and had nothing to do with deeds. While studying Saint Paul's Epistle to the Romans (1:17), Luther achieved a breakthrough that freed him from his torment: By the grace of God alone could one be saved, and this salvation was obtained only through faith in Christ. Neither good works nor indulgences could have anything to do with salvation. This stand called into question the very foundation of established Christian belief. Was the pope the true Vicar of Christ who spoke the words of God? If so, why did he advocate indulgences as a means of salvation? Was he in fact infallible on such matters of faith? The corruption of the papacy was also troubling, yet Luther's objective was not to overthrow the church, but to reform it from within.

The church replied to such a challenge with what it considered swift and appropriate action. Luther was excommunicated and his writings were condemned as heretical. It became evident to Luther that his desire to reform the church could be achieved only by defying the authority of the pope and starting a new church. Supported by the Holy Roman Emperor Charles V, the church sought to eliminate the root of the controversy. However, Luther was hidden, protected by the secular princes in Germany who, because of their location and traditional independence, were willing to defy their emperor and promote a religion that to them served a secular purpose. Yet Luther's movement was spiritual in nature, and he decried such political connections even as he sought the aid of the princes and nobility.

This chapter seeks to explore the spiritual and political foundations of the Reformation and the Protestant movement, from its inception by Martin Luther through its development under John Calvin to its royal imposition in England under Henry VIII and Elizabeth I. The Reformation era must also be viewed in its proper context, noting that during this period the Catholic Church made significant strides toward reform in its own right. The themes presented in this chapter include the role of the individual in changing history and the impact of religion on the political framework and social fabric of the times. The Reformation era was one of transition and instability that eventually led to war and bloodshed as nations fought during the sixteenth and seventeenth centuries in support of the "true religion." This bloody future was far from Martin Luther's mind when he nailed his *Ninety-five Theses* on the Wittenberg church door in 1517 and thus started a movement that shook the spiritual foundations of Christendom and altered the political face of Europe for centuries to come.

The State of the Papacy

The Criticism of the Northern Humanists

Humanism, the state of mind that formed the cornerstone of the Italian Renaissance, spread to the north in the late fifteenth and sixteenth centuries and became popular in the courts of France and England. The emphasis on the wonder, versatility, and individuality of humankind was evident in the art and literature of the period. Humanism also fostered scholarship which, in the north especially, tended to criticize the abuses within the church. The first selection is a response from the German humanist Jacob Wimpheling to a letter written by Enea Silvio Piccolomini (a cardinal and later Pope Pius II) that recounts grievances against the church in 1515, just two years before the Reformation began in earnest. The second piece is a satire written by the most famous of all northern humanists,

Desiderius Erasmus. In it he criticizes abuses within the church and thereby expresses the hope of promoting a greater spirituality in religion.

The Pope's Special Mission (1515)

JACOB WIMPHELING

The Council of Basel [1431–1449] pointed out that our sacred church fathers had written their canons for the purpose of assuring the Church of good government, and that honor, discipline, faith, piety, love, and peace reigned in the Church as long as these regulations were observed. Later however, vanity and greed began to prevail; the laws of the fathers were neglected, and the Church sank into immorality and depravity, debasement, degradation and abuse of office. This is principally due to papal reservations of prelacies and other ecclesiastical benefices, also to the prolific award of expectancies to future benefices, and to innumerable concessions and other burdens placed upon churches to clergy. To wit:

Church incomes and benefices are given to unworthy men and Italians.

High offices and lucrative posts are awarded to persons of unproven merit and character.

Few holders of benefices reside in their churches, for as they hold several posts simultaneously they cannot reside in all of them at once. Most do not even recognize the faces of their parishioners. They neglect the care of souls and seek only temporal rewards.

The divine service is curtailed.

Hospitality is diminished.

Church laws lose their force.

Ecclesiastical buildings fall into ruin.

The conduct of clerics is an open scandal.

Able, learned, and virtuous priests who might raise the moral and professional level of the clergy abandon their studies because they see no prospect of advancement.

The ranks of the clergy are riven by rivalry and animosity; hatred, envy, and even the wish for the death of others are aroused.

Striving after pluralities of benefices is encouraged.

Poor clerics are maltreated, impoverished, and forced from their posts.

Crooked lawsuits are employed to gather benefices.

Some benefices are procured through simony.

Other benefices remain vacant.

"The Pope's Special Mission" is from Gerald Strauss, *Manifestations of Discontent in Germany on the Eve of the Reformation* (Bloomington: Indiana University Press, 1971), pp. 43–45. Reprinted by permission of the publisher.

Able young men are left to lead idle and vagrant lives.

Prelates are deprived of jurisdiction and authority.

The hierarchical order of the Church is destroyed.

In this manner, a vast number of violations of divine and human law is committed and condoned. . . . "It is the pope's special mission," writes Enea, "to protect Christ's sheep. He should accomplish this task in such a way as to lead all men to the path of salvation. He must see that the pure Gospel is preached to all, that false doctrines, blasphemies, and unchristian teachings are eradicated, and that all enemies of the faith are driven from the lands of Christendom. He must heal schisms and end wars, abolish robbery, murder, arson, adultery, drunkenness and gluttony, spite, hatred and strife. He must promote peace and order, so that concord might reign among men, and honor and praise be given to God."

So Enea. My question is: Does a court of ephebes and muleteers and flatterers help the pope prevent schism and abolish blasphemy, wars, robbery, and the other crimes mentioned by Enea? Would he not be better served by men learned in canon law and Scripture, by men who know how to preach and can help the faithful ease their conscience in the confessional? The Council of Basel was surely inspired when it decreed that a third of all benefices should go to men versed in the Bible. . . . If I am not mistaken, the conciliar fathers wished to see the true Gospel of Christ preached everywhere. They wished honor and glory given to God. Ourselves want nothing else. We would rejoice if many men were to praise God, if every priest in his sufficiently endowed benefice were to serve God and celebrate the Eucharist, if popes and emperors, if the whole Church were to draw rich benefit from this holy work, the most efficacious office of them all.

The Praise of Folly (1509)

DESIDERIUS ERASMUS

The next to be placed among the regiment of fools are such as make a trade of telling or inquiring after incredible stories of miracles and prodigies. Never doubting that a lie will choke them, they will muster up a thousand several strange relations of spirits, ghosts, apparitions, raising of the devil, and such like bugbears of superstition; which the farther they are from being probably true, the more greedily they are swallowed, and the more devoutly believed. And these absurdities do not only bring an empty pleasure and cheap divertisement, but they are a good trade and procure a comfortable income to such priests and friars as by this craft get their gain.

To these again are nearly related such others as attribute strange virtues to the shrines and images of saints and martyrs, and so would make their

"The Praise of Folly" is from Desiderius Erasmus, *The Praise of Folly* (London: Hamilton Adams and Company, 1887), pp. 90–96, 143–149, 164–169.

credulous proselytes believe that if they pay their devotion to St. Christopher in the morning, they shall be guarded and secured the day following from all dangers and misfortunes. If soldiers, when they first take arms, shall come and mumble over such a set prayer before the picture of St. Barbara, they shall return safe from all engagements. Or if any pray to Erasmus on such particular holidays, with the ceremony of wax candles and other fopperies, he shall in a short time be rewarded with a plentiful increase of wealth and riches. The Christians have now their gigantic St. George, as well as the pagans had their Hercules; they paint the saint on horseback, and drawing the horse in splendid trapping very gloriously accoutred, they scarce refrain in a literal sense from worshipping the very beast.

What shall I say of such as cry up and maintain the cheat of pardons and indulgences? That by these compute the time of each soul's residence in purgatory, and assign them a longer or shorter continuance, according as they purchase more or fewer of these paltry pardons and saleable exemptions? Or what can be said bad enough of others, who pretend that by the force of such magical charms, or by the fumbling over their beads in the rehearsal of such, and such petitions; which some religious imposters invented, either for diversion, or, what is more likely, for advantage; they shall procure riches, honor, pleasure, health, long life, a lusty old age, nay, after death a sitting at the right hand of our Saviour in His kingdom.

By this easy way of purchasing pardons, any notorious highwayman, any plundering soldier, or any bribe-taking judge shall disburse some part of their unjust gains, and so think all their grossest impieties sufficiently atoned for. So many perjuries, lusts, drunkenness, quarrels, bloodsheds, cheats, treacheries, shall all be, as it were, struck a bargain for, and such a contract made, as if they had paid off all arrears and might now begin upon a new score.

From the same principles of folly proceeds the custom of each country's challenging their particular guardian-saint. Nay, each saint has his distinct office alloted to him and is accordingly addressed to upon the delivery in childbirth, a third to help persons to lost goods, another to protect seamen in a long voyage, a fifth to guard the farmer's cows and sheep, and so on. For to rehearse all instances would be extremely tedious.

And now for some reflections upon popes, cardinals and bishops, who in pomp and splendour have almost equalled if not [outdone] secular princes. Now if any one consider that their upper crotchet of white linen is to signify their unspotted purity and innocence; that their forked mitres, with both divisions tied together by the same knot, are to denote the joint knowledge of the Old and New Testament. That their always wearing gloves represents their keeping their hands clean and undefiled from lucre and covetousness; that the pastoral staff implies the care of a flock committed to their charge; that the cross carried before them expresses their victory over all carnal affection. He that considers this, and much more of the like nature, must needs conclude they are entrusted with a very weighty and difficult office. But alas, they think it sufficient if they can but feed themselves, and as to their flock, either commend them to the care of Christ Himself, or commit them to the guidance of some inferior vicars and curates. [They do] not so much as remember what their name of bishop imports, to wit, labor, pains and diligence, but by base simoniacal contracts, they are in a profane sense . . . overseers of their own gain and income.

The popes of Rome . . . pretend themselves Christ's vicars; if they would but imitate His exemplary life . . . an unintermitted course of preaching [and] attendance with poverty, nakedness, hunger and a contempt of this world; if they did but consider the import of the word pope, which signifies a father; or if they did but practice their surname of most holy, what order or degrees of men would be in a worse condition? There would be then no such vigorous making of parties and buying of votes in the conclave upon the vacancy of that see.

And those who, by bribery or other indirect courses, should get themselves elected would never secure their sitting firm in the chair by pistol, poison, force and violence. How much of their pleasure would be abated if they were but endowed with one dram of wisdom? Wisdom, did I say? Nay, with one grain of salt which our Saviour bid them not lose the savor of. All their riches, all their honor, their jurisdictions, their Peter's patrimony, their offices, their dispensations, their licenses, their indulgences, their long train and attendants, see in how short a compass I have abbreviated all their marketing of religion; in a word, all their perquisites would be forfeited and lost; and in their [place] would succeed watchings, fastings, tears, prayers, sermons, hard studies, repenting sighs and a thousand such like severe penalties. . . . The very Head of the Church, the spiritual prince, would then be brought from all his splendour to the poor equipage of a scrip and staff.

The Lutheran Reformation

The Indulgence Controversy

The controversy over the sale of indulgences was the spark that set the Reformation in motion. In 1515, Pope Leo X made an agreement with Archbishop Albert to sell indulgences in Mainz and other areas of northern Germany, with half the proceeds going to support Leo's construction of Saint Peter's Basilica in Rome and half going to pay for the debts that Albert had incurred in securing his church offices. In the first selection, Archbishop Albert gives instructions to those subcommissioners who actually sold the indulgences in 1517. One of the most successful subcommissioners was Johann Tetzel, prior of the Dominican monastery at Leipzig. His oratorical ability is evident in the second passage.

Instructions for the Sale of Indulgences (1517)
ARCHBISHOP ALBERT

Here follow the four principal graces and privileges, which are granted by the apostolic bull, of which each may be obtained without the other. In the matter of these four privileges preachers shall take pains to commend each to believers with the greatest care, and, in-so-far as in their power lies, to explain the same.

The first grace is the complete remission of all sins; and nothing greater than this can be named, since no man who lives in sin and forfeits the favor of God, obtains complete remission by these means and once more enjoys God's favor: moreover, through this remission of sins the punishment which one is obliged to undergo in Purgatory on account of the affront to the divine Majesty, is all remitted, and the pains of Purgatory completely blotted out. And although nothing is precious enough to be given in exchange for such a grace—since it is a free gift of God and grace is beyond price—yet in order that Christian believers may be the more easily induced to procure the same, we [offer them the following guidance]. . . . Because the conditions of men, and their occupations, are so various and manifold, and we cannot consider and assess them individually, we have therefore decided that the rates can be determined thus, according to recognized classifications: [Then follows a graded schedule of rates: kings and their families, bishops, etc., 25 Rhenish gold guilders; abbots, counts, barons, etc., 10; lesser nobles and ecclesiastics and others with incomes of 500, 6 guilders; citizens with their own income, 1 guilder; those with less, ½. Those with nothing shall supply their contribution with prayer and fasting, "for the kingdom of heaven should be open to the poor as much as the rich."]

The second grace is a confessional letter containing the most extraordinarily comforting and hitherto unheard of privileges, and which also retains its virtue even after our bull expires at the end of eight years, since the bull says: "they shall be participators now and for ever. . . ."

The third most important grace is the participation in all the possessions of the church universal, which consists herein, that contributors toward the said building, together with their decreased relations, who have departed this world in a state of grace, shall from now and for eternity be partakers in all petitions, intercessions, alms, fasting, prayers, in each and every pilgrimage, even those to the Holy Land; furthermore, in the stations at Rome, in the masses, canonical hours, flagellations, and all other spiritual goods which have brought forth or which shall be brought forth by the universal most holy church militant or by any of its members. Believers will become participants in all these things who purchase confessional letters.

"Instructions for the Sale of Indulgences" is from James H. Robinson, ed., *Translations and Reprints from the Original Sources of European History*, vol. 2, no. 6 (Philadelphia: University of Pennsylvania, 1902), pp. 4–9.

The fourth distinctive grace is for those souls which are in purgatory, and is the complete remission of all sins, which remission the pope brings to pass through his intercession to the advantage of said souls, in this wise; that the same contribution shall be placed in the chest by a living person as one would make for himself. . . . Moreover, preachers shall exert themselves to give this grace the widest publicity, since through the same, help will surely come to departed souls, and the construction of the Church of St. Peter will be abundantly promoted at the same time.

"How Many Sins Are Committed in a Single Day?" (1517)

JOHANN TETZEL

Venerable Sir, I pray you that in your utterances you may be pleased to make use of such words as shall serve to open the eyes of the mind and cause your hearers to consider how great a grace and gift they have had and now have at their very doors. Blessed eyes indeed, which see what they see, because already they possess letters of safe conduct by which they are able to lead their souls through that valley of tears, through that sea of the mad world, where storms and tempests and dangers lie in wait, to the blessed land of Paradise. Know that the life of man upon earth is a constant struggle. We have to fight against the flesh, the world and the devil, who are always seeking to destroy the soul. In sin we are conceived,—alas! what bonds of sin encompass us, and how difficult and almost impossible it is to attain to the gate of salvation without divine aid; since He causes us to be saved, not by virtue of the good works which we accomplish, but through His divine mercy, it is necessary then to put on the armor of God.

You may obtain letters of safe conduct from the vicar of our Lord Jesus Christ, by means of which you are able to liberate your soul from the hands of the enemy, and convey it by means of contrition and confession, safe and secure from all pains of Purgatory, into the happy kingdom. For know that in these letters are stamped and engraven all the merits of Christ's passion there laid bare. Consider, that for each and every mortal sin it is necessary to undergo seven years of penitence after confession and contrition, either in this life or in Purgatory.

How many mortal sins are committed in a day, how many in a week, how many in a month, how many in a year, how many in the whole course of life! They are well-nigh numberless, and those that commit them must needs suffer endless punishment in the burning pains of Purgatory.

"'How Many Sins Are Committed in a Single Day?'" is from James H. Robinson, ed., *Translations and Reprints from the Original Sources of European History,* vol. 2, no. 6 (Philadelphia: University of Pennsylvania, 1902), pp. 9–10.

Caricature of Johann Tetzel, the indulgence preacher who spurred Luther to publish his *Ninety-five Theses.* The last line of the caption reads: "As soon as gold in the basin rings, right then the soul to heaven springs." *(Wilfried Kirsch/Foto Kirsch)*

But with these confessional letters you will be able at any time in life to obtain full indulgence for all penalties imposed upon you, in all cases except the four reserved to the Apostolic See. Therefore throughout your whole life, whenever you wish to make confession, you may receive the same remission, except in cases reserved to the Pope, and afterwards, at the hour of death, a full indulgence as to all penalties and sins, and your share of all spiritual blessings that exist in the church militant and all its members.

Do you not know that when it is necessary for anyone to go to Rome, or undertake any other dangerous journey, he takes his money to a broker and gives a certain percent—five or six or ten—in order that at Rome or elsewhere he may receive again his funds intact, by means of the letter of this same broker? Are you not willing, then, for the fourth part of a florin, to obtain these letters, by virtue of which you may bring, not your money but your divine and immortal soul safe and sound into the land of Paradise?

Salvation Through Faith Alone
MARTIN LUTHER

Martin Luther's transformation from monk to reformer was not a preconceived act; it developed gradually not only as a result of corruption around him, but especially because of a spiritual awakening. Luther struggled with the need to imitate the perfection of Christ, which was important in the eyes of the church for salvation. Luther realized that because of his nature as a human, he was too sinful, and that no amount of prayer or good works could help him achieve the Kingdom of Heaven. After much study and pain, he concluded that salvation was a free gift of God and that a person was saved by faith in Christ alone. In the first selection, Luther explains his enlightenment. The second document is his answer to the indulgences being sold by Johann Tetzel. When Luther posted the Ninety-five Theses *on the church in Wittenberg, the Reformation began in earnest.*

I, Martin Luther, entered the monastery against the will of my father and lost favor with him, for he saw through the knavery of the monks very well. On the day on which I sang my first mass he said to me, "Son, don't you know that you ought to honor your father?" . . . Later when I stood there during the mass and began the canon, I was so frightened that I would have fled if I hadn't been admonished by the prior. . . .

When I was a monk I was unwilling to omit any of the prayers, but when I was busy with public lecturing and writing I often accumulated my appointed prayers for a whole week, or even two or three weeks. Then I would take a Saturday off, or shut myself in for as long as three days without food and

"Salvation Through Faith Alone" is from Theodore Tappert and H. Lehmann, eds., *Luther's Works, vol. 54: Table Talk* (Philadelphia: Fortress Press, 1965), pp. 85, 193–194, 234, 264–265. Copyright © 1965 by Fortress Press. Reprinted by permission of Augsburg Fortress.

drink, until I had said the prescribed prayers. This made my head split, and as a consequence I couldn't close my eyes for five nights, lay sick unto death, and went out of my senses. Even after I had quickly recovered and I tried again to read, my head went 'round and 'round. Thus our Lord God drew me, as if by force, from that torment of prayers. . . .

The words "righteous" and "righteousness of God" struck my conscience like lightning. When I heard them I was exceedingly terrified. If God is righteous [I thought], he must punish. But when by God's grace I pondered, in the tower and heated room of this building, over the words, "He who through faith is righteous shall live" [Rom. 1:17] and "the righteousness of God" [Rom. 3:21], I soon came to the conclusion that if we, as righteous men, ought to live from faith and if the righteousness of God should contribute to the salvation of all who believe, then salvation won't be our merit but God's mercy. My spirit was thereby cheered. For it's by the righteousness of God that we're justified and saved through Christ. These words [which had before terrified me] now became more pleasing to me. The Holy Spirit unveiled the Scriptures for me in this tower.

God led us away from all this in a wonderful way; without my quite being aware of it he took me away from that game more than twenty years ago. How difficult it was at first when we journeyed toward Kemberg after All Saints' Day in the year 1517, when I first made up my mind to write against the crass errors of indulgences! Jerome Schurff advised against this: "You wish to write against the pope? What are you trying to do? It won't be tolerated!" I replied, "And if they have to tolerate it?" Presently Sylvester, master of the sacred palace, entered the arena, fulminating against me with this syllogism: "Whoever questions what the Roman church says and does is heretical. Luther questions what the Roman church says and does, and therefore [he is a heretic]." So it all began.

The Ninety-five Theses (1517)
MARTIN LUTHER

In the desire and with the purpose of elucidating the truth, a disputation will be held on the underwritten propositions at Wittenberg, under the presidency of the Reverend Father Martin Luther, Monk of the Order of St. Augustine, Master of Arts and of Sacred Theology, and ordinary Reader of the same in that place. He therefore asks those who cannot be present and discuss the subject with us orally, to do so by letter in their absence. In the name of our Lord Jesus Christ, Amen. . . .

"The Ninety-five Theses" is from H. Wace and C. A. Buchheim, eds., *First Principles of the Reformation* (London: John Murray, 1883), pp. 6–13.

5. The Pope has neither the will nor the power to remit any penalties except those which he has imposed by his own authority, or by that of the canons.

6. The Pope has no power to remit any guilt, except by declaring and warranting it to have been remitted by God; or at most by remitting cases reserved for himself; in which cases, if his power were [disregarded], guilt would certainly remain. . . .

20. Therefore the Pope, when he speaks of the plenary remission of all penalties, does not really mean of all, but only of those imposed by himself.

21. Thus those preachers of indulgences are in error who say that by the indulgences of the Pope a man is freed and saved from all punishment.

22. For in fact he remits to souls in Purgatory no penalty which they would have had to pay in this life according to the canons.

23. If any entire remission of all penalties can be granted to any one it is certain that it is granted to none but the most perfect, that is to very few.

24. Hence, the greater part of the people must needs be deceived by his indiscriminate and high-sounding promise of release from penalties.

25. Such power over Purgatory as the Pope has in general, such has every bishop in his own diocese, and every parish priest in his own parish. . . .

27. They are wrong who say that the soul flies out of Purgatory as soon as the money thrown into the chest rattles.

28. It is certain that, when money rattles in the chest, avarice and gain may be increased, but the effect of the intercession of the Church depends on the will of God alone. . . .

32. Those who believe that, through letters of pardon, they are made sure of their own salvation will be eternally damned along with their teachers.

33. We must especially beware of those who say that these pardons from the Pope are that inestimable gift of God by which man is reconciled to God. . . .

35. They preach no Christian doctrine who teach that contrition is not necessary for those who buy souls (out of Purgatory) or buy confessional licenses.

37. Every true Christian, whether living or dead, has a share in all the benefits of Christ and of the Church, given by God, even without letters of pardon.

42. Christians should be taught that it is not the wish of the Pope that buying of pardons should be in any way compared to works of mercy.

43. Christians should be taught that he who gives to a poor man, or lends to a needy man, does better than if he bought pardons.

45. Christians should be taught that he who sees any one in need, and, passing him by, gives money for pardons, is not purchasing for himself the indulgences of the Pope but the anger of God. . . .

50. Christians should be taught that, if the Pope were acquainted with the exactions of the Preachers of pardons, he would prefer that the Basilica

of St. Peter should be burnt to ashes rather than that it should be built up with the skin, flesh, and bones of his sheep. . . .

62. The true treasure of the Church is the Holy Gospel of the glory and grace of God.

66. The treasures of indulgences are nets, wherewith they now fish for the riches of men.

86. Again; why does not the Pope, whose riches are at this day more ample than those of the wealthiest of the wealthy, build the Basilica of St. Peter with his own money rather than with that of poor believers. . . .

94. Christians should be exhorted to strive to follow Christ their head through pains, deaths, and hells.

95. And thus not trust to enter heaven through many tribulations, rather than in the security of peace.

Breaking with Rome

Within a period of six months in 1520, Luther finished three important treatises that sealed his break with the Roman church. Excerpts from two of these treatises are presented below. In the Address to the Christian Nobility of the German Nation, *Luther advocated that the secular authorities in Germany undertake the reform that the church would not. The treatise* On Christian Liberty *describes the liberating effect that pure faith in Christ has on an individual. Luther had written an accompanying letter to Pope Leo X stating that his writings were directed at the false doctrine and corruption surrounding the church and not meant as a personal slight against Leo; nevertheless, the break with Rome was complete, as events in the next year proved.*

Address to the Christian Nobility of the German Nation (1520)

MARTIN LUTHER

The Romanists have, with great adroitness, drawn three walls round themselves, with which they have hitherto protected themselves, so that no one could reform them, whereby all Christendom has fallen terribly.

Firstly, if pressed by the temporal power, they have affirmed and maintained that the temporal power has no jurisdiction over them, but on the contrary that the spiritual power is above the temporal.

"Address to the Christian Nobility" is from H. Wace and C. A. Buchheim, eds., *First Principles of the Reformation* (London: John Murray, 1883), pp. 20–21, 23, 25–26, 28–30. Translation modernized by the editor.

Secondly, if it were proposed to admonish them with the Scriptures, they objected that no one may interpret the Scriptures but the Pope.

Thirdly, if they are threatened with a Council, they pretend that no one may call a Council but the Pope.

Thus they have secretly stolen our three rods, so that they may be unpunished, and entrenched themselves behind these three walls, to act with all wickedness and malice, as we now see. . . .

Now may God help us, and give us one of those trumpets, that overthrew the walls of Jericho, so that we may blow down these walls of straw and paper, and that we may set free our Christian rods, for the chastisement of sin, and expose the craft and deceit of the devil, so that we may amend ourselves by punishment and again obtain God's favor.

The First Wall

Let us, in the first place, attack the first wall.

It has been devised, that the Pope, bishops, priests and monks are called the Spiritual Estate; Princes, lords, [artisans] and peasants are the Temporal Estate; which is a very fine, hypocritical device. But let no one be made afraid by it; and that for this reason: That all Christians are truly of the Spiritual Estate, and there is no difference among them save of office alone. As St. Paul says (I Cor. 12), we are all one body, though each member does its own work, to serve the others. This is because we have one baptism, one gospel, one faith, and are all Christians alike; for baptism, gospel and faith, these alone make Spiritual and Christian people. . . .

It follows then, that between layman and priests, princes and bishops, or as they call it, between spiritual and temporal persons, the only real difference is one of office and function, and not of estate: for they are all of the same Spiritual Estate, true priests, bishops and Popes, though their functions are not the same: just as among priests and monks every man has not the same functions. . . . Christ's body is not double or twofold, one temporal, the other spiritual. He is one head, and he has one body. . . .

The Second Wall

The second wall is even more tottering and weak: that they alone pretend to be considered masters of the Scriptures; although they learn nothing of them all their life, they assume authority, and juggle before us with impudent words, saying that the Pope cannot err in matters of faith, whether he be evil or good; [yet] they cannot prove it by a single letter. That is why the canon law contains so many heretical and unchristian, [even], unnatural laws. . . . If I had not read it, I could never have believed, that the Devil should have put forth such follies at Rome and find a following. . . .

The Third Wall

The third wall falls of itself, as soon as the first two have fallen; for if the Pope acts contrary to the Scriptures, we are bound to stand by the Scriptures, to punish and to constrain him, according to Christ's commandment: ["If your brother sins against you, go and tell him his fault. . . . If he does not listen, . . . tell it to the church (Matt. 18, 15–17)."] . . . If then I am to accuse him before the church, I must collect the church together. Moreover they can show nothing in the Scriptures giving the Pope sole power to call and confirm councils; they have nothing but their own laws; but these hold good only so long as they are not injurious to Christianity and the laws of God. . . .

Therefore when need requires and the Pope is a cause of offence to Christendom, in these cases whoever can best do so, as a faithful member of the whole body, must do what he can to procure a true free council. . . .

And now I hope we have laid bare the false, lying spectre with which the Romanists have long terrified and stupefied our consciences. And we have shown that, like all the rest of us, they are subject to the temporal sword; that they have no authority to interpret the Scriptures by force without skill; and that they have no power to prevent a council or to pledge it in accordance with their pleasure, or to bind it beforehand, and deprive it of its freedom; and that if they do this, they are verily of the fellowship of Antichrist and the Devil, and have nothing of Christ but the name.

On Christian Liberty (1520)

MARTIN LUTHER

That I may open, then, an easier way for the ignorant—for these alone I am trying to serve—I first lay down these two propositions, concerning spiritual liberty and servitude.

A Christian man is the most free lord of all, and subject to none; a Christian man is the most dutiful servant of all, and subject to every one.

Although these statements appear contradictory, yet, when they are found to agree together, they will be highly serviceable to my purpose. They are both the statements of Paul himself, who says: "Though I be free from all men, yet have I made myself servant unto all" (I Cor. 9.19), and: "Owe no man anything, but to love one another." (Rom. 13.8) Now love is by its own nature dutiful and obedient to the beloved object. Thus even Christ, though Lord of all things, was yet made of a woman; made under the law; at once free and a servant; at once in the form of God and in the form of a servant.

Let us examine the subject on a deeper and less simple principle. Man is composed of a two-fold nature, a spiritual and a bodily. As regards the

---

"On Christian Liberty" is from H. Wace and C. A. Buchheim, eds., *First Principles of the Reformation* (London: John Murray, 1883), pp. 104–125. Translation modernized by the editor.

spiritual nature, which they name the soul, he is called the spiritual, inward, new man; as regards the bodily nature, which they name the flesh, he is called the fleshly, outward, old man. The Apostle speaks of this: "Though our outward man perish, yet the inward man is renewed day by day." (II Cor. 4.16) The result of this diversity is that in the Scriptures opposing statements are made concerning the same man; the fact being that in the same man these two men are opposed to one another; the flesh lusting against the spirit, and the spirit against the flesh. (Gal. 5.17) . . .

And, to cast everything aside, even speculations, meditations, and whatever things can be performed by the exertions of the soul itself, are of no profit. One thing, and one alone, is necessary for life, justification, and Christian liberty; and that is the most holy word of God, the Gospel of Christ, as He says: "I am the resurrection and the life; he that believeth in me shall not die eternally" (John 11.25); and also (John 8.36) "If the Son shall make you free, ye shall be free indeed"; and (Matt. 4.4) "Man shall not live by bread alone."

Let us therefore hold it for certain and firmly established that the soul can do without everything, except the word of God, without which none at all of its wants are provided for. But having the word, it is rich and wants for nothing; since that is the word of life, of truth, of light, of peace, of justification, of salvation, of joy, of liberty, of wisdom, of virtue, of grace, of glory, and of every good thing. . . .

Therefore, the first care of every Christian ought to be, to lay aside all reliance on works, and strengthen his faith alone more and more, and by it grow in the knowledge, not of works, but of Christ Jesus, who has suffered and risen again for him. . . . And yet there is nothing of which I have need—for faith alone suffices for my salvation—unless that, in it, faith may exercise the power and empire of its liberty. This is the inestimable power and liberty of Christians.

Nor are we only kings and the freest of all men, but also priests for ever, a dignity far higher than kingship, because by that priesthood we are worthy to appear before God, to pray for others, and to teach one another mutually the things which are of God. For these are the duties of priests, and they cannot possibly be permitted to any unbeliever. Christ has obtained for us this favor, if we believe in Him, that, just as we are His brethren, and co-heirs and fellow kings with Him, so we should be also fellow priests with Him, and venture with confidence, through the spirit of faith, to come into the presence of God, and cry "Abba, Father!" and to pray for one another, and to do all things which we see done and figured in the visible and corporeal office of priesthood. But to an unbelieving person nothing renders service or works for good. He himself is in servitude to all things, and all things turn out for evil to him, because he used all things in an impious way for his own advantage, and not for the glory of God. And thus he is not a priest, but a profane person, whose prayers are turned into sin; nor does he ever appear in the presence of God, because God does not hear sinners. . . .

Here you will ask: "If all who are in the Church are priests, by what character are those, whom we now call priests, to be distinguished from the laity?" I reply: By the use of these words, "priest," "clergy," "spiritual person," "ecclesiastic," an injustice has been done, since they have been transferred from the remaining body of Christians to those few, who are now, by a hurtful custom, called ecclesiastics. For Holy Scripture makes no distinction between them, except that those, who are now boastfully called popes, bishops, and lords, it calls ministers, servants, and stewards, who are to serve the rest in the ministry of the World, for teaching the faith of Christ and the liberty of believers. For though it is true that we are all equally priests, yet we cannot, nor, if we could, ought we all to minister and teach publicly. Thus Paul says: "Let a man so account of us as of the ministers of Christ, and stewards of the mysteries of God." (I Cor. 4.1)

This bad system has now issued a pompous display of power, and such a terrible tyranny, that no earthly government can be compared to it, as if the laity were something else than Christians. Through this perversion of things it has happened that the knowledge of Christian grace, of faith, of liberty, and altogether of Christ, has utterly perished, and has been succeeded by an intolerable bondage to human works and laws; and, according to the Lamentations of Jeremiah, we have become the slaves of the vilest men on earth, who abuse our misery to all the disgraceful and ignominious purposes of their own will. . . .

True then are these two sayings: Good works do not make a good man, but a good man does good works. Bad works do not make a bad man, but a bad man does bad works. Thus it is always necessary that the substance or person should be good before any good works can be done, and that good works should follow and proceed from a good person. As Christ says: "A good tree cannot bring forth evil fruit, neither can a corrupt tree bring forth good fruit." (Matt. 7.18) Now it is clear that the fruit does not bear the tree, nor does the tree grow on the fruit; but, on the contrary, the trees bear the fruit and the fruit grows on the trees. . . .

Here is the truly Christian life; here is faith really working by love; when a man applies himself with joy and love to the works of that freest servitude, in which he serves others voluntarily and for naught; himself abundantly satisfied in the fullness and riches of his own faith.

Address at the Diet of Worms (1521)

MARTIN LUTHER

After his excommunication by Leo X in June 1520, Luther was summoned to appear before a diet (assembly) of prelates and officials of the Holy Roman Empire in the city of Worms to answer questions about his heretical writings. His safe conduct to the meeting was guaranteed by the Holy Roman Emperor Charles V, who presided over the Diet. Accompanied by his secular protector, Frederick the

"Address at the Diet of Worms" is from J. Pelikan, ed., *Luther's Works, vol. 2: Career of the Reformer* (Saint Louis: Concordia Publishing House, 1958), pp. 109–112. Copyright © 1958 by Concordia Publishing House. Used by permission.

Wise, Elector of Saxony, Luther appeared on April 17, 1521. When asked whether he wished to defend all his writings or retract some, Luther delivered this famous speech. On April 23, Luther secretly left Worms and was hidden by friends at Wartburg castle. Charles V's edict against Luther is the second selection.

"Most serene emperor, most illustrious princes, most clement lords, obedient to the time set for me yesterday evening, I appear before you, beseeching you, by the mercy of God, that your most serene majesty and your most illustrious lordships may deign to listen graciously to this my cause—which is, as I hope, a cause of justice and truth. If through my inexperience I have either not given the proper titles to some, or have offended in some manner against court customs and etiquette, I beseech you to kindly pardon me, as a man accustomed not to courts but to the cells of monks. I can bear no other witness about myself but that I have taught and written up to this time with simplicity of heart, as I had in view only the glory of God and the sound instruction of Christ's faithful. . . .

"[A] group of my books attacks the papacy and the affairs of the papists as those who both by their doctrines and very wicked examples have laid waste the Christian world with evil that affects the spirit and the body. For no one can deny or conceal this fact, when the experience of all and the complaints of everyone witness that through the decrees of the pope and the doctrines of men the consciences of the faithful have been most miserably entangled, tortured, and torn to pieces. Also, property and possessions, especially in this illustrious nation of Germany, have been devoured by an unbelievable tyranny and are being devoured to this time without letup and by unworthy means. [Yet the papists] by their own decrees . . . warn that the papal laws and doctrines which are contrary to the gospel or the opinions of the fathers are to be regarded as erroneous and reprehensible. If, therefore, I should have retracted these writings, I should have done nothing other than to give strength to this [papal] tyranny and I should have opened not only windows but doors to such great godlessness. It would rage further and more freely than ever it has dared up to this time. Yes, from the proof of such a revocation on my part, their wholly lawless and unrestrained kingdom of wickedness would become still more intolerable for the already wretched people; and their rule would be further strengthened and established, especially if it should be reported that this evil deed had been done by me by virtue of the authority of your most serene majesty and the whole Roman Empire. Good God! What a cover for wickedness and tyranny I should have then become.

"I have written a third sort of book against some private and (as they say) distinguished individuals—those, namely, who strive to preserve the Roman tyranny and to destroy the godliness taught by me. Against these I confess I have been more violent than my religion or profession demands. But then, I do not set myself up as a saint; neither am I disputing about my life, but about the teachings of Christ. It is not proper for me to retract these works, because by this retraction it would again happen that tyranny and godlessness

Martin Luther by Lucas Cranach the Elder (1521). This picture of Luther was painted in the same year that he defied the pope and the Holy Roman Emperor at the Diet of Worms. His complete break with Rome ushered in an age of religious reform. *(Lucas Cranach, "Martin Luther," Firenze, Galleria degli Uffizi)*

would, with my patronage, rule and rage among the people of God more violently than ever before.

"However, because I am a man and not God, I am not able to shield my books with any other protection than that which my Lord Jesus Christ himself offered for his teaching. When questioned before Annas about his teaching and struck by a servant, he said: 'If I have spoken wrongly, bear witness to the wrong' [John 18:19–23]. If the Lord himself, who knew that he could not err, did not refuse to hear testimony against his teaching, even from the lowliest servant, how much more ought I, who am the lowest scum and able to do nothing except err, desire and expect that somebody should want to offer testimony against my teaching! Therefore, I ask by the mercy of God, may your most serene majesty, most illustrious lordships, or anyone at all who is able, either high or low, bear witness, expose my errors, overthrowing them by the writings of the prophets and the evangelists. Once I have been taught I shall be quite ready to renounce every error, and I shall be the first to cast my books into the fire.

"From these remarks I think it is clear that I have sufficiently considered and weighed the hazards and dangers, as well as the excitement and dissensions aroused in the world as a result of my teachings, things about which I was gravely and forcefully warned yesterday. To see excitement and dissension arise because of the Word of God is to me clearly the most joyful aspect of all in these matters. For this is the way, the opportunity, and the result of the Word of God, just as He [Christ] said, 'I have not come to bring peace, but a sword. For I have come to set a man against his father, etc.' [Matthew 10:34–35]. . . . Therefore we must fear God. I do not say these things because there is a need of either my teachings or my warnings for such leaders as you, but because I must not withhold the allegiance which I owe my Germany. With these words I commend myself to your most serene majesty and to your lordships, humbly asking that I not be allowed through the agitation of my enemies, without cause, to be made hateful to you. I have finished."

When I had finished, the speaker for the emperor said, as if in reproach that I had not answered the question, that I ought not call into question those things which had been condemned and defined in councils; therefore what was sought from me was not a horned response, but a simple one, whether or not I wished to retract.

Here I answered:

"Since then your serene majesty and your lordships seek a simple answer, I will give it in this manner, neither horned nor toothed: Unless I am convinced by the testimony of the Scriptures or by clear reason (for I do not trust either in the pope or in councils alone, since it is well known that they have often errored and contradicted themselves), I am bound by the Scriptures I have quoted and my conscience is captive to the Word of God. I cannot and I will not retract anything, since it is neither safe nor right to go against conscience.

"I cannot do otherwise, here I stand, may God help me, Amen."

The Edict of Worms (1521)

EMPEROR CHARLES V

In view of . . . the fact that Martin Luther still persists obstinately and perversely in maintaining his heretical opinions, and consequently all pious and God-fearing persons abominate and abhor him as one mad or possessed by a demon . . . we have declared and made known that the said Martin Luther shall hereafter be held and esteemed by each and all of us as a limb cut off from the Church of God, an obstinate schismatic and manifest heretic. . . .

And we publicly attest by these letters that we order and command each and all of you, as you owe fidelity to us and the Holy Empire, and would escape the penalties of the crime of treason, and the ban and over-ban of the Empire, and the forfeiture of all regalia, fiefs, privileges, and immunities, which up to this time you have in any way obtained from our predeccessors, ourself, and the Holy Roman Empire—commanding, we say, in the name of the Roman and imperial majesty, we strictly order that immediately after the expiration of the appointed twenty days, terminating on the fourteenth day of May, you shall refuse to give the aforesaid Martin Luther hospitality, lodging, food, or drink; neither shall any one, by word or deed, secretly or openly, succor or assist him by counsel or help; but in whatever place you meet him, you shall proceed against him; if you have sufficient force, you shall take him prisoner and keep him in close custody; you shall deliver him, or cause him to be delivered, to us or at least let us know where he may be captured. In the meanwhile you shall keep him closely imprisoned until you receive notice from us what further to do, according to the direction of the laws. And for such holy and pious work we will indemnify you for your trouble and expense. . . .

And in order that all this may be done and credit given to this document we have sealed it with our imperial seal, which has been affixed in our imperial city of Worms, on the eighth day of May, after the birth of Christ 1521, in the second year of our reign over the Roman Empire, and over our other lands the sixth.

By our lord the emperor's own command.

Social and Political Aspects of the Lutheran Reformation

The Lutheran Reformation was not simply spiritual or corrective in nature, for it had many political and social repercussions as well. In response to the celibacy demanded of priests by the church, Luther advocated that clergy be allowed to marry. He himself married a former nun. Such defiance in one sphere was confusing for

"The Edict of Worms" is from James H. Robinson, ed., *Readings in European History*, vol. 2 (Boston: Ginn and Company, 1906), pp. 87–88.

certain elements of society that saw Luther as their champion as well. In 1524, a major peasant revolt broke out in Germany as social and economic conflicts came to a head. The peasants demanded freedom from the long-standing feudal obligations of serfdom. Luther understood that the survival of his movement depended on the political influence and protection of the nobility. Although Luther sympathized with the peasants, he clearly sided with the nobility, and they savagely crushed the revolt.

On Celibacy and Marriage

MARTIN LUTHER

First, not every priest can do without a woman, not only on account of the weakness of the flesh but much more because of the needs of the household. If, then, he is to keep a woman, and the pope grants him permission to do so, but he may not have her in marriage, what is this but leaving a man and a woman alone and forbidding them to fall? It is like putting fire and straw together and commanding that there shall be neither smoke nor fire. Secondly, the pope has as little power to give this command as he has to forbid eating, drinking, the natural process of bodily elimination or becoming fat. No one, therefore, is in duty bound to keep this commandment and the pope is responsible for all the sins that are committed against this ordinance, for all the souls lost thereby, and for all consciences thereby confused and tortured. Consequently, he undoubtedly has deserved long ago that someone should drive him out of the world, so many souls has he strangled with this devilish snare; although I hope that God has been more gracious to many of them at their end than the pope had been during their life. Nothing good has ever come out of the papacy and its laws, nor ever will.

Listen! In all my days I have not heard the confession of a nun, but in the light of Scripture I shall hit upon how matters fare with her and know I shall not be lying. If a girl is not sustained by great and exceptional grace, she can live without a man as little as she can without eating, drinking, sleeping, and other natural necessities. Nor, on the other hand, can a man dispense with a wife. The reason for this is that procreating children is an urge planted as deeply in human nature as eating and drinking. That is why God has given and put into the body the organs, arteries, fluxes, and everything that serves it. Therefore what is he doing who would check this process and keep nature from running its desired and intended course? He is attempting to keep nature from being nature, fire from burning, water from wetting, and a man from eating, drinking, and sleeping.

Whoever intends to enter married life should do so in faith and in God's name. He should pray that it may prosper according to His will and that marriage may not be treated as a matter of fun and folly. It is a hazardous matter and as serious as anything on earth can be. Therefore we should not rush into it as the world does, in keeping with its frivolousness and wantonness and in pursuit of its pleasure; but before taking this step we should consult God, so that we may lead our married life to His glory. Those who do not go about it in this way may certainly thank God if it turns out well. If it turns out badly, they should not be surprised; for they did not begin it in the name of God and did not ask for His blessing.

Condemnation of the Peasant Revolt (1524)
MARTIN LUTHER

In my preceding pamphlet [on the "Twelve Articles"] I had no occasion to condemn the peasants, because they promised to yield to law and better instruction, as Christ also demands (Matt. 7.1). But before I can turn around, they go out and appeal to force, in spite of their promises and rob and pillage and act like mad dogs. From this it is quite apparent what they had in their false minds, and that what they put forth under the name of the gospel in the "Twelve Articles" was all vain pretense. In short, they practice mere devil's work, and it is the arch-devil himself who reigns at Muhlhausen, indulging in nothing but robbery, murder, and bloodshed; as Christ says of the devil in John 8.44, "he was a murderer from the beginning." Since, therefore, those peasants and miserable wretches allow themselves to be led astray and act differently from what they declared, I likewise must write differently concerning them; and first bring their sins before their eyes, as God commands (Isa. 58.1; Ezek. 2.7), whether perchance some of them may come to their senses; and, further, I would instruct those in authority how to conduct themselves in this matter.

With threefold horrible sins against God and men have these peasants loaded themselves, for which they have deserved a manifold death of body and soul.

First, they have sworn to their true and gracious rulers to be submissive and obedient, in accord with God's command (Matt. 22.21), "Render therefore unto Caesar the things which are Caesar's," and (Rom. 13.1), "Let every soul be subject unto the higher powers." But since they have deliberately and sacrilegiously abandoned their obedience, and in addition have dared to oppose their lords, they have thereby forfeited body and soul, as perfidious, perjured, lying, disobedient wretches and scoundrels are wont to do. Wherefore St. Paul judges them saying (Rom. 13.2), "And they that resist shall receive to themselves damnation." The peasants will incur this sentence, sooner or later; for God wills that fidelity and allegiance shall be sacredly kept.

Second, they cause uproar and sacrilegiously rob and pillage monasteries and castles that do not belong to them, for which, like public highwaymen

"Condemnation of the Peasant Revolt" is from James H. Robinson, ed., *Readings in European History,* vol. 1 (Boston: Ginn and Company, 1904), pp. 106–108.

and murderers, they deserve the twofold death of body and soul. It is right and lawful to slay at the first opportunity a rebellious person, who is known as such, for he is already under God's and the emperor's ban. Every man is at once judge and executioner of a public rebel; just as, when a fire starts, he who can extinguish it first is the best fellow. Rebellion is not simply vile murder, but is like a great fire that kindles and devastates a country; it fills the land with murder and bloodshed, makes widows and orphans, and destroys everything, like the greatest calamity. Therefore, whosoever can, should smite, strangle, and stab, secretly or publicly, and should remember that there is nothing more poisonous, pernicious, and devilish than a rebellious man. Just as one must slay a mad dog, so, if you do not fight the rebels, they will fight you, and the whole country with you.

Third, they cloak their frightful and revolting sins with the gospel, call themselves Christian brethren, swear allegiance, and compel people to join them in such abominations. Thereby they become the greatest blasphemers and violators of God's holy name, and serve and honor the devil under the semblance of the gospel, so that they have ten times deserved death of body and soul, for never have I heard of uglier sins. And I believe also that the devil foresees the judgment day, that he undertakes such an unheard-of measure; as if he said, "It is the last and therefore it shall be the worst; I'll stir up the dregs and knock the very bottom out." May the Lord restrain him! Lo, how mighty a prince is the devil, how he holds the world in his hands and can put it to confusion; who else could so soon capture so many thousands of peasants, lead them astray, blind and deceive them, stir them to revolt, and make them the willing executioners of his malice. . . .

And should the peasants prevail (which God forbid!),—for all things are possible to God, and we know not but that he is preparing for the judgment day, which cannot be far distant, and may purpose to destroy, by means of the devil, all order and authority and throw the world into wild chaos,—yet surely they who are found, sword in hand, shall perish in the wreck with clear consciences, leaving to the devil the kingdom of this world and receiving instead the eternal kingdom. For we are come upon such strange times that a prince may more easily win heaven by the shedding of blood than others by prayers.

In the Wake of Luther

John Calvin and the Genevan Reformation

Although Lutheranism formed the basis of the Reformation, by the mid-sixteenth century it had lost much of its energy and was confined to Germany and Scandinavia. The movement was spread throughout Europe by other reformers, the most influential of whom was John Calvin (1509–1564).

A trained lawyer and classical scholar, Calvin had been a convert to Luther's ideas and was forced to leave France, eventually settling in Geneva in the 1530s. There in the 1540s, he established a very structured society that can best be described as a theocracy. Calvin's strict adherence to biblical authority and his singular strength of personality can be seen in his treatise, On the Necessity of Reforming the Church. *In it he defines the church as "a society of all the saints, a society spread over the whole world, and existing in all ages, yet bound together by the one doctrine and the one Spirit of Christ." In the words of Saint Cyprian, which Calvin often quoted, "We cannot have God for our Father without having the Church for our mother." The importance of this idea cannot be overestimated in Calvin's understanding of doctrine and of the reform of the church. In the following excerpt from his famous treatise, which was addressed to the Holy Roman Emperor Charles V in 1544, Calvin expressed disgust that the church had become divorced from the society of saints it was supposed to serve. The continuity of the church as a universal embodiment of all believers had to be reestablished through clerical reform and a reconceptualization of Spirit.*

On the Necessity of Reforming the Church (1544)

JOHN CALVIN

In the present condition of the empire, your Imperial Majesty, and you, Most Illustrious Princes, necessarily involved in various cares, and distracted by a multiplicity of business, are agitated, and in a manner tempest-tossed.... I feel what nerve, what earnestness, what urgency, what ardor, the treatment of this subject requires.... First, call to mind the fearful calamities of the Church, which might move to pity even minds of iron. Nay, set before your eyes her squalid and unsightly form, and the sad devastation which is everywhere beheld. How long, pray, will you allow the spouse of Christ, the mother of you all, to lie thus protracted and afflicted—thus, too, when she is imploring your protection, and when the means of relief are at hand? Next, consider how much worse calamities impend. Final destruction cannot be far off, unless you interpose with the utmost speed. Christ will, indeed, in the way which to him seems good, preserve his Church miraculously, and beyond human expectation; but this I say, that the consequence of a little longer delay on your part will be, that in Germany we shall not have even the form of a Church. Look round, and see how many indications threaten that ruin which it is your duty to prevent, and announce that it is actually at hand. These things speak loud enough, though I were silent....

Divine worship being corrupted by so many false opinions, and perverted by so many impious and foul superstitions, the sacred Majesty of God is insulted with atrocious contempt, his holy name profaned, his glory only not trampled under foot. Nay, while the whole Christian world is openly polluted with idolatry, men adore, instead of Him, their own fictions. A thousand

"On the Necessity of Reforming the Church" is from John Calvin, *Tracts and Treatises on the Reformation of the Church,* trans. by Henry Beveridge, vol. 1 (Edinburgh: Calvin Translation Society, 1844), pp. 231–234.

superstitions reign, superstitions which are just so many open insults to Him. The power of Christ is almost obliterated from the minds of men, the hope of salvation is transferred from him to empty, frivolous, and insignificant cere- monies, while there is a pollution of the Sacraments not less to be execrated. Baptism is deformed by numerous additions, the Holy Supper [communion] is prostituted to all kinds of ignominy, religion throughout has degenerated into an entirely different form. . . .

In the future, therefore, as often as you shall hear the croaking note— "The business of reforming the Church must be delayed for the present"— "there will be time enough to accomplish it after other matters are trans- acted"—remember, Most Invincible Emperor, that the matter on which you are to deliberate is, whether you are to leave to your posterity some empire or none. Yet, why do I speak of posterity? Even now, while your own eyes behold, it is half bent, and totters to its final ruin . . .

But be the issue what it may, we will never repent of having begun, and of having proceeded thus far. The Holy Spirit is a faithful and unerring witness to our doctrine. We know, I say, that it is the eternal truth of God that we preach. We are, indeed, desirous, as we ought to be, that our ministry may prove salutary to the world; but to give it this effect belongs to God, not to us. If, to punish, partly the ingratitude, and partly the stubbornness of those to whom we desire to do good, success must prove desperate, and all things go to worse, I will say what it befits a Christian man to say, and what all who are true to this holy profession will subscribe: We will die, but in death even be conquerors, not only because through it we shall have a sure passage to a bet- ter life, but because we know that our blood will be as seed to propagate the Divine truth which men now despise.

Predestination: Institutes of the Christian Religion (1536)

JOHN CALVIN

Calvin's doctrines were primarily Lutheran in nature, but Calvin went a step beyond and stressed the doctrine of predestination: One's salvation had already been deter- mined by God, and those elect who had been "chosen" gave evidence of their calling by living exemplary lives. Calvinism became popular in the Netherlands and Scotland and it formed the core of the Puritan belief that was to be so influential in the colo- nization of America. The following excerpts reveal Calvin's justification for reform, his concept of predestination, and his strict regulation of lives and beliefs in Geneva.

The covenant of life is not preached equally to all, and among those to whom it is preached, does not always meet with the same reception. This diversity

"Predestination" is from John Calvin, *Institutes of the Christian Religion*, vol. 2, trans. Henry Bev- eridge (Edinburgh: Calvin Translation Society, 1845), pp. 529, 534, 540.

displays the unsearchable depth of the divine judgment, and is without doubt subordinate to God's purpose of eternal election. But it is plainly owing to the mere pleasure of God that salvation is spontaneously offered to some, while others have no access to it, great and difficult questions immediately arise, questions which are inexplicable, when just views are not entertained concerning election and predestination. . . .

By predestination we mean the eternal decree of God, by which he determined with himself whatever he wished to happen with regard to every man. All are not created on equal terms, but some are preordained to eternal life, others to eternal damnation; and, accordingly, as each has been created for one or other of these ends, we say that he has been predestined to life or to death. . . .

We say, then, that Scripture clearly proves this much, that God by his eternal and immutable counsel determined once for all those whom it was his pleasure one day to admit to salvation, and those whom, on the other hand, it was his pleasure to doom to destruction. We maintain that this counsel, as regards the elect, is founded on his free mercy, without any respect to human worth, while those whom he dooms to destruction are excluded from access to life by a just and blameless, but at the same time incomprehensible judgment. In regard to the elect, we regard calling as the evidence of election, and justification as another symbol of its manifestation, until it is fully accomplished by the attainment of glory. But as the Lord seals his elect by calling and justification, so by excluding the reprobate either from the knowledge of his name or the sanctification of his Spirit, he by these marks in a manner discloses the judgment which awaits them. I will here omit many of the fictions which foolish men have devised to overthrow predestination. There is no need of refuting objections which the moment they are produced abundantly betray their hollowness. I will dwell only on those points which either form the subject of dispute among the learned, or may occasion any difficulty to the simple. . . .

Genevan Catechism (1541): Concerning the Lord's Supper
JOHN CALVIN

The minister: Have we in the supper simply a signification of the things above mentioned, or are they given to us in reality?

The child: Since Jesus Christ is truth itself there can be no doubt that the promises he has made regarding the supper are accomplished, and that what is figured there is verified there also. Wherefore according as he promises

"Genevan Catechism" is from James H. Robinson, ed., *Translations and Reprints from the Original Sources of European History,* vol. 3 (Philadelphia: University of Pennsylvania, 1902), pp. 8–9.

and represents I have no doubt that he makes us partakers of his own substance, in order that he may unite us with him in one life.

The minister: But how may this be, when the Body of Jesus Christ is in heaven, and we are on this earthly pilgrimage?

The child: It comes about through the incomprehensible power of his spirit, which may indeed unite things widely separated in space.

The minister: You do not understand then that the body is enclosed in the bread, or the blood in the cup?

The child: No. On the contrary, in order that the reality of the sacrament be achieved our hearts must be raised to heaven, where Jesus Christ dwells in the glory of the Father, whence we await him for our redemption; and we are not to seek him in these corruptible elements.

The minister: You understand then that there are two things in this sacrament: the natural bread and wine, which we see with the eye, touch with the hand and perceive with the taste; and Jesus Christ, through whom our souls are inwardly nourished?

The child: I do. In such a way moreover that we have there the very witness and so say a pledge of the resurrection of our bodies; since they are made partakers in the symbol of life.

Ordinances for the Regulation of Churches (1547)
JOHN CALVIN

Blasphemy

Whoever shall have blasphemed, swearing by the body or by the blood of our Lord, or in similar manner, he shall be made to kiss the earth for the first offence; for the second to pay 5 sous, and for the third 6 sous, and for the last offence be put in the pillory for one hour.

Drunkenness

1. That no one shall invite another to drink under penalty of 3 sous.
2. That taverns shall be closed during the sermon, under penalty that the tavern-keeper shall pay 3 sous, and whoever may be found therein shall pay the same amount.
3. If any one be found intoxicated he shall pay for the first offence 3 sous and shall be remanded to the consistory; for the second offence he shall

"Ordinances for the Regulation of Churches" is from James H. Robinson, ed., *Translations and Reprints from the Original Sources of European History,* vol. 3 (Philadelphia: University of Pennsylvania, 1902), pp. 10–11.

be held to pay the same sum of 6 sous, and for the third 10 sous and be put in prison.

Songs and Dances

If any one sing immoral, dissolute or outrageous songs, or dance the virollet or other dance, he shall be put in prison for three days and then sent to the consistory.

Usury

That no one shall take upon interest or profit more than five percent, upon penalty of confiscation of the principal and of being condemned to make restitution as the case may demand.

Games

That no one shall play at any dissolute game or at any game whatsoever it may be, neither for gold nor silver nor for any excessive stake, upon penalty of 5 sous and forfeiture of stake played for.

How Soon Marriage Must Be Consummated After the Promise Is Made

After the promise is made the marriage shall not be deferred more than six weeks; otherwise the parties shall be called before the consistory, in order that they may be admonished. If they do not obey they shall be remanded to the council and be constrained to celebrate the marriage.

Concerning the Celebration of the Marriage

That the parties at the time when they are to be married shall go modestly to the church, without drummers and minstrels, preserving an order and gravity becoming to Christians; and this before the last stroke of the bell, in order that the marriage blessing may be given before the sermon. If they are negligent and come too late they shall be sent away.

Of the Common Residence of Husband and Wife

That the husband shall have his wife with him and they shall live in the same house, maintaining a common household, and if it should happen that one should leave the other to life apart they shall be summoned in order that they may be remonstrated with and constrained to return, the one to the other.

The Spread of Calvinism (1561)

GIOVANNI MICHIEL

*Giovanni Michiel was the Venetian ambassador to the French court when he of-
fered this appraisal of the dangerous spread of Calvinism in France. Notice his
comparison of Calvinism to a contagious disease. In Michiel's view, religious
disputes would inevitably result in civil war and political chaos.*

Unless it otherwise please the Almighty, religious affairs will soon be in an evil
case in France, because there is not one single province uncontaminated....
This contagion has penetrated so deeply that it affects every class of persons,
and, what appears more strange, even the ecclesiastical body itself. I do not
mean only priests, friars, and nuns, for there are but few monasteries that are
not corrupted, but even bishops and many of the principal prelates, who
hitherto had not shown any such disposition.... But you Serenity must learn
that while the people and the populace show fervent devotion by frequenting
the churches and observing the Catholic rites, all other classes are supposed
to be disaffected, and the nobility perhaps more than any other class, and,
particularly, persons of forty years of age and under.... It has now been determined not to proceed against any disaffected persons unless they venture
to preach, persuade, and to take part publicly in congregations and assemblies. All other such persons are allowed to live, and some have been set at
liberty, and released from the prisons of Paris and of other parts of the kingdom. A great number of these last have still remained in the kingdom,
preaching and speaking publicly, and boasting that they have gained their
cause against the Papists, as they delight to style their adversaries; so that,
now, every one of them is assured against the fear of being questioned; and
there exists thus a silent truce because while formerly all suspected persons
had to quit the kingdom, and to retire some to Geneva, some to Germany,
and some to England, now they not only do not leave the country, but a large
number of those who had already emigrated have returned....

Your Serenity will hardly believe the influence and the great power which
the principal minister of Geneva, by name Calvin, a Frenchman, and a native
of Picardy, possesses in this kingdom; he is a man of extraordinary authority,
who by his mode of life, his doctrines, and his writings, rise superior to all the
rest; and it is almost impossible to believe the enormous sums of money
which are secretly sent to him from France to maintain his power. It is sufficient to add that if God does not interfere, there is great and imminent danger that one of two things will happen in this kingdom; either that the truce
which is desire and sought publicly, will end by the heretics having churches
wherein they can preach, read, and perform their rites, according to their

"The Spread of Calvinism" is from *Calendar of State Papers, Venetian VII*, pp. 322–323.

doctrine, without hindrance; . . . or else, that we shall see an obedience to the Pope and to the Catholic rites enforced, and shall have resort to violence and imbrue our hands in noble blood. For these reasons I foresee a manifest and certain division in the kingdom, and civil war as a consequence; and this will be the cause of the ruin both of the kingdom and of religion, because upon a change in religion a change in the state necessarily follows.

The Radical Reformation: Anabaptism

It is somewhat misleading to speak of the "radical Reformation" as a distinct entity because in a sense the Reformation movement by its very nature was a radical departure from the doctrines of the western Christian church. Still, within a period of great religious upheaval and change, personal insight and interpretation of Holy Scripture often resulted in the establishment of congregations, which were formed around derivative issues and channeled through dynamic leadership. These new ideas and leaders, working within a fluid spiritual and political environment, became immediate and even radical threats to authority figures like Luther and Calvin. Indeed, this points up the relative nature of "radicalism." After Luther and Calvin had established their "radical" doctrines and congregations in defiance of papal and Imperial decrees, they sought to protect their gains and thus became defenders of their own status quo, suspicious and resistant to alternate interpretations of the Bible. One of the most dramatic movements of the period that challenged both the Catholic and Protestant religious landscape was that of Anabaptism.

Anabaptism arose within the cradle of the Swiss reformation in Zurich. The most influential local reformer during the 1520s was the contentious Ulrich Zwingli (1484–1531). He and Luther had their own disagreements about the nature of the Eucharist that were never resolved. But Zwingli's influence within Zurich was substantial and thus he became concerned when in 1523, a few members of the congregation proposed the idea that baptism should not be administered to infants who were unaware of the significance of the act. Baptism, they argued, should be reserved for adults who had made a conscious decision to receive it. Therefore, adults in the community must be "rebaptized" in order to be truly cleansed of original sin. After much discussion, Zwingli and the Zurich city council pronounced that infant baptism was scriptural and ordered the baptism of all unbaptized children and the prohibition of radical meetings. Anabaptists would not be tolerated in Zurich.

Although Anabaptists believed theirs to be a righteous cause with scriptural support, city governments in southern Germany and Austria disagreed and revived ancient decrees forbidding rebaptism as adults, under penalty of death. After 1529, Anabaptists could be sent to prison and even burned at the stake in some communities. Anabaptists, spiritually unified by persecution and driven together by economic need, saw themselves in the mold of early Christians, migrating and endeavoring to found the "true church" in the New Jerusalem.

One such group of Anabaptists succeeded in establishing itself in the town of Münster, Germany and actually assumed control of the city in 1534. All those who refused to be rebaptized were ordered to leave the city. Under the leadership of two Dutchmen, Jan Matthijs and Jan van Leyden, radical steps were taken to convert Münster to its biblical image as the New Jerusalem. This rather unrepresentative group of radical Anabaptists ordered all books except the Bible to be burned and even introduced communism and polygamy. Condemned by both Catholics and Protestants alike, the town was seized by the forces of Charles V. The Anabaptist leaders were slowly tortured and eventually executed.

The Münster debacle served to cast suspicions on all Anabaptists, since it was thought that the inherent doctrine would lead to immorality and social chaos. Amidst a savage European persecution, the movement was refocused by the exhaustive and moderate efforts of Menno Simons, who died in 1561. Anabaptism would later arrive in America through the influence of the Mennonites.

The following sources recount the spiritual premise and struggles of this tragic radical sect. Ultimately, their fate confirmed the intolerance of the Reformation era.

On the Mystery of Baptism
HANS HUT

Now we will speak further about the baptism of rebirth, which is not an exterior sign that Christ shows, but a bath of souls that washes and rinses them clean from all lusts and desires of the heart. That is, baptism is an obliteration of all the lusts and disobedience which are in us and which incite us to oppose God. . . . The whole world . . . is baptized in the same way. But all people do not emerge from baptism alike, nor is baptism equally useful to all. The wicked certainly come to it but do not emerge again, because with their lusts they sink to the very bottom in creaturely things. They have not been able to let go of either worldly things or themselves. But they live continually and happily in lust and the love of creaturely things. . . .

So, to those who live for a renewal of their lives, baptism is not only a submersion and drowning, but a joyous departure from the wavering wishes and impulses of our own desires. We once lived hectically—for these desires and this vehemence are the conflict of the spirit—and the flesh which is in a person. In this conflict, if the desires of the flesh, the lusts, the impulses, and the attraction and repulsions are to be stilled and overcome, then the sweet waters—that is, lust and the desires of the flesh—must become, by contrast and to the same degree, acrid and bitter through the movement of divine justice that sweeps out everything. For the desires were sweet in a creaturely way—coming not from God but from the person himself, for he was inclined to them. Then the vehement conflict in one's consciousness between spirit and flesh arises. Oh, the way to life gets narrow at this point! Then the person, through the dying-out of the old man, must turn to a new life in God. And this is the rebirth in baptism. Here such fears, trembling, and shuddering attack the person as those of a woman in childbirth. When God directs such waters through one's soul, one must be patient, until he has been taught and understand. And peace from the impulses of the flesh is born on this earth. Them, in the patient waiting of his time, in the endurance of God's hand, a person becomes a prepared residence of God. Then, just as the troubled waters become clear, the bitter sweet, and the turbulent calm, the son of God appears on the waters, stretches out his hand, pulls a person from the turbulence, and lets him se that he unlocks our darkness through his truth—that is, the flow of the living water that is concealed in us. Christ does this in order to prepare us sinful, earthly people for eternal life. The waters which rush into the soul are tribulation, affliction, fear, trembling, and worry. So baptism is suffering. So Christ was also constricted by his baptism before it was perfected in his death. True baptism is nothing but conflict with sin through one's whole life. So the waters of adversity wash from the soul all the lasciviousness and lust which defile and cling to it. . . .

Therefore, baptism has its time and goal and age, just as our first birth has its goal and time and also its age. And thus all creatures are born to their essence and perfection through water; and without baptism nothing is able to live fully and be blessed. Infant baptism, the practice of the existing world, is a pure invention of man, without the word and commandment of God. It is a defrauding of simple people, a pernicious trick on all Christendom, and an arch-villain's cloak for all the godless. For not a single verse in all of Scripture can be brought forth to defend it. Infant baptism is so totally without foundation that the godless must all remain silent about it, no matter how eloquent they wax. According to the words of Christ in the context of Scripture, no one should baptize another unless the baptized person is able, in passionate fidelity, to account for his faith and trust. If this sign of baptism is accepted, it points to the true baptism of suffering which follows, about which I have spoken and without which no one is able to be saved. But the contrived baptism of children is not only useless, it is also the greatest hindrance to truth.

"They Should Be Drowned Without Mercy": Measures Against Anabaptists

18th January 1525

Erroneous opinion has arisen concerning baptism, that young children should not be baptized until they reach years of discretion and know the

"They Should Be Drowned Without Mercy" is from Hans J. Hillerbrand, *The Reformation* (New York: Harper & Row, Publishers, 1964), p. 229–230, 232–233. Copyright © 1964 by SCM Press Ltd., and Harper & Row Inc. Used by permission.

meanings of faith. Some have accordingly left their children unbaptized. Out Lords, the Mayors, Council and Great Council, called the Two Hundred of Zurich, held a disputation concerning this matter to learn the view of the Holy Scripture. It was agreed that, contrary to such erroneous opinion, children should be baptized as soon as they are born. Therefore all those who have recently left their children unbaptized must have them baptized within eight days. Whoever does not want to do this must leave our town, jurisdiction and domain with his wife, children and property, or await further action against him. Everyone will know how to conduct himself.

7ᵗʰ March 1562

Our Lords . . . have for some time earnestly endeavored to turn the misguided and erring Anabaptists from their errors. None the less, some of them, hardened against their oaths, vows and promises, have appeared disobedient to the detriment of public authority and government and the destruction of the common weal and true Christian institution. Several of them, both men, women and girls, were harshly punished and imprisoned by order of the Lords. It is therefore the earnest commandment, order and warning of these our Lords that no one in town, country and domain, whether man, woman or girl, shall henceforth baptize another. Whoever hereafter baptizes someone will be apprehended by our Lords and, according to this present decree, be drowned without mercy. It is hoped that everyone will know to avoid this lest he cause his own death. This pronouncement is to be proclaimed in the three parishes on Sunday.

Communism In Münster (1535)

HEINRICH GRESBECK

The prophets, preachers and the entire council deliberated and felt that everything should be held in common. It was first ordered that everyone who had copper money should bring it to the City Hall, where he would receive a different currency. This was done. After the prophets and the preachers had reached an agreement with the council in this matter, it was announced in the sermons that all things should be held in common. Thus they said in the sermon: "Dear Brothers and sisters, inasmuch as we are one people, and are brothers and sisters one to another, it is God's will that we should bring our money, silver and gold together. Each one of us should

"Communism In Münster" is from Hans J. Hillerbrand, *The Reformation* (New York: Harper & Row, Publishers, 1964), p. 257. Copyright © 1964 by SCM Press Ltd., and Harper & Row Inc. Used by permission.

have as much as any other. Therefore everyone is to bring his money to the chancellery near the City Hall. There the council will be present and receive the money." Likewise preacher Stutenbernt said: "A Christian should not have any money; everything which Christian brothers and sisters possess belongs to one as well as the other. You shall not lack anything, be it food, clothes, house, or goods. What you need, you shall receive, God will not suffer you to lack anything. One thing shall be held as much in common as the other. It belongs to all of us. It is mine as well as yours, and yours as well as mine." Thus they persuaded the people so that some of them brought their money, silver and gold, indeed everything they owned. But there was much inequality in Münster, where one supposedly had as much as any other.

Some people in the city turned in all their money, silver and gold and did not keep anything. Others turned in part and kept part. Still others did not turn in anything.

"The Devil Laughed Hard": Polygamy in Münster (1535)

HEINRICH GRESBECK

Thus [Anabaptist leader] Jan van Leiden—together with the bishop, the preachers and the twelve elders—proclaimed concerning the married estate that it was God's will that they should inhabit the earth. Everyone should take three or four wives, or as many as were desired. However, they should live with their wives in a divine manner. This pleased some men and not others. Husbands and wives objected that the marital estate was no longer to be kept.

Jan van Leiden was the first to take a second wife in addition to the one he had married in Münster. It was said that there was still another wife in Holland. Jan van Leiden continued to take more wives until he finally had fifteen. In similar fashion all the Dutchmen, Frisians, and true Anabaptists had additional wives. Indeed, they compelled their first wives to go and obtain second wives for them. The devil laughed hard about this. Those who had old wives and wanted to take young ones had their way. . . . The Anabaptists in Münster, especially the leaders, such as Jan van Leiden and the twelve elders, were planning it well. They had done away with money, gold and silver, and had driven everyone from his property. They sat in the houses, held the property, and also wanted to have ten or twelve wives. I presume they called this the "right baptism."

The English Reformation

The Protestant Reformation has often been viewed as essentially a spiritual move-ment which had fundamental political and social impact throughout Europe. But the motives of some reformers were not purely spiritual, and they sought a more expedient premise. As the Reformation spread to Switzerland, northern Ger-many, and Scandinavia, it met with little organized opposition. But England, it seemed, was prepared to resist any incursion. Its monarch, Henry VIII, was a gregarious and dynamic king who had grown up amidst political intrigue and international power plays in the court of his father, Henry Tudor (VII). Henry VIII knew how to handle himself politically and sought to maintain domestic tranquility by promoting secure alliances abroad.

Henry VIII had himself been a pawn in his father's political accommoda-tions. In order to preserve an alliance with Spain, Henry had been allowed to marry his brother's widow, Catherine of Aragon, through a special papal dis-pensation. For a time, this arrangement seemed to work all around. Henry VIII had proved a dutiful son of the church by writing a religious tract supporting the pope which earned him the title "Defender of the Faith." But Henry became concerned when Catherine suffered a series of miscarriages and was unable to provide a male heir to the Tudor throne. Although she bore Henry a daughter named Mary, this did not conciliate the English king. To secure the succession, he needed a male heir, so he turned to a young favorite at court named Anne Boleyn. When Henry wanted an annulment of his marriage to Catherine on the grounds that his union with his brother's widow was incestuous and accursed by God, the pope could not renege on his earlier dispensation. The pathway to a workable solution seemed closed. Henry became increasingly consumed with the need to stabilize the future of England with a male heir. He finally decided to break with Rome and found the Church of England with himself as head. He granted himself a divorce from Catherine and married Anne in 1533. He was excommunicated by the pope "with the sword of eternal damnation" that same year. Henry did not buckle. The Protestant Reformation had come to England, although through political expediency rather than through spiritual commit-ment.

The following sources are essential in understanding the English Reforma-tion. The first is the Act of Supremacy (1534), which recognized Henry VIII as the supreme head of the Church of England. He had already extorted from the English bishops, abbots, and priests written declaration that the pope had no more authority in England than any other foreign bishop. The next source is an excerpt from "The Act of Succession" (1534), which declared his marriage with Catherine void and provided for the royal succession: Anne's daughter, the princess Elizabeth, would succeed unless Anne should have sons by the king. Note the harsh provisions should anyone not accept the arrangement. Anne, in-deed, failed to produce a son and paid for it with her life as Henry accused her of adultery and moved on to more fertile pastures. Elizabeth was then bumped down the succession ladder.

The Supremacy Act (1534): "The Only Supreme Head of the Church of England"

Albeit the king's majesty firstly and rightfully is and ought to be the supreme head of the Church of England, and so is recognized by the clergy of this realm in their Convocations . . . ; be it enacted by authority of this present Parliament, that the king our sovereign lord, his heirs and successors, kings of this realm, shall be taken, accepted, and reputed the only supreme head in earth of the Church of England . . . and shall have and enjoy, annexed and united to the imperial crown of this realm, as well the title and style thereof, as all honors, dignities, pre-eminences, jurisdictions, privileges, authorities, immunities, profits, and commodities to the said dignity of supreme head of the same Church . . . ; and that our said sovereign lord, his heirs and successors, kings of this realm, shall have full power and authority from time to time to visit, repress, redress, reform, order, correct, restrain, and amend all such errors, heresies, abuses, offenses, contempts, and enormities, whatsoever they be . . . to the pleasure of Almighty God, the increase of virtue in Christ's religion, and for the conservation of the peace, unity, and tranquility of this realm. . . .

The Act of Succession (1534)

If any person or persons, of what estate, dignity, or condition whosoever they be, maliciously, by writing, print, deed, or act, procure or do any thing or things to the prejudice, slander, or derogation of the said lawful matrimony solemnized between your Majesty and the said Queen Anne, or to the peril or slander of any of the heirs of your Highness, being limited by this act to inherit the crown of this realm, every such person and persons, and their aiders and abettors, shall be adjudged high traitors, and every such offense shall be adjudged high treason, and the offenders . . . shall suffer pain of death, as in cases of high treason.

All are to be sworn truly, firmly, and constantly, without fraud or guile, to observe, fulfill, maintain, and keep, . . . to the utmost of their powers, the whole effects and contents of this present act.

"The Supremacy Act" is from *Statutes of the Realm*, vol. 3, no. 492, in Henry Gee and W. J. Hardy, eds., *Documents Illustrative of English Church History* (London: Macmillan and Co., Ltd., 1896), pp. 243–244.

"The Act of Succession" is from *Statutes of the Realm*, vol. 3, no. 471, in Henry Gee and W. J. Hardy, eds., *Documents Illustrative of English Church History* (London: Macmillan and Co., Ltd., 1896), p. 240.

The Execution of Bishop Fisher and Sir Thomas More (1535): "When I Come Down, Let Me Shift for Myself"

The break with the Catholic church had its advantages. Henry confiscated all the wealth and land of the English churches, which helped him stabilize his economy and reward his supporters. Clergy who resisted his authority were executed, and England entered a difficult period of religious and political instability. Two of the most famous dissenters were John Fisher, who served as the bishop of Rochester, and Sir Thomas More, the scholar and lawyer who was known for his honesty, fidelity, and wit. More had served as Henry's chancellor before refusing to deny the legitimacy of Henry's first marriage to Catherine and the authority of the pope as Vicar of Christ.

The twenty-second day of the same month John Fisher, Bishop of Rochester, was beheaded, and his head set upon London Bridge. This bishop was of very many men lamented; for he was reported to be a man of great learning, and a man of very good life, but therein wonderfully deceived, for he maintained the pope to be supreme head of the Church, and very maliciously refused the king's title of supreme head. It was said that the pope, for that he held so manfully with him and stood so stiffly in his cause, did elect him cardinal, and sent the cardinal's hat as far as Calais, but the head it should have stood on was as high as London Bridge before the hat could come to Bishop Fisher. . . .

Also the sixth day of July was Sir Thomas More beheaded for the like treason before rehearsed, which, as you have heard, was for the denying of the king's Majesty's supremacy. This man was also counted learned, and, as you have heard before, he was lord chancellor of England, and in that time a great persecutor of such as detested the supremacy of the bishop of Rome, which he himself so highly favored that he stood to it until he was brought to the scaffold on the Tower Hill, where on a block his head was stricken from his shoulders and had no more harm.

I cannot tell whether I should call him a foolish wise man, for undoubtedly he, beside his learning, had a great wit, but it was so mingled with taunting and mocking. . . . When he went up the stair on the scaffold he desired one of the sheriff's officers to give him his hand to help him up, and said, "When I come down again let me shift for myself as well as I can."

"The Execution of Bishop Fisher and Sir Thomas More" is from James H. Robinson, *Readings in European History*, vol. 2 (Boston: Ginn and Company, 1906), pp. 142–143.

Good Queen Mary (1553): "Loving Subjects and Christian Charity"

Henry VIII was certainly no Protestant, although he utilized the political and economic advantages of declaring himself a Protestant. He enforced Catholic doctrine in his Church of England while rejecting the control of the pope. But after his death, his son Edward VI (1547–1553), embraced Protestantism and issued an official Book of Common Prayer *and several statutes establishing the primacy of Protestant doctrine. But upon Edward's death in 1553, Henry VIII's daughter by Catherine, Mary Tudor, became queen. She had been raised a Catholic and was married to Philip II, King of Spain. Her brutal attempts to reinstate Catholicism in England by burning heretics earned her the epithet "Bloody Mary." The following accounts offer two perspectives on her reign from 1553 to 1558.*

The queen's highness well remembering what great inconvenience and dangers have grown to this her highness's realm in times past through the diversity of opinions in questions of religion, and hearing also that now of late, since the beginning of her most gracious reign, the same contentions be again much renewed, through certain false and untrue reports and rumors spread by some light and evil-disposed persons, has thought good to do to understand to all her highness's most loving and obedient subjects her most gracious pleasure in manner and form following.

First, her majesty being presently by the only goodness of God settled in her just possession of the imperial crown of this realm . . . cannot now hide that religion, which God and the world know she has ever professed from her infancy; which as her majesty is minded to observe and maintain for herself by God's grace during her time, so does her highness much desire, and would be glad, the same were of all her subjects quietly and charitably embraced.

And yet she does signify unto all her majesty's loving subjects, her most gracious disposition and clemency; . . . forbidding nevertheless all her subjects of all degrees, at their perils, to move seditions or stir unquietness in her people; . . . and therefore wills and charges and commands all her said good loving subjects to live together in quiet sort and Christian charity, leaving those new-found devilish terms of papist or heretic and such like, and applying their whole care, study, and travail to live in the fear of God, exercising their conversations in such charitable and godly doing, as their lives may indeed express that great hunger and thirst of God's glory and holy word. . . .

"Good Queen Mary" is from Henry Gee and W. J. Hardy, eds., *Documents Illustrative of English Church History* (London: Macmillan and Co., Ltd., 1896), pp. 373–374.

Bloody Mary: "To Be Burned According to the Wholesome Laws of Our Realm"

Whereas John Hooper, who of late was called bishop of Rochester and Gloucester, by due order of the laws ecclesiastic, condemned and judged for a most obstinate, false, detestable heretic, and committed to our secular power, to be burned according to the wholesome and good laws of our realm in that case provided; forasmuch as in those cities, and the diocese thereof, he has in times past preached and taught most pestilent heresies and doctrine to our subjects there, we have therefore given order that the said Hooper, who yet persists obstinate, and has refused mercy when it was graciously offered, shall be put to execution in the said city of Gloucester, for the example and terror of such as he has there seduced and mistaught, and because he has done most harm there. . . .

The Enforcement of the Elizabethan Settlement (1593): "Divine Service According to Her Majesty's Laws"

After the unsettling reign of Mary Tudor, Henry VIII's daughter by Anne Boleyn came to the throne as Elizabeth I (1558–1603). A talented and diligent queen, she became one of the greatest of all English monarchs, and her reign established England as the most formidable political power of its age. Her religious solution to the struggle between Catholicism and Protestantism was a compromise: The Church of England would be Protestant in doctrine and Catholic in ritual. This "Anglican Settlement" would endure, though Catholic dissent and Protestant attempts at "purifying" or purging Catholic elements from the Church of England would not be settled for nearly two centuries. The following selection demonstrates Elizabeth's commitment to enforcing her religious compromise by demanding Catholic allegiance to the authority of the English crown. Other statutes demanding Puritan obeisance were likewise initiated.

For the better discovering and avoiding of all such traitorous and most dangerous conspiracies and attempts as are daily devised and practiced against our most gracious sovereign lady the queen's majesty and the happy estate of this commonweal, by sundry wicked and seditious persons, who, terming themselves Catholics, and being indeed spies and intelligencers, not only for her majesty's foreign enemies, but also for rebellious and traitorous subjects

---

"Bloody Mary" is from James H. Robinson, *Readings in European History,* vol. 2 (Boston: Ginn and Company, 1906), pp. 151–152.

"The Enforcement of the Elizabethan Settlement" is from Statutes of the Realm, vol. 4, pt. 2, p. 843, in Henry Gee and W. J. Hardy, eds., *Documents Illustrative of English Church History* (London: Macmillan and Co., Ltd., 1896), pp. 499, 506.

born within her highness's realms and dominions, and hiding their most detestable and devilish purposes under a false pretext of religion and conscience, do secretly wander and shift from place to place within this realm, to corrupt and seduce her majesty's subjects, and to stir them to sedition and rebellion: Be it ordained and enacted by our sovereign lady the queen's majesty, and the Lords spiritual and temporal, and the Commons, in this present Parliament assembled, and by the authority of the same, that every person above the age of sixteen years, born within any of the queen's majesty's realms and dominions . . . shall come to some parish church on some Sunday or other festival day, and then and there hear divine service, and . . . make public and open submission and declaration of his and their conformity to her majesty's laws and statutes. . . .

The Catholic Reformation

The Society of Jesus

> *During the Protestant movement, the Catholic church was active in its own efforts to reform from within. The Society of Jesus (Jesuits) was a religious order founded by Ignatius Loyola in 1540. Loyola (1491–1556) was a soldier who had turned to religion while recovering from wounds. Under Loyola's firm leadership, the Jesuits became a disciplined organization that was dedicated to serving the pope with unquestioned loyalty. The next two selections from the constitution of the society and the famous spiritual exercises of Loyola demonstrate the purity and determination of these Catholic reformers.*

Constitution (1540)

He who desires to fight for God under the banner of the cross in our society,—which we wish to distinguish by the name of Jesus,—and to serve God alone and the Roman pontiff, his vicar on earth, after a solemn vow of perpetual chastity, shall set this thought before his mind, that he is a part of a society founded for the especial purpose of providing for the advancement of souls in Christian life and doctrine and for the propagation of faith through public preaching and the ministry of the word of God, spiritual exercises and deeds of charity, and in particular through the training of the young and ignorant in Christianity and through the spiritual consolation of the faithful of Christ in hearing confessions; and he shall take care to keep first God and next the purpose of this organization always before his eyes. . . .

"Constitution" is from James H. Robinson, ed., *Readings in European History*, vol. 1 (Boston: Ginn and Company, 1904), pp. 162–163.

All the members shall realize, and shall recall daily, as long as they live, that this society as a whole and in every part is fighting for God under faithful obedience to one most holy lord, the pope, and to other Roman pontiffs who succeed him. And although we are taught in the gospel and through the orthodox faith to recognize and steadfastly profess that all the faithful of Christ are subject to the Roman pontiff as their head and as the vicar of Jesus Christ, yet we have adjudged that, for the special promotion of greater humility in our society and the perfect mortification of every individual and the sacrifice of our own wills, we should each be bound by a peculiar vow, in addition to the general obligation, that whatever the present Roman pontiff, or any future one, may from time to time decree regarding the welfare of souls and the propagation of the faith, we are pledged to obey without evasion or excuse, instantly, so far as in us lies, whether he send us to the Turks or any other infidels, even to those who inhabit the regions men call the Indies; whether to heretics or schismatics, or, on the other hand, to certain of the faithful.

Spiritual Exercises (1548)

IGNATIUS LOYOLA

1. Always to be ready to obey with mind and heart, setting aside all judgement of one's own, the true spouse of Jesus Christ, our holy mother our infallible and orthodox mistress, the Catholic Church, whose authority is exercised over us by the hierarchy.
2. To commend the confession of sins to a priest as it is practised in the Church; the reception of the Holy Eucharist once a year, or better still every week, or at least every month, with the necessary preparation.
4. To have a great esteem for the religious orders, and to give the preference to celibacy or virginity over the married state.
5. To approve of the religious vows of chastity, poverty, perpetual obedience, as well as the other works of perfection and supererogation. Let us remark in passing, that we must never engage by vow to take a state (such e.g. as marriage) that would be an impediment to one more perfect.
6. To praise relics, the veneration and invocation of Saints: also the stations, and pious pilgrimages, indulgences, jubilees, the custom of lighting candles in the churches, and other such aids to piety and devotion.
9. To uphold especially all the precepts of the Church, and not censure them in any manner; but, on the contrary, to defend them promptly, with reasons drawn from all sources, against those who criticize them.

"Spiritual Exercises" is from Henry Bettenson, ed., *Documents of the Christian Church*, 2nd ed. (London: Oxford University Press, 1963), pp. 364–365. Reprinted by permission of the publisher.

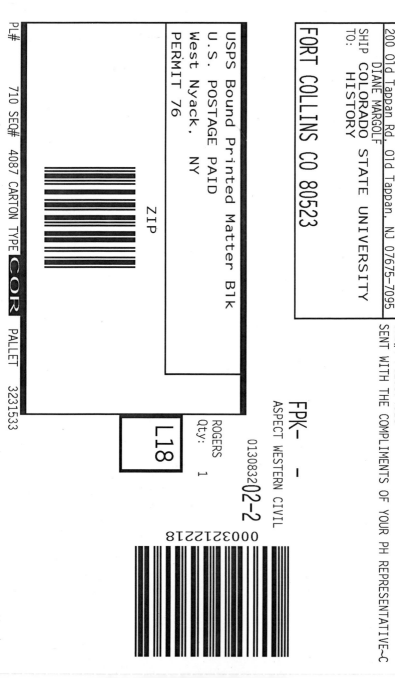

PRENTICE HALL

FROM:
200 Old Tappan Rd, Old Tappan, NJ 07675-7095
DIANE MARGOLF
SHIP COLORADO STATE UNIVERSITY
TO: HISTORY

FORT COLLINS CO 80523

PO#: 005020202913
ORD#: FC20874618
SENT WITH THE COMPLIMENTS OF YOUR PH REPRESENTATIVE~C

USPS Bound Printed Matter Blk
U.S. POSTAGE PAID
West Nyack, NY
PERMIT 76

ZIP

PL# 710 SEQ# 4087 CARTON TYPE COR PALLET 3231533

L18

ROGERS
Qty: 1

FPK- -
ASPECT WESTERN CIVIL

01308320 02-2

000321 2218

W 5

10. To be eager to commend the decrees, mandates, traditions, rites and conduct; although there may not always be the uprightness of conduct that there ought to be, yet to attack or revile them in private or in public tends to scandal and disorder. Such attacks set the people against their princes and pastors; we must avoid such reproaches and never attack superiors before inferiors. The best course is to make private approach to those who have power to remedy the evil.

The Way of Perfection:
"Prayer Is the Mortar Which Keeps Our House Together"

SAINT TERESA OF AVILA

The Catholic Reformation was advanced not only by those, like Ignatius Loyola, who advocated an active and disciplined resistance to Protestantism in the world at large. Others, like Saint Teresa of Avila, struggled in poverty behind convent walls to guide her nuns to a pureness of thought in order to achieve the "Way of Perfection." By writing her autobiography in 1565, she hoped to influence others to choose a simple life of faith and commitment to God.

You see, daughters, upon how great an enterprise we have embarked.... Clearly we must work hard; it is a great help to have high aspirations that may cause our actions to become great also. If we endeavor to observe our Rule and Constitutions very faithfully, I hope that God will grant our petitions. I ask you nothing new, my daughters, but only that we should keep what we have professed, which is our vocation and our duty, although there are very diverse ways of observing it.

The first chapter of our Rule bids us "Pray without ceasing": we must obey this with the greatest perfection possible for it is our most important duty; then we shall not neglect the fasts, penances, and silence enjoined by the Rule. As you know, these are necessary if the prayer is to be genuine; self-indulgence and prayer do not go together. Prayer is the subject of which you have asked me to speak; I beg of you, in return, to practice and to read, again and again, what I have already told you. Before speaking of interior matters, that is of prayer, I will mention some things that must be done by those who intend to lead a life of prayer....

"'Prayer is the Mortar Which Keeps Our House Together'" is from Saint Teresa of Jesus, *The Way of Perfection*, 6th ed., ed. Father Benedict Zimmerman (Westminster: The Newman Press, 1961), pp. 20–21, 22, 24, 115–117. Reprinted by permission.

The first of these is love for one another: the second, detachment from all created things: the third is true humility, which, though I mention it last, is chief of all and includes the rest. The first, that is of fervent mutual charity, is most important, for there is no annoyance that cannot easily be borne by those who love one another: anything must be very out of the way to cause irritation. If this commandment were observed in this world as it ought to be, I believe it would be a great help towards obeying the others, but whether we err by excess or by defect we never succeed in keeping it perfectly.

You might think there could be no harm among us in excessive love for one another, but no one would believe what evil and imperfections spring from this source unless she had seen it herself. The devil sets many snares here which are hardly detected by those who are content to serve God in a superficial way—indeed, they take such conduct for virtue—those however who are bent on perfection understand the evil clearly, for little by little, it deprives the will of strength to devote itself entirely to the love of God. I think this injures women even more than men, and does serious damage to the community. It prevents a nun from loving all the others equally, makes her resent any injury done to her friend, causes her to wish she had something to give her favorite, to seek for opportunities to talk to her often, to tell her how much she loves her and other nonsense of the sort, rather than of how much we should love God. These close friendships rarely serve to forward the love of God; in fact, I believe the devil originates them so as to make factions among the religious. . . .

In order to guard against these partialities great care must be taken from the very first, and this more by watchfulness and kindness than by severity. A most useful precaution is for the nuns, according to our present habit, never to be with one another nor talk together except at the appointed times, but that, as the Rule enjoins, the sisters should not be together, but each in her own cell. Let there be no work-room in St. Joseph's for although it is a praiseworthy custom, silence is better kept when one is alone. To accustom ourselves to solitude is a great help to prayer, and since prayer is the mortar which keeps our house together and we came here to practice it, we must learn to like what promotes it. . . .

Take my advice, and let no one mislead you by pointing out any other way than prayer. I am not discussing here whether mental and vocal prayer are necessary for everybody, but I say that you require them both. This is the work of the religious; if anyone tells you it is dangerous, look upon him as your greatest danger and shun his company. Keep my words in mind, for you may need them. A want of humility, of the virtues, may endanger you, but prayer—prayer! Never would God permit that the way of prayer should be a dangerous way! The devil must have originated these fears and so brought about, by crafty tricks, the fall of certain souls that practiced prayer. See how blind men are! . . .

Therefore, sisters, banish these misgivings: take no notice of public opinion. This is no time to believe everything you hear. Be guided only by those who conform their lives to that of Christ; try to keep a good conscience and humility; despise all earthly things; firmly believe that teaching of our holy Mother the Church—then you may feel sure you are on the right way. Cast aside these causeless fears. If anyone tries to frighten you, humbly explain the way to him: tell him that our Rule bids us pray constantly and that you are bound to obey it.

The Council of Trent (1545–1563)

The Council of Trent was an involved effort by the Catholic church to clarify its doctrine and bring about internal reform. The Church sought to make its own stand in the face of the Protestant threat, and thus its traditional doctrinal views are set forth with firmness and confidence, as the first excerpt indicates. The second excerpt is from the oration by Bishop Jerome Ragozonus, which was delivered during the last session of the Council of Trent and summarized its accomplishments. One of the most significant actions of Trent was its reorganization and codification of laws concerning censorship and the prohibition of books. The last selection, published after the Council closed, sets out some of the restrictions. These general rules were in force until they were replaced with new decrees in 1897.

The Profession of Faith

I profess . . . that true God is offered in the Mass, a proper and propitiatory sacrifice for the living and the dead, and that in the most Holy Eucharist there are truly, really and substantially the body and blood together with the soul and divinity of Our Lord Jesus Christ, and that a conversion is made of the whole substance of bread into his body and of the whole substance of wine into his blood, which conversion the Catholic Church calls transubstantiation. I also confess that the whole and entire Christ and the true sacrament is taken under the one species alone.

I hold unswervingly that there is a purgatory and that the souls there detained are helped by the intercessions of the faithful; likewise also that the Saints who reign with Christ are to be venerated and invoked; that they offer prayers to God for us and that their relics are to be venerated. I firmly assert that the images of Christ and of the ever-Virgin Mother of God, as also those of the older Saints, are to be kept and retained, and that due honour and veneration is to be accorded them; and I affirm that the power of

"The Profession of Faith" is from Henry Bettenson, ed., *Documents of the Christian Church,* 2nd ed. (London: Oxford University Press, 1963), pp. 364–365. Reprinted by permission of the publisher.

indulgences has been left by Christ in the Church, and that their use is very salutary for Christian people.

I recognize the Holy Catholic and Apostolic Roman Church as the Mother and mistress of all churches; and I vow and swear true obedience to the Roman Pontiff, the successor of blessed Peter, the chief of the Apostles and the representative [vicarius] of Jesus Christ.

I accept and profess, without doubting the traditions, definitions and declarations of the sacred Canons and Oecumenical Councils and especially those of the holy Council of Trent. . . .

The Closing Oration at Trent (1563)

BISHOP JEROME RAGOZONUS

"Hear these things, all you nations; give ear all inhabitants of the world!"

The Council of Trent which was begun long ago, was for a time suspended, often postponed and dispersed, now at last through a singular favor of almighty God and with a complete and wonderful accord of all ranks and nations has come to a close. This most happy day has dawned for the Christian people; the day in which the temple of the Lord, often shattered and destroyed, is restored and completed, and this one ship, laden with every blessing and buffeted by the worst and most relentless storms and waves, is brought safely into port. Oh, that those for whose sake this voyage was chiefly undertaken had decided to board it with us; that those who caused us to take this work in hand had participated in the erection of this edifice! Then indeed we would now have reason for greater rejoicing. But it is certainly not through our fault that it so happened.

For that reason we chose this city, situated at the entrance to Germany, situated almost at the threshold of their homes. We have, in order to give them no ground for suspicion that the place is not entirely free, employed no guard for ourselves; we granted them that public security which they requested and which they themselves had drawn up. For a long time we awaited them and never did we cease to exhort them and plead with them to come here and learn the truth. Indeed, even in their absence we were, I think, sufficiently concerned about them. In a twofold respect medicine had to be applied to their weak and infirm spirits, one, the explanation and confirmation of the teaching of the Catholic and truly evangelical faith in those matters upon which they had cast doubt and which at this time appeared opportune for the dispersion and destruction of all the darkness of errors; the other, the restoration of ecclesiastical discipline, the collapse of which they claim was the chief cause of their severance from us. We have amply accomplished both so far as the conditions of the times would permit.

"The Closing Oration at Trent" is from J. Barry Colman, ed., *Readings in Church History,* rev. ed., vol. 2 (Westminster, Md.: Christian Classics, Inc., 1985), pp. 699–703.

At the beginning, [the Council of Trent] . . . made a profession of faith, in order to lay a foundation, as it were, for subsequent transactions and to point out by what witnesses and evidence the definition of articles of faith must be supported. . . . Through this most extraordinary decree in the memory of man, well-nigh all heresies are strangled and, as darkness before the sun, dispersed and dissipated, and the truth appears with such clearness and splendor that no one can any longer pretend not to see so great a light.

[Most esteemed fathers,] you have thereby removed from the celebration of the Mass all superstition, all greed for lucre and all irreverence; forbidden vagrant, unknown and depraved priests to offer this holy sacrifice; removed its celebration from private homes and profane places to holy and consecrated sanctuaries. You have banished from the temple of the Lord the more effeminate singing and musical compositions, promenades, conversations and business transactions; you have thus prescribed for each ecclesiastical rank such laws as leave no room for the abuse of the orders divinely conferred. You have likewise removed some matrimonial impediments which seemed to give occasion for violating the precepts of the Church, and to those who do not enter the conjugal union legitimately, you have closed the easy way of obtaining forgiveness. And what shall I say about furtive and clandestine marriages? For myself I feel that if there had been no other reason for convoking the council, and there were many and grave reasons, this one alone would have provided sufficient ground for its convocation. For since this is a matter that concerns all, and since there is no corner of the earth which this plague has not invaded, provision had to be made by which this common evil might be remedied by common deliberation. By your clear-sighted and well-nigh divine direction, most holy fathers, the occasion for innumerable and grave excesses and crimes has been completely removed, and the government of the Christian commonwealth most wisely provided for. To this is added the exceedingly salutary and necessary prohibition of many abuses connected with purgatory, the veneration and invocation of the saints, images and relics, and also indulgences, abuses which appeared to defile and deform in no small measure the beautiful aspect of these objects.

The other part, in which was considered the restoration of the tottering and well-nigh collapsed ecclesiastical discipline, was most carefully performed and completed. In the future only those who are known for their virtues, not for their ambition, who will serve the interests of the people, not their own, and who desire to be useful rather than invested with authority, will be chosen for the discharge of ecclesiastical offices. The word of God, which is more penetrating than any two-edged sword, will be more frequently and more zealously preached and explained.

The bishops and others to whom the *cura animarum* [care of the soul] has been committed, will remain with and watch over their flocks and not wander about outside the districts entrusted to them. Privileges will no longer avail anyone for an impure and wicked life or for evil and pernicious teaching; no crime will go unpunished, no virtue will be without its reward. The multitude of poor and mendicant priests have been very well provided for; everyone will be assigned to a definite church and to a prescribed field of labor whence he may obtain sustenance.

Avarice, than which there is no vice more hideous, especially in the house of God, will be absolutely banished therefrom, and the sacraments, as is proper, will be dispensed gratuitously. From one Church many will be established and from many One, according as the welfare of the people and circumstances demand. Questors of alms, as they are called, who seeking their own and not the things of Jesus Christ, have brought great injury, great dishonor upon our religion, will be completely removed from the memory of men, which must be regarded as a very great blessing. For from this our present calamity took its beginning; from it an endless evil did not cease to creep in by degrees and daily take a wider course, nor have precautionary and disciplinary measures of many councils thus far been able to suppress it. Wherefore, who will not agree that for this reason it was a very prudent undertaking to cut off this member, on whose restoration to health much labor had been vainly spent, lest it corrupt the remainder of the body?

Moreover, divine worship will be discharged more purely and promptly, and those who carry the vessels of the Lord will be so chastened that they will move others to follow their example. In connection with this point plans were skillfully devised whereby those who are to be promoted to sacred orders might in every church be from their youth up instructed in the habits of Christian life and knowledge, so that in this way a sort of seminary of all virtues might be established. In addition, . . . visitations [were] reintroduced for the welfare of the people, not for the disturbance and oppression of them; greater faculties granted to the pastors for guiding and feeding their flocks; . . . plurality of benefices abolished; the hereditary possession of the sanctuary of God prohibited; excommunication restricted and the manner of its imposition determined; . . . a sort of bridle put on the luxury, greed and licentiousness of all people, particularly the clergy, which cannot be easily shaken off; kings and princes diligently reminded of their duties, and other things of a similar nature were enacted with the greatest discernment. . . .

Let [the Protestant Reformers] read with humility, as becomes a Christian, what we have defined concerning our faith, and if some light should come upon them, let them not harden their hearts, and if they should wish to return to the common embrace of mother Church from which they severed themselves, they may rest assured that every indulgence and sympathy will be extended to them. . . .

The Tridentine Index of Books (1564)

The holy council in the second session, celebrated under our most holy Lord, Pius IV, commissioned some fathers to consider what ought to be done concerning various censures and books either suspected or pernicious and to report to this holy council. . . .

"The Tridentine Index of Books" is from J. Barry Colman, ed., *Readings in Church History*, rev. ed., vol. 2 (Westminster, Md.: Christian Classics, Inc., 1985), pp. 705–706, 708.

1. All books which have been condemned either by the supreme pontiffs or by ecumenical councils before the year 1515 and are not contained in this list, shall be considered condemned in the same manner as they were formerly condemned.

2. The books of those heresiarchs, who after the aforesaid year originated or revived heresies, as well as those who are or have been the heads or leaders of heretics, as Luther, Zwingli, Calvin, Balthasar Friedberg, Schwenkfeld, and others like these, whatever may be their name, title or nature or their heresy, are absolutely forbidden. The books of other heretics, moreover, which deal professedly with religion are absolutely condemned. Those on the other hand, which do not deal with religion and have by order of the bishops and inquisitors been examined by Catholic theologians and approved by them, are permitted. Likewise, Catholic books written by those who afterward fell into heresy, as well as by those who after their fall returned to the bosom of the Church, may be permitted if they have been approved by the theological faculty of a Catholic university or by the general inquisition.

3. The translations of writers, also ecclesiastical, which have till now been edited by condemned authors, are permitted provided they contain nothing contrary to sound doctrine. Translations of the books of the Old Testament may in the judgment of the bishop be permitted to learned and pious men only. . . . Translations of the New Testament made by authors of the first class of this list shall be permitted to no one, since great danger and little usefullness usually results to readers from their perusal. . . .

4. Since it is clear from experience that if the Sacred Books are permitted everywhere and without discrimination in the vernacular, there will by reason of the boldness of men arise therefrom more harm than good, the matter is in this respect left to the judgment of the bishop or inquisitor, who may with the advice of the pastor or confessor permit the reading of the Sacred Books translated into the vernacular by Catholic authors to those who they know will derive from such reading no harm but rather an increase of faith and piety, which permission they must have in writing. Those, however, who presume to read or possess them without such permission may not receive absolution from their sins until they have handed them over to the authorities. . . .

5. Those books which sometimes produce the works of heretical authors, in which these add little or nothing of their own but rather collect therein the sayings of others, as lexicons, concordances, apothegms, parables, tables of contents and such like, are permitted if whatever needs to be eliminated in the additions is removed and corrected in accordance with the suggestions of the bishop, the inquisitor and Catholic theologians.

7. Books which professedly deal with, narrate or teach things lascivious or obscene are absolutely prohibited, since not only the matter of faith but also that of morals, which are usually easily corrupted through the reading of such books, must be taken into consideration, and those who possess them are to be severely punished by the bishops. Ancient books written by heathens may by reason of their elegance and quality of style be permitted, but may by no means be read to children.

8. Books whose chief contents are good but in which things have incidentally been inserted which have reference to heresy, ungodliness, divination or superstition, may be permitted if by the authority of the general inquisition they have been purged by Catholic theologians. . . .

Finally, all the faithful are commanded not to presume to read or possess any books contrary to the prescriptions of these rules or the prohibition of this list. And if anyone should read or possess books by heretics or writings by any author condemned and prohibited by reason of heresy or suspicion of false teaching, he incurs immediately the sentence of excommunication. . . .

Resolution:
The Bloody Wars of Religion

The Abdication of Charles V (1556):
"The Wretched Condition of the Christian State"

EMPEROR CHARLES V

As the Reformation expanded its influence in Germany, Switzerland, and France during the 1530s and 1540s, the Holy Roman Emperor Charles V made several abortive attempts to enforce compromise agreements between Catholics and Protestants. As discussions broke down, he even tried to effect a military solution in 1547 by crushing the Protestant Schmalkaldic League. But the Reformation had become too entrenched to be resolved by brute force. The Emperor was finally forced to relent and accepted the Peace of Augsburg in 1555. This compromise established that the ruler of a region would determine its religion. Lutheranism was finally recognized as a legal form of Christian belief. Lutherans were allowed to retain church lands seized before 1552 and were permitted to migrate from one area to another without restriction.

But by 1556 Charles V, who had served as King of Spain and Holy Roman Emperor since 1519 at the outset of the Reformation, had become a tired and disappointed man. His abdication speech that follows gives insight into his struggles and some political consequences of the Reformation.

Soon came the death of my grandfather Maximilian, in my nineteenth year [1519], and although I was still young, they conferred upon me in his stead the imperial dignity. I had no inordinate ambition to rule a multitude of kingdoms, but merely sought to secure the welfare of Germany, to provide for the defence of Flanders, to consecrate my forces to the safety of Christianity

---

"'The Wretched Condition of the Christian State'" is from James H. Robinson, ed., *Readings in European History*, vol. 2 (Boston: Ginn and Company, 1906), pp. 165–167.

against the Turk and to labor for the extension of the Christian religion. But although such zeal was mine, I was unable to show so much of it as I might have wished, on account of the troubles raised by the heresies of Luther and the other innovators of Germany and on account of serious war into which the hostility and envy of neighboring princes had driven me, and from which I have safely emerged, thanks to the favor of God.

This is the fourth time that I go to Spain, there to bury myself. I wish to say to you that nothing I have ever experienced has given me so much pain or rested so heavily upon my soul as that which I experience in parting from you today, without leaving behind me that peace and quiet which I so much desired. . . . I am no longer able to attend to my affairs without great bodily fatigue and consequent detriment to the affairs of the state. The cares which so great a responsibility involves; the extreme dejection it causes; my health already ruined; all these leave me no longer the strength sufficient for governing the states which God has confided to me. The little strength that remains to me is rapidly disappearing. So I should long ago have put down the burden if my son's immaturity and my mother's incapacity had not forced both my spirit and my body to sustain the weight until this hour.

The last time that I went to Germany I had determined to do what you see me do today, but I could not bring myself to do it when I saw the wretched condition of the Christian state, a prey to such a multitude of disturbances, of innovations, of singular opinions as to faith, of worse than civil wars, and fallen finally into so many lamentable disorders. I was turned from my purpose because my ills were not yet so great, and I hoped to make an end of all these things and restore the peace. In order that I might not be wanting in my duty I risked my strength, my goods, my repose and my life for the safety of Christianity and the defence of my subjects. From this struggle I emerged with a portion of the things I desired. . . .

I have carried out what God has permitted, since the outcome of our efforts depends upon the will of God. We human beings act according to our powers, our strength, our spirit, and God awards the victory and permits defeat. I have ever done as I was able, and God has aided me. I return to Him boundless thanks for having succored me in my greatest trials and in all my dangers.

I am determined then to retire to Spain, to yield to my son Philip the possessions of all my states, and to my brother, the king of the Romans, the Empire. I particularly commend to you my son, and I ask of you in remembrance of me, that you extend to him the love which you have always borne towards me; moreover I ask you to preserve among yourselves the same affection and harmony. Be obedient towards justice, zealous in the observance of the laws, preserve for all that merits it, and do not refuse to grant authority the support of which it stands in need.

Above all, beware of infection from the sects of neighboring lands. Extirpate at once the germs, if they appear in your midst, for fear lest they may spread abroad and utterly overthrow your state, and lest you may fall into the direst calamities.

The Saint Bartholomew's Day Massacre (1572): "A Thousand Times More Terrible Than Death Itself"

THE DUKE OF SULLY

It is important to note that Calvinism was not recognized as a legal and therefore protected form of Christianity by the Peace of Augsburg in 1555. After the Council of Trent in 1563, Catholic forces, led by Jesuit-inspired activists, began an offensive against equally dogmatic and aggressive Calvinists, who were determined to secure full religious toleration. The wars of religion that followed were both internal conflicts and international struggles that engaged virtually every major European nation from the 1560s until the resolution of the Thirty Years War in 1648.

The first selection is an eyewitness account of the Saint Bartholomew's Day Massacre in 1572. Catherine De Medici, as French regent for her son Charles IX, sought to maintain a precarious balance between Protestant and Catholic influence within her court. When it appeared that the scale was tilting in favor of the Protestants and that her position might be threatened, she convinced Charles that a Huguenot plot against the monarchy was afoot.

On the eve of Saint Bartholomew's Day in 1572, three thousand Huguenots were butchered in Paris and over twenty thousand died throughout France during the ensuing three-day massacre. After this, Protestant leaders became convinced that an international struggle to the death must be pursued against a brutal Catholic foe. The Duke of Sully (1560–1641), who later became ambassador and finance minister to King Henry IV and architect of the Edict of Nantes, was only twelve when he viewed the massacre firsthand—but he never forgot it.

If I were inclined to increase the general horror inspired by an action so barbarous as that perpetrated on the 24th of August, 1572, and too well known by the name of the *massacre of St. Bartholomew*, I should in this place enlarge upon the number, the rank, the virtues, and great talents of those who were inhumanly murdered on that horrible day, as well in Paris as in every other part of the kingdom; I should mention at least the ignominious treatment, the fiend-like cruelty, and savage insults these miserable victims suffered from their butchers, whose conduct was a thousand times more terrible than death itself.

I have writings still in my hands which would confirm the report, of the court of France having made the most pressing solicitations to the courts of England and Germany, to the Swiss and the Genoese, to refuse an asylum to

"The Saint Bartholomew's Day Massacre" is from Bayle St. John, ed., *Memoirs of the Duke of Sully*, Vol. 1 (London: George Bell and Sons, 1877), pp. 85–87.

those Huguenots who might fly from France; but I prefer the honor of the nation to the satisfying of a malignant pleasure. . . .

Intending on that day to wait upon the king my master [Henry of Navarre, who became King Henry IV of France], I went to bed early on the preceding evening; about three in the morning I was awakened by the cries of people, and the alarm-bells, which were everywhere ringing. . . . I was determined to escape to the College de Bourgogne, and to effect this I put on my scholar's gown, and taking a book under my arm, I set out. In the streets I met three parties of the Life-guards; the first of these, after handling me very roughly, seized my book, and, most fortunately for me, seeing it was a roman Catholic prayer-book, suffered me to proceed, and this served me as a passport with the two other parties. As I went along I saw the houses broken open and plundered, and men, women, and children butchered, while a constant cry was kept up of, "Kill! Kill! O you Huguenots! O you Huguenots!" This made me very impatient to gain the college, where, through God's assistance, I at length arrived, without suffering any other injury than a most dreadful fright.

The Edict of Nantes (1589)

Henry IV of France came to the throne in 1589, weary of war and religious tur-moil. He was a politique, *who believed that political accommodation and sta-bility could only be obtained through religious toleration. Accordingly, one of his first acts of reconciliation was the Edict of Nantes, which assured Huguenots at least partial religious freedom within an officially Catholic France. This truce produced a "cold war" of sorts between religious factions within France. But the "hot war" continued throughout northern Europe from 1614 to 1648. This Thirty Years War, which reflected the hatred and distrust between Protestants and Catholics, was perhaps the worst European catastrophe since the Black Death of the fourteenth century. But at its conclusion with the Treaty of West-phalia, the Calvinists obtained their long-sought recognition.*

We ordain that the Catholic, Apostolic, and Roman faith be restored and re-established in all those districts and places of this our Realm . . . in which its exercise has been interrupted, there to be freely and peaceably exercised. . . .

And to leave no occasion for trouble or difference among our subjects: We permit those of the so-called Reformed Religion to live and abide in all the towns and districts of this our Realm . . . free from inquisition, molestation or compulsion to do anything in the way of Religion, against their conscience . . . provided that they observe the provisions of this Edict. . . .

We also permit those of the aforesaid Religion to practise it in all the town and districts of our dominion, in which it had been established and publicly observed by them on several distinct occasions during the year 1596 and the year 1597 up to the end of August, all decrees and judgements to the contrary notwithstanding.

We most expressly forbid to those of this religion the practice thereof, in respect of ministry, organization, discipline or the public instruction of children, or in any respect, in our realm and dominion, save in the places permitted and granted by this edict.

The practice of this religion is forbidden in our court and suite, in our domains beyond the mountains, in our city of Paris, or within five leagues thereof.

CHRONOLOGY: The Reformation Era

1509	Desiderius Erasmus, a northern humanist, writes *The Praise of Folly*, a satire that criticizes abuses within the Church.
1517	Martin Luther posts his *Ninety-five Theses*, a list of grievances against indulgences, on the door of Wittenberg church in hopes of engaging clerical authorities in debate.
1519	Luther challenges authority of the pope and the inerrency of Church councils at the Leipzig Debate.
1520	Luther publishes two works: *Address to the Christian Nobility of the German Nation* and *On Christian Liberty*.
1521	Luther is excommunicated by order of the pope. Diet of Worms called to question him about his heretical writings. Luther is condemned and secretly leaves Worms.
1521–1522	Edict of Worms issued imposing the "ban of Empire" on Luther. Luther is hidden by friends at Wartburg Castle, where he translates the New Testament into German.
1523	Ulrich Zwingli active as Protestant reformer in Switzerland. Issues Sixty-seven Articles.
1524–1525	Peasant Revolt breaks out in Germany as peasants demand freedom from the long-standing feudal obligations of serfdom. Luther sides with aristocracy and condemns violence of peasants.
1529	Marburg Colloquy called by Philip of Hesse, who sought to unite Luther and Zwingli. Luther leaves thinking Zwingli a dangerous fanatic.

1534	Act of Supremacy declares Henry VIII of England "the only supreme head of the Church of England." Henry's political need for an heir forces his religious break with the Catholic church.
1534–1535	Anabaptists assume political power in the city of Münster. Theocracy imposed and polygamy practiced. Shocked Protestant and Catholic armies unite to crush the radicals.
1536	John Calvin arrives in Geneva. Publishes Institutes of the Christian Religion, which contains the doctrine of predestination.
1540	Jesuit order formed by Ignatius Loyola is recognized by the pope. The Jesuits became a disciplined organization that was dedicated to serving the pope with unquestioned loyalty.
1545–1563	Council of Trent is called to clarify Catholic doctrine and bring about internal reform.
1546	Death of Martin Luther.
1553–1558	Mary I restores Catholic doctrine to England.
1555	Peace of Augsburg recognizes the rights of Lutherans to worship as they please. Principle of *cuius regio, eius religio* is established: "The ruler of a land would determine the religion of the land."
1558–1603	Elizabeth I of England fashions an Anglican religious compromise settlement.
1572	Saint Bartholomew's Day Massacre in which 3,000 Huguenots in Paris and 20,000 throughout France are killed.
1588	Destruction of the Spanish Armada by English navy.
1589	Edict of Nantes legally recognizes the legitimacy of Calvinism.
1618–1648	The Thirty Years' War fought between Catholic and Protestant forces primarily in northern Europe.

STUDY QUESTIONS

1. Discuss the abuses within the church during the fifteenth and sixteenth centuries. What specifically are the criticisms of Jacob Wimpheling and Desiderius Erasmus? Is there any evidence that the church tried to reform itself during this period?
2. Why were indulgences so detested by critics of the church? Can you construct a logical argument in support of indulgences with which the church could have satisfactorily defended itself against criticism? Is the principle of indulgences at issue here, or just the manner in which they were sold?

3. What would you identify as the underlying causes for the Reformation, and what is the "spark" that set things in motion? To what extent was Martin Luther's action directed against abuses within the church?

4. What do you consider the most significant passages from Luther's *Address to the Christian Nobility of the German Nation* and treatise *On Christian Liberty*? Why? What was Luther trying to accomplish by writing them? Why did Luther finally break completely with the Roman church?

5. What were Luther's arguments against the peasants in 1524? Are they persuasive? What does Luther's condemnation of the Peasants' Revolt tell you about his reform movement? Do you regard Luther as a hypocrite or not?

6. In the treatise *On the Necessity of Reforming the Church,* what is John Calvin's primary message to the Holy Roman Emperor Charles V? Do you think Calvin was exaggerating when he reminded the Emperor that "the matter on which you are to deliberate is, whether you are to leave to your posterity some empire or none"?

7. How would you define the concept of predestination and why is it so efficient as a device for controlling a congregation? What is the basis for the success of the Calvinist movement?

8. After reading the selections on the catechism and the regulation of churches in Geneva, do you think that Calvin was a "control-freak" or a brilliant organizer? What was the basis for the success of Calvinism? Why did the spread of Calvinism seem so dangerous to Giovanni Michiel, the Venetian ambassador to France?

9. The nature and process of baptism was a particularly divisive issue during the Reformation. Why? According to Hans Hut in the "Mystery of Baptism," what is the purpose of baptism and why is it important to be "patient" in the process of becoming baptized? Do his arguments seem dangerous? What measures were taken against Anabaptists and why were they so harsh?

10. What did communism and polygamy have to do with Anabaptist doctrine? Was the Anabaptist community in Münster an aberration that afforded justification for the persecution of Anabaptists by both Catholics and Protestants alike? Did the intolerance toward Anabaptists actually serve as a unifying factor for Catholic and Protestant factions?

11. Did the English Reformation involve personal conscience or political expediency? How was the religious authority of the monarch achieved?

12. Read carefully the selection on the Society of Jesus and the Council of Trent. What specifically do Loyola and the Council of Trent demand from the Catholic faithful? How did Saint Teresa of Avila's approach differ? Does the closing oration at the Council of Trent seem to be progressive in its message? Why then does the Tridentine Index of Books seem so repressive? Can faith be enforced in this manner? Some historians have called the Catholic reform movement the "Counter Reformation." Do you think a reformation of the church would have occurred without Martin Luther? How important was Luther in changing history?

13. A critical issue of the Reformation era centered on the diverse means of attaining salvation. How is this issue reflected in the sources? According to Luther,

Calvin, Loyola, and the Catholic church, how is one saved? Be specific in your documentation.

14. One of the most important questions of this period which separated the reformers from the church centered on religious authority. In spiritual matters, did religious authority rest in the church (as dictated by the pope), in church councils (such as Trent), in scripture, or in individual conscience? How is this problem reflected in the sources?

15. Some historians have maintained that the success of the Reformation was dependent on the forces arrayed against it. Without the opposition of figures like Ignatius Loyola and Emperor Charles V, would the Reformation have succeeded? Does opposition help a political or religious movement better define and clarify its doctrine? Does opposition actually strengthen the organization of the movement? In his abdication speech, why does Charles V seem so dejected?

16. Intolerance is a primary theme during the Reformation era. How was it reflected in the primary sources? Pay particular attention to the Anabaptist episode and the Saint Bartholomew's Day massacre. To what extent was the Edict of Nantes a progressive vehicle for tolerance?

17. Edward Bulwer-Lytton once said, "A reform is a correction of abuses; a revolution is a transfer of power." Under this definition, would you consider the Protestant Reformation to be a revolution?

10

"An Embarrassment of Riches": The Interaction of New Worlds

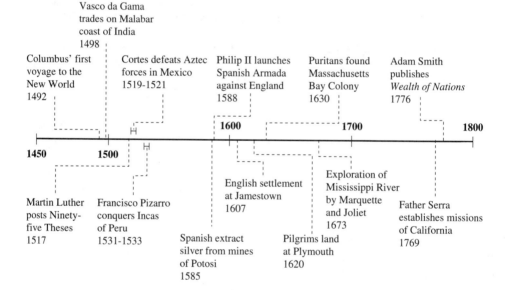

Vasco da Gama
trades on Malabar
coast of India
1498

Columbus' first
voyage to the
New World
1492

Cortes defeats Aztec
forces in Mexico
1519-1521

Philip II launches
Spanish Armada
against England
1588

Puritans found
Massachusetts
Bay Colony
1630

Adam Smith
publishes
Wealth of Nations
1776

1450　　　1500　　　1600　　　1700　　　1800

Martin Luther
posts Ninety-
five Theses
1517

Francisco Pizarro
conquers Incas
of Peru
1531-1533

English settlement
at Jamestown
1607

Exploration of
Mississippi River
by Marquette
and Joliet
1673

Father Serra
establishes missions
of California
1769

Spanish extract
silver from mines
of Potosi
1585

Pilgrims land
at Plymouth
1620

They are poor discoverers who think that there is no land when they see nothing but sea.

—Sir Francis Bacon

Discovery! To know that you are walking where no others have walked; that you are beholding what the human eye has not seen before; to give birth to an idea, to discover a great thought. To be the first—that is the idea!

—Mark Twain

The destiny of nations depends on how they nourish themselves.

—Jean Anthelme Brillat-Savarin

It should be noted that when he seizes a state, the new ruler ought to determine the injuries that he will need to inflict. He should then inflict them all at once, and not have to renew them everyday.

—Niccolò Machiavelli

The use of force is but temporary. It may subdue for a moment; but it does not remove the necessity of subduing again—and a nation is not governed, which is perpetually to be conquered.

—Edmund Burke

CHAPTER THEMES

- *Systems of Government:* How did political and economic rivalry among European powers provide motives for exploration and conquest? How did the centralization of absolute monarchies and mercantile economies contribute to the maintenance of empire and the development of a restrictive colonial policy?

- *Imperialism:* Why did Europeans conquer and settle lands in the new worlds of America, Africa, and Asia? Why were they particularly successful in suppressing natives? How important is technology as a factor in progress and destruction? Is imperialism a process that inherently carries the seeds of genocide? What are these components?

- *Propaganda:* How did Europeans justify their exploitation of the Americas? In order to justify conquest or genocide, must the conquered be methodically dehumanized? How has this process been repeated throughout history?

- *Church/State Relationships:* What role did the Catholic Church and Protestant religious exiles play in the settlement of the Americas? Are missionary motives simply another justification for conquest? Or did religious representatives work for accommodation and coexistence? Were they a positive force in the settlement of the Americas?

- *Historical Change and Transition:* What impact did the European exploration and conquest of the Americas have on the cultures of both regions? What are some of the "seeds of change" that ultimately linked these continents? Is the interaction between cultures both a beneficial and dangerous process? In our modern world, can a culture be truly homogeneous? What are the challenges of cultural integration and diversity?

- ***The Big Picture:*** Must exploration always result in exploitation? How have the European and American worlds been changed through "first contact" over five hundred years ago?

"In 1492, Columbus sailed the ocean blue." Often our childhood education is linked to simple, expressive phrases like this that encapsulate important events or ideas adults think are worth remembering. This rhyme does little beyond connecting an event with a date, but the ramifications of Columbus's voyages are vast indeed, for they changed the course of world history. The cultures of Europe and America each existed in old worlds with established societies, religions, and political organizations. Columbus's first contact with Native Americans in the Bahamas began a process of interaction and development that transformed each hemisphere and created a New World where cultures were blended, products exchanged, and societies redefined. This is a story of the transfer of plants and animals that affected the nutrition and movement of peoples, and it is a tragic saga of the decimation of whole Indian populations, the enslavement of African peoples, and the destruction of natural ecosystems. It is difficult to simplify in a phrase what was a complex human drama.

Since the Renaissance, European contact with the world has gone through distinct phases. The first stage, which ended by the seventeenth century, was one of exploration, conquest, and consolidation of territory in recently discovered lands. The second phase during the seventeenth and eighteenth centuries was characterized by colonial trade rivalry between England, France, Spain, and the Netherlands. The third stage of European contact with the world occurred in the nineteenth century and saw the establishment of European empires in Africa, India, and Asia. These empires disintegrated in the final stage after 1945 as Britain, France, and Germany, reduced by the destruction of World War II, retreated from control of their empires and acknowledged the sovereign legitimacy of indigenous governments. This chapter will focus on the first two stages.

There is perhaps no more important or tragic example of the debilitative effects of imperialism than the European domination of the Americas. We often regard the concept of exploration as a positive venture: Europeans took a courageous and imaginative step when Columbus, following the thirteenth century accounts of Marco Polo, set out to find Chipangu, an outer island of Japan. But exploration was only a means to an end as Portuguese and Spanish explorers were motivated by the lure of wealth, the spice trade in India, the gold and silver in the Americas, and the slaves of Africa. After Hernando Cortés and Francisco Pizarro conquered, respectively, the Aztecs in 1519 and the Incas in 1531, the door lay open for the European domination of a continent. Spanish conquistadores, French trappers, Dutch traders, and English religious refugees all sought to establish themselves on territory that was already occupied by indigenous peoples. Europeans ravaged their land, mocked their gods, banished their languages, decimated their populations through disease, and subjugated their children to a subservient and dependent status that is still in evidence today.

This dominance was certainly disproportionate to the geographic size or population of Europe. Although European apologists would concoct theories that explained and justified the domination of "inferior races," their conquest was not the result of racial superiority, but of technological supremacy. Gunpowder and naval power proved to be the decisive forces in the eradication of Native American cultures.

The contact between Europeans and American natives also changed the nature of both cultures. Europeans introduced horses, cows, pigs, wheat, barley, and sugar cane to the Americas. Horses alone proved instrumental in extending the horizons and altering the way of life for Indian tribes on the North American plains. Sugar cane has often been seen as the most detrimental contribution of the European world, since the human craving for sweetness resulted in the defoliation of the tropical environment for the establishment of cane plantations, and the methodical integration of slavery into the economies and societies of Africa and the Americas.

American crops such as maize took root in Africa and contributed to better nutrition and higher population that perhaps promoted the slave trade itself. Likewise, the American potato was introduced to Europe and became the dominant food staple in Ireland. When the potato blight hit that country in 1854, the result was starvation and a new migration of Irish to America.

This interactive relationship might best be noted in the specter of disease. Although there is continuing controversy about what diseases were introduced by outsiders into the Americas, it is generally held that smallpox, cholera, measles, diphtheria, typhoid fever, some strains of influenza, and the plague came from Europe and Africa. The affect of these diseases on American populations without previous exposure or immunity was devastating. Indian populations may have declined by 75 percent.

The influx of spices into Europe from the Malabar coasts of India and the precious metals delivered by the Spanish treasure fleets from the Americas proved to be a mixed blessing for the economy of Europe and highlights the importance of interdisciplinary study. The increase in gold and silver bullion certainly paid for innovations in printing, shipping, mining, textile manufacturing, and weapons development. The influx of bullion alone allowed Spain to launch its powerful naval Armada against England in 1588, France to develop its silk industry, and all of Europe to gorge on the bloody seventeenth-century wars of religion. But it also contributed to serious inflation that saw prices doubling in Spain by 1600, and the cost of food and clothing increasing by 100 percent in Germany by 1540.

By the eighteenth century, European trade rivalries for the products and labor of the Americas intensified. European empires existed to enrich the coffers of government and the pockets of the commercial elite. The Americas also provided new opportunities for Europe's disaffected and dispossessed, and a "pressure valve" for the home government that drained excess population from competitive domestic economies.

The competition between the French and British in Canada, on the North Atlantic seaboard, and along the Saint Lawrence and Mississippi rivers was particularly vicious as Indians and colonists alike fought in bitter rivalry. Although its supremacy on the west coast of North America and in much of South America was secure during the eighteenth century, Spain competed with both France and England for the lucrative sugar trade in the Carribean. The lesson was clear: National prosperity was directly linked to the protection of foreign trade and the efficient management of overseas empire.

The regulation of these empires in the seventeenth and eighteenth centuries was managed through an informal economic system called mercantilism. Mercantilist businessmen believed that the world contained a very limited amount of natural resources and that each country was in dire competition with the other. A country could only call itself wealthy if it could amass more bullion, grow more crops, and manufacture more goods than any other. The economic well-being of a country was therefore directly tied to the vitality of its colonies and the ability of each nation to control its colonial markets. Laws regulated just what goods colonists could produce and in what quantity. Colonists had to purchase certain raw materials from Europe and all colonial goods had to be transported by ships from the mother country. National monopoly was the prime directive.

But mercantilism was an inherently awkward economic system. Ultimately, the home and colonial markets did not mesh and the colonial governments, especially in America, chafed at the restrictions and grew restive. And there were new economic theories on the horizon. In 1776, Adam Smith in his treatise, *The Wealth of Nations,* envisioned a world of limitless resources, where the only restrictions were tied to ability and ambition—capitalism was born.

This chapter will explore the political, social, economic, and cultural interactions between different worlds in conflict during the sixteenth through eighteenth centuries. This is not a simple story to be summed up in a cute phrase. History reflects the complexity of human environments and as such is necessarily interactive. This is a bloody tale of the European encounter with the new worlds of Africa, Asia, and America. It is a story of greed, destruction, and ultimately of cultural awareness that affords perspective and presents new possibilities for the progress of World Civilization.

First Contact:
Exploration and Encounter

Christopher Columbus: "Admiral of the Ocean Sea"

The adventures and achievements of Christopher Columbus have stirred contro-
versy among historians for over a century. The 1992 quincentenary recognition
of his four voyages to the New World reignited debate between those who regard
him as a great explorer and true embodiment of the Renaissance spirit of discov-
ery and others who regard him as an exploiter, leader of the first invasion of Eu-
ropean barbarians, which resulted in the sixteenth-century conquests of the Aztecs
under Hernando Cortés and the Incas at the hands of Francisco Pizarro. Colum-
bus remains an enigmatic figure. His reputation as a skilled navigator has been
challenged, and his handling of his men was inept at best. Still, he provides an
important example of an individual who, through a supreme confidence in his
abilities and in the rightness of his vision, altered the course of history. But just
what was his vision, and how positive were his contributions to history?

Columbus expected that since the world was round, he could sail west and arrive
at Chipangu, the Japan mentioned by Marco Polo. There the wealth of the East
would justify his risk and hardship. Columbus's principle illusion, that he had suc-
cessfully made the voyage to Asia, was fostered by his need to provide evidence of a
wealth that would in turn justify the backing for future exploration. But the islands
in the Caribbean that he "discovered" were not rich. The gold he claimed to be just
about ready to discover was always on the next island. Ultimately, he was arrested
in Santo Domingo for misgovernment and sent home in chains. Yet even this
turned to his advantage as Columbus was viewed, even by his enemies, as a man of
destiny who had vastly extended the domain of Christianity.

The first selection from Columbus's initial voyage in 1492 is a digest of his
lost logbook made by Bartolome dé Las Casas, a friend of the Columbus family.
The second source is a letter written by Columbus to various supporters in Spain
on his return journey from the New World. These documents justify his actions
but also provide insight into this controversial historical figure.

Logbook of the First Voyage (1492)
BARTOLOMÉ DE LAS CASAS

On 2 January in the year 1492, when your Highnesses had concluded their
war with the Moors [Muslims in Spain] who reigned in Europe, I saw your
Highnesses' banners victoriously raised on the towers of the Alhambra, the

---

"Logbook of the First Voyage" is from *The Four Voyages of Christopher Columbus*, trans. J. M. Cohen (Baltimore, Md., and Harmondsworth, Middlesex: Penguin Books, 1969), pp. 37–38, 43,
51–53. Copyright © J. M. Cohen, 1969. Reprinted by permission.

citadel of that city, and the Moorish king come out of the city gates and kiss the hands of your Highnesses and the prince, My Lord. And later in that same month, on the grounds of information I had given your royal Highnesses concerning the lands of India and a prince who is called the Great Khan—which means in Spanish 'King of Kings'—and of his and his ancestors' frequent and vain application to Rome for men learned in the holy faith who should instruct them in it, your Highnesses decided to send me, Christopher Columbus, to see these parts of India and the princes and peoples of those lands and consider the best means for their conversion. For, by the neglect of the Popes to send instructors, many nations had fallen to idolatry and adopted doctrines of perdition, and your Highnesses as Catholic princes and devoted propagators of the holy Christian faith have always been enemies of the sect of Mahomet [Muhammad] and of all idolatries and heresies.

Your Highnesses ordained that I should not go eastward by land in the usual manner but by the western way which no one about whom we have

Portrait of Christopher Columbus, "Admiral of the Ocean Sea," by Ridolfo del Ghirlandaio (1483–1561). The exploits of this mythic adventurer continue to inspire controversy over the benefits and human tragedy associated with his linking of the European and American civilizations. *(Museo Navale di Pegli, Genoa, Italy. Scala/Art Resource, N.Y.)*

positive information has ever followed. Therefore having expelled all the Jews from your dominions in that same month of January, your Highnesses commanded me to go with an adequate fleet to those parts of India. In return you granted me great favors bestowing on me the titles of Don and High Admiral of the Ocean Sea and Viceroy and perpetual governor of such islands and mainland as I should discover and win or should in future be discovered and won in the Ocean Sea, and that these rights should be inherited by my eldest son and so on from generation to generation.

I departed from the city of Granada on Saturday, 12 May, and went to the seaport of Palos, where I prepared three ships very suitable for such a voyage and set out from that port well supplied both with provisions and seamen. Half an hour before sunrise on Friday, 3 August, I departed on a course for the Canary Islands, from which possession of your Highnesses I intended to set out and sail until I reached the Indies, there to deliver your Highnesses' letters to their princes and to fulfil your other commands. . . .

TUESDAY, 18 SEPTEMBER

During that day and night they made more than fifty-five leagues but he reckoned only forty-eight. On these days the sea was as smooth as the river at Seville. That day Martin Alonso called ahead in the Pinta, which was a fast ship; because, as he called to the Admiral from his ship, he had seen a great flock of birds flying westward and hoped to sight land that night; this was his reason for not holding back. To the north there appeared a great bank of clouds, which is a sign that land is near. . . .

WEDNESDAY, 10 OCTOBER

He sailed west-south-west, making ten miles an hour but sometimes dropping to seven and sometimes rising to twelve, and in the day and night together they went fifty-nine leagues, which he counted as no more than forty-four for the men. Here the men could bear no more; they complained of the length of the voyage. But the Admiral encouraged them as best he could, holding out high hopes of the gains they could make. He added that it was no use their complaining, because he had reached the Indies and must sail on until with the help of Our Lord he discovered land.

THURSDAY, 11 OCTOBER

He sailed west-south-west. They ran into rougher seas than any they had met with on the voyage. They saw petrels and a green reed near the ship. The men of the Pinta saw a cane and a stick and picked up another small stick, apparently shaped with an iron tool; also a piece of cane and some land-grasses and a small board. Those on the caravel Nina saw other indications of land and a stick covered with barnacles. At these signs, all breathed again and were rejoiced. That day they went twenty-seven leagues before sunset and after sunset he resumed his original western course. They made twelve miles an hour and up to two hours before midnight had gone ninety miles, which are twenty-two leagues and a half. The caravel Pinta, being swifter and sailing ahead of the Admiral, now sighted land and gave the signals which the Admiral had commanded.

The first man to sight land was a sailor call Rodrigo from Triana, who afterwards vainly claimed the reward, which was pocketed by Columbus. The Admiral, however, when on the sterncastle at ten o'clock in the night, had seen a light, though it was so indistinct he would not affirm that it was land. He called Pero Gutierrez, butler of the King's table, and told him that there seemed to be a light and asked him to look. He did so and saw it. He said the same to Rodrigo Sanchez of Segovia, whom the King and Queen had sent in the fleet as accountant, and he saw nothing because he was not in a position from which anything could be seen. After the Admiral spoke, this light was seen once or twice and it was like a wax candle that went up and down. Very few thought that this was a sign of land, but the Admiral was quite certain that they were near land. Accordingly, after the recitation of the Salve in the usual manner by the assembled sailors, the Admiral most seriously urged them to keep a good lookout from the forecastle and to watch carefully for land. He promised to give a silk doublet to the first sailor who should report it. And he would be entitled also to the reward promised by the sovereigns, which was an annual payment of ten thousand maravedis [a small copper coin].

Two hours after midnight land appeared, some two leagues away. They took in all sail, leaving only the mainsail, which is the great sail without bonnets, and lay close-hauled waiting for day. This was Friday, on which they reached a small island of the Lucayos, called in the Indian language Guanahani [Watling Island in the Bahamas]. Immediately some naked people appeared and the Admiral went ashore in the armed boat, as did Martin Alonso Pinzon and Vincente Yanez his brother, captain of the Nina. The Admiral raised the royal standard and the captains carried two banners with the green cross which were flown by the Admiral on all his ships. On each side of the cross was a crown surmounting the letters F and Y (for Ferdinand and Isabella [Ysabela]). On landing they saw very green trees and much water and fruit of various kinds.

The "New World"

CHRISTOPHER COLUMBUS

All these islands are very beautiful, and distinguished by a diversity of scenery; they are filled with a great variety of trees of immense height, and which I believe to retain their foliage in all seasons. . . . The inhabitants of both sexes in this island, and in all the others which I have seen, or of which I have received information, go always naked as they were born, with the exception of some of the women, who use the covering of a leaf or small bough, or an apron of cotton which they prepare for that purpose. None of them . . . are possessed of any iron, neither have they weapons, . . . [for] they are timid and full of fear. They

---

"The 'New World'" is from R. H. Major, ed., *Select Letters of Christopher Columbus* (London: The Hakluyt Society, 1847), pp. 5–9.

carry however in lieu of arms canes dried in the sun, on the ends of which they fix heads of dried wood sharpened to a point, and even these they dare not use habitually. . . . As soon as they see that they are safe, and have laid aside all fear, they are very simple and honest and exceedingly liberal with all they have. . . . They exhibit great love towards all others in preference to themselves; they also give objects of great value for trifles, and content themselves with very little or nothing in return. I however forbade that these trifles and articles of no value (such as pieces of dishes, plates, and glass, keys, and leather straps) should be given to them, although if they could obtain them, they imagined themselves to be possessed of the most beautiful trinkets in the world. . . . Thus they bartered, like idiots, cotton and gold for fragments of bows, glasses, bottles, and jars; which I forbade as being unjust, and myself gave them many beautiful and acceptable articles which I had brought with me, taking nothing in return. I did this in order that I might the more easily conciliate them, that they might be led to become Christians, and be inclined to entertain a regard for the King and Queen, our Princes and all Spaniards, and that I might induce them to take an interest in seeking out, and collecting, and delivering to us such things as they possessed in abundance, but which we greatly needed. They practice no kind of idolatry, but have a firm belief that all strength and power, and indeed all good things would come to them after they had thrown aside their fears. Nor are they slow or stupid, but of very clear understanding; and those men who have crossed to the neighboring islands give an admirable description of everything they observed; but they never saw any people clothed, nor any ships like ours. On my arrival at that sea, I had taken some Indians by force from the first island that I came to, in order that they might learn our language, and communicate to us what they knew respecting the country; this plan succeeded excellently, and was a great advantage to us, for in a short time, either by gestures and signs, or by words, we were enabled to understand each other. These men are still travelling with me, and although they have been with us now a long time, they continue to entertain the idea that I have descended from heaven; and on our arrival at any new place they published this, crying out immediately with a loud voice to the other Indians, "Come, come and look upon beings of a celestial race": upon which both women and men, children and adults, young men and old, when they got rid of the fear they at first entertained, would come out in throngs, crowding the roads to see us.

The Portuguese in Africa and India

Portugal was to play a primary role in the exploration of new worlds. The Portuguese had traditionally made their living on the sea both as fishermen and as traders, but the leadership of Prince Henry the Navigator (reigned 1394–1468) organized and intensified Portuguese exploration. Henry, inspired both by mercenary motives and missionary ideals, sponsored a series of explorations of the African coast in an effort to compete with Muslims who controlled the land routes of the gold trade. In addition to the lure of gold, the Portuguese saw opportunity in the spice trade of the East and sought to establish outposts that would provide access to new markets and the possibility of commercial dominance.

Explorers such as Bartholomew Dias in 1487 and Vasco da Gama in 1498, rounded the Cape of Good Hope at the tip of Africa and sailed east to India. The first ventures were especially lucrative; da Gama returned with a cargo worth sixty times the cost of the voyage. The Portuguese soon established themselves on the Malabar coast of western India with colonies in Goa and Calcutta. So effective were they in organizing and exploiting commercial links that by the sixteenth century, the Portuguese had successfully challenged the Arabs and Venetians for control of the European spice trade. By the next century, Portuguese contact extended to Japan and other lands in the Far East.

But the establishment of these commercial colonies came at a distinct price for the inhabitants of those regions. In the following selection, Duarte Barbosa (ca. 1480–1521), an agent of the Portuguese government who helped establish commercial contacts along the east African coast, describes the people and products of the area, and Portuguese methods for controlling trade.

The East Coast of Africa
DUARTE BARBOSA

Sofala

Going forward in the direction of India there is a river of no great size upon which up the stream is a town of the Moors [African Muslims] which they call Sofala, close to which the King our Lord [Portuguese King Manuel I] possesses a fort. These Moors have dwelt there a long time by reason of the great traffic which they carried on with the heathen of the mainland. The Moors of this place speak Arabic and have a king over them who is subject to the King our Lord.

And the manner of their traffic was this: they came in small vessels named zambucos from the kingdoms of Kilwa, Mombasa, and Malindi, bringing many cotton cloths, some spotted and others white and blue; also some of silk, and many small beads, grey, red, and yellow, which things come to the said kingdoms from the great kingdom of Cambay [on the coast of northwest India] in other greater ships. And these wares the said Moors who came from Malindi and Mombasa paid for in gold at such a price that those merchants departed well pleased . . .

Kilwa

Going along the coast from the town of Mozambique, there is an island hard by the mainland which is called Kilwa, in which is a Moorish town with many

"The East Coast of Africa" is from *The Book of Duarte Barbosa: An Account of the Countries Bordering the Indian Ocean*, 2 vols. (London: Hakluyt Society, 1918, 1921).

fair houses of stone and mortar, with many windows after our fashion, very well arranged in streets, with many flat roofs. The doors are of wood, well carved, with excellent joinery. Around it are streams and orchards and fruit-gardens with many channels of sweet water. It has a Morrish king over it. . . . Before the King our Lord sent out his expedition to discover India, the Moors of Sofala, Cuama, Angoya and Mozambique were all subject to the King of Kilwa, who was the most mighty king among them. And in this town was great plenty of gold, as no ships passed toward Sofala without first coming to this island . . .

This town was taken by force from its king by the Portuguese, as, moved by arrogance, he refused to obey the King our Lord. There took many prisoners and the king fled from the island, and His Highness ordered that a fort should be built there, and kept it under his rule and governance. . . .

Mombasa

Further on, an advance along the coast toward India, there is an isle hard by the mainland, on which is a town called Mombasa. . . . This Mombasa is a land very full of food. Here are found many very fine sheep with round tails, cows and other cattle in great plenty, and many fowls, all of which are exceedingly fat. There is much millet and rice, sweet and bitter oranges, lemons, pomegranates, Indian figs, vegetables of diverse kinds, and much sweet water. The men are often times at war . . . but at peace with those of the mainland, and they carry on trade with them, obtaining great amounts of honey, wax, and ivory.

The king of this city refused to obey the commands of the King our Lord, and through this arrogance he lost it, and our Portuguese took it from him by force. He fled away, and they slew many of his people and also took captive many, both men and women, in such sort that it was left ruined and plundered and burned. Of gold and silver great booty was taken here, bangles, bracelets, earrings and gold beads, also great store of copper with other rich wares in great quantity, and the town was left in ruins.

The City of Brava

Yet further along the coast, beyond these places, is a great town of Moors, of very fine stone and mortar houses, called Brava. It has no king, but is ruled by elders, and ancients of the land, who are the persons held in the highest esteem, and who have the chief dealings in merchandise of diverse kinds. And this place was destroyed by the Portuguese, who slew many of its people and carried many into captivity, and took great spoil of gold and silver and goods. Thenceforth many of them fled away toward the inland country, forsaking the town; yet after had been destroyed the Portuguese again settled and peopled it, so that now it is as prosperous as it was before.

"Our Kingdom Is Being Lost"

NZINGA MBEMBA (AFONSO I)

The next selection is a letter from the African King of Kongo, Nzinga Mbemba, who had converted to Christianity and adopted the name Afonso I (reigned ca. 1506–1543). Afonso had hoped to develop a prosperous state by cooperating with the Europeans. But by the time of his death, his kingdom had almost disintegrated. His concerns are expressed in a letter to the Portuguese king, Joao III, in 1526. It was evident that Portuguese exploitation and aggressive pursuit of slaves resulted in dissension and instability throughout the region.

Sir, Your Highness should know how our Kingdom is being lost in so many ways that it is convenient to provide for the necessary remedy, since this is caused by the excessive freedom given by your agents and officials to the men and merchants who are allowed to come to this Kingdom to set up shops with goods and many things which have been prohibited by us, and which they spread throughout our Kingdoms and Domains in such an abundance that many of our vassals, whom we had in obedience, do not comply because they have the things in greater abundance than we ourselves; and it was with these things that we had them content and subjected under our vassalage and jurisdiction, so it is doing a great harm not only to the service of God, but the security and peace of our Kingdoms and State as well.

And we cannot reckon how great the damage is, since the mentioned merchants are taking every day our natives, sons of the land and the sons of our noblemen and vassals and our relatives, because the thieves and men of bad conscience grab them wishing to have the things and wares of this Kingdom which they are ambitious of; they grab them and get them to be sold; and so great, Sir, is the corruption and licentiousness that our country is being completely depopulated, and Your Highness should not agree with this nor accept it as in your service. And to avoid it we need from your Kingdoms no more than some priests and a few people to teach in schools, and no other goods except wine and flour for the holy sacrament. That is why we beg of Your Highness to help and assist us in this matter, commanding your factors [agents] that they should not send here either merchants or wares, because it *our will that in these Kingdoms there should not be any trade of slaves nor outlet for them.* Concerning what is referred [to] above, again we beg of Your Highness to agree with it, since otherwise we cannot remedy such an obvious damage. Pray Our Lord in his mercy to have Your Highness under His guard and let you do forever the things of His service. . . .

Moreover, Sir, in our Kingdoms there is another great inconvenience which is of little service to God, and this is that many of our people, keenly

---

"Our Kingdom Is Being Lost" is from Basil Davidson, trans., *The African Past* (London: Curtis Brown Ltd., 1964), pp. 191–193. Reprinted by permission of Curtis Brown, Ltd., London. Copyright © 1964 by Basil Davidson.

desirous as they are of the wares and things of your Kingdoms, which are brought here by your people, and in order to satisfy their voracious appetite, seize many of our people, freed and exempt men, and very often it happens that they kidnap even noblemen and the sons of noblemen, and our relatives, and take them to be sold to the white men who are in our Kingdoms; and for this purpose they have concealed them; and others are brought during the night so that they might not be recognized.

And as soon as they are taken by the white men they are immediately ironed and branded with fire, and when they are carried to be embarked, if they are caught by our guards' men the whites allege that they have bought them but they cannot say from whom, so that it is our duty to do justice and to restore to the freemen their freedom, but it cannot be done if your subjects feel offended, as they claim to be.

And to avoid such a great evil we passed a law so that any white man living in our Kingdoms and wanting to purchase goods in any way should first inform three of our noblemen and officials of our court whom we rely upon in this matter, and these are Dom Pedro Manipanza and Dom Manuel Manissaba, our chief usher, and Gocalo Pires our chief freighter, who should investigate if the mentioned goods are captives or free men, and if cleared by them there will be no further doubt nor embargo for them to be taken and embarked. But if the white men do not comply with it they will lose the aforementioned goods. And if we do them this favor and concession it is for the part Your Highness has in it, since we know that it is in your service too that these goods are taken from our Kingdom, otherwise we should not consent to this. . . .

"Cut Off Their Ears, Hands and Noses!"
GASPAR CORREA

The following selection is an excerpt from the journals of Gaspar Correa, who sailed with Vasco da Gama in 1502. This incident occurred after a group of Portuguese had been killed in the trading station of Calcutta. Vasco da Gama sought to control the situation by exacting a bloody vengeance.

The captain-major [Vasco da Gama], on arriving at Calecut, was in the passion because he found the port cleared, and in it there was nothing to which he could do harm, because the Moors, knowing of his coming, had all fled, and hid their vessels and sambuks in the rivers. . . . The King of Calecut thought that he might gain time, so that the captain-major should not do him harm; and when his fleet arrived he sent him a Brahman [religious official] of his in a boat with a white cloth fastened to a pole, as a sign of peace. This Brahman came dressed in the habit of a friar, one of those who had been killed in the country; and on

"Cut Off Their Ears, Hands and Noses!" is from H.E.J. Stanley, ed., *The Three Voyages of Vasco de Gama* (London: The Hakluyt Society, 1869), pp. 328–332.

reaching the ship, he asked for a safe conduct to enter. When it was known that he was not a friar—for the captain-major and everyone had been joyful, thinking that he was one of our friars—seeing that he was not, the captain-major gave him a safe conduct, and bade him enter the ship. . . . He then ordered all the fleet to draw in close to the shore, and all day, till night, he bombarded the city, by which he made a great destruction. . . .

While they were doing this business, there came in from the offing two large ships and twenty-two sambuks and Malabar vessels, which came from Coromandel laden with rice, which the Moors of Calecut had ordered to be laden there; . . . but our fleet having sighted them, the [Portuguese] caravels went to them, and the Moors could not fly, as they were laden, and the caravels brought them to the captain-major, and all struck their sails. . . .

Then, the captain-major commanded them to cut off the hands and ears and noses of all the crews, and put all that into one of the small vessels, into which he ordered them to put the friar, also without ears, or nose, or hands, which he ordered to be strung round his neck, with a palm-leaf for the King, on which he told him to have a curry made to eat of what his friar brought him. When all the Indians had been thus executed, he ordered their feet to be tied together, as they had no hands with which to untie them: and in order that they should not untie them with their teeth he ordered them to strike upon their teeth with staves, and they knocked them down their throats; and they were thus put on board, heaped up upon the top of each other, mixed up with the blood which streamed from them; and he ordered mats and dry leaves to be spread over them, and the sails to be set for the shore, and the vessel set on fire; and there were more than eight hundred Moors; and the small vessel with the friar, with all the hands and ears, was also sent on shore under sail, without being fired. These vessels went at once on shore, where many people flocked together to put out the fire, and draw out those whom they found alive, upon which they made great lamentations.

Domination and Destruction

Hernando Cortés and the Conquest of Mexico

A primary area of historical controversy and dissension in the twentieth century concerns the Spanish conquest of Mexico and Peru and the subsequent administration of Spanish domains in the Western Hemisphere collectively called "New Spain." The role of the Spanish explorers and conquistadors as agents of destruction or purveyors of progress has been hotly disputed in recent years. Subsidized by Spanish royalty, explorers such as Hernando Cortés and Francisco Pizarro landed in Mexico (1519) and Peru (1531), respectively, with lofty dreams and visions of enormous wealth to be extracted from the inhabitants of this mythic land. The Spanish monarchy itself sought the wealth and geopolitical advantage that such a presence in the New World could bring, while the church saw an opportunity to spread the Christian faith to new lands without the stifling competition and dissension that the Protestant Reformation had engendered in Europe.

But it is dangerous to narrow the perspective, and the Spanish presence in New Spain surely combined national interest, religious zealotry, and personal greed. This was an encounter of unparalleled importance, and in the process of consolidating their claims, the Spanish destruction of native peoples and their cultures reflected a European arrogance and confirmation of the Machiavellian principle that the "ends justify the means." Indeed, the Catholic Church had difficulty tolerating the exploitation of native populations it was trying to convert. A "Black Legend" of Spanish abuse and butchery soon developed and, through the propaganda of Anglo-Dutch rivals, colored the Spanish national profile for centuries. This encounter between forces of the Old World and the New inaugurated centuries of exploitation and rigid consolidation that set precedents for slaughter and fueled competition among European powers.

The first source describes the initial encounter of the Aztecs with the Spanish explorers in 1519. The Franciscan friar Bernardino de Sahagún was instrumental in preserving information about Aztec culture and the history of this period. His intention was to understand native culture and religious beliefs in order to more effectively convert the Indians to Christianity. His General History of the Things of New Spain *was based on information gained from Aztec eyewitnesses and surviving participants to the conquest of Mexico from 1519 to 1521.*

The succeeding sources are excerpted from letters by Mexico's Spanish conqueror, Hernando Cortés. They lend a valuable perspective to the motives and methods of Spanish conquest in the New World.

The Aztec Encounter: "This Was Quetzalcoatl Who Had Come to Land"

BERNARDINO DE SAHAGÚN

When the first Spanish ships were seen in this land, Montezuma's stewards and captains who lived along the coast of Veracruz immediately assembled and took counsel among themselves, deciding whether they should give this news to their lord Montezuma, who was in the city of Mexico. The chief among them said, "In order for us to take an accurate report of this matter, it seems to me proper that we should see with our own eyes what this is; this we can do if we go to them on the pretext of selling them some things that they have need of." This seemed like a good idea to the others, and at once they took articles of food and clothing, and loaded into canoes what they were going to sell them and went to them by water. When they arrived at the

"The Aztec Encounter" is from Bernardino de Sahagún, *The Conquest of New Spain*, trans. Howard F. Cline (Salt Lake City: University of Utah Press, 1989), pp. 34–35. Copyright © 1989 University of Utah Press. Reprinted by permission. Editor's Note: the spelling of Montezuma has been standardized throughout this section.

flagship (to which they directed their canoes because of the banner they saw on it), immediately upon arriving they paid homage and gave signs that they came in peace to sell them food and clothing. [It was thought that this was Quetzalcoatl who had come to land.] The Spaniards asked them where they were from and what they came for. They said, "We are Mexicans." The Spaniards said, "If you are Mexicans, tell us who the lord of Mexico is."

The Indians said, "Gentlemen, the lord of Mexico is called Montezuma." Then the Spaniards answered, "Well, come and sell us some things that we need; climb up here and we shall look at them. Have no fear that we shall do you harm." . . . Then [the Indians] climbed into the ship and took with them certain bundles of rich [capes] that they had brought.

They spread them out in front of the Spaniards, who liked them and agreed to buy them, for which they gave the Indians strings of fake precious stones, some red, others green, some blue, others yellow. As they seemed to the Indians to be precious stones, they accepted them, and gave them the capes. . . . Finally the Spaniards said to them, "God go with you and take those stones to your master and tell him that we are unable to see him now . . . ; we will come again and go to see him in Mexico."

With this they departed in their canoes, and upon reaching land they got ready and departed for Mexico to give the news to Montezuma. . . .

Montezuma: "We Shall Obey You and Hold You As Our God"

HERNANDO CORTÉS

After we had crossed this bridge, Montezuma came to greet us and with him some two hundred lords, all barefoot and dressed in a different costume, but also very rich in their way and more so than the others. They came in two columns, pressed very close to the walls of the street, which is very wide and beautiful and so straight that you can see from one end to the other. . . . Montezuma came down the middle of this street with two chiefs, one on his right hand and the other on his left. . . . When we met I dismounted and stepped forward to embrace him, but the two lords who were with him stopped me with their hands so that I should not touch him; and they likewise all performed the ceremony of kissing the earth. . . .

When at last I came to speak to Montezuma himself I took off a necklace of pearls and cut glass that I was wearing and placed it round his neck; after we had walked a little way up the street a servant of his came with two necklaces, wrapped in a cloth, made from red snails' shells, which they hold in

"Montezuma" is from Hernando Cortés, *Letters from Mexico*, trans. and ed. A. R. Pagden, (New York: Grossman Publishers, 1971), pp. 84–86. Copyright © 1971 by A. R. Pagden. Reprinted by permission.

Hernando Cortés: "Montezuma came to greet us and with him some two hundred lords, all barefoot and dressed in a different costume, but also very rich in their way and more so than the others." *(Engraving by Theodor de Bry taken from a sixteenth-century Dutch edition of the* Short Account of the Destruction of the Indies *by Bartolome de las Casas. Reproduced by permission of the British Library)*

great esteem; and from each necklace hung eight shrimps of refined gold almost a span in length. . . . [Montezuma] took me by the hand and led me to a great room facing the courtyard through which we entered. And he bade me sit on a very rich throne . . . and addressed me in the following way:

"For a long time we have known from the writings of our ancestors that neither I, nor any of those who dwell in this land, are natives of it, but foreigners who came from very distant parts; and likewise we know that a chieftain, of whom they were all vassals, brought our people to this region. And he returned to his native land and after many years came again, by which time all those who had remained were married to native women and had built villages and raised children. And when he wished to lead them away again they would not go nor even admit him as their chief; and so he departed. And we have always held that those who descended from him would come and conquer this land and take us as their vassals. So because of the place from which you claim to come, namely from where the sun rises, and the things you tell us of the great lord or king who sent you here, we believe and are certain that he is our natural lord, especially as you say that he has known of us for some time. So be assured that we shall obey you and hold you as our lord in place of that great sovereign of whom you speak; and in this there shall be no offense or betrayal whatsoever. And in all the land that lies in my domain, you may command as you will, for you shall be obeyed; and all that we own is for you to dispose of us as you choose. Thus, as you are in your own country and your own house, rest now from the hardships of your journey and the battles which you have fought. . . ."

Human Sacrifice: "A Most Horrid and Abominable Custom"

HERNANDO CORTÉS

JULY 10, 1519

Most High, Mighty and Excellent Princes, Most Catholic and Powerful Kings and Sovereigns:

[The Aztecs] have a most horrid and abominable custom which truly ought to be punished and which until now we have seen in no other part, and this is that, whenever they wish to ask something of the idols, in order that their plea may find more acceptance, they take many girls and boys and even adults, and in the presence of the idols they open their chests while they are still alive and take out their hearts and entrails and burn them before the idols, offering the smoke as sacrifice. Some of us have seen this, and they say it is the most terrible and frightful thing they have ever witnessed.

This these Indians do so frequently that . . . not one year passes in which they do not kill and sacrifice some fifty persons in each temple. . . . Your Majesties may be most certain that, as this land seems to us to be very large, and to have many temples in it, not one year has passed, as far as we have been able to discover, in which three or four thousand souls have not been sacrificed in this manner.

Let Your Royal Highnesses consider, therefore, whether they should not put an end to such evil practices, for certainly Our Lord God would be well pleased if by the hand of Your Royal Highnesses the people were initiated and instructed in our Holy Catholic Faith, and the devotion, trust and hope which they have in these their idols were transferred to the divine power of God. . . . And we believe that it is not without cause that Our Lord God has been pleased that these parts be discovered in the name of Your Royal High-

"Human Sacrifice" is from Hernando Cortés, *Letters from Mexico*, trans. and ed. A. R. Pagden (New York: Grossman Publishers, 1971), pp. 35–36. Copyright © 1971 by A. R. Pagden. Reprinted by permission.

nesses so that Your Majesties may gain much merit and reward in the sight of God by commanding that these barbarous people be instructed and by Your hands be brought to the True Faith. For, as far as we have been able to learn, we believe that had we interpreters and other people to explain to them the error of their ways and the nature of the True Faith, many of them, and perhaps even all, would soon renounce their false beliefs and come to the true knowledge of God; for they live in a more civilized and reasonable manner than any other people we have seen in these parts up to the present.

The Destruction of Tenochtitlán:
"And Their Mothers Raised a Cry of Weeping"
BERNARDINO DE SAHAGÚN

The following accounts of the brutal destruction of the Aztec capital of Tenochtitlán, first from the native perspective and then from that of Cortés, demonstrate the advantages that the Spanish enjoyed with their armor, weaponry, horses, and sophisticated manipulation of the rivalries and animosities of Aztec enemies. Cortés had difficulty controlling the anger and brutality of his native allies who were released to fight against their Aztec rulers.

The greatest evil that one can do to another is to take his life when [the victim] is in mortal sin. This is what the Spaniards did to the Mexican Indians because they provoked them by being faithless in honoring their idols. [The Spaniards], catching [the Indians] enclosed [in the courtyard] for the feast [of Huitzilopochtli], killed them, the greater part of whom were unarmed, without their knowing why.

When the great courtyard of the idol, Huitzilopochtli, god of the Mexicans, was full of nobles, priests, and soldiers, and throngs of other people, intent upon the idolatrous songs to that idol, whom they were honoring, the Spaniards suddenly poured forth ready for combat and blocked the exits of the courtyard so that no one could escape. Then they entered with their weapons and ranged themselves all along the inner walls of the courtyard. The Indians thought that they were just admiring the style of their dancing and playing and singing, and so continued the style of their dancing and playing and singing, and so continued with their celebration and songs.

At this moment, the first Spaniards to start fighting suddenly attacked those who were playing the music for the singers and dancers. They chopped off their hands and their heads so that they fell down dead. Then all the other Spaniards began to cut off heads, arms, and legs and to disembowel the

"The Destruction of Tenochtitlán" is from Bernardino de Sahagún, *The Conquest of New Spain*, trans. Howard F. Cline (Salt Lake City: University of Utah Press, 1989), pp. 76–78. Copyright © 1989 University of Utah Press. Reprinted by permission.

Indians. Some had their heads cut off, others were cut in half, and others had their bellies slit open, immediately to fall dead. Others dragged their entrails along until they collapsed. Those who reached the exits were slain by the Spaniards guarding them; and others jumped over the walls of the courtyard; while yet others climbed up the temple; and still others, seeing no escape, threw themselves down among the slaughtered and escaped by feigning death.

So great was the bloodshed that rivers of blood ran through the courtyard like water in a heavy rain. So great was the slime of blood and entrails in the courtyard and so great was the stench that it was both terrifying and heartrending. Now that nearly all were fallen and dead, the Spaniards went searching for those who had climbed up the temple and those who had hidden among the dead, killing all those they found alive. . . .

Seeing themselves hotly pursued by the Mexicans, the Spaniards entered the royal houses and fortified and barricaded themselves as best they could to keep the Indians out. From inside they began to defend themselves, firing off crossbows, [rifles], and cannon, and even aiming stones from the rooftop to drive off the Indians struggling to break down the wall and force their way in.

Having a convenient opportunity, the Spaniards conferred with each other, and also with Montezuma and his courtiers, and decided to put them in irons. Meanwhile, the Mexicans were busy performing burial ceremonies for those who had been killed in the ambush and so delayed a few days before returning to do battle with the Spaniards. Great was the Indians' mourning over their dead. . . . [And their mothers, their fathers raised a cry of weeping. There was weeping for them. There was weeping.]

"We Could No Longer Endure the Stench of Dead Bodies"
HERNANDO CORTÉS

AUGUST 12, 1521

On leaving my camp, I had commanded Gonzalo de Sandoval to sail the brigantines [ships] in between the houses in the other quarter in which the Indians were resisting, so that we should have them surrounded, but not to attack until he saw that we were engaged. In this way they would be surrounded and so hard pressed that they would have no place to move save over the bodies of their dead or along the roof tops. They no longer had nor could find any arrows, javelins or stones with which to attack us; and our allies fighting with us were armed with swords and bucklers, and slaughtered so many of them on land and in the water that more than forty thousand were killed or taken that day. So loud was the wailing of the women and children that there was not one man among us whose heart did not bleed at the sound; and indeed we had more trouble in preventing our allies from killing with such cruelty than we had in fighting the enemy. For no race, however savage, has ever practiced such fierce and unnatural cruelty as the natives of these parts. Our allies also took many spoils that day, which we were unable to prevent, as they numbered more than 150,000 and we Spaniards were only some nine hundred. Neither our precautions nor our warnings could stop their looting, though we did all we could. One of the reasons why I had avoided entering the city in force during the past days was the fear that if we attempted to storm them they would throw all they possessed into the water, and, even if they did not, our allies would take all they could find. For this reason I was much afraid that Your Majesty would receive only a small part of the great wealth this city once had, in comparison with all that I once held for Your Highness. Because it was now late, and we could no longer endure the stench of the dead bodies that had lain in those streets for many days, which was the most loathsome thing in all the world, we returned to our camps.

Disease and the Encounter of New Worlds

Small pox was the captain of the men of death . . . in that war, typhus fever the first lieutenant, and measles the second lieutenant. More terrible than the conquistadores on horseback, more deadly than the sword and gunpowder, they made the conquest [of the Americas] . . . a walkover as compared with what it would have been without their aid. They were the forerunners of civilization, the companions of Christianity, the friends of the invader.

—P. M. Ashburn

It would be narrow and simplistic to view the Spanish conquest of Mexico and Peru from a military or even cultural perspective alone. For there were even more encompassing societal changes that affected both Europe and the Americas as a result of the encounter. Recent research has noted the importance of the Spanish introduction of horses to the Americas and especially the impact of these horses on the Native American cultures of the Southwest and Plains. In addition, the crops that poured into Europe from the Americas after 1492 included maize, potatoes, sweet potatoes, tomatoes, peanuts, and various kinds of peppers, beans, and squashes. When one considers that the four chief staples of the human diet in our contemporary world are wheat, rice, maize, and potatoes, the impact of the Old World on the New becomes apparent.

But perhaps the most immediate factor in the exchange of European and American cultures was disease. It has been proposed by scholars that syphilis, a disease unknown in Europe before the end of the fifteenth century, was brought to Europe by the Spaniards from America. The Indians suffered from it in a mild form, but it attacked the Spanish more severely. Next to tobacco, it may have been the most harmful gift of the Old World to the New. By the same token, the Spanish brought with them diseases against which the Indians had no resistance.

The smallpox as described in the first selection by Sahagún certainly devastated the Aztecs and may have been the pivotal factor in Cortés's success. The noted scholar William McNeill addresses these topics and offers a broader perspective in the second excerpt from his book Plagues and Peoples.

The Devastation of Smallpox
BERNARDINO DE SAHAGÚN

After the previously mentioned hardships that befell the Spaniards in the year 1519, at the beginning of the year 1520 the epidemic of smallpox, measles, and pustules broke out so virulently that a vast number of people died throughout this New Spain. This pestilence began in the province of Chalco and lasted for sixty days. Among the Mexicans who fell victim to this pestilence was the lord Cuitlahuactzin, whom they had elected a little earlier. Many leaders, many veteran soldiers, and valiant men who were their defense in time of war, also died.

During this epidemic, the Spaniards, rested and recovered, were already in Tlaxcala. Having taken courage and energy because of the ravages of the [Mexican] people that the pestilence was causing, firmly believing that God was on their side, being again allied with the Tlaxcalans, and attending to all the necessary preparations to return against the Mexicans, they began to construct the brigantines [ships] that they would need in order to wage war by water.

Spanish Success and Epidemic Disease
WILLIAM H. MCNEILL

Wholesale demoralization and simple surrender of will to live certainly played a large part in the destruction of the Amerindian communities. Numerous recorded instances of failure to tend newborn babies so that they died unnecessarily, as well as outright suicide, attest the intensity of

"The Devastation of Smallpox" is from Bernardino de Sahagún, *The Conquest of New Spain*, trans. Howard F. Cline (Salt Lake City: University of Utah Press, 1989), p. 103. Copyright © 1989 University of Utah Press. Reprinted by permission.

"Spanish Success and Epidemic Disease" is from William H. McNeill, *Plagues and Peoples* (New York: Doubleday, 1976), pp. 206–209. Copyright © 1976 by William H. McNeill. Reprinted by permission of Doubleday, a division of Bantam Doubleday Dell Publishing Group, Inc.

Amerindian bewilderment and despair. European military action and harsh treatment of laborers gathered forcibly for some large-scale undertaking also had a role in uprooting and destroying old social structures. But human violence and disregard, however brutal, was not the major factor causing Amerindian populations to melt away as they did. After all, it was not in the interest of the Spaniards and other Europeans to allow potential taxpayers and the Indian work force to diminish. The main destructive role was certainly played by epidemic disease.

The first encounter came in 1518 when smallpox reached Hispaniola and attacked the Indian population so virulently that Bartolomé de Las Casas believed only a thousand survived.

From Hispaniola, smallpox traveled to Mexico, arriving with the relief expedition that joined Cortés in 1520. As a result, at the very crisis of the conquest, when Montezuma had been killed and the Aztecs were girding themselves for an attack on the Spaniards, smallpox raged in Tenochtitlán. The leader of the assault, along with innumerable followers, died within hours of compelling the Spaniards to retreat from their city. Instead of following up on the initial success and harrying the tiny band of Spaniards from the land, therefore, as might have been expected had the smallpox not paralyzed effective action, the Aztecs lapsed into a stunned inactivity. Cortés thus was able to rally his forces, gather allies from among the Aztecs' subject peoples, and return for the final siege and destruction of the capital. Clearly, if smallpox had not come when it did, the Spanish victory could not have been achieved in Mexico. . . .

Two points seem particularly worth emphasizing here. First, Spaniards and Indians readily agreed that epidemic disease was a particularly dreadful and unambiguous form of divine punishment. Interpretation of pestilence as a sign of God's displeasure was a part of the Spanish inheritance, enshrined in the Old Testament and in the whole Christian tradition. The Amerindians, lacking all experience of anything remotely like the initial series of lethal epidemics, concurred. Their religious doctrines recognized that superhuman power lodged in deities whose behavior toward men was often angry. It was natural, therefore, for them to assign an unexampled effect to a supernatural cause, quite apart from the Spanish missionary efforts that urged the same interpretation of the catastrophe upon dazed and demoralized converts.

Secondly, the Spaniards were nearly immune from the terrible disease that raged so mercilessly among the Indians. They had almost always been exposed in childhood and so developed effective immunity. Given the interpretation of the cause of pestilence accepted by both parties, such a manifestation of divine partiality for the invaders was conclusive. The gods of the Aztecs as much as the God of the Christians seemed to agree that the white newcomers had divine approval for all they did. And while God thus seemed to favor the whites, regardless of their mortality and piety or lack thereof, his wrath was visited upon the Indians with an unrelenting harshness that often puzzled and distressed the Christian missionaries who soon took charge of the moral and religious life of their converts along the frontiers of Spain's American dominions. . . .

From the Amerindian point of view, stunned acquiescence in Spanish superiority was the only possible response. No matter how few their numbers or how
brutal and squalid their behavior, the Spaniards prevailed. Native authority
structures crumbled; the old gods seemed to have abdicated. The situation was
ripe for the mass conversions recorded so proudly by Christian missionaries.
Docility to the commands of priests, viceroys, landowners, mining entrepre-
neurs, tax collectors, and anyone else who spoke with a loud voice and had a
white skin was another inevitable consequence. When the divine and natural
orders were both unambiguous in declaring against native tradition and belief,
what ground for resistance remained? The extraordinary ease of Spanish conquests and the success a few hundred men had in securing control of vast areas
and millions of persons is unintelligible on any other basis.

The Advantages of Empire

The Spanish Empire in America

*With the exploration of America by Christopher Columbus in 1492, the subse-
quent Spanish conquest of the Aztecs by Hernando Cortés in 1519, and the Incas
by Juan Pizarro in 1531, perspectives suddenly changed. This "New World"
fired the imagination with the abstraction of discovery—the encounter with
strange peoples of different color, perspective, customs and religions. But it also
presented unique tangible opportunities to realize immense national and personal power through regional conquest and consolidation, and of untold, mythic
wealth through the exploitation and extraction of natural resources.*

*Thus began one of the most brutal episodes in modern Western history. The
Spanish* conquistadores *("conquerors") methodically organized the region in
order to extract the gold and silver that would allow Spain to surpass its rivals for
European power. This was an economy of exploitation that was primarily focused
on mining, agriculture, and shipping. There was little accommodation to the native population on the part of the Spanish as European language, values, and religion became the dominant culture of what would be called Latin America.*

*Although the Spanish were particularly attracted to gold, silver became the
primary metal of Mexico and Bolivia. Since the Spanish crown received one-fifth
(the* quinto*) of all mining revenues, it imposed a monopoly over the production
and sale of mercury, which was essential in the process of mining silver. The extraction of silver was such a labor-intensive process that the Spanish developed
various systems to compel and organize native workers.*

One of the most important was the encomienda*. Influential businessmen (encomenderos) received formal grants to the labor of a specified number of Indians
for a limited time. In the silver mines of Potosi, Bolivia, the* mita *or "labor tax"
placed on Indians required that they contribute a certain number of days of labor
annually to the Spanish authorities. Many of these Indians did not survive their*

mita *as conditions in the mines were dangerous and the overseers harsh in their demands.*

The following selection is from the meticulous Spanish government records on tribute assessments for the encomienda *of Nestalpa, a district north of Mexico City in 1565.*

The *Encomienda* System

In the city of Mexico on April 2, 1565, the [officials] of the royal audiencia of New Spain, having seen the account and visitation that was made of the town of Nestalpa, which Pedro Moreno and Pedro Valdovinos are said to have in encomienda, in view of what appears there and in view of the number of people that there are in the said town, ordered that the natives give in tribute each year 964 pesos and seven tomines . . . of common gold, the payments to be made three times a year, and also 410 1/2 fanegas of maize at harvest time, placed in the cabecera of the said town; of this the said encomenderos are to receive 821 common gold pesos and all the maize, and the 153 pesos and seven tomines remaining are for the community of the said town, and this amount is to be placed in a box of three keys, of which the governor is to have one, one alcalde [government magistrate] another, and a mayordomo [government steward] the third, and all three are to be present when funds are taken out for necessary and convenient expenditures for the republic. They are to keep accounts so that these can be shown on demand. And in order to pay the said tribute each married tributary is to pay each year nine and one-half silver reales and one-half fanega of maize, and each widower, widow, bachelor, and spinster possessing and living on lands outside the parental jurisdiction is to pay [half that]; and they are not to be taxed or assessed or required to pay more tribute, service, or anything else under penalty of the ordinances, cedulas, and provisions of his majesty. Under the said penalties no tribute is to be collected from the unmarried young men who are with their parents so long as they do not marry or go out to live by themselves, nor from the old people, the blind, the crippled, and the sick, who are exempt for the said count; and they are to keep this assessment and it is to be entered in the book of tributes; and it is charged to the said encomenderos that they provide what is necessary for the maintenance of the divine cult and support of the clergy who are in charge of the religion of the natives of the said town. And thus it was pronounced and ordered, marked as by the royal audiencia.

The Extraction of Mercury

ANTONIO VASQUEZ DE ESPINOSA

Antonio Vasquez de Espinosa (d. 1630) was a Spanish friar and missionary in the Americas, who sought to convert the Indians to Christianity. He returned to Spain in 1622 and wrote several accounts of his experiences. In the following excerpt, he describes the mita *system of forced Indian labor used in the dangerous process of extracting mercury from the mines. He then describes Potosi, the richest silver mine in the world. Such wealth allowed the Spanish government to wage wars in Europe against Protestant forces and contributed to the stability of the Spanish crown.*

And so at the rumor of the rich deposits of mercury . . . in the years 1570 and 1571, they started the construction of the town of Huancavelica de Oropesa in a pleasant valley at the foot of the range. It contains 400 Spanish residents, as well as many temporary shops of dealers in merchandise and groceries, heads of trading houses, and transients, for the town has a lively commerce. . . .

Every two months His Majesty sends by the regular courier from Lima 60,000 pesos to pay for the mita of the Indians, for the crews are changed every two months, so that merely for the Indian mita payment (in my understanding of it) 360,000 pesos are sent from Lima every year, not to speak of much besides, which all crosses at his risk that cold and desolate mountain country which is the puna [high plateau] and has nothing on it but llama ranches.

Up on the range there are 3,000 or 4,000 Indians working in the mine; it is colder up there than in the town, since it is higher. The mine where the mercury is located is a large layer which they keep following downward. When I was in that town (which was in the year 1616) I went up on the range and down into the mine, which at that time was considerably more than 130 stades deep [about 104 miles]. The ore was very rich black flint, and the excavation so extensive that it held more than 3,000 Indians working away hard with picks and hammers, breaking up that flint ore; and when they have filled their little sacks, the poor fellows, loaded down with ore, climb up those ladders or rigging, some like masts and others like cable, and so trying and distressing that a man empty-handed can hardly get up them. That is the way they work in this mine, with many lights and the loud noise of the pounding and great confusion. Nor is that the greatest evil and difficulty; that is due to thievish and undisciplined superintendents. As that great vein of ore keeps going down deeper and they follow its rich trail, in order to make sure that no section of that ore shall drop on top of them, they keep leaving supports or pillars of the ore itself, even if of the richest quality, and they necessarily help to sustain and insure each section with less risk. This being so, there are men so heartless that for the sake of stealing a little rich ore, they go down out of hours and deprive the innocent Indians of this protection by hollow-

"The Extraction of Mercury" is from Antonio Vasquez de Espinosa, *Compendium and Description of the West Indies* (Washington D.C.: Smithsonian Institution, 1942), pp. 621–625.

ing into these pillars to steal the rich ore in them, and then a great section is apt to fall in and kill all the Indians, and sometimes the unscrupulous and grasping superintendents themselves, as happened when I was in that locality; and much of this is kept quiet so that it shall not come to the notice of the manager and cause the punishment of the accomplices. . . .

This is how they extract the mercury. On the other side of the town there are structures where they grind up the mercury ore and then put it in jars with molds like sugar loaves on top of them, with many little holes, and others on top of them, flaring and plastered with mud, and a channel for it to drip into and pass into the jar or place where it is to fall. Then they roast the ore with a straw fire. . . . Under the onset of this fire it melts and the mercury goes up in vapor . . . until it cools and coagulates and starts falling downward again. Those who carry out the reduction of this ore have to be very careful and test cautiously; they must wait till the jars are cold before uncovering them for otherwise they may easily get mercury poisoning and if they do, they are of no further use; their teeth fall out, and some die. After melting and extracting the mercury by fire, they put it in dressed sheepskins to keep it in His Majesty's storehouses, and from there they usually transport it on llamaback to the port of Chincha . . . where there is a vault and an agent appointed by the royal Council, and he has charge of it there; then they freight it on shipboard to the port of San Marcos de Arica, from which it is carried by herds of llamas and mules to Potosi.

The Silver Mines of Potosi

ANTONIO VASQUEZ DE ESPINOSA

The famous Potosi range, so celebrated all over the world for the great wealth which God has created unique in its bowels and veins, lies in the Province of the Charcas, 18 leagues from the city of Chuquisaca, which was later called La Plata, on account of the great richness of this range. . . .

According to His Majesty's warrant, the mine owners on this massive range have a right to the mita of 13,300 Indians in the working and exploitation of the mines, both those which have been discovered, those now discovered, and those which shall be discovered. It is the duty of the Corregidor of Potosi [a district military officer] to have them rounded up and to see that they come in from all the provinces between Cuzco over the whole of El Collao and as far as the frontiers of Tarija and Tomina; this Potosi Corregidor [official] has power and authority over all the Corregidors in those provinces mentioned; for if they do not fill the Indian mita allotment assigned each of them in accordance with the capacity of their provinces as indicated to them, he can send them, and does, salaried inspectors to report upon it, and when the remissness is great or remarkable, he can suspend them, notifying the Viceroy of the fact.

"The Silver Mines of Potosi" is from Antonio Vasquez de Espinosa, *Compendium and Description of the West Indies* (Washington D.C.: Smithsonian Institution, 1942), pp. 631–634.

These Indians are sent out every year under a captain whom they choose in each village or tribe, for him to take them and oversee them for the year each has to serve; every year they have a new election, for as some go out, others come in. This works out very badly, with great losses and gaps in the quotas of Indians, the villages being depopulated; and this gives rise to great extortions and abuses on the part of the inspectors toward the poor Indians, ruining them and thus depriving the chief Indians of their property and carrying them off in chains because they do not fill out the mita assignment, which they cannot do, for the reason given and for others which I do not bring forward.

These 13,300 are divided up every four months into three mitas, each consisting of 4,443 Indians, to work in the mines on the range and in the 120 smelters in the Potosi and Tarapaya areas; it is a good league [three miles] between the two. These mita Indians earn each day, or there is paid each one for his labor, four reals [Spanish silver coins]. . . .

After each [Indian] has eaten his ration, they climb up the hill, each to his mine, and go in, staying there from that hour until Saturday evening without coming out of the mine; their wives bring them food, but they stay constantly underground, excavating and carrying out the ore from which they get the silver. They all have tallow candles, lighted day and night; that is the light they work with, for as they are underground, they have need of it all the time. . . .

So huge is the wealth which has been taken out of this range since the year 1545, when it was discovered, up to the present year of 1628, which makes 83 years that they have been working and reducing its ores, that merely from the registered mines, as appears from an examination of most of the accounts in the royal records, 326,000,000 pesos have been taken out.

Over and above that, such great treasure and riches have come from the Indies in gold and silver from all the other mines in New Spain and Peru, Honduras, the New Kingdom of Granada, Chile, New Galicia, New Vzcaya [north central and northwestern Mexico], and other quarters since the discovery of the Indies, that they exceed 1,800 millions.

The Barbarians of the New World: "They Are Slaves By Nature"
JUAN GINES DE SEPULVEDA

Juan Gines de Sepulveda (1490–1573) was a scholar and apologist for the Spanish treatment of Indians in the Americas. His argument, in essence, is one that would be echoed by conquerors of later ages, from the nineteenth century British imperialists and American Social Darwinists, to the Nazis of the twenti-

"The Barbarians of the New World" is from Charles Gibson, editor and translator, *The Spanish Tradition in America* (Columbia, South Carolina: University of South Carolina Press, 1968), pp. 116–120. Copyright © 1968 by Charles Gibson. Reprinted by permission.

eth century: Superior peoples had the right to enslave inferior peoples. For Sepul-
veda, the Aztecs were stupid, cruel, immoral, and deserved destruction; they were
"natural slaves." Note how his argument is countered by Bartolomé de Las Casas
in the succeeding source.

Turning then to our topic, whether it is proper and just that those who are
superior and who excel in nature, customs, and laws rule over their inferiors,
you can easily understand . . . if you are familiar with the character and moral
code of the two peoples, that it is with perfect right that the Spaniards exercise their dominion over those barbarians of the New World and its adjacent
islands. For in prudence, talent, and every kind of virtue and human senti-
ment they are as inferior to the Spaniards as children are to adults, or women
to men, or the cruel and inhumane to the very gentle, or the excessively intemperate to the continent and moderate. . . .

And what shall I say of [Spanish] moderation in rejecting gluttony and lasciviousness, inasmuch as no nation or very few nations of Europe can compare with the frugality and sobriety of the Spaniards? I admit that I have observed in these most recent times that through contact with foreigners luxury
has invaded the tables of our nobles. Still, since this is reproved by good men
among the people, it is to be hoped that in a short while they may return to
the traditional and innate sobriety of our native custom. . . .

As for the Christian religion, I have witnessed many clear proofs of the
firm roots it has in the hearts of Spaniards, even those dedicated to the military. . . . What shall I say of the Spanish soldiers' gentleness and humanitarian
sentiments? Their only and great solicitude and care in the battles, after the
winning of the victory is to save the greatest possible number of vanquished
and free them from the cruelty of their allies. Now compare these qualities of
prudence, skill, magnanimity, moderation, humanity, and religion with those
of those little men [of America] in whom one can scarcely find any remnants
of humanity. They not only lack culture but do not even use or know about
writing or preserve records of their history—save for some obscure memory
of certain deeds contained painting. They lack written laws and their institutions and customs are barbaric. And as for their virtues, if you wish to be informed of their moderation and mildness, what can be expected of men committed to all kinds of passion and nefarious lewdness and of whom not a few
are given to the eating of human flesh. Do not believe that their life before
the coming of the Spaniards was one of . . . peace, of the kind that poets sang
about. On the contrary, they made war with each other almost continuously,
and with such fury that they considered a victory to be empty if they could
not satisfy their prodigious hunger with the flesh of their enemies. . . . But in
other respects they are so cowardly and timid that they can scarcely offer any
resistance to the hostile presence of our side, and many times thousands and
thousands of them have been dispersed and have fled like women, on being
defeated by a small Spanish force scarcely amounting to one hundred. . . .

Could there be a better or clearer testimony of the superiority that some
men have over others in talent, skill, strength of spirit, and virtue? Is it not

proof that they are slaves by nature? For the fact that some of them appear to have a talent for certain manual tasks is no argument for their greater human prudence. We see that certain insects, such as the bees and the spiders, produce works that no human skill can imitate. . . .

I have made reference to the customs and character of the barbarians. What shall I say now of the impious religion and wicked sacrifices of such people, who, in venerating the devil as if he were God, believed that the best sacrifice that they could placate him with was to offer him human hearts? . . . Opening up the human breasts they pulled out the hearts and offered them on their heinous altars. And believing that they had made a ritual sacrifice with which to placate their gods, they themselves ate the flesh of the victims. These are crimes that are considered by the philosophers to be among the most ferocious and abominable perversions, exceeding all human iniquity. . . .

How can we doubt that these people—so uncivilized, so barbaric, contaminated with so many impieties and obscenities—have been justly conquered by . . . a nation excellent in every kind of virtue, with the best law and best benefit for the barbarians? Prior to the arrival of the Christians they had the nature, customs, religion, and practice of evil sacrifice as we have explained. Now, on receiving with our rule our writing, laws, and morality, imbued with the Christian religion, having shown themselves to be docile to the missionaries that we have sent them, as many have done, they are as different from their primitive condition as civilized people are from barbarians, or as those with sight from the blind, as the inhuman from the meek, as the pious from the impious, or to put it in a single phrase, in effect, as men from beasts.

The "Black Legend" of Spain
BARTOLOMÉ DE LAS CASAS

More than any other single individual, the Dominican friar Bartolomé de Las Casas was responsible for the birth of the "Black Legend," the vicious Spanish reputation that developed during the sixteenth and seventeenth centuries. Although the Black Legend became primarily an instrument of Anglo-Dutch propaganda against the Spanish which Las Casas probably would never have accepted, his influence in its creation is undeniable. After witnessing the ravages and atrocities of Spanish colonists, Las Casas dedicated himself to the protection and defense of the Indians. He wrote the Short Account of the Destruction of the Indies *in 1542 and dedicated it to the Spanish king Philip II in an effort to inform the crown of atrocities in the New World which, if not curtailed, would result in God's destruction of Spain. This book, a fierce and deeply atmospheric anatomy of genocide, established the image of the Spanish conquest of*

"The 'Black Legend' of Spain" is from Bartolomé de Las Casas, *A Short Account of the Destruction of the Indies,* trans. and ed. Nigel Griffin (New York and Harmondsworth, Middlesex: Penguin Books, 1967), pp. 14–15. Copyright © Nigel Griffin, 1992. Reprinted by permission.

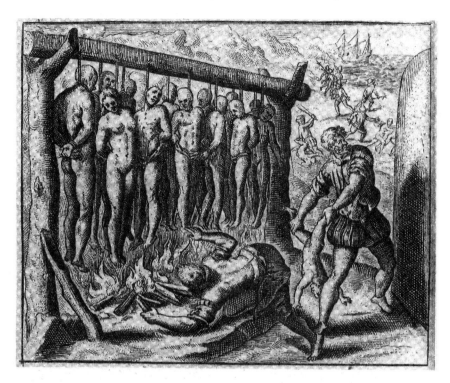

Bartolomé de Las Casas: "[The Spaniards] spared no one, erecting especially wide gibbets on which they could string their victims up with their feet just off the ground and then burn them alive." *(Illustration by the Flemish engraver Theodor de Bry taken from a sixteenth-century Dutch edition of the* Short Account of the Destruction of the Indies *by Bartolomé de las Casas. Reproduced with permission of the British Library)*

America for the next three centuries. It is testimony to the persuasive and endur-ing influence of the Black Legend that the Spanish government hoped to amend this pejorative image by hosting the 1992 Olympics in Barcelona.

As we have said, the island of Hispaniola was the first to witness the arrival of Europeans and the first to suffer the wholesale slaughter of its people and the devastation and depopulation of the land. It all began with the Europeans taking native women and children both as servants and to satisfy their own base appetites; then not content with what the local people offered them of their own free will (and all offered as much as they could spare), they started taking for themselves the food that natives contrived to produce by the sweat of their brows, (which was in all honesty little enough). . . . Some of them started to conceal what food they had, others decided to send their women and children into hiding, and yet others took to the hills to get away from the brutal and ruthless cruelty that was being inflicted on them. The Christians punched them, boxed their ears and flogged them in order to track down the local leaders, and the whole shameful process came to a head when one of the European commanders raped the wife of the paramount chief of the entire island. It was then that the locals began to think up ways of driving the Europeans out of their lands and to take up arms against them. Their weapons, however, were flimsy and ineffective both in attack and in defence (and, indeed, war in the Americas is no more deadly than our jousting, or than many European children's games) and, with their horses and swords and lances, the Spaniards easily fended them off, killing them and committing all kind of atrocities against them.

They forced their way into native settlements, slaughtering everyone they found there, including small children, old men, pregnant women, and even women who had just given birth. They hacked them to pieces, slicing open their bellies with their swords as though they were so many sheep herded into a pen. They even laid wagers on whether they could manage to slice a man in two at a stroke, or cut an individual's head from his body, or disembowel him with a single blow of their axes. They grabbed suckling infants by the feet and, ripping them from their mothers' breasts, dashed them headlong against the rocks. . . . They slaughtered anyone and everyone in their path, on occasion running through a mother and her baby with a single thrust of their swords. They spared no one, erecting especially wide gibbets on which they could string their victims up with their feet just off the ground and then burn them alive thirteen at a time, in honor of our Savior and the twelve Apostles, or tie dry straw to their bodies and set fire to it. Some they chose to keep alive and simply cut their wrists, leaving their hands dangling, saying to them: "Take this letter"—meaning that their sorry condition would act as a warning to those hiding in the hills. The way they normally dealt with the native leaders and nobles was to tie them to a kind of griddle consisting of sticks resting on pitchforks driven into the ground and then grill them over a slow fire, with the result that they howled in agony and despair as they died a lingering death.

The Colonization and Settlement of the New World

Although the Portuguese and the Spanish took the lead in exploring and methodically exploiting new worlds for economic gain in the fifteenth and sixteenth centuries, other European nations did not stand idly by. England, France, and the Netherlands often staked their competitive claims to the same regions in North America. A race of sorts was on to occupy and explore the forests and waterways of Canada and the east coast of North America. Early explorers such as Jacques Cartier, Samuel de Champlain, and Henry Hudson would establish bases for economic gain and religious freedom that became important in the "planting" of colonists in the New World.

Although most governments gave their sanction and even economic support to these activities, the English proved hesitant. The first selection is by Richard Hakluyt (1552–1616), a passionate geographer and churchman who sought to convince Queen Elizabeth I in 1584 of the political and economic advantages of establishing colonies in Norumbega, the east coast of North America. Hakluyt hoped to gain government sponsorship of Sir Walter Raleigh's project in Virginia, but Elizabeth declined and English colonization became the focus of private enterprise or religious commitment as reflected in the second selection. This is William Bradford's account of the Pilgrim landing at Plymouth in 1620. Religious freedom would become a primary inspiration for English colonization. Note Bradford's concerns as the colonists faced the dangerous unknown.

The Advantages of Colonization (1584)

RICHARD HAKLUYT

Chapter XX: A brief collection of certain reasons to induce her Majesty and the state to take in hand the western voyage [to America] and the planting [of colonies] there:

1. The soil yields and may be made to yield all the several commodities of Europe. . . .
2. The passage [there] and home is neither too long nor too short, but easy, and to be made twice in the year.
3. The passage does not cut near the trade of any prince, nor near any of their countries or territories, and is a safe passage, and not easy to be [interfered with] by prince or potentate whatsoever.
6. This enterprise may stay the Spanish king from flowing over all the face of that [uninhabited land] of America, if we seed and plant there in time. . . . And England possessing the purposed place of planting, her Majesty may, by the benefit of the seat, having won good and royal havens, have plenty of excellent trees for masts, of goodly timber to build ships and to make great navies, of pitch, tar, hemp, and all things incident for a navy royal, and that for no price, and without money or request. How easy a matter may it be to this realm, swarming at this day with valiant youths, trusting and hurtful by lack of employment, and having good makers of cable and of all sorts of [ship rigging], and the best and most cunning shipwrights of the world, to be lords of all those seas, and to spoil [King Philip of Spain's American] navy, and to deprive him of yearly passage of his treasure to Europe, and consequently to abate the pride of Spain and the supporter of the great Anti-Christ of Rome [the pope], and to pull him down in equality to his neighbor

"The Advantages of Colonization" is from Charles Deane and Leonard Woods, eds., *Documentary History of the State of Maine* (Collections of the Maine Historical Society, 2nd series, Volume 2, 1877). Text modernized by the editor.

princes, and consequently to cut off the common mischiefs that come to all Europe by the peculiar abundance of his Indian [American] treasure, and this without difficulty.

11. At the first traffic with the people of those parts, the subjects of this realm for many years shall change many cheap commodities of these parts for things of high value [which are not esteemed there]; and this to the great enriching of the realm, if common use [holds true].

12. By the great plenty of those regions the merchants and their [agents] shall lie there cheap, buy and repair their ships cheap, and shall return at pleasure without stay or restraint of foreign prince; whereas upon stays and restraints the merchant raises his charge in sale over his [expenses] . . .

15. The substances serving, we may out of those parts receive the mass of [manufactured] wares that now we receive out of France, Flanders, Germany, etc.; and so we man [subdue] the pride of some enemies of this realm, or at the least in part purchase those wares, that now we buy dearly of the French and Flemish, better cheap; and in the end, for the part that this realm was [going] to receive, drive them out of trade to idleness [because of the employment of our people].

16. We shall by planting there enlarge the glory of the Gospel, and from England plant sincere religion, and provide a safe and a sure place to receive people from all parts of the world that are forced to flee for the truth of God's word.

18. The Spaniards govern in the Indies [America] with all pride and tyranny; and like as when people of contrary nature at sea enter into galleys, where men are tied as slaves, all yell and cry with one voice, *Liberta, Liberta,* as desirous of liberty and freedom, so no doubt whensoever the Queen of England, a prince of such clemency, shall seat upon that firmament of America, and shall be reported throughout all that tract to use the natural people there with all humanity, courtesy, and freedom, they will yield themselves to her government, and revolt clean from the Spaniard. . . .

21. Many soldiers, in the end of the wars, that might be hurtful to this realm, may there be unladen [deposited], to the common profit and quiet of this realm, and to our foreign benefit there, as they may be employed.

22. The [class] of wandering beggars of England, that grow up idly, and hurtful and burdenous to this realm, may there be unladen, better bred up, and may people waste countries to the home and foreign benefit, and to their own more happy state.

23. If England cry out and affirm that there are so many in all trades that one cannot live for another, as in all places they do, this [land in America] offers the remedy.

The Landing at Plymouth (1620)

WILLIAM BRADFORD

Being thus arrived in a good harbor and brought safe to land, [the colonists] fell upon their knees and blessed the God of Heaven, who had brought them over the vast and furious ocean, and delivered them from all the perils and miseries thereof, again to set their feet on the firm and stable earth, their proper element. And no marvel if they were thus joyful. . . .

But here I cannot but stay and make a pause, and stand half amazed at this poor people's present condition; and so I think the reader will too, when he well considers the same. Being thus passed the vast ocean, and a sea of troubles before in their preparationp . . . , they had now no friends to welcome them, nor inns to entertain or refresh their weatherbeaten bodies, no houses or much less towns to [inhabit], to seek for aid. . . . And since the season was winter, and they that know the winters of [their own] countries know them to be sharp and violent, and subject to cruel and fierce storms, dangerous to travel to known places, much more to search an unknown coast. Besides, what could they see but a hideous and desolate wilderness, full of wild beasts and wild men? . . . [Because summer was over], all things stood upon them with a weatherbeaten face; and the whole country, full of woods and thickets, represented a wild and savage [terrain]. If they looked behind them, there was the mighty ocean which they had passed, and was now a [primary] bar and gulf separate them from all the civilized parts of the world. . . .

What could now sustain them but the spirit of God and his grace? May not and ought not the children of these fathers rightly say: Our fathers were Englishmen who came over this great ocean, and were ready to perish in this wilderness; but they cried unto the Lord, and he heard their voice, and looked on the adversity. Let them therefore praise the Lord, because He is good and His mercies endure forever. Yea, let they who have been redeemed of the Lord, show how He has delivered them from the hand of the oppressor. When they wandered in the desert wilderness, and found no city to dwell in, both hungry and thirsty, their soul was overwhelmed in them. Let them confess before the Lord His loving kindness, and His wonderful works before the sons of men.

"Murdered in Cold Blood" (1643)

DAVID PIETERZEN DE VRIES

The early Dutch colonists settled primarily in New York along the banks of the Hudson River. New Netherland, as it was called by its founder Henry Hudson

"The Landing at Plymouth" is from William Bradford, *History of the Plymouth Plantation*, contained in James Harvey Robinson and Charles A. Beard, *Readings in Modern European History* (Boston: Ginn and Company, 1908), vol. 1, pp. 123–125. Text modernized by the editor.

"Murdered in Cold Blood" is from David Pieterzen de Vries, *Voyages from Holland to America* (New York: Billin and Brothers, 1853), pp. 114–117.

in 1609, was settled through large grants of land to wealthy Dutchmen called patroons, who in turn agreed to settle fifty tenants within four years. David Pieterzen de Vries was a landowner in the Netherlands who settled in New Amsterdam (New York City) as a patroon in the 1640s. Relations with the Algonquin and Raritan Indian tribes had generally been cordial until the arrival of Governor Willem Kieft in 1642. When Kieft tried to tax the natives and force them off their land, the relationship degenerated as de Vries relates in his account of a vicious massacre.

The 24th of February, sitting at a table with the Governor, he began to state his intentions, that he had a mind to *wipe the mouths* of the savages; . . . Moreover, as I was the first to come from Holland or Zeeland to plant a colony, [I requested] that he should consider what profit he could derive from this business, as he well knew that on account of trifling with the Indians we had lost our colony in the South River at Swanendael, in the Hoere-kil, with thirty-two men, who were murdered in the year 1630; and that in the year 1640, the cause of my people being murdered on Staten Island was a difficulty which he had brought on with the Raritan Indians, where his soldiers had for some trifling thing killed some savages. . . . But it appeared that my speaking was of no avail. He had, with his co-murderers, determined to commit the murder, deeming it a [glorious] deed, and to do it without warning the inhabitants in the open lands that each one might take care of himself against the retaliation of the savages, for he could not kill all the Indians.

When I had expressed all these things in full, sitting at the table, and the meal was over, he told me he wished me to go to the large hall, which he had been lately adding to his house. Coming to it, there stood all his soldiers ready to cross the river to Pavonia to commit the murder. Then spoke I again to Governor Willem Kieft: "Let this work alone; you wish to break the mouths of the Indians, but you will also murder our own nation, for there are none of the settlers in the open country who are aware of it. My own dwelling, my people, cattle, corn, and tobacco will be lost." He answered me, assuring me that there would be no danger; that some soldiers should go to my house to protect it. But that was not done. So was this business begun between the 25th and 26th of February in the 1643.

I remained that night at the Governor's, sitting up. I went and sat by the kitchen fire, when about midnight I heard a great shrieking, and I ran to the ramparts of the fort, and looked over to Pavonia. I saw nothing but firing, and heard the shrieks of the savages murdered in their sleep. I returned again to the house by the fire. Having sat there awhile, there came an Indian with his squaw, whom I knew well, and who lived about an hour's walk from my house, and told me that they two had fled in a small skiff, which they had taken from the shore at Pavonia; that the Indians from Fort Orange had surprised them; and that they had come to conceal themselves; that they who had killed their people at Pavonia were not Indians, but the Swannekens, as they call the Dutch, had done it. They then asked me how they should get out of the fort. I took them to the door, and there was no sentry there, and so they betook themselves to the woods. When it was day the soldiers returned to the fort, having massacred or murdered eighty Indians, and considering they had done a deed of [glorious] valor, in murdering so many in their sleep; where infants were torn from their mother's breasts, and hacked to pieces in the presence of the parents, and the pieces thrown into the fire and in the water, and other sucklings, being bound to small boards, were cut, stuck, and pierced, and miserably massacred in a manner to move a heart of stone.

Some were thrown into the river, and when the fathers and mothers endeavored to save them, the soldiers would not let them come on land but made both parents and children drown—children from five to six years of age, and also some old and decrepit persons. Those who fled from this onslaught, and concealed themselves in the neighboring sedge, and when it was morning, came out to beg a piece of bread, and to be permitted to warm themselves, were murdered in cold blood and tossed into the fire or the water. Some came to our people in the country with their hands, some with their legs cut off, and some holding their entrails in their arms, and others had such horrible cuts and gashes, that worse than they were could never happen. And these poor simple creatures, as also many of our own people, did not know any better than that they had been attacked by a party of other Indians—the Maquas. After this exploit, the soldiers were rewarded for their services, and Director Kieft thanked them by taking them by the hand and congratulating them. . . .

This is indeed a disgrace to our nation, who have so generous a governor in our Fatherland as the Prince of Orange [Frederick Henry], who has always endeavored in his wars to spill as little blood as possible.

As soon as the savages understood that the Swannekens had so treated them, all the men whom they could surprise on the farmlands, they killed; but we have never heard that they have ever permitted women or children to be killed. They burned all the houses, farms, barns, grain, haystacks, and destroyed everything they could get hold of. So there was an open destructive war begun. They also burnt my farm, cattle, corn, barn, tobacco-house, and all the tobacco. . . . While my people were in alarm, the savage whom I had aided to escape from the fort in the night came there, and told the other Indians that I as a good chief, that I had helped him out of the fort, and that the killing of the Indians took place contrary to my wish. Then they all cried out together to my people that they would not shoot them; that if they had not destroyed my cattle they would not do it, nor burn my house; . . . but hearing now that it had been done contrary to my wish, they all went away, and left my house unbesieged. When now the Indians had destroyed so many farms and men in revenge for their people, I went to Governor Willem Kieft, and asked him if it was not as I had said it would be, that he would only effect the spilling of Christian blood. Who would now compensate us for our losses? But he gave me no answer. He said he wondered that no Indians came to the fort. I told him that I not wonder at it: "why should the Indians come here where you have so treated them?"

The Missions of California (1769)

FATHER JUNIPERO SERRA

*Although it often seems that the relationship between colonists and the indige-
nous populations of America were strained and destructive, this was certainly
not always the case. One of the most important moderating forces against the exploitation of forced labor and the economy of extraction so dominant in the Spanish experience was the Franciscan friar, Father Junipero Serra (1713–1784). His
was a vision, not of conquest, but of peaceful coexistence through conversion of
the native population to Christianity. Although the process of conversion itself
can be considered a form of intolerance, Father Serra sought to engage Indians as
children of God. His sensitivity to their humanity contrasts sharply with the brutal realities of life in the silver mines of Bolivia or on the sugar cane plantations
of the Carribean.*

*In 1769, Father Serra set out from Loreto, Mexico to establish a string of mis-
sions which would eventually extend north to San Francisco and beyond. Although this could be dangerous work, for the Indians were sometimes hostile to
the presence of churchmen accompanied by soldiers, Father Serra proved to be a
positive force in the establishment of humane values in early California. In the
following account from his journals, Father Serra discusses the land, the dangers, and his vision for the missions of California.*

As to my own experiences, the whole trip was a very happy one without
mishap or change in my health. As I crossed the frontier my leg and foot
were in bad shape. But God was good to me. Every day I felt better, and kept
up with the day's marches just as if nothing were wrong with me. At the present time the foot is as completely well as the other; but from the ankle half
way up the leg, it is like the foot was before—one large wound, but without
swelling or pain except a certain amount of itching. Anyway it is a matter of
little moment.

I never went short of food or of anything; neither did the Indian neophytes with us; and so they all arrived in good health and in good condition. I
kept a diary and I will send a copy of it to Your reverence at the first opportunity. The missions, in the country we have seen, will all be very good, as there
is good land, good water supply, and neither here nor in much of the country
behind us is it very rocky or choked with thorns. Mountains, yes, plenty of
them—and big ones too—but of pure soil. The roads are both good and bad;
the latter most of the time. But that is of no importance. Halfway on our journey or even before that, all the arroyos [rivers] and valleys were dotted with
groves of trees. Vines grow well and plentifully and in some places, they are
laden with grapes. In various arroyos along the way, and in the place where

Retrato del Rev. Padre Fray Junipero Serra. Apostol de la Alta California, tomado del original que se conserva en su Convento de la Santa Cruz de Querétaro.

Portrait of Father Junipero Serra who established a string of missions along the "King's Highway" from Mexico to northern California. *(From the painting at Mission Santa Barbara, Archive/Library)*

we are, besides the vines there are various kinds of Castilian roses. In short, it is a good country—distinctly better than Old California [Mexico]. . . .

After having established the mission in San Diego in July, 1769, Father Serra noted the poor condition of the Indians living in the countryside and regretted the fact that the missionaries did not have an interpreter to communicate with them. On August 15, the situation deteriorated into violence.

When these natives, with whom the soldiers from the very beginning showed much familiarity, noticed how small our numbers were, and that we were continually burying a great number, and that many besides were prostrate in bed on the Assumption Day of Our Blessed Lady, they imagined they could kill us all very easily. The more so when out of our very limited number they saw four going to the beach to change escort and bring back Father Fernando. He had gone on the preceding Saturday to say Mass for those on the boat.

They broke in all of a sudden; and the only four soldiers present, seeing their ugly mood, immediately snatched up their arms. The fight was on. There were wounded both on our side and theirs. The one worst hurt was a young Spanish lad from the diocese of Guadalajara. He came to me in Loreto to be my servant on the road, and to be with me wherever I should be established.

At the first shot he darted into my hut, spouting so much blood at the mouth and from his temples, that I had hardly time to absolve him and help him to meet his end. This came in less than a quarter of an hour. He expired on the ground before me bathed in his own blood. And so I was quite a while with him there dead, and my little apartment a pool of blood. Still the exchange of shots—bullets and arrows—went on. There were only four on our side against more than twenty on theirs. And there I was with the dead man, thinking it most probable I would soon have to follow him, but at the same time praying to God that the victory would be for our catholic Faith without losing a single soul.

And so it turned out, thank God, for seeing many of their companions covered with blood, they all fled. . . . they are all by this time recovered from their wounds, and we are all, since then, living in peace. . . .

In this letter from Monterrey dated June, 1771, Father Serra reviewed his activity and offered plans for future missionary work in northern California.

I can tell you that, over and above the ten new [missions] that are going to be founded—five between San Fernando de Velicata and San Diego, and five, counting San Buenaventura, between San Diego and Monterey—and afterwards that of San Francisco . . . , it is of vital interest that, as soon as possible, almost as many more should be founded, since from here to San Francisco at least two more are needed.

In the stretch between San Luis Obispo and San Buenaventura, three more are needed. They may be all on the Channel itself, to provide for that immense [Indian] population, living in so many large pueblos, and to prepare the way for the conversion of the islands facing them whose people maintain by means of their canoes a frequent intercourse with the inhabitants of the mainland, and vice versa; or at least two missions on the Channel and the third midway between the Channel and El Buchon, or San Luis. Furthermore, between San Buenaventura and San Gabriel, one, or better still, two. Another between San Gabriel and San Diego. The rest should be placed in the empty space between San Diego and Velicata.

Such a plan would mean—over and above the great increase in Christianity, and an almost uninterrupted chain of missions covering an immense stretch of country, and that is our principal aim—that the religious who have to come would be saved by the hardship of the ocean trip; the journey would be by land, and they would sleep at least every third day in a mission belonging to the College. This would make the whole trip easy, even if they had to go as far as San Francisco. There would only be the short sea crossing from San Blas to Loreto.

The gentleness and peaceful dispositions of the Indians are an incentive to travel by that route, and although in some parts they show signs of being troublesome, it is a matter of small importance; we all have to put up with some annoyance for God.

The Mercantile Economy

Since the Renaissance, Europeans had sought new economic horizons. The commercial revolution of the sixteenth century and the exploration of the Americas had resulted in the establishment of colonies that engendered competition among imperial powers. Dominance and success in this commercial rivalry required that nations such as Spain, France, Great Britain, and the Netherlands become efficient producers and resourceful traders. To this end, governments focused their domestic economies and strictly regulated their foreign colonies in order to produce profit at each turn. This was especially important because these powers were constantly at war with each other in the eighteenth century, often squandering the precious wealth that they had accumulated.

To the extent that there was any formal economic theory behind this process of accumulating wealth, it was called mercantilism. Mercantilism gradually became a structured economic system based on the notion that the world was an arena of scarce resources. Since gold, silver and other products were limited, governments had to regulate trade with protective tariffs, navigation laws that restricted trade with rivals, and domestic monopolies on salt and gunpowder. Mercantilist statesmen believed that their economies could grow only at the expense of others.

Although this economic system developed in the seventeenth century, it became more pronounced in the eighteenth as the wars in Europe and North America forced each country to become even more heavy-handed. The first selection by the French King Louis XIV reflects the suggestions of his Finance Minister Jean Colbert. Colbert wanted to structure and strengthen the domestic economy of France so that it might be more competitive abroad. He was willing to use the treasury of the French state in order to regulate and support an efficient commercial base.

The next two selections by the West Indies merchant Fayer Hall and Sir William Keith, English Governor of Pennsylvania from 1712–1726, encapsulate the tenets of mercantilism and the "Old Colonial System" that drew every ounce of profit from the colonies. But there were also critics and the reaction to this economic regulation reached a climax in the late eighteenth century with the ideas of Adam Smith.

The Efficiency of the Domestic Economy (1664)
KING LOUIS XIV

Very Dear and Well Beloved:

Considering how advantageous it would be to this realm to reestablish its foreign and domestic commerce, . . . we have resolved to create a council particularly devoted to commerce, to be held every fortnight in our presence, in which all the interests of merchants and the means conducive to the revival of commerce shall be considered and determined upon, as well as all that which concerns manufactures.

We also inform you that we are setting apart, among the expenses of our State, a million livres each year for the encouragement of manufactures and the increase of navigation, to say nothing of the considerable sums which we cause to be raised to supply the companies of the East and West Indies;

That we are working constantly to abolish all the tolls in which are collected on the navigable rivers;

That there has already been expended more than a million livres for the repair of the public highways, to which we shall also devote our constant attention;

That we will assist by money from our royal treasury all those who wish to reestablish old manufactures or to undertake new ones; . . .

That all the merchants and traders by sea who purchase vessels, or who build new ones, for traffic or commerce shall receive from us subsidies for each ton of merchandise which they export or import on the said voyages.

We desire, in this present letter, not only to inform you concerning all these things, but to require you, as soon as you have received it, to cause to be assembled all the merchants and traders of your town of Marseilles, and explain to them very particularly our intentions in all matters mentioned above, in order that, being informed of the favorable treatment which we desire to give them, they may be the more desirous of applying themselves to commerce. Let them understand that for everything that concerns the welfare and advantage of the same they are to address themselves to Sieur Colbert. . . .

"The Efficiency of the Domestic Economy" is from James Harvey Robinson and Charles A. Beard, *Readings in Modern European History* (Boston: Ginn and Company, 1908), vol. 1, pp. 13–14.

The "Clear Profit" of the Old Colonial System (1731)

FAYER HALL

Hence may be perceived the excellence of our economy and government, that in [climates] less temperate and kind [than the Spanish Indies], on Lands less luxurious and fruitful, unacquainted with mines of gold or silver, our own people enjoy happiness and pleasures, are comparatively more wealthy, are justly esteemed more considerable, their productions from their labour infinitely more valuable, and their trade more beneficial to their native kingdom, as well as themselves.

In pursuance of my design, I shall consider the advantages we receive from our sugar islands: and first I shall begin with Barbados. Of what consequence the island of Barbados is to this Kingdom, might in a great measure be estimated from the amount of the 4½ percent [tax] on their sugars only, which sum has amounted many years to upwards of £10,000 a year, as I have been informed. And the vast advantage it is to this Kingdom will further appear, when we consider the numbers of people which are constantly employed for the supplying of that island with almost all sorts of our own manufactures: and if it be farther considered and allowed that not less than 1000 of our own seamen are constantly employed, on account of that island only; at a time too when 200 tons of craft, or shipping, do not require above 20 men; so that there is not less than 10,000 tons of shipping constantly employed: which shipping, or at least three fourths of the whole, if not built in England are always repaired, refitted, [stocked] and constantly paid here; and it never yet was suggested that one penny of money or bullion was ever carried there from England. . . .

Bermudas, though a small island, or rather a great many small islands, lies . . . about two hundred leagues distant from the continent of America. In Queen Ann's War [1702–1713] there was upwards of a hundred sail of brigantines and sloops [war ships] belonging to this island; but at present I am assured that there is not above half that number. This island, which was formerly one of the most fruitful, is now near worn out; and such is and will be the fate of all small islands, where people increase so fast, and so constantly keep their lands tilled. Such in part is the case of the island of Barbados already, yet the planters there are not willing to remove to places where twice the quantity of sugars may be made by the same labor as there. The people of Bermudas too are not easily persuaded to remove to a better country, where the same degree of industry and frugality, which these people are remarkable for, would soon enrich them. These people are extremely civil and kind to strangers; and when they have a

"The 'Clear Profit' of the Old Colonial System" is from Fayer Hall, *The Importance of the British Plantations in America to this Kingdom* (London, 1731) in *English Historical Documents* (London, 1957), Vol. X (1714–1783), pp. 764–765, 768.

good governor, as it is universally allowed they had by Governor Bennet, no people are more happy. They have very few priests, very few physicians, and fewer lawyers. All the necessaries which they want, such as apparel and household goods, they are furnished with from hence; for which they send us money, and fine [material] for making women's hats, etc. together with whatever they can spare, of any commodities which bear a price here. The Bermudians in general are excellent hands on board of sloops [ships], and the best fishermen that I ever knew. They navigate their vessels at less expense than any other people, and consequently can get by smaller freights.

To conclude, I am of opinion that this Kingdom gains clear profit by our American colonies yearly, the sum of one million sterling, exclusive of what we get by any trades for Negroes or dry goods by the Spaniards; and that in and by our colonies only, we maintain and employ at least eighteen thousand seamen and fishermen.

Economic Regulation: "The Maxim of All Polite Nations"

SIR WILLIAM KEITH

When either by conquest or increase of people, foreign provinces are possessed, and colonies planted abroad, it is convenient, and often necessary, to substitute little dependant provincial governments, whose people being enfranchised, and made partakers of the liberties and privileges belonging to the original Mother State, are justly bound by its laws, and become subservient to its interests, as the true end of their incorporation.

Every act of a dependant provincial government therefore ought to terminate in the advantage of the Mother State, unto whom it owes its being, and by whom it is protected in all its valuable privileges: hence it follows, that all advantageous projects or commercial gains in any colony, which are truly prejudicial to, and inconsistent with the interest of the Mother State, must be understood to be illegal, and the practice of them unwarrantable, because they contradict the end for which the colony had a being, and are incompatible with the terms on which the people claim both privilege and protection. . . .

It has ever been the maxim of all polite nations, to regulate their government to the best advantage of their trading interest. . . . By this short view of trade in general we may plainly understand that those colonies can be very beneficially employed both for Great Britain and themselves, without interfering with any of the staple manufactures in England.

But in order to set this point yet in a clearer light, we will proceed to consider some of the obvious regulations on the American trade, for rendering the colonies truly serviceable to Great Britain.

"Economic Regulation" is from Sir William Keith, *A Collection of Papers and Other Tracts, Written Occasionally on Various Subjects* (London: J. Mechell, 1740), pp. 169–170, 173–175.

1. That all the product of the colonies, for which the manufacture and trade of Britain has a constant demand, be enumerated among the goods which by law must be first transported to Britain, before they can be carried to any other market.
2. That all kinds of woollen manufactures for which the colonies have a demand, shall continue to be brought from Britain only, and linens from Great Britain and Ireland.
3. All other European commodities to be carried to the colonies, (salt excepted) entry thereof to be first made in Britain, before they can be transported to any of the English colonies.
4. The colonies to be absolutely restrained in their several governments from laying any manner of duties on shipping or trade from Europe, or upon European goods transported from one colony to another.

Supposing these things to be done, it will evidently follow that the more extensive the trade of the colonies is, the greater will be the advantages accruing to Great Britain therefrom; and consequently, that the enlargement of the colonies, and the increase of their people, would still be an addition to the national strength. . . .

From what has been said of the nature of colonies, and the restriction that ought to be laid on their trade, it is plain that none of the English plantations in America can with any reason or good sense pretend to claim an absolute legislative power with themselves; so that let their several Constitutions be founded by Charters, Royal Patents, . . . or what other legal authority you please; yet still they cannot be possessed of any rightful capacity to contradict, or evade the true intent and force of any Act of Parliament, wherewith the wisdom of Great Britain may think fit to affect them from time to time.

The Wealth of Nations (1776)

ADAM SMITH

Adam Smith can rightly be considered one of the most influential thinkers of the Enlightenment. He studied moral philosophy at Oxford and in his mid-twenties conceived of an economic philosophy of "the obvious and simple system of natural liberty," which the world would come to know as capitalism. In response to the restrictive emphasis of mercantilism, Smith conceived of an expansive universe, full of opportunity for the individual or nation to exercise initiative, accumulate wealth, and serve others in the process.

The following selection is an excerpt from his major work, The Wealth of Nations. *It focuses on Smith's view of human nature and the "invisible hand" of competition as guide to an economic system based on individual self-interest.*

"The Wealth of Nations" is from Adam Smith, *An Inquiry into the Nature and Causes of the Wealth of Nations,* ed. Edwin A. Seligman (London: J.M. Dent, 1901), pp. 12–15, 400–401, 436–437.

If one views the Industrial Revolution of the early nineteenth century and the birth of Marxism in 1848 as being directly influenced by Smith's theories, then his impact on the history of the twentieth century is immeasurable.

Human Nature and the Division of Labor

This division of labour, from which so many advantages are derived, is not originally the effect of any human wisdom, which foresees and intends that general opulence to which it gives occasion. It is the necessary, though very slow and gradual, consequence of a certain propensity in human nature which has in view no such extensive utility; the propensity to truck, barter, and exchange one thing for another.

Whether this propensity be one of those original principles in human nature, of which no further account can be given; or whether, as seems more probable, it be the necessary consequence of the faculties of reason and speech, it belongs not to our present subject to enquire. It is common to all men, and to be found in no other race of animals, which seem to know neither this nor any other species of contracts. . . . In civilized society, [man] stands at all times in need of the cooperation and assistance of great multitudes, while his whole life is scarce sufficient to gain the friendship of a few persons. In almost every other race of animals each individual, when it is grown up to maturity, is entirely independent, and in its natural state has occasion for the assistance of no other living creature. But man has almost constant occasion for the help of his brethren, and it is in vain for him to expect it from their benevolence only. He will be more likely to prevail if he can interest their self-love in his favour, and show them that it is for their own advantage to do for him what he requires of them. Whoever offers to another a bargain of any kind, proposes to do this. Give me that which I want, and you shall have this which you want, is the meaning of every such offer; and it is in this manner that we obtain from one another the far greater part of those good offices which we stand in need of. It is not from the benevolence of the butcher, the brewer, or the baker, that we expect our dinner, but from their regard to their own interest. We address ourselves, not to their humanity but to their self-love, and never talk to them of our own necessities but of their advantages. . . .

The difference of natural talents in different men is, in reality, much less than we are aware of; and the very different genius which appears to distinguish men of different professions, when grown up to maturity, is not upon many occasions so much the cause, as the effect of the division of labour. The difference between the most dissimilar characters, between a philosopher and a common street porter, for example, seems to arise not so much from nature, as from habit, custom, and education. When they came into the world, and for the first six or eight years of their existence, they were, perhaps, very much alike, and neither their parents nor playfellows could perceive any remarkable difference. About that age, or soon after, they come to be employed in very different occupations. The difference of talents comes then to be taken notice of, and widens by degrees, till at last the vanity of the philosopher is willing to acknowledge scarce any resemblance. . . . By nature a philosopher is not in genius and disposition half so different from a street porter, as a mastiff is from a grey-hound, or a greyhound from a spaniel, or this last from a shepherd's dog. . . . Among men, on the contrary, the most dissimilar geniuses are of use to one an-other; the different produces of their respective talents, by the general disposi-tion to truck, barter, and exchange, being brought, as it were, into a common stock, where every man may purchase whatever part of the produce of other men's talents he has occasion for. . . .

The Invisible Hand

As every individual, therefore, endeavors as much as he can both to employ his capital in the support of domestic industry, and so to direct that industry that its produce may be of the greatest value; every individual necessarily labours to render the annual revenue of the society as great as he can. He generally, indeed, neither intends to promote the public interest, nor knows how much he is promoting it. . . . He intends only his own security; and by di-recting that industry in such a manner as its produce may be of the greatest value, he intends only his own gain, and he is in this, as in many other cases, led by an invisible hand to promote an end which was no part of his inten-tion. Nor is it always the worse for the society that it was no part of it. By pur-suing his own interest he frequently promotes that of the society more effec-tually than when he really intends to promote it. I have never known much good done by those who affected to trade for the public good. . . . The states-man, who should attempt to direct private people in what manner they ought to employ their capitals, would not only load himself with a most unnecessary attention, but assume an authority which could safely be trusted, not only to no single person, but to no council or senate whatever, and which would nowhere be so dangerous as in the hands of a man who had folly and pre-sumption enough to fancy himself fit to exercise it.

Unreasonableness of Restraints

Each nation has been made to look with an invidious eye upon the prosperity of all nations with which it trades, and to consider their gain as its own loss. Commerce, which ought naturally to be, among nations, as among individu-als, a bond of union and friendship, has become the most fertile source of discord and animosity. . . . The violence and injustice of the rulers of mankind is an ancient evil, for which, I am afraid, the nature of human af-fairs can scarce admit of a remedy. But the mean rapacity, the monopolising spirit of merchants and manufacturers, who neither are, nor ought to be, the rulers of mankind, though it cannot perhaps be corrected, may very easily be prevented from disturbing the tranquility of anybody but themselves.

That it was the spirit of monopoly which originally both invented and propagated this doctrine cannot be doubted; and they who first taught it were by no means such fools as they who believed it. In every country it always is and must be the interest of the great body of the people to buy whatever they want of those who sell it cheapest. The proposition is so very manifest that it seems ridiculous to take any pains to prove it; nor could it have ever been called in question had not the interested sophistry of merchants and manufacturers confounded the common sense of mankind. Their interest is, in this respect, directly opposite to that of the great body of the people. As it is the interest of the freemen of a [guild] to hinder the rest of the inhabitants from employing any workmen but themselves, so it is the interest of the merchants and manufacturers of every country to secure to themselves the monopoly of the home market. Hence in Great Britain, and in most other European countries, the extraordinary duties upon almost all goods imported by alien merchants. Hence the high duties and prohibitions upon all those foreign manufactures which can come into competition with our own. Hence, too, the extraordinary restraints upon the importation of almost all sorts of goods from those countries . . . whom national animosity happens to be most violently inflamed. . . . This very competition, however, is advantageous to the great body of the people, who profit greatly besides by the good market which the great expense of such a nation affords them in every other way.

The Legacy of Cultural Interaction

In commemoration of the 500th anniversary of Christopher Columbus's first voyage to the Americas in 1492, the Smithsonian Institution sponsored a 1992 exhibit entitled "Seeds of Change" that revealed the impact Columbus's voyages had on the subsequent history of the world. Herman J. Viola, Director of the Quincentenary Programs at the National Museum of Natural History, defined the "seeds of change" as plants, animals, and diseases that established interactive links between the European and American worlds. Scholars working on the project chose five examples to represent the Columbian exchange: sugar, maize, disease, the horse, and the potato. Each of these seeds incorporated an expansive human story, whether positive or negative, that truly transformed the biological landscape and contributed to new foundations of political, social, and economic life. This excerpt from the commemorative volume accompanying the exhibition illustrates these intercultural links.

"Seeds of Change"

HERMAN J. VIOLA

What Columbus had really discovered was . . . another old world, one long populated by numerous and diverse peoples with cultures as distinct, vibrant, and worthy as any to be found in Europe. Tragically, neither Columbus nor those who followed him recognized this truth. The Europeans regarded the

peoples whom they encountered in North and South America more as natural objects—another form of the fauna to be discovered and exploited—
than as human beings with histories as rich and ancient as their own. They
could not imagine that these peoples could offer anything of aesthetic or cultural value. Only recently, in fact, have we come to realize that what Columbus did in 1492 was to link two old worlds, thereby creating one new world.

Another tragedy of 1492 was the failure of the Europeans to recognize the
fragility of the American environment. They set to work despoiling the resources of the New World as quickly as they began destroying its peoples.
What had taken nature thousands of centuries to create was largely undone
in less than five, beginning in September 1493, when the Admiral of the
Ocean Sea returned to America at the head of an armada of seventeen ships.
These disgorged on Hispaniola some fifteen hundred would-be empire
builders and a Noah's ark of Old World animals and plants including horses,
cows, pigs, wheat, barley, and shoots of sugarcane, which was, next to disease,
perhaps the most detrimental contribution of the Old World to the New.

Sugarcane merits censure because it harmed both man and the environment. With sugarcane came the plantation system and the initial assault on
the tropical rain forests of the New World. Sugarcane was a labor-intensive
crop that absorbed huge human resources, beyond what was needed for altering the landscape, to make large-scale production both possible and profitable. Although American Indians were readily enslaved, they just as readily
died—in vast numbers from the diseases the Europeans introduced to the
New World along with their plants and animals.

Consider, for example, what occurred on the island of Hispaniola, where
Columbus established Santo Domingo, the first permanent colony in the
New World. In neither Haiti nor the Dominican Republic, which share this island today, are there any descendants of the original Indian inhabitants. Indeed, the native peoples had disappeared by 1600. Although no one knows
what their numbers were in 1492, current estimates range from sixty thousand to as many as eight million. Columbus himself remarked that "the Indians of this island . . . are its riches, for it is they who dig and produce the
bread and other food for the Christians and get the gold from the mines . . .
and perform all the services and labor of men and of draft animals." . . .

When there were no longer sufficient Indians to maintain the New World
plantations, Europeans turned to Africa for labor. The exact number of
Africans kidnapped and sold into New World slavery will never be known, but
estimates range from ten to thirty million. Despite the enormous loss of life,
both in the transatlantic passage and in the New World, that slavery entailed—
perhaps the life of one slave for each ton of sugar produced—Africans not only
made sugar production profitable but they also replaced Indians as the dominant ethnic group in the Caribbean. Ironically, it may have been maize, a New
World food taken to Africa by Europeans, that underlaid population growth on
that continent and enabled Atlantic slavers to keep the sugar, cotton, and tobacco plantations of the New World supplied with labor. . . .

Although literally hundreds of examples could have been chosen to represent the Columbian exchange, the scholars working on this project selected

five: sugar, maize, disease, the horse, and the potato. Many will argue effectively that alternative plants and animals—tobacco, quinine, rubber, cattle, or a dozen others—were more important. Nonetheless, each of these seeds was chosen because of the human dimension in its story. Sugar led directly to the enslavement of Africans and the transformation of New World ecosystems; maize fed the Africans that provided the manpower for American plantations; the potato, like maize, was developed by American Indians and has become a basic food of people around the globe; disease, especially smallpox, measles, even the common cold, wrought havoc with New World peoples. Exact figures will never be known, but scholars believe that fifty to ninety percent of the Indians in North and South America died of diseases introduced from Europe. Most of those who died never saw a European; the diseases radiated throughout the New World much like ripples in a pond. The demoralization and psychological devastation caused by Old World diseases also worked in favor of the European settlers in displacing the native peoples. . . .

The horse, the fifth seed of change, was one gift from the Old World that Indians came to embrace and cherish. At first amazed by these strange creatures, the Indians of North and South America eventually became some of the finest riders the world has known. Even today members of many North American tribes regard the horse as a vital part of their culture.

"Seeds of Change," . . . is an attempt to interpret the true meaning of Columbus five hundred years after that fateful day when the Admiral of the Ocean Sea stepped ashore in the Bahamas and unwittingly changed the course of world history.

CHRONOLOGY: "An Embarrassment of Riches": The Interaction of New Worlds

1394–1468	Reign of Portuguese Prince Henry the Navigator, who organized and sanctioned Portuguese exploration on the coasts of Africa and India.
1478–1492	Florence ruled by Lorenzo d'Medici, called "The Magnificent." Florence at height of political and artistic influence.
1487	Bartholomew Dias opens spice routes to the East.
1492	Columbus' first voyage to the eastern Bahamas in search of a route to India.
1498	Vasco da Gama trades on Malabar coast of India.
1498–1512	Florence survives as a true republic. Niccolò Machiavelli looks toward a strong, practical rule and writes *The Prince* (1513).
1503–1513	Papacy of Julius II, "Warrior Pope" and patron of the arts (commissions Michelangelo's painting of the Sistine Chapel, among other works).

1517	Protestant reformer Martin Luther posts Ninety-five Theses on Wittenberg church door in hopes of engaging clerical authorities in debate.
1519–1521	Hernando Cortés lands on the coast of Mexico and brutally defeats Aztec forces.
1526	Afonso I, King of Kongo, writes to Portuguese King Joao III requesting him to condemn slavery.
1531–1533	Francisco Pizarro conquers Incas in Peru.
1558–1603	Reign of Queen Elizabeth of England, last Tudor monarch.
1584	Colonization of North America proposed to Elizabeth I by Richard Hakluyt and Sir Walter Raleigh
1585	Silver mines of Potosi, Bolivia bring extraordinary wealth to Spain.
1588	King Philip II launches Spanish Armada against England.
1607	English settlement of Jamestown.
1608	Samuel de Champlain founds Quebec.
1610–1625	Reign of English King James I.
1620	Pilgrims land at Plymouth.
1624	Dutch colony New Netherland founded.
1628–1630	Puritans establish Massachusetts Bay Colony near Boston.
1642–1649	English Civil War and establishment of the Commonwealth.
1643–1715	Reign of French King Louis XIV.
1673	Exploration of the Mississippi River by Jacques Marquette and Louis Joliet.
1754–1763	French and Indian War in America.
1769	Father Junipero Serra begins establishment of California missions.
1776	Adam Smith publishes *The Wealth of Nations*.

STUDY QUESTIONS

1. In the logbook of Columbus's first voyage to the New World, what are the primary reasons he gives for wanting to sail to "the lands of India"? Do you think he was revealing the truth? What other motives might have influenced his decision to sail? Can you find evidence of them in this source? How did Columbus treat the inhabitants of the islands? Was Columbus a great explorer who reflected the adventurous spirit of the Renaissance, or an exploiter of peoples?

2. In the description of the east coast of Africa by Duarte Barbosa, what does he find most important and impressive? What is the Portuguese method of doing business? How does Barbosa justify the destruction of African cities?

3. In his correspondence with the Portuguese king, what matters were of the gravest concern to the King of Kongo, Afonso I? Why was his kingdom "out of balance" and what reforms did he suggest? Does Afonso's predicament reveal a Portuguese policy of political and commercial exploitation consistent with the description given by Duarte Barbosa in the previous selection? What does the account of mutilation in the following selection by Gaspar Correa say about Portuguese methods of control? Is a trading relationship based on fear a good commercial policy?

4. Analyze the sources in the section on the conquest of Mexico. What were Cortés' motives in sailing to Mexico? Why did he decide to destroy the Aztecs after having been accepted as conqueror by Montezuma? Compare the two accounts of Cortés and Sahagún regarding the destruction of Tenochtitlán by the Spanish. How do you explain Cortés's statements that "there was not one man among us whose heart did not bleed at the sound" of the slaughter? Who bears the primary responsibility for the Aztec destruction? Cortés? His Indian allies? Or Montezuma himself? Is Cortés's attitude toward the Amerindians consistent with that of Columbus'? Were they explorers or exploiters?

5. How was Cortés able to defeat thousands of Aztec warriors with only a few hundred soldiers? What role did smallpox play in the destruction of the Aztec civilization in Mexico? Do you agree with William McNeill that "the main destructive role was certainly played by epidemic disease"? How important is disease as an agent of change in history?

6. What was the *encomienda* system and how was it and the *mita* used to exploit Indian labor? How was the mercury extracted from the mines and why was this a dangerous process? Why were the silver mines of Potosi so important to the Spanish and what made them such a lucrative operation?

7. What was the "Black Legend" of Spain? What types of atrocities were committed by the Spanish conquistadores? Study the pictures accompanying the accounts of Bartolomé de Las Casas. Was this an attempt at genocide, or have these atrocities been blown out of proportion by Las Casas and inflated as anti-Spanish propaganda? Do the arguments of Juan Gines de Sepulveda effectively counter those of Las Casas? How does Sepulveda justify Spanish treatment of the Indians?

8. Analyze the arguments of Richard Hakluyt in support of English colonization in the New World. Do you find them to be persuasive? What do they tell you about the European competition for empire in the Americas?

9. How does William Bradford's account of the Pilgrim landing at Plymouth reflect the dangers of colonization? What were his primary concerns and how did religious faith sustain these early settlers?

10. Compare the account of David Pieterzen de Vries entitled "Murder in Cold Blood" with that of Bernardino de Sahagún on the destruction of Tenochtitlán. What were the motives for slaughter and what did the perpetrators hope to gain? Why was it more important for the Europeans to dominate the Native

Americans than to coexist with them? How does Father Serra's account of the establishment of the missions of California compare? What was his reaction to the Indian attack and how was he, like William Bradford at Plymouth, sustained by religious faith? Was Father Serra's establishment of missions still a form, albeit less brutal, of foreign domination?

11. What are the primary tenets of mercantilism as noted by Fayer Hall in his account of the "Old Colonial" system and by Sir William Keith in the selection entitled "The Maxim of All Polite Nations"? As the ruler of a state, would you find their arguments compelling? Why might mercantilism develop naturally in response to the European competition for empire in the Americas and in the East? How do the mercantilist arguments differ from those of Adam Smith as expounded in the selection entitled *The Wealth of Nations*? Do you find his view of human nature and self-interest to be persuasive? According to Smith, what are the primary ingredients of success in the world? How do you define the principle of the "invisible hand?"

12. According to Herman Viola, what were the cultural ramifications of Columbus' first contact with the New World of America? Was it a "New World" in the sense that the cultures of America were young and not developed? How did the Europeans affect the Native Americans and what influence did American crops and products have on Europe and Africa? Do you believe that Columbus's voyages really changed the history of the world?